PERSONAL FINANCE

PERSONAL
FINANCE
An Integrated Planning Approach

Bernard J. Winger

Ralph R. Frasca
University of Dayton

3rd

Edition

Prentice Hall
Upper Saddle River, NJ 07458

Library of Congress Cataloging-in-Publication Data

Winger, Bernard J.
   Personal finance : an integrated approach / Bernard J. Winger,
Ralph R. Frasca.—3rd ed.
     p.   cm.
   Includes bibliographical references and index.
   ISBN 0-02-428601-X
   1. Finance, Personal. I. Frasca, Ralph R. II. Title.
IN PROCESS

92-12421
CIP

Editor: Jill Lectka
Production Supervisor: Dora Rizzuto
Production Manager: Nick Sklitsis
Text Designer: A Good Thing, Inc.
Cover Designer: Russ Maselli
Cover photograph: Copyright 1992 Comstock
Photo Researcher: Cindy Lee Fairfield
Illustrations: Rolin Graphics, Inc.

This book was set in 10/12 Berling by York Graphic Services, Inc.

 © 1993 by Prentice-Hall, Inc.
A Simon & Schuster Company
Upper Saddle River New Jersey 07458

Earlier editions copyright © 1989 and 1986 published by
Merrill Publishing Company

Printed in the United States of America

10 9 8 7 6 5 4

ISBN 0-02-428601-X

Prentice-Hall International (UK) Limited, *London*
Prentice-Hall of Australia Pty. Limited, *Sydney*
Prentice-Hall Canada Inc., *Toronto*
Prentice-Hall Hispanoamericana, S.A., *Mexico*
Prentice-Hall of India Private Limited, *New Delhi*
Prentice-Hall of Japan, Inc., *Tokyo*
Simon & Schuster Asia Pte. Ltd., *Singapore*
Editora Prentice-Hall do Brasil, Ltda., *Rio de Janeiro*

To those we love:
Sue, Mike, and Bob
Crystal, Matthew, Anthony, Michael, and Christina

Preface

Our primary aim in writing this text is to help the reader plan for a successful financial future. Planning has never been easy and in recent years it has grown increasingly difficult. A lingering recession, corporate restructures and downsizing, and an ever-changing tax law are among the many factors influencing today's personal financial plans. Moreover, a change in attitude seems to have taken place—the high-flying 1980s are giving way to a somber and cautious 1990s.

As with previous editions, we attempt to reflect changes in the financial environment throughout the text. Again, this edition is a collaborative effort of many people—teachers, students, and financial planners—who have contributed numerous suggestions, criticisms, and helpful insights. While many changes have been made to reflect the conservative mood, update the material, clarify explanations, and sharpen the decision-making focus, the general outline remains intact.

Part One begins with the foundation of decision making: setting goals. The first two chapters discuss personal and financial goals for both career and day-to-day living. Measuring performance and budgeting for success are discussed in Chapters 3 and 4, while Chapter 5 presents effective methods for reducing tax obligations. Part Two deals with ways to make the right decisions in the marketplace. Deciding upon savings plans, choosing among credit alternatives, selecting consumer goods, and evaluating housing options are among the topics covered. Part Three discusses how insurance works to protect individuals and families from the potential loss of income, health, and property. Investing money to achieve future objectives is the subject of Part Four. This section examines the relationship between risk and return, and explains how to devise an investment portfolio consistent with net-worth goals. Finally, Part Five focuses on long-term planning, showing how to plan for retirement and how to arrange for an estate to be economically distributed after death.

DISTINGUISHING FEATURES

Decision-Making Approach We continue using a four-part approach to decision making that involves setting goals, listing alternatives, measuring performance, and evaluating achievement. Important in this process are the concepts of opportunity costs and marginal analysis. These topics are introduced and explained in Chapter 1 and are used extensively throughout the text.

An Emphasis on Risk and Return At the core of financial decision making is the balancing of risk and return. While this concept applies in particular to investments, it is also useful in other decisions that involve uncertainty; thus, there is an expanded discussion of risk management in the insurance section. In the investment section, we treat risk in such a way that students can use the concept when making investment decisions. Readers thus gain a practical tool as well as an understanding of the basic principles.

The Use of Action Plans An action plan is a written, step-by-step approach to solving a financial problem. This concept is explained in detail in Chapter 4 and is then employed at appropriate points in the chapters that follow. The use of action plans encourages students to think analytically about problems, rather than memorizing answers. *New to this edition:* All action plans developed in previous editions have been revised and updated to reflect changes in the financial environment.

An Illustrative Family As part of the decision-making approach, we continue to highlight a typical American family, the Steeles. Their financial situation is far from perfect, and, like most of us, they make mistakes. *New to this edition:* The Steeles' financial situation has been updated and revised. While they still manage to live a reasonably comfortable and financially secure life, they are encountering growing financial pressures as they consider their future needs to educate their children and to provide an income for themselves in retirement. The Steele family appears in nearly every chapter, where they encounter problems common to most families. As they deal with them and make decisions, so does the reader. In many cases, an action plan details a concrete approach to the problem, allowing the student to participate in solving it.

Vignettes Each chapter opens with a vignette (many are new to this edition) that describes a real-life situation, the pitfalls in a particular financial planning area, or a unique solution to a financial problem. Each vignette invites the student immediately into the chapter and encourages enthusiasm and interest in the topics the chapter covers. The vignettes touch on such topics as lemon laws, tax strategies, and the changing financial values within an American family.

Boxed Features Each chapter contains three featured items that have been selected specifically for this edition to add interest and to provide background. *New to this edition:* All boxes have been selected to fit into three themes: "Saving Money," "Simplifying Financial Planning," and "What's New in Personal Finance?" These themes focus student attention and often include practical and useful information.

Marginal Notes The text is enhanced by marginal notes. *New to this edition:* All margin notes provide key term definitions, which should benefit students in understanding concepts and preparing for exams.

The Use of Color, Graphics, and Other Visual Aids The sophisticated graphic treatment in this text is meant to heighten interest in the topic at hand and to illustrate the concept in a concrete and effective way. The illustrations are both analytical and inviting, and the photographs add a practical tone by illustrating real-life financial situations in detail.

An Informal Writing Style To help the reader comprehend the many complex aspects of personal finance, we employ an informal writing style that brings the student into the discussion without simplifying the concepts involved. We have been careful to explain new or un-familiar terms, to use examples where appropriate, and to speak engagingly to the student.

A Complete Complement of End-of-Chapter Learning Aids Each chapter concludes with the follow-ing study aids:

Summary. A brief review of the major topics discussed.

Key Terms. A list of important concepts in each chapter, accompa-nied by the page number where each key term is introduced and defined. To help the reader locate them, the key terms appear in bold-face type within the chapter.

Problems and Review Questions. A list of questions meant to provide the basis for a review of textual material and to stimulate thought and discussion on the chapter's content. *New to this edition* is an expanded list of questions and problems. Also, all items have been updated to reflect changes in the financial environment.

Cases in Personal Finance. Two cases that, when completed, pro-vide additional insight into the top-ics covered. These study aids are more challenging than the problems and review questions, requiring a firm grasp of the fundamentals and more computation. *New to this edi-tion:* All cases have also been re-vised to reflect changes in the fi-nancial environment.

Helpful Readings. A brief list of informative sources and survey arti-cles. *New to this edition:* Along with helpful readings, each chapter now contains a list of "Helpful Contacts." These provide names, addresses, and phone numbers of

institutions providing help in finan-cial planning.

Supplementary Materials This text is accompanied by a complete list of supplementary teaching aids for both the instructor and the student.

Student Study Guide. Paul Allen of Sam Houston State University has prepared the Study Guide to assist students in completing this course. For each chapter of the text, the guide contains highlights, a review of key terms, and test questions. The self-test items consist of match-ing concepts, sentence completions, true-false statements, multiple-choice questions, and learning exer-cises.

Instructor's Manual and Test Bank. The Instructor's Manual, also by Paul Allen, includes extensive sum-maries that highlight essential points in each chapter. Also included are answers to the end-of-chapter questions and sample solutions for the cases.

New to this edition is a test bank of over 1,400 questions (all written by the authors). The questions vary in rigor and type, from term identi-fication to problem solving, and they should provide adopters a wide array of choices in preparing tests. For those adopting this text, the test bank is also available on a computer disk, along with comple-mentary software for generating examinations keyed to chapters in the text.

Spreadsheet Templates. Several spreadsheet programs are available for use on personal computers. These programs may be used for planning and forecasting, and as decision-making aids. To help the instructor in this area, we have taken many of the examples and problems in the text and placed the data on templates for use in conjunction with the commercial spreadsheet programs that are compatible with *Lotus 1-2-3*® on the IBM-PC.

We usually learn by doing, and this text gives students plenty of opportunities to both do and learn. The decision-making approach enlivens the classroom, simplifies the teaching process, and encourages independent analysis on the part of the student. *Personal Finance: An Integrated Planning Approach* presents personal finance in a way that is easy to understand, easy to teach, and interesting to learn. We hope that you enjoy this text.

ACKNOWLEDGMENTS

To complete a work of this scope requires the assistance of many dedicated professionals. To begin with, we are grateful to Paul R. Allen (Sam Houston State University), Patrick J. Cusatis (Pennsylvania State University), and Jerry Mason (Texas Tech University) for reviewing this edition. We wish to acknowledge again the many reviewers for the first and second edition. This text is unquestionably strengthened by their contributions and we welcome this opportunity to publicly thank them and acknowledge their efforts.

We also wish to thank George Euskirchen and Thomas E. Davidson for their contributions and Laura Abrams for her assistance.

Finally, the members of Macmillan's staff should be recognized for their work and, more importantly, for their enthusiasm for the project. Special thanks are due Jill Lectka, Teresa A. Cohan, and Dora Rizzuto who directed the revision from beginning to end. Their commitment to its successful completion went beyond what an author usually expects from a publisher.

Bernard J. Winger
Ralph R. Frasca

Brief

Contents

Detailed

Contents

**PART 2
SPENDING, BORROWING,
AND SAVING**

PART 4
INVESTING FOR THE
FUTURE

PERSONAL FINANCE

The Basic Framework

We usually think of financial success as making the most of what we have. We can achieve it through planning: setting goals, establishing priorities, and making effective decisions. Our goals are likely to be both financial and nonfinancial. Indeed, nonfinancial goals, those pertaining to love, family, and religion, are probably more important. But our success in achieving financial goals often enables us to enrich the nonfinancial aspects of our lives.

Part One deals with effective planning techniques, the key to financial success. We begin, in Chapter 1, by outlining the planning process and presenting you with several basic concepts that can help you effectively evaluate financial choices. Among other issues, we consider the uneven match between income and needs during the life cycle, which requires us to respond by shifting resources through time to accommodate present and future needs.

Effective planning of your career, perhaps your most valuable resource, is extremely important to both nonfinancial and financial success. Career planning takes into account a complex system of needs and goals, and Chapter 2 looks at ways all of these personal considerations can be focused to make effective career decisions.

Long-run financial success is usually accomplished by achieving short-run goals. Budgets and financial statements, the subjects of Chapters 3 and 4, help you do just that. Financial statements show you where you are now so that you can plan effectively for the future; they help determine your existing worth and show how you managed your income in the past. Budgeting, on the other hand, helps you manage your future income, thereby increasing your net worth.

Planning to minimize taxes is not just an annual task. It should be thought of as part of a long-term financial scheme. Part One concludes with a discussion of taxes, emphasizing the federal personal income tax. Chapter 5 familiarizes you with tax law, as well as tax-minimizing strategies.

Part 1

Personal Financial Planning: Why It's Important to You

Objectives

1 To understand why setting goals is an important first step in financial planning

2 To see why life-cycle financial planning is important and to understand the nature of a planning approach

3 To understand what is meant by marginal analysis, opportunity costs, and time value of money and to know how these concepts are used in financial decision making

4 To appreciate that factors in the financial environment—inflation, interest rates, and economic cycles—affect financial success and enhance the need for planning

5 To know the Steele family, a family we will follow through the text

Turning Conservative: New Values for the American Middle Class

The American middle class has been repeating the same cycle for decades: Wanting to feel prosperous and successful, it goes on a binge of conspicuous consumption. Then, debt-laden and disillusioned, it retreats to traditional values of financial security and a simpler life. Sometimes a recession acts as a catalyst.

Already changing spending habits is Kenneth Jacobsmeyer, a 37-year-old father of four who now is obsessed with paying off debt. What he wants, he says, is more control over his life. Over pizza and beer in the family room of his suburban St. Louis home, Mr. Jacobsmeyer admits to feeling uneasy about the future. Though he believes his job is secure—he is loss-prevention director for a Midwest supermarket chain—he has heard enough horror stories about layoffs to wonder "What if?" His wife, Michele, has grown anxious watching three friends lose children to cancer, and deplete their savings in the process.

"You've got to look to the future and be prepared to deal with things if an emergency should arise," Mr. Jacobsmeyer asserts. He wants to retire early but recognizes that the nest egg in his company profit-sharing plan "isn't going to amount to peanuts." He plans eventually to raise his contribution to his tax-deferred 401(k) savings plan to the maximum of 15% of his income.

Such thinking is a big change for Mr. Jacobsmeyer, who used to justify buying new cars every few years with the motto "You only live once." In the freewheeling 1980s, he didn't give saving a thought. He and his wife racked up big credit-card balances, fixing up their house and splurging on Christmas gifts. They even borrowed cash from Mr. Jacobsmeyer's mother.

"We were able to live like that and feel somewhat comfortable and not think about down the road," Mr. Jacobsmeyer says incredulously.

The Jacobsmeyers aren't alone. Charles "Skip" Lowe and his wife, Janet, can still afford to buy almost anything striking their fancy, but they no longer do. Now the Mansfield Center, Conn., couple get satisfaction from relationships with family and friends—a satisfaction that lasts "a longer time," says Mr. Lowe, a 48-year-old psychology professor and marketing consultant who earns about $100,000 a year. Adds his wife: "You cannot buy security, love and friends."

The Lowes were jolted into action by their belief that their sons' materialism had got out of hand. The boys knew all the trendy brand names and how much each item cost. Mrs. Lowe felt they had lost sight of intrinsic values and were just trying to impress their friends. "We saw our kids getting exactly the way we were, and we didn't like it," Mr. Lowe says.

SOURCE: Adapted from Francine Schwadel, "Growing Up: Turning Conservative, Baby Boomers Reduce Their Frivolous Buying." *The Wall Street Journal*, June 19, 1991, p. A1. Reprinted by permission of *The Wall Street Journal*, © 1991 Dow Jones & Company, Inc. All Rights Reserved Worldwide.

Personal financial planning is obviously changing for the Jacobsmeyer and Lowe families. Would you prefer their high-consumption style in the 1980s—or does the more cautious approach seem more in step with your life-style? Actually, the question isn't important, and you don't have to choose one approach over others to be a financial success. However, success often requires thorough planning and familiarity with the financial institutions serving us. And, perhaps most importantly, it demands effective decision making. This chapter and those to follow are designed to help you in these efforts.

Why Study Personal Finance

You are probably reading this text because financial success is important to you and you realize that in most cases it doesn't come easily. But what is financial success and how is it measured? To some, it means making a lot of money—the sooner, the better. If that is your goal, then we are afraid this text won't help you very much; nor, we might add, will any other. You might as well save your time and go to Las Vegas or Atlantic City and hope for the best. **Financial success,** often elusive to define, is usually thought of as *obtaining the maximum benefits from limited financial resources.* This means you can be a financial success (or failure) regardless of your income level. A widow with many children and an income below the poverty line may be quite successful in allocating her very limited resources to achieve the goals her family feels are important, while a millionaire might misallocate most of his resources and achieve nothing. We're not suggesting the poor widow is more comfortable or lives a happier life than the millionaire, but she does achieve her goals while he does not. Actually, personal finance has little to do with happiness other than the fact that most of us feel content and proud when we achieve important personal goals.

Your Goals in Life

If personal finance deals with achievement of goals, then you might ask: What goals does it try to achieve? Does it suggest, for example, that we all should save as much as we can? Do we measure success in terms of our weekly contributions to the bank account? Not necessarily. Obviously, what we plan to do during our lifetimes differs considerably. You may want to have a big family and enjoy entertainment activities with the kids while they are young and growing; you might also want to provide for their education. We, on the other hand, might be skinflints who love money for money's sake and have virtually no other interests in life. (We're really not.) As Figure 1.1 indicates, we can categorize goals as either nonfinancial or financial.

NONFINANCIAL GOALS   We should realize that many of our aspirations in life are nonfinancial. We hold moral, family, social, religious, or political ideals that have little or no connection to finance. You can't put a price tag on these goals, and you don't try. In fact, an attempt to buy a vote or a preferred position in the hereafter is considered sacrilegious. Oscar Wilde once defined a cynic as someone who knows the price of everything and the value of nothing. As students of personal finance, let us not become cynics. On the other hand, the extent to which we succeed in achieving our financial goals might determine how much time and energy are available to pursue the nonfinancial. Sociologists tell us, for example, that one of the primary reasons for divorce is financial stress in the family. Achieving financial goals doesn't assure a happy life, but the evidence suggests that it helps more than it hinders.

FINANCIAL GOALS   Financial goals form the basis for financial planning. Indeed, without financial goals, planning is impossible. Setting goals and incorpo-

FIGURE 1.1

Life's goals.

Nonfinancial	Financial
• Moral	• Current consumption
• Family	• Future consumption
• Social	• Savings
• Religious	
• Political	

Financial independence:
Having sufficient income
or resources to be self-
reliant.

rating them in annual budgeting are important topics discussed in depth in Chapter 4. However, it is useful to introduce the topics here.

Very broadly, one might list the most important financial goal as **financial independence;** that is, to have enough income or resources to be self-reliant. However, a goal defined this broadly really doesn't help us plan for the future. What does self-reliant mean? You might understand it as having a job with little threat of a layoff, while someone else sees it as never going into debt. Actually, there are two more concrete goals to shape financial plans: a consumption goal—current and future—and a savings goal.

Current consumption:
Goods and services used in
a current time period.

Current Consumption.   **Current consumption** refers to goods and services that we use in a current period of time, such as this year. These goods and services measure our scale of living. A low consumption budget means we use fewer of them and (probably) have a lower level of satisfaction than someone with a high consumption budget. If Mary's consumption budget is twice that of John's, chances are very good she has more consumption satisfaction than he. But she might not have twice as much. Economists often point out the **principle of diminishing marginal satisfaction,** which means that current consumption satisfaction increases as current income increases but usually at a decreasing rate. This principle explains why we begin to look more favorably at future consumption after we have achieved reasonable levels of current consumption.

Principle of diminishing
marginal satisfaction: A
decreasing *rate* of
satisfaction in relation to
increasing income.

Future consumption:
Goods and services to be
used in future periods.

Future Consumption.   **Future consumption** refers to goods and services to be used in future periods. By itself, future consumption is less desirable than current consumption. Would you rather enjoy a good meal today or 20 years from today? In fact, if your annual income were to remain constant throughout your life, you might very well choose to spend a higher proportion on consumption while you are young, rather than waiting until you are old. But our incomes are seldom the same from year to year. Usually, they are quite low when we start our careers, increase substantially as we move into our most productive years, and then decline as we enter retirement. If we were forced to consume all our income each year, a very uneven consumption pattern would result. Fortunately, there is no such requirement. We try to smooth current consumption over time in order to get the highest overall consumption satisfaction throughout our lifetimes. This means we borrow heavily when we are young and repay our debts in later years.

Savings: The portion of
current income *not*
consumed.

Savings.   **Savings** is simply the portion of our income not spent on current consumption. We have just mentioned one important reason for saving—to enjoy future consumption—but there are others. One of the more important of these is to leave an estate to our heirs. Another might be to increase our investment assets, thereby gaining greater financial independence.

Achieving Financial Goals Through Planning

Planning is the key to personal financial success. Without it, your situation resembles that of an empty, rudderless ship floating on a lake. You can't tell where the ship has been or where it's going. While few people live this aimlessly, many have only very hazy and poorly defined ideas about what they hope to accomplish financially. Waking up one morning in your mid-forties and realizing you'd better do something about retirement is a poor approach. You may not have enough

7

time to accumulate an adequate retirement nest egg, and you also lose all the income tax advantages that were available during the lost years, plus the earnings that earlier investments could have provided. A dollar saved and properly invested in your twenties could easily be the equivalent of $10 saved and improperly invested during your forties. This view of planning as a lifelong process is called **life-cycle planning.**

Life-cycle planning: A view of financial planning as a lifelong process.

Life-Cycle Planning

People go through different phases during their lives, as Figure 1.2 shows. Goals change in importance as we enter different phases, but the key to life-cycle planning is that _all_ our lifelong goals are recognized and attended to at _each_ phase in the cycle. The sooner a goal is stated and solidified, the better. Retirement (as in the preceding example) or the children's educations, or a trip to Tahiti, are more easily and effectively accomplished when lead times are longer.

Major Planning Areas

Certain areas require constant attention in all life-cycle phases. These areas are: career planning, consumption and savings planning, debt planning, insurance planning, investment planning, retirement planning, and estate planning. Threaded throughout all of these areas is income tax planning. The government's share of your success is a fact of life that is probably already familiar to you. It certainly will become more familiar as this course progresses. The sections that follow discuss each type of planning and identify the chapter in the text where the discussion will be developed more fully.

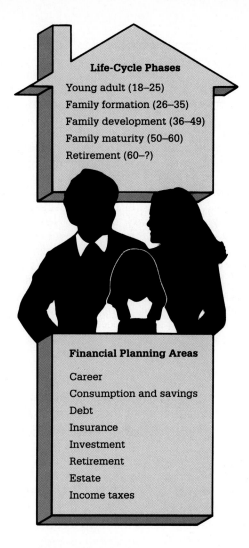

Life-Cycle Phases

Young adult (18–25)

Family formation (26–35)

Family development (36–49)

Family maturity (50–60)

Retirement (60–?)

Financial Planning Areas

Career

Consumption and savings

Debt

Insurance

Investment

Retirement

Estate

Income taxes

FIGURE 1.2

Life-cycle financial planning.

CAREER PLANNING Career planning is obviously important in your youth—particularly during your college years—but its importance may resurface later in life. You may find your first career choice falls short of your expectations, either in advancement opportunities or in personal fulfillment, leading you to search for another career. People in the family maturity stage often aspire to a midlife career change, or the spouse who assumed the larger share of household duties might decide to reenter the work force after the children have become self-sufficient. Career planning is discussed in detail in the next chapter.

CONSUMER AND SAVINGS PLANNING Consumption and savings planning is an integral part of your strategy to achieve lifelong goals. As mentioned previously, you must decide each year how much of your income to allocate to current consumption and how much to save for the future. Two important activities related to consumption and savings planning are preparing periodic personal financial statements—an income statement and a balance sheet—and an annual budget. The latter is the instrument you use most often to make sure you are

9

moving toward your goals. Financial statements are covered in Chapter 3, and budgeting is the topic of Chapter 4. Also, the most important consumption expenditures, those for consumer durables and housing, are discussed in Chapters 8 and 9.

DEBT PLANNING Very few people avoid debt throughout their lives—nor should they. Debt is the vehicle that allows us to even our lifelong consumption. In addition, it is a shopping convenience, and it can help us hedge against inflation by permitting us to buy assets that match or beat the inflation rate. But debt must be managed carefully. We must avoid excessive debt and make sure we tap the lowest-cost sources of credit. Why borrow at 18 percent if you have access to funds costing 14 percent or less? Unfortunately, many Americans do. Debt management is discussed in Chapter 7.

INSURANCE PLANNING Life's uncertainties create continuous insurance needs. As a young adult with few obligations and no dependents, your primary asset is your ability to work and earn income. Therefore, you must protect yourself against the loss of that ability; that is, you need disability insurance. As you go through later phases of the life cycle, other insurance needs increase in importance. The needs of your dependents in the event of your death create a demand for life insurance, and as you accumulate assets—a house, automobiles, household furnishings, and others—you need more property and personal liability insurance. And, most importantly, you need medical insurance to protect against health or accident problems. The "average" illness can lead to hospital and doctor bills large enough to wipe out your entire savings, and then some. Insurance planning is explained in Chapters 10, 11, and 12.

INVESTMENT PLANNING While saving part of our income each year, we must decide how to invest it. Choices here seem almost limitless, ranging from simply letting our bank account grow to speculating in raw land or commodity futures contracts. Successful investment often spells the difference between achieving our lifelong goals (and maybe even exceeding them), and failing to do so. An important first investment goal is to provide sufficient liquidity; this topic is discussed in Chapter 6. You can then turn your attention to more risky investments offering potentially higher returns, discussed in Chapters 13, 14, 15, and 16.

RETIREMENT PLANNING Retirement planning consists primarily of estimating future consumption and other needs and then determining how you will meet these needs when you are no longer working. Most of us rely upon Social Security and employer-sponsored retirement plans for retirement income, but we also realize that supplemental sources may be necessary to maintain a suitable lifestyle in retirement. We must invest during our working years to accumulate a retirement nest egg. The federal government has recognized these supplemental retirement efforts and has enacted favorable tax legislation to help achieve them. Retirement planning is the subject of Chapter 17.

ESTATE PLANNING If you live forever, you can avoid the problem of estate planning: how to minimize taxes while giving away your wealth. Since the odds in favor of earthly immortality are not encouraging, your next best strategy is to make sure you have your financial house in order when you make the grand exit. Essential to this plan are a proper will and a sound tax strategy, which might mean distributing part of your wealth in the form of gifts while you are still alive. Estate planning is, appropriately enough, our final subject, and it appears in Chapter 18.

INCOME TAX PLANNING Almost no aspect of our financial lives is untouched by federal income taxes. The federal government will become a partner in all the income you earn. There are ways to minimize the tax bite, but it is up to you to find out what they are, and how and when to use them. Two people with identical incomes and family situations could wind up with a $100,000 difference in their assets after 30 years or so because of effective versus ineffective tax planning. With this much at stake, it's worth your effort to become familiar with the income tax law, and Chapter 5 will give you a good start.

A Planning Approach

As shown in Figure 1.3, planning involves four steps. First, you must state your broad goals in specific and concrete terms. For example, if buying a home is an important goal, you must decide eventually when you will buy it, how much to pay for it, the size of your down payment, and how to finance it. The second step is to create an action plan, which sets out in detail how you will achieve your goal. To achieve the goal of buying a home, you must save a portion of your income each year and invest the funds temporarily. After you have set a specific date to buy a home, you can decide which temporary investments are best suited to help achieve the goal. If the purchase date is relatively far in the future (say,

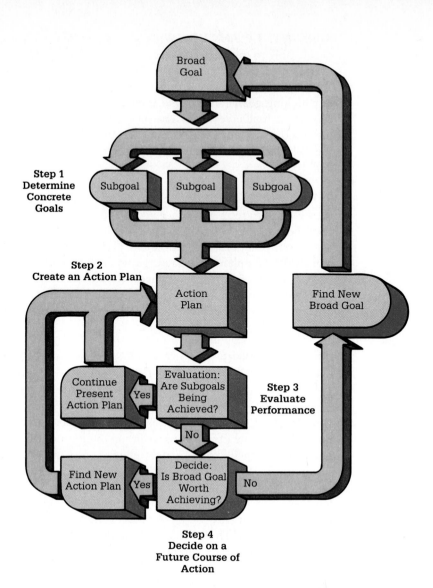

Step 1
Determine
Concrete
Goals

Step 2
Create an Action Plan

Step 3
Evaluate
Performance

Step 4
Decide on a
Future Course of
Action

Broad
Goal

Subgoal   Subgoal   Subgoal

Action
Plan

Find New
Broad Goal

Continue
Present
Action Plan

Evaluation:
Are Subgoals
Being
Achieved?

Yes

No

Find New
Action Plan

Decide:
Is Broad Goal
Worth
Achieving?

Yes

No

FIGURE 1.3

Steps in the planning
approach.

five years or longer), you might choose investments that are somewhat riskier
(with potentially higher yields) than you would choose if you intend to buy next
year. The third step in the planning process involves evaluating your performance
toward the goal. This step would be unnecessary if we lived in an unchanging
world—but we do not. The type of home you want might increase in price, or
financing costs might go up, or other changes could frustrate your effort to buy
the home. The fourth and final planning stage forces us to decide if the goal is still
worth achieving, or if we should abandon it and search for another broad goal. If
you decide the home is still worth the effort, for example, you must then revise
your action plan, by increasing the annual savings or perhaps by choosing other
temporary investments offering higher returns. (The latter approach could be
very risky, though.)

Using the above four steps does not guarantee success, but you will certainly
achieve goals far more easily if you use this method rather than a haphazard

The Basic
Framework

approach. Effective planning puts you at the rudder of the ship on the lake, and it gives you the navigational aids you need to bring the ship to its destination.

The Building Blocks of Success

An important part of financial planning is setting priorities. All through life you will encounter both opportunities and risks, and you need to put them in perspective. Suppose you are a young person with family obligations and very little savings. A friend, who has recently become a securities salesperson, calls and tells you how you can double your money in a speculative investment. There is a strong temptation to take the offer, even though you know if it fails you will have to give up or delay other important goals. But if it succeeds, you can do so much more! Most financial advisers will tell you to forget risky propositions such as this until you have satisfied those goals you have already decided are the most important.

Building-block approach to personal finance: Sequential investing, starting with a low-risk foundation and then moving to more risky investments.

Setting priorities and sticking to the long-run plan suggests a **"building-block" approach to personal finance,** as illustrated in Figure 1.4. You begin with the lowest blocks, which means you first build a strong foundation of support. You proceed to the first investment level *after* the lowest blocks are secure. Likewise, go to riskier investments only after you have a suitable level of safe ones, deferring the very riskiest until last. Remember that if you fail at a higher level, the goals supported by success at the lower levels will not be achieved. You might have decided, for example, to invest in government bonds that will guarantee enough future return to put your kids through the state university. If you abandon this plan and put the money instead in speculative growth stocks, you might eventually have enough to put them through Harvard—or you might have to tell

FIGURE 1.4

The building blocks of success.

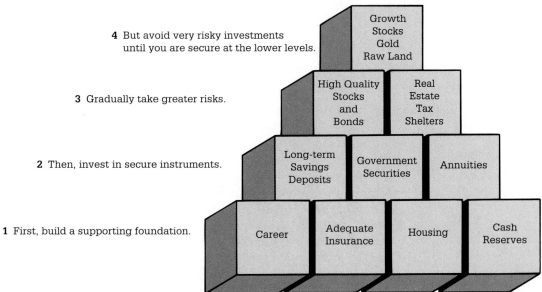

4 But avoid very risky investments until you are secure at the lower levels.

3 Gradually take greater risks.

2 Then, invest in secure instruments.

1 First, build a supporting foundation.

them there is very little available to support their educations anywhere. You must make the choice, but at least understand the risks involved and the potential consequences of your choice.

Making Financial Decisions

Making a decision is a complex process. To decide is to choose among alternatives. You probably have encountered many situations where making a choice was difficult; indeed, your biggest problem may have been simply identifying what choices were available. Then you had to find some basis for evaluating the expected outcomes of each alternative. With all that done, you must pick one alternative as the best. Consider how difficult choosing a major in college can be; unfortunately, we face equally difficult financial decisions most of our lives. While each decision is made in its own set of circumstances, all of them involve techniques that can help you. Each technique—using marginal analysis, determining opportunity costs, and considering the time value of money—is explained below.

Marginal analysis: Evaluating *changes* in important variables in relation to controllable decision inputs.

MARGINAL ANALYSIS   **Marginal analysis** means looking at *changes* in important variables that are related to changes in decision inputs you can control. For example, suppose you are ready to graduate and you are investing in a wardrobe you will need for your first job. You know that two good business suits are a must but a third might be a luxury. To decide whether to buy the third suit requires that you compare the benefits it provides to its cost. If you think the added benefits are worth it, buy the third suit; if not, then don't buy it. But definitely do not consider benefits that the first and second suits provide, because they are totally irrelevant to the decision.

Marginal analysis should always be employed whenever a decision involves comparing different approaches to a problem. For example, suppose you are considering buying two different automobile insurance policies that differ with respect to coverage and cost. They each have the same basic coverage, but one includes protection against certain perils while the other does not. It also has a higher yearly premium. In deciding between the two, it isn't necessary to look at the total coverages and total premiums of each; all that must be done is to compare the extra (marginal) coverage with the extra (marginal) premium. Then decide if the more comprehensive policy is worth the extra cost.

Opportunity costs: Benefits given up when one alternative is chosen over another.

OPPORTUNITY COSTS   **Opportunity costs** are benefits that you give up when you choose one alternative over another. If you decide to work during the Christmas holidays, you might give up a skiing trip to Colorado. The opportunity cost of the job is the fun you lose by not choosing the skiing trip; and the opportunity cost of the skiing trip is the income you won't earn by turning down the job. Sometimes opportunity costs are obvious, while at other times they are identified only by thoughtful consideration. For example, what is your opportunity cost of taking a course in personal finance, assuming you need the hours for graduation? It is not the tuition cost of the course; rather, it is the information and learning offered by another course that you can't take because you are taking this one.

These examples might seem trivial, but opportunity costs arise in big decisions as well as small. Examples: What are the opportunity costs of choosing one career over another? What are the opportunity costs of your undergraduate education? What are the opportunity costs of renting versus buying a home? Consider carefully your responses to these questions. Some of the costs are clearly economic and probably easy to measure, while others involve personal preferences and can be measured only by expressing personal value judgments. To get on the right track when using this technique, ask the following question: What do I give up if I choose one alternative over another? The answer will give you the opportunity cost for the alternative under consideration.

The Time Value of Money

Many financial decisions involve paying or receiving sums of money over future periods of time. This is called a **future value.** For example, you might be considering an investment that costs $1,000 today and returns the same amount to you at the end of three years. Is it a good investment? Of course not! Why be content just to get your money back when other investments pay interest? If someone wishes to use our money, we insist on a return—one at least as good as those available on equal-risk, alternative investments. Suppose the borrower offered to give your $1,000 back at the end of three years along with $200 in interest. Is that acceptable, if you think you could earn 10 percent annual interest somewhere else? To answer the question we must calculate the future value, *FV,* of $1,000 invested elsewhere. This calculation is shown below.

FV at end of year 1 = $1,000 + 0.10($1,000) = $1,100

FV at end of year 2 = $1,100 + 0.10($1,100) = $1,210

FV at end of year 3 = $1,210 + 0.10($1,210) = $1,331

An alternative quick calculation is:

$$FV = (\$1,000)(1.0 + i)(1.0 + i)(1.0 + i)$$

where i = your required investment rate each period. Then

$$FV = (\$1,000)(1.1)(1.1)(1.1) = (\$1,000)(1.331) = \$1,331$$

An even quicker calculation (assuming you use a calculator) is:

$$FV = (\$1,000)(1.0 + i)^n$$

where n = the number of periods you earn the rate i. Then,

$$FV = (\$1,000)(1.1)^3 = (\$1,000)(1.331) = \$1,331$$

In the above example, your $1,000 grows to $1,331 if you can invest it (and all the subsequent interest earned) at 10 percent. Comparing $1,331 to the $1,200 offered by the other investment tells us the other investment should be rejected.

The $331 of interest calculated above is called **compound interest.** It includes "interest on interest," which means that interest earned in earlier periods is as-

Future value: A sum of money received or paid in the future.

Compound interest: A future value that includes interest on interest.

15

sumed to be reinvested to earn interest in future periods. **Simple interest** assumes that interest earned in each period is withdrawn and not reinvested. The formula below is used to calculate simple interest:

$$\text{Simple interest} = (\text{principal}) \times (\text{rate}) \times (\text{time})$$

Using the above data, simple interest would be $300 as calculated below:

$$\$300 = (\$1{,}000) \times (0.10) \times (3)$$

You can use either method to calculate interest, depending upon which one is more appropriate to what you actually will do with earned interest. However, in most financial planning illustrations the compound method is used.

THE IMPORTANCE OF ADDITIONAL YIELD   The future values of different investments are crucial to many financial decisions. For example, suppose you are considering investments A and B. A offers an 8 percent yield and has virtually no risk on either a short- or long-term basis. B offers a 10 percent yield and is about as risky as A on a long-term basis, but somewhat riskier short-term. (You might pay a penalty for early withdrawal, for example.) Since you plan to hold each investment for a long period of time, B's added risk is not of major concern to you. On the other hand, you aren't sure that a mere two percentage points is enough marginal yield to pick B over A. By looking only at the difference of two percentage points, you may fail to see the substantial difference in future values between the two. Figure 1.5 shows this difference in dramatic detail. (The

FIGURE 1.5

Future value of $1,000 invested at 8 and at 10 percent.

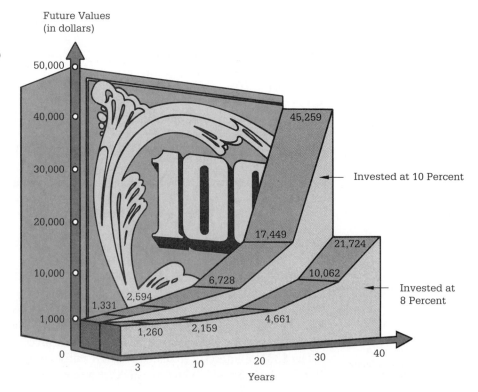

amounts were calculated using the compound interest techniques explained above.) At the end of three years, you will have only $71 ($1,331 minus $1,260) more with investment *B*, but at the end of 40 years you will have an extra $23,535—more than twice as much!

THE IMPORTANCE OF ADDITIONAL TIME Figure 1.5 also dramatizes the importance of investing early to achieve certain goals, such as retirement. Suppose you are 25 and plan to retire at age 65. You are considering investing now for retirement but wonder how much difference it would make if you waited 10 years to start. Assuming the 10 percent investment rate, the answer is $27,810 ($45,259 minus $17,449). You accumulate considerably more in the last 10 years than you do in the first 30!

TIME VALUE OF MONEY TABLES Future value calculations are easy to make with a hand calculator, following the procedures just explained. As an alternative, many people use a *future value of $1 table*. A portion of such a table is shown as Table 1.1. (More detailed tables and a discussion of both present and future value techniques are given in Appendix A. These techniques are not required to understand the examples given in this text but will serve as a handy reference if you need to make complex financial decisions in the future.)

A future value table shows the future value of $1 invested for a specified number of periods and at a specified investment rate each period. To use the table, simply multiply the future value of $1 by the number of dollars you invest. If you invest $100, multiply $100 times 1.3310; if $200, multiply $200 times 1.3310 and so forth. You can see from Table 1.1 how the values in Figure 1.5 were determined.

Professional Financial Planner

Financial planner: A professional person with a broad financial background who offers planning advice to clients.

The growing complexities of financial planning over the past 20 years have created a demand for a new professional—the **financial planner**. This person has a broad understanding of tax laws, insurance, investments, and finance in general. He or she is not necessarily an expert in any one area, but is sufficiently knowledgeable in all to recognize problems and to suggest specialized professional help, if it is needed. The planner's main function is to create a financial plan to help clients achieve their goals. This profession is not yet as organized and regulated as other professions, such as medicine, law, or accounting, and anyone can adopt the title of professional planner. But there is a growing trend toward regulation

TABLE 1.1 • Portion of a Future Value of $1 Table

Periods n	Values of i			
	6%	8%	10%	20%
1	1.0600	1.0800	1.1000	1.2000
3	1.1910	1.2597	1.3310	1.7280
10	1.7908	2.1589	2.5937	6.1917
20	3.2071	4.6610	6.7275	38.3370
30	5.7435	10.0620	17.4490	237.3700
40	10.2850	21.7240	45.2590	1,469.7000

Fee-Based Versus Commission-Based Financial Planners

An enduring controversy in the financial planning industry is whether planners should be compensated by client fees or by commissions on the investment and insurance products they sell. On the surface, fee-only planners appear to be more expensive, since product commissions are often not revealed to clients. But commissions can be stiff—often ranging between 4 and 9 percent on amounts invested.

Apart from cost considerations, some critics charge that commission-based planners face an inherent conflict of interest. Rather than recommending what's best for you, they push the products with the largest commissions for them. Proponents of the system argue, though, that without receiving commissions from product sponsors, planners could not provide their services to consumers with limited funds.

What to do? Here's a checklist of important items to consider.

- Since many commission-based planners specialize in selling particular products, they may not be qualified to provide broad financial advice or to create a comprehensive financial plan.

- Ask how much commission the planner will earn on the transaction. Such information can help you make comparisons among both types of planners—and do not hesitate to do comparative shopping.

- Seek low- or no-cost planning advice that might be provided by your employer or your local bank.

- If you are seeking life insurance or mutual fund investments, be aware that there are many providers with low or no commissions. But you must locate them. (This text will help in the effort.)

- Absolutely never use a planner or adviser (investment, insurance, or other) without determining the person's background and experience. Ask for references and, if possible, try to find other clients whose names the adviser does not provide.

and, as Figure 1.6 shows, there are a number of self-regulatory organizations that are active in establishing standards and a professional code of ethics.

Do you need a professional planner? Of course, the answer to that question depends upon the complexity of your financial situation and how much of your own time you are willing to devote to the job. Assuming you have an average financial situation and you complete carefully this text (and the course, if you are using the text as part of a course), you should be able to develop your own

FIGURE 1.6

Organizations active in personal financial planning.

Organization	Certification/Membership
International Board of Standards and Practices	Certified Financial Planner (CFP)
American College	Chartered Financial Consultant (ChFC)
International Association of Financial Planning	Member of the Registry
International Association of Registered Planners	Registered Financial Planner (RFP)
National Association of Personal Financial Advisors	Association of Fee-Only Planners
American Institute of Certified Public Accountants—Personal Financial Planning Division	Certified Public Accountant— Accredited Personal Financial Planning Specialist (CPA—APFS)

financial plans. However, the professional planner may be able to add insights to a problem, or use a computer to develop and evaluate your financial plans. These services could be worth their costs, which usually start at about $300 for a simple evaluation and could go to several thousand dollars for someone with complex financial problems.

The Financial Environment

Even the best financial plans may not be successful. This is so because financial success depends as much upon environmental factors as it does on good planning. You have no control over the rate of inflation or the rate of interest or the rate of economic growth; yet these are important. However, your apparent helplessness argues for more rather than less planning. Only with adequate contingency planning can you adjust to a changing economic environment.

Inflation

If you were asked to identify one economic constant in that environment, it probably would be inflation. Prices go up, but they rarely seem to come down. In both our own and our parents' experiences, inflation has been a fact of life.

Inflation: A general rise in prices.

Consumer Price Index (CPI): A broad measurement of prices.

Inflation is usually defined as a general rise in prices, and it is measured by the changing cost over time of a market basket of goods. The **Consumer Price Index (CPI),** one of the broadest measurements of prices, is shown in Figure 1.7. What it illustrates is what we probably already know: The period after World War II has seen an almost continuous increase in the price level, also called the cost of living.

FIGURE 1.7

The Consumer Price Index, 1953–1992, and annual rates of inflation, measured by the percentage change in the CPI.

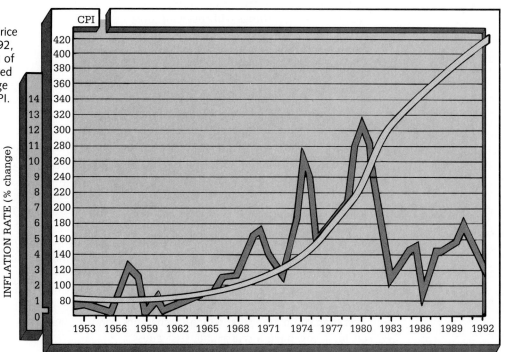

While the general trend is upward, prices have risen at a faster pace in some years than in others. The **inflation rate**—a term you usually hear on the evening news—is simply the annual percentage change in the CPI. As Figure 1.7 shows, rates of inflation during the 1970s and early 1980s were generally higher than rates in all preceding decades except the 1940s. Does this mean we are in for even higher rates of inflation in coming decades? Some forecasters think there is a direct relationship between big government, big deficits, and high rates of inflation. Their guess is that all three will continue to increase. But our recent experiences don't completely confirm this; rather, they show rates of inflation far below the highs of the 1970s and early 1980s. Is this only a temporary reduction? Unfortunately, nobody really knows. What rate of inflation should you use in financial planning? Be flexible: For short-run plans, use a rate that appears most realistic. For long-run plans, follow a similar approach, but be quick to change your figure if the economy seems to be undergoing a fundamental change. A figure of 3 to 4 percent for 1993, if you were planning in 1992, would seem reasonable. In Chapter 4, we'll show how inflation adjustments are considered in budgeting.

Interest Rates

The interest rate experience of the U.S. economy is shown in Figure 1.8. It appears to parallel the movement in inflation rates, with substantial increases in the 1970s and early 1980s. This relationship is what you might expect, and it is explained in terms of our previous discussion on the time value of money.

An **interest rate** is called the cost of money. It determines how much you will be paid for investing and postponing present consumption. When the rate of inflation is high, things will cost a lot more in the future. If you forego purchasing today, you must earn a substantial return on your money to compensate you for tomorrow's higher prices. So, when the rate of inflation is high, investors will demand and get higher interest rates. Otherwise, they won't invest, even in securities they know won't default, such as U.S. Treasury securities. Furthermore, because an adequate interest return depends upon the rate of inflation, the rate of interest in future years will be just as uncertain as the rate of inflation in those years. As Figure 1.9 shows, investors recognize that an interest rate consists of at least three components: (*a*) a return for postponing consumption, (*b*) a return for expected inflation, and (*c*) a return for undertaking risk. The risk component is higher for longer-term investments because the chances are greater that your inflation estimate will be wrong. (Would you feel more sure of your estimate for next year, or for the next ten years?) That is why longer-term investments often pay higher interest rates—they're simply riskier.

What interest rates should you use in financial planning? Again, that's a hard question to answer. We *can* say that your figures should be consistent with your expectations of inflation. If you think inflation will be 3 percent, it would be realistic to expect at least 5 to 7 percent on your safe short-term investments and maybe 8 to 12 percent on safe ones with long maturities. You might get more or less than these amounts, which is why contingency planning is so necessary, but at least you have a reasonable first guess.

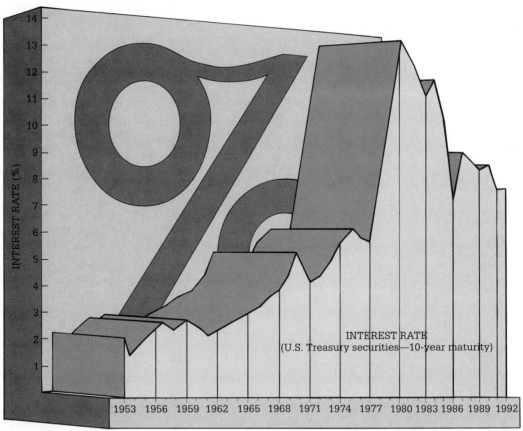

FIGURE 1.8

Interest rates, 1953–1991. (Source for 1953–1983 figures: *Economic Report of the President,* 1984, p. 298. Others from *Federal Reserve Bulletin,* December, 1991.)

Business Cycles

Business cycle: A fluctuation in economic activity consisting of four distinct phases.

Economic growth is seldom uniform over time; rather, it tends to come in cycles. A **business cycle** is a fluctuation in economic activity. The four usual phases of a business cycle—peak, recession, trough, and recovery—are illustrated in Figure 1.10. At the peak the economy is operating close to full capacity with a low rate of unemployment. As the economy moves into a recession, unemployment increases, business activity declines, and consumers generally become more pessimistic. If the decline in economic activity is especially severe, the recession phase may be replaced by depression. The difference between a recession and a depression is really only a question of the magnitude of the decline in production.

When economic activity is at its lowest, the cycle is in the trough. From there, the economy enters the expansionary phase with rapid increases in output and employment. This is accompanied by a rise in the rate of inflation as the additional demands generated by expansion strain limited resources and push up prices. The economy may then reach its peak, thus completing the cycle. Can identifying the stage of an economic cycle help in financial planning? Not as

21

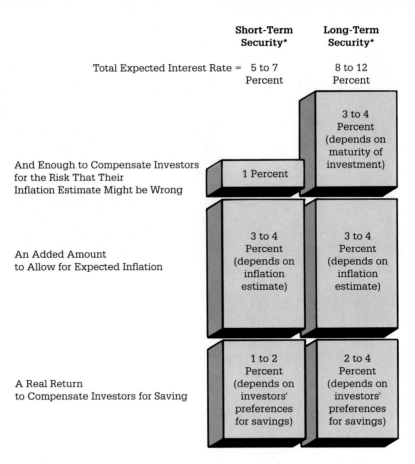

	Short-Term Security*	Long-Term Security*
Total Expected Interest Rate =	5 to 7 Percent	8 to 12 Percent

And Enough to Compensate Investors for the Risk That Their Inflation Estimate Might be Wrong — 1 Percent — 3 to 4 Percent (depends on maturity of investment)

An Added Amount to Allow for Expected Inflation — 3 to 4 Percent (depends on inflation estimate) — 3 to 4 Percent (depends on inflation estimate)

A Real Return to Compensate Investors for Saving — 1 to 2 Percent (depends on investors' preferences for savings) — 2 to 4 Percent (depends on investors' preferences for savings)

FIGURE 1.9

What investors expect in an interest rate.

*Assumes a security that will not default, such as a U.S. Treasury security. If there is a chance of default, investors will expect an even higher interest rate.

much as you might think, because it is very difficult to know *in advance* the dates when each stage takes place. Perhaps the most valuable lesson we can learn is to be suspicious of forecasts, particularly in the area of investments. At a cycle's peak, for example, you will find no shortage of "experts" forecasting prosperity or high inflation forever. While history can't tell us the exact date the cycle will end, it does at least suggest that an end will come.

Planning Versus Forecasting

Forecasting: Science (or art) of predicting future events.

Planning: Science of preparing for future events.

Planning and forecasting are two distinct activities, and one does not necessarily require the other. **Forecasting** is the science—some would call it an art—of predicting future events. **Planning** is the science of preparing for future events. Obviously, if you could forecast inflation, interest rates, and the direction of the economy, you could more adequately and easily plan for the future. You could also become a millionaire almost instantly. But nobody seems to do a very good job at predicting any of these variables. Realizing this, financial planners try to minimize the adverse effects of unforeseen changes in the economic environment.

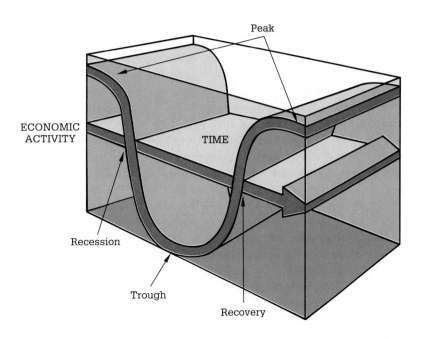

Peak

ECONOMIC
ACTIVITY

TIME

Recession

Trough

Recovery

FIGURE 1.10

The four phases of the
business cycle.

As we confront uncertainty, planning grows more important. But don't despair: There are appropriate methods for answering such important financial questions as the ones below.

- How do you decide whether to invest your money in the stock market or place it in a savings account when you don't know in what direction the economy is headed?
- How do you decide how much to save for college, if you don't know how much interest your savings will earn?
- How do you decide on amounts to set aside for retirement, if you don't know how much things will cost thirty years from now?

You probably agree these are interesting questions. That's why you're reading this book.

The Steele Family

Before we conclude this introductory chapter, we would like to introduce you to the Steele family. You will meet them from time to time in the succeeding chapters as they help us illustrate the application of financial planning techniques. The Steeles represent a composite of the characteristics of a typical American middle-class family. Sharon and Arnold are both professionals in their mid-thirties with two children, two cars, and a dog.

By most measures, the Steeles have achieved a certain level of success. Arnold, 37, is a chemist with a major paint manufacturer and is currently next in line for vice president of plant operations. Sharon, 35, is a CPA and works part time at a local accounting firm. As the time demanded by the two children, Nancy, 9 and John, 7, has declined, her part-time work has steadily expanded. In a few years she hopes to return to full-time employment.

23

Personal
Financial
Planning

Like many people, the Steeles are not experiencing any unusual financial stress. They live a comfortable life in their own home near a relatively large Midwestern city. Also, like most of us, they have achieved all this without much in the way of serious financial planning. Of course, they have some general idea of what their monthly inflows and outflows are, but they never really sat down as a family to specify their financial goals and come up with an orderly plan for achieving them.

Lately, they have come to the conclusion that a casual review of their expenditures and income might not adequately prepare them for future and long-term needs. As of now, they have not yet fully considered how they will provide for the children's college educations, or for their own support in retirement. These and other related questions are too important for the casual planning they have done so far. The tools developed in this text will help them plan for whatever may be on their financial horizon.

Summary

Planning for personal finance needs is necessary for all of us. In this chapter we have introduced you to the planning process, a process that involves setting concrete goals, devising action plans to achieve goals, evaluating performance, and deciding which goals are worth continuing to pursue. We have also explored several basic techniques and concepts that form the framework for making financial decisions—marginal analysis, opportunity cost, and the time value of money. Finally, we have considered the changing nature of the financial environment and how financial plans should respond by reducing economic risk rather than by relying on accurate forecasting.

Key Terms

"building-block" approach to personal finance (p. 13)

business cycle (p. 21)

compound interest (p. 15)

Consumer Price Index (CPI) (p. 19)

current consumption (p. 7)

financial independence (p. 7)

financial planner (p. 17)

financial success (p. 6)

forecasting (p. 22)

future consumption (p. 7)

future value (p. 15)

inflation (p. 19)

inflation rate (p. 20)

interest rate (p. 20)

life-cycle planning (p. 8)

marginal analysis (p. 14)

opportunity costs (p. 14)

planning (p. 22)

principle of diminishing marginal satisfaction (p. 7)

savings (p. 7)

simple interest (p. 16)

Problems and Review Questions

1 Give a definition of financial success and discuss how it may be measured.
2 Discuss the choice of financial and nonfinancial goals and the part each may play in personal financial planning.
3 What are the phases of the life cycle and how do they relate to financial planning?
4 Explain the steps involved in financial planning and list the eight major planning areas.
5 What does a building-block approach to success entail, and how does it reduce the risk of failure?
6 Explain marginal analysis and opportunity cost and then indicate why they are important concepts in financial decision making.

7 How would you measure the cost of spending a night at home watching television?

8 How does simple interest differ from compound interest?

9 You deposit $100 in a bank account earning 8 percent a year compounded once *annually*. Assuming you have not withdrawn anything, how much do you have in the account after two years? How much would you have if you withdrew each year's interest? Calculate your interest earned in each case.

10 What organizations certify individuals as qualified financial planners? Is it necessary to be certified as a financial planner to practice financial planning? Explain.

11 What is the relationship between the rate of inflation and the rate of interest? Explain.

12 Why do longer-term investments tend to earn a higher annual rate of return than shorter-term investments?

13 If you expect the inflation rate next year will be 10 percent, what do you think a short-term (one-year) investment in U.S. Treasury securities should yield? Defend your answer.

14 What are the four common phases of the business cycle? Which phase is sometimes replaced by a depression? High rates of inflation usually occur in which phase?

15 How does planning differ from forecasting?

Case 1.1
The Haggertys' Financial Planning

Jan and Mickey Haggerty graduated from college several years ago. Each majored in biology, and they were fortunate to receive good job offers at graduation; their combined income last year was over $50,000. The Haggertys enjoy a high level of current consumption, but they also have saved about $6,000, which is invested in a bank savings account. They would like to buy a house eventually, but they are not certain when. Jan thinks they should have a definite plan for buying the house. This plan would indicate the date of purchase, the down payment, the expected purchase price, and other important details. Jan is so enthusiastic over the purchase that she thinks they should take their money out of savings and invest it in growth stocks. She has heard that you ought to get 20 percent on these stocks, which certainly beats the 6 percent they are getting at the bank.

Mickey thinks Jan worries too much about buying a house. He questions the necessity of a financial plan, believing instead that they should just continue saving in the future as they have in the past. Besides, he heard at work that a recession could be coming, and if it does, he thinks it might be a good idea to delay buying stocks until their prices come way down. He heard you make money in the stock market by buying low and selling high. While Jan would like to buy the house within five years, Mickey thinks setting a date is not wise. If the stocks work out well, they get it sooner; if not, they have to wait. Besides, a friend of Mickey's told him he should worry more about all the income taxes he and Jan are paying, since they already are in a 28 percent tax bracket.

Questions
1 Without knowing more about the Haggertys, would you say they might benefit from financial planning? Cite specific examples.
2 What do you think of Jan's idea of investing in growth stocks? What additional information about the Haggertys would you like to have before you give a final answer to this question?
3 What is your opinion of Mickey's idea to delay buying common stocks until their prices fall? Do you think his source of information at work is a reliable forecaster? And do you think it's a good idea in general to base the success of your financial plans on accurately forecasting future economic events? Explain.

Case 1.2
Lou Pirella and Vicki Wright: Two College Students

Lou Pirella and Vicki Wright are taking a course in computer science together. They have been good friends for some time, and each will graduate at the end of the current term. Lou is going directly into the work force, while Vicki plans to earn an MBA degree at a university near her hometown. She is trying to convince Lou to join her, but he feels four years of college is enough—at least for a while.

Lou and Vicki have been talking quite a bit about their plans after graduation. Vicki is relying on her MBA to earn a good income in the future, although she also plans to invest, but only in very secure investments. Lou will take a more aggressive approach to investing, and he told Vicki he will probably earn two percentage points more than she each year. Vicki hardly thinks that's worth the effort; after all, 2 percent on a thousand dollars is only $20. Big deal. Both agree, though, they will take care of their insurance, housing, and liquidity needs before they start investing.

Questions

1 How should Vicki look at the opportunity costs of her MBA degree? Explain.
2 Do you agree that an extra 2 percent return is trivial and hardly worth taking any additional risk for? Illustrate your answer with a good example.
3 Suppose that when Vicki registers at the university, she learns that she can pay a flat tuition of $3,000 a semester and take up to 15 credit hours (but no more). Or she can elect simply to pay $250 per credit hour and take as many hours as she wants each semester. Assuming it takes 60 hours to graduate and also assuming she could handle 20 hours a semester without threatening her grades, what is the marginal cost of the second option—that is, paying $250 per credit hour? What might be the opportunity costs of the first option? Explain.

Helpful Reading

Changing Times

Bodnar, Janet. *"Rethinking the American Dream."* March 1991, pp. 27–33.

Money

Bodnar, Janet. *"5 Crucial Financial Crossroads."* April 1990, pp. 31–41.

Koblinger, Beth. *"Tight Times for Twentysomethings."* August 1991, pp. 54–59.

Willis, Clint. *"Americans and Their Money."* April 1991, pp. 74–76.

The Wall Street Journal

Gottschalk, Earl C., Jr. *"CPAs Find Investment Role Too Taxing."* January 16, 1991, p. C1.

Malabre, Alfred L., Jr. *"Under Pressure."* June 17, 1991, p. A1.

Schultz, Ellen. *"Is a Financial Planner Really Necessary?"* May 13, 1991, p. C1.

———. *"Financial Planners Blur Their Price Tags."* May 29, 1991, p. C1.

Slater, Karen. *"Conflict of Interest Issues Cloud Financial Planning."* March 21, 1990, p. C1.

Helpful Contacts

American College
270 Bryn Mawr Avenue, Bryn Mawr, PA 19010

American Institute of Certified Public Accountants
1211 Avenue of the Americas, New York, NY 10036 (telephone 1-800-969-7371)

The International Board of Certified Financial Planners
5445 DTC Parkway, Englewood, CO 80111 (telephone 303-850-0333)
(If you are interested in a career in financial planning, ask for their publication, "Financial Planning as a Career." If you are thinking of using a financial planner, ask for their publication, "How to Select a Financial Planner.")

2

Career Planning and Preparation: Your Long-Term Goals

Objectives

1 To undertake an ordered approach to career planning
2 To obtain information on career opportunities
3 To describe important factors determining income levels
4 To discuss the evolving job market
5 To review the costs of higher education
6 To state the most successful job search method
7 To evaluate fringe benefits

From the Ring to the Pits

Even if Jack Sandner, at five feet 7½ inches, didn't wear Lucchese cowboy boots with 1½ inch heels, the other traders who shout, shove, and speculate their days away in the pits of the Chicago Mercantile Exchange would still look up to him. A boxer turned lawyer, Sandner, 44, uses both backgrounds to win big in the hyperaggressive world of commodity futures trading. For 11 years the wiry blond, who raises his hands in Rocky-style clenched fists when he trades, has been scoring knockouts in cattle, currency, and index futures. Today he is a self-described multimillionaire who lives in top-of-the-line Lake Forest in the mansion once inhabited by the Swift meat-packing dynasty. That's 60 miles and worlds away from the squalid South Side streets where he was raised.

James Cagney could have played Sandner. The fiery-tempered son of an Irish father and an Italian mother, he dropped out of high school and started sparring at a Catholic Youth Organization gym. After a strong 58–2 amateur record, Sandner was recruited by several colleges. Applying the discipline he had learned in the ring, Sandner graduated in 1965 in the top 5% of his Southern Illinois University class. Then Notre Dame Law School rejected his late application, but Sandner appealed to the dean in person. Won over—and tired out—by an hour and a half of pleadings, the dean admitted Sandner. He graduated with honors in 1968.

After law school, the South Side friends who had stolen cars as teenagers now came to him to defend them for auto theft and even murder. In 1973 he won a personal-injury case for the wife of Everette Harris, the chairman of the Mercantile Exchange. Harris saw in Sandner's spunk and preparation a one-two combination that would make him a great trader. He encouraged Sandner to scrape together $80,000 and buy an exchange seat.

Trading on his lunch hour, Sandner soon became obsessed. After a profitable year and a half, he began trading full time.

Sandner works 14-hour days, but he devotes his weekends to his family—his wife of 17 years, Carole, and five adopted children, ages two to 17. After the children have gone to bed, he works on a suspense novel about a conspiracy to suppress a cure for cancer. Several agents have offered to supply a ghostwriter, but Sandner won't give in. His long-considered viewpoint: "It's the journey, not the destination, that's important."

SOURCE: Excerpted from "Trading's Diminutive Rocky," *Money*, July 1986, pp. 58–60. The excerpts are reprinted from MONEY Magazine by special permission; copyright 1986, The Time Inc. Magazine Company.

Jack Sandner's story demonstrates that a career is a process. It is a path that may twist and turn, taking you from boxer to lawyer to trader. It's part luck (an understanding dean) and part ability (a 58–2 record). Those who succeed are able to draw upon seemingly unrelated experiences and prosper from them.

You can actively select a career or fall into one inadvertently. Whether you choose or not, you will eventually find yourself in an occupation. Some argue that selecting an appropriate career today can help you avoid wasting time and money on unnecessary education and training. Others suggest that you put off career choices until you have sampled various disciplines and occupations. As usual, the best advice is to avoid extremes and choose a path somewhere between these two points of view.

We believe that every individual can benefit from financial planning. Moreover, a complete financial plan must take account of expected future income, which is highly dependent upon your choice of career. Thus, career planning is a prerequisite to successful financial planning.

Choosing a Career

Career planning can be looked upon as a three-step process. First, engage in a self-evaluation of your likes, dislikes, and aptitudes, and in a survey of those occupations that most closely match your own personal characteristics. Second, gather additional information on job opportunities and requirements for those occupations that are likely career choices. Third, set career goals and devise a plan for achieving those goals. Throughout this process, remain flexible and be ready to return to any of the previous three steps when new information and new opportunities arise. The best goals and plans are those that can be adapted to an uncertain and changing environment.

Self-Evaluation

When choosing a career, you should start by listing your interests and abilities. Does science or art interest you? Is money or recognition important to you? Once you have answered these and other relevant questions, you will be better able to choose a career that matches your personal characteristics. It should be obvious that the better the match between occupational requirements and your own likes and aptitudes, the more likely you are to achieve satisfaction and success.

If you have trouble determining your likes and aptitudes, you may want some professional help. The guidance counselor at the school you attend can provide testing that may help you better understand your own desires and find occupations that most closely fulfill those needs. If you are not in school, these same services may be available for a minimal fee at a local state or city school, or at your state employment service. Before employing a private counselor, be sure to seek recommendations and check credentials. The International Association of Counseling Services accredits counseling services throughout the nation and can provide a list of accredited services in your area.

Information on the abilities and skills needed for success in numerous occupations can be found in the *Occupational Outlook Handbook*, published by the U.S. Department of Labor. This information can prove helpful if you have identified your interests but are uncertain about which careers might best fulfill them.

Obtaining Information on Career Opportunities

Information on careers can be found at your school's placement office and at the library. The reference department at most libraries will have publications on career opportunities. The *Occupational Outlook Handbook* is also helpful in providing information on educational and training requirements, advancement possibilities, earnings, and job outlooks for about 250 occupations that represent about 86 percent of all jobs in the economy.

A related publication, the *Occupational Outlook Quarterly*, has timely articles that usually summarize the most recent information the Labor Department has collected on labor market prospects. It also contains some very good articles that survey various occupations and attempt to match up personal characteristics with career choices.

If you desire further information on a particular profession or industry, contact the professional or trade association representing that group. Most will be pleased to provide additional materials on job opportunities and salaries in their field. In addition, many of these organizations publish periodicals that provide information on current industry conditions. The addresses for many trade and professional groups can be found in the *Occupational Outlook Handbook*, or the *Encyclopedia of Associations*.

Setting and Revising Goals

Goals are meant to be achieved. They are not simply daydreams. As you acquire additional information and your tastes change, you may find that your original goals are no longer attainable or desirable. If you created flexible goals, you can easily revise them in light of new information. It is thus to your advantage to avoid specializing in any one area until it appears beneficial to do so.

The sooner you specialize, the harder it is to change career plans. Economists who deal with human-resource planning generally prefer systems that provide for specialization only at the later stages of training, because these systems tend to be more flexible. For example, suppose all college students were forced to pick a specific major in their freshman year and then could not change majors throughout the rest of their four years of undergraduate training. The educational system would then require four years to respond to changes in industry demands for a specific major. In most programs, however, specialization occurs largely in the junior and senior years, cutting the response lag to two years.

Specialization cannot be put off indefinitely, because most occupations require some level of specialized training. Like all problems in personal finance, determining the best time to move from generalist to specialist can be solved by examining the **marginal** (or additional) **benefits** against the **marginal** (or additional) **costs**. Specialization provides additional benefits because it allows you to prepare more adequately for a given occupation. Specialization provides additional costs because it limits your choices. When the additional benefits outweigh the costs, you have found the best time for a specific career choice.

No matter what career you choose, you must set goals that accurately encompass your likes, aptitudes, opportunities, and financial resources. The purpose of financial planning is to maximize your welfare. This is not necessarily the same as maximizing your bank account. To choose a career that appears to enhance your wealth, but does not satisfy your own likes or desires, may lead to disappointment and financial failure. If your goal setting does take these characteristics into account, you have more than a daydream—you have an achievable objective.

Marginal benefits and marginal costs: Benefits and costs that depend upon the current decision. They represent additional benefits and costs.

Income Considerations

While potential income should not be the only piece of information on which you base your career decision, it is nevertheless an important consideration. If you choose an occupation that ranks low on the income scale, be sure that the nonmonetary rewards compensate you adequately for the reduced earnings.

A prime example of the trading off of monetary for nonmonetary benefits is in college teaching. This profession requires the greatest amount of formal training, yet average salaries of college professors are significantly below those of other professionals with comparable training, such as medical doctors and lawyers. The most cited reason for this discrepancy is that the nonmonetary rewards from college teaching outweigh the income loss. For example, college teachers have substantial control of their working hours, giving them the opportunity to concentrate on topics of personal academic interest with little or no control from superiors. In addition, they receive a high degree of respect from the rest of the community. It is the willingness of teachers to work for low salaries in order to capture the nonmonetary rewards that lowers average salaries in this occupation.

EDUCATION Table 2.1 shows average annual earnings by selected characteristics of full-time workers. As can be seen, there is an apparent positive relationship between education and earnings. For example, those with four years or more of college earn over 80 percent more than those full-time workers with less than four years of high school.

Note that the data in Table 2.1 represent average earnings for an entire group of workers. Experiences of particular occupations and individuals can vary widely. For example, an individual with a high school education working on the Alaskan pipeline is likely to earn more than the typical college graduate.

You should also recognize that a positive relationship between earnings and education does not mean that more education is necessarily financially profitable. The cost of higher education, including the explicit costs of tuition, room, board, and books, and the implicit cost of lost income while in school, can be substantial. Each year the College Board collects information on the costs of going to college. For the 1990–1991 academic year, they found that the annual cost of tuition and fees, room and board, books and supplies, transportation, and personal expenses for a resident student attending a four-year public college averaged $6,991. As shown in Figure 2.1, the annual cost at four-year private colleges was even higher, averaging $15,318.

TABLE 2.1 · Median Earnings for Year-Round, Full-Time Workers in 1991 Dollars

	Male	Female
Total	$31,212	$21,433
Age		
15–24	16,914	14,897
25–34	27,268	21,502
35–44	35,320	23,457
45–54	38,588	22,810
55–64	37,649	21,708
65 years and over	37,218	23,465
Education		
Elementary:		
8 years or less	19,155	13,299
High school:		
1 to 3 years	22,985	15,192
4 years	29,034	19,125
College:		
1 to 3 years	34,161	23,602
4 years	42,079	29,143
5 years or more	51,111	34,971
Race		
White	32,566	21,684
Black	22,593	19,540
Hispanic origin	20,262	17,465

SOURCE: U.S. Department of Commerce, Bureau of the Census, *Current Population Reports*, Consumer Income, Series P-60, No. 168, Money Income and Poverty Status in the U.S.: 1989. Adjusted to 1991 dollars by authors.

The Basic Framework

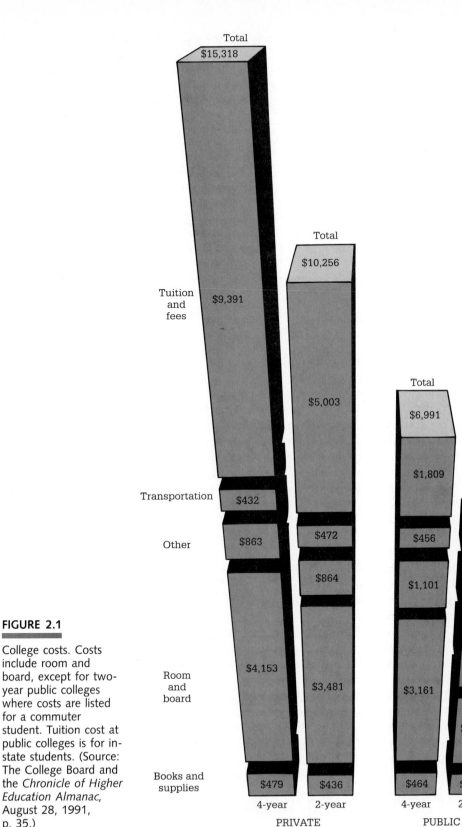

Total
$15,318

Total
$10,256

Total
$6,991

Total
$4,654

Tuition and fees: $9,391 | $5,003 | $1,809 | $456

$884

Transportation: $432 | $472 | $456 | $857

Other: $863 | $864 | $1,101 | $941

Room and board: $4,153 | $3,481 | $3,161 | $1,520

Books and supplies: $479 | $436 | $464 | $452

4-year | 2-year | 4-year | 2-year
PRIVATE | PUBLIC

FIGURE 2.1

College costs. Costs include room and board, except for two-year public colleges where costs are listed for a commuter student. Tuition cost at public colleges is for in-state students. (Source: The College Board and the *Chronicle of Higher Education Almanac,* August 28, 1991, p. 35.)

33

Educational costs weren't much lower for most students who commuted to school. The College Board survey found that their costs were only $1,400 to $2,100 lower than an average resident student's. Thus, even the least expensive college education will represent a major financial burden for most families. Furthermore, the costs listed in Figure 2.1 represent only the direct out-of-pocket expenses, or what may be called **explicit costs.**

By going to college after high school, instead of entering the work force directly, you are giving up some market wages you could have earned. These foregone market earnings represent the **implicit** or hidden **cost** of a college education, which can be quite large. The concept of opportunity cost, explained in Chapter 1, includes both explicit and implicit costs. A high school graduate employed full time will average about $65,600 over the four years immediately following graduation. If we add this implicit cost of lost income to the preceding explicit costs, even at a public institution a four-year college education can cost more than $93,000.

The educational investment is financially profitable only when the additional income generated by the education exceeds the cost of the education. Economic studies have shown that the benefits from higher education through four years of college typically outweigh the cost.

AGE AND EXPERIENCE   Not all training is received through formal education. Much can be learned from on-the-job experience. For this reason we would expect to see earnings positively related to age. Table 2.1 also contains an age–earnings profile for full-time workers. The data show a rapid increase in earnings between the early twenties and the mid-thirties, after which earnings appear to level off. Thereafter, earnings are relatively constant during the forties and into the fifties, and begin a preretirement decline before age 60.

A financial plan meant to accompany you over your life cycle should take this age–earnings profile into account. Your current level of savings and spending will depend not only upon your current earnings but also upon your age and your expected future earnings. For example, college students typically spend more than they earn by borrowing against expected future earnings.

SEX, RACE, AND DISCRIMINATION   In Table 2.1 we can also observe earnings differences by sex and by race. Some of the differential in wages may be explained by factors that influence worker productivity, such as educational attainment or intermittent participation in the labor force because of child rearing. Productivity may not explain all of the wage differential, however, and the unexplained residual may be attributed to discrimination. It exists whenever earnings are based upon characteristics unrelated to one's true market worth.

DEMAND AND SUPPLY   An employer is not likely to pay you more than necessary, and those workers who can most readily find jobs elsewhere are more likely to receive pay increases. This phenomenon is simply the common-sense outcome of the forces of demand and supply. Accordingly, your earnings prospects are better if you are in an expanding industry rather than a stagnant or declining one.

An analysis of wages shows that increases in earnings are closely tied to expansions in demand. When the Bureau of Labor Statistics ranked 247 occupations in terms of weekly earnings, they found that roughly half of the 20 jobs expected to grow the fastest had earnings in the top third of the ranking. Furthermore, as indicated in Table 2.2 and later, in Table 2.3, growth is likely to be fastest in occupations requiring the most education.

Job Opportunities

It is easy to find information on current job openings and income levels, but a career choice should depend upon other factors as well. Although you may be able to change careers later in life, the later the change, the more costly it will be. You would be better off to choose an occupation that will remain in demand over your entire work life, or at least until you finish your formal education.

The problem is that nobody can forecast the future perfectly. In fact, those who pride themselves on this ability are more often wrong than right. As a case in point, read the forecasts that appeared during the oil shortage of the 1970s. None of the disastrous consequences predicted by the futurists materialized.

Despite the inaccuracy of forecasting, certain general trends are worth considering because they give us some insight into what jobs might be in demand in the coming years. Four generally accepted trends will be discussed below:

1. The expansion of the services sector relative to the manufacturing and agricultural sectors
2. The aging of the population
3. The increasing educational attainment of the work force
4. The movement of the population to the Sunbelt and nonurban areas

TABLE 2.2 · Fastest Growing and Fastest-Declining Occupations

Occupation	Percent Change in Employment 1988–2000
Fastest growing	
Medical assistant	70
Home health aide	68
Radiologic technologist and technician	66
Medical secretary	58
Securities and financial services sales worker	55
Travel agent	54
Computer systems analyst	53
Computer programmer	48
Human services worker	45
Correction officer and jailer	41
Electrical and electronics engineer	40
Receptionist and information clerk	40
Fastest declining	
Electrical and electronic equipment assembler	−44
Farmer	−23
Stenographer	−23
Telephone and cable TV line installer and repairer	−21
Sewing machine operator	−14
Crushing and mixing machine operator and tender	−14
Textile machine operator	−13
Machine feeder and offbearer	−13
Hand packer and packager	−12

SOURCE: U.S. Department of Commerce, Bureau of the Census, *Statistical Abstract of the United States: 1990.*

Career Planning and Preparation

The Changing Nature of Production

The economic development of a nation may be divided into three phases. In the first phase the agricultural sector dominates the economy. In the second phase the nation industrializes, and manufacturing comes to the forefront. The last phase consists of rapid growth in the service sector and a dwindling importance for both manufacturing and agriculture. The U.S. economy is in this last stage of economic development.

Figure 2.2 illustrates the changes that occurred over a major part of this century. If we look back at the U.S. economy in the 1920s, we find that about 33 percent of the labor force was engaged in the agricultural sector. Labor market projections undertaken by the U.S. Department of Labor indicate that by 2000 only about 2 percent of the labor force will remain in agriculture.

The U.S. economy was already highly industrialized by the 1920s. At that time, the goods-producing sector—consisting of mining, construction, and manufacturing—employed slightly over 30 percent of the work force. This percentage share remained relatively constant until about 1970. Since then it has declined slightly. The Labor Department expects this trend to continue until at least 2000, at which time the goods-producing sector will employ only about 21 percent of the work force.

Where are these workers moving? No doubt, you have heard statements that the U.S. economy is entering the information age, in which most workers will either handle or manipulate data. This prediction may not be entirely correct. What does seem certain, however, is that most jobs will be service related. The decline in agriculture and goods production has been offset by the growth in the service-producing sector of the economy. This sector includes workers in government, transportation, communications, sales, and personal service. From less than 40 percent of the work force in 1920, this sector has grown to encompass about 74 percent of all workers. Labor market projections indicate it should increase still further, to about 77 percent by 2000. Consequently, look for expanding job opportunities in the service sector and declining opportunities in the manufacturing and agricultural sectors.

FIGURE 2.2

Labor force employment in the U.S. economy. (Source: U.S. Department of Labor, *Outlook 2000*.)

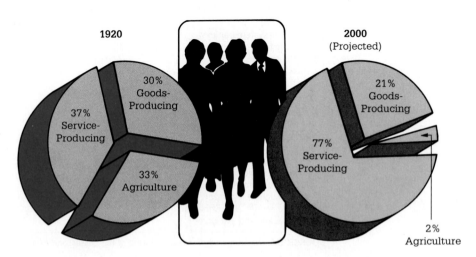

The Changing Age Structure of the Population

Baby boom generation:
The generation born
between World War II and
the mid 1960's.

After World War II, the U.S. birth rate increased dramatically. The persons born during this postwar period have become known as the **baby boom generation.** The annual number of births rose steadily, until they reached a peak of 4.4 million in 1957. For each of the years between 1954 and 1964, births topped 4 million, before declining and then stabilizing at about 3.7 million. The effect of these high birth rates on the age structure of the population is illustrated in Figure 2.3.

As a percent of the total population, those in the 24–44 age group reached a peak around 1990 at about one-third of the population. From this point onward their relative share will continue to decline, as the baby boom generation ages and enters the next age grouping in Figure 2.3. The final impact of the baby boom will occur with the expansion of the percentage share of those aged 64 and older. If the birth rate continues at its currently low level, this group's percentage share should increase rapidly during the first quarter of the twenty-first century.

As the population ages, its demands and needs will greatly influence the system of production and the provision of social services. In addition, we can expect an echo effect as the children of the baby boom mature. Look for job opportunities in industries serving the baby boom generation or their offspring.

The Changing Educational Structure of the Labor Force

The baby boom generation has also had a significant impact on the educational structure of the labor force. As Figure 2.4 indicates, with the entry of those new

FIGURE 2.3

Age Distribution of the U.S. Population from 1970 to 2000.

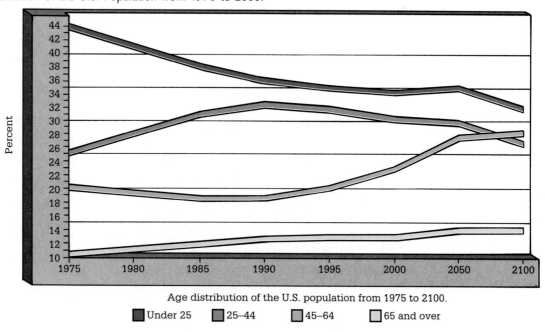

Age distribution of the U.S. population from 1975 to 2100.

■ Under 25   ■ 25–44   ■ 45–64   ■ 65 and over

FIGURE 2.4

Educational attainment
of employed civilians 25
to 64 years of age.
(Source: U.S.
Department of Labor,
Bureau of Labor
Statistics.

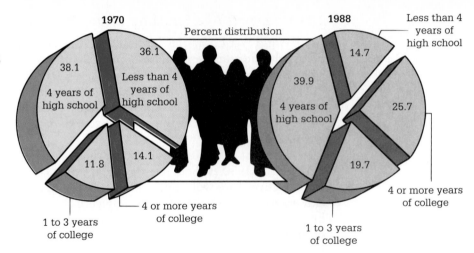

workers into the labor force, the proportion of workers without a high school diploma declined to less than half its original size between 1970 and 1988. During the same period, those with some education beyond the high school level rose from less than 26 percent to more than 45 percent of the labor force.

During the 1970s and 1980s, the baby boom generation pushed the supply of college graduates beyond the demand for them. This forced many of these graduates to accept jobs in occupations that did not traditionally require a college degree. With the decline in the number of births from the mid-1960s to the late 1970s, the U.S. Department of Labor predicts a more promising outlook for college graduates in the 1990s. In this decade the supply of college graduates should just slightly exceed the demand.

Given a surplus of graduates, employers may prefer to higher those with a college degree even when the job does not require one. In addition, the chances for promotion may be greater for college graduates than for their co-workers without degrees. This may help explain why, despite the excess of graduates in the 1980s, the gap in real incomes between those with and without a college degree continued to widen in the 1980s. In 1978, college graduates earned on average 30 percent more than high school graduates; whereas in 1988, college graduates earned a little over 50 percent more. This gap is expected to continue to widen during the 1990s as a result of limited opportunities for those without some advanced education.

The Changing Geographic Concentrations

Numerous articles have been written on the migration toward the Sunbelt. *Sunbelt* is an unfortunate term, because the population has been migrating not only toward the sunny states of the South, but also toward the Pacific and Mountain states. It is estimated that, during the 1980s, while the entire nation experienced a population increase of 10.3 percent, the Northeast expanded by 3 percent, and the Midwest increased by only 1.5 percent. During this same period the South had an above-average increase of 15.8 percent. However, the fastest-growing region was not the traditional Sunbelt, but rather the Pacific and Mountain states, with a remarkable 21 percent surge in population. Accordingly, the dominant pattern of migration may be described more accurately as being from the older, agricultural and industrial regions of the country toward the South and the more recently settled Western regions.

Figure 2.5 illustrates the changes in population forecasted for the 1990s. The overall increase in population is expected to decline to 7.2 percent during the current decade as the baby boom leaves the child-bearing ages. However, those regions in Figure 2.5 that are expected to grow at rates exceeding 7.2 percent are again located in the southern and western parts of the United States. In the near future, at least, the pattern should mirror that of the recent past.

The U.S. population is moving not only between regions but also within them. An exodus from the central cities toward the surrounding beltway areas continues, even though governments have pumped funds into the downtown areas in an attempt to revitalize them. Free publicity from the media has supported these ventures, and increases in the time and cost of commuting have encouraged workers to live closer to their jobs in the cities. Despite all this, the public has continued to vote with its feet for what they perceive as a more pleasurable life in the suburbs. The odds are very high that this trend will continue.

FIGURE 2.5

Projected percent change in state populations, 1990 to 2000. (Source: Signe I. Wetrogan, *Projections of the Population of States by Age, Sex, and Race: 1988 to 2000*, U.S. Department of Commerce, Bureau of the Census, 1988, p. 5.)

Projected Percent Change in State Populations: 1990 to 2000

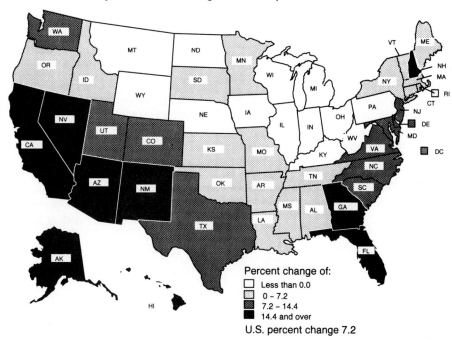

Percent change of:
- ☐ Less than 0.0
- ▨ 0 – 7.2
- ▦ 7.2 – 14.4
- ■ 14.4 and over

U.S. percent change 7.2

Career
Planning and
Preparation

Geographically, the most rapid expansion in job opportunities should continue to occur in the West and South, and in the areas surrounding large and medium-size cities. This expansion is expected to continue in the 1990s, although perhaps at a moderating pace.

The Jobs Forecast

Pumping the above and other information into their computers, the Bureau of Labor Statistics forecasts the growth in employment for over 340 occupations, a few of which are listed in Table 2.2. Their forecast to the year 2000 by major occupational group is presented in Table 2.3. Those occupations that require the highest level of educational attainment are expected to grow most rapidly. The fastest-growing grouping—professional specialty occupations—consists of such occupations as engineer, computer specialist, lawyer, health worker, and grade school teacher. Due to the continued decline in the manufacturing sector, operators, fabricators and laborers are expected to grow by only 1.3 percent, far below the growth in all employment of 15.3 percent.

The implication is that job prospects for white-collar and service workers should be favorable, with job prospects for blue-collar workers generally lagging behind, and jobs for farm workers actually declining. The most promising job market appears to exist for personal-service workers. These are workers who serve the public directly. Within this group, the food service and health service occupations are predicted to grow the fastest. The demand for these workers will increase because of the rise in two-income families, and because of the aging baby boom generation.

The Job Search

You have the experience and education for the career of your choice. You are going to find a job. The objective is to find the best one for you. This can be achieved by starting with a personal data inventory, including the information you will need to complete resumes and application forms.

According to job-search consultants, the personal data inventory should contain the following:

TABLE 2.3 • Actual 1988 and Projected 2000 Employment

Occupational Title	Percent of Employment		Percentage Growth in Employment
	1988	2000	1988–2000
Total, all occupations	100.0	100.0	15.3
Executive, administrative, and managerial	10.2	10.8	22.0
Professional specialty	12.4	13.3	24.0
Technicians and related support	3.3	3.7	31.6
Marketing and sales	11.3	11.7	19.6
Administrative support, including clerical	17.8	17.3	11.8
Service occupations	15.6	16.6	22.6
Agricultural, forestry, fishing, and related occupations	3.0	2.4	−4.8
Precision craft and repair occupations	12.0	11.4	9.9
Operators, fabricators, and laborers	14.4	12.6	1.3

SOURCE: U.S. Department of Labor, Bureau of Labor Statistics, *Outlook 2000*.

- Current address and phone number, as well as a phone number where messages can be left for you during business hours
- Job sought and career goal
- Experience, including your employment history, with the name and full address of each employer and your job title, starting and finishing salary, and reason for leaving each position
- Education, including the school's name and address, the years attended, the degree earned, and the course of studies pursued
- Other qualifications, including work-related hobbies, organizations you belong to, honors you have received, and leadership positions you have held
- Office machines, tools, and equipment you have used and skills that you possess
- Languages, both foreign and computer, and proof of proficiency

Your next step is to acquire information on the job market. Accumulate information on the jobs you are applying for and the companies offering those jobs. Figure 2.6 lists the usual sources of information on job openings. The best source, however, appears to be employers. Contact directly those businesses that might employ workers in jobs that interest you. Studies have shown that direct inquiries of prospective employers have been the most effective method of job search.

Direct contact means more than just sending out a letter of inquiry. It means calling up prospective employers and, whenever possible, going out to the job site to talk with potential employers and others associated with potential employers. Personal contact increases your chance of success. It is easy to turn down a written application. It is much more difficult to refuse someone a position in a face-to-face meeting. All other things being equal, the job applicant with the personal contact is going to get the job.

Although the direct application method appears to be the most promising, you should not commit yourself exclusively to any one method. Developing job-related personal contacts, called **networking,** is an important job-search tool. Ask friends and relatives about job openings where they work, register with a state or school placement office, contact professional societies and trade organizations, and answer promising newspaper ads. Studies have also shown that most successful job seekers have tried several methods before finding a job. Be resourceful, and don't let rejection get you down.

Networking: Developing personal contacts for career advancement.

The Resume

Resume: A short written account of your job-related qualifications and experience.

Whatever job-search method you use, you will likely need a **resume.** This is a short written account of your qualifications and experience. Much has been published on the subject, and you will find numerous articles stating authoritatively the exact format for a successful resume. These discussions may prove helpful, but in the end you should rely on your own common sense.

The resume is both an introduction and an advertisement. It should be no longer than one or two pages. When you have a lot of information to present, try listing your accomplishments rather than using a narrative approach. An employer with numerous applicants to screen is unlikely to read a ten-page biography. Additional information may be offered in a cover letter. If you pass the

41

Where to Learn About Job Openings
- State employment offices.
- Civil service announcements (federal, state, local.
- Classified advertisements:
  Local and out-of-town newspapers.
  Professional journals.
  Trade magazines.
- Labor unions.
- Professional associations (state and local chapters).
- Libraries and community centers.
- Women's counseling and employment programs.
- Youth programs.
- School or college placement services.
- Employment agencies and career consultants.
- Employers.
- Parents, friends, and neighbors.

Interview Preparation
- Learn about the organization.
- Have a specific job or jobs in mind.
- Review your job qualifications.
- Be prepared to answer general questions about yourself.
- Review your resume.
- Arrive before the scheduled time.

Personal Appearance
- Do not chew or smoke.
- Dress appropriately.
- Be well groomed.

At the Interview
- Answer each question concisely.
- Be prompt in giving responses.
- Use good manners.
- Use proper English and avoid slang.
- Be cooperative and enthusiastic
- Ask questions about the position and the organization.

Test (if employer gives one)
- Listen carefully to instructions.
- Read each question carefully.
- Write legibly and clearly.
- Budget your time wisely.

Information to Take with You
- Social Security number.
- Driver's license number.
- Resume contain information on your
- Education, including school name or number and address; curriculum; dates of attendance; highest grade completed or date or graduation.
- Employment, including for each job: name of employer; address of job; job title; dates of employment.
- References. Usually an employer requires three references. Get permission from people before using their names. If you can avoid it, do not use the names of relatives. For each reference, give the following information: name, address, telephone number, and occupation.

FIGURE 2.6

Tips for job seekers. (Source: Adapted from U.S. Department of Labor, Bureau of Labor Statistics, *Occupational Outlook Handbook,* 1990–91 ed., Bulletin 2350, p. 6.)

initial screening based on your resume, the reviewer may be willing to spend some time reading your cover letter.

You should already have the information needed for the resume listed on your personal data inventory. It must now be organized and presented in the most attractive way. The typical method is to organize the information into logical categories such as education, experience, and special talents. Within each category it is best to list the most recent information first. Although something you accomplished ten years ago may be of interest, the employer is probably more concerned about what you are doing now.

Organize the resume in a way that emphasizes your most significant category of achievements. If you think an employer would be most impressed by your educational background, start by listing that. If your educational record is not particularly impressive but your work experiences are, list your work history first.

Box 2.1
Simplifying Personal Finance

Letter of Application

In many fields of work, writing a letter of application is the customary way to ask for a personal interview. This is particularly true in the following cases:

- When the employer you wish to contact lives in another city or town

- As a cover letter when you are mailing resumes

- When you are answering an ad

The following guidelines may help you write a letter of application:

- Type neatly, using care in sentence structure, spelling, and punctuation.

- Use a good grade of letter-sized white bond paper.

- Address your letter to a specific person, if possible (use city directories or other sources).

- State exactly the kind of position you are seeking and why you are applying to the particular firm.

- Be clear, brief, and businesslike.

- Enclose a resume.

Letters of application will vary considerably depending on the circumstances in which they are used. The sample illustrates one way of writing such a letter.

(This letter refers to the accompanying resume, which uses a narrative approach successfully.)

---

304 Amen St.
San Francisco, CA 94102
(415) 778-0000

[date]

Mr. Wilbert R. Wilson
President, XYZ Company
3893 Factory Boulevard
Cleveland, Ohio 44114

Dear Mr. Wilson:

Recently I learned through Dr. Robert R. Roberts of Atlantic and Pacific University of the expansion of your company's sales operations and your plans to create a new position of sales director. If this position is open, I would appreciate your considering me.

Starting with over-the-counter sales and order service, I have had progressively more responsible and diverse experience in merchandising products similar to yours. In recent years I have carried out a variety of sales promotion and top management assignments.

For your review I am enclosing a resume of my qualifications. I would appreciate a personal interview with you to discuss my application further.

Very truly yours,

John W. Doe

Enclosure

John W. Doe
304 Amen St.
San Francisco, Calif. 94102
778-0000

[date of resume]

OBJECTIVE: Sales Executive

SALES PROMOTION

Devised and supervised sales promotion projects for large business firms and manufacturers, mostly in the electronics field. Originated newspaper, radio, and television advertising and coordinated sales promotion with public relations and sales management. Analyzed market potential and developed new techniques to increase sales effectiveness and reduce sales costs. Developed sales training manuals. As sales executive and promotion consultant handled a great variety of accounts. Sales potentials in these firms varied from $100,000 to $5 million per annum. Was successful in raising the volume of sales in many of these firms 25 percent within the first year.

SALES MANAGEMENT

Hired and supervised sales staff on a local, area, and national basis. Established branch offices throughout the United States and developed uniform systems of processing orders and sales records. Promoted new products as well as improving sales of old ones. Developed sales training program. Developed a catalog system involving inventory control to facilitate movement of scarce stock between branches.

MARKET RESEARCH

Devised and supervised market research projects to determine sales potentials, as well as need for advertising. Wrote detailed reports and recommendations describing each step in distribution, areas for development, and plans for sales improvement.

SALES

Retail and wholesale. Direct sales to consumer, jobber, and manufacturer. Hard goods, small metals, and electrical appliances.

ORDER CLERK

Received, processed, and expedited orders. Trouble shooter. Set up order control system which was adopted for all branches.

FIRMS

1983–1992	B.B. Bowen Sales Development Co., San Francisco, Calif.	Sales Executive
1975–1983	Appex Sales Research Corp. Oakland, Calif.	Sr. Sales Promotion Mgr.
1970–1975	Dunnock Brothers Electronics Co., San Francisco, Calif.	Order Clerk, Salesworker, Sales Mgr.

EDUCATION

University of California, B.S. 1970; *Major:* Business Admin.

PERSONAL DATA

Birth date, January 4, 1948. Married, three children.

SOURCE: U.S. Department of Labor, Employment, and Training, *Merchandising Your Job Talents.* pp. 12–13.

You might even consider having more than one resume if you are applying for more than one type of job or contacting employers who appear to emphasize different qualifications.

Your resume should answer an employer's unspoken questions, not create them. If your background and training do not appear to coincide with the needs of the employer, you must somehow explain this in either the cover letter or the resume. Likewise, don't leave large blocks of time unexplained. If you spent a year sailing around the world, state so.

The gravest harm you can do to yourself is to submit a messy resume. Proofread what you write, have a friend proofread it, and then have a third person proofread it. A sloppy resume reflects on the person who wrote it. If this person can't take the time to prepare a presentable resume, will he or she devote adequate effort to the job?

The Interview

At your initial interview, first impressions are inevitably important. In such situations it is best to be prepared and to be yourself.

If you have engaged in the career planning process, you will have given some thought to your objectives and goals. During your interview, you will likely be asked to verbalize those thoughts. Be prepared to express yourself in as clear and precise a manner as possible. Besides knowing yourself, you should also know the employer. Find out all you can, perhaps by going to the library and reviewing financial reports on the firm, or by talking with current employees or people who do business with this firm. Knowledge of what the organization does and what its objectives are will enable you to carry on an intelligent conversation.

Be prepared for the 21 most-often-asked questions listed in Figure 2.7. Don't attempt to memorize answers. Rather, review how you might answer the questions during the interview. When you feel you can handle them comfortably, you should be ready. This preparation is important, because the answers to many of these questions will tell the employer whether or not you have given adequate consideration to your choice of career and your choice of employer.

It's a mistake to try to give the impression that you are someone you are not. Most of us are poor actors, and an experienced interviewer will easily detect an attempted coverup. Remember, should you gain the job based upon a false impression, you will have to continue that act every day.

The primary purpose of the interview is to provide the employer with information on your background and personality. Given the opportunity, you may also use it to gain information on the opening and the company. *Occupational Outlook Quarterly* suggests that you might ask the following questions of the interviewer.

- What would a day on the job be like?
- Would I supervise anyone? May I meet them?
- How important is this job to the company?
- What training programs are offered?
- What advancement opportunities are offered?
- Why did the last person leave this job?
- What is that person doing now?

FIGURE 2.7

Be prepared for the interview: 21 questions. (Source: Price, Waterhouse & Co. and the Career Resource Center at the University of Florida, The Accounting Interview.)

1. Why would you like to work for our firm?
2. What are your career ambitions?
3. Tell me about your work experiences! What did you gain from them?
4. How did you like your university courses?
5. Tell me about your extracurricular activities.
6. What made you choose your major?
7. What makes you think you could be successful in this job?
8. What leadership experience do you have?
9. What course did you like best? Least? Why?
10. What are your geographic preferences? Why?
11. How do your work experiences relate to our job openings?
12. What made you choose this university?
13. What do you know about our firm?
14. Do you plan to go to graduate school?
15. What, in your opinion, are the personal characteristics neccessary for success in your chosen field?
16. What do you want to be doing five years from now?
17. What two or three things are most important to you for an initial job assignment?
18. What criteria are you using to interview employers?
19. What are your strengths? Weaknesses?
20. How do you get along with your fellow workers?
21. Why should we hire you?

- What is the greatest challenge of this position?
- What plans does the company have with regard to . . . ? (Mention some development of which you have read or heard.)
- Is the company growing?

After the interview, analyze what went right and what went wrong. Write out responses to questions that were difficult to answer, and make a list of ways in which you might improve your performance on the next interview. Finally, be sure to send the interviewer a follow-up letter thanking him or her for the job consideration. The letter serves to reinforce your impression on the interviewer. Furthermore, it is a convenient instrument for expanding upon topics discussed at the meeting. For example, if you forgot to state certain aspects of your background that might interest the employer, mention them in the letter. Or if you are still uncertain of all the conditions surrounding the prospective position, include your questions.

Salary

Your research, undertaken before the interview, should have provided you with some idea about the going market wage rate for the position you are seeking. If the interviewer asks for your salary requirements, don't sell yourself short. Moreover, be prepared to explain why you're worth every penny of that salary. The interview, however, is really not the place to negotiate your wage. This can be accomplished better after you are offered the position.

You may find yourself in the lucky position of having more than one employer bidding for your services. You will then have to decide among competing job offers. It is unwise to base your decision on the highest salary offer unless all other things are equal. Consideration should be given to relative working conditions, opportunities for advancement, job-related learning experiences, and most importantly, nonwage fringe benefits.

FRINGE BENEFITS As Figure 2.8 indicates, over 27 percent of total employee compensation consists of fringe benefits in addition to wages and salaries. A **fringe benefit** is a benefit received other than direct wages for time worked. It may include any of the items surveyed by the Bureau of Labor Statistics and

Fringe benefit: A job-related benefit other than straight wages and salary for time worked.

FIGURE 2.8

Fringe Benefits. Employer cost for employee compensation as a percent of total compensation, March 1990. (Source: U.S. Department of Labor, Bureau of Labor Statistics, *Employment Cost Indexes and Levels, 1975–90*, Bulletin 2372, October 1990.)

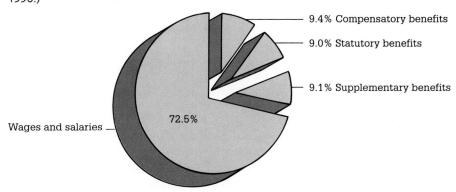

9.4% Compensatory benefits

9.0% Statutory benefits

9.1% Supplementary benefits

Wages and salaries — 72.5%

listed in Figure 2.8. Fringe benefits may also include perquisites. A **perquisite** is a nonsalary benefit provided to select employees as a sign of prestige. "Perks," as they are commonly called, may include a fancy office, an expensive company car, a paid membership in an exclusive country club, or free use of a company vacation home. Such perks are not surveyed by the Bureau of Labor Statistics and, therefore, are not reflected in the percentages in Figure 2.8.

Fringe benefits can be separated into three categories: statutory, compensatory, and supplementary. *Statutory benefits* are legally required benefits, including Social Security, workers' compensation, and unemployment insurance. These programs are jointly paid for by contributions from both employers and employees. *Compensatory benefits* are payments for time not worked, such as paid leave for vacations, holidays, or sickness. Some firms provide a leave bank that allows you to accumulate days of leave based upon your time on the job. These days may be withdrawn from the bank and taken as sick leave, personal leave, or vacation time. Plans that do not place restrictions on how the leave is used permit greater flexibility in arranging vacations or coping with emergencies.

All other benefits are classified as *supplementary benefits*. These usually consist of health insurance, pension plans, and life insurance. Employer-sponsored programs that provide for each of these coverages will be discussed in subsequent chapters of this text. For now you should realize that these items usually represent an important part of the compensation package, and that these benefits are usually tax advantaged.

Most supplementary benefits are either tax deferred or tax exempt. **Tax-deferred benefits** are those on which taxes come due only at some future date. The most common tax-deferred benefits are employer contributions to pension plans. The tax on such contributions does not become due until some future date, when you, as a retiree, are likely to be in a lower tax bracket.

Usually, employer contributions to health and life insurance plans are tax exempt. On **tax-exempt benefits,** the tax is permanently forgiven. Thus, the dollar value of fringe benefits will understate their actual value to the employee. For example, suppose you are in the 28 percent marginal tax bracket. This means that if you earn another dollar, you will have to pay the government 28 cents. You get to keep only 72 cents as after-tax income. Now suppose the prospective employer offers to provide $1,000 of medical insurance payments. In the 28 percent marginal tax bracket, you would have to earn $1,388.89 before taxes in order to undertake the identical insurance payments privately. The before-tax cost may be calculated using the following formula:

$$\text{Before-tax cost} = \frac{\text{tax-free fringe benefit}}{(1 - \text{marginal tax rate})}$$

$$\$1,388.89 = \frac{\$1,000}{(1 - 0.28)}$$

When two salary offers are compared, one with the medical insurance and one without, the salary offer without the fringe benefit must be at least $1,388.89 higher for it to be equally attractive in before-tax dollars. Thus, when comparing alternative salary offers, be sure to value the fringe benefits accompanying the direct salary payments. If the fringe benefits provide tax advantages, remember to value them at their before-tax cost to you.

Employers would like to see their dollars go into benefits that are most valued by their employees. **Flexible benefit plans,** also called cafeteria plans, permit workers to choose from a menu of benefits and benefit options, thus ensuring that the employer's dollars are allocated so as to provide the greatest benefit. In families with two market workers, it is unnecessary for both to carry employer-sponsored family health insurance, because one is covered on the other's policy. Under a flexible benefit plan, one worker may substitute alternative benefits, such as employer-sponsored child care, additional life insurance, or a tax-deferred savings plan.

Of all the fringe benefits, the one that is of the most concern to employers and employees is health insurance. The cost of employer-sponsored group insurance is often much less than an individually purchased policy. However, even group policies have dramatically risen in cost over the last decade. In order to hold down rising health-care costs, many firms have integrated "wellness" programs with their health insurance. These programs provide free or heavily subsidized training and exercise programs aimed at improving the health of the work force and decreasing medical expenses. More controversial are attempts made under some of these programs to regulate your off-the-job life-style by making your employment contingent on losing weight, lowering your cholesterol, or quitting smoking. The ability of employers to enforce such life-style changes is currently being argued in the courts.

COST-OF-LIVING ADJUSTMENTS About 41 percent of collective bargaining contracts in private industry contain cost-of-living adjustments (cola). Under an unrestricted **cola clause,** your wage base is adjusted each year to reflect the annual percentage change in the Consumer Price Index discussed in Chapter 1. Consequently, if consumer prices rose by 6 percent last year, then the wage base would be increased by 6 percent.

Many cola clauses, however, place restrictions upon when and how the inflation adjustment will be made. For example, some place a cap on the cost-of-living adjustment, while others require that inflation exceed a certain percentage before cost-of-living adjustments are made. Cola agreements also differ on what is included in the wage base. When health insurance benefits are included in the wage base, the rising employer cost of health insurance may offset increases in take-home pay even after a cola adjustment.

REGIONAL COST-OF-LIVING ADJUSTMENTS If your job search is not limited to a specific area of the country, you must take into consideration differences in regional costs. A dollar does not purchase as much in Chicago, Illinois, as it does in Indianapolis, Indiana. Fortunately, the Inter-City Cost of Living Index, published by the American Chamber of Commerce and found in many libraries, can be used to evaluate regional salary offers. For example, suppose you are trying to compare a salary offer of $30,000 from an employer in Chicago with a competing salary offer of $25,000 from a company in Indianapolis. The Chicago offer is higher, but so are prices in the larger city. Is the Chicago salary high enough to compensate you adequately for the relative higher cost of living there? Given the index values in Table 2.4, the following formula can be used to answer that question.

49

Metropolitan Area	Cost-of-Living Index
Atlanta, GA	100.9
Chicago, IL	128.7
Dayton–Springfield, OH	98.6
Denver, CO	101.6
Huntsville, AL	98.1
Indianapolis, IN	97.7
Miami–Hialeah, FL	113.9
Nassau–Suffolk, NY	152.1
Orlando, FL	102.7
Phoenix, AZ	102.0
San Diego, CA	131.4

SOURCE: American Chamber of Commerce Researchers Association, *Cost of Living Index: Comparative Data for 291 Urban Areas,* Vol. 24, No. 1.

$$\text{Salary offer city } A \times \frac{\text{index city } B}{\text{index city } A} = \text{equivalent salary city } B$$

Equivalent salary in Chicago to $25,000 Indianapolis offer:

$$\$25,000 \times \frac{128.7}{97.7} = \$32,932$$

Equivalent salary in Indianapolis to $30,000 Chicago offer:

$$\$30,000 \times \frac{97.7}{128.7} = \$22,774$$

As you can see the higher salary offer in Chicago does not cover the higher relative cost of living. This does not mean that you should necessarily reject the Chicago position. It does mean, however, that if you decide to move to Chicago, you should make sure that other, nonmonetary benefits compensate you adequately for the lower comparative real salary.

Self-Employment

Don't overlook the possibility of starting up your own business. Each year about 250,000 new firms are formed. Unfortunately, about 55 percent of these fail within five years. The risks are high, but so are the potential rewards.

The Small Business Administration, created by the Small Business Act of 1953, is designed to provide special assistance to newly formed small businesses. If you are thinking of going into business, you should contact the local office of the SBA. They can provide useful counseling and training for the new entrepreneur, in addition to much-needed financial assistance.

Summary

Financial and career planning are necessarily intertwined, because your choice of career will significantly affect your financial plans. Successful career planning is a three-step process consisting of self-evaluation, information gathering, and goal setting and revision. In this chapter we have examined several factors that are likely to have an important influence on your choice of career, such as income, future demand, and educational costs. Given adequate career planning and preparation, you should be able to make profitable use of the job-search techniques we have examined.

Box 2.2
What's New in Personal Finance

Fringe-Benefit Coverage

The Bureau of Labor Statistics regularly surveys fringe benefits provided by firms with 100 or more employees. The data from the most recent survey are in the accompanying table.

Retirement and health care represent the most important fringe benefits for most workers. Such benefits were offered by most firms, with 81 percent of those surveyed providing retirement benefits and 92 percent providing health-care benefits.

Among recently added benefits have been unpaid parental leave for mothers and fathers of newborn or newly adopted children. The maximum leave available averages 20 weeks. Paid parental leave is much more rare, with only 3 percent of firms reporting paid maternity leave.

A few firms, 3 percent of those surveyed, have begun to make available long-term-care insurance which would cover a stay in a nursing home. This is a service that is typically not included under traditional medical insurance. In most cases the cost of this additional insurance is paid entirely by the employee; however, the employee does get the benefit of group rates.

With regard to retirement plans, defined-contribution plans have been growing in importance. In these plans the employer and the employee make pretax contributions to an investment account. The amount available to the employee at some future date, such as the employee's retirement, will depend upon initial contributions and future earnings and losses on the account's investments.

The statistics in the accompanying table are for medium and large-size firms. Fringe benefits in firms with fewer than 100 employees are on average less generous than those in larger companies. For example, only 62 percent of full-time workers in smaller establishments are covered by medical insurance, whereas 92 percent of similar employees in larger firms have employer-sponsored medical benefits.

Full-Time Employees Participating in Selected Employee Benefit Programs in Medium and Large Private Firms, 1989

Employee Benefit Program	Percent
Paid	
Holidays	97
Vacations	97
Personal leave	22
Lunch period	10
Rest time	71
Funeral leave	84
Jury-duty leave	90
Military leave	53
Sick leave	68
Maternity leave	3
Paternity leave	1
Unpaid	
Maternity leave	37
Paternity leave	18
Health-care benefits	
Sickness and accident insurance	43
Long-term disability insurance	45
Medical care	92
Dental care	66
Life insurance	94
Retirement benefits	
All retirement plans	81
Defined-benefit plans	63
Defined-contribution plans	48
Other benefits	
Flexible benefits plans	9
Reimbursement accounts	23

SOURCE: Cathy A. Cooley, ''1989 Employee Benefits Address Family Concerns,'' *Monthly Labor Review*, June 1990, p. 61.

Key Terms

baby boom generation (p. 37)

career planning (p. 30)

cola clause (p. 49)

explicit cost (p. 34)

flexible benefit plan (p. 49)

fringe benefit (p. 47)

implicit cost (p. 34)

marginal benefits (p. 31)

marginal costs (p. 31)

networking (p. 41)

perquisite (p. 48)

resume (p. 41)

tax-deferred benefits (p. 48)

tax-exempt benefits (p. 48)

Problems and Review Questions

1 Discuss the three steps to career planning.

2 Suppose you decide to switch careers during your last year of college. What are the relevant explicit and implicit costs?

3 List several important factors influencing lifetime earnings.

4 The U.S. economy is experiencing significant changes. List and discuss the four trends examined in this chapter.

5 Over what approximate time period did the baby boom occur? How might the baby boom affect the economy over the next 30 years?

6 Describe some of the explicit and implicit opportunity costs of a college education.

7 Suppose you were considering two engineering programs. One is a straight four-year program, and the other is a cooperative five-year program. In the cooperative program you can earn $10,000 each year while working in a career-related job. Assuming that all other aspects of the programs are identical, what factors should you consider in choosing between the two programs?

8 List five sources of information on job opportunities.

9 Discuss some of the *dos* and *don'ts* of writing a resume.

10 What is the difference between a fringe benefit and a perquisite?

11 Explain why fringe benefits are an important component of total compensation.

12 Why is a dollar in tax-exempt benefits to be preferred to a dollar of tax-deferred benefits?

13 Given tax-exempt, employer-paid medical insurance benefits of $2,000, and a marginal tax rate of 28 percent, find the amount of taxable income necessary to purchase the same insurance benefit individually.

14 How does a flexible benefit plan enhance the value of fringe benefits?

15 If a job recruiter in San Diego were trying to match the real purchasing power of a $50,000 job offer made by another employer in Orlando, Florida, how much would the recruiter have to pay a potential employee?

Case 2.1 Joan Brady Decides Her Next Step

Joan Brady graduated from college four years ago with a B.A. in history. At that time, she had no employment prospects and had to settle for a job as a sales clerk. Fortunately, the department chain that employs her has a policy of fostering internal advancement. Because of her excellent on-the-job performance, she has been moved into a management position. Joan enjoys her new responsibilities and would like to move further up the management ladder. However, she feels that without formal business training, future advancement might be difficult. Therefore, she is considering returning to school for a master's degree in business.

If she returns to school as a full-time student, she could receive the degree in a year and a half. However, she would have to quit her current job. If she attends a night program, it will take her about five years to graduate. Of course, by going nights she could remain with her current employer. In order to make an informed decision, she would like to set out the explicit and implicit costs associated with each of the choices.

Questions

1 List the explicit costs associated with each choice.
2 List and discuss the implicit costs associated with each choice.
3 Discuss the potential benefits associated with each of the choices.

Case 2.2
Jim Vukovic Reviews His Career Alternatives

Jim Vukovic has been considering a career as a stockbroker. His primary responsibility would be to sell a variety of financial instruments to individuals. If he is successful with individual clients, he is likely to receive larger corporate accounts.

The brokerage houses offer on-the-job training lasting four to six months. During that time he will receive a salary ranging from $1,000 to $1,400. After the training period, his salary will be based primarily on sales commissions. Data from 1988 indicate that brokers with individual accounts averaged $71,000 a year, and those with corporate accounts averaged $240,000 a year. Jim also knows, however, that not all individuals who become stockbrokers remain in the profession long enough to earn these high salaries. A significant number leave the profession by the fifth year.

Questions

1 In order to become a successful stockbroker, certain personality traits are essential. Discuss the ones you think are important.
2 Explain how Jim might go about getting further information on a career as a stockbroker.

Helpful Reading

American Chamber of Commerce Researchers Associations. *ACCRA Cost of Living Index.* (Quarterly). ACCRA, P.O. Box 6749, Louisville, KY.

Baxter, Neale. *"Resumes, Application Forms, Cover Letters and Interviews,"* Occupational Outlook Quarterly, Spring 1987, pp. 17–23.

Bolles, Richard Nelson. *What Color Is Your Parachute? A Practical Manual for Job-Hunters and Career Changers.* (Annual Edition.) Ten Speed Press, P.O. Box 7123, Berkeley, CA 94707.

College Placement Annual. (Latest edition.) College Placement Council, Inc., 62 Highland Avenue Bethlehem, PA 18017.

Encyclopedia of Associations. (Annual Edition). Gale Research, Inc., New York.

Fountain, Melvin. *"Matching Yourself with the World of Work,"* Occupational Outlook Quarterly, Fall 1986, pp. 3–12. U.S. GPO, Washington, D.C. Also available as a reprint.

Mitchell, Joyce Slayton. *The College Board Guide to Jobs and Career Planning.* (Annual Edition.) College Board Publications, New York.

Stelluto, George, and Deborah P. Klein. *"Compensation Trends into the 21st Century,"* Monthly Labor Review, February 1990, pp. 39–45.

U.S. Department of Labor, Bureau of Labor Statistics. *Employee Benefits in Medium and Large Firms,* 1990.

U.S. Department of Labor, Bureau of Labor Statistics. *Employee Benefits Survey: An MLR Reader*, Bulletin 2362, June 1990.

U.S. Department of Labor, Bureau of Labor Statistics. *Occupational Outlook Handbook.* (Latest edition.)

U.S. Department of Labor, Bureau of Labor Statistics. *Outlook 2000*, Bulletin 2352. April 1990.

U.S. Department of Labor, Employment and Training Administration. *Merchandising Your Job Talents.* 1986 (revised).

Helpful
Contacts

International Association of Counseling Services, 5999 Stevenson Ave., 3rd Floor, Alexandria, VA 22304. Tel: (703)823-9800—accredits counseling services.

Chapter 3

Financial Statements: Where Are You Now?

Objectives

1 To understand the importance of the balance sheet as a tool for measuring personal wealth

2 To prepare a balance sheet by identifying and valuing assets and liabilities

3 To see that financial strength is measured by net worth and to understand how net worth changes over time

4 To prepare an income statement and to recognize its role in measuring financial performance

5 To appreciate that contributions to savings each year are more likely to happen when they are planned

6 To evaluate financial performance by using appropriate financial ratios

You learned in Chapter 1 that financial planning is a four-stage process: First, financial goals are set; second, action plans are devised for achieving these goals; third, a system is developed to measure the degree to which success is achieved; and fourth, based on an evaluation of achievement, goals and action plans are reexamined to determine whether they should be dropped, modified, or left unchanged. In this chapter and the next, our attention is directed toward the third task—measuring achievement. We are helped in this effort by accountants, who have devised three particularly useful statements that measure success. These are the balance sheet, the income statement, and the cash budget. Each is structured to answer a specific question about financial performance. The balance sheet determines your financial position *at a particular point in time*, usually at the end of the year. The income statement shows your income, expenses, and contribution to savings *over a past period of time*, usually the preceding year. The cash budget details estimates of your income, expenses, and contribution to savings *in the upcoming period*, usually the next year. As you can tell, the income statement and the cash budget are virtually the same. The important difference is that the income statement reviews historical events, while the cash budget focuses on events to come. From a planning point of view, the cash budget is the more important of the two, and it receives detailed coverage in the next chapter.

The Balance Sheet

Personal balance sheet: A statement designed to measure someone's wealth.

What are you worth? It's a good practice to ask yourself this question periodically. A loan officer at a bank most certainly will ask it if you apply for a loan. She will also ask you to prepare a **personal balance sheet** to aid her in determining whether or not you should get the loan. The balance sheet is designed to determine someone's wealth. It has three components: **assets,** items that are owned and are measured by their fair market values; **liabilities,** bills and other obligations owed creditors that must be paid in the future; and **net worth,** the difference between assets and liabilities. (Net worth is actually the accounting term for wealth.) A simple balance sheet for Mike Mason, a second-year college student, appears in Figure 3.1. Mike has only a few assets, the most important being his stereo unit and tape and record albums, and he has only two liabilities—$20 he owes Ed Bates and the balance due on his Visa card. Since the total value of Mike's assets is $1,311, and his liabilities are only $96, he has a net worth of $1,215 ($1,311 − $96) on December 31, 1992.

The word "balance" in balance sheet suggests a particular relationship among its three components. As Figure 3.1 shows, the balance is between assets on the one hand and the sum of liabilities and net worth on the other. Arithmetically, it is shown by the equation

$$\text{Assets} = \text{liabilities} + \text{net worth}$$

The equality always holds, because net worth can be either positive or negative. It is positive when the market values of assets are greater than the total value of all liabilities; it is negative when the reverse is true.

Listing liabilities ahead of net worth on the right-hand side of the balance sheet is done for a purpose, too: it reflects the legal claims creditors have in assets. Specifically, it means that in most cases (except bankruptcy), their claims to your assets rank before your own claims. This relationship can be seen with an example. Suppose you purchase a new car for $10,000, putting down $2,000 and financing $8,000 with a local bank. Ignoring all other balance sheet items, immediately after the purchase your balance sheet would appear as below:

$$\begin{array}{ccc} \$10,000 = & \$8,000 & + & \$2,000 \\ \text{(assets)} & \text{(liabilities)} & \text{(net worth)} \end{array}$$

After the first year of ownership, you may have paid off $2,000 of the loan, but if the car depreciated by $3,000, the new balance sheet would be:

$$\begin{array}{ccc} \$7,000 = & \$6,000 & + & \$1,000 \\ \text{(assets)} & \text{(liabilities)} & \text{(net worth)} \end{array}$$

If the car had to be sold at this point to raise cash, the bank's $6,000 loan balance would be satisfied first. After that is taken care of, then you can take what is

FIGURE 3.1

A balance sheet for Mike Mason prepared as of December 31, 1992.

Assets		Liabilities and Net Worth	
Cash on hand	$ 18.00	Loan from Ed Bates	$ 20.00
Balance in the checking account	75.00	End-of-month balance on Visa card	76.00
Clothing inventory	237.00		
Textbooks, school supplies, and similar items	81.00	Total liabilities	$ 96.00
Stereo unit and tape and record albums	900.00	Net worth	$1,215.00
Total assets	$1,311.00		
		Total liabilities and net worth	$1,311.00

left—in the above example, $1,000. You should also be able to see how negative net worth arises. If the car depreciated by $5,000 in the first year while the loan payoff remained at $2,000, net worth would now be a negative $1,000. Before we look more closely at assets, liabilities, and net worth, it should be remembered that financial planning aims to maximize net worth; it does not attempt to maximize assets. As you can see, regardless of how much your assets are worth, if your liabilities are greater, you have negative net worth. Technically and legally, you're insolvent.

Assets

Assets are things you own that have market value. They might have physical substance, such as jewelry or a house; or they may be pieces of paper, such as stocks and bonds, that give you rights to receive income or other benefits. Determining the total value of your assets takes two steps. First, you must identify and count all the items you own, and secondly, you need to determine each item's market value. This second step is often harder, even though some assets' values are easily determined: For example, a quick glance at the morning newspaper will tell you what a share of IBM stock is worth. But other assets, such as a diamond engagement ring purchased many years ago, have market values that can be only roughly approximated unless an expert is consulted. It is probably apparent that the usefulness of a balance sheet depends directly on how carefully it is prepared. If identifying or counting assets is done sloppily, or if market values are pulled out of a hat with little concern for their appropriateness, then the balance sheet isn't worth much—if anything. On the other hand, if identifying and counting are done accurately, and if time and care are given to determining market values, then the balance sheet is a useful instrument for measuring net worth and evaluating financial performance.

Assets and liabilities are often grouped on the balance sheet to make-evaluation easier. A balance sheet for a business firm, for example, normally lists assets according to their liquidity, beginning with the most liquid assets and progressing towards the least liquid. This approach is appropriate for a personal balance sheet as well, but it is also helpful to group assets according to their use. In this respect, there are three main categories: assets to satisfy liquidity needs, assets that are a part of our life-styles, and investment assets that can increase net worth or provide income for current use or for retirement. We now take a closer look at these three categories.

Liquid asset: Cash or any other asset converted to cash easily and with no loss in market value.

LIQUID ASSETS A **liquid asset** is cash or any other asset that can be converted to cash with a minimum amount of inconvenience and with no loss in market value. Currency and coins, of course, are the most liquid of all assets, and most people carry them to meet daily expenses, such as lunch, the dry cleaning bill, and many others. Since currency and coins provide no return and are easily lost or stolen, we usually try to minimize the amount held. To pay larger bills, and possibly to earn interest on daily balances, checking accounts are used; and finally, after we determine our minimum requirement here, we then can place our funds into many other kinds of liquid deposits that offer potentially higher returns. Examples of these are deposits offered by banks and other financial institutions, such as savings accounts, money market deposits, and certificates of deposit. Other examples are money market mutual funds and U.S. Series EE savings bonds. The total amount of liquid assets that you should hold and the specific kinds of deposits to hold depend upon your income level and your disposition towards risk.

Figure 3.2 shows a comprehensive balance sheet for the Arnold and Sharon Steele family that you met in Chapter 1. You will become better acquainted with them in this chapter and the next as we use their financial situation in 1992 to explain the balance sheet and income statements in this chapter and the budget in the next chapter. (Before going on, though, notice that further discussion of the various assets and liabilities can be found in the chapters indicated in the left-hand margin of Figure 3.2.) Arnold and Sharon have $16,240 in liquid assets, with most of it being held in their passbook savings account and certificates of deposit.

LIFE-STYLE ASSETS   Things that help us achieve the quality of life we want are our **life-style assets** (also called use assets.) Most families hold the greatest percentage of their total assets in them. This is particularly true if a house is purchased, since it is such a large investment; but many other similar assets are also "big ticket" items, such as household furniture and furnishings, appliances, automobiles, and possibly hobbies like coin and stamp collections. Naturally, ownership of these assets varies considerably from one family to another, depending upon family members' interests and activities. As indicated before, market values of some of these assets, such as a coin collection or an antique, may not be easily determined. Although you might be able to look up such values in appropriate manuals, the actual amount received in the marketplace could be very different from the prices listed. Marketplace prices are usually lower, reflecting selling costs and perhaps poorer physical conditions. For this reason, it is generally good practice to value assets of this type conservatively. You could start with a listed price, but then reduce it by 20 to 40 percent to reflect what the asset might actually bring if it had to be sold. The Steeles used a conservative approach to value all their life-style assets. They have quite a bit invested in their furniture ($20,000), since several items are fairly valuable and were given to Arnold and Sharon by their parents. The $16,000 value for the Voyager and $11,000 for the Honda were determined by referring to the "blue book" of used-car values available at their bank.

Referring to Figure 3.2, you can see that of the Steeles' total life-style assets of $261,500, $205,000 is in their home. They determined this value by observing the selling prices of homes similar to theirs and then deducting 7 percent to allow for a realtor's commission. The Steeles have done quite well with their investments in personal residences. They paid $65,000 for their first home in 1980 with a down payment of $7,000. They were fortunate to sell this home in 1986 for $90,000. They bought their current place in the same year for $180,000, taking out a $160,000 mortgage on it. At the end of 1992, their mortgage balance was down to $152,829, giving them an equity (current net market value minus the mortgage balance) in the home of $52,171 ($205,000 − $152,829).

INVESTMENT ASSETS   **Investment assets** are purchased for the purpose of providing additional income or increasing your net worth over time. Certain other assets, such as your house (as we have just seen), may also fulfill this function.

Life-style assets: Things that help us achieve our desired quality of life.

Investment assets: Assets that provide income or increase our net worth.

Financial
Statements

Discussion in Chapters	
	BALANCE SHEET at _December 21, 1992_
	For _Arnold & Sharon Steele_
	ASSETS
	Liquid Assets
6	Coins and currency on hand — $ 240
6	Checking account balances — 2,400
6	Other deposits at financial institutions:
	Savings Account — 5,600
	42-month certificate of deposit — 5,000
	—
6	Money market mutual funds — —
6	U.S. Series EE or HH bonds — 3,000
6	Other liquid assets:
	none — —
	none — —
	Total liquid assets — $ 16,240
	Life-Style Assets
9	Residence — 205,000
16	Vacation home — —
8	Furniture, household furnishings, and appliances — 20,000
8	Automobiles and recreational vehicles:
	1991 Voyager Van — 16,000
	1989 Honda Sedan — 11,000
	1987 Coleman Camper — 2,100
16	Jewelry — 4,000
8	Clothing — 1,400
8	Sporting equipment — 600
16	Hobbies and collections _(stamp collection)_ — 400
	Other life-style assets:
	1990 Toro riding mower — 1,000
	Total life-style assets — $ 261,500
	Investment Assets
13, 14	Preferred stocks — $ —
13, 14	Common stocks — 16,000
14	Corporate bonds — —
14	Government bonds — —
15	Mutual funds _400 shares of Fidelity Fund_ — 6,800

FIGURE 3.2

Balance sheet for the Steele family.

16	Business interests	—
10	Cash value of life insurance	4,000
10, 17	Cash value of annuities	—
17	Cash value of retirement fund	21,000
5, 6, 17	Individual retirement accounts (IRAs):	

Arnold — none —

Sharon - none —

	Total investments assets	(c)	47,800
	TOTAL ASSETS = (a) + (b) + (c) =	(d)	325,540

LIABILITIES

Current Liabilities

7	Unpaid bills Gas and Electric, Telephone		460
7	Credit card balances due		1,720
5	Estimated taxes due		1,750
7, 8	Installment loan balances due in one year:		
	Autos		4,424
	Others:		
	none		—
7, 8	Other current liabilities:		
	none		—
	Total current liabilities	(e)	8,354

Noncurrent liabilities

7, 8	Installment loan balances due after one year:		
	Autos		4,966
	Others:		
	none		—
9	Mortgage loans		152,829
7	Loans on life insurance policies		2,000
7, 13	Debit balances on margin accounts with stockbrokers		—
	Other noncurrent liabilities:		
	none		—
	Total noncurrent liabilities	(f)	159,795
	TOTAL LIABILITIES = (e) + (f) =	(g)	168,149
	NET WORTH = (d) − (g) =	(h)	157,391
	TOTAL LIABILITIES AND NET WORTH = (g) + (h) =	(i)	325,540

FIGURE 3.2

Continued.

Your ultimate goal might be to provide adequate funds for retirement, or to accumulate an estate to pass on to your heirs. You may also be investing for shorter-range purposes, such as providing for your children's college education. Whatever the reason, you need to invest your funds in assets that will provide a return that is at least equal to the inflation rate. Naturally, you would like to do even better than this, if you can.

A wide variety of assets can be held for investment purposes: stocks, bonds, business interests, real estate, cash values of insurance, annuities and retirement funds, and many others. These investments range from very liquid assets, such as high-grade, short-term Treasury bonds, to those that are virtually illiquid and extremely risky, such as a limited partnership interest in a private venture wildcatting for oil.

The Steeles have accumulated a reasonable amount of investment assets. They own 400 shares of a mutual fund and have invested in other common stocks, including those of the company Arnold is with, InChemCo. The stocks are quoted on the financial pages of their local newspaper, so finding their values at December 31, 1992, was quite simple. It was also easy to determine the cash surrender value of Arnold's life insurance policy, because this value is printed in the policy. To find the cash value of Arnold's retirement fund at InChemCo, however, he had to call the company's personnel office. The Steeles realize they must increase their investment assets if they are to achieve their retirement goal and the goals they have for educating John and Nancy.

Adding the total of investment assets to the total of life-style assets and liquid assets determines total assets. As you can see in Figure 3.2, for the Steeles this was $325,540.

Liabilities

At any point in time, most people have debt obligations. These obligations arise for a variety of reasons. You might use a bank credit card because of its convenience. If you don't want to use all your liquid assets to pay for one item, you might arrange an installment loan. Because you simply don't have enough resources, you obtain a mortgage loan to buy a house. Liabilities such as these are usually arranged on the balance sheet as current or noncurrent.

Current liability: A debt that must be paid within one year.

CURRENT LIABILITIES A **current liability** is any debt that must be paid within one year. There are two sources of current liabilities. First are unpaid bills. These come from your use of credit cards, or from direct purchases, as in the case of gas, electric, and telephone bills. The Steeles had $2,180 ($460 + $1,720) of these items. The second source consists of portions of installment loans that are due within one year. The Steeles are paying off two car loans over four years. The current liability portion is $4,424. We distinguish between current and noncurrent liabilities in order to better evaluate the Steeles' liquidity position, a topic we'll explain in more detail later in this chapter.

Noncurrent liabilities: Debt obligations beyond one year.

NONCURRENT LIABILITIES **Noncurrent liabilities** are all debt obligations beyond one year, and they are also of two types. The first type represents the noncurrent portion of loans with specific repayment schedules. Examples are installment loans on automobiles, furniture, and major appliances, or credit card balances being paid off on an installment basis. To illustrate, one of the Steeles' car loans extends into 1995 with portions payable in 1994 and 1995, which explains their $4,966 noncurrent liability. Another important example is a mortgage loan on a house or other property. The second kind of noncurrent liability consists of loans that do not have repayment schedules. A loan on your life insurance policy, such as the $2,000 loan the Steeles have on Arnold's policy, is one example. Another is a loan you arrange through a stockbroker, using securities you own as collateral (backing) to support the loan. This type of loan is called a broker's loan, and it is available with a specific type of account you can have with the broker, called a margin account. While these latter two kinds of loans do not require repayment, you do pay interest on them either at the end of the year (the life insurance policy loan) or at the end of each week, or even each day (the broker's loan). Adding noncurrent and current liabilities gives total liabilities; for the Steeles, this figure is $168,149 ($8,354 + $159,795).

Net Worth

As indicated previously, net worth is the difference between total assets and total liabilities. Even though this form of measurement has its problems, it is still the single best estimate of one's wealth. The Steeles' net worth at December 31, 1992, was $157,391. This figure was calculated in Figure 3.2 by subtracting total liabilities (item *g*) from total assets (item *d*). Net worth plays a crucial role in estimating financial strength, so we need to understand how it can change from one period to the next. Net worth can be changed in two ways: by cash flow changes and by market value changes.

Positive contribution to savings: Increase in net worth.

Dissavings: Reduction in net worth.

CASH FLOW CHANGES IN NET WORTH   Net worth increases whenever cash income exceeds cash expenses during a period. This situation is called a **positive contribution to savings;** conversely, if expenses exceed income, a negative contribution—call it **dissavings**—occurs, and it reduces net worth. The balance sheet illustration in Figure 3.3 shows the relationship of income, expenses, and a positive contribution to savings. The person in this case is paid a salary of $800 on June 1, which she deposits in her checking account and then uses to pay expenses of $600 during the month. When she receives her salary, her net worth increases by the amount of her income, but it is then reduced each time an expense is paid. By the end of the month, assuming there are no other income or expense items, the increase in her net worth—$200—is exactly equal to the difference between her income and expenses, which is her positive contribution to savings. Notice further that this contribution has increased her checking account balance by $200, but the funds may not remain there. She may use them eventually to acquire other assets or reduce her liabilities.

You should see that a positive contribution to savings leads to an increase in net worth that must be accompanied by either an increase in assets (as in the above example) or a decrease in liabilities, or a combination of the two. Conversely, a negative contribution means that assets are reduced or liabilities increased. Of course, a negative contribution can continue only as long as there are remaining assets to convert to cash or creditors willing to increase their loans.

Checking Account		Liabilities	
June 1 balance	$1,000	June 1 balance	$ 700.00
June 1: receive salary	+ 800	June 30 balance	$ 700.00
June 5: pay the rent	− 300		
June 9: pay food	− 200		
June 20: pay insurance bill	− 100	June 1 balance	
Change in the checking account during June	+ 200	**Net Worth**	$4,300
		Positive contribution to savings during month of June	+ 200
June 30 balance	$1,200		$4,500
Other Assets		June 30 balance	
June 1 balance	4,000		
June 30 balance	4,000		
		Total liabilities and net worth	
Total assets:			
June 1	$5,000	June 1	$5,000
June 1	$5,200	June 30	$5,200

FIGURE 3.3

Income, expenses, and a positive contribution to savings illustrated on the balance sheet.

MARKET VALUE CHANGES IN NET WORTH   Changes in net worth also occur when the market values of assets you own at the beginning of a period increase or decrease during the period. We saw previously the good fortune the Steeles have had in this respect with their personal residences; it has provided a major part of their total increase in net worth since their marriage. Several other of the Steeles' assets have shown steady increases in value each year; these are the cash values of their life insurance and retirement fund. The latter is especially important to them, since they are counting on it for a large portion of their retirement income.

While the value of many properties has followed the Steeles' experience, other assets often decline in market value over time and thereby reduce net worth. This is especially true of most automobiles and other consumer durables. It is also true of clothing, sporting equipment, and similar items. Of course, most of us want to own and use these things, but we should realize that a heavy investment in any or all of them may lead eventually to substantial decreases in net worth.

The Income Statement

Income statement: Detailed breakdown of cash income and expenses over a past period.

The **income statement** (sometimes called the statement of cash flows) presents a detailed breakdown of cash income and expenses over a past period. In doing this, it also provides a figure for the period's contribution to savings, and thus it becomes an important companion statement to the balance sheet. The income statement provides the opportunity to review how well you have done financially in the past period, and also to help you budget your income and expense items for the upcoming period.

In personal financial planning, the income statement is prepared on a cash basis, which means it does not follow strict accounting rules for determining net income. In this way it differs from the kind of income statement most businesses

Box 3.1
What's New in Personal Finance

Sources of Household Net Worth

What is the median net worth of a U.S. household, and in what assets is it held? Questions such as these have interested researchers for some time, and thanks to studies completed by the Bureau of the Census, we now are getting some definitive answers. But the studies probably don't surprise us very much or give information that we didn't guess before the data became available. What they show is that if you are a middle-aged, white, upper-income household, you will have considerably greater net worth than if you are a young, black or Hispanic-origin, low-income household. As the data below indicate, the overall median net worth in 1988 was $35,752, with differences from the median strongly correlated with age, race, and income of the household.

You might have guessed also that equity in the family residence is by far the major source of net worth (about 43.0 percent) and that most American households (86.3 percent) have some net worth in the family car(s). Also, a fairly large number have checking accounts (48.3 percent) but apparently keep rather small balances in them, because they represent less than 1.0 percent of net worth. Interest-earning deposits are the most important investment assets, and equity in a business or profession is

second. Real estate is also important as an investment, since 12.2 percent of net worth is represented by rental property and other real estate. Finally, although stocks and mutual fund shares are held by a fairly large number of households (21.8 percent), they account for only 6.5 percent of net worth.

SOURCE: U.S. Department of Commerce, Bureau of the Census, *Household Wealth and Asset Ownership: 1988.* Current Population Reports, Household Economic Studies, Series P.70, No. 22.

Median Household Net Worth (1988 overall median = $35,752) and:		
A. Age	Less than 35 years	$ 6,421
	35 to 44 years	40,264
	45 to 54 years	64,346
	55 to 64 years	83,750
	over 64 years	68,600
B. Race	White	$ 43,279
	Black	4,169
	Hispanic origin	5,524
C. Monthly income	Less than $939	$ 4,324
	$939 to $1,699	19,694
	$1,699 to $2,568	28,044
	$2,568 to $3,883	46,235
	$3,883 or more	111,700

Sources of Net Worth

Asset Type	Percent of Households That Own Asset Type	Source of Net Worth (adjusted for reporting error)	
		$	%
1. Own home	63.6	$15,296	43.0
2. Interest-earning assets at financial institutions	72.9	5,016	14.1
3. Business or profession	12.5	3,130	8.8
4. Rental property	9.0	2,810	7.9
5. Stocks and mutual fund shares	21.8	2,312	6.5
6. Vehicles	86.3	2,063	5.8
7. Other financial investments	6.6	1,067	3.0
8. Other real estate	10.5	1,530	4.3
9. Other interest-earning assets	9.4	1,494	4.2
10. IRA or Keogh accounts	24.2	1,490	4.2
11. Checking accounts	48.3	213	0.6
12. U.S. savings bonds	17.5	213	0.6
13. Unsecured liabilities	5.9	−882	−3.0
Totals	—	$35,752	100.0

show in their annual financial reports, which is prepared on an accrual basis. This difference does not diminish the statement's usefulness; on the contrary, it puts it more in line with the way most of us think of our incomes (or losses), which is in terms of cash flows. The Steeles' income statement for 1992 is shown in Figure 3.4 and discussed in the sections below.

INCOME STATEMENT for the Period _____ *Year Ended 12/31/92*

For _____ *the Arnold and Sharon Steele Family*

INCOME			Percent
Wages and Salaries:			
Arnold – InChem Co.		# 60,200	
Sharon – Todd and Talbot, CPAs		15,400	
Total wages and salaries	(a)	75,600	97.4%
Other Income:			
Interest		# 937	
Dividends		1,090	
Capital gains or (losses)		none	
Others		none	
Total other income	(b)	# 2,027	2.6%
TOTAL INCOME = (a) + (b)	(c)	# 77,627	100.0%
EXPENSES			
Housing:			
Rent		# none	
Mortgage payments		18,285	
Maintenance fees on condo or cooperative		none	
Maintenance and home furnishings		3,500	
Total housing expenses	(d)	# 21,785	28.0%
Transportation:			
Automobile loan payments		# 5,688	
Gas, oil, other maintenance and repairs		2,100	
Licenses, parking, and other auto		210	
Other transportation		none	
Total transportation expenses	(e)	# 7,498	10.3%
Food and Other Consumption Items:			
Food and household supplies		# 6,300	
Meals eaten out		1,210	
Personal care—barbers and beauticians		720	
Others		none	
Total food and other consumption items	(f)	# 8,230	10.6%
Utilities:			
Telephone		# 540	
Gas and electric		2,280	
Water and sanitation		510	
Garbage pickup		none	
Cable TV		420	
Others		none	
Total utilities	(g)	# 3,750	4.8%

FIGURE 3.4

Income statement for the Steele family.

				Percent
Taxes:				
Payroll		$	14,570	
Real estate and personal property			3,500	
Others			none	
Total taxes	(h)	$	18,070	23.3%
Insurance:				
Health and medical withheld from wages		$	none	
Life			480	
Property and liabilty			570	
Automobile			1,470	
Disability			none	
Others			none	
Total insurance	(i)	$	2,520	3.3%
Leisure and Entertainment:				
Theater and sporting events		$	870	
Health club memberships			none	
Newspapers, magazines, etc.			430	
Vacations			2,380	
Hobbies			280	
Sporting equipment			160	
Others _Family Christmas gifts_			890	
Total leisure and entertainment	(j)	$	5,010	6.5%
Clothing:				
New clothing		$	1,830	
Laundry and dry cleaning			290	
Others			none	
Total clothing	(k)	$	2,120	2.7%
Others:				
Gifts and charitable contributions		$	2,080	
Dues and subscriptions			200	
Tuition, books, other education expenses			390	
Babysitters			540	
Family members' personal allowances			1,300	
Unreimbursed medical–dental			1,040	
			—	
			—	
			—	
Total others	(l)	$	5,550	7.2%
TOTAL EXPENSES = (d) + (e) + (f) + (g) + (h) + (i) + (j) + (k) + (l) =	(m)	$	75,033	96.7%
CONTRIBUTION TO SAVINGS = (c) − (m) =	(n)	$	2,594	3.3%

FIGURE 3.4

Continued.

Income

Income: Cash inflows, consisting primarily of salaries and wages.

Income usually consists of cash inflows. As Figure 3.4 shows, there are many potential sources of income. For many people, Arnold and Sharon included, by far the largest percentage of their total income consists of wages and salaries. Arnie has a full-time position with InChemCo, but Sharon works only during the tax season—roughly January through April—with a CPA firm. The data arrangement in Figure 3.4 shows gross wages rather than after-tax, or take-home, wages. While you probably will do your financial planning with the take-home figure, it is also instructive to detail the actual amount of taxes you pay. This puts the total expense in perspective and underscores the need for effective tax planning. It is surprising how few people actually know how much in total taxes they pay—much less their effective tax rates—because they focus attention exclusively on take-home pay. You should look carefully at both.

The Steeles' total wages in 1992 were $75,600. Deducting from this the total payroll taxes of $14,570 leaves their combined take-home salary of $61,030. Arnold's and Sharon's salaries have increased rather nicely in the last several years, making it easier for them to achieve their financial goals.

The Steeles' $937 of interest income came from their passbook savings account, certificates of deposit, and U.S. Series EE bonds. They did not actually withdraw the interest earned on any of these deposits (you have limited access to the latter two), but instead allowed it to accumulate. The $1,090 of dividend income was earned on their common stocks and Fidelity Fund shares, and they did receive these dividends in cash. Adding the interest and dividends to their wages and salaries gives their total income of $77,627.

Expenses

Expenses: Cash outflows that sustain our scale of living.

Expenses are cash outflows that sustain our scale of living. They do not include all cash outlays, however. You would not, for example, consider the purchase of investment assets as expenses. Payments made on installment and mortgage loans are viewed as expenses even though formal accounting rules would probably require us to distinguish between payments of interest and principal in measuring income. (We are required to do this for tax purposes, because interest is an itemized deductible expense while principal payments are not. But our focus here is not on taxes.)

The breakdown of expenses in Figure 3.4 is typical of most income statements you are likely to encounter in loan applications and elsewhere. The list of expenses is fairly comprehensive, although you might prefer to arrange them differently. We'll distinguish between inflexible and flexible expenses when budgeting is discussed in the next chapter, but it is useful to introduce and explain these terms here.

Inflexible expenses: Expenses that are hard to control in the short run.

INFLEXIBLE EXPENSES   **Inflexible expenses** (also called fixed expenses) are often defined as those over which you have very little control in the short run. Some expenses are perfectly inflexible, meaning they never change in amount. Such expenses arise typically from contractual arrangements requiring payments of so much per period. As you review the expense categories in Figure 3.4, you most likely would pinpoint the following as examples: the mortgage payments of

$18,285, the automobile loan payments of $5,688, and maybe the life insurance premiums of $480. These expenses are often called **sunk costs** because the fixed amount must be paid regardless of what happens in the future; the only way out of them is to drop, pay off, or renegotiate the underlying contracts. Other inflexible expenses are not fixed in amount from period to period, but are nevertheless difficult to control. The Steeles' taxes of $18,070 are a good example of this type; we know they must be paid each year, but the actual amounts might differ each year, or even in each month of the year.

FLEXIBLE EXPENSES   **Flexible expenses** (also called variable expenses) are those over which you have some control, at least in the short run. A good example is home maintenance. Of course, some of these expenses are more flexible than others. Home maintenance expenses, along with doctors' and dentists' bills, are very irregular and are the most troublesome to deal with in budgeting. Others, however, are far more predictable, such as purchases of food and household supplies. Some flexible expenses might be paid in such a way that they become inflexible expenses. For example, gas and electric usage can be billed in equal monthly payments regardless of seasonal variations. Also, some flexible expenses go up or down along with your income. For example, if you use your car on the job, and you work more hours during a period, your car expenses will increase as your income rises.

Figure 3.5 shows a breakdown of the Steeles' $75,033 of total expenses in 1992. As you can see, the larger percentage is in the inflexible category, indicating that quite a bit of their expenses were set and predictable during the year.

Contribution to Savings

As explained earlier in this chapter, the excess of income over expenses is a positive contribution to savings (or savings, for short). It increases net worth and

FIGURE 3.5

A breakdown of the Steeles' 1992 expenses.

Inflexible Expenses		Flexible Expenses	
Mortgage payments	$18,285	Family members' allowances	$ 1,300
Automobile loan payments	5,688	Leisure and entertainment	5,010
Car licenses	210	Home maintenance and furnishings	3,500
All utilities	3,750	Gas, oil, and car repairs	2,100
All taxes	18,070	All food and other consumption items	8,230
All insurance	2,520	Clothing, laundry, and dry cleaning	2,120
Dues to professional societies	200	Gifts and charitable contributions	2,080
Tuition and books	390	Babysitters	540
		Medical-dental expenses	1,040
Totals	$49,113		$25,920
Total Expenses			

$75,033

Percentages
Inflexible = $49,113/$75,033 = 0.66, or 66%
Flexible   = $25,920/$75,033 = 0.34, or 34%

is a source of increases in assets or reductions in liabilities. In 1992, the Steeles made a positive contribution to savings of $2,594. Placing the contribution to savings figure last in the income statement seems to foster the notion that savings are something left over after everything else has been bought. Actually, this is a poor view toward savings that frequently leads to no savings at all, since there is usually some expenditure offering a quicker and more immediately satisfying return than savings. Placing savings last is meant to highlight its importance, not diminish it. Like all other expense items, savings should be planned. It also helps to determine just how much you should save in relation to your income.

PLANNED SAVINGS   Many people view savings as a fixed expense; that is, each period they make sure the amount they wish to save is placed into an investment vehicle. A helpful technique is to establish specific savings goals and to open an investment account for each goal. Although it is relatively inconvenient, this approach does have merit in that it allows for goals that are expected to be achieved at different dates in the future. A deposit appropriate for a goal you hope to achieve next year may not be appropriate for a goal targeted for ten years in the future. You may want to put your money in a very safe place for next year's goal, while the goal ten years away might call for a riskier and potentially more profitable investment. The key piece of advice is: Set specific goals and use specific savings instruments to achieve them.

HOW MUCH SHOULD YOU SAVE?   The amount you save depends upon two factors: the importance of savings in your overall financial plan, and your level of income. This text's approach to the first factor does not promote savings over all other activities in life. Your long-run health may depend as much on an enjoyable vacation in the mountains as it does on a "mountain" of savings. Each should be evaluated by you and your family members as to their relative importance. With respect to the second factor, it is probably self-evident that more income usually leads to more savings. What is less obvious is that as your income increases, the *percentage of income saved* also rises. For example, if your income is $20,000 a year, you might save $1,000 of it, or 5 percent ($1,000/$20,000). Now, if your income were to increase to $30,000, you might save $3,000, and your percentage saved would increase to 10 percent ($3,000/$30,000). Economists call this phenomenon an *increasing marginal propensity to save.* What is means to consumers is that saving becomes much easier at higher incomes, usually because many expenses (food, for example) do not increase at the same pace as income. As a result, it becomes relatively easier to save.

The average savings rate for all U.S. families has changed from time to time, but in recent years it has been around 4 percent of disposable (after-tax) income. Thus, if the average family income in 1992 is $40,000, the annual contribution to savings for the average family should be $1,600. In 1992, the Steeles saved 3.3 percent of their $77,627 gross income and 4.1 percent of their after-tax income.

THE STEELES' SAVINGS   The Steeles are quite unhappy with their savings performance in recent years, and they realize that attaining education and retirement goals may be impossible unless they save more. Accordingly, they plan to increase savings substantially in 1993. Their planned savings depends upon their income levels, shown in Table 3.1. Since both Arnold's and Sharon's incomes are uncertain for 1993, the Steeles thought it important to plan savings based on a sliding scale. There was a very slim chance Sharon would not work at all, and if Arnie's salary fell for some reason—also a very remote possibility—their 1993 income could go as low as $60,000. On the brighter side, if Sharon works more than expected, or if Arnie's income rises because of a promotion or extra bonus, their income could reach $95,000. By looking at the range of possible incomes and working with reasonable savings rates, the Steeles are in a position to set realistic and achievable savings goals. (We'll see the importance of goals in the next chapter.) So, even under the poorest set of possible conditions, they plan to save $4,800, and if the best take place, they will increase their savings to $12,350. As you see, the most likely situation in their view is an income between $80,000 and $85,000 and savings between $7,200 and $8,500.

Evaluating Financial Performance

Ultimately, your financial performance can be judged successful or unsuccessful only within the framework of your personal goals. If your plans call for buying a house or a new car, or saving $5,000, then you are successful if you achieve these goals. Apart from this personal evaluation, however, there also are objective yardsticks, called **financial ratios,** to measure present financial strength and its

TABLE 3.1 · The Steeles' Planned Savings for 1993

Range of Income	Range of Savings Rates	Range of Dollar Savings
$60,000 to $75,000	6% to 8%	$4,800 to $ 6,000
75,000 to 80,000	8 to 9	6,000 to 7,200
80,000 to 85,000	9 to 10	7,200 to 8,500
85,000 to 90,000	10 to 11	8,500 to 9,900
90,000 to 95,000	11 to 13	9,900 to 12,350

Financial ratios: Yardsticks to measure financial strength and progress.

growth over time. Actually, to an outsider, such as a bank from which you are seeking a loan, your personal goals are not important. The bank must evaluate your request with an impersonal, objective attitude, asking whether or not you are a good credit risk. In attempting to answer this question, the bank relies upon, among other things, certain ratios that can be calculated from the balance sheet and income statement. Even if your financial picture is not being evaluated by outsiders, it is a worthwhile effort for you to use similar objective criteria to assess your situation. Three areas that are particularly important to evaluate are your financial performance as compared to the annual inflation rate, the liquidity of your assets, and your level of debt.

Matching or Beating the Inflation Rate

It is always sound financial management to compare the annual inflation rate to annual changes in both your income and net worth. In periods of high inflation, such as the early 1980s, it is doubly important, because failure to match inflation will lead to an eroding scale of living and a diminished real net worth.

Nominal income: Actual income received.

Real income: Nominal income adjusted for inflation.

INCOME AND THE INFLATION RATE   Let us suppose your **nominal income** (the amount you actually receive) increases by 5 percent during a year when prices in general are increasing by 10 percent. In real terms—that is, in terms of what your nominal income buys—your **real income** (the amount your nominal income is worth) has declined by 5 percent. You are worse off this year because you have not kept up with the inflation rate. You may not feel much worse off, at least not immediately, because some items in your budget are fixed, as we explained earlier. So, you will continue to make the same payments on your auto or furniture loans, or on your home loan, as you did in the past, and you may perhaps continue to meet your savings goals. But eventually many of the items being financed will need to be replaced, and we then confront the reality of a deteriorated financial condition. This happened with such regularity in the late 1970s and early 1980s that a phrase was coined to describe it: **sticker shock.** It referred to the surprise of consumers who hadn't looked at a price sticker on a new automobile for five or six years.

Sticker shock: Consumers' surprise at the amount of price inflation when a durable item, such as a car, is replaced.

An important first test, then, is to compare your increase in nominal income with the inflation rate for the year. The simplest approach is first to calculate a percentage change in nominal income, as shown below:

$$\% \text{ change in nominal income} = \left(\frac{\text{this year's nominal income}}{\text{last year's nominal income}}\right) - 1.0$$

After you have this figure, compare it to the inflation rate (which is frequently reported in the newspaper and on television) to judge your relative performance. Using the Steeles as an example, and assuming the 1992 inflation rate was 4.0 percent, we have

$$\begin{array}{c}\% \text{ change in} \\ \text{nominal income}\end{array} = \frac{\$77,627}{\$71,788} - 1.0 = 1.0813 - 1.0 = 0.0813, \text{ or } 8.13\%$$

Thus, we know that the 8.13 percent increase in the Steeles' nominal income was about twice the inflation rate.

You may also want to calculate your real income for the year. To do this, simply divide your nominal income by 1.0 plus the inflation rate. We have for the Steeles:

$$\text{Real income} = \frac{\$77,627}{1.0 + 0.04} = \$74,641$$

Thus, of the $5,839 increase in nominal income for 1992 ($77,627 − $71,788), only $2,853 ($74,641 − $71,788) represented real progress; $2,986 ($5,839 − $2,853) was needed just to maintain last year's scale of living.

NET WORTH AND THE INFLATION RATE Inflation's impact is not limited to your income. If the market values of your assets do not increase at inflation's rate, your real net worth will decline. The same arithmetic procedures shown above can be used to calculate the change in real—as opposed to nominal—net worth. To prevent a decline in net worth, you must own assets that appreciate in value equal to the inflation rate. During most of the 1970s, many people held the bulk of their savings in deposits in financial institutions yielding 5½ percent or less. In many of those years, the inflation rate exceeded the earning rate on the deposit, meaning that if the annual interest earned was left to accumulate, the real value of the deposits declined during the year. The depositors' real financial positions worsened.

The Steeles' net worth of $157,391 at December 31, 1992, is a fairly substantial amount, but not outstanding. Back in 1978, it might have been described as spectacular, because very few families then had a net worth in excess of $100,000. The Steeles are pleased in achieving their net-worth goals, but they should not delude themselves about their real financial progress.

Maintaining Adequate Liquidity

Adequate liquidity means having sufficient liquid assets to pay your bills on time. You may have a very high net worth, but if most of it is represented by assets with poor liquidity, such as your house, you still could be illiquid. To prevent this from happening, we often hold a portion of our total assets in cash or other liquid assets, such as savings accounts. While you want to avoid illiquidity, it is certainly possible to hold excessive liquidity. How liquid should you be? Unfortunately, there is no pat answer to this question. It would simplify things if liquid assets always offered the highest returns on our investments. Unfortunately, the reverse is usually true: the more liquid the asset, the poorer its return. Currency and coin, for example, are perfectly liquid but have a zero return.

Lacking a perfect standard to assess the optimal amount of liquidity, we must rely upon rules of thumb. Two ratios are frequently used in this effort: the ratio of liquid assets to take-home pay, and the ratio of liquid assets to current liabilities.

LIQUID ASSETS TO TAKE-HOME PAY We usually pay current bills from current income. If we could match the two uniformly, we would have little reason to hold more than a very minimal amount of liquid assets. For example, if we routinely incurred $100 a day in expenses and earned $100 a day in income, we wouldn't need to hold any cash: One day's expenses would be met with one day's income. But things seldom work this smoothly. We may get a heavy and unpredictable inflow of bills that is not matched by our current income. Then, too, we may temporarily lose some or all of our income because of a layoff or illness. Reasons such as these are why a liquidity reservoir is needed to serve as a buffer against periods of unanticipated shortages in cash. Financial advisers often use the rule of thumb that you should hold liquid assets equal to three to six months of take-home pay to serve as such a buffer. If you have good loss-of-income protection through your employer or union, then the low figure might be adequate. If protection is poor, you should strive for the higher amount.

Liquid assets to take-home pay ratio: A liquidity measurement.

Using data for the Steeles, we can calculate their **liquid assets to take-home pay ratio.** Recalling (from page 68) that their 1992 take-home pay was $61,030 and their liquid assets at December 31, 1992, were $16,240 (see Figure 3.2), we have:

$$\frac{\text{Liquid assets to}}{\text{take-home pay ratio}} = \frac{\text{liquid assets}}{\text{take-home pay}} = \frac{\$16,240}{\$61,030} = 0.266$$

The number can then be expressed as months of the year; for example, 0.266 means about 27 percent of 12 months, or about 3.2 months. (Notice that an answer of 0.5 indicates half the year, or six months.) Thus, the Steeles fall at the lower rule-of-thumb figure of three months, suggesting they should build their liquid reserves. Since Arnold does have rather good loss-of-income protection at InChemCo. the lower figure is the more appropriate one for them to use. (We should note that take-home pay is an appropriate value to use if there are no other major sources of income, as in the Steeles' case. If there are other major sources, they should be included in the denominator, after allowing for related income taxes.)

LIQUID ASSETS TO CURRENT LIABILITIES   The ratio of liquid assets to take-home pay does not consider the level of existing liabilities. Another family may show an identical ratio to the Steeles' but be in far worse shape because their existing current liabilities are much greater. To augment the first ratio, then, it is helpful to calculate another ratio, called the **liquidity ratio,** which measures liquid assets against current liabilities. For the Steeles, it is:

Liquidity ratio: Liquid assets divided by current liabilities.

$$\text{Liquidity ratio} = \frac{\text{liquid assets}}{\text{current liabilities}} = \frac{\$16,240}{\$8,354} = 1.94$$

This number tells us the Steeles have $1.94 of liquid assets for every $1.00 of existing current liabilities. There is no hard-and-fast rule indicating what this ratio should be, but any number greater than 1.0 shows fairly good strength, assuming the ratio of liquid assets to take-home pay is also adequate. Of course, the larger the number, the better the liquidity. With a ratio of 1.94, the Steeles are in reasonable shape.

Home Financial Statement and Budgeting Software

When personal computers became popular some years ago, it didn't take long for software firms to offer home financial planning programs. Unfortunately, they were expensive, and worse, they were difficult to learn and use. Not so today. There are a number of inexpensive and truly user-friendly programs. Most have help menus that lead us by the hand and pop-up calculators and note pads to assist with calculations. They also can be integrated directly with other software that prepares year-end income tax returns.

The big advantage of computeriz-ing the family finances is not the time you might save (although that can be considerable), but the ability to *analyze* your financial situation and measure your progress (or lack thereof) in achieving budgeted goals. For example, the programs have check-writer features, so, as you pay bills or record deposits, information is stored that can be used to prepare financial statements and update budget evaluations. And, if the traditional statements bore you, press a key and you can view results in dramatic graphics (pie charts and the like).

The five programs listed below are widely used. While it is the most expensive, *Managing Your Money* has the most powerful software and is probably the most popular; however, the less-expensive offerings are highly regarded, even by professional financial planners who use them in their practice. Even if you consider yourself a computer illiterate, you should consider buying a program. The only qualifier is that you need access to a computer, and in that regard make sure the software and computer are compatible.

Program	Manufacturer	Sugg. Retail
Managing Your Money	Meca, Inc.	$220.00
DACEasy	DAC Software Technology	69.95
MoneyCounts	Parsons Technology	35.00
Dollars $ Sense	Monogram, Inc.	99.95
Quicken	Intuit, Inc.	59.95

Avoiding Excessive Amounts of Debt

Adequate liquidity protects you from temporary cash emergencies, and liquidity ratios are designed to warn you of liquidity problems. However, they do not tell us whether total debt is being used properly, or if it is excessive. In many instances, as you increase your total assets, you also increase your total liabilities. We saw earlier how the Steeles purchased a second home by using profit from the sale of their first home as a down payment and increasing their mortgage loan. In this instance they added a considerable amount of debt, but not necessarily an excessive amount. *Excessive* doesn't mean too much debt in absolute dollars, but rather, in relation to your underlying assets and income that support the debt. Two important ratios are often used to evaluate total debt: the ratio of total liabilities to total assets, and the ratio of take-home pay to debt repayment obligations.

TOTAL LIABILITIES TO TOTAL ASSETS Technically, you are judged insolvent when your total liabilities exceed your total assets. Being insolvent doesn't automatically mean you are illiquid; you might still have sufficient cash to pay your bills for a while. What it does mean is that, unless the situation changes, you will ultimately not have enough assets to pay all your bills. Many people in this position eventually file bankruptcy as a means of settling with creditors or establishing an orderly plan for paying their bills over an extended period of time.

Bankruptcy (discussed more fully in Chapter 7) is not to be taken lightly or viewed as a convenience to avoid paying obligations. You should look for early signals of impending troubles. The **debt ratio,** which measures total liabilities against total assets, is one such signal. Using the Steeles' data from Figure 3.2 as an example, it is calculated below:

$$\text{Debt ratio} = \frac{\text{total liabilities}}{\text{total assets}} = \frac{\$168,149}{\$325,540} = 0.517$$

This number tells us the Steeles have about $0.52 in total debts for each $1.00 of total assets. Looking at it in another way, the value of their assets could shrink up to 48 percent (1.00 − 0.52) before the Steeles would encounter insolvency problems. The smaller the ratio, the better from a safety point of view, but again, there is no iron-clad rule telling us what the ratio should be in every instance. The less volatile the market prices of your assets, the higher the ratio could be, all other things considered. Generally, we like to see ratios below 0.5, to be on the relatively safe side. The Steeles are right at the margin.

DEBT SERVICE COVERAGE   Your capacity to carry debt is reflected not only in the market value of assets you own, but also by the relationship of your take-home pay to your total debt-servicing charges. By debt service, we mean monthly (or yearly) payments of both principal and interest on those loans requiring periodic repayment. The debt service coverage ratio measures take-home pay against total debt service charges. The Steeles have two auto loans and their home mortgage. In addition, they borrowed $2,000 on Arnold's life insurance policy. Although this loan does not require periodic repayments, they pay interest of $160 each year. The total annual payments are $24,133 ($18,285 + $5,688 + $160), and the following **debt service coverage ratio** can be calculated:

$$\text{Debt service coverage ratio} = \frac{\text{take-home pay}}{\text{debt service charges}} = \frac{\$61,030}{\$24,133} = 2.53$$

This number indicates the Steeles earned $2.53 in take-home pay for each $1.00 of required debt repayment and interest. Higher ratios, of course, indicate greater debt-carrying capacity than low ones. A ratio of 1.0 means all of your after-tax income is needed to repay existing debts, and a ratio less than 1.0 indicates your income will not even cover your existing repayments. (Again, if other major sources of income exist, they should be included, on an after-tax basis, in the numerator.)

A single number is never enough to distinguish strength from weakness, but it is usually felt that a ratio of 3.0 or better signals adequate strength and reasonable flexibility in future budgeting. In such a situation, a large portion of your income will not be committed to repaying existing debt. The Steeles' ratio of 2.53 indicates some weakness in this area.

Review of the Steeles' Financial Situation

Now that you have learned about financial statements and have seen them applied to the Steeles' financial situation for 1992, what impression do you have?

Are they a wealthy family? Are they "sailing right along" with few financial concerns? Actually, their situation is not quite so successful as it might first appear.

True, they have a net worth of over $157,000. But there are a number of areas of concern. First, their residence of $205,000 is almost two-thirds of their total assets. While housing prices often increase over time at the inflation rate, or greater, real estate markets can become very soft in the short run. A decline of 10 or 20 percent over several years, while not likely, would decrease their net worth substantially.

Second, Arnie and Sharon have $27,000 invested in late-model automobiles, which depreciate in value rather rapidly. If they continue to turn over their cars after three or four years, they will perpetually carry a rather high amount of expensive installment debt. As our ratio analysis revealed, they are probably already at their debt limit, and it would be helpful to reduce debt somewhat.

Third, and most important, the Steeles are enjoying a high-consumption budget that produces very little savings in relation to their income. At their current pace, they will not accumulate sufficient funds to educate Nancy and John or to achieve other important future goals. Put simply, the Steeles must rethink their priorities, or become smarter consumer-investors, or do both. We will follow them in this process as the remaining chapters unfold.

Summary

Financial statements are prepared to measure financial performance and to assist in future planning. There are three major financial statements: the balance sheet, the income statement, and the cash budget (discussed in the next chapter). A balance sheet measures your net worth, which is the difference between the market values of all the assets you own and your liabilities. Net worth is the best measurement of your wealth, even though it is difficult to place market values on some assets. It is important to understand not only the level of net worth, but also how net worth changes over time. These changes can come about if your income exceeds your expenses, or if the market values of assets held at the beginning of a period increase during the period. An income statement shows income, expenses, and contribution to savings over a period of time. Income is cash inflow from wages or salaries, interest, dividends, gains or losses on sale of securities, business or partnership profits, and other sources, while expenses are cash outflows that sustain a living scale. Financial performance is evaluated periodically to objectively assess one's financial strength. A first test is a comparison of percentage changes in income and net worth to changes in the cost of living—the CPI. A second test measures one's liquidity, and a third evaluates a person's total debt to see if it is being used excessively.

Key Terms

assets (p. 57)

current liability (p. 62)

debt ratio (p. 76)

debt service coverage ratio (p. 76)

dissavings (p. 63)

expenses (p. 68)

financial ratios (p. 72)

flexible expenses (p. 69)

income (p. 68)

income statement (p. 64)

inflexible expenses (p. 68)

investment assets (p. 59)

liabilities (p. 57)

life-style assets (p. 59)

liquid asset (p. 58)

liquid assets to take-home pay ratio (p. 74)

liquidity ratio (p. 74)

net worth (p. 57)

nominal income (p. 72)

noncurrent liabilities (p. 62)

personal balance sheet (p. 56)

positive contribution to savings (p. 63)

real income (p. 72)

sticker shock (p. 72)

sunk costs (p. 69)

1 Explain the following elements of a balance sheet and give an example of each (a) liquid assets, (b) investment assets, (c) life-style assets, (d) current liabilities, and (e) noncurrent liabilities.

2 Explain how asset values are determined on the balance sheet and whether or not these valuations are made easily.

3 What is net worth? Does it have anything to do with wealth? Explain two factors that can change net worth from one period to the next.

4 Explain the difference between a current and a noncurrent liability. Give an example of each. Explain if liability amounts are difficult or easy to determine.

5 Lisa Rich spent every cent she had and then borrowed $1,000 to purchase an elaborate wardrobe worth $2,000. Ignoring all of Lisa's other assets and liabilities, construct her balance sheet after the purchase. Suppose that, a year later, Lisa's wardrobe—now completely out of style—is worth only $100. If Lisa has paid off $500 of her loan, what does her balance sheet look like now? Comment on her present financial position.

6 What is an income statement and what are its component parts? In your answer, distinguish between flexible and inflexible expenses.

7 Would you classify the following expense items as flexible or inflexible? Which one(s) would you consider "sunk costs"? (a) property taxes, (b) house mortgage payments, (c) clothing, (d) car licenses, (e) insurance, and (f) family members' personal allowances.

8 Explain two factors that determine a person's savings. Also, how does planned savings differ from savings as something "left over"?

9 The following items, arranged alphabetically, belong to either the income statement or the balance sheet. Put them in their correct place and then construct each statement. (You must also calculate net worth and contribution to savings.)

Automobile (1990 Ford)	$ 6,000
Automobile loan payments	1,200
Cash value of life insurance	2,000
Coins and currency	300
Credit card balances due	500
Federal income taxes withheld from wages	4,000
Food and household supplies	6,000
Gas and electric expenses	2,200
Gifts	400
Hobbies and collections	650
Installment loan balances due in one year	1,200
Interest	700
Jewelry	850
Mortgage loan on residence	60,000
Mortgage payments	6,200
Property and liability insurance	300
Real estate taxes	1,200
Residence	80,000
Telephone	240
Theater and sporting events	700
Tuition	1,100
U.S. Series EE bonds	1,600
Unpaid bills	700
Wages and salaries	26,000

10 You are given the following data for Kim Zerussen:

	1991	1992
Income during the year	$30,000	$32,000
End of year: Assets	50,000	60,000
Liabilities	40,000	49,000

Assuming inflation, as measured by the CPL, was 10 percent during 1992, evaluate Kim's financial performance for that year.

11 Explain a financial ratio and then identify the ratios below, indicating what they are supposed to test. How would you evaluate each, given their specific numbers? After you complete that assignment, discuss whether or not you think the person to whom these ratios apply is a good credit risk.
(a) liquid assets to take-home pay = 0.08
(b) liquidity ratio = 0.75
(c) debt ratio = 1.20
(d) debt service coverage ratio = 1.10

Case 3.1
Can Arnold and Sharon Afford a Vacation Condominium?

At the end of 1991, Arnold and Sharon Steele were considering buying a condominium in Gatlinburg, Tennessee. Gatlinburg is a resort town next to the Great Smoky Mountain National Park area, where the Steeles have often camped. The condo they particularly liked was priced at $67,000, and the seller offered to finance 90 percent of the purchase price with a first mortgage loan requiring monthly payments of $597 during the first year. To make the $6,700 down payment, the Steeles planned to sell both their Coleman camper (which would have been worth $1,700 at that time) and their U.S. Series EE bonds (then worth $1,400). The balance of $3,600 would be borrowed from Sharon's parents, who would not expect regular repayments of the loan but would charge interest of $288 each year. Arnold and Sharon decided against the purchase for a number of reasons, one of which involved finances. They felt the condo would have placed an excessive strain on their budget, given their alternative goal of adding to their investments and liquid assets.

Questions

1 Using the data given above and elsewhere in this chapter, calculate what the Steeles' contribution to savings would have been in 1992, assuming they bought the condo on January 1, 1992. (Assume expenses, including income taxes, not related to the purchase remain the same.)
2 Prepare a new balance sheet at December 31, 1992, for the Steeles, again assuming they made the purchase on January 1, 1992, and that total interest payments on the mortgage loan were $6,935, and payments of principal were $229 for the year.
3 Using the four ratios given in this chapter to evaluate liquidity and total debt, make new calculations for the Steeles, assuming the condo purchase, and compare them to those calculated in the chapter. Comment on and discuss the comparisons.
4 Do you agree with the Steeles that the purchase would have been a financial strain for them? Explain your answer.

Bill Strawser, an engineering major at a Western university, has very little background in personal financial matters. He expects to graduate in June and has a job offer from Apex, Inc., a machine tool manufacturer, to start at $32,000 a year. Bill thinks this is a good offer, and he has heard from a friend that Apex has averaged about 5 percent a year in salary increases. Bill's net worth at graduation will be about $2,000 (represented by $1,000 in cash and $1,000 in clothing and jewelry, and no liabilities), and he then plans to buy a $25,000 sports car, putting down $1,000 and financing the balance over three years with monthly payments of about $808. As he sees it, he can afford $9,700 a year, although it will reduce his potential savings to zero. Linda Leese, Bill's girlfriend, has recently completed a course in personal financial planning. She is not trying to talk Bill out of his sports car, but she is urging him to take time to watch his financial situation carefully as he embarks on his career.

Questions

1 Suppose Bill's sports car loses each year 20 percent of its beginning-of-year market value. Also, assume the price of a new car identical to Bill's increases by 7 percent a year. At the end of three years—when Bill makes his last payment on the present car loan—what will his car be worth? How much will a new, identical car cost? And assuming he uses the old car as a down payment on a new one, how much must he then borrow? After Linda makes these calculations, she intends to explain "sticker shock" to Bill. Complete Linda's task.
2 Explain specific steps you think Linda should discuss with Bill for evaluating his financial performance relative to the annual inflation rate.
3 Using the liquidity and debt service coverage ratios, evaluate Bill's debt position.

Helpful Reading

Changing Times
"Our Bad Rap as Spendthrifts." April 1991, pp. 30–31.

Money
Feinberg, Andrew. "Where Are Wall Street's Yuppies Now?" October 1990, pp. 107–116.

Fenner, Elizabeth. "14 Terrific Moves That Can Save Plenty." December 1991, pp. 77–82.

Reid, Jeanne L. "Twelve Steps to Financial Security." January 1988, pp. 66–74.

Willis, Clint. "The Ten Mistakes to Avoid with Your Money." June 1990, pp. 85–94.

The Wall Street Journal
Graven, Kathryn. "Reformed Spenders." April 22, 1991, p. A1.

Schwadel, Francine. "Growing Up." June 19, 1991, p. A1.

Helpful Contacts

The National Foundation for Consumer Credit (a nonprofit organization, telephone 1-800-388-2227). This organization can help if you are having credit problems.

Budget Management: Where Are You Going?

Objectives

1 To understand why setting goals is important and why broad goals must be reduced to specific targets before budgeting can be effective

2 To explain the details of an action plan and to see why action plans must be linked to the annual budget and updated on a regular basis

3 To prepare an annual budget by constructing a master budget worksheet and a monthly income and expense plan

4 To monitor monthly activities by creating a system for recording actual income and expenses, and then comparing them with budgeted amounts

5 To evaluate and control expenses during the year through a monthly review process

Ask Kay and Larry Emmons what they think about budgeting and they'll tell you, "Forget it." The two married right after college and each had the good luck to find a well-paying job. Their combined incomes exceeded $4,500 a month, but after six months it dawned on them that none of it was finding its way into their savings account. First, they rented an apartment for more than they had planned; then, they bought a new car, memberships to a health club, and the list goes on; and in addition they dined out so often that eating at home was an adventure. While all this added up to the good life, it didn't add up to savings.

Kay and Larry were disappointed, but like a prize fighter who has been mauled in the first nine rounds but somewhere finds the inspiration to KO his opponent in the tenth, they resolved to put things right by saving $5,000 before their first year of marriage came to an end. The key to success? A budget. A tight one, and no deviations from it. And to get things going, Larry spent $25 on an elaborate journal, the fancy kind you see in a stationery store with a hard cover and lots of columns on each page, one for each expense category. Larry planned to have many expense categories to keep a close track on where the money went.

After the first week, the Emmons were thrilled. Each night they did their homework by dutifully recording expenses for the day. They spent about a half-hour on this activity, even though they didn't have much to record because they were living like monks who take vows of poverty. But they saved $200 that week. The budget was working. It also worked in the second week, and their savings account jumped another $200. By the middle of the third week, Larry's journal was in the back of the bookshelf (he couldn't bring himself to throw it in the trash can, despite Kay's urging to do so), and the Emmons celebrated their liberation from economic servitude with a $500 weekend at Lake Tahoe. Budgets, they agreed as they toasted with their wine glasses at dinner, belong to governments and big corporations—not families or real people.

SOURCE: Kay and Larry Emmons' diary.

The Emmons' feelings are typical of many families who start, and ultimately fail at, budgeting. Some years ago there was an advertising slogan for a nonprescription remedy that said, "Medicine doesn't have to taste bad to be good." The same can be said of budgeting: It doesn't have to leave a bad taste in your mouth in order to be effective. But what is a **budget?** Put very simply, a budget is any plan—simple or complex—that expresses your financial goals and how you will allocate your limited resources to achieve them. A budget can be so simple that you keep it on the back of an envelope to monitor your monthly progress with checkmarks. Or it can be as complex as the one the federal government prepares each year, detailing how over 2 trillion dollars will be spent. But size is no guarantee of success. Your envelope approach might work, and there are many critics who feel the federal budget never has. We'll discuss principles of effective budgeting in this chapter, but before doing so, we will set forth some simple rules for budgeting success. Our discussion will revolve around these rules:

Budget: A plan indicating financial goals and how resources will be allocated to achieve them.

- *Set realistic budget goals.* The plural is important here. The budget is a device for achieving all your important goals; it is not a straitjacket to produce only savings, as the Emmons hoped to do.
- *Stick to simple procedures.* A $25 journal like the Emmons' is nice if you use it, but a waste of money if you don't. Trying to categorize every conceivable expense misses the whole point of budgeting and creates an unnecessary work burden that makes budgeting "taste bad." In passing, let us

note that personal computers are not used in home financial planning to make budgeting more complex; on the contrary, computers simplify things and reduce the work load.

- *Use the budget to control and direct expenses.* The main strength of a budget does not lie with its record-keeping function, although that is a necessary part. A budget allocation, say, for dining out, is a commitment you and your family make to an underlying activity. If you exceed the budget amount, ask yourself why. If the answer is because you want to, then you need to reexamine your goals to see if more funds should be allocated to this activity and less to others. If the answer reflects a temporary "overindulgence," then cut back next month to bring the activity back within budget. The simple acts of knowing you have exceeded budget and then deciding what to do about it are the essence of successful budgeting.

Goal Setting

Perhaps one reason we feel uncomfortable with budgeting is that it forces us to determine our important financial goals and, more generally, what we really hope to achieve in life. Often, we are not sure of the answers to these questions. But we must choose, and the budget forces us to do so. It forces us, for example, to choose among many current consumption goals: Do we spend $50 for a nice dinner, or do we buy a new pair of shoes with the money? Equally important, it forces us to choose between current and future goals: Do we give up both the dinner and the shoes and choose instead to save for our retirement years? One of the earliest lessons learned in life is that we cannot have everything, so we must choose. A budget, then, is a reflection of those choices, expressed as goals to be accomplished. As you review it, you should say, Here is the upcoming year's installment of my (or my family's) lifelong plan for financial well-being.

Management by Objective

Goal setting: A complex process that involves a hierarchy of wants—abstract at the top and tangible at the bottom.

When you set goals, you are effectively managing your finances rather than merely letting them take place as you go about your routine activities. Actually, **goal setting** is a rather complex process, and it has been studied by professionals from many disciplines, including social psychology, economics, and behavioral management. Goals can be viewed in a type of hierarchy, with very general and abstract goals at the top and more specific and tangible ones at the bottom. Figure 4.1 illustrates such a hierarchy of financial goals. At the top is the general goal of attaining financial independence for each member of the family. But what does this mean? You might understand it to mean sufficient wealth to be self-reliant, while another might understand it as having a job free of possible firing or other layoffs. To be meaningful, the general goals must be expressed in specific terms. For example, in Figure 4.1 financial independence is structured into three distinct goals: to enjoy a current living scale that reflects a moderate to high level of consumption, to provide a college education for the children, and to achieve a scale of living in retirement that is on a par with the current living scale. As we move to the lowest level on the triangle, goals become even more specific and can be broken down to yearly savings and current consumption targets. Things to be acquired in the future—the children's education and retirement funds—must be

"Brown-Bagging: It's for the Professional"

Striding out of her office on the way to lunch, Elizabeth McBride passes up the company cafeteria, the sandwich shops, the Chinese restaurants and the hot-dog stand.

"You can't get out of those places for less than five bucks," said the promotions director of the United Way in Atlanta, pulling a chicken sandwich and a container of pasta salad out of a brown paper sack. "So I pack my own."

And the money she saves adds up: a brown-bagger can save $676 a year by packing a lunch.

On the eleventh floor at Mead Corp.'s headquarters in downtown Dayton, La-Rinda Saylor pulls some leftover pizza from her bag and heats it up in a microwave. "There are quite a few brown-baggers here," says Ms. Saylor, a secretary in the company's government affairs office.

She brings her lunch to work at least four times a week. "Sometimes three or four of us get together in the conference room and, if we have er-

rands to do, we eat and run." Saylor also saves a minimum of $15 a week compared to what she'd pay at the least expensive fast-food restaurants.

At a downtown Atlanta building, attorney Roger Murray dines at his desk. "I bring my lunch religiously," says Murray, who does so despite ribbing from his peers. He brown-bags lunch so he has time to work out at the end of the day. "It's usually tuna, two or three pieces of fruit and, depending on my weight at the time, a cookie."

Judging from the sack-lunch set, the profile and palate of the typical brown-bagger have come a long way from the factory worker who put a bologna sandwich and a thermos in a metal lunch box.

Indeed, today's adult brown-baggers are mostly office workers and professionals, says David Lyon, founder of the Brown Bag Institute in Green Farms, Conn., a marketing and research company that bases its figures on nationwide phone surveys.

Only 25 percent of the nation's estimated 60 million brown-baggers are blue-collar workers, Lyon says. "They're not the core of the brown-bag crowd, just like they're not the core of America anymore," he says.

As a group, brown-baggers earn higher salaries and are better edu-

cated than the population as a whole, according to a 1987 survey of 1,500 Americans conducted by Strategic Alternatives, Inc., in Norwalk, Conn., which polls Americans on their eating habits. People who pack their lunch are twice as likely to be college-educated and to have household incomes of more than $30,000.

It seems like a small hedge against the recession, but you'll save more than $650 a year on the brown-bag variety of sandwiches alone.

For example, a deli turkey sandwich on wheat costs about $3.50, with or without chips. If you were to purchase the sliced roasted turkey from the supermarket at $3.99 a pound and slip it between two slices of bread with lettuce, tomato and condiments, you would spend 90 cents.

That's a savings of $2.60 per sandwich, or $13 per week, or, better yet, $676 a year.

Plus, you save the headaches of deciding where to dine, and if you're dieting, you can tote low-calorie foods such as carrot sticks, hard-cooked eggs, fruit and graham crackers for snacking at your desk.

SOURCE: *Dayton Daily News,* April 12, 1991, p. 10b. Reprinted with permission of the *Dayton Daily News.*

saved for out of current income. Savings must be budgeted if these goals are to be achieved.

Since all our goals are not achieved in the current year, you could also classify goals in terms of when they are expected to be achieved. Thus, we have short-range goals that might span, say, the next five years; intermediate-range goals that arrive in 5 to 15 years; and long-range goals that mature beyond 15 years. Referencing goals to the year when we hope to accomplish them allows us to plan for the use of funds we must accumulate during the waiting period. Table 4.1 shows important goals of the Arnold and Sharon Steele family and when they expect these goals to be accomplished. They prepared this list at the end of 1992 in connection with their planning for 1993 and beyond. Keep in mind that these are their major goals that will require savings to be achieved, and they do not include

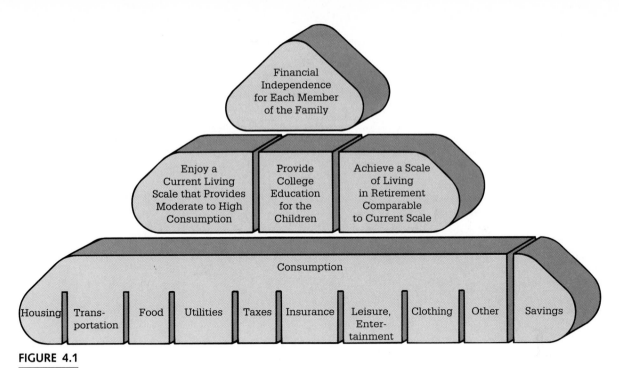

FIGURE 4.1

A hierarchy of personal goals.

those goals that are a part of their annual consumption expenditures. For example, their cars must be replaced periodically, but this will be a part of their annual expenditure budget. As you can see in Table 4.1, Arnold and Sharon must save an average of $9,500 a year to accomplish all their major goals. However, they expect their savings to be somewhat below this average in the earlier years and above it later on. For simplicity they are assuming savings will start at $8,000 and increase by $500 over each four-year period. Also for simplicity, they are not including their current investment assets (the common stocks and mutual fund shares). If they considered these, the total required savings would be approximately $23,000 less, or $243,000.

Along with the amount that must be saved each year, the balance in savings and investments assets should also be estimated. If this balance ever turns negative, it means the Steeles must borrow to achieve their goals. Table 4.2 shows estimates for the Steeles and indicates that their balance grows steadily to $55,000 in the year 2001 (the year before Nancy starts college), but falls to $14,500 in the year 2007 (John's last year in college); it then builds to the required $100,000 in the year 2020, when Arnold plans to retire.

It should be pointed out that the above figures are not adjusted for inflation, but on the other hand, they do not include any earnings on the investment assets. Obviously, for greater accuracy, the Steeles should review both of these factors each year and make appropriate adjustments, if they are necessary. These adjustments are done best through individual action plans.

Budget Management

TABLE 4.1 • The Steeles' Major Goals

Goal	Approximate Amount Required	Year Goal Will Be Accomplished	Ages at That Time	
			Arnold's	Sharon's
1 Down payment on a vacation condo in the Smoky Mountain area	$ 15,000	1995	40	38
2 Family vacation in Hawaii	5,000	1997	42	40
3 College expenses for Nancy and John	96,000	2002–2007	47–53	45–51
4 Add patio and greenhouse to home; also do major landscaping	40,000	2012	57	55
5 European vacation for Arnold and Sharon	10,000	2015	60	58
6 Accumulate additional investment assets to supplement retirement income	100,000	2020	65	63

Total required savings	$266,000
Remaining years	28
Average savings per year	$ 9,500

Estimated savings by four-year periods:

1993–1996	$ 8,000
1997–2000	8,500
2001–2004	9,000
2005–2008	9,500
2009–2012	10,000
2013–2016	10,500
2017–2020	11,000

Achieving Goals Through Action Plans

If a goal is really important, you should be willing to devote your time and effort to planning how to achieve it. It is best to have a specific plan—on paper—detailing what you hope to accomplish, when, and how. You then have an **action plan,** which has the advantage of being specific and concrete rather than general and hazy. It allows you to monitor progress toward your goal.

Action plan: A specific plan detailing what you hope to accomplish, when, and how.

DETAILS OF AN ACTION PLAN An action plan can be prepared for any objective. In Chapter 6 we illustrate an action plan for the Steeles with respect to how they might manage their liquid assets. On page 89 is another illustration: in this case, we examine the Steeles' action plan for purchasing a vacation condominium in the Smoky Mountain area. The Steeles had decided to buy in this region as opposed to somewhere else, and their only decision in 1993 was whether to buy immediately or to wait three more years. As you see in the action plan, they chose the latter, primarily because of the heavy financial strain involved with buying now. They also believed that more favorable financing would be available in the future, particularly if they had a substantial down payment.

This action plan indicates the deposits the Steeles plan to make in 1993, 1994, and 1995 to accumulate the needed $15,000. They are assuming their deposits will earn 6 percent interest each year, and if this assumption proves correct, they will make their goal. Of course, the earned interest helps them in their saving effort, and you should see that it adds almost $1,260 over the three years. (The Steeles' contributions are $4,400, $4,600, and $4,800, a total of $13,800; the amount accumulated is $15,059, with the difference being interest.) The last part

TABLE 4.2 · How the Steeles Plan to Achieve Their Major Goals

Year	Annual Contribution to Savings	Outflow	Balance in Savings and Investment Assets
1993	$8,000	—	$8,000
1994	8,000	—	16,000
1995	8,000	$15,000	9,000
1996	8,000	—	17,000
1997	8,500	5,000	20,500
1998	8,500	—	29,000
1999	8,500	—	37,500
2000	8,500	—	46,000
2001	9,000	—	55,000
2002	9,000	12,000	52,000
2003	9,000	12,000	49,000
2004	9,000	24,000	34,000
2005	9,500	24,000	19,500
2006	9,500	12,000	17,000
2007	9,500	12,000	14,500
2008	9,500	—	24,000
2009	10,000	—	34,000
2010	10,000	—	44,000
2011	10,000	—	54,000
2012	10,000	40,000	24,000
2013	10,500	—	34,500
2014	10,500	—	45,000
2015	10,500	10,000	45,500
2016	10,500	—	56,000
2017	11,000	—	67,000
2018	11,000	—	78,000
2019	11,000	—	89,000
2020	11,000	—	100,000

of this action plan provides space for an annual review of progress in achieving the goal. Assume, for example, the Steeles actually earned 8—rather than 6—percent interest on the deposits made in 1993. This means they would have earned a bit more interest than planned and their deposits for 1994 and 1995 could be a little less. But they might also find the price of the condo increased in 1993. This, too, should be noted and a new schedule of required deposits prepared. If the price increased substantially, it might mean they need to delay the purchase for one or more years. As a last possibility, they might decide the goal is no longer worth pursuing, in which case the action plan is discarded and the funds are made available for another goal.

LINKING ACTION PLANS TO THE ANNUAL BUDGET The action plan tells what you must do to achieve a goal. The "bottom line" of most action plans, such as the one just reviewed, is the amount of savings that is required to achieve the goal. This figure, then, becomes part of your total savings effort for the year. In the previous example, the Steeles needed to save $15,000 over the next three years for the down payment on their condo. It should be noted that the required savings figure is not the same as the required investment deposits, if any interest is earned. In this case, the savings figure is the higher of the two. But keep in mind that we are always assuming that interest earned on the deposits is left in the account to earn additional interest and not withdrawn for current consumption uses. If the latter course of action is taken, then the deposit required each period will be the same as the required savings. To keep things simple and avoid excessive discussion on technical details, just think of the savings figure as being the same as the cost of the item for which you are saving. As savings funds accumulate and are subsequently invested in earning deposits, the interest earned will be recorded as part of your income—and eventually savings—on the income statement. Meanwhile, your actual investment of cash as it becomes available should follow the investment guidelines set up in each action plan.

UPDATING ACTION PLANS An action plan should be evaluated at least once a year, and possibly more often. As we saw before, this evaluation involves comparing what your action plan predicted and what actually happened. It also includes an explanation of any major differences. The annual review provides you and your family an opportunity to express views about a goal's continuing appeal. It might also include alternative courses of action to achieving the broad goal. So if the Steeles' condominium proves to be financially out of reach, they might consider alternatives, such as purchasing a more elaborate travel trailer, or even a motor home. The point to remember is there are usually alternatives to achieving a broad goal, and these should not be discarded after one course of action has been selected.

What the Steeles really might want to accomplish is to have a comfortable vacation spot they can enjoy over the years, along with an investment that potentially increases in value and possibly offers periodic rental income. The first part of their dual goal can be accomplished in a variety of ways, from camping to staying in motels, and the second part should be evaluated along with all other investment opportunities available to them. If the potential return here is far below what they can earn on other investments, then it would be foolish for the Steeles to continue with the condo goal just for the sake of enjoying several weeks' vacation each year. In short, the opportunity cost of not investing their funds in their best use might make the condominium vacation a very expensive one relative to what they would pay vacationing in some other way.

Preparing the Annual Budget

Master budget worksheet: Budget allocations detailing planned income, expenses, and contribution to savings.

Monthly income and expense plan: A monthly breakdown of amounts listed on the master budget worksheet.

Armed with a set of action plans and a clear understanding of the importance of expressing goals, you are in position to prepare the annual budget. It is this budget and your willingness to stick with it that will determine your success in goal achievement. There are two parts to budget preparation: the **master budget worksheet,** which details planned income, expenses, and contribution to savings in total for the budget year; and the **monthly income and expense plan,** which shows how each month's income, expenses, and contribution to savings will take place.

The Master Budget Worksheet

Budgeting begins each year by trying to forecast what your total income and expenses will be in the budget year. Some income and expense items are easy to forecast because they are known in advance (recall our discussion of fixed ex-

Date   December 1992

Objective   Purchase a vacation condominium within 40 miles of the Great Smoky Mountain National Park. The condo should be in the $65,000-to-$75,000 range.

Present Alternatives   (*a*) Purchase the condo immediately, using financing provided by the developer; or (*b*) defer purchase until 1995 in order to accumulate a $15,000 down payment.

Advantages/Disadvantages of the Alternatives

	Item	Alternative a	Alternative b
1	Financing flexibility—possibly lower interest rate	Poor. Locked into seller's financing arrangement with high current rate of 11.5 percent.	Good. A substantial down payment will allow financing from a number of lending institutions, possibly at a lower rate.
2	Use of the property	Good. You can use it for the three years.	Poor. However, the camper can still be used during the waiting period.
3	Impact on present financial position	Very poor. A down payment of $6,000 would deplete present cash reserves.	Good. The down payment could be saved over the next three years and not impair present liquidity.
4	Price increases over next three years	Good. Buying now avoids any future higher price.	Moderately bad. Waiting might mean a higher price, but that could be greatly offset by lower financing costs over the 30-year life of the loan.

The Choice   Alternative *b*, primarily because of item 3 above. This choice entails making deposits shown below into a money market mutual fund presumed to earn 6 percent interest each year:

Year	Amount in the Account at Beginning of the Year	Deposit Required During the Year	Amount in the Account at the End of the Year
1993	–0–	$4,400	$ 4,400 + (0.06)(0.5)*($4,400) = $4,532
1994	$4,532	4,600	9,132 + (0.06)(4.532) + (0.06)(0.5)*($4,600) = $9,542
1995	9,542	4,800	14,342 + (0.06)($9,542) + (0.06)(0.5)*($4,800) = $15,059

*Assumes deposits are made uniformly during the year; thus, the average balance for the year is one-half the total deposit.

penses in Chapter 3): your mortgage payments on the house, for example. Others can vary widely and will be much more difficult to estimate: Dentist or doctor bills are good examples here, as is home maintenance. Despite the difficulties, estimates must be made and the budget finished.

Figure 4.2 illustrates a master budget worksheet the Steele family prepared for 1993. You probably recognize immediately that the budget has the same format as the income statement discussed in the previous chapter. Indeed it does. The budget for a year should lead directly to the same kind of actual income and expense items after the year is over. In fact, budgeted and actual figures should be compared very closely at the end of a budget year, both for evaluating results for the year just ended and for preparing a budget for the upcoming year.

MAKING REALISTIC ESTIMATES   It goes almost without saying that budget figures should be determined as realistically as possible. Each line item should be reviewed and some reason found for making the estimate; that is, your figure should be defensible. A common mistake made by the Emmons (whom we met at the beginning of this chapter) and many others is to set a consumption item unrealistically low. If you think there is a good chance you will spend $40 a week on dining out, and if that is what you want to do, then don't budget this activity at $20 a week. It will only lead to frustration and eventual discarding of the budget.

A common approach for estimating an expense item is to look at the previous year's figure as a starting point. Then this figure is adjusted for any anticipated inflation (and on rare occasions, deflation) to arrive at a preliminary estimate for the current year. As an example, suppose you spent $900 on entertainment last year and expect an overall inflation rate of 6 percent. Your budget estimate would be $954 ($900 × 1.06), and by allocating this much, you are in effect saying that you would like to maintain the same level of real consumption in this area. Naturally, keeping the real level constant takes $54 more this year because of inflation. Now, if your intention is to increase (or decrease) the real consumption level, then more (or fewer) budget dollars would be needed. Various economic forecasters, including those employed by the federal government, make forecasts of the overall inflation rate, usually measured by the consumer price index. These numbers are frequently published in newspaper and magazine articles. Good sources for the latter are U.S. *News and World Report, Newsweek, Money,* and *Changing Times.*

Making budget estimates will be more difficult if you are doing it for the first time, particularly if you are just starting housekeeping. Some help is available in the form of family budget statistics, such as those shown in Figure 4.3, but it probably will take several months' experience to determine expense patterns you feel comfortable with.

We will discuss here how the Steeles arrived at their budget figures for 1993. For their salaries, they thought Arnold would most likely get a 5 percent increase over his 1992 salary, while Sharon would probably get a 10 percent increase and work more hours than she did in 1992. Interest income was expected to average 7 percent on their average balances, and dividends on the InChemCo stock were estimated to increase by 10 percent.

The Steeles used a number of approaches to estimate expenses. The mortgage payments on their home and automobile were fixed, as were the premiums on

MASTER BUDGET WORKSHEET for the period _Upcoming Year, 1993_

For _the Arnold and Sharon Steele Family_

INCOME

Wages and Salaries:

    Arnold — expect 5% raise this year $ 63,216

    Sharon — expect 10% raise and more hours   18,000

      Total wages and salaries   (a)   81,216

Other Income:

    Interest _Should be about 7% on average balance_ $ 984

    Dividends _expect 10% increase_   1,200

    Capital gains or (losses)   none

    Others   none

      Total other income   (b) $ 2,184

TOTAL INCOME = (a) + (b)   (c) $ 83,400

EXPENSES

Housing:

    Rent $ none

    Mortgage payments _fixed_   18,285

    Maintenance fees on condo or cooperative   none

    Maintenance and home furnishings _Cut back a bit_   2,400

      Total housing expenses   (d) $ 20,685

Transportation:

    Automobile loan payments _fixed_ $ 5,688

    Gas, oil, other maintenance and repairs _say $200 a month_   2,400

    Licenses, parking, and other auto _should be about $20 a month_   240

    Other transportation   none

      Total transportation expenses   (e) $ 8,328

Food and Other Consumption Items:

    Food and household supplies _about $550 a month_ $ 6,600

    Meals eaten out _let's budget $80 a month_   960

    Personal care—barbers and beauticians _about $60 a month_   720

    Others   none

      Total food and other consumption items   (f) $ 8,280

Utilities:

    Telephone _this should be $45 a month_ $ 540

    Gas and electric _last year was $190 a month; go higher_   2,400

    Water and sanitation _last year was $128 a quarter; go higher_   720

    Garbage pickup   none

    Cable TV _$35 a month last year; will go higher_   480

    Others   none

    Total utilities   (g) $ 4,140

FIGURE 4.2

Master budget worksheet for the Steeles.

Taxes:

Payroll *estimates based on 1992 estimated income* $ 15,600

Real estate and personal property *last years; didn't go up*   3,500

Others   none

  Total taxes   (h) $ 19,100

Insurance:

Health and medical withheld from wages *InChem Co pays* $ none

Life *fixed; don't anticipate more insurance*   480

Property and liabilty *budget 5% over last year*   600

Automobile *budget 5% over last year*   1,560

Disability *InChem Co. pays*   none

Others   none

  Total insurance   (i) $ 2,640

Leisure and Entertainment:

Theater and sporting events *budget $70 a month* $ 840

Health club memberships *not interested*   none

Newspapers, magazines, etc. *budget $40 a month*   480

Vacations *count on four weeks camping*   1,800

Hobbies *buy one small antique*   240

Sporting equipment *soccer shoes; tennis equipment*   240

Others *Christmas gifts*   800

  Total leisure and entertainment   (j) $ 4,400

Clothing:

New clothing *let's budget $150 a month* $ 1,800

Laundry and dry cleaning *estimate $20 a month*   240

Others   none

  Total clothing   (k) $ 2,040

Others:

Gifts and charitable contributions *budget $180 a month* $ 2,160

Dues and subscriptions *last years amount*   200

Tuition, books, other education expenses *expect big increase*   480

Babysitters *estimate at $50 a month*   600

Family members' personal allowances *we agree on this*   1,200

Unreimbursed medical–dental   —

InChem Co. pays all,   —

figure the worst on braces   1,200

  —

  Total others   (l) $ 5,840

TOTAL EXPENSES = (d) + (e) + (f) + (g) + (h)

     + (i) + (j) + (k) + (l) =   (m) $ 75,453

CONTRIBUTION TO SAVINGS = (c) − (m) =   (n) $ 7,947

FIGURE 4.2

Continued.

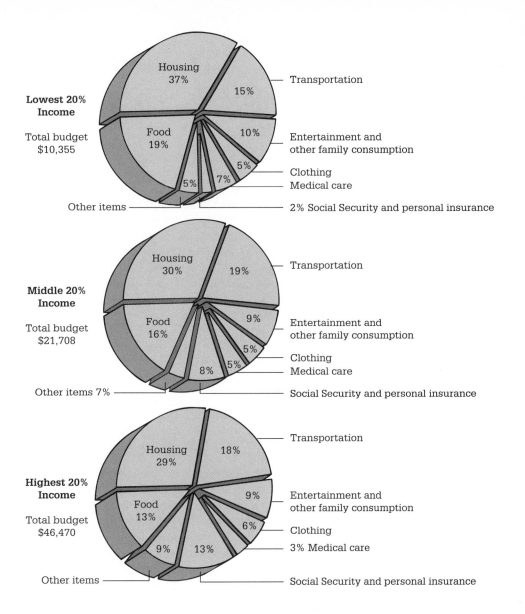

FIGURE 4.3

Expenditures by income levels (quintiles), 1987. (SOURCE: U.S. Department of Labor, *Consumer Expenditure Survey, 1987*, Bulletin 2354.)

Arnold's life insurance. Next were items the Steeles expected to consume rather uniformly throughout the year, and estimating the year's total consisted of making a realistic estimate for one month (around the middle of the year to allow for inflation) and then multiplying this figure by twelve. As you see, many expenses—such as all the line items under *Food and Other Consumption Items*—were estimated in this fashion. The third kind of estimate consisted of looking at what happened in the previous year and then making an intelligent guess as to what might happen in the budget year. For example, the Steeles expect a big increase in education expenses. Finally, some figures were determined through family

Budget
Management

agreement. This was true of *Vacations* expense and *Family members' personal allowances*. Actually, these latter current consumption goals were used to reconcile the budget, as we now explain.

RECONCILING GOALS   The budget amounts you see in Figure 4.2 did not come about on the first budget draft. Actually, the first draft for the Steeles left them somewhat short of their savings goal. Thus, the budget had to be reconciled, which simply means that the sum of expenses and contribution to savings must equal total income. Since their savings goal was the most important budget priority to them in 1993 (they felt it was vitally important to build their investment and liquid assets), reconciliation required some cutting of current consumption. To illustrate the give-and-take among the family members in current consumption, we have left some of the initial expense estimates on the worksheet in crossed-out form. Notice that they planned to spend $2,500—rather than $1,800—on their vacations, and personal allowances were also cut from $1,400 to $1,200. These allowances, by the way, are personal funds available to each member of the family to do with as he or she pleases. Their main purpose is to give each member a little independence from the family budget. Of course, each is expected to live within the yearly allowance and to understand that if anyone requests more, he or she is asking other members of the family to sacrifice, since some other line item must be reduced to meet the request. It's one way to learn the meaning of "either-or," although you may disagree with the practice of individual allowances.

The Monthly Income and Expense Plan

After the master budget worksheet has been prepared, the next budgeting step is to determine how income and expense items will occur during the year. Usually, this is done on a monthly basis. Some expenses occur sporadically and in rather large amounts. It is important to plan for these expenses so that sufficient funds are available when these expenses must be paid. The monthly income and expense plan details income, expenses, and contributions to savings on a month-to-month basis. Arnold and Sharon Steele programmed their personal computer to show their monthly income and expense plan; it is shown in Figure 4.4.

ESTIMATING THE MONTHLY ACTIVITY   As mentioned above, some of the expense items were estimated in total by determining a budget monthly figure and then multiplying by twelve. The monthly allocation, then, is this same monthly figure. For example, the Steeles' telephone bill was budgeted at $45 a month, so that figure is entered for each month. Notice in Figure 4.4 those expenses that do not occur uniformly. For example, all the insurance bills come in January and February; real estate taxes are paid in February and August, and dentist bills are also expected in these two months. Notice further that Sharon's salary comes only in January through June and again in December, and that dividends are received quarterly. In planning the monthly activity, you should try to determine as well as you can when the expected income or expense will occur.

Budgeting in the Year 2022

Few people give much thought to what their budget will look like next year, so why worry about it for the year 2022? Actually, we're not worried about the budgets, as such; our main concern is whether or not our income will increase enough to allow the same standard of living we enjoy today. Clearly, both overall inflation and relative inflation of individual budget items will be important in the income–expenditure equation.

Within the past decade there have been periods of high and low inflation. For example, in the four-year period from 1978 to 1981 most prices rose very rapidly; however, in the four following years, 1982 to 1985, inflation was rather mild.

What will the next 30 years hold? No one knows, but it is interesting to project budget items based upon high-inflation and low-inflation scenarios. The data below result from such an exercise.

Suppose we spend $15,000 in 1992 in the six budget categories as indicated. Now, if each category experiences future inflation at the same rate that occurred in the high-inflation years, the budget in 2022 will total $350,000, which reflects an overall average *annual* inflation rate of 11.1 percent. But, as you see, the categories do not inflate at equal rates. In 2022 we will spend almost 55 percent of our budget dollars on housing and only about 1 percent on clothing (it's practically a free good!).

However, if the low-inflation scenario holds, the overall inflation rate falls to 4.0 percent. Now, it takes *only* $48,100 to be as well off in 2022 as we are today. But again, the relative inflation rates change the budget allocations: medical care increases considerably; entertainment increases moderately; housing stays about the same; and food, apparel, and transportation decline.

Should we worry about the 2022 budget? Losing sleep over it might be a mistake, but the exercise shows clearly the ravages of inflation. If its fires begin to heat up, we'd better look more closely at all our financial plans—not just future budgets.

Category	1992 Expenditures		Growth Factor: High Inflation[1]	2022 Expenditures		Growth Factor: Low Inflation[2]	2022 Expenditures	
Food	$ 4,000	26.6%	13.2	$ 52,800	15.1%	2.5	$10,000	20.7%
Housing	6,000	40.0	31.8	190,800	54.5	3.2	19,200	39.9
Apparel	1,000	6.7	4.0	4,000	1.1	2.0	2,000	4.2
Transportation	2,000	13.3	37.4	74,800	21.4	2.3	4,600	9.6
Medical	1,000	6.7	19.2	19,200	5.5	8.8	8,800	18.3
Entertainment	1,000	6.7	8.4	8,400	2.4	3.5	3,500	7.3
Totals	$15,000	100.0	—	$350,000	100.0	—	$48,100	100.0

[1]Based on annual inflation rates, 1978–1981.

[2]Based on annual inflation rates, 1982–1985.

SOURCE: Data for inflation rates from *Monthly Labor Review*, April 1986, p. 18.

GETTING THROUGH THE LEAN MONTHS Because of the irregularity of some income and expense items, it is possible that your expenses will exceed your income in a given month. Of course, you must have the funds available to meet the deficit, and you may have to borrow to do so. In looking at Figure 4.4 you see the Steeles will have four deficit months. The other eight months show positive contributions to savings. By knowing they are likely to need extra funds in these four months, the Steeles can be alert to the need for effective cash management. For example, if we assume their checking account balance is at a bare minimum as they begin 1993, then they should be careful how they deposit the expected surplus of $1,157 in January. It would not be wise to put all of it into some type

FIGURE 4.4

Monthly income and expense plan for the Steele family for 1993.

INCOME	JAN	FEB	MAR	APR	MAY	JUNE	JULY	AUG	SEPT	OCT	NOV	DEC	TOTAL
Arnold's salary	5,268	5,268	5,268	5,268	5,268	5,268	5,268	5,268	5,268	5,268	5,268	5,268	63,216
Sharon's salary	2,000	3,000	4,000	4,000	2,000	1,000					2,000	2,000	18,000
Interest	82	82	82	82	82	82	82	82	82	82	82	82	984
Dividends	—	300	300	—	—	300	—	—	300	—	—	300	1,200
Total Income	7,350	8,350	9,650	9,350	7,350	6,650	5,350	5,350	5,650	5,350	5,350	7,650	83,400
EXPENSES													
House mortgage	1,524	1,524	1,524	1,524	1,524	1,524	1,524	1,524	1,524	1,524	1,524	1,524	18,285
Maintenance and furnishings	200	200	200	200	200	200	200	200	200	200	200	200	2,400
Auto loan	474	474	474	474	474	474	474	474	474	474	474	474	5,688
Gas, oil, maintenance	200	200	200	200	200	200	200	200	200	200	200	200	2,400
Licenses, parking	20	20	20	20	20	20	20	20	20	20	20	20	240
Food, household items	550	550	550	550	550	550	550	550	550	550	550	550	6,600
Meals eaten out	80	80	80	80	80	80	80	80	80	80	80	80	960
Personal care	60	60	60	60	60	60	60	60	60	60	60	60	720
Telephone	45	45	45	45	45	45	45	45	45	45	45	45	540
Gas and electric	200	200	200	200	200	200	200	200	200	200	200	200	2,400
Water, garbage	180	—	—	180	—	—	180	—	—	180	—	—	720
Cable TV	120	—	—	120	—	—	120	—	—	120	—	—	480
All payroll taxes	1,400	1,500	1,700	1,600	1,400	1,200	1,100	1,100	1,100	1,100	1,100	1,300	15,600
Real estate taxes	—	1,800	—	—	—	—	—	1,700	—	—	—	—	3,500
Life insurance	480	—	—	—	—	—	—	—	—	—	—	—	480
Property insurance	—	600	—	—	—	—	—	—	—	—	—	—	600
Auto insurance	—	1,560	—	—	—	—	—	—	—	—	—	—	1,560
Theater, sports	70	70	70	70	70	70	70	70	70	70	70	70	840
Newspapers, magazines	40	40	40	40	40	40	40	40	40	40	40	40	480
Vacations	—	—	—	300	—	400	600	—	—	—	—	500	1,800
Hobbies, Christmas gifts	—	—	—	120	—	—	—	120	—	—	—	800	1,040
Sporting equipment	—	—	—	120	—	—	—	120	—	—	—	—	240
New clothing	150	150	150	150	150	150	150	150	150	150	150	150	1,800
Laundry, dry cleaning	20	20	20	20	20	20	20	20	20	20	20	20	240
Gifts, contributions	180	180	180	180	180	180	180	180	180	180	180	180	2,160
Dues and Subscriptions	50	—	—	—	50	—	25	25	25	25	—	—	200
Tuition, books, etc.	—	—	—	—	—	—	—	480	—	—	—	—	480
Baby sitters	50	50	50	50	50	50	50	50	50	50	50	50	600
Personal allowances	100	100	100	100	100	100	100	100	100	100	100	100	1,200
Dental–medical	—	600	—	—	—	—	—	—	600	—	—	—	1,200
Total Expenses	6,193	10,023	5,663	6,403	5,413	5,563	5,988	7,508	5,688	5,388	5,063	6,563	75,453
Contribution to Savings	1,157	−1,673	3,987	2,947	1,937	1,087	−638	−2,158	−38	−38	287	1,087	7,947

of account—say, a certificate of deposit—that is not readily available for withdrawals, because they will need $1,673 in the next month. Unquestionably, the year's activity will not unfold exactly as the Steeles see it in Figure 4.4; there are sure to be some surprises along the way to change things, but the Steeles are now in a far better position to cope with these changes than they would be without their monthly income and expense plan.

Monitoring and Controlling Activities

With the master budget worksheet and the monthly income and expense plan finished, the first phase of budgeting is completed. You now have a road map to guide your financial activities through the year. The second phase of budgeting begins as the year unfolds and events take place. This phase involves three separate tasks: First, you need a system to record your actual income and expenses. Second, you must periodically update your income and expense accounts to see if actual amounts received and spent are in line with amounts planned. (This is usually done on a monthly basis.) Third, you need to evaluate and control activities as the year progresses.

Recording Income and Expenses

Record keeping is perhaps the most unpleasant aspect of budgeting, but it is necessary. Our concern should be primarily with how to do it most efficiently. Like the Emmons, most people resent doing extensive bookkeeping each evening or weekend. The following list of suggestions might help you simplify the work:

DON'T USE CASH Pay as many bills as you can with checks or by charges to your credit cards (assuming neither method induces you to spend more). These will give you a written record of expenses that can be recorded at the end of the month. Paying bills with cash means, in effect, you must create your own record, by either saving invoices or writing things on odd pieces of paper. Both of these activities are time-consuming, and the records are easily lost. Whenever you do pay with cash, standardize the recording by creating your own little "voucher," which can be a small piece of paper like the one shown in Figure 4.5. You can make many of these if you have access to a copying machine. Stick a few of these in your pocket each day and get in the habit of using them.

CODE INCOME AND EXPENSE ACCOUNTS Assign an account number to each line item (particularly those used frequently), and as you pay a bill, code the check stub with the appropriate number. This will facilitate summing expenses by category each month. Also, code your income items as you make bank deposits in order to identify the income source. If you receive a check from someone and cash it instead of depositing it, you also will have to record the amount received and identify the source. It is almost always better to deposit all checks and cash to your checking (or other) account so they can be identified; if you need cash, write a check to get it.

SEE IF YOUR BANK CAN HELP Ask if your bank provides computerized services in summarizing your checks and deposit slips. Some banks do (and the trend is

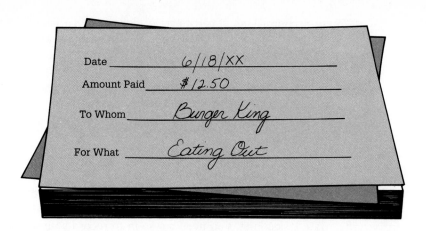

FIGURE 4.5

A simple voucher to record cash expenses.

growing), and if you simply number-code your checks and deposits for each income and expense classification, the bank's monthly statement can provide you with the following information: (*a*) income and expense by each code number, (*b*) number of entries in each code number, (*c*) a percentage breakdown of income and expenses by code number for the month, and (*d*) an update of income and expense items by code number for the year. There probably will be a modest charge (say, $6 to $12 a month) for this service.

USE A PERSONAL COMPUTER   If, like the Steeles, you have a personal computer, determine if a home budgeting software package will be helpful. These vary in capability, but all provide data manipulation similar to the bank's service mentioned above. In addition, your personal computer has capabilities to store all the data and make it readily available for other purposes, such as comparing one month's expenses in a given category to similar monthly expenses of the previous year. And much more can be done; for example, the budget can be connected directly to your year-end balance sheet and income statement, so that making entries on the computer keyboard is virtually all you ever have to do for the entire financial recording process. All data manipulation and storage—and even printed copies—are provided automatically by the computer.

Updating Income and Expense Accounts

Variance: Actual income or expense item compared to the budgeted amount.

Income variance: Income item variance—favorable when actual exceeds budget; unfavorable in the reverse situation.

Expense variance: Expense item variance—favorable when actual is less than budget; unfavorable in the reverse situation.

Cumulative variance: Monthly accumulation of variances.

After all income and expense items have been accounted for, the next step is to update your monthly income and expense plan by recording actual amounts and then comparing them to the budget. This is usually done monthly, and it is done best with an income and expense plan update, such as the one shown in Figure 4.6. If the actual amount for a line item differs from the budgeted figure, it is called a **variance**. Variances can then be either favorable—meaning they assisted in the saving effort—or unfavorable—meaning they detracted from it. An **income variance** is favorable whenever actual exceeds budget; it is unfavorable when the reverse is true. An **expense variance** is favorable whenever actual is less than budget, and it is unfavorable in the reverse case. Unfavorable variances are indicated in Figure 4.6 by parentheses around the amount. The **cumulative variance** figure results from adding the current month's variance to variances of

FIGURE 4.6

Monthly budget update for the Steeles for the first quarter, 1993.

	JANUARY				FEBRUARY				MARCH			
INCOME	Budget	Actual	Variance	Cumulative Variance	Budget	Actual	Variance	Cumulative Variance	Budget	Actual	Variance	Cumulative Variance
Arnold's salary	$5,268	$5,268	$ 0	$ 0	$ 5,268	$ 5,268	$ 0	$ 0	$5,268	$ 5,268	$ 0	$ 0
Sharon's salary	2,000	2,375	375	375	3,000	3,475	475	850	4,000	4,425	425	1,275
Interest	82	84	2	2	82	80	−2	0	82	77	−5	−5
Dividends	0	0	0	0	0	0	0	0	300	300	0	0
Total Income	$7,350	$7,727	$ 377	$ 377	$ 8,350	$ 8,823	$ 473	$ 850	$9,650	$10,070	$ 420	$1,270
EXPENSES												
House mortgage	$1,524	$1,524	$ 0	$ 0	$ 1,524	$ 1,524	$ 0	$ 0	$1,524	$ 1,524	$ 0	$ 0
Maintenance and furnishings	200	188	12	12	200	160	40	52	200	230	−30	22
Auto loan	474	474	0	0	474	474	0	0	474	474	0	0
Gas, oil, maintenance	200	210	−10	−10	200	225	−25	−35	200	232	−32	−67
Licenses, parking	20	23	−3	−3	20	27	−7	−10	20	24	−4	−14
Food, household items	550	548	2	2	550	596	−46	−44	550	593	−43	−87
Meals eaten out	80	88	−8	−8	80	102	−22	−30	80	91	−11	−41
Personal care	60	73	−13	−13	60	66	−6	−19	60	63	−3	−22
Telephone	45	41	4	4	45	43	2	6	45	43	2	8
Gas and electric	200	195	5	5	200	208	−8	−3	200	176	24	21
Water, garbage	180	188	−8	−8	0	0	0	−8	0	0	0	−8
Cable TV	120	120	0	0	0	0	0	0	0	0	0	0
All payroll taxes	1,400	1,531	−131	−131	1,500	1,647	−147	−278	1,700	1,910	−210	−488
Real estate taxes	0	0	0	0	0	0	0	0	0	0	0	0
Life insurance	480	480	0	0	0	0	0	0	0	0	0	0
Property insurance	0	0	0	0	600	620	−20	−20	0	0	0	−20
Auto insurance	0	0	0	0	1,560	1,630	−70	−70	0	0	0	−70
Theater, sports	70	62	8	8	70	80	−10	−2	70	76	−6	−8
Newspapers, magazines	40	37	3	3	40	37	3	6	40	56	−16	−10
Vacations	0	0	0	0	0	0	0	0	0	0	0	0
Hobbies, Christmas gifts	0	0	0	0	0	0	0	0	0	0	0	0
Sporting equipment	0	40	−40	−40	0	0	0	−40	0	0	0	−40
New clothing	150	161	−11	−11	150	133	17	6	150	174	−24	−18
Laundry, dry cleaning	20	27	−7	−7	20	28	−8	−15	20	26	−6	−21
Gifts, contributions	180	180	0	0	180	178	2	2	180	173	7	9
Dues and subscriptions	50	50	0	0	0	0	0	0	0	0	0	0
Tuition, books, etc.	0	0	0	0	0	0	0	0	0	0	0	0
Baby sitters	50	67	−17	−17	50	64	−14	−31	50	79	−29	−60
Personal allowances	100	100	0	0	100	100	0	0	100	100	0	0
Dental-medical	0	0	0	0	600	470	130	130	0	0	0	130
Total Expenses	$6,193	$6,407	$ −214	$ −214	$10,023	$10,212	$ −189	$ −403	$5,663	$ 6,044	$ −381	$ −784
Contribution to Savings	$1,157	$1,320	$ 163	$ 163	$ −1,673	$ −1,389	$ 284	$ 447	$3,987	$ 4,026	$ 39	$ 486

previous months; thus, the cumulative variance for maintenance—the second expense item—in February is a favorable $52, which is the sum of the favorable $40 variance in February added to the favorable variance of $12 in January. In March, maintenance showed an unfavorable variance of $30, and subtracting this from February's cumulative variance gives a new cumulative variance of $22 at the end of March.

Figure 4.6 shows the Steeles' activity for the first three months of 1993. Although you see all three months at once, you should assume each month's activities were recorded separately. The flow of data gives you a fairly good picture of how the Steeles' financial events took place during the quarter. Sharon began working more hours than she anticipated, which led to most of the favorable income variance in January, and this continued in February and March. By the end of the quarter, Sharon had earned $1,275 more than budget. The estimates for Arnold's salary and dividends were accurate, and the interest variance is trivial.

While the Steeles were pleased with the extra income, it was also the source of many of their unfavorable expense variances during the quarter. The first and most obvious of these is the extra $488 of payroll taxes. Sharon's increased work activity meant she used the car more than planned, had a bit higher personal care expense, hired baby sitters more frequently, and incurred larger dry cleaning bills. If we assume all the increases in these expense accounts are attributable to the Steeles' added income, this means a total of $651 ($488 + $67 + $14 + $22 + $60) of the added income went to cover the additional expenses associated with it. This left them with $769 ($1,420 − $651) of discretionary income to be spent or saved. We saw in the previous chapter that the Steeles had a sliding scale with respect to their planned contributions to savings for the year (Table 3.1), so they then implemented that plan by setting a higher savings goal for the rest of the year. Their revised savings goal was $8,200 for all of 1993. However, they did not save *all* the added discretionary income, which means by implication that they also planned to increase their consumption in 1993. They began doing so in January, when Arnie and Sharon bought some racquetball equipment. Also, the family started eating out more frequently.

The remainder of the expense variances are relatively minor on a month-to-month basis; you seldom will budget more accurately during a period as short as a month. The only exception—a pleasant one—is the dentist's bill was far less than expected.

Evaluating and Controlling Activities

Being able to stay within budget means you are continuously adjusting your expenses during the year. Evaluating and controlling activities really make the budget work; an elaborate recording system does little good if we choose to ignore the information it provides. Actually, recording, evaluating, and controlling should be activities that go on simultaneously; however, it is convenient to have monthly reviews and a year-end summary that ties the budget to the year's income statement.

Monthly review: End-of-month evaluation of budgeting performance.

THE MONTHLY REVIEW AND CONTROL   The **monthly review** begins by looking at the expense variances, and the control starts in the following month. After

The Basic
Framework

Box 4.3
Simplifying Financial Planning

Budgeting with Envelopes and Play Money

At first glance, the bulletin board in Mark and Carla Spielman's kitchen looks pretty much like anyone else's—but there's a difference. Along with the reminders, recipes, and other assorted notes usually adorning theirs are nine letter-size envelopes, one for each of the most important ways the Spielmans spend money; there's also a red envelope for savings, red meaning: "Stop before entering." In each of the ten envelopes Mark and Carla put a predetermined amount of play money at the beginning of each month, which represents their monthly allotment for the activity marked on the envelope; for example, the "Entertainment" envelope starts each month with $100 in it.

These envelopes are the Spielmans' complete budgeting system. Every evening they go together to the bulletin board and withdraw money from the appropriate envelopes to represent the money they spent that day, whether by check or cash. At the end of the month all the envelopes should be empty, except those that include things like vacations, where

funds are being temporarily saved for later use. If all goes exactly to plan, every envelope should be empty, except savings, on December 31. But what happens if the money runs out before a month is over? Unless they come up with a good reason for transferring from one envelope to another (but never from the red one unless it's an absolute emergency), that activity is shot for the month. So if $100 is taken out of the entertainment envelope by mid-month, the Spielmans watch a lot of television, or find other things to do for the rest of the month.

The envelope system of budgeting probably dates back to the time envelopes were invented. Of course, the system itself doesn't guarantee success, but supposedly the discipline you gain by touching and feeling the money as you slip it out of the envelope makes you more budget-conscious than do other approaches, like writing things down on a budget worksheet, or, in today's environment, punching data into your home computer. But what about play money: will you have the same emotional reservations about spending it? Some financial planners think so, and if you haven't done well at budgeting in the past, it's worth a try. It has several big advantages over the real thing: it's not that important if you lose some and hardly anyone wants to steal it. And, just as important, you can leave your actual cash in the bank to earn interest. Don't take this last advantage lightly. If you have an expense budget of $3,000 a month and pay expenses uniformly over a month, your average balance for the month—and for the year as a whole—is $1,500. If you have a NOW account earning 4 percent, you would give up $60 a year by stuffing cash in those envelopes. So, use play money and sleep at night—and have a good night on the town with the interest you earn.

each monthly expense variance is calculated, you must decide what to do about it in the months ahead. Assuming no major variances in income (which is not the Steeles' case) and no changes in budget goals, then your next month's activities should be managed (as well as they can) to reduce a cumulative expense variance, if one exists. For example, the Steeles went $11 over their budget for new clothing in January. This tells them they have only $139 ($150 − $11) to spend in February. You must subtract the cumulative variance (add, if it's favorable) from the current monthly budget figure to determine how much current funds are available for a given line item. In February, the Steeles went $17 under budget for new clothing, which offset the unfavorable $11 variance, leaving a $6 favorable variance for March. However, March's figure was $24 over budget, meaning the

Steeles ended the first quarter with a cumulative unfavorable variance of $18 in this account. Unless their goal is changed here, they should try to reduce this variance to zero by the end of June.

If your income has changed considerably from the planned amount, or if you have changed your goals, then the budget should also be changed. Of course, this means some extra work since you are actually starting all over. A personal computer along with a home budgeting software program is very helpful in revising budgets, since only a few new entries on your part are needed to automatically adjust all the spreadsheets, such as those illustrated in Figures 4.4 and 4.6. If you do not have a personal computer, you can make revised estimates of your income and some expense items for the balance of the year. These revisions can be kept on a separate worksheet, which should be included in the year-end review. As we saw previously, the Steeles have already decided to increase some of their discretionary consumption activities.

Year-end review: End-of-year evaluation of budgeting performance.
THE YEAR-END REVIEW   Assuming you are monitoring activities and calculating cumulative variances at the end of each month, the **year-end review** can be brief. It serves mainly to assist in making budget estimates for the next year. It also provides an opportunity to prepare the current year's income statement, because the figure for each line item here is simply the budget amount for the year plus its cumulative variance at December 31.

A Concluding Note on Budgeting

At the beginning of this chapter, we indicated that budgeting doesn't have to be "bad-tasting medicine." Despite all the worksheets you have seen that seem to contradict our statement, budgeting is simple and really doesn't take that much time, even if you don't have a computer. Once you start you will probably agree that the most time is spent deciding on goals and evaluating performance. Bookkeeping time can be kept to a minimum. You should reconcile your bank statement (see Chapter 6) each month anyway, so coding each check and deposit and then summing them by code numbers can be done at the same time. It shouldn't add more than an hour of work each month. If the work seems excessive, cut down on the number of codes. You lose a little control over where the money is going, but it does save time. The main thing is to have some kind of budget. (For the sake of showing a wide variety of income and expense items, our budget and income statement have more categories than are needed for effective control.)

Many financial advisers agree that the most often cited factor explaining a lack of savings and eventual financial problems is the absence of concrete plans to indicate where a person wants to be and how to get there. Very often a petitioner in bankruptcy will be asked to work with a court-appointed financial adviser to prepare a budget showing how he or she will liquidate remaining debts in the coming years. If that person had learned to budget earlier, there might never have been the need to file bankruptcy.

Keeping and Storing Records

Over your lifetime you will accumulate a mass of financial and personal data. Much of it will have to do with the tax returns you file, particularly if you itemize deductions. General guidelines on what information to keep for the government and for how long are explained in Chapter 5. Figure 4.7 provides some insights on keeping and storing other records.

It's a good idea to have a simple set of files that can be kept in a drawer or other convenient place. Some advisers suggest having one large manila envelope for tax-related items. As you accumulate documents during the year supporting your tax return, put them in the envelope. Then, at tax time, everything is in one place. Other envelopes or folders can be set up for other documents—stock records, insurance policies, birth certificates, and so on—which are filed as soon as you get them. After you file your tax return, you should get a folder or envelope and mark the tax year on it, and save all supporting documents in it. Your income statements, balance sheets, and budgets (and any other financial planning statement) can be kept in a three-ring binder. Many people keep copies of their

FIGURE 4.7

Keeping and storing records.

ATTORNEY / SAFE DEPOSIT / HOME

Records to Keep at Home

- Tax returns for every year a return is filed
- Documents supporting tax returns—at least the past three years
- Social Security—as a worker, you should file Social Security Form 7004 every three years to make sure contributions are reported correctly
- Confirmation slips for all securities purchased, to show what you paid for the securities and when they were purchased. (If you sell the securities, the slips then become part of your tax records.)
- All information related to your house. In particular, keep records of any improvements: how much and when made
- All insurance policies; it's a good idea to have an insurance folder to keep the policies in one place.
- Education documents—SAT scores, grade transcripts, any scholastic honors
- A copy of your will; include with this the name of a person who can advise your spouse about employer death benefits (of course, this assumes you arrange such an adviser)
- All bank statements, credit statements, and other invoices should be reviewed for accuracy when received and saved for one year; if they support your tax return, save at least three years
- Monthly statements from your stockbroker; save as needed for tax-filing purposes, although many investors keep them permanently.

Records to Keep in Your Safe Deposit Box

- Marriage contract
- Dissolution (or divorce) decree
- Stock and bond certificates, including U.S. Savings bonds
- Military records
- Jewelry or precious coins; keep in mind, though, safe deposit boxes are not insured; if the dollar value of these items is substantial, other storage arrangements should be found.
- Birth and death certificates—also keep copies at home

Records Your Lawyer Should Have

- Your will
- Any burial instructions—keep a copy at home
- Details of any trust arrangements—keep a copy at home

Budget
Management

tax returns in this binder, although some prefer keeping the copies in the tax-year envelope mentioned above. One last tip: If any document is extremely important to you, consider keeping it in the refrigerator. It's probably the safest place in the house in case of a disaster. Of course, a safe deposit box is better, if you have one.

Summary

A budget is a plan expressing goals and allocations of limited resources to achieve them. Whether simple or complex, budgeting is likely to be successful if it (a) sets realistic goals, (b) sticks to simple procedures, and (c) serves to control and direct expenses. In order to be useful for budgeting, goals must be set in specific terms. It is important to have a schedule of major future goals showing when the goal will be accomplished and the amount of annual savings required for accomplishment. Each major goal should have an action plan, which expresses in specific terms how the goal will be achieved. The action plan, in turn, should be linked to the annual budget, and all action plans should be reviewed and updated annually. An annual budget is usually prepared with the aid of two schedules: the master budget worksheet and the monthly income and expense plan. The master budget worksheet lists all expected income and expenses for the upcoming year. The monthly income and expense plan takes the total income or expense for the year and shows the individual amounts received or spent in each month. These monthly amounts are useful because they pinpoint how funds will be used each month, thereby helping to control future activities. Monitoring and controlling activities make up an important phase of budgeting, which begins by recording monthly income and expenses. After these are recorded, it is then necessary to update each income and expense account by comparing the actual amount with the budget; any difference is called a *variance*, which is favorable if it assists the savings effort and unfavorable if it detracts from it. An account's budget variance for one month is combined with budget variances of preceding months to arrive at a cumulative variance for the year. This figure is then used to evaluate performance as the year progresses. Controlling activities brings an expense back within the budget if its variance is unfavorable. It can also indicate that extra funds are available in the current month if a variance is favorable. The year-end review completes budgeting activities for the year.

Key Terms

action plan (p. 86)	income variance (p. 98)	monthly review (p. 100)
budget (p. 82)	master budget worksheet (p. 88)	variance (p. 98)
cumulative variance (p. 98)		year-end review (p. 102)
	monthly income and expense plan (p. 88)	
expense variance (p. 98)		
goal setting (p. 83)		

Problems and Review Questions

1 Explain three simple rules that often lead to success in budgeting. Do you agree that the more complex a budget is, the more successful it will be? Explain.

2 Discuss the process of setting goals. List several general goals that you think will be important to you after graduation and then indicate what specific goals you will use in your annual budgets.

3 Describe details of an action plan and explain why they are important. Also, discuss why they should be reviewed periodically.

4 Describe the master budget worksheet, indicating some expenses you believe might be easy to forecast and some that are more difficult.

5 Explain how you would forecast the following expense items for an upcoming budget year: (a) mortgage payments; (b) food and household items; (c) income and other payroll taxes; and (d) family members' personal allowances.

6 How does a monthly income and expense plan help in managing your cash and checking account?

7 Suppose you are preparing your first budget. Explain briefly how you will estimate expense items.

8 Explain what is meant by reconciling the budget.

9 Briefly describe four procedures that might simplify bookkeeping activities connected with recording monthly income and expense amounts.

10 Explain the relationship among the budget, the income statement, and cumulative variances. Also, discuss possible situations that might warrant making changes in your budget during the year.

11 Discuss what is done in a year-end review, explain if such a review is really necessary if you are monitoring activities monthly.

12 Below are budget and actual figures for selected income and expense accounts for the month of June, and cumulative variances for each account through May. (Parentheses indicate an unfavorable variance.)

	Cumulative Variance Through May	June Budget	June Actual
Salaries	$(1,600)	$3,000	$3,400
Expenses:			
Rent	(100)	300	320
Transportation	85	200	215
Food	125	550	575
All others	(160)	850	780
Payroll taxes	400	900	1,000

Assuming the accounts listed above are all that need to be considered, answer the following questions. (a) Calculate June's variances and the cumulative variances through June. (b) If the budgeter planned at the beginning of the year to save an equal amount each month and has not revised that plan, how much has he or she actually saved through June? (Show your work.)

13 Refer to the data in Question 12, and suppose the budgeter expects his or her salary to be the same as June's for the balance of the year. Make specific suggestions the budgeter can follow in order to achieve the savings goal set up at the beginning of the year.

Case 4.1 Future Planning for the Ingrams

Joseph and Mary Jean Ingram are a young couple in their late twenties with three children: two girls—ages four and six—and a boy, age two. They currently rent a condominium in the suburban area of a large Midwestern city but are planning to buy their own detached home within the next three years. Except for this plan, the Ingrams haven't given much thought to what their intermediate and long-range goals are. They expect their kids will want to go to college—at least they would like them to have the opportunity to do so—and they feel they will surely need more retirement funds than those provided by Social Security and Joe's retirement plan at work.

As a financial analyst for a stockbrokerage firm, Joe is making about $42,000 a year. Mary Jean is currently limiting her activities to the household, but she is a registered nurse and expects to resume nursing activities when all the children are in school. The Ingrams have about $7,200 in liquid assets but feel they need at least $18,000 more in order to have an adequate down payment on their home. They would also like to have about $12,000 for furniture and other furnishings within four years after they move into the new home.

Questions

1 Discuss how various action plans might help the Ingrams in achieving their goals.
2 Joe's father has suggested they might buy a place somewhat sooner than they planned; in fact, he has come across a property where the seller might provide second-mortgage financing if Joe and Mary Jean could come up with about $6,000 now. Prepare an action plan for the objective of buying a home and listing as alternatives (a) *buy now* and (b) *buy later.*
3 Assuming it is the beginning of 1993, and Joe would like to retire at age 62 (he is now 28), and that educating the children will cost $10,000 a year for each, prepare a schedule of required savings for the Ingrams up to retirement. Include all the goals mentioned in the case and assume they will wait to buy a home rather than buying one immediately.

Case 4.2
The Terrels' Budget for 1993

Donna and Sherman Terrel are preparing a budget for 1993. Donna is a systems analyst with an airplane manufacturer, and Sherman is working on a master's degree in educational psychology. The Terrels do not have any children or other dependents. Donna estimates her salary will be about $36,000 in 1993, while Sherman expects to work only during the summer months, doing painting and remodeling work for a building contractor. He anticipates an income from these activities of $2,400 a month in June, July, and August. Sherman does have a scholarship that pays his tuition and also provides $2,400 a year, payable in equal amounts in October and February. The Terrels don't expect to have any other income in 1993.

Donna and Sherman have listed their expected total expenses in 1993 below:

Housing (rent)	$ 5,760
Transportation	4,800
Food (includes dining out)	7,920
Utilities	2,880
Payroll taxes:	
Donna	10,800
Sherman	1,200
Insurance:	
Life—payable in May	600
Auto—payable in January	1,320
Leisure and entertainment:	
Vacation in May	1,152
All others	1,728
Clothing	1,296
Others	3,840
Total Expenses	$43,296

The Terrels will begin 1993 with about $1,200 in liquid assets, and they prefer not to draw this balance below $600 at any time during the year.

Questions

1 Prepare a monthly income and expense plan for the Terrels in 1993.
2 Based upon the plan you have just prepared, discuss the Terrels' expected financial situation in 1993. Explain if you foresee any difficulties.
3 During the quarter break in April, Sherman's employer landed a major remodeling project and asked for Sherman's help. Sherm agreed, and he expects to earn $1,800 from the job before taxes, but probably won't receive a check until early June. Discuss how this unexpected event might affect the Terrels' activities and their budget for the balance of 1993. It is not necessary to prepare a revised monthly income and expense plan, but do refer to specific accounts and amounts (make appropriate assumptions) in your discussion.

Helpful Reading

Changing Times

Davis, Kristin. "We Tracked Every Penney for 32 Years." November 1990, pp. 70–74.

Giese, William. "Do Your Investments Fit Your Goals?" February 1991, pp. 51–55.

Money

Luciano, Lani. "How to Cut Your Expenses by 20%." December 1991, pp. 71–75.

Parade

Lemley, Brad. "How to Save a Buck." March 17, 1991, pp. 4–6.

The Wall Street Journal

Ansberry, Clare. "Autumn Years." November 13, 1990, p. A1.

Myers, Henry F. "Why Consumer Debt May Not Be Too High." October 22, 1989, p. A1.

Schultz, Ellen E. "When It's the Wrong Time for Big Financial Decisions." October 29, 1991, p. C1.

Helpful Contacts

The National Foundation for Consumer Credit (cited in Chapter 3's *Helpful Contacts*) assists people with credit problems in preparing budgets.

Chapter 5

Taxes: The Government's Share of Your Rewards

Objectives

1 To understand the basic approach used by the Internal Revenue Service to determine your yearly federal income tax liability

2 To be able to calculate your yearly federal income tax liability following directions and guidelines provided by the Internal Revenue Service

3 To recognize the role the Internal Revenue Service plays in enforcing the income tax law, and to know when to seek professional help in income tax matters

4 To understand and use important strategies that help you save federal income taxes, or defer them to later years

5 To identify other important taxes that you currently pay, or will pay in future years

Taxes are an important part of our everyday lives. We pay sales and excise taxes on many items that we purchase to consume. Our houses, automobiles, and other assets—tangible and intangible—are subject to property taxes. The income we earn is taxed, and when we die, our estates are taxed. Figure 5.1 indicates the size of the "tax bite" in relation to income; it should be noted that the table considers only so-called direct taxes levied on households. When all taxes are considered, the percentages are considerably higher. Indeed, the average family must work about five months each year to support government services. The largest single tax is the federal income tax, and Figure 5.1 gives a clear indication of the federal government's role in American society. Not only does its size make it important, but it is structured in such a fashion—as the Contadinos learned— that most people can reduce their tax liability through effective tax planning. But planning is difficult. Despite the good intentions of many past Presidents and Congresses, the tax law grows increasingly complex, as evidenced by the comprehensive 1986 Tax Reform Act and the more recent Revenue Reconciliation Act of 1990. Some call these tax laws the "full employment acts for accountants," a description they probably deserve. Despite their compexities, you can become aware of simple strategies to reduce your tax liability. With effort, you too can find "tax scholarships" or other tax-minimizing devices. This chapter will help you.

FIGURE 5.1

Money Income Before Taxes	State and Local Taxes[a]	Federal Taxes[b]	Total Taxes	Total Taxes, Percent of Income[c]
Under $5,000	$ 677	$ 350	$ 1,027	25.7
$ 5,000–$ 9,999	780	741	1,531	20.4
$10,000–$14,999	946	2,123	3,069	24.6
$15,000–$19,999	1,136	3,246	4,382	25.0
$20,000–$24,999	1,267	4,504	5,771	25.6
$25,000–$34,999	1,644	6,499	8,143	27.1
$35,000–$49,999	2,338	9,787	12,125	28.5
$50,000 and over	4,917	21,454	26,371	35.2

[a]Consists of property taxes and state income taxes.

[b]Consists of federal income taxes, FICA payroll taxes, and federal retirement taxes.

[c]Percentages calculated using the midpoint of the range, except for the first group (base = $4,000) and the last group (base = $75,000).

FIGURE 5.1

1986 taxes and income. (Source: U.S. Department of Commerce, Bureau of the Census, *Statistical Abstract of the United States—1990*, 110th ed., p. 447.)

Determining Your Federal Income Tax

The federal income tax follows the approach—or formula—illustrated in Figure 5.2. To begin with, many items that you might look upon as income are not considered taxable income by the Internal Revenue Service (the IRS). From the total of the included gross income items, you then are allowed certain deductions to arrive at adjusted gross income. From this total, two other deductions are allowed: personal and dependency exemptions and personal deductions, either itemized or taken as a standardized amount. You now have taxable income, which is then subjected to specific tax rates to arrive at your tax liability before tax credits for the year. From this amount, tax credits are deducted to arrive at your tax liability. Since most of us have income taxes withheld (or paid in advance, using estimates), this liability may have been paid before filing time. In this case, a refund is claimed when the return is filed. If withholding falls short of the liability, as shown in Figure 5.2, we must pay the balance due along with the return. The entire process is explained in greater detail in the following sections, and later we'll illustrate the topic by showing Arnold and Sharon Steele's income tax.

Gross Income Items

Gross income items: Sources of income that are subject to the federal income tax.

Nontaxable exclusions: Items that are *not* includable as gross income.

Basically, any compensation you receive for the use of your labor or capital is a taxable income item. If you take the time to enter a contest and are fortunate enough to win, the prize is income and not a gift, which you would prefer because gifts are not taxable. A partial list of **gross income items** is shown in Figure 5.3, and a partial list of **nontaxable exclusions** is shown in Figure 5.4.

Some of the excluded items are important in tax strategy and should be identified and explained here. Notice that municipal bond interest is an excluded item. All other factors the same, it is to your advantage to own municipal bonds as opposed to those whose interest payments are fully taxable. Also, such items as group term life insurance and health insurance are often offered as fringe benefits by employers (or as part of a salary-reduction plan). You should see that if you must provide these benefits yourself, it will take more of your income than if you

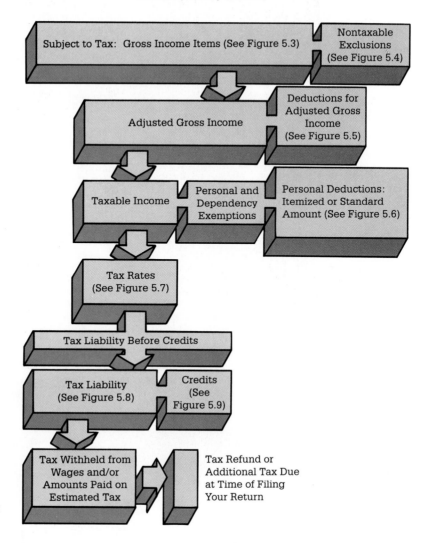

Income (Broadly Defined)

Subject to Tax: Gross Income Items (See Figure 5.3)

Nontaxable Exclusions (See Figure 5.4)

Adjusted Gross Income

Deductions for Adjusted Gross Income (See Figure 5.5)

Taxable Income

Personal and Dependency Exemptions

Personal Deductions: Itemized or Standard Amount (See Figure 5.6)

Tax Rates (See Figure 5.7)

Tax Liability Before Credits

Tax Liability (See Figure 5.8)

Credits (See Figure 5.9)

Tax Withheld from Wages and/or Amounts Paid on Estimated Tax

Tax Refund or Additional Tax Due at Time of Filing Your Return

FIGURE 5.2

The federal income tax formula.

receive them as fringes. Why? Because you cannot deduct such payments in calculating your tax liability and, therefore, they are bought with after-tax dollars. For example, if you are in a 28 percent tax bracket and purchase $1,000 of such insurance, you must earn $1,389 to net the $1,000. [You get this figure by dividing the $1,000 by 1.00 minus the tax bracket; that is, $1,389 = 1,000/(1.00 − 0.28)$.] Clearly, if your employer gives you a choice between the $1,000 or the insurance, choose the latter if you intend to buy the insurance anyway.

Adjustments to Income

Adjusted gross income: Gross income plus or minus certain adjustments.

The tax law requires certain adjustments to arrive at **adjusted gross income.** Most of these adjustments are expenses related to earning income, but some simply reflect the intent of Congress to provide equity or incentives in the tax law. A

Alimony	Hobby income
Awards	Interest
Back Pay	Jury duty fees
Bargain purchase from employer	Living quarter, meals (unless
Bonuses	furnished for employer's
Breach of contract damages	convenience)
Business income	Mileage allowance
Clergy fees and contributions	Military pay (unless combat pay)
Commissions	Partnership income
Compensation for services	Pensions
Death benefits in excess of $5,000	Prizes
Debts forgiven	Professional fees
Director's fees	Punitive damages
Dividends	Reimbursement for moving
Embezzled funds	expenses
Employee awards	Rent
Employee benefits (exception certain	Retirement pay
fringe benefits)	Rewards
Estate and trust income	Royalties
Farm income	Salaries
Fees	Severance Pay
Free tour	Strike and lockout benefits
Gains from illegal activities	Supplemental unemployment
Gains from sale of property	benefits
Gambling winnings	Tips and gratuities
Group term life insurance, premium	Travel allowance
paid by employer (coverage over	Wages
$50,000)	

FIGURE 5.3

A partial list of gross income items.

listing of the adjustments is shown in Figure 5.5, and a discussion of the more important ones follows.

EXCESS REIMBURSEMENT OF EMPLOYEE BUSINESS EXPENSES   Some employees incur expenses in their jobs. Such expenses might include the use of your car, telephone calls, storage facilities in your home, and others. It is important to keep good records to support these items, since employers often reimburse the outlays. If reimbursement exceeds actual expenses, the excess must be reported as income. However, if reimbursement falls short of actual expenses, the deficiency can be taken only as an itemized deduction.

IRAs and Keogh plans: Retirement plans that reduce gross income.

IRAS AND KEOGH PLANS   IRAs and Keogh plans will be explained in greater detail in Chapter 17; however, a few words about each are appropriate here. A

The Basic Framework

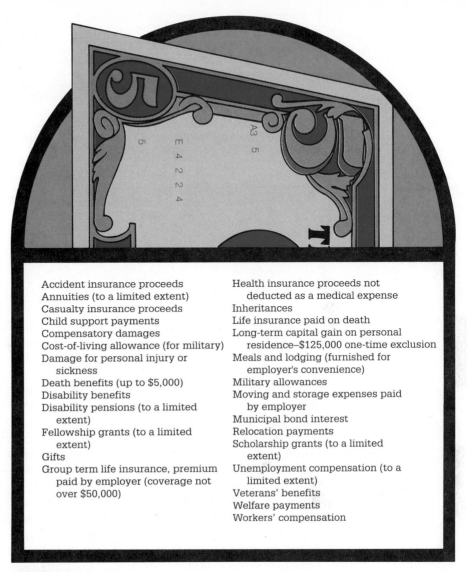

Accident insurance proceeds
Annuities (to a limited extent)
Casualty insurance proceeds
Child support payments
Compensatory damages
Cost-of-living allowance (for military)
Damage for personal injury or
    sickness
Death benefits (up to $5,000)
Disability benefits
Disability pensions (to a limited
    extent)
Fellowship grants (to a limited
    extent)
Gifts
Group term life insurance, premium
    paid by employer (coverage not
    over $50,000)

Health insurance proceeds not
    deducted as a medical expense
Inheritances
Life insurance paid on death
Long-term capital gain on personal
    residence–$125,000 one-time exclusion
Meals and lodging (furnished for
    employer's convenience)
Military allowances
Moving and storage expenses paid
    by employer
Municipal bond interest
Relocation payments
Scholarship grants (to a limited
    extent)
Unemployment compensation (to a
    limited extent)
Veterans' benefits
Welfare payments
Workers' compensation

FIGURE 5.4

A partial list of exclusions from gross income.

Keogh Plan can be established by anyone with self-employed income; that is, income from a business. Such plans are used by many small business operators and professionals, such as artists and writers. Allowable contributions to a Keogh are considerably greater than IRA contributions, so if you earn self-employed income, you should become familiar with the Keogh provisions.

The IRA (Individual Retirement Account) can be used by anyone (employed or self-employed) whose income does not exceed certain limitations. IRAs became extremely popular in 1982, after Congress liberalized its provisions in the 1981 Tax Act. Its intent is to encourage individual retirement planning, and it

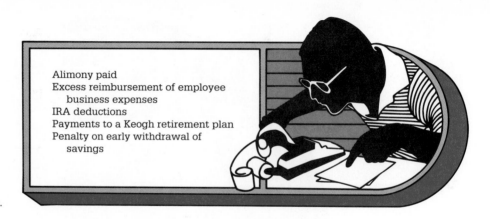

FIGURE 5.5

Adjustments to income.

Inside figure:
Alimony paid
Excess reimbursement of employee
  business expenses
IRA deductions
Payments to a Keogh retirement plan
Penalty on early withdrawal of
  savings

accomplishes this aim by allowing deductions to qualified IRA investments. Most investments people make—such as deposits in banks and savings and loans, common and preferred stocks, bonds, certain partnership interests, and more—are qualified investments. A single taxpayer (or each spouse) can deduct up to $2,000 invested in these each year if he or she (or each) has that much in wages, alimony, or other earned income, which does not include interest, dividends, or other items (all these are defined as unearned income). A married couple in which one spouse has all the earned income can deduct up to $2,250. It goes almost without saying that the IRA is one of the easiest and most generous tax concessions provided by Congress. Many tax advisers call it the best tax shelter for the middle-income family.

Not only is the IRA a generous deduction, it's virtually the only one you can take even after the tax year is over, since you have until April 15 of the following year to make your investment. Unfortunately, if your income exceeds certain limits, the deductibility of an IRA is gradually eliminated. Specifically, the income limits are $40,000 for a married couple filing a joint return and $25,000 for a single filer (see Chapter 17 for more details).

Alimony payments: Added to gross income to the receiver, but a reduction of the payer's gross income.

ALIMONY PAID   In general, **alimony payments** must be included as income by the person receiving them and are deductible by the ex-spouse making them. Such payments must be the result of a court decree of divorce or separation, and also must satisfy all of the following requirements: They must be based on your marital status or family relationship, paid after the decree, and paid periodically instead of in a lump sum. Divorce or separation often involves deep emotional feelings, and the last thing on the spouses' minds is how to structure the divorce to minimize future tax liabilities. This is unfortunate, because a cooperative approach can benefit each partner. You need good tax advice in this area, and it's usually worth retaining an attorney or CPA to help with the settlement.

Box 5.1
Simplifying Financial
Planning

Adjusted Gross Income (thousands)	Medical– Dental	State–Local Taxes	Interest	Contri- butions
$ 25–30	$ 3,128	$ 1,975	$ 4,314	$ 1,109
30–40	2,849	2,342	4,887	1,184
40–50	3,546	2,947	5,400	1,318
50–75	4,713	3,943	6,271	1,607
75–100	6,448	5,713	8,531	2,108
100–200	10,090	9,020	12,150	3,532
200–500	24,134	19,645	19,853	7,213
500–1,000	40,556	43,499	29,758	18,374
Over 1,000	66,478	148,529	68,303	83,929

How Do Your Deductions Compare?

At right are average amounts written off by taxpayers who claimed these deductions on 1989 returns filed in 1990. Note: This does not mean that taxpayers with $40,000 to $50,000 in income averaged $3,546 in medical deductions. Most such persons did not qualify for medical write-offs. The figure instead is the average deduction among those who *could* deduct medical expenses.

Adjusted Gross Income

Making all the adjustments to income from the total gross income items leaves adjusted gross income. It is an important figure because some itemized deductions have maximum limits based upon it.

Taxable Income

Taxable income: Adjusted gross income less personal and dependency exemptions and allowable personal expense deductions.

Taxable income consists of adjusted gross income less **personal and dependency exemptions** and deductions for personal expenses. This latter item consists of either taking a standardized amount or itemizing allowable deductions.

Personal and dependency exemptions: Deductions from adjusted gross income based on the number of people in a household, their ages, and eyesight quality.

PERSONAL AND DEPENDENCY EXEMPTIONS The law allows each taxpayer a personal exemption. The amount was $2,150 in 1991 and $2,300 in 1992. Each spouse on a joint return is entitled to the exemption, and it also applies to any of the taxpayer's dependents. Therefore, a married couple with four dependents could claim $12,900 in exemptions for tax year 1991. It is important to note that someone claimed as a dependent on another's return, such as parents claiming a dependent child, cannot also take the personal exemption. A working college student, for example, might provide most of his or her own support, thereby earning the exemption amount but preventing the parents from taking it. If the parents are in a higher tax bracket, this is poor tax strategy.

Finally, the exemption amount is *indexed* for all years beyond 1989. This means the amount will be adjusted upward each year by the year's inflation rate. So, if inflation was 5 percent in 1992, the amount would be $2,415 ($2,300 × 1.05) in 1993.

We should note that personal and dependency exemption deductions are gradually eliminated when taxable income exceeds certain limits. For a married couple filing a joint return the threshold income was $157,900 for 1992 returns; and, at an income level of $272,500 all exemption deductions were eliminated. Comparable figures for a single filer were $105,250 and $227,750.

THE STANDARD DEDUCTION   In addition to personal and dependency exemptions, the law also allows a **standard deduction** for personal expenses. The deductible amount depends upon taxpayer filing status as indicated below.

Standard deduction: Deduction from adjusted gross income based on the taxpayer's filing status.

		Standard Deduction Amounts	
If you are:		**1991**	**1992**
1 Married filing jointly, or a qualifying widow or widower		$5,700	$6,000
2 Head of a household		5,000	5,250
3 Single		3,400	3,600
4 Married filing separately		2,850	3,000

Standard deduction amounts also are inflation indexed for years beyond 1989.

Age and impaired sight allow taxpayers *additional* standard deduction amounts beyond those just described. For the 1992 tax year, an unmarried taxpayer 65 or older was allowed an additional $900; if he or she was also blind, the amount was increased another $900. For a married couple, the deduction was $700 for each spouse 65 or older or blind. For example, for a married couple with both spouses over 65 and one blind, the additional amount was $2,100 and the total 1992 standard deduction was $8,100 ($6,000 + $2,100).

ITEMIZED DEDUCTIONS   In general, the IRS does not allow personal expenses as deductions except in those cases where the tax law clearly indicates to the contrary. Most allowable personal deductions reflect activities regarded as socially desirable (giving to charity, for example), or alleviating undue financial hardship (medical expenses). Some are allowed probably because strong vested interests were influential in having them included in the tax law. Figure 5.6 indicates the more common deductions. The total of **itemized deductions** is taken as an offset to adjusted gross income. While it is important to keep good records to support all items on your tax return, it is particularly so in the case of itemized deductions. A lack of supporting evidence—canceled checks, invoices, or carefully written logs—will often lead to a disallowance of the claimed deduction.

Itemized deductions: Deductions from adjusted gross income based on actual amounts spent by a taxpayer.

There are limits on the amounts you can deduct for medical expenses, charitable contributions, casualty losses, and miscellaneous expenses. You can take only amounts greater than 7.5 percent of your adjusted gross income for medical expenses, which include hospital and doctor bills, payments to health insurance plans, and drugs and medicines. Special rules apply if charitable contributions exceed 20 percent of adjusted gross income. Also, for a charitable contribution to qualify, it must be made to an IRS-recognized charity; gifts made to individuals do not count as deductions. The limitations on casualty losses are explained in

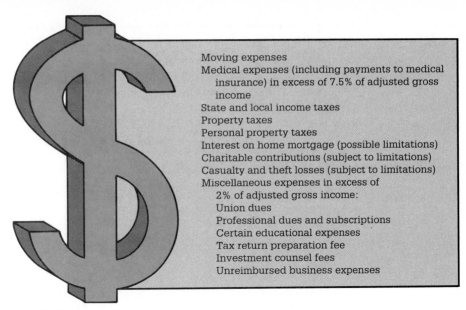

Moving expenses
Medical expenses (including payments to medical insurance) in excess of 7.5% of adjusted gross income
State and local income taxes
Property taxes
Personal property taxes
Interest on home mortgage (possible limitations)
Charitable contributions (subject to limitations)
Casualty and theft losses (subject to limitations)
Miscellaneous expenses in excess of 2% of adjusted gross income:
    Union dues
    Professional dues and subscriptions
    Certain educational expenses
    Tax return preparation fee
    Investment counsel fees
    Unreimbursed business expenses

FIGURE 5.6

Frequently claimed itemized deductions.

detail in Chapter 12, and possible limitations on mortgage interest are discussed in Chapter 8. As is the case with personal and dependency exemptions, taxpayers lose a portion of itemized deductions when their incomes exceed certain limits. The law becomes somewhat involved here, and if you are fortunate to have a taxable income in excess of $105,000 you should refer to an appropriate tax publication or consult with a tax professional.

Determining Your Tax Liability Before Tax Credits

After taxable income has been calculated, you are ready to determine your tax liability before tax credits. To do this you will use either the tax table or Tax Rate Schedules X, Y, or Z. You must use the tax table—a portion of which is shown in Figure 5.7—if your taxable income is less than $50,000. To find the tax, simply find the appropriate income bracket and move over to the column corresponding to your filing status. For example, if your taxable income is $37,220 and you are married filing a joint return, the tax is $6,003.

If your taxable income is greater than $50,000, you must use one of the tax rate schedules shown in Figure 5.8. You will calculate your tax by following directions in the schedule. For example, suppose you are a single taxpayer with a taxable income of $60,000. Your tax would be calculated from Schedule X as follows:

$$\text{Tax} = \$11,158.50 + 0.310(\$60,000 - \$49,300)$$
$$= \$11,158.50 + \$3,317.00$$
$$= \$14,475.50$$

If line 37 (taxable income) is—		And you are—			
At least	But less than	Single	Married filing jointly *	Married filing separately	Head of a household
			Your tax is—		
37,000					
37,000	37,050	7,722	5,947	8,157	6,818
37,050	37,100	7,736	5,961	8,171	6,832
37,100	37,150	7,750	5,975	8,185	6,846
37,150	37,200	7,764	5,989	8,199	6,860
37,200	37,250	7,778	6,003	8,213	6,874
37,250	37,300	7,792	6,017	8,227	6,888
37,300	37,350	7,806	6,031	8,241	6,902
37,350	37,400	7,820	6,045	8,255	6,916
37,400	37,450	7,834	6,059	8,269	6,930
37,450	37,500	7,848	6,073	8,283	6,944
37,500	37,550	7,862	6,087	8,297	6,958
37,550	37,600	7,876	6,101	8,311	6,972
37,600	37,650	7,890	6,115	8,325	6,986
37,650	37,700	7,904	6,129	8,339	7,000
37,700	37,750	7,918	6,143	8,353	7,014
37,750	37,800	7,932	6,157	8,367	7,028
37,800	37,850	7,946	6,171	8,381	7,042
37,850	37,900	7,960	6,185	8,395	7,056
37,900	37,950	7,974	6,199	8,409	7,070
37,950	38,000	7,988	6,213	8,423	7,084

Example ⟶ (row 37,200–37,250)

Steeles' taxable income ⟶ (row 37,700–37,750)

FIGURE 5.7

A portion of the 1991 tax table.

Tax Credits

Tax credit: A dollar-for-dollar offset against the tax liability.

A **tax credit** is a direct deduction against your tax liability. There are a number of such credits, which are shown in Figure 5.9. Most tax credit calculations follow specific formulas established in the tax law. It is necessary to follow these formulas to determine both whether you qualify for a credit and how much you can claim.

Your tax liability for the year is determined by subtracting the total of your credits from the taxes you calculated using the tax table or one of the schedules. This tax liability is an important figure—one you should be very much aware of as you make financial decisions. An even more important figure to know is your marginal tax rate, which we'll explain shortly. The withholding system, although convenient, very often does not show in bold terms either what our actual liability is or at what rates our incomes are being taxed.

Do You Get a Refund or Owe More Taxes?

The amount you receive or pay depends upon how much tax has been withheld from your wages. (Or, if you earned income not subject to withholding, how much you have paid in estimated taxes. By the way, if you expect to earn such

1991
Tax Rate
Schedules

Caution: Use **only** if your taxable income (Form 1040, line 37) is $50,000 or more. If less, use the **Tax Table.** (Even though you cannot use the tax rate schedules below if your taxable income is less than $50,000, all levels of taxable income are shown so taxpayers can see the tax rate that applies to each level.)

Schedule X—Use if your filing status is **Single**

If the amount on Form 1040, line 37, is: Over—	But not over—	Enter on Form 1040, line 38	of the amount over—
$0	$20,350	.... 15%	$0
20,350	49,300	$3,052.50 + 28%	20,350
49,300	....	11,158.50 + 31%	49,300

Text example

Schedule Y-1—Use if your filing status is **Married filing jointly or Qualifying widow(er)**

If the amount on Form 1040, line 37, is: Over—	But not over—	Enter on Form 1040, line 38	of the amount over—
$0	$34,000	.... 15%	$0
34,000	82,150	$5,100.00 + 28%	34,000
82,150	....	18,582.00 + 31%	82,150

Steeles' bracket

Schedule Y-2—Use if your filing status is **Married filing separately**

If the amount on Form 1040, line 37, is: Over—	But not over—	Enter on Form 1040, line 38	of the amount over—
$0	$17,000	.... 15%	$0
17,000	41,075	$2,550.00 + 28%	17,000
41,075	....	9,291.00 + 31%	41,075

Schedule Z—Use if your filing status is **Head of household**

If the amount on Form 1040, line 37, is: Over—	But not over—	Enter on Form 1040, line 38	of the amount over—
$0	$27,300	.... 15%	$0
27,300	70,450	$4,095.00 + 28%	27,300
70,450	....	16,177.00 + 31%	70,450

FIGURE 5.8

Partial tax schedules for 1991.

income you are required to file an estimated tax. Failure to do this can lead to both penalties and interest.) If withholding was greater than your tax liability, you are entitled to a refund; if the reverse is true, you must pay additional tax. Every employer is required to provide employees an annual report of their wages

FIGURE 5.9

Tax credits.

W-2 form: A form prepared by an employer showing an employee's earnings and withholdings.

W-4 form: A form signed by an employee to claim exemption allowances for payroll withholding purposes.

and all the taxes (and possibly other items) withheld from their wages. This report is called a **W–2 form,** and you should review yours each year to make sure it is correct. Also, you need the carbon copies to attach to your federal and state income tax returns.

Keep in mind that the IRS does not pay interest on excess withholding. Despite this fact, many taxpayers claim fewer exemptions than they need to on withholding forms filed with their employers (called a **W–4 form**). They do this because it is a form of forced savings or because they enjoy getting a big refund. Actually, this is very poor financial management. In many cases, it is just as easy to have your employer withhold from your salary each week and invest the money in a way that offers you a return. Savings plans with Series EE bonds, for example, are very popular; there are many others. Before you allow excess withholding, see if any plans are available and select one that fits your investment objectives.

Determining the Steeles' 1991 Income Tax

In 1992, Arnold and Sharon Steele had the following items to consider in preparing their 1991 income tax return. Arnold earned $55,380 at InChemCo and had $5,400 of federal income tax withheld from his salary. Sharon earned $13,800 at

The Basic Framework

Todd and Talbot and had $728 of such taxes withheld. They received $861 in interest on savings accounts and $812 in dividends on stocks they owned. During the year they sold some stocks Sharon received from her parents as a gift. There was a $935 gain on the sale. The Steeles itemized their deductions and arrived at an allowable total of $25,476.55. They also paid $600 in child-care expenses. With the above information, the Steeles are ready to prepare their return. They used form 1040 (the so-called long form), which is shown in Figure 5.10.

Filing Status and Exemptions

The Steeles are filing a joint return, and they are claiming four exemptions. They could have filed under option 3—married filing separate returns—but they found their tax liability would have been greater. This isn't always the case, so you should check your liability each way to determine the appropriate option.

Total Income

The Steeles' total income was $71,788.

Adjustments to Income

None.

Tax Computation

The Steeles' adjusted gross income is reduced first by their net itemized deductions of $25,476.55. Then this subtotal of $46,311.45 is further reduced by the $8,600 of exemptions (four exemptions claimed times $2,150 per exemption) to arrive at their taxable income of $37,711.45. Their tax liability before tax credits is $6,143, which is found in the tax table.

Credits and Refund

The Steeles had one credit in 1991. It is the credit for child and dependent care expenses. The amount of this credit is related to your total qualifying expenses and level of adjusted gross income. The maximum is $720 if you have one qualifying dependent, and $1,440 if you have two or more. The Steeles' credit in 1991 was 20 percent of the $600 of qualifying expenses, or $120.

At this point, Arnold and Sharon reflect upon their tax situation. Their tax liability is $6,023.00 out of their pretax total income of $71,788. Therefore, they paid 8.39 percent ($6,023.00/$71,788.00) of their income in 1991 in federal income taxes. This is their **average tax rate,** but a far more useful figure is their **marginal tax rate.** This rate is more or less buried in the tax table, so Arnold and Sharon found it by using Schedule Y to calculate their tax (see Figure 5.8). This schedule clearly highlights their marginal rate, which is 28 percent. The marginal rate, as you should see, is the rate being applied to the bracket in which taxable income falls. If the Steeles' taxable income rose enough to put them in the next

Average tax rate: Total tax liability divided by total income.

Marginal tax rate: Additional tax liability divided by additional income.

U.S. Individual Income Tax Return **1991** (B)

For the year Jan.–Dec. 31, 1991, or other tax year beginning , 1991, ending , 19 | OMB No. 1545-0074

Label

(See instructions on page 11.)

Use the IRS label. Otherwise, please print or type.

Your first name and initial: Arnold S. | Last name: Steele

Your social security number: 000 : 00 : 0000

If a joint return, spouse's first name and initial: Sharon R. | Last name: Steele

Spouse's social security number: 000 : 00 : 0000

Home address (number and street). (If you have a P.O. box, see page 11.): 496 Mulberry Lane | Apt. no.

City, town or post office, state, and ZIP code. (If you have a foreign address, see page 11.): Middleburg, Missouri 64131

For Privacy Act and Paperwork Reduction Act Notice, see instructions.

Presidential Election Campaign (See page 11.)

Do you want $1 to go to this fund? — Yes ✓ / No — **Note:** Checking "Yes" will not change your tax or reduce your refund.

If joint return, does your spouse want $1 to go to this fund? — Yes / No ✓

Filing Status

Check only one box.

1 ☐ Single
2 ✓ Married filing joint return (even if only one had income)
3 ☐ Married filing separate return. Enter spouse's social security no. above and full name here. ▶
4 ☐ Head of household (with qualifying person). (See page 12.) If the qualifying person is a child but not your dependent, enter this child's name here. ▶
5 ☐ Qualifying widow(er) with dependent child (year spouse died ▶ 19). (See page 12.)

Exemptions

(See page 12.)

6a ✓ **Yourself.** If your parent (or someone else) can claim you as a dependent on his or her tax return, do not check box 6a. But be sure to check the box on line 33b on page 2.

b ✓ **Spouse**

| No. of boxes checked on 6a and 6b | 2 |

c **Dependents:**

(1) Name (first, initial, and last name)	(2) Check if under age 1	(3) If age 1 or older, dependent's social security number	(4) Dependent's relationship to you	(5) No. of months lived in your home in 1991
Nancy T. Steele		000 : 00 : 0000	D	12
John L. Steele		000 : 00 : 0000	S	12

If more than six dependents, see page 13.

No. of your children on 6c who:
• lived with you: 2
• didn't live with you due to divorce or separation (see page 14):
No. of other dependents on 6c:

d If your child didn't live with you but is claimed as your dependent under a pre-1985 agreement, check here ▶ ☐

e Total number of exemptions claimed

Add numbers entered on lines above ▶ 4

Income

Attach Copy B of your Forms W-2, W-2G, and 1099-R here.

If you did not get a W-2, see page 10.

Attach check or money order on top of any Forms W-2, W-2G, or 1099-R.

7	Wages, salaries, tips, etc. (attach Form(s) W-2)	7	69,180 00
8a	**Taxable** interest income (also attach Schedule B if over $400)	8a	861 00
b	**Tax-exempt** interest income (see page 16). DON'T include on line 8a. 8b		
9	Dividend income (also attach Schedule B if over $400)	9	812 00
10	Taxable refunds of state and local income taxes, if any, from worksheet on page 16	10	—
11	Alimony received	11	—
12	Business income or (loss) (attach Schedule C)	12	—
13	Capital gain or (loss) (attach Schedule D)	13	935 00
14	Capital gain distributions not reported on line 13 (see page 17)	14	—
15	Other gains or (losses) (attach Form 4797)	15	—
16a	Total IRA distributions 16a	16b Taxable amount (see page 17)	16b	—
17a	Total pensions and annuities 17a	17b Taxable amount (see page 17)	17b	—
18	Rents, royalties, partnerships, estates, trusts, etc. (attach Schedule E)	18	—
19	Farm income or (loss) (attach Schedule F)	19	—
20	Unemployment compensation (insurance) (see page 18)	20	—
21a	Social security benefits 21a	21b Taxable amount (see page 18)	21b	—
22	Other income (list type and amount—see page 19)	22	—
23	Add the amounts shown in the far right column for lines 7 through 22. This is your **total income** ▶	23	71,788 00

Adjustments to Income

(See page 19.)

24a	Your IRA deduction, from applicable worksheet on page 20 or 21	24a —	
b	Spouse's IRA deduction, from applicable worksheet on page 20 or 21	24b —	
25	One-half of self-employment tax (see page 21)	25 —	
26	Self-employed health insurance deduction, from worksheet on page 22	26 —	
27	Keogh retirement plan and self-employed SEP deduction	27 —	
28	Penalty on early withdrawal of savings	28 —	
29	Alimony paid. Recipient's SSN ▶	29 —	
30	Add lines 24a through 29. These are your **total adjustments** ▶	30	—

Adjusted Gross Income

| 31 | Subtract line 30 from line 23. This is your **adjusted gross income.** If this amount is less than $21,250 and a child lived with you, see page 45 to find out if you can claim the "Earned Income Credit" on line 56. ▶ | 31 | 71,788 00 |

FIGURE 5.10

Arnold and Sharon Steele's 1991 income tax return.

The Basic Framework

Tax Compu-tation	32	Amount from line 31 (adjusted gross income)	32	71,788	00

33a Check if: ☐ **You** were 65 or older, ☐ Blind; ☐ **Spouse** was 65 or older, ☐ Blind.
Add the number of boxes checked above and enter the total here . . . ▶ **33a** ☐

If you want the IRS to figure your tax, see page 24.

b If your parent (or someone else) can claim you as a dependent, check here ▶ **33b** ☐

c If you are married filing a separate return and your spouse itemizes deductions, or you are a dual-status alien, see page 23 and check here . . . . . ▶ **33c** ☐

34 Enter the larger of your:
{ Itemized deductions (from Schedule A, line 26), **OR**
Standard deduction (shown below for your filing status). **Caution:** If you checked **any** box on line 33a or b, go to page 23 to find your standard deduction. If you checked box 33c, your standard deduction is zero.
• Single—$3,400   • Head of household—$5,000
• Married filing jointly or Qualifying widow(er)—$5,700
• Married filing separately—$2,850

34	25,476	55
35	Subtract line 34 from line 32	35	46,311	45
36	If line 32 is $75,000 or less, multiply $2,150 by the total number of exemptions claimed on line 6e. If line 32 is over $75,000, see page 24 for the amount to enter	36	8,600	00
37	**Taxable income.** Subtract line 36 from line 35. (If line 36 is more than line 35, enter -0-.)	37	37,711	45
38	Enter tax. Check if from **a** ☑ Tax Table, **b** ☐ Tax Rate Schedules, **c** ☐ Schedule D, or **d** ☐ Form 8615 (see page 24). (Amount, if any, from Form(s) 8814 ▶ e _____ .)	38	6,143	00
39	Additional taxes (see page 24). Check if from **a** ☐ Form 4970 **b** ☐ Form 4972 . . .	39	–	
40	Add lines 38 and 39 . . . . ▶	40	6,143	00

Credits (See page 25.)	41	Credit for child and dependent care expenses *(attach Form 2441)*	41	120	00			
	42	Credit for the elderly or the disabled *(attach Schedule R)* .	42	–				
	43	Foreign tax credit *(attach Form 1116)*	43	–				
	44	Other credits (see page 25). Check if from **a** ☐ Form 3800 **b** ☐ Form 8396 **c** ☐ Form 8801 **d** ☐ Form (specify)_____	44	–				
	45	Add lines 41 through 44				45	120	00
	46	Subtract line 45 from line 40. (If line 45 is more than line 40, enter -0-.) . . . . ▶				46	6,023	00

Other Taxes	47	Self-employment tax *(attach Schedule SE)*	47	–	
	48	Alternative minimum tax *(attach Form 6251)*	48	–	
	49	Recapture taxes (see page 26). Check if from **a** ☐ Form 4255 **b** ☐ Form 8611 **c** ☐ Form 8828 .	49	–	
	50	Social security and Medicare tax on tip income not reported to employer *(attach Form 4137)* .	50	–	
	51	Tax on an IRA or a qualified retirement plan *(attach Form 5329)*	51	–	
	52	Advance earned income credit payments from Form W-2	52	–	
	53	Add lines 46 through 52. This is your **total tax** . . . . ▶	53	–	

Payments Attach Forms W-2, W-2G, and 1099-R to front.	54	Federal income tax withheld (if any is from Form(s) 1099, check ▶ ☐)	54	6,128	00			
	55	1991 estimated tax payments and amount applied from 1990 return .	55	–				
	56	**Earned income credit** *(attach Schedule EIC)*	56	–				
	57	Amount paid with Form 4868 (extension request)	57	–				
	58	Excess social security, Medicare, and RRTA tax withheld (see page 27) .	58	–				
	59	Other payments (see page 27). Check if from **a** ☐ Form 2439 **b** ☐ Form 4136 .	59	–				
	60	Add lines 54 through 59. These are your **total payments** . . . . ▶				60	6,128	00

Refund or Amount You Owe	61	If line 60 is more than line 53, subtract line 53 from line 60. This is the amount you **OVERPAID**. . ▶	61	105	00
	62	Amount of line 61 to be **REFUNDED TO YOU** . . . . ▶	62	105	00
	63	Amount of line 61 to be **APPLIED TO YOUR 1992 ESTIMATED TAX** ▶	63		
	64	If line 53 is more than line 60, subtract line 60 from line 53. This is the **AMOUNT YOU OWE**. Attach check or money order for full amount payable to "Internal Revenue Service." Write your name, address, social security number, daytime phone number, and "1991 Form 1040" on it.	64	–	
	65	Estimated tax penalty (see page 28). Also include on line 64. **65**			

Sign Here
Keep a copy of this return for your records.

Under penalties of perjury, I declare that I have examined this return and accompanying schedules and statements, and to the best of my knowledge and belief, they are true, correct, and complete. Declaration of preparer (other than taxpayer) is based on all information of which preparer has any knowledge.

Your signature *Arnold Steele*	Date 4/2/92	Your occupation *Chemical Engineer*
Spouse's signature (if joint return, BOTH must sign) *Sharron Steele*	Date 4/2/92	Spouse's occupation *Accountant*

Paid Preparer's Use Only

Preparer's signature ▶	Date	Check if self-employed ☐	Preparer's social security no.
Firm's name (or yours if self-employed) and address ▶		E.I. No.	
		ZIP code	

☆ U.S. GOVERNMENT PRINTING OFFICE: 1991-285-035

FIGURE 5.10

Continued.

Box 5.2
Saving Money

Do Your Own Tax Return

Why do so many Americans not prepare their own tax returns? Completing the 1040EZ usually takes no more time and is no more challenging than completing a credit application. The 1040A is only a bit more involved, and even the so-called long form—the 1040—should be relatively simple for most taxpayers, considering that 60 percent of 1040 users do not itemize deductions. Is it fear of the IRS, unwillingness to undertake an unpleasant task, or simple year-to-year inertia? Some people feel that the signature of a professional preparer on the return lessens their chance of being audited, although there is no evidence to support this belief. Why you use an outsider is unimportant; what matters is that

you will pay anywhere from $25 to $2,000 when you go for outside help.

If you have used outsiders in the past, the trick is to break the cycle by deciding to go it alone this year. It is extremely helpful to have a copy of your previous year's return when you begin. In most cases, doing this year's return is no more involved than following last year's return but using this year's numbers. (If your preparer did not give you a copy of last year's return, call and ask for one.) Along with "plugging in" the new numbers, you should read the information booklet mailed to you along with your return. This will alert you to any current-year changes.

Actually, the IRS booklets are easy to read and reasonably clear in indicating the steps to take in preparing a return. They are keyed to the line items on the returns, which makes it easy to start at the beginning and work toward the end. If you have a question and cannot find a suitable answer in the booklet, you can call

the IRS assistance line (1–800–829–1040). *Money* magazine annually tests the correctness of IRS responses and finds the service has improved substantially.

Whether you go it alone or use an outsider, it is important to keep good records along with the documents provided by your employer or financial institutions. These latter items indicate your wages and interest or dividends earned during the year. They also will show any mortgage interest that can be deducted. It's a good idea to put the documents in a large envelope or box as soon as you receive them; also, put your tax returns there when they arrive.

Finally, file your return early. You should have all your needed documents by January 31, so set mid-February as your target. Waiting until April accomplishes nothing and may create a feeling of desperation that you won't be able to finish the return on time by yourself.

---

higher bracket, their marginal rate would jump to 31 percent; if their taxable income fell to a lower bracket, the marginal rate would be 15 percent. The marginal rates are the ones to consider in making financial decisions concerning future sources of income or deductions, because additional income will be taxed, or additional deductions will save taxes, at the marginal rate. For example, suppose Sharon has considered working additional hours at Todd and Talbot, and she could earn $1,000 more by doing so. Should she work the additional hours? If she does, the Steeles' taxable income will increase by $1,000. Assuming that everything else remains the same, they will pay $280 more in taxes, and their after-tax income will increase by only $720. Of course, they must decide if the additional $720 is worth the extra time and effort on Sharon's part.

Finally, since the Steeles had $6,128 of taxes withheld from their wages, they overpaid their 1991 tax liability by $105. They could have applied this overpayment to a 1992 estimated tax, but chose a refund instead.

Other Aspects of the Federal Income Tax

In addition to understanding how the federal income tax formula is used to determine your tax liability, it is important to be familiar with other aspects of the tax. In the sections below, we will explain capital gains and losses, loss limitation rules, and the role of the Internal Revenue Service (the IRS). Finally, we discuss the issue of seeking outside help in preparing your return.

Capital Gains and Losses

As your income and wealth increase, you can expect to have a growing number of transactions involving the sale or exchange of capital assets. Almost always, an exchange results in either a gain or a loss that may have to be reported in filing your annual return.

WHAT IS A CAPITAL GAIN OR LOSS?   A **capital gain or loss** results whenever you sell a capital asset for more or less than what you paid for it (or your "basis" in the asset if you received it as a gift). The next logical question is: What are **capital assets**? For the most part, everything you own and use for personal purposes, pleasure, or investment is a capital asset. Examples are stocks, bonds, and other securities; your house, car, and household goods; or your hobbies, such as stamp and coin collections, and fishing gear.

TAX TREATMENT OF CAPITAL GAINS AND LOSSES   Important provisions apply to the tax treatment of capital gains and losses. To begin with, any gain on the sale of property held for personal use—your car, for example—must be reported and is taxed in full. Any losses on the sale of such assets, however, cannot be deducted against other income. Of course, you seldom sell personal property at a gain, but it is possible.

Investment assets are treated similarly to personal-use assets, but with one distinction: you can deduct up to $3,000 of any losses (all gains are reported in full). Moreover, if losses in a year exceed $3,000, the unused portion can be carried forward to future years and taken as deductions. However, the maximum allowable deduction in any year is $3,000. This includes carry-forward amounts and current-year losses.

SELLING YOUR HOME   Your home is a personal property, so it is also subject to capital gain taxation. However, special provisions have been written into the law to soften the tax's impact. To begin with, you can defer any gain from selling your existing home by buying (or having built) another one within 24 months from the time you sold the first one. Second, you are allowed a one-time exclusion of $125,000 ($62,500 if you are married and filing an individual return) if you are 55 or older at the time of sale (and if you meet other tests). For example, suppose Alice Dean buys a home in 1966 for $20,000; she then sells it in 1986 for $90,000 and buys another three months later for $95,000. In 1992, when she is 60 years old, she sells this home for $155,000 and retires to Florida. Alice has a $70,000 gain in 1986, but she doesn't pay tax on this gain in 1986 because she purchased another home at a higher price within 24 months. In 1992, she realizes a $60,000 gain on the sale of the second home, which, combined with the deferred gain of $70,000, gives her a $130,000 total gain. Her one-time exclusion of $125,000 reduces the taxable gain to $5,000.

It is obvious that a home is a tax-advantaged investment. This feature, coupled with the fact that home prices have increased considerably over the years, has made home ownership a very attractive investment. This aspect is explained more fully in Chapter 9.

Loss Limitation Rules

Many investment and business activities produce income or losses other than capital gains and losses. The tax law also has special provisions dealing with their treatment for tax purposes.

EARNED, PORTFOLIO, AND PASSIVE INCOME   First, there are important distinctions depending on the source of your income. **Earned income** refers to income received through employment or in the direct operation of a business. Common forms of this income are wages, salaries, bonuses, commissions, and business profits. **Portfolio income** describes income earned on investment assets such as stocks, bonds, and deposits at financial institutions. Dividends and interest are common forms of this income. **Passive income** (or losses) is any income that results from passive activities. These activities include the conduct of any trade or business in which the taxpayer does not materially participate, including the rental of tangible property (such as real estate). It is your responsibility to provide evidence of active participation; without such proof, the IRS will assume you are inactive.

The distinctions are critical because you cannot use any passive losses to offset earned or portfolio income. This was a common practice before the 1986 Tax Reform Act. Investors with high tax rates often invested in so-called tax shelters to earn substantial losses that were used to offset other income. Although such shelters are still available under limited conditions in the oil and gas industry, they have been eliminated everywhere else.

MAXIMUM ALLOWABLE LOSS   Even if you are active in managing your business, you cannot offset more than $25,000 of losses against earned or portfolio income. Moreover, the maximum deduction is gradually eliminated—$0.50 for each $1.00—as income exceeds $100,000, being fully exhausted at $150,000. To illustrate: Suppose you earn $120,000 in wages and interest. You also run a business that shows a $40,000 loss. Your loss offset is $15,000, determined as follows: $25,000 (maximum) less 0.5 × $20,000 (amount over $100,000) = $25,000 less $10,000 = $15,000. Taxable income is then $105,000 ($120,000 less $15,000). Again, keep in mind that if you were an inactive owner, there would be no loss offset.

The Role of the Internal Revenue Service

The **Internal Revenue Service (IRS)** a division of the Treasury Department, is the federal agency assigned the task of administering the federal income tax. Two of its most important functions are providing taxpayer assistance and auditing tax returns. In addition to understanding these functions, you should be aware of the filing deadline and extensions, and the statute of limitations as it applies to the federal income tax.

TAXPAYER ASSISTANCE   The IRS attempts to make filing your return as easy as possible. (Don't blame the IRS if the return itself is difficult to complete; blame Congress, because the tax law is its responsibility.) If you have filed a return in the past, you are automatically sent a tax form for the current year. If you have never filed a return, or if you need to file one different from the previous year, you can find forms at practically every public library and many banks or savings and loans. The IRS may have an office in your town, which you can call or visit for forms or taxpayer assistance. If an office is not convenient, you can call 1–800–829–1040 for assistance. In addition to form 1040 (illustrated with the Steeles' example), there are two simpler forms—1040A and 1040EZ—that many taxpayers can use.

It is often helpful to read IRS publications to handle a tax item properly. The instruction booklet that accompanies your tax return contains a list of IRS publications and forms, and shows where to write in your state to get them. We strongly recommend Publication 17, *Your Federal Income Tax*, as a handy and reliable general reference on many tax matters. All IRS publications are free, so don't hesitate to ask for any that you might need.

If you file Form 1040EZ or Form 1040A, the IRS will figure the tax for you, if you wish. You must provide all the relevant information, however. The IRS will also figure your tax on Form 1040 if you meet certain tests. These are too involved to discuss here, but if you file a 1040 you can read the instructions guide that comes with it to see if you meet these tests. Actually, once you have gathered all the necessary information, filing the return involves very little extra work. As a tip, we suggest you do it in pencil (assuming you'll make a mistake or two) and then make photocopies to send the IRS.

IRS AUDITS   The strength of our tax system rests upon the integrity of millions of taxpayers to file an honest and reasonably correct return. An important function—the IRS audit—is to ensure that such filing takes place. Actually, the IRS has three basic audit approaches: the field audit—where an IRS agent visits your premises to examine your return; the office audit—where you visit an IRS center; and the self audit—where the IRS essentially questions some aspect of your return and asks you to examine the item again to determine its appropriateness.

An audit may involve questioning just one item on your return, or the whole return might be audited, which means you must have documentary support for each line item. Returns selected for audit are determined by a formula (known only to the IRS) and random procedures. But, as Figure 5.11 shows, your odds of

Adjusted Gross Income	Audit Chance (number out of 1,000)
Under $10,000 (1040-A)	4.5
Under $10,000 (non-1040-A)	3.5
$10,000 to $25,000:	
With itemized deductions	12.5
Without itemized deductions	6.1
$25,000–$50,000	12.1
Over $50,000	23.2
Self-employed income: gross receipts:	
Under $25,000	14.5
$25,000–$100,000	21.2
Over $25,000	42.0

FIGURE 5.11

Adjusted gross income and chances of an audit—1988 tax returns. (Source: IRS data.)

being audited increase substantially with your income and if you are self-employed.

It is illegal to file a fraudulent return, or not to file a return at all, and stiff penalties can be assessed in each case. A mistake or an alternative interpretation of the law may not lead to a penalty, but you will pay interest on any deficiency. The interest rate changes periodically, depending on market rates of interest. For assessments of additional taxes, the interest period begins on the due date of the return—not from the time the deficiency is found.

FILING DEADLINE AND EXTENSIONS   Your tax return must be filed before April 16. If you can't meet that deadline, you can get an **automatic extension** for four months. However, before April 15 you must file Form 4868 asking for the extension. Remember, though, an automatic filing extension does not extend the time you have to pay your tax. You must estimate your tax for the year and pay any tax due along with Form 4868. There is a penalty for late payment unless you have reasonable cause for not paying your tax when due. You can request extensions beyond the automatic four-month extension, but you must meet certain tests before the IRS will grant them.

ELECTRONIC FILING   As an alternative to mailing your tax return, you can have it filed electronically. To do this, take your return and W-2 forms to a qualified tax preparer and sign Form 8453, which authorizes transmission of the tax data. Note: You are not required to use the preparer's assistance in preparing the return—you can do the return yourself. A number of preparers also will make you a **refund anticipation loan** of $300 to $3,000. With this loan you receive your refund within six days, rather than the usual three to four weeks. Naturally, you should determine if there are any fees associated with electronic filing or the refund anticipation loan. Unless you need the refund desperately, determine the equivalent annual interest on the latter item, and if it exceeds, say, 12 percent, consider foregoing the loan.

THE STATUTE OF LIMITATIONS   The **statute of limitations,** as it generally applies to the federal income tax law, gives the IRS three years from the time a return is filed to impose additional tax liabilities. This fact suggests that tax records should be kept at least this long. But a special six-year limitation applies if you omit a gross income item that is greater than 25 percent of reported total gross income. Moreover, the statute of limitations does not apply if a return is never filed or if a fraudulent return is filed.

Also, be forewarned that if you overpaid taxes in a given year, you must file a claim for a refund within three years from the date the return was filed or two years from the date the tax was paid, whichever is later. Failure to file within these periods usually leads to loss of the refund.

Getting Outside Help

Preparing returns has become a very big business, and you are probably familiar with H & R Block, the largest tax preparation service in the United States. Should you use an outside firm? The answer to that question depends upon several factors. If you have a rather complex tax question that cannot be answered by

Automatic extension: An extension of time for filing an income tax return, given automatically by the IRS.

Refund anticipation loan: A loan provided by a tax preparation service based on a taxpayer's refund.

Statute of limitations: A period of three years given the IRS to impose additional taxes on a filed return.

referring to Publication 17 or a tax reference manual at the public library, and if the item is large enough to matter, then an expert's opinion is needed. Second, you may not care to spend the time doing your return. There are two broad types of preparers: the tax service companies such as H & R Block and professionals such as CPAs and attorneys.

TAX SERVICE COMPANIES   Many tax service companies open their offices in January and close them in May. Others remain open all year in some of their locations. Fees for their services vary, but a Form 1040 with several supporting schedules will usually cost between $50 and $100. The short forms cost less, but there are additional charges for state and local income tax returns. While most of these companies do a good job in filing your return, you should know that most of their work consists of simply entering the data you give them in appropriate places on the return. While they claim their staff is instructed to ask the right questions to save you taxes, you shouldn't count on it.

After you finish this chapter, if you get Publication 17 and also keep reasonably alert to newspaper and magazine articles on how to reduce your taxes, you will have a good chance of doing a better job on your return than many of these preparers will. Actually, you're more likely to save taxes by planning throughout the year rather than finding clever loopholes at year's end. You're not likely to get effective tax planning from these companies for the modest fees involved. And if you want such planning, you must either inform yourself or turn to the experts.

CPAS AND ATTORNEYS   CPAs and attorneys with specialized training in federal income taxation are the tax experts. If you are fortunate to have a high income, or if you are involved in activities with many income tax implications (running a business, for example), you probably need a professional. As just mentioned, you may want his or her services to guide you throughout the year. You most likely want assistance not only in preparing the return but also in setting up trusts or gifts, or advising you about the income tax implications of various investments, including self-employed retirement plans (if they are applicable). Fees for these services are very high: Count on $60 to $120 an hour, or an annual retainer of $500 as a minimum.

FINANCIAL PLANNERS   Many financial planners do not specialize in income tax advice, although they may have contact with people who do. Also, a number of business firms are now engaging financial planners to advise their employees on financial planning. Their services are offered as a fringe benefit to employees. You might ask if this service is available at your company and, of course, take advantage of it if it is. The financial planner may not do tax returns, but he or she should be able to help with tax planning.

TAX PUBLICATIONS AND SOFTWARE   If you decide to prepare your own return, you might want to consider buying books that offer tax advice. A classic is *J. K. Lasser's Your Income Tax* (around $15). Written in an easy-to-read style, the publisher, J. K. Lasser Institute, offers buyers a free 24-hour consultation hotline.

If you have access to a personal computer, consider using income tax software. A number of very good programs are available at relatively low cost. For example, the *Andrew Tobias' Tax Cut* (around $90) uses a question–answer format that is very easy to follow, and it also provides tax advice. If you have a lengthy return with a number of separate schedules, the time you can save in manipulating data may by itself be worth the software's cost. There are less expensive programs (between $30 and $60) that also perform this function very well.

Planning to Reduce Your Income Taxes

Effective tax planning is an ongoing process. Among other things, it requires selecting investments carefully, holding them for a sufficient length of time, and then selling them at the most opportune time for tax purposes. It also means that you must use provisions of the income tax law that are specifically designed to lower your tax liability. Tax planning attempts to either avoid taxes altogether or defer them to a later time. It works within the tax law, not outside of it, as is the case with tax evasion. Some of the more common and useful tax-planning techniques are described below.

Invest Where You Receive Tax-Advantaged Income

The tax law favors some forms of income over others. You can reduce your taxes by investing first in those favored investments, which are discussed below.

Municipal bonds: Bonds paying interest that is exempt from federal income tax.

BUY MUNICIPAL BONDS   All interest on **municipal bonds** is tax-exempt. These bonds are explained in more detail in Chapter 14, but you should see at this point that the after-tax yield on a municipal bond is the same as its pretax yield.

BUY A HOME   We have already explained the income tax treatment of your personal residence. In effect, you can enjoy a $125,000 tax-free, long-term capital gain. It's hard to beat that anywhere. Also, most mortgage interest is deductible as an itemized expense. The investment quality of a personal residence is explained in depth in Chapter 9.

BE AN ACTIVE INVESTOR IN REAL ESTATE   Despite the disadvantage of limited deductibility of business losses, actively managing your own business, such as real estate, offers certain tax advantages to taxpayers with incomes under $150,000. As discussed, you can deduct up to $25,000 if your income is under $100,000. The appeal of real estate rests in the fact that a large portion of many losses is represented by a noncash charge called depreciation. This means that even though the property shows a loss for tax purposes, you might still have a decent cash return. The Steeles were considering a real estate investment, and their experiences are described in Chapter 16. If you have further interest in the topic, you should review the details in that chapter.

Take Capital Losses Quickly

If you have a capital loss, it is usually to your advantage to take it before a tax year ends. Even if you believe the security's price might rebound and eliminate the loss, you should consider selling the security you own and replacing it with a similar security. For example, suppose you buy Exxon common stock, and after your purchase its price falls to half of what it was. You believe the international

Get Ready for the Self-Audit

The letter from the IRS is reasonably friendly: Some aspect of your return doesn't seem quite right and you now have the chance to audit the return, assessing yourself for any unpaid taxes, penalties, and interest. Does the IRS really expect you to respond something like this: "You were right. I caught myself for overstating travel and entertainment expenses. I reported a $2,000 deduction but half of that actually was for entertaining my family—not business clients." Yes, in a way that is exactly what the IRS expects. Or at least it hopes that its friendly letter will scare you enough to come clean.

The self-audit is an attempt by the IRS to use its resources more efficiently since Congress has limited its budget allocations. The program is currently being evaluated for effectiveness, and if it passes muster it will likely be continued. At best, the IRS now can audit only around 1 percent of all returns; but the self-audit could be administered to a far greater number.

What characteristics of your return might invite the self-audit? While the IRS does not disclose its formula for spotting potential underreporters, the following are generally recognized as "red flags":

- Itemized deductions in excess of average amounts deducted

- Operation of a business that typically has cash transactions—a restaurant, for example

- Operation of a business that continuously shows losses, or very meager profits in relation to sales

- Claiming a business loss on an activity that appears more like a hobby. Even a hobby with profit might be a flag, since it can be used to write off expenses that have nothing to do with the hobby. For example, you restore old cars and sell them, so you write off a family vacation to Disney World because you "consult" with an expert in Orlando on how to repair a 1965 Mustang

- Claiming a dependent who does not live with you, or a dependent who is not your child

- Showing less dividend or interest earned on your return than the amount shown on 1099 returns provided by financial institutions (this is almost sure to be questioned)

- Failing to report an IRA distribution (another sure questioning)

- Reporting a large amount of travel and entertainment expenses

If your return features one or more of the above items, you have nothing to fear if you reported correctly on the return and if you have good documentation supporting the item. If you don't, and if your self-audit seems uninspiring to the IRS, they may send an agent to show you how an audit should be conducted—on your return.

oil companies will do well in the future, but the year is about to end. Consider selling Exxon and buying Mobil, another international oil. You will then be able to deduct all the loss in Exxon (up to $3,000), and the tax savings will enable you to buy that many additional shares of Mobil. Why not just sell Exxon and buy it right back? You can't; that's called a *wash sale*. You must wait at least 30 days, which also may not be a bad idea if you think Exxon is a far better stock than Mobil over the long run. This strategy works well for stocks, but it works even better with bonds since their characteristics are more similar from one bond to another.

Split Your Income

Dividing income among family members so that it is taxed at a collectively lower marginal rate is a favorite tax-avoidance technique. If you are in a 28 percent tax bracket and your child is in a 15 percent tax bracket, then the family will save 13 cents on each dollar of income earned by the child rather than the parent. This approach is used often when people wish to establish educational funds for their children, as the Contadinos did in the vignette that opened this chapter. It can also be used to create retirement income for aging parents, who may also have high medical expenses. The two most frequently used techniques are making outright gifts and setting up trusts.

GIFTS   A husband and wife can give someone as much as $20,000 a year without incurring any gift tax; and since it is a gift, it is not income to the recipient. Regardless of the amount given, any future earnings on the invested funds become income of the recipient. Suppose you are interested in providing funds for your child's education. It's a simple matter to set up a **custodial account** (at a bank or other financial institution) and make a gift each year, the amount depending on how much you wish to accumulate.

For minors under 14 years of age, the first $500 of income from gifted assets (or any assets) is tax free by virtue of a modified standard deduction. The next $500 of income is taxed at the minor's rate, which is usually 15 percent; then, all amounts over $1,000 are taxed at the parents' rate. Even though only $1,000 of income receives favorable tax treatment, shifting income still can result in substantial tax savings, as indicated in the Contadinos' case. Savings are greatest if a gifting arrangement is started early—ideally, when a child is born. Also, for minors 14 years of age or older, all income is taxed at their rates, and not the parents'; thus, it makes sense to increase gift amounts for these individuals.

Be careful when you set up a custodial account to name as legal custodian someone who will not make contributions to the account: a friend or relative, for example. Also, keep in mind that once you make gifts to your children, they become the children's property. In effect, you lose control of the money and cannot legally get it back. Finally, anyone who sells securities that have appreciated in value to finance their children's college costs is simply throwing money down the drain. At the very least, they should give the securities to the children, who can then sell them.

TRUSTS   A trust is a legal arrangement that allows assets to be managed by a trustee for the benefit of individuals called beneficiaries. Trusts are more expensive to establish than a gifting program, but they can be structured in many ways, making it wise to seek legal advice in establishing one. Trusts are often used to provide income for someone who is aged or infirm and in need of medical or other care. Funds provided the beneficiary are derived from income earned on trust assets, which is taxed at a lower rate than the one applying to the trust creator. For example, if your marginal rate is 28 percent and the beneficiary's rate is 15 percent, 13 percent savings can be realized on income earned.

A popular trust frequently used to provide funds for college expenses is a 2503(c) trust, also called a minor's trust. With it, the first $5,000 of trust income is taxed at a 15 percent rate, regardless of the minor's age. As with gifts, at some time, assets in the trust become the property of the beneficiary.

Stagger Income and Expenses

If you can control the timing of expenses and income, you may be able to reduce taxes. For example, you may have a very large doctor or hospital bill that can be paid in either 1992 or 1993. But you might find that even by paying the bill in

1992, you don't have enough other itemized expenses to exceed the standard deduction. If you pay the bill in 1992 anyway, you may lose benefit of the deduction in 1993. By delaying payment, you hold the expense until 1993, when you may be able to itemize.

Even if you itemize in both years, it could be advantageous to stagger as many itemized expenses as you can into one of the two years. Again, this difference results from the income tax's progressive rate structure: a large total in one year could put you in a lower tax bracket that year, whereas taking an approximately even amount each year might leave you in the same bracket each year. As the months of November and December get closer, you should review your tax situation and see if expenses can be staggered profitably. Of course, staggering income—if that's possible—should also be considered.

Defer Income to Later Years

Deferring income to be taxed in later years is different from avoiding taxes altogether. However, deferring can be as attractive as avoidance, for several reasons. First, deferred income is free to accumulate, and it will grow to a substantially larger sum than income that is taxed each year. Second, your marginal tax rate when you recognize the income (usually during retirement) might be lower than your current marginal rate. Some commonly used income-deferring investments are IRAs and Keogh and 401(k) plans; tax-deferred annuities; and U.S. Treasury Series EE bonds. In addition to these formal plans, any investment that defers your return to the future offers tax advantages. For example, a growth stock typically pays little or no current dividends that would be taxable. Rather, you can enjoy your total return as a capital gain when you sell the stock in the future. True, you might pay the same amount of tax as you would with, say, a savings account; but with the growth stock, taxes are deferred until the stock is sold. The "saved" taxes can be invested and earn a return during the entire investment period.

IRAS, KEOGHS, AND 401(K) PLANS   We explained IRAs and Keoghs earlier in this chapter. A 401(k) is an optional retirement plan many employers make available to their employees. It also may be better than an IRA, depending upon the options offered. We will discuss each of these in far greater depth in Chapter 17. Certainly one of the major advantages of these plans is the deduction against current income of amounts invested.

With IRAs, you should be aware you can always take your money out of an IRA before retirement. If you do, though, you must pay a 10 percent penalty on amounts withdrawn, and you also must include the withdrawals in determining taxable income in the withdrawal year. (Remember: You excluded the IRA investment in the year you made it.) Even with the penalty, though, it may be to your advantage to use the IRA if your funds can remain invested for a sufficient period of time. But what period of time is sufficient? This is a rather difficult question to answer, so we'll defer the response to Chapter 17.

Tax-deferred annuity: An investment, usually sold by insurance companies, that allows tax deferral on current interest earned.

TAX-DEFERRED ANNUITIES   A **tax-deferred annuity** is an investment that is usually written by an insurance company. It also defers income to later years, but in contrast to IRAs, Keoghs, and 401(k)s, you cannot take a deduction on your current return for amounts invested, which makes them less attractive. More-over, the financial collapse of Baldwin United—one of the leaders in writing tax-deferred annuities—in 1983 created doubts in the minds of many investors about their safety. However, the 1986 Tax Reform Act rekindled interest in annuities because so many other tax shelters were eliminated.

U.S. TREASURY SERIES EE BONDS   Series EE bonds give you the option of reporting income as it accrues on the bond each year, or reporting it when you cash the bond. The main advantage of this bond is its flexibility. You choose when to cash it and pay the tax, and choosing a year when your marginal tax rate is low can save taxes. These bonds are explained further in Chapter 6.

Income Tax Planning for the Steeles

Arnold and Sharon Steele have done virtually no income tax planning. They hope to help John and Nancy with college costs, and they should already be considering making gifts or using trusts for that purpose, even though funds won't be needed for about eight more years. The Steeles are interested in purchasing a vacation condominium which they hope to rent for most of the year; and are considering buying a rental property. Each of these investments has certain tax-sheltering aspects that must be reviewed in depth, and we'll look at them in Chapter 16, giving detailed attention to the rental property.

The Steeles also intend to accumulate about $100,000 for a retirement nest egg. This means they should begin taking advantage of tax deferrals as soon as possible. While most of their savings through 2002 will be earmarked for the vacation condo and the children's education, they will still have some savings that can be invested for retirement. To date, the Steeles have invested in a mutual fund, Fidelity, and have bought $16,000 of InChemCo common stock through the company's share-purchase plan. They might consider selling the Fidelity shares and some of the InChemCo shares and reinvest the funds in tax-deferred annuities, although advantages from this switch seem minimal. The Steeles have not clearly identified the purposes for buying the InChemCo and Fidelity shares—something they really should do—but if retirement is one of those purposes, they need to examine the expected future accumulations with the shares versus accumulations with tax-deferred annuities.

Other Important Taxes

While the federal income tax is the most important tax to most of us, others should also be understood. For example, people in low- or middle-income brackets might pay more in Social Security taxes than personal income taxes; if you are very wealthy, you will pay substantial estate and inheritance taxes when you die, or gift taxes if you try to give the estate away before you die. The growing fiscal needs of state and local governments have brought forth an array of income, sales, and property taxes at these levels.

Social Security Taxes

Most of us are familiar with the Social Security system. We are counting on it as an important part of our retirement income or for survivor benefits to our families if something happens to us. But, as you probably also know, it has come under financial stress because benefits seem to be outpacing revenues. As a result, Social Security taxes have escalated rapidly and will continue to do so in the future.

FICA taxes: Taxes collected for Social Security purposes.

The taxes withheld from your wages for Social Security are called **FICA taxes**; FICA means Federal Insurance Contributions Act. Your FICA taxes depend upon the tax rate and the base amount of your wages subject to the tax. Each of these has changed over time, as Table 5.1 indicates. It is important to realize that you might overpay FICA taxes. This could happen if you change employers during the year or if you work for two or more employers. You can claim excess payments as a credit against your federal income tax liability at the time you prepare your return. By all means, check the W–2 forms your employer gives you in January to make sure you have not overpaid. However, both spouses must pay the full amount of the tax, so you cannot have an overpayment simply because the sum of the two exceeds the maximum.

Also, you should be aware that your employer must pay FICA tax equal to the amount withheld from your wage. This is an expensive payroll cost for employers. Self-employed individuals must also pay FICA tax, and their rates have been extremely high in recent years: 15.3 percent in 1991.

Estate and Gift Taxes

Federal estate tax: A tax levied on a decedent's estate.

The **federal estate tax** is levied on the value of a decedent's estate at the time of death. The tax follows a fairly complicated formula that is explained in greater detail in Chapter 18. Provisions of the federal estate tax have been liberalized in recent years, and in 1991 your estate must have exceeded $600,000 before any tax would have been levied.

Inheritance taxes: State taxes levied on the heirs to an estate.

In addition to the federal estate tax, each state has its own inheritance and estate tax. **Inheritance taxes** are levied somewhat differently than estate taxes, in that heirs are classified according to their relationship to the decedent. The tax depends on this classification, with more distant relationships leading to greater taxes.

Federal gift tax: Excise tax levied on the transfer of property; supplements the federal estate tax.

The **federal gift tax** is an excise tax charged on the transfer of property. A gift tax is necessary to supplement an estate tax, but otherwise you would be able to transfer wealth during your lifetime and so avoid the estate tax. Like the federal estate tax, the federal gift tax follows a specific formula, but it does permit a

TABLE 5.1 · FICA Taxes: Selected Years

Year	Rate (%)	Base Amount Subject to Tax	Maximum Tax[a]
1978	6.05	$17,700	$1,070.85
1980	6.13	25,900	1,587.67
1982	6.70	32,400	2,170.80
1984	6.70	37,800	2,532.60
1986	7.15	42,000	3,003.00
1988	7.51	45,000	3,379.50
1991	——[b]	——[b]	5,123.00

[a]This is the most tax any taxpayer should have paid. Amounts paid in excess of the maximum can be claimed as credits on the federal income tax return.

[b]A split rate: 6.2% on $53,400 and 1.45% on $125,000.

135

"modest" gift each year of $10,000 per donee ($20,000 for husband and wife donors). For most families the "modest" gift provision allows a substantial transfer of their wealth each year.

State and Local Taxes

The maze of state and local taxes in most states not only takes a fairly large amount from your bank account but also creates considerable confusion as to what is being taxed and for how much. Very few people thoroughly understand all these taxes; in fact, some of the taxes are buried in the prices of items that we buy. There is little that can be done about the situation except to make the best of it. Table 5.2 gives an indication of how tax burdens vary among different cities. Of course, governments that collect high taxes may also provide high levels of services. In this sense, then, high taxes aren't necessarily bad.

INCOME TAXES All the states except Florida, Alaska, Nevada, South Dakota, Texas, Washington, and Wyoming levy income taxes. These are usually withheld from your wages, but you must file an annual return, similar to the federal return, to calculate your tax liability and to determine any over- or underpayment. The tax bases and rates vary among the states, and they can be quite high. A New York City resident whose income is in the highest bracket will pay over 20 percent in combined state and city income tax.

Many local governments—mostly cities and villages—impose income taxes. While these are often called payroll taxes, they are imposed on all forms of income. These also require filing an annual return if you have taxable income not subject to withholding. It is not uncommon for someone in Ohio or Pennsylvania (such as a sales representative) to file more than a dozen returns if he or she earned income in 12 different communities. To make matters more confusing, there is always the question of whether you pay tax to the city where the income was earned or the city in which you live, assuming they are different. Generally, the tax follows the place of employment unless the city of residence imposes a higher tax rate; then you usually pay the difference between the two rates to the city of residence. Of course, you must file a tax return with that city.

TABLE 5.2 ·
Estimated State and
Local Taxes Paid by a
Family of Four in
Selected Large Cities,
by Income Level: 1989

	Total Tax Paid by Income Level		
	$25,000	$50,000	$100,000
Atlanta	$ 2,651	$5,181	$ 9,679
Baltimore	2,861	5,758	11,701
Chicago	1,931	3,791	7,972
Detroit	3,016	6,091	12,478
Milwaukee	3,546	7,409	15,063
New York City	2,654	6,154	14,001
Portland, OR	3,496	7,288	15,139
St. Louis	2,164	4,303	8,883
Salt Lake City	2,313	4,784	10,083
Washington, DC	2,602	5,381	9,446

SOURCE: U.S. Department of Commerce, Bureau of the Census, *Statistical Abstract of the United States, 1991*, p. 304.

The Basic
Framework

PROPERTY TAXES Property taxes are still the mainstay of local governments, particularly school districts. All states have taxes on real property (houses and buildings), and most also tax personal property (equipment, furniture, fixtures, and the like) of businesses; some also tax household personal property. Many impose taxes on intangible property, such as stocks and bonds. The property tax rate that you pay depends very much upon the community where the property is located. Rates can vary widely even within a county or other geographical area. One city's rate might be $60 per $1,000 valuation, while a neighboring city might charge only $30 per $1,000. And comparisons between states show even more dramatic differences: You'll pay about $50 per $1,000 in Boston and $8.00 per $1,000 in Phoenix.

SALES TAXES Forty-five states and the District of Columbia have sales taxes. Some tax all consumption items—services as well as commodities—while others omit services. Some tax necessities, such as food, while others do not. The sales tax rates vary among states, and even within states when local governments enact their own taxes to ''piggyback'' the state tax.

Summary

The federal income tax is the largest source of revenue for the federal government. As applied to individuals, it follows a specific formula that begins with gross income items and ends with additional taxes due the IRS, or with a refund for overpayments. A gross income item is any compensation you receive for the use of your labor or capital. From the total of gross income items, you may make certain adjustments; the balance is called adjusted gross income. Taxable income is calculated by subtracting personal deductions—by either itemizing or using the standard amounts—and exemption allowances from adjusted gross income. Your tax liability is then determined by finding the tax associated with your taxable income and subtracting from it any allowable tax credits. Your tax liability is then compared to the amount of taxes withheld from your wages and estimated taxes paid during the year to determine if you overpaid or underpaid during the year.

Other aspects of the federal income tax should also be understood. Only $3,000 of capital losses can be deducted each year. Also, other loss limitation rules apply to investments and business interests. The Internal Revenue Service (the IRS) is the federal agency responsible for administering the income tax. In so doing, it provides taxpayer assistance and periodic audits of returns. You can get outside help in preparing your return from either the tax service companies, such as H & R Block, or CPAs and attorneys, and effective planning can reduce your income taxes.

The federal income tax is not the only important tax you must pay. Social Security (FICA) taxes are growing rapidly, and many people pay more in these taxes than they do in federal income taxes. Estate and gift taxes are levied by both the federal and state governments. State and local governments also have many other taxes, such as income taxes, property taxes, and sales taxes. The amounts collected by states and local areas vary considerably throughout the United States.

Key Terms

adjusted gross income (p. 111)

alimony payments (p. 114)

automatic extension (p. 128)

average tax rate (p. 121)

capital assets (p. 125)

capital gain or loss (p. 125)

custodial account (p. 132)

earned income (p. 126)

federal estate tax (p. 135)

federal gift tax (p. 135)

FICA taxes (p. 135)

gross income items (p. 110)

inheritance taxes (p. 135)

Internal Revenue Service (IRS) (p. 126)

IRAs and Keogh plans (p. 112)

itemized deductions (p. 116)

marginal tax rate (p. 121)

municipal bonds (p. 130)

nontaxable exclusions (p. 110)

passive income (p. 126)

personal and dependency exemptions (p. 115)

portfolio income (p. 126)

refund anticipation loan (p. 128)

standard deduction (p. 116)

statute of limitations (p. 128)

taxable income (p. 115)

tax credit (p. 118)

tax-deferred annuity (p. 133)

W–2 form (p. 120)

W–4 form (p. 120)

Problems and Review Questions

1   Arrange the following items in their appropriate sequence according to the federal income tax formula: (*a*) adjusted gross income, (*b*) adjustments to income, (*c*) itemized deductions, (*d*) tax credits, (*e*) gross income items, (*f*) nontaxable exclusions, (*g*) federal income taxes withheld, and (*h*) exemptions.

2   What is the amount allowed for each exemption? Is the exemption amount indexed? Explain what this means.

3   Suppose you and your spouse work and have wages of $16,000 and $5,000, respectively. Calculate the maximum deduction for IRAs. Calculate it if your income was $21,000 and your spouse's was zero.

4   Chrissy, Jack, and Janet share an apartment. Jack and Janet have grown fond of each other and are thinking of marrying. Chrissy has told them, however, that if they do, their income taxes will increase. Jack and Janet don't see how that's possible. Assume each made $37,000 and took the standard deduction in 1991. Using the tax table or tax schedules given in this chapter, determine whether Chrissy is right.

5   John is 66 years old and blind. He lives with his wife Clara, who is also 66 but has good vision. John had $8,000 of income in 1992. Will he and Clara pay any tax? If so, how much?

6   Steve has a 28 percent marginal tax rate. What is it worth to him to have: (*a*) an additional itemized deduction of $100, (*b*) an additional $100 invested in an IRA, and (*c*) an additional tax credit of $100?

7   Explain how capital losses are treated. Also, explain the loss limitation rules as they apply to actively—and inactively—managed investments.

8   Miguel purchased a home in 1969 for $30,000. He sold it in 1979 for $70,000 and immediately purchased another one for $80,000, which he sold in 1992 for $135,000. How much taxable capital gain, if any, does Miguel have?

9   Identify, explain, or elaborate upon the following items: (*a*) functions of the IRS, (*b*) automatic extension of time for filing, (*c*) statutes of limitations, (*d*) assistance in tax-return preparation, (*e*) income splitting, (*f*) staggering expenses, (*g*) avoiding taxes, and (*h*) deferring taxes.

10 How are FICA taxes calculated? Is it possible to overpay them? If your answer is yes, what should you do?

11 What are estate, gift, and inheritance taxes?

12 Identify frequently levied state and local taxes.

Case 5.1
Preparing Becky Sell's First Tax Return

Becky Sell graduated from a Midwestern college in 1991 and immediately began work as a marketing manager trainee for a large consumer products company. Becky had never prepared her own tax return before, but she was determined to do it for the first time. Becky got all pertinent information together in February 1992, and it appears below.

1 Data on two W–2 forms (Becky worked part-time prior to graduation) showed wages of $18,000 and federal income tax withheld of $1,600. In addition, they showed she paid $600 in state and city income taxes and $1,287 in FICA taxes.
2 Becky paid most of her bills with checks and kept all cancelled receipts for purchases. Examination of these and her check stubs shows the following major classifications of expenses: rent = $3,000; charitable contributions = $500; interest on installment loans = $1,900; food and clothing = $7,000; dues to professional marketing society = $200; hospital and doctor's bills = $900; state sales tax = $600; contributions to a political candidate in her hometown = $110; contributions to a panhandler she often sees outside the office of the political candidate = $50.
3 Becky received $12,000 in gifts at graduation, and with it she purchased shares of GM stock in April. Three months later she sold these shares for $8,500.

Becky wants to file a return that will minimize her 1991 tax liability. She has cash from the GM stock sale that could be used for an IRA investment, but she isn't sure of the maximum allowed.

Questions

1 If Becky itemized personal expenses, how much can she deduct? How much is her standard deduction?
2 Using the tax form and tax schedules presented in this chapter, and taking the standard deduction, determine Becky's 1991 tax liability. (Assume she will make a maximum IRA investment.) How much will Becky owe or have refunded?
3 Determine Becky's marginal tax rate and explain to her what this rate means.
4 Becky worked for two employers; did she overpay her FICA taxes? Explain.

Case 5.2
The Brittens' Investment Alternatives

Bernie and Pam Britten are a young married couple beginning careers and establishing a household. They will each make about $30,000 next year and will have about $40,000 to invest. They now rent an apartment but are considering purchasing a condominium for $60,000. If they do, a down payment of $10,000 will be required.

They have discussed their situation with Lew McCarthy, an investment adviser and personal friend, and he has recommended the investments detailed below:

1 The condominium—expected annual increase in market value = 10 percent.
2 Municipal bonds—expected annual yield = 8 percent.
3 High-yield corporate stocks—expected dividend yield = 12 percent.
4 Savings account in a commercial bank—expected annual yield = 9 percent.
5 High-growth common stocks—expected annual increase in market value = 12 percent; expected dividend yield = 0.

Questions

1 Calculate the after-tax yields on the above investments, assuming the Brittens have a 28 percent marginal tax rate.
2 How would you recommend the Brittens invest their $40,000? Explain your answer.

Helpful Reading

Changing Times

Kosnett, Jeff. *"Time to Wake Up Your IRA."* October 1991, pp. 36–40.

McCormally, Kevin. *"Taxes: Software to the Rescue."* February 1991, pp. 56–58.

———. *"How to Boost Your Take-Home Pay."* May 1991, pp. 33–35.

———. *"How to Pay Lower Taxes."* October 1991, pp. 36–40.

Money

Sims, John. *"Is Your State a Haven or a Hell?"* January 1991, pp. 87–91.

Smith, Marguerite T. *"Who Cheats on Their Income Taxes."* April 1991, pp. 101–107.

———. *"How to Avoid 13 Costly Tax Errors."* March 1991, pp. 84–93.

Tritch, Teresa, and Deborah Lohse. *"The Pros Flub Our Tax Test Again."* March 1991, pp. 96–107.

———. *"Cut Your Taxes."* August 1991, pp. 83–95.

The Wall Street Journal

Schultz, Ellen E. *"Beware of Accountants Promising Riches."* May 31, 1990, p. C1.

Mason, Todd. *"Mama, Don't Let Your Babies Grow Up to Work for the Tax Boys."* January 29, 1991, p. C1.

Helpful Contacts

IRS Assistance Line: 1–800–829–1040.

Spending, Borrowing, and Saving

Now that you have established a sound financial framework, it is time to consider some of the basics of household financial management. In the past, our finances were much simpler. Most of us had the same kind of checking account, if we had one at all, and we avoided consumer credit. We placed our savings in the neighborhood savings and loan, and, when the time came, we went there for our home mortgages, too. Today? Your checking account might be with a New York bank even though you live in Manhattan, Kansas; and your real estate broker (who is also affiliated with a stock brokerage firm) can arrange your home mortgage with a savings and loan in Los Angeles. Do you benefit from these changes? Yes, if you take the time to become an informed consumer; no, if you do not.

Chapter 6, *Cash Management*, presents several ways you may hold your cash balances, and the advantages of each. Strategies for allocating deposits among financial institutions and instruments will be discussed. Studying this chapter should give you a basic understanding of how deposits grow and how liquidity is important in your asset portfolio.

You will examine methods for establishing and using credit in Chapter 7. Furthermore, you will learn the proper use and the real cost of these financial obligations by examining how interest is charged and paid on consumer loans.

Given an understanding of credit management, you may then evaluate methods for finding "best buys" in Chapter 8, *Consumer Durables*. You will learn where to find information on products, how to compare that information, and what to do if the product doesn't live up to your expectations.

The last topic in Part Two is the housing decision, which is considered in Chapter 9. The chapter begins with a discussion of the alternatives. Various types of shelter are examined. In addition, methods for deciding whether to rent or buy are presented, along with a comprehensive discussion of the many kinds of home mortgages.

Part

2

Cash Management: Funds for Immediate Needs

Objectives

1 To identify the important deposits for holding cash balances, and the advantages and disadvantages of each

2 To determine how much liquidity is usually necessary, given your income and preferences for safety

3 To understand the various kinds of financial institutions offering deposits and check-writing privileges

4 To decide on the appropriate type of checking account, and to learn how to make transactions with your account and reconcile it each month

5 To understand how compounding makes your deposits grow over time, and why deposits with long maturities are riskier than those with short maturities

6 To devise a strategy for managing your total liquid asset portfolio

"Wilma, I Wouldn't Sell You Anything That Isn't Safe"

At 70, with only $20,000 to her name, Wilma Goodman wasn't the kind of person who would have thought of risking a cent on some S&L's uninsured bonds. But when she accompanied an acquaintance to a Germania branch in O'Fallon, Ill. and saw signs touting the security's 11% yield, the idea of earning extra interest to supplement her $440-a-month Social Security was too attractive to pass up.

"We spoke to a saleslady," Goodman recalls, "and she said we had nothing to worry about."

And when Goodman agreed to invest $5,000 in the bonds, the sales rep pushed her to redeem a $10,000 federally insured CD she had at Germania and put that money into the bonds as well. As a sweetener, the rep offered to waive the CD's early-withdrawal penalty. Goodman hesitated, "I told her that this was my life savings," she says. But the representative swept away Goodman's fears by saying: "Wilma, I wouldn't sell you anything that isn't safe."

In June, Goodman received a notice from the RTC saying it had frozen the bonds. Shortly afterward, she suffered a slight stroke, which she believes was triggered by the strain of her financial loss. Goodman is now part of a pending class action suit on behalf of all 876 bondholders that will try to reclaim their savings.

SOURCE: Excerpted from Walter L. Updegrave, "Keep Your Cash Safe." *Money,* February 1991, pp. 68–75. © 1991, Time, Inc. All rights reserved.

Cash management strategy: A plan determining how much cash to hold, in what form, and in which financial institutions.

An error in judgment, such as the one in the vignette, is easy to make in dealing with banks. Above all, you must develop a sound **cash management strategy.** That is, you must decide how much cash to hold, in what forms, and in which financial institutions.

Cash is the most liquid asset you hold. Because it is so liquid and can be used so readily for paying bills or other obligations, it often offers either no return or one below what might be available on other investments, such as stocks and bonds. This difference in return is the price (opportunity cost) you pay to be liquid, and it makes sense to keep this price as low as possible. Sound cash management, then, is minimizing cash balances while maintaining an adequate level of liquidity, which means safety. This chapter discusses the important aspects of cash management.

Meeting Cash Needs

Few of us hold the same amount of cash. Your income might be far greater than mine, or you might be more conservative in your financial outlook. Despite such differences, people share some very common characteristics that determine their cash needs. And to satisfy them, most of us keep some pocket money and hold the rest of our cash in either checking or savings accounts.

Why Hold Cash?

In a barter system, cash would be unnecessary, but life would be much more difficult. If you had fish and wanted corn, you would have to find someone who had corn and wanted fish. And if you didn't consume or trade all your fish, you would find it difficult to hold—or save—the excess supply. All developed countries eventually evolve very complex monetary systems in order to facilitate trade

145

Cash
Management

and commerce. After a while, these systems appear so complicated that people without training in finance usually give up trying to understand them. These people usually deposit their cash based on the advice of a friend or relative. Before looking at the kinds of deposits available, though, it is helpful to understand the primary reasons why cash must be held in the first place. These reasons are threefold: to undertake transactions, to have a cash reserve in case of an emergency, and to have a temporary store of value. Each of these will now be examined.

UNDERTAKE TRANSACTIONS   Each day you make small transactions. You may have bought lunch at the cafeteria; perhaps you stopped at a vending machine to buy a candy bar or some other item. It took cash—specifically, **pocket money** (coins and currency)—to do these things. How much pocket money do most people have on hand? Normally, they keep enough to get through a week or two; so, if you spend an average of $10 a day, you might cash a check each week for $70. Or if you have access to an automated teller machine (an ATM), you can use your bank card to make withdrawals, and this method is usually more convenient than cashing a check. Actually, it is convenience, along with safety, that dictates how much pocket money to have on hand: The more convenient it is to get it, the less you need to hold. Since pocket money is easily lost or stolen, it is usually worthwhile to put up with some inconvenience to keep your balance low.

These inconveniences lead most people to open a **checking account** to pay larger monthly bills, such as the rent or utilities. You wouldn't want the risk of losing currency in the mail, or the inconvenience of visiting the creditor just to pay the bill in cash. Moreover, a cancelled check serves as evidence of having paid the bill. The advantages of checking accounts so heavily outweigh any of their disadvantages, that a much larger portion of our total liquid assets are held in them than in coins and currency.

EMERGENCY RESERVES   In addition to needing cash for everyday transactions, most people want to hold a portion of their assets in liquid form in case of emergencies. An illness, the loss of a job, or any other unfortunate event can severely strain a family's budget, and without some liquid assets, the family could be forced to sell other assets, such as the house or automobile, to meet daily living expenses. While most people agree that some cash should be held for **emergency reserves,** *how much* should be held isn't clear. Individual circumstances must dictate the amount. If you have disability income insurance or other protection that would maintain your income at close to its previous level while you are unemployed, you need a smaller emergency reserve than does someone whose income stops altogether. Important, too, is the amount of medical insurance carried: The more you have, the less cash you need. Many financial planners recommend a reserve equivalent to three to five months' after-tax income; so if you take home $2,000 a month, a reserve of $6,000 to $10,000 is suggested. Remember, though, this is only a rule of thumb.

Since emergency reserves are not intended to be used for making transactions, they should be held in deposits that offer the highest potential return consistent with reasonable liquidity. Holding them in a checking account that pays no interest, for example, would be a mistake.

Pocket money: Coins and currency a person holds.

Checking account: Funds held with a financial institution and available upon demand.

Emergency reserve: Liquid deposits held to meet unexpected cash needs.

Spending, Borrowing, and Saving

STORE OF VALUE   You may be saving to make a major purchase in the future: a house, a new automobile, a personal computer, or a vacation. Until you have enough money, you need to save each pay period and then hold your savings in a form that will earn a return. You should be aware, though, that if you are holding funds for a fairly long period of time, the return on your deposits may not match the inflation rate on the item you are saving to buy. In this case, the deposit has not served well as a store of value. It is important to balance earnings against liquidity in the savings effort; in order to achieve your target, you may have to give up some liquidity to capture a higher return.

In addition to saving for a major purchase, some people hold cash balances as temporary ''parking places'' for their money. They really plan to reinvest their funds in less liquid investments in the future but are waiting for the investment environment to improve. Whatever the motive for holding cash, it must be held in specific kinds of deposits, to which we now turn our attention.

Fundamental Deposits

Many people meet their cash needs by holding deposits in checking and NOW accounts and passbook savings accounts. These are the basic deposits, but other types are often used as well. Table 6.1 shows how the relative importance of the most frequently used deposits has changed over the period indicated. In this section and the next we will explain these deposits, but first, remember that what makes a deposit liquid is your ability to withdraw it easily, with no delays or other complications, and your ability to withdraw it with *no loss in principal*. This last feature rules out many kinds of investments for serving liquidity needs. Common stocks, for example, can be sold quickly and relatively inexpensively—but there is never a guarantee they can be sold without loss, so they fail the liquidity test. Some of the deposits examined below are much more liquid than others. Certificates of deposit are the least liquid because of their interest penalties for early withdrawal.

TABLE 6.1 ·
Composition of Liquid
Deposits

	Average Daily Balances		
	June 1990	June 1991	June 1991 Average per Capita
Currency and checks	$234 bil.	$258 bil.	$1,080
Traveler's checks	8	8	33
Checking accounts[a]	276	281	1,176
NOW accounts[b]	294	312	1,305
Savings deposits:			
Passbook accounts	412	439	1,837
Others (mostly CDs)[c]	1,155	1,129	4,724
Money market deposit			
accounts	502	542	2,268
Money market mutual			
funds	328	364	1,523
Savings bonds	124	128	536

SOURCE: *Federal Reserve Statistical Release*, various issues.

[a]Deposits at commercial banks.

[b]Deposits at commercial banks, mutual savings banks, and savings and loans.

[c]Certificates of deposit in excess of $100,000 are excluded.

Closely related to the issue of losing principal is the question of safety. Many depositors view safety as their most crucial concern because a large portion of their total investments may be in liquid accounts. Certainly a major advantage of holding deposits in most banks, savings and loans, and credit unions is the availability of federal insurance. (See Table 6.2.)

Keep in mind that federal insurance is far different from so-called state-provided insurance, which is actually privately funded. Such "state" insurance is weaker, as depositors in Ohio and, more recently, Rhode Island, sadly learned. In the Ohio case, the failure of one large savings and loan, Home State, threatened the entire insurance fund, leading the governor to order a bank holiday for all "state-insured" S&Ls (about 70 in all) until other insurance arrangements could be made for them. Home State depositors faced weeks of uncertainty, unable to withdraw their funds and not knowing when, if ever, their institution would reopen. This incident prompted questions about the safety of any deposit system that is not federally insured. You should inquire as to how your accounts are insured, and you must then decide whether they are adequately protected.

CHECKING AND NOW ACCOUNTS   Checking and NOW accounts are used to satisfy transaction needs. In June 1991, an average daily balance of $593 billion was held in these accounts. While there is a slight technical difference between a regular checking and a **NOW (negotiated order of withdrawal) account,** for all practical purposes they are identical. Their major difference to you is that a NOW account pays interest on balances in the account, while a regular checking account does not. The only reason you should consider not having a NOW account is if you do not meet the requirement for a minimum monthly balance. Most banks advertise their NOW accounts and **super NOW accounts** (these pay higher interest) with names such as *Checking Plus* or *Checking Plus More,* to indicate that interest is earned on the account. The interest may be paid in several ways. Amounts below a minimum (usually between $500 and $5,000) earn interest at what is referred to as the passbook rate (explained below), while amounts above the limit earn higher rates. The higher rates are usually pegged to current money market rates, which means the interest you receive depends upon the level of interest rates in general; as these go up, so does the amount earned.

NOW (negotiated order of withdrawal) account: Interest-earning checking account, usually with a minimum balance requirement.

Super NOW account: NOW account paying high interest but with a large minimum balance requirement.

TABLE 6.2 ·
Federally Insured
Financial Institutions

	Insuring Federal Agency		
	Federal Deposit Insurance Corporation (FDIC)	Savings Association Insurance Fund (SAIF)	National Credit Union Administration (NCUA)
Institutions insured	Commercial banks and mutual savings banks	Savings and loan associations	Federally chartered credit unions
Approximate number of insured institutions	13,000	2,900	15,000
Amount of insurance per depositor[a]	$100,000	$100,000	$100,000
Insured deposits, Dec. 1990	$2.3 trillion	$858 billion	$178 billion

[a]It is important to note that insurance is for each depositor and not for each account. If the amount held by one depositor exceeds $100,000, another account should be opened with a different institution, or additional deposits with the same institution could be made in another person's name.

Of course, the reverse is also true, but the NOW rate never goes below the passbook rate.

To determine the appropriate checking account for you, you must compare the costs of maintaining the account and the interest you can earn on it with what might be earned on an alternative liquid account, called the side account. Table 6.3 contrasts four checking account plans based on data provided by a Midwestern bank in mid-1991. As you see, the most effective account is the NOW, based on the situation described in Table 6.3. Notice that the special checking account would be preferred to the regular checking account only if fewer than ten checks were written each month. Actually, the dollar differences between the alternatives are not that great, and perhaps the best advice is (a) make sure you don't have a restricted checking account if you write more than ten checks a month (and most people do), and (b) don't keep excessive balances in your regular checking if it offers no interest or less interest than is available on alternative accounts. It is important to realize that the illustration in Table 6.3 assumes any amount over $200 in regular checking is immediately invested in the side account; if you fail to do this, the opportunity cost of maintaining the regular checking account increases substantially.

Savings account: Account with virtually no restrictions but with no check-writing privileges.

Passbook rate: Interest rate on a savings account; usually the lowest savings rate offered by a financial institution.

SAVINGS ACCOUNTS   Many Americans have had a **savings account** at one time or another. They were often called passbook accounts because a record of your activity in the account was recorded in a passbook. These books are now mostly replaced by the type of statements used for checking accounts. However, the rate of interest earned on passbook accounts is still called the **passbook rate.** Because these accounts require no minimum balances, they are used frequently when only small deposits can be made, and about $439 billion was still held in them (average daily balance) in June 1991. The passbook rate is generally the lowest rate of interest available, and it may be to your advantage to invest funds in alternative liquid accounts if you have enough cash to qualify for one of them. But shopping around may be to your advantage, even with savings accounts. For

TABLE 6.3 · A Comparison of Four Checking Account Plans

	Alternatives			
	Special Checking	Regular Checking	NOW (4% rate)	Super NOW (4½% rate)
1. Service charges: Rates	$1.00/month + $0.15/check	$2.50/month	none	none
Amount per year	$ 57.00	$ 30.00	-0-	-0-
2. Minimum monthly balance	200.00	200.00	$1,000.00	$3,000.00
3. Interest earned on the account	-0-	-0-	40.00	135.00
4. Amount deposited in the side account (assumed to earn 6.5%)	2,800.00	2,800.00	2,000.00	-0-
5. Interest earned on the side account	182.00	182.00	130.00	-0-
6. Total interest earned	182.00	182.00	170.00	135.00
7. Net interest earned (line 6 less service changes)	$ 125.00	$ 152.00	$ 170.00	$ 135.00

ASSUMPTIONS: 1. The depositor has an average balance of $3,000 for liquid deposits.
      2. A balance of $200 will be maintained for checking account needs.
      3. Twenty-five checks are written each month, or 300 a year.
      4. Amounts above minimum requirements are deposited in an alternative interest-earning, liquid account (the side account).

Cash Management

example, your credit union might offer a higher rate than your bank or savings and loan.

Other Deposits

Major legislation, specifically the Financial Institutions Deregulation and Monetary Control Act, was passed in 1980 to affect financial institutions and the types of deposits they can offer. This legislation, along with very high interest rates in the late 1970s and early 1980s, created a competitive environment among financial institutions as each attempted to attract deposits. The result has been a number of alternatives to the traditional passbook savings account.

Money market deposit account (MMDA): Savings account whose interest rate is tied to money market rates of interest.

MONEY MARKET DEPOSIT ACCOUNTS Money market deposit accounts **(MMDAs)** came into being in December 1982. By June 1991 they had attracted an average daily balance of $542 billion. They were popular almost at once, and for good reason. They offered current money market rates and easy access through check-writing privileges, usually limited to three checks (or six transfers in total) a month. Federal depository insurance also enhances their appeal, as does access through automated teller machines. Unfortunately for small depositors, they have minimum deposit balances. Also, in very recent years, banks have lowered the rates on MMDAs substantially below market rates. It remains to be seen if this trend will continue. If it does, you should consider using money market mutual funds instead of MMDAs.

Money market mutual fund: Pooling arrangement that invests in money market securities having very large denominations.

MONEY MARKET MUTUAL FUNDS Money market mutual funds were introduced in the middle 1970s, and $364 billion was invested in them in June 1991. Mutual funds will be explained in greater detail in Chapter 15, so the discussion here is brief. Essentially, these funds pool the resources of many investors to purchase short-term securities issued by the U.S. Treasury, large commercial banks, and financially strong corporations. Most people cannot afford to purchase such securities directly because they are sold only in very large denominations, such as $10,000 for a U.S. Treasury Bill and $100,000 for a commercial bank certificate of deposit. Since most of these investments are very safe, so too are the money market mutual funds that invest in them. Nevertheless, your deposit is not insured as it is in a money market account or other federally insured deposit. A unique money market fund is one that invests in municipal bonds with very short maturities. Such funds appeal to depositors in high tax brackets, because the earnings are exempt from federal income tax. All money market mutual funds have a minimum balance requirement, which is usually $1,000, although some are as low as $500.

Certificate of deposit (CD): Savings account with a set maturity and restricted access to funds until maturity.

CERTIFICATES OF DEPOSIT Certificates of deposit (CDs) are somewhat different from money market deposit accounts or money market mutual funds. When you buy CDs, you are in effect freezing your money for the maturity of the deposit, which can vary from seven days to eight years, or even longer. For instance a 60-month deposit of $1,000 might be purchased to yield 8 percent. At the end of 60 months you will get $1,469.33, which is the principal plus interest (assuming annual compounding). But suppose you need the money before the 60 months end? You will then pay an interest penalty, the amount depending upon

Has the Bank Supermarket Finally Arrived?

For at least a decade now, we have been hearing of the bank of the future—one that offers not only traditional bank products and services but new ones, such as money market and other mutual funds, insurance, tax preparation, real estate listings, and even travel and legal services. Until recently, most of what we heard was only talk.

Now, however, there are indications that the new bank has arrived. Congress is considering legislation which, if passed, would remove most legal barriers that currently slow or prevent bank expansion along the new lines. If the legislation is approved, we should see a proliferation of new products and services.

Not that banks are sitting back waiting for Congress to act. Indeed, some are already moving aggressively in new directions, which seem to take one of two paths. Dollar Dry Dock, the nation's ninth largest savings bank, characterizes one path. It features neon lights, television monitors, and person-to-person sales pitches to sell everything from six-month CDs to travel cruises. Also following this path is Banc One of Ohio, one of the nation's largest bank groups.

The second path, characterized by LaSalle National Bank of Chicago, is that of a personal financial consultant—someone that can help you make financial decisions, such as choosing appropriate investments or insurance. This approach is an at-

tempt to capitalize on the trust many people apparently have in a banker's advice as opposed to advice offered by stock brokers or insurance sales agents.

Do you need or want the bank of the future? There are some advantages, convenience being the most notable. Research indicates that banks attract customers primarily because of convenience. What could be more convenient, then, than satisfying your other financial needs while at the bank? Another advantage would be a monthly statement showing on one form all your financial assets and liabilities. A potential disadvantage is placing so much confidence in your local banker. Is he or she truly qualified to offer so much financial advice and so many financial products? Our recent history suggests a note of caution.

when withdrawal takes place. A very early withdrawal can mean you get less back than your initial deposit. Naturally, this penalty discourages investors from using these deposits indiscriminately to obtain higher rates. The interest rate at the time of purchase is locked in for the entire term of the deposit. If interest rates fall during that period, you benefit by having your money invested at the higher rate. But if interest rates rise, the certificates will have been a poor choice. During June 1991, the average daily investment in CDs was $1,129 billion.

U.S. Series EE bonds: Treasury-issued bonds with indexed interest rates, low denominations, and other attractive features.

U.S. SERIES EE BONDS With recent changes, **U.S. Series EE bonds** have become very attractive short-term investments, particularly for small investors. They now offer a minimum rate of 6 percent (if they are held five years), which certainly makes them more attractive than passbook deposits. If they are held longer than five years, the interest they pay will be 85 percent of the actual average interest earned on an index of Treasury securities for the five-year period prior to their redemption. This feature ties the yield on Series EE bonds to floating rates and protects their holders against inflation losses that typically occur to fixed-rate securities when interest rates rise. The interest you earn on Series EE bonds is free of state and local income taxes and can be deferred for federal income tax purposes until you redeem the bonds. Moreover, federal income taxes may be avoided altogether if interest on the bond is used to pay for a child's college or vocational education. Currently, single individuals earning $40,000 or less and married couples jointly earning $60,000 or less earn a full exclusion of all

Series EE bond interest. For incomes from $40,000 to $50,000 (single return) and $60,000 to $90,000 (joint return), partial exclusion is available; and for incomes over $50,000 and $90,000, no exclusion is allowed. Clearly, this possible avoidance of taxes on Series EE bonds makes them very attractive.

Interest is earned on the Series EE bond by redeeming it for an amount greater than what was paid to purchase it. Another important consideration in purchasing Series EE bonds is their widespread availability. They can be bought or redeemed at most federally insured commercial or mutual savings banks or savings and loans. Outstanding Series EE and HH bonds totaled $128 billion in June 1991. Some basic information about U.S. Series EE bonds is shown in Figure 6.1.

U.S. Series HH bonds: Treasury-issued bonds that pay a fixed semiannual interest; available only through exchange of U.S. Series EE bonds.

U.S. SERIES HH BONDS **U.S. Series HH bonds** are also issued by the Treasury. You cannot buy them, however; you can acquire them only by exchanging Series EE bonds (or series E bonds, an older version of Series EE). The HH series differs from the EE series in that interest is paid semiannually at a fixed 6 percent rate and the bonds mature in ten years (but can be extended to 30 years). An appealing feature of HH bonds is that deferred interest on EE bonds can be continued by the exchange. However, semiannual interest is taxable.

A SUMMARY OF LIQUID DEPOSITS AND ACCOUNTS We have discussed the most popular deposits and accounts held for liquidity. Table 6.4 presents a convenient summary of their important characteristics. *Availability* refers to a minimum balance requirement, *safety* refers to potential default risk, and *liquidity* means how easily you can withdraw your funds. Keep in mind, there are usually restrictions on an account—yield, minimum balance, withdrawals, or whatever—

PURCHASE PRICE	• $25 to $5,000; maximum investment is $30,000 per individual
YOUR RETURN	• No less than 4.27% if held one year
	• No less than 6.0% if held five years or longer
	• Actual return after five years indexed to returns on U.S. Treasury securities (six-month annualized yield beginning November 1, 1991 = 6.38%; this rate changes every six months)
WHERE TO BUY	• Through payroll deduction plans
	• At most banks and other financial institutions
	• Through the mail from Bureau of Public Debt, Washington, DC 20226
REDEMPTION	• Must wait six months, unless there is an emergency
	• Redeem at any bank, but be careful not to redeem immediately before an interest date (there are two a year), since you can lose several months' interest even if you redeem only several days too early
OTHER ADVANTAGES	• No buying or selling charges, fees, or commissions
	• Income taxes can be deferred until redemption, or possibly avoided altogether if bond interest is used for a child's education
	• No state or local income taxes

FIGURE 6.1

Important facts about U.S. Series EE savings bonds.

TABLE 6.4 · A Scorecard for Liquid Deposits and Accounts

Deposit	Availability	Safety	Liquidity	Yield (Average Rate)[a]
Regular checking account	A+ (no minimum)	A+	A+	F (-0-)
Savings account	A+ (no minimum)	A+	B+	D (4.0–5.0%)
NOW account	A (small minimum)	A+	A+	D (4.0–5.0%)
Super NOW account	C (fairly large minimum)	A+	A+	C (4.7%)
Money market deposit account	C (fairly large minimum)	A+	B+	B− (5.3%)
Money market mutual fund	B+ (minimum varies)	A to C (depending on securities held)	A+ to B (depending on checkwriting privileges)	B− (5.5%)
Certificates of deposit	A (minimum varies)	A+	C (early withdrawal penalties)	A (7.2%)[b]
Series EE bonds	A (small minimum)	A+	B	B+ (6.6%)

[a]Approximate amounts at mid-July, 1991.

[b]On 60-month CDs; longer maturities offered higher rates, shorter maturities less.

imposed by the financial institution. These restrictions will vary among the institutions, which means it's a good idea to shop around, paying particular attention to those characteristics important to you. Also, be careful of advertising: Some of it is anything but clear and helpful to the consumer. If a bank advertises a high interest rate, for example, be sure it applies to your entire deposit and not to just a small part of it. In short, be sure to read the fine print. And be extra careful to understand the early withdrawal penalties on CDs.

Financial Institutions

Perhaps no segment of American business has undergone as much change in recent years as have financial institutions. In the past, lines of distinction among the various types of institutions were clear. For example, only banks offered checking accounts. If you wanted a mortgage loan on your house, you borrowed from the neighborhood savings and loan. All that has changed. Now, the savings and loan will provide you with a checking account as well as a mortgage loan, and the commercial bank might combine your checking account with a stock brokerage account and even act as a broker in buying or selling your stocks and bonds.

Banks and "Almost Banks"

Bank: Any institution that accepts deposits and allows checks to be written against those deposits.

The term **bank** can be used to describe any institution that accepts deposits and then allows checks to be written against those deposits as a means of making payments. It doesn't matter if the written document used to make payment is called a check, a share draft, a negotiated order of withdrawal, or anything else;

153

the function it performs is exactly the same. Commercial banks dominate the industry in terms of size and are also the most rapidly growing, in terms of attracting new deposits.

COMMERCIAL BANKS   As indicated above, the traditional role of the **commercial bank** was to provide check-writing services, referred to as *demand deposits*. This function was an outgrowth of goldsmithing practices during the Middle Ages, when goldsmiths made loans on the basis of customers' gold deposits. Often, these loans were worth quite a bit more than the gold in the vault. This is the origin of *fractional reserve banking*, which continues today. While gold is no longer a part of our monetary system, commercial banks are still required to have deposits with the Federal Reserve Bank in proportion to their total checking and savings deposits. This reserve requirement varies from time to time in response to Federal Reserve policy and differs for checking and for savings deposits. While reserves probably provide some added protection to bank deposits, their primary purpose is to give the Federal Reserve a means of controlling deposit expansion or contraction, which is the way it controls the nation's money supply.

> Commercial bank: A financial institution that offers a wide array of financial products and services.

Many commercial banks, and certainly all the larger ones, are called *full-service banks* because they offer a wide array of financial services. You can expect to be charged for these services, and the trend of such charges is clearly upward. The average charge for a bounced check, for example, has nearly tripled: jumping from $5.07 in 1979 to $15.00 and more in 1991. Other services subject to these rapidly rising charges include overdraft protection, balance inquiries, and rental of safe deposit boxes, as well as routine checking services. Moreover, these charges vary from bank to bank, so ask about them before selecting one.

SAVINGS AND LOAN ASSOCIATIONS   The local **savings and loan association (S&L)** is still the most favored institution when consumers look for loans to finance their homes. There are two kinds of S&Ls: mutual and corporate. The mutual savings and loan, the most common, is actually owned by its depositors, who receive dividends on their deposits, theoretically out of the S&L's profits. Although not guaranteed, these dividends are virtually the same as interest, and very rarely are they cut or not paid at all. Moreover, the Internal Revenue Service calls them interest payments, not dividends, for federal income tax purposes. A corporate S&L is a profit-seeking corporation similar to any commercial bank; its deposit payments are unquestionably interest, not dividends. Although found primarily in California, Ohio, and Texas, their growth in other areas is likely, given the merger and acquisition changes taking place in the financial institutions industry. As this evolution continues, less emphasis will be placed on distinguishing the firm as an S&L or as a commercial bank. Most will simply be called "banks." Regardless of what they are called, the important task of providing funds to the real estate industry will remain and will require servicing by these institutions.

> Savings and loan association (S&L): A financial institution that typically offers limited services, usually specializing in home mortgage loans.

The choice of a commercial bank or an S&L to meet your financial needs should depend primarily on factors such as costs (as mentioned above), deposit interest, convenience, personal courtesy, and last (but not least)—safety. The number of S&L (and bank) failures in recent years has been so large as to pose a threat to our entire financial system. Before opening an account at any institution, you should try to determine its solvency, although this may not be an easy task.

Mutual savings bank: A financial institution more similar to an S&L than a commercial bank.

MUTUAL SAVINGS BANKS   In terms of the services provided, a **mutual savings bank** is more closely related to an S&L than to a commercial bank. Mutual savings banks are geographically concentrated in the Northeast, with about 75 percent of them in New York and Massachusetts. The word *mutual* tells us they are depositor-owned, and, as indicated above, the payments on their deposits are called dividends even though they are interest payments for all practical purposes.

Other Financial Institutions

Although commercial banks and S&Ls dominate the financial institutions industry, other organizations are also important. Credit unions have been serving their members' financial needs for a long time; recent newcomers to the banking business are stock brokerage firms and insurance companies.

Credit union: A financial institution similar to an S&L but not specializing in home mortgages, often serving a limited customer base, such as employees of a particular company.

CREDIT UNIONS   Credit unions are the most convenient financial institution for many people, because the credit union is usually associated with their place of work. As a result, payroll deductions can be made for both savings and loan servicing. In addition, the credit union office is probably located conveniently near the plant or office. But credit unions have traditionally offered their members much more than just convenient service. Their dividend rates are usually as high as, or higher than, passbook rates, and loan charges are usually competitive with those of commercial banks and S&Ls. In addition, many credit unions offer free life insurance protection up to a maximum of $2,000 and free insurance that pays off a loan in the event of death or disability. As noted previously in this chapter, if the credit union is federally chartered, deposits are insured by the National Credit Union Administration up to $100,000. The larger credit unions also provide check-writing privileges with some accounts, and they offer the same package of savings plans as do large commercial banks and S&Ls. With the possible exception of real estate loans, you very likely will find that your credit union—if it is a large one—can service all your financial needs. However, smaller credit unions are a different story. You should be very careful if they lack NCUA protection, and you can expect their interest rates, on both loans and deposits, to lag somewhat behind market rates.

STOCK BROKERAGE FIRMS   In the mid-1970s, Merrill Lynch, a large stock brokerage firm, began offering its customers the most comprehensive financial account ever seen in the industry. Called the *Cash Management Account*, it combined checking, borrowing, and security buying into one account. Moreover, management of the account was automatic. For example, if you sold securities for, say, $10,000, the funds were automatically invested in a money market fund, rather than lying idle in a checking account. Also, if you happened to buy securities for an amount greater than your cash available, credit was automatically extended on what is called a *margin account*, which will be explained in more detail in Chapter 13. The Cash Management Account required a minimum deposit of $20,000, which many people thought would limit its popularity. In fact, it became the most popular account of its type ever offered. Motivated by its success, other large stock brokerage firms have introduced their own versions of the Cash Management Account.

INSURANCE COMPANIES   Very large insurance companies are also offering services to consumers. Prudential Insurance, one of the largest, acquired Bache and Company, a large stock brokerage firm, to form Prudential-Bache. Since the merger, they have developed their "Total Financial Planning Program," which is supposed to take care of a family's total financial needs. Their promotional material indicates that it includes over 65 financial alternatives. Linking insurance to investments and cash management makes sense, since all three are part of the broader picture of providing funds for immediate liquidity and also for the future.

CONSUMER BANKS   A consumer bank is a financial institution that limits its activities to individuals; that is, it does not offer services to businesses. Consumer banks usually offer savings—but not checking—accounts and make consumer loans. You might find their rates very attractive in comparison to commercial banks or S&Ls, but keep in mind that federal deposit insurance is not offered by these institutions (it's really a misnomer to call them banks), which increases your risk substantially.

Using Your Checking Account

The convenience of paying bills by checks, rather than with cash, was noted earlier in this chapter. Maintaining a checking account properly, however, involves some work. Care must be taken in making deposits and writing checks, and it is important to keep an adequate balance in the account, both to avoid overdrafts and to stay above the minimum, if one applies to the account. In addition, each month the bank will provide a statement of activity in the account, which you should reconcile with your activity records to insure that neither you nor the bank has made a mistake. The first order of business, though, is to select a bank.

Selecting a Bank

Your choice of bank is usually determined by a variety of factors. Perhaps the most important of these is convenience, but very often the range of services provided by the bank is also considered. Finally, what the bank charges to service the account and what it offers in interest on average balances must be evaluated. Shop around to find a checking account that fills your needs best. Many alternative accounts, as we discussed previously, have come into the marketplace, and the various features they offer should be compared.

GEOGRAPHIC CONVENIENCE   Depositors often cite geographic convenience as the single most important factor in choosing one bank over another. While many transactions can be made indirectly through such means as preauthorized savings or bill payments, people nevertheless still conduct most of their banking business by direct contact with the bank. They visit it frequently to cash checks, make deposits, pay off loans, and so forth. It's not surprising, then, that geographic convenience still matters the most. But closely related to the geographic convenience of the main office and branches is the existence of automated teller machines at convenient locations. Many people now rely upon them as a source of cash and as a means of making other transactions. Finally, convenience and courtesy at the bank will probably influence your choice to open or keep an account there. Drive-in window facilities are obviously important to many of us, judging by the long lines of automobiles we often see at banks.

BANK SERVICES   Full-service banks and many other institutions now offer a wide array of services to their depositors, as Figure 6.2 shows. You might notice the items of convenience, such as the arrangements available for paying bills and transferring funds. A particularly intriguing service is the "Answer Bank," which provides useful information about many personal financial questions.

SERVICE CHARGES AND EARNED INTEREST   Earlier in this chapter we compared four different checking account plans offered by a Midwestern bank. While this bank did not provide interest on daily balances unless a $1,000 minimum was maintained, other financial institutions in the area were offering interest on all balances, in addition to free checking. There is little reason to pay any fee, no matter how small, for a service, when you can get the same service free elsewhere. However, if a bank's charges are low for some services, they might be high for others. Decide what services are important and then do your shopping.

Savings

- Passbook accounts
- Money market deposit accounts
- Certificates of deposit—maturities of one week to ten years
- Savings reserve, to protect against accidental overdrafts
- IRAs

Loans

- Personal loans—autos, trucks, recreational vehicles, home improvements
- Business loans—lines of credit, term loans
- Mortgage loans—business and residential (conventional, FHA, VA)

Major Credit Cards

- American Express Gold Card/Executive Credit
- Mastercard/Visa

Other Services

- Automated teller machines
- Safe deposit boxes
- Trust services
- Business services—payroll, accounting, leasing, direct deposit
- "Answer Bank"—free personal financial advice to 50 commonly asked questions
- Preauthorized savings—automatic transfers from checking to savings
- Direct deposit of retirement checks (Social Security, Civil Service, or Railroad Retirement)
- Direct deposit of payroll checks
- Wire transfers
- Bank by mail
- Money orders, cashier's checks, traveler's checks
- Utility payments
- Home banking by personal computer

FIGURE 6.2

A partial list of services offered by a large Midwestern bank.

Spending,
Borrowing,
and Saving

Checking Account Procedures

Using a checking account is a relatively simple process if you are careful. Once an account is opened, you will make periodic deposits to increase your balance, and you will draw it down by writing checks. A record of these transactions is kept in a check register, which may be a journal but is more often simply stubs to the checks written. Regardless of what forms are used to keep records, it is a good idea to take a little extra time to record all pertinent data. Very often a check is written in haste at a crowded checkout line, for example, and the stub is left for our memory to fill in later. Unfortunately, memories fade with time, particularly with respect to the exact amount of the check, and after several such instances, we have no idea how much is in the account. Along with filling out the stub completely as the check is written, it is also a good idea to earmark certain expenditures if they have particular importance. For example, many people use a check mark or other symbol to identify tax-deductible expenses. This identification helps when next year's tax return needs to be filed.

As more people buy and use personal computers (PCs), they will also begin using them to store and evaluate banking data as part of their overall financial planning. All transactions within the checking account will be recorded on disk to be available for any form of processing the user desires. In some areas it is now possible to connect your PC with the bank by way of a telephone line and to make transactions by phone and record them simultaneously. In short, you can call the bank on the phone, hook it to your PC monitor, and conduct business on the screen; meanwhile, everything is stored for later use.

OPENING THE ACCOUNT Opening a checking or savings account requires nothing more than filling out a simple signature card. If a joint account is opened, both (or all) signatures are required. It is important to use your legal name on any account. A married couple should consider a joint account rather than separate accounts for several reasons. First, the monthly service charges on two accounts are generally higher than for only one account. Second, and more important, if one of the spouses were to die, the funds in a joint account would pass immediately to the remaining spouse. This **right of survivorship** is associated with most bank accounts. However, in some states a joint account that does not specifically state right of survivorship will presume that **tenants in common** applies, in which case the survivor receives only his or her share of the account. Be sure to inquire about right of survivorship when you open an account.

Right of survivorship: An owner of an account has access to all funds upon the death of a co-owner.

Tenants in common: An owner of an account has a legal claim only to his or her share of an account upon the death of a co-owner.

MAKING ADDITIONAL DEPOSITS AND ENDORSING CHECKS Making deposits to a checking account is a regular activity. These deposits consist of currency, coins, and checks written to you. Deposits are made with a deposit slip, such as the one illustrated in Figure 6.3. Notice the deposit is for $600, consisting of $100 in currency and a check for $500. The arrangement of numbers 01–4/435 is the bank transit number on the check deposited. This number is of no particular importance to you, but it is used in the Federal Reserve's check-clearing process, and it should be listed carefully to help this process. Also, use a separate line for each check deposited even if they are from the same bank.

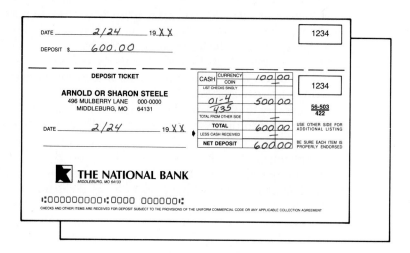

FIGURE 6.3

A deposit slip.

Blank endorsement:
Unrestricted endorsement
of a check; anyone
possessing the check can
cash it.

Restrictive endorsement:
Limits the use of a check
to a single purpose, usually
to make a deposit.

Special endorsement:
Using a check to pay a
third party.

Checks can be endorsed (signed on the back) in three different ways, as shown in Figure 6.4. You use a **blank endorsement** when withdrawing cash from the account, but remember that once you sign a check it becomes a negotiable instrument and can be used as such by anyone. If you happen to lose the check, all the finder needs to do is sign it under your signature and cash it. As a safeguard, don't sign the check until you are at the bank and ready to make the withdrawal. A **restrictive endorsement** limits the use of the check to a single purpose. "For deposit only" is written on a check when it is deposited by mail. If the check is lost in the mail and subsequently found, it cannot be cashed. A **special endorsement** is used when you use the check to pay someone else. All that you need do is indicate the payee and sign, as shown in Figure 6.4. It is usually not a good idea to pay bills in this manner, however, since you will not have a record of the payment unless you take the time to make one. Remember, the check will be returned to the person who issued it, not to you.

WRITING CHECKS   Writing a check is a simple procedure illustrated in Figure 6.5. As mentioned above, the stub should be filled in at the same time the check is written and, naturally, they should be in agreement. Your account number is printed on the bottom of the check, as well as the deposit slip. This number identifies the account and is needed whenever inquiries about the account are made. As a safeguard, the amount of the check is indicated both numerically and in written form. Be particularly careful about the written amount, because it is the legally binding figure. Also, your signature should appear exactly as you signed the signature card to open the account.

Overdraft (bounced
check): A check lacking
sufficient funds to cover it.

"BOUNCING A CHECK"   If you happen to write a check without sufficient funds to cover it, you will have an **overdraft,** commonly referred to as a **bounced check.** It's an expensive oversight, since most banks charge about $15.00 for each such check. Moreover, it can lead to a poor credit rating. Either of these factors

160

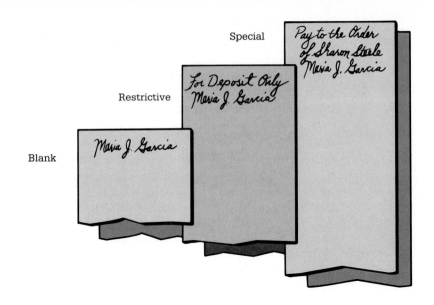

FIGURE 6.4

Ways to endorse a check.

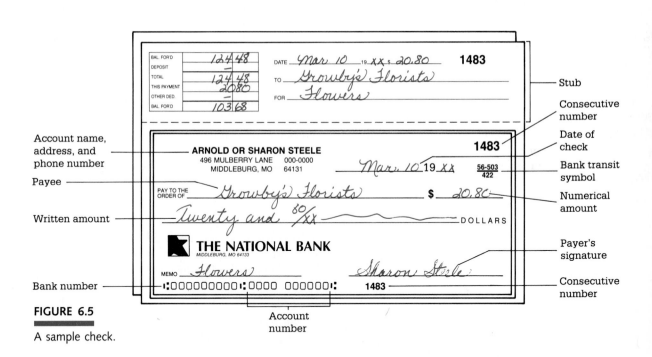

FIGURE 6.5

A sample check.

should motivate you to balance your account accurately on a timely basis. After writing one or two overdrafts, some people go to the opposite extreme and keep an excessive balance to avoid the problem in the future. But this practice is costly if the account does not pay interest. Another precautionary step is to arrange a savings reserve that ties the checking account to a savings account and automatically transfers funds from the latter to the former whenever an overdraft takes place. Although this arrangement is better than "overloading'" the checking account, it too has a drawback if interest earned on the savings account is only at the passbook rate. You might get a better rate than this in another account. A third alternative is to arrange for a loan that will cover the overdraft. This is the worst alternative, since interest is typically charged at your credit-card rate, which is usually 18 percent or more.

AVAILABILITY OF FUNDS   A 1987 federal law requires all banks to comply with the following standards in making funds available after deposits have been made to the account: Cash, wire transfers, government checks, cashier's checks, and certified checks must be available on the next business day. Checks written on a local bank or other local financial institution must be available two business days after the deposit day, while checks written on a nonlocal financial institution must be available five business days after the deposit day.

STOPPING PAYMENT ON A CHECK   Sometimes it is necessary to stop payment on a check already issued. Perhaps you paid someone for merchandise and after inspection found it defective or incomplete. You simply go to the bank and fill out a form, called a **stop-payment order,** directing the bank not to pay the check. You are charged for this service, so it shouldn't be used casually. It's a better idea not to issue a check until you are satisfied with the service or merchandise in question.

Stop-payment order: Directive to a bank not to pay a check.

You should not issue a stop-payment order for a lost or stolen check. Contrary to what you may have heard, such checks are the bank's responsibility and not yours; that is, the bank is supposed to verify your signature before honoring a check. So there is no reason for you to incur a charge to benefit the bank. Naturally, you should inform the bank—both as a courtesy and to close the old account while opening a new one (which may involve a charge). The same advice applies to a check you forgot to sign. Let it process and the bank may honor the check anyway. If it doesn't, write another check to the payee.

End-of-Month Activities

At the end of each month, the bank will send you a monthly statement showing all transactions the bank has recorded in your account. It is important to reconcile this statement each month, both to update and audit your records for accuracy and to make sure the bank hasn't made a mistake.

Bank reconciliation: End-of-month analysis comparing the cash balance per bank statement with the cash balance per checkbook.

BANK RECONCILIATION   A **bank reconciliation** means the end-of-month balance as shown on the bank statement is reconciled to the end-of-month balance shown in the check record. Figures 6.6, 6.7, and 6.8 illustrate the steps in the reconciliation process. Figure 6.6 shows the stubs from a series of checks, numbers 1483 through 1488, written from the account. Notice that the running balance is maintained and that the end-of-month balance is $134.48. Figure 6.7 shows the bank statement sent to the depositor at the end of the month. A glance at it reveals several bits of information. First, the bank has deducted a service charge of $2.00, which wasn't known and therefore was not recorded up to now. So the first task is to reduce the book balance from $134.48 to $132.48. Second,

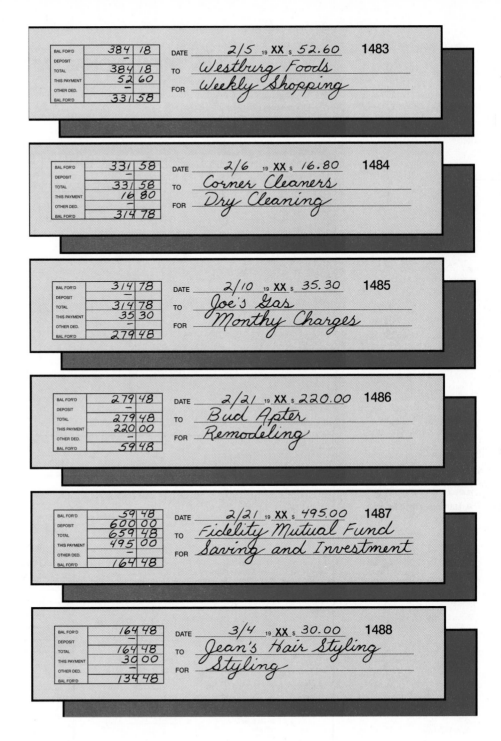

FIGURE 6.6

Sample check stubs.

you can see that of the six checks written during the month, only four have cleared; checks 1486 and 1488 are still outstanding. That is why the bank's balance is so much greater than the book balance. Figure 6.8 is a reconciliation form that appears on the back of this particular bank statement. By following steps one

FIGURE 6.7

Sample bank statement.

THE NATIONAL BANK

ARNOLD OR SHARON STEELE
496 MULBERRY LANE
MIDDLEBURG, MO 64131

YOUR BANKING NO.   211 4003

STATEMENT PERIOD   PAGE
FROM 2/04/XX TO 3/07/XX   1

TYPE	PREVIOUS BALANCE	DEPOSITS & CREDITS		CHECKS & DEBITS		NOW INTEREST	SERVICE CHARGE	CURRENT BALANCE
		NUMBER	AMOUNT	NUMBER	AMOUNT			
FREE&EASY 02	384.18		600.08	I	601.70		2.00	382.48

DAY	AMOUNT	CHECK NO. OR DESCRIPTION	DAY	AMOUNT	CHECK NO. OR DESCRIPTION	DAY	AMOUNT	CHECK NO. OR DESCRIPTION
07	2 00	SERVICE CHARGE						
05	52 60	1483						
08	16 80	1484						
16	35 30	1485						
24	600 00	DEPOSIT						
25	495 00	1487						

FIGURE 6.8

A bank reconciliation.

To balance your checking account:

Step 1.   Subtract from your checkbook balance all charges or other transfers that are shown in the checking section on the front of this statement such as, Service Charges, Automatic Transfers, Reorder of Checks or Others. Your Checking Plus Loan Payment is shown in the bottom right section on the front of your banking statement. Subtract only the payment amount from your checkbook balance. Add your NOW Account interest to your checkbook balance.

Step 2.   Compare checks shown on this statement to your checkbook records and list checks outstanding by dollar amount.

Check Outstanding		
Date or No.	1486	$ 220.00
	1488	30.00
Total		$ 250.00

Step 3.   Enter Current Balance shown on this statement $ 382.48

Add Deposits make after Statement Period $ —

TOTAL $ 382.48

Subtract total of checks outstanding $ 250.00

Step 4.   This Balance should agree with your checkbook $ 132.48

through four, you should be able to reconcile the statement. Notice that after the outstanding checks are deducted from the bank's balance, the book balance (after the service charge has been deducted) of $132.48 is confirmed. This reconciliation is a fairly simple one, since there are only six checks to review, no deposits in transit, and no other activity to make things more difficult. However, before you start a reconciliation, it is a good idea to compare each cleared check to the data recorded on the stub, because errors seem to occur no matter how carefully we try to keep our books. Cross-checking before you start to reconcile can prevent a headache later on if the two balances fail to agree after a first reconciliation attempt.

FILING AND STORAGE   After reconciliation, the bank statement can be filed for later reference. Most banks will return the cancelled checks along with your statement, although the trend today is toward **truncation,** which simply means the payer's bank retains the checks and forwards only a bank statement. This statement, however, does indicate the name of the payee on each check, along with the check number and dollar amount. Many depositors prefer truncation because it reduces the bulky records they must keep. The stock brokerage accounts, such as Merrill Lynch's cash management account mentioned earlier, are structured in this manner. Be careful to save whatever documents the bank returns to you. These items—not your check stubs or other documents that you generate—are necessary to support a claim that payment has been made. For example, the Internal Revenue Service requires these source documents to support your personal income tax deductions.

Checks That Guarantee Payment

On occasion you may need a check that guarantees payment. Maybe you are buying something from a person who doesn't know you and is also not familiar with your bank. Conversely, there are instances when you want to be sure a check you are receiving will not bounce. There are three popular approaches to guaranteeing a check: have a personal check certified, buy a cashier's check, and buy traveler's checks.

CERTIFIED CHECK   A person can take a personal check to his or her bank and ask to have it certified, making it a **certified check.** This means the bank will verify that sufficient funds are in the account to cover the check. After this verification, the bank deducts the amount of the check from the account, making the funds immediately available to the payee. A certification is then stamped on the check.

Certified check: Bank verification that a payer has sufficient funds to cover a specific check.

CASHIER'S CHECK   People without checking accounts often use a **cashier's check** to pay bills. Such a check is also used when the amount involved is very large. It is written by a bank against itself and is accordingly much more acceptable than a personal check. There is a small service charge for a cashier's check unless you are a special customer to the bank, in which case it might be waived.

Cashier's check: A check issued by a bank against itself.

Understanding the Blizzard of New Service Charges

Before opening a checking or savings account, make sure you understand how the account works with respect to service charges. You might be surprised to learn that such charges often apply to services that once were provided free or at low cost. Some potential trouble spots are indicated below. Consider them and how you intend to use your account. If it seems likely that you will run up a sizable monthly total, you should consider a simpler account, even though it may offer fewer services.

ATM Users

If you use an ATM, you are likely to be charged if you use a "foreign" machine (one that's not part of the bank's system). These charges can be as high as $2 a transaction. Even if you use an in-system machine, expect to pay charges for many regularly made transactions such as cash advances. While many banks levy a 2 percent charge, most cap the charge at $10 or $20; however, some do not, and this means an exorbitant fee for a cash advance. Also, if you open an ATM-only account, expect to pay a stiff fee if you make a teller-assisted transaction.

Credit Cards

Most banks charge an annual fee of $20 or so for a credit card. In addition, you may face a similar charge if you exceed your credit limit or if your monthly payment is late. Of course, the big cost is the high rate of interest charged on most cards—from 18 to 21 percent. The persistence of these high rates is remarkable considering that interest rates in general have declined substantially in recent years and are now considered low.

Handling Mistakes

Transactions involving the bank often lead to mistakes that can be costly. If you overdraw your account, expect a charge of $10 to $20. Issuing a stop-payment order on a check is likely to incur a similar fee. Finally, you might be charged $5 (or more) if you are unsure of the current account balance and ask the bank for such information.

Traveler's check: Checks purchased from a bank, usually when a payer is traveling away from home.

TRAVELER'S CHECKS   A **traveler's check** is generally used when you are traveling away from home. These checks can be purchased at any bank or other financial institution in denominations that usually range from $10 to $100. At the time you buy these checks, you sign each one in the presence of a bank officer; later, when you cash one of them, you sign again in the presence of the person cashing it. The payees can thus compare signatures to guard against forgery. You also get a small journal to record the check serial numbers and other pertinent information. It's a good idea to keep this journal somewhere other than where you keep the checks, since theft or loss of the checks must be reported to the bank to stop payment. If the journal and checks are lost or stolen together, you may not know what specific checks are actually missing. Traveler's checks are accepted practically everywhere throughout the world. They are a wise purchase (some banks will provide them free) whenever you travel.

Electronic Banking

Growing computer and electronics technologies have created important changes in the way banking transactions can be made. As mentioned before, it is now possible to do much of your banking business with your telephone hooked up to your personal computer. Most of us are already familiar with **automated teller machines (ATMs).** With these, you use a plastic ID card and a personal access code to conduct a number of bank activities such as withdrawing cash (in limited amounts only), transferring funds from one account to another, or paying routine monthly bills. You should exercise care in using an ATM, because it is a fertile area for consumer fraud and theft. For example, don't leave your access card in

Automated teller machines (ATMs): Machines that perform certain banking functions.

the machine or in other unprotected places, and don't use obvious code numbers such as your street address or phone number.

Electronic funds transfer systems (EFTs) extend beyond ATM services. The same access card can also be used to pay bills at stores that have point-of-sale terminals. In this way, funds are transferred automatically from your account to the vendor's. There are still other forms of electronic transfers: You may have an arrangement whereby your payroll check is wired directly to your bank; or if you are a retiree, you may receive your Social Security check through an electronic transfer. While electronic banking lacks a personal touch, it does add convenience.

Electronic funds transfer systems (EFTS): Electronic payment of bills and other transfers of cash.

Understanding How Your Account Earns Interest

What does a financial institution mean when it offers to pay you, say, 12 percent interest on your account? On the surface, this looks like a simple enough calculation: If you put $1,000 in the account, you get back $1,120 a year later, which is the initial $1,000 plus $120 (0.12 × $1,000) of earned interest. Simple as it seems, complications can arise if your account is structured differently from the one above. Suppose, for example, that the quoted interest rate applies for a period of time shorter than a year. For instance, when the new money market deposit accounts were introduced, many financial institutions advertised them with very high interest rates, such as 15 and even 20 percent. Sounds good, but buried in the fine print was a notice that the rate was effective for only a limited period of time, in some cases just a week. So while the ads were true, they were nevertheless confusing because they touted an *annual rate* that was effective for less than a year. This advertising created an impression of a much greater increase in interest earned by switching funds into one of these accounts than would actually have taken place. On a $1,000 deposit, for example, you would have earned $1.92 more by switching to an account that paid 20 percent for one week from one that paid 10 percent. An amount this small would hardly have been worth the inconvenience of opening a new account. So, in addition to knowing the interest rate on an account, you also need to ask: To what period of time does the rate apply?

Another source of confusion in the simple interest calculation is that it assumes interest is paid only once—at the very end of the year. But you probably have seen accounts that advertise interest paid weekly, daily, or even continuously. Do you earn more with these accounts? If so, how much more? To answer these questions we need an understanding of basic interest calculations. Finally, suppose you make periodic deposits and withdrawals to and from an account. Will interest be earned on the deposit balance at the beginning of the month, the end of the month, the average for the month, or just what? Clearly, these questions, too, must be asked before you open an account.

How Interest Is Calculated

The actual interest dollars (I) earned on a deposit depend on three factors: the amount you invest (P); a stated interest rate (i), expressed in decimal form; and the length of time (t) the deposit is held, expressed as a fraction or multiple of a year. This relationship is shown below:

$$\$I = (\$P)\,(i)\,(t)$$

Thus, in the earlier example we have

$$\$120 = (\$1{,}000)\,(0.12)\,(1)$$

And if the deposit was held for only six months, then the interest earned is

$$\$60 = (\$1{,}000)\,(0.12)\left(\frac{6}{12}\right)$$

The future value (FV) of any deposit is simply the sum of principal invested and interest earned; that is,

$$\$FV = \$P + \$I$$

The FV for the deposit held 12 months is $1,120 ($1,000 + $120), and it is $1,060 ($1,000 + $60) for the six-month deposit. Which of these two deposits would you rather have? If you thought that at the end of six months you could take the $1,060 and reinvest it at a 12 percent annual rate for another six months, you would clearly prefer the two six-month deposits to the one 12-month. Why? To see this, calculate the FV of the six-month deposit at the end of the second six months. You must first calculate I, which is

$$\$63.60 = (\$1{,}060)\,(0.12)\left(\frac{6}{12}\right)$$

Then, FV is $1,123.60 ($1,060 + $63.60). What you have determined is the future value of a deposit with a 12 percent stated interest rate (also called the *nominal rate*) *compounded semiannually.* In comparison to the annual compounding, it provided $3.60 more over the one-year holding period. From this illustration, you probably also recognize that the more often compounding takes place, the greater is the future value of any given deposit for any given stated interest rate. Table 6.5 shows future values for a $1,000 deposit and an 8 percent stated rate for various compounding periods, assuming the deposit is held for 1, 2, 4, 8, or 16 years. As you see, more frequent compounding leads to greater future values. The table also shows a fairly common phenomenon in compounding.

TABLE 6.5 · Future Values of $1,000 Invested at 8 Percent Stated Rate with Interest Calculated Under Various Compounding Periods

Frequency of Compounding	Years Deposit Is Held				
	1	2	4	8	16
Annually	$1,080.00	$1,166.40	$1,360.49	$1,850.93	$3,425.94
Semiannually	1,081.60	1,169.86	1,368.57	1,872.98	3,508.06
Quarterly	1.082.43	1,171.66	1,372.79	1,884.54	3,551.49
Weekly	1,083.22	1,173.37	1,376.79	1,895.55	3,593.11
Daily	1,083.28	1,173.49	1,377.08	1,896.35	3,596.13
Continuously	1,083.30	1,173.51	1,377.13	1,896.48	3,596.62

Small differences compounded over a long period of time eventually become a big difference. For example, daily compounding added only $3.28 more than annual compounding for one year, but over 16 years the difference grows to $170.19 ($3,596.13 − $3,425.94). *Continuous compounding* may not be familiar to you. It assumes interest is calculated even more frequently than every second of every day. It sounds impressive but, as Table 6.5 shows, adds little above daily or weekly compounding.

Determining Interest on Your Account

All savings accounts are not alike in the way interest is determined on them. Differences arise with respect to the length of time balances in the account are judged to qualify for earning interest. In some cases, if a deposit is not held for an entire quarter, it earns no interest at all, even if it was withdrawn on the very last day of the quarter. Four different methods are in general use: (*a*) day of deposit to day of withdrawal (or daily interest), (*b*) minimum balance, (*c*) FIFO, and (*d*) LIFO. Table 6.6 illustrates those four methods. It is assumed that a deposit of $1,000 is made on the first day of the quarter; another $1,000 is made on the 30th day; and a $900 withdrawal takes place on the 60th day. The account has a stated interest rate of 6 percent.

Day-of-deposit to day-of-withdrawal method: Pays interest on the average daily balance in an account.

DAY-OF-DEPOSIT TO DAY-OF-WITHDRAWAL METHOD The **day-of-deposit to day-of-withdrawal method** is the fairest method to a depositor, and, fortu-

TABLE 6.6 · Quarterly Interest Earned Under Four Different Determination Methods with a 6 Percent Stated Interest Rate

Activity in the Account		
Day	Deposit (Withdrawal)	Balance
1	$1,000	$1,000
30	1,000	2,000
60	(900)	1,100
90	Closing	1,100
Interest Calculations		

1. Day of deposit to day of withdrawal:
   a. $1,000 × 30/360 × 0.06 = $ 5.00
   b. $2,000 × 30/360 × 0.06 = $10.00
   c. $1,100 × 30/360 × 0.06 = $ 5.50
   Total $20.50

2. Minimum balance:
   $1,000 × 90/360 × 0.06 = $15.00

3. FIFO:
   a. $ 100 × 90/360 × 0.06 = $ 1.50
   b. $1,000 × 60/360 × 0.06 = $10.00
   Total $11.50

4. LIFO:
   a. $1,000 × 90/360 × 0.06 = $15.00
   b. $ 100 × 60/360 × 0.06 = $ 1.00
   Total $16.00

Cash
Management

nately, competition is forcing most institutions to offer it. In effect, interest is computed on the account each day; but notice, this method is not the same as daily compounding. As we saw above, daily compounding would mean each day's interest is reinvested at the stated rate. The calculations in Table 6.6 do not assume daily compounding. The $20.50 of total interest results from having $1,000 invested for 30 days; then, after the second deposit is made, $2,000 is invested for another 30 days; and after $900 is withdrawn, $1,100 is invested for the final 30 days. With this method, you earn the actual stated rate of interest on the account. With the other methods, you might earn something less, but never more, than the stated rate.

MINIMUM-BALANCE METHOD The **minimum-balance method** pays interest for the entire quarter—but only on the minimum balance in the account during the quarter. The minimum balance in our example is the beginning deposit of $1,000; thus, all deposits made after that, in effect, earn nothing. Similarly, withdrawals that do not reduce the minimum balance do not enter into the interest

Minimum-balance method: Pays interest only on the minimum (lowest) balance in an account.

Action Plan for the Steeles: Cash Management

Background In late December 1992, the Steeles had about $16,000 in liquid deposits, which equaled roughly three months of their combined take-home pay. This seemed a reasonable amount, given their medical insurance coverage and loss-of-income protection at Arnie's job. They always kept a rather sizable balance in their checking account because they are antique buffs and never know when they might come upon an attractive purchase and need the funds to buy it. They used a regular checking account with a $300 minimum balance requirement, but no service charges. Their actual balance in the account, however, was never below $1,000 and averaged about $2,000 a month. They also had $5,600 in a savings account they opened when they married and added to over the years. Arnie also purchased U.S. Series EE bonds through payroll withholding and had approximately $3,000 in these, measured at current market value. The balance of their liquid deposits was in 42-month certificates of deposit that were about to mature.

The Problem The Steeles wanted to arrange their deposits to get a maximum yield consistent with reasonable safety and liquidity. They were hesitant to forecast future interest rates but felt the chances were high that rates would increase over the planning period. They realized this was only a guess, but it was the best they could do. They were willing to take some risks to capture a higher return.

The Plan The first step was to gather information on what deposits were available and their current rates. These are shown in the schedule of deposits, which also indicates the suggested arrangement of new deposits. As you see, the financial planner recommended the following changes: (*a*) eliminate the savings account and transfer these funds to a newly opened money market account; (*b*) reduce the balance in regular checking by about $600 and transfer these funds also to the new money market account; (*c*) as the CDs mature, use the funds to acquire additional U.S. Series EE savings bonds.

determination. In the example, then, interest earned is simply 6 percent of the opening balance for 90 days, or $15.00. With an account such as this, it would make no sense whatsoever to add deposits *except* right before the beginning of a quarter.

FIFO method: Withdrawals from an account reduce the earliest account balance.

FIFO METHOD   FIFO stands for *first in, first out*. It is an assumption as to how withdrawals are deducted against account balances. Specifically, the **FIFO method** assumes that any withdrawal reduces your earliest balance first and then works toward the more recent balances. This assumption works to your disadvantage, as Table 6.6 illustrates. Here, the $900 withdrawal made on the 60th day goes back and reduces the opening $1,000 deposit. As a result, you have only $100 invested for the full 90 days. The $1,000 deposit on the 30th day, however, is undisturbed and continues to earn interest for the full 60 days it is on deposit. Only $11.50 was earned with the FIFO method in this example, and it is usually the most undesirable method. It should be avoided if you expect to make withdrawals from your account.

Schedule of Deposits

		Rates Assumed to Exist at December 31, 1992	Current Balances	Suggested Balances
1	Regular checking	-0-%	$2,400	$ 500
2	Savings account	4.0	5,600	-0-
3	42-Month CDs	7.0	5,000	-0-
4	U.S. Series EE bonds	6.4	3,000	8,000
5	Money market account	5.0	-0-	7,500
	Total		$16,000	$16,000

Rationale for the Plan   The Steeles have sufficient resources to avoid the low-yielding savings account, and replacing it was to be their first priority. The money market account gave them a far better yield and, in fact, easier access to their funds than did the savings account. It also provided sufficient cash reserves (for the occasional antique uncovered at a garage sale), thereby allowing them to reduce their checking account balance to a more sensible level.

The CDs would be a bad choice if interest rates were expected to increase. The savings bonds are a better choice because their rates are indexed to market rates on other Treasury securities. Moreover, the bonds offer far better liquidity, since there are no early withdrawal penalties. Overall, the plan involved very little liquidity risk. This is desirable if interest rates are expected to rise. By maintaining liquidity, the Steeles will be in a position to invest in the future at the expected higher rates. And if rates do not rise, they still will earn reasonable returns on the money market account and savings bonds.

LIFO METHOD   In contrast to FIFO, LIFO means *last in, first out*. The **LIFO method** presumes that any withdrawal reduces the most recent deposit first and then works backward until the entire balance is exhausted. It is an improvement over FIFO, but is still not a fair representation of actual funds on deposit during the period. In the example, the $900 withdrawal reduced the last $1,000 deposit to $100, which then earned interest for 60 days. The first $1,000 deposit was undisturbed and continued to earn interest for the full 90 days. The total interest earned is $16.00, which comes closest to the true interest of $20.50 but is still quite short of it.

Cash Management Strategy

At the beginning of this chapter we said that the object of cash management is to minimize cash balances while maintaining an adequate level of liquidity. By now you can see that the problem is made more complex by the many forms of liquid deposits. No one would argue against keeping currency and coin holdings to a minimum, but differences of opinion arise over how other cash should be held. If you want to manage your cash actively, rather than putting it all into one account, then you should follow these steps:

1. Resolve to your own satisfaction which direction you think interest rates will move in the planning period.
2. Obtain current information about various deposit accounts, particularly current interest rates and possible account restrictions.
3. Allocate your liquid funds among the accounts to satisfy your preferences for yield, safety, and liquidity.

Keep in mind: The more yield you want, the less safety and liquidity you must take. These three aspects will be brought together in an action plan for the Steele family, but first we should recognize the instability of interest rates.

Interest Rate Volatility

The advent of money market funds introduced many of us to the volatile behavior of interest rates. Up to that time, most saving deposits were in passbook accounts with their virtually constant rates. However, when yields on money market funds rose into the double-digit range in 1979 and then almost to 18 percent by mid-1981, deposits by the billions flowed out of passbook accounts and into the funds. But these exceptionally high rates didn't last, and by the end of 1982 they were down to around 8 percent. Figure 6.9 illustrates how widely short-term interest rates have varied. The U.S. Treasury bill rate is often used as a barometer of such rates. It represents the yield on a perfectly safe security, and, to that extent, it is the lowest rate in the market. Rates on money market funds, for example, are about one to two percentage points above the three-month U.S. Treasury bill rate, depending upon the specific short-term securities held by the fund; one that holds only these Treasury bills would have an almost identical rate.

There are several key points in Figure 6.9. First, you should see that deposits linked to money market rates will show quite different returns over time. And, you really can't do a great deal about it without adding risk. When rates begin to

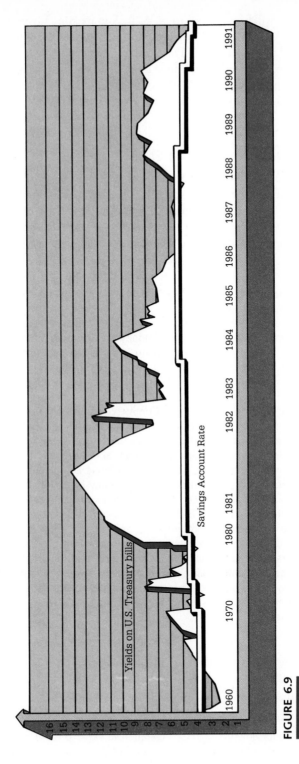

FIGURE 6.9

Three-month U.S. Treasury bills market yields and rates on savings accounts at commercial banks.

fall, you will be tempted to try to lock in existing higher rates by switching funds into CDs with long maturities, or even buying long-term bonds (these will be covered in Chapter 14). This strategy works so long as rates do indeed fall; but if they rise, then you would have been better off staying in short-term deposits. The second point, and one that is clearly visible, is how much better off you would have been in U.S. Treasury bills over the period.

An Action Plan for the Steele Family

Sharon and Arnie Steele are like many Americans who were caught in the volatility of inflation and interest rates. Not paying attention to the new types of deposits, they held relatively large balances in their traditional passbook and checking accounts. The action plan on pages 170–171 describes their situation and the changes suggested by one financial planner.

Summary

People hold cash to meet three liquidity needs: to undertake transactions, to have emergency reserves, and to have a store of value. Fundamental deposits for meeting these needs are checking, NOW, and savings accounts. Other major deposits are money market deposit accounts, money market mutual funds, certificates of deposit, and U.S. Series EE savings bonds. An important consideration to depositors is the availability of federal insurance on deposits up to $100,000 at federally insured commercial banks, mutual savings banks, savings and loan associations, and credit unions.

Financial institutions are undergoing important changes, with the trend being toward the large financial supermarket. Commercial banks offer a wide range of services and have traditionally been the sole issuers of checking accounts, but that is no longer true. Savings and loans and mutual savings banks also offer NOW accounts, as do credit unions. In very recent years, other financial institutions, such as stock brokerage firms and insurance companies, have begun offering complete financial service accounts.

A checking account is used primarily to pay bills. Geographic convenience and the package of services offered are usually important criteria to depositors in selecting a bank. Interest earned on a checking or savings account depends on two key factors: first, the frequency of compounding; and second, the method the financial institution uses to determine which balances qualify for interest. A cash management strategy considers how much total cash should be held and in what forms. The expected rates of interest over the holding period determines whether deposits should be held in accounts with floating interest rates, or whether they should be held in CDs with fixed rates. The volatility of interest rates over the last 20 years has made this decision a difficult one.

Key Terms

automated teller machine (ATM) (p. 166)

bank (p. 153)

bank reconciliation (p. 162)

blank endorsement (p. 160)

cash management strategy (p. 145)

cashier's check (p. 165)

certificates of deposit (CDs) (p. 150)

certified check (p. 165)

checking account (p. 146)

commercial bank (p. 154)

credit union (p. 155)

day-of-deposit to day-of-withdrawal method (p. 169)

electronic funds transfer systems (EFTS) (p. 167)

emergency reserves (p. 146)

FIFO method (p. 171)

LIFO method (p. 172)

minimum-balance method (p. 170)

money market deposit accounts (MMDAs) (p. 150)

money market mutual funds (p. 150)

mutual savings bank (p. 155)

NOW (negotiated order of withdrawal) account (p. 148)

overdraft (bounced check) (p. 160)

passbook rate (p. 149)

pocket money (p. 146)

restrictive endorsement (p. 160)

right of survivorship (p. 159)

savings account (p. 149)

savings and loan association (S&L) (p. 154)

special endorsement (p. 160)

stop-payment order (p. 162)

super NOW account (p. 148)

tenants in common (p. 159)

traveler's check (p. 166)

truncation (p. 165)

U.S. Series EE bonds (p. 151)

U.S. Series HH bonds (p. 152)

Problems and Review Questions

1 Explain the reasons for holding cash. How much pocket money (coins and currency) do most people hold? What advantages does a checking account have over pocket money?

2 List and briefly explain three fundamental deposits and five other popular types of deposits, ranking them according to availability, safety, and liquidity.

3 What is a *federally insured* deposit? Is deposit insurance important to you? Explain.

4 Explain all the advantages of U.S. Series EE bonds. Identify several advantages that are most important to you.

5 A local bank offers a "free" checking account if you maintain a minimum balance of $1,000. Is the account really "free"? Explain.

6 What institutions are banks and "almost banks," and what is the difference between a mutual and a corporate savings and loan?

7 Discuss factors that should be considered in choosing a bank.

8 Identify or explain the following items: (a) Series EE rollover; (b) "bank"; (c) right of survivorship; (d) bounced check; (e) stop-payment order; (f) truncation; (g) certified check, cashier's check, or traveler's check; (h) ATM; (i) EFTS.

9 Explain three ways to endorse a check; explain which is the riskiest and why.

10 Explain what is meant by interest rate volatility and then discuss the volatility history of the interest rate on U.S. Treasury bills. Finally, explain the risk of investing in CDs in periods of interest rate volatility.

11 Juan Mendez has just opened a savings account that pays interest at a 4 percent annual stated rate, compounded semiannually. If he puts $1,000 in the account, how much will he get back a year later? After he opened the account, Juan learned that another account was also available that quoted a rate of 4.25 percent, compounded annually; now he isn't sure whether he got the best deal. Did he?

12 Lori Shaw opened a savings account at her credit union that paid interest at 4 percent a year, compounded annually; it used the minimum balance method for computing interest. Activity in her account for the quarter was as follows:

Opening balance at day 1	$1,000
Deposit, 60 days after day 1	500
Withdrawal, 75 days after day 1	600
Balance at end of the quarter	900

Calculate Lori's interest earned. Also, calculate the interest she would have earned under the other methods of determining interest: (a) day of deposit to day of withdrawal; (b) FIFO; (c) LIFO.

Case 6.1
Mark's First
Checking
Account

During his junior year in college, Mark Sutherland opened a checking account at the First National Bank of Westerly, Nebraska. His account does not have a minimum balance requirement, but he does pay a monthly service charge of $3.00. Mark has just received his first monthly bank statement and notices that the end-of-month balance on the statement is quite different from the end-of-month balance he shows in his check record. He has asked your help in explaining this difference and has provided you with the bank statement and his check record shown below.

ACCOUNT: Mark J. Sutherland		PERIOD:	January 3, 1992 through January 31, 1992
ACCOUNT #: 43967			

ACTIVITY THIS MONTH

Beginning Balance	Deposits and Other Credits to Your Account	Checks and Other Charges to Your Account	Ending Balance
00.00	300.00	163.80	136.20

		Deposits and Other Credits	Checks and Other Charges
03	Deposit	300.00	
05	100		16.50
07	101		20.00
12	103		42.96
14	104		16.87
17	105		5.00
17	106		11.43
19	107		25.00
24	108		14.04
28	109		9.00
31	Service Chg.		3.00

MARK'S CHECK RECORD

Date	No.	Payee	For	Amount	Balance
1/3		Deposit		300.00	300.00
1/3	100	Harmon Foods	food	16.50	283.50
1/4	101	Cash		20.00	263.50
1/5	102	VOID			
1/7	103	Mel's Sporting Goods	gym shoes	42.96	220.54
1/10	104	Valley Cleaners	dry cleaning	18.67	201.87
1/13	105	Sharon Mackey	birthday present	5.00	196.87
1/14	106	University Bookstore	supplies	11.43	190.44
1/14	107	Cash		25.00	175.44
1/19	108	Harmon Foods	food	14.04	161.40
1/24	109	Mom	repay loan	9.00	152.40
1/25	110	Poindexter's Cafe	Sharon's birthday party	20.00	132.40
1/26		Deposit		50.00	182.40
1/28	111	Exxon	monthly statement	12.96	169.44

Questions

1 Reconcile Mark's account for him and explain the difference between his balance of $169.44 and the bank's of $136.20.
2 How careful was Mark in keeping a record of his checking activities? Discuss.

Case 6.2
Choosing Liquid
Accounts for
Marcia and
Philip Helms

Marcia and Phil Helms have been married for several years. They have no children and each has a professional career. Marcia is a trainee for a management position at a large department store, and Phil is an engineer at an electronics firm. While their careers have promising futures, neither has exceptionally good income protection in the event of a layoff. The Helms have saved around $8,000 and $7,400 of it is in a 3.5 percent savings account at the credit union where Phil works. They have about $600 in a regular checking account (with Mid-City Bank) that doesn't have a service charge or monthly minimum requirement, but also doesn't pay any interest. The Helms' combined take-home pay is about $2,500 a month, and Phil thinks they should take the $7,400 out of their savings and invest in the stock market to earn a better return. He points out that, excluding their life insurance policies, they have no other investments. Marcia thinks this plan might be too risky, but she does agree that the 3.5 percent yield is not very good. Recently, at a party, a friend suggested they take out certificates of deposit (CDs) with long maturities, since they were paying around 6 percent. The Helms liked her advice and stopped at Phil's credit union to get more information on the CDs. After talking with the office manager for a while, though, they became even more confused. He didn't favor CDs, although the union had them available. He pointed out that interest rates on the new money market accounts were around 4 percent and didn't require "freezing" your money for a year or more. He also indicated the union could offer a super NOW account that would allow the Helms to close their current unproductive checking account with Mid-City. This account would give them unlimited check-writing privileges with no service charges and would pay 3 percent interest; however, it would require a minimum balance of $2,500. If their balance went below the minimum in a month, interest would be only 2 percent.

The Helms left the credit union without taking any action. They have asked you for advice on managing their liquid deposits.

Questions

1 Explain the relative risks and potential advantages of CDs. Explain under what condition(s) you would recommend them for the Helms.
2 Do you agree with Phil that some of their funds should be invested in the stock market? Explain.
3 Prepare and defend a cash management plan that you think suits the Helms' situation most appropriately.

Helpful Reading

Changing Times

Bodnar, Janet, and Kevin McManus. *"What If Your Bank Fails?"* February 1991, pp. 27–35.

———. *"Supercharge Your Savings."* October 1990, pp. 28–33.

Davis, Kristin. *"Deposit Insurance: Are You Covered?"* April 1991, pp. 43–44.

Kosnett, Jeff. *"Top Yields: Yours for the Taking."* June 1991, pp. 24–28.

Schiffres, Manuel. *"Your Investments: The March to Safety."* January 1991, pp. 36–39.

Money

Kobliner, Beth. *"How to Protect Yourself in the Bank Crisis."* March 1991, pp. 112–130.

Updegrave, Walter L. *"The Bank of the Future."* 1990 Extra Edition, pp. 66–71.

_____. *"Keep Your Cash Safe."* February 1991, pp. 68–74.

The Wall Street Journal

Asinof, Lynn. *"How to Survive a Bank Failure: Be Prepared."* January 11, 1991, p. C1.

Gottschalk, Earl C., Jr. *"How Safety Can Mean Investment Disaster."* September 5, 1991, p. C1.

Schultz, Ellen. *"What If Your Banker Offers an Annuity?"* July 1, 1990, p. C1.

_____. *"College Savings Plans That May Not Make the Grade."* November 4, 1991, p. C1.

Helpful Contacts

1. Disputes or other issues involving commercial banks, federally chartered savings and loans, and federally chartered credit unions:
   a. Comptroller of the Currency, Consumer Affairs Division, Washington, DC 20219 (if the bank is nationally chartered)
   b. Board of Governors of the Federal Reserve System, Division of Consumer Affairs, Washington, DC 20551 (if the bank is state chartered but a member of the Federal Reserve System)
   c. Federal Deposit Insurance Corporation, Office of Bank Consumer Affairs, Washington, DC 20429 (if the bank is state chartered but not a member of the Federal Reserve System and offers Federal Deposit Insurance)
   d. Federal Home Loan Bank Board, Washington, DC 20552 (federally insured savings and loan)
   e. National Credit Union Administration, Division of Consumer Affairs, Washington, DC 20456 (federally chartered credit unions)

2. U.S. Savings Bonds:
   a. Legal or technical questions: Bond Consultant Branch, Bureau of the Public Debt, Parkersburg, WV 26106 (telephone 304–420–6102)
   b. Current rate information: 1–800–US-Bonds
   c. Commercial banks provide information; a particularly helpful publication is *The Savings Bonds Question and Answer Book.*

7

Consumer Credit: Buying Now and Paying Later

Objectives

1 To evaluate reasons for and against using credit and decide whether or not credit is appropriate for you

2 To be able to take the necessary steps to establish credit and develop a credit history

3 To identify what is meant by sales credit and how it is used

4 To understand how to use credit cards properly and to know your legal rights as a borrower against credit mistakes

5 To identify what is meant by cash credit and how it is used, and to learn the important characteristics of installment loans

6 To compare the various sources of credit and to learn what to do if you experience credit problems

Christmas at the Wards' house this year wasn't quite as merry as it once was.

Seven-year-old Brendan didn't get the Nintendo video game he wanted. His five-year-old sister Amanda settled for a second-hand Christmas dress. Their parents, Peter and Pam Ward, accepted a frail donated Christmas tree for the living room.

The Wards weren't Scrooges by choice: They're haunted by the ghost of credit cards past. Once they spent freely, by middle-class standards, dashing off to Disneyland on the spur of the moment with pockets full of cash and wallets full of plastic. Then they lost control. Now they are on the edge of bankruptcy, with tens of thousands of dollars in credit-card debt and a large mortgage. "It never crossed my mind that I'd have to pay it all back," says Mr. Ward.

With combined incomes of more than $60,000, the Wards were confident they could handle their mortgage debt, which now amounts to $152,000 and their

new, homeowners' life style. Then the credit-card spiels started coming in the mail. They offered automatic approval and $5,000 credit lines for new homeowners. Over a period of 18 months, Mr. Ward secretly amassed 25 cards, many in his wife's name without her knowledge. "It was like candy," says Mr. Ward.

The Wards rented a cottage in Rhode Island every summer and took a babysitter for a vacation in Maine. Once Mr. Ward came home with a 1967 Mustang he had bought on impulse. Another time he bought his wife a ring and a gold chain—and put them on her credit card. They bought pricey Osh-Kosh clothes for the children, spent $600 a month on day care, and stayed at the best hotels on shopping trips to Boston.

By the summer of 1989, the debt was becoming unmanageable. Until then, Mrs. Ward had guessed the family owed no more than $5,000 on credit cards. The true total came to $35,000, all debt with annual interest rates in

the high teens. "It still makes me cry," she says. "Imagine finding out that you owe twice what you make in a year." Mr. Ward adds: "And we don't have anything to show for it." The trips are over, he says, and the clothes are getting old.

The future seems precarious. The Wards put money in an Individual Retirement Account in 1989 but had to withdraw it in 1990 despite the penalty. They have no savings. College and retirement funds are a distant dream for now. So is the dream of a bigger house.

Mr. Ward, who had a heart attack five years ago, has just $20,000 of life insurance. "He can only be dead for three months," Mrs. Ward jokes.

SOURCE: Excerpted from Dana Milbank, "Hooked on Plastic: Middle-Class Family Takes a Harsh Cure for Credit-Card Abuse," *The Wall Street Journal*, January 8, 1991, pp. A1, A10.

A Federal Reserve Bank survey indicated that most people report no problems in meeting their debt-repayment obligations. However, a significant minority, about 14 percent of households, missed at least one scheduled debt payment during the last 12 months.

The Wards' are an unfortunate example of those who have let credit work against them, rather than for them. With some care, credit can become a useful instrument in financial planning. Borrowing to purchase assets, such as a home, which are likely to increase in value, can be a wise investment strategy. On the other hand, borrowing to increase present consumption, or to purchase assets that will decrease in value, places a burden on our future ability to consume. Too much, and it can result in a vicious cycle, with an ever-increasing burden of obligations as we attempt to repay old debts with new loans.

All of us use credit in one form or another. When the paper boy or girl delivers your newspaper each day and stops by only at the end of the month to collect, he or she extends credit to you for the month's bill. The same is true for the local gas and electric company or any other business that does not demand immediate payment for its product or service. Much of this credit—called **service credit**—

Service credit: Credit extended by the merchant from whom you have purchased the good or service.

we take for granted, probably because it is readily available and usually provided without cost. The forms of credit we are more aware of—sales credit and cash credit—are more difficult to obtain and often carry interest and other expenses; these forms of credit are the topics of this chapter.

We live in an era of what appears to be abundant credit: about $8,000 for each household in the United States, not including home mortgages. It is hard to imagine that not too many years ago you probably would have been advised to avoid all forms of credit, with the possible exception of a mortgage loan to buy a home. Borrowing was a sign of financial weakness: If you had cash to buy something, you shouldn't have to borrow; and if you didn't have the cash, then you couldn't afford the item and you shouldn't buy it. This thinking led to the popular observation that only those who don't need credit can get it. We still experience a similar type of contradiction. If you fail to qualify for credit, you will feel it is in short supply; but once you qualify, you will be swamped by lending institutions willing to loan you funds almost at the drop of a hat. So, there always seems to be either too much or too little of it. But in either case, credit must be planned and managed effectively.

Arranging and Using Credit

Before applying for credit, you should consider carefully why you want it in the first place and what possible disadvantages are connected with its use. It is important to avoid too much debt, as this often leads to serious financial problems, including the possibility of bankruptcy.

Reasons for Using Credit

People sometimes think that the only reason for using credit is a lack of sufficient cash to pay for a purchase. While this factor can be important, it may not be the only one. Furthermore, your lack of sufficient cash does not necessarily mean that the item's cost exceeds all the cash you have. You may have more than enough to pay for it, but in so doing you would reduce your cash reserves below what you consider a safe level. Furthermore, you would give up the potential earnings on those reserves. So you may choose not to use cash in order to maintain adequate liquidity and earnings. You might choose credit over cash for other reasons, too, and these are discussed below.

AS A SHOPPING CONVENIENCE Using credit instead of cash can make shopping much more convenient. You avoid the risks of loss or theft associated with carrying cash, and your end-of-month statement provides a clear and complete record of expenses to help with budgeting and income tax preparation. Moreover, if you are one of a store's credit customers, you will receive information about its future sales or other promotional events. A credit card also simplifies shopping by phone or returning merchandise. A national credit card, such as Visa or MasterCard, allows you to enjoy many of these advantages throughout the entire United States, even throughout the world.

TO INCREASE TOTAL CONSUMPTION BENEFITS Borrowing allows people to consume in a given year at a level greater than their incomes would otherwise permit. This consumption in turn can lead to a higher scale of living and greater satisfaction from total consumption over time. This point is illustrated in Figure 7.1, in which we show a four-year period to keep things simple. Assume you would like to have an even amount of consumption in each year, as indicated by the line *AB*, and also assume your total consumption for the four years equals your total income; that is, assume zero savings over the four years. If your income is low at the beginning and then rises, as shown by the line *CD*, and if your consumption is tied to your income, it would also be low at the start and higher at the end. However, borrowing allows you to even out consumption and achieve your goal. You borrow in years 1 and 2 and repay the loans in years 3 and 4. The illustration does not consider interest, which would reduce total consumption, since part of your income would be needed to pay it, but the added satisfaction you gain from an even level of consumption might far outweigh the satisfaction you lose by paying interest.

AS AN INFLATION HEDGE When the rate of inflation increases, many people tend to use credit in an effort to soften its impact. We hear such expressions as "paying back your debt with cheap dollars," and "buy now and avoid higher future prices." All too often, these words have been true and symbolic of a high-consumption approach towards life. Credit makes this approach possible. Buying now to avoid higher future prices, however, is not often as simple as it appears, since a high inflation rate is almost always accompanied by a high rate of interest on money borrowed.

Table 7.1 illustrates the "buy now or buy later" purchase decision. In columns 1 and 2 we are assuming a shopper is trying to decide whether to use consumer credit to buy an item now or wait one year until she has sufficient cash to buy it without borrowing. Because she does not yet have enough cash, using credit is the only way she can buy it now. As you can see in column 2, the item is expected to increase 10 percent in price over the year, so waiting will add another $10 to the cost of the item. In this case, the inflation rate must be weighed against the cost of borrowing, the interest expense of $18 in column 1. In effect, the net

FIGURE 7.1

Consumption and credit over time.

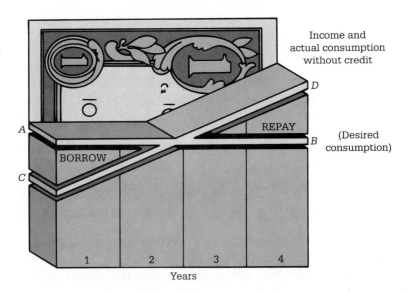

Spending, Borrowing, and Saving

TABLE 7.1 · Deciding
Whether to Buy Now
or Buy Later

	Cash Is Not Available Now		Cash Is Available Now	
	Buy Now (1)	Buy Later (2)	Explicit Cost (3)	Opportunity Cost (4)
Cost of item to be purchased	$100.00	$110.00	$100.00	$100.00
Interest expense at 18%	18.00			
Interest earned on investment fund at 9%				9.00
Less income tax on interest earned (marginal tax rate = 28%				(2.52)
Net cost	$118.00	$110.00	$100.00	$106.48

marginal cost of borrowing now is $8 ($18 − $10), therefore the shopper must decide if the $8 saving is worth not having the use of the item for one year.

In columns 3 and 4 we are assuming that the shopper has sufficient cash to buy the item now. However, to do so she would have to give up the opportunity of placing those funds in an investment, assumed to be earning a taxable return of 9 percent. The shopper now has three options; she can either buy now and pay cash, buy now and finance the purchase, or delay the purchase for one year. If the shopper wants to purchase the item now, her next decision is whether to pay cash or finance it. If she looks only at the $100 explicit cash cost in column 3, she might conclude that she saves $18, the total interest expense in column 1, by paying cash now rather that borrowing to finance the purchase. This does not take into account, however, the entire opportunity cost of paying cash. The opportunity cost listed in column 4 incorporates the cost of all lost opportunities. This includes not only the explicit cash expense of $100, but also the implicit after-tax income she could have earned had she not used these funds.

Her marginal tax rate is the tax rate on an additional dollar of earnings. If she could have earned $9 on a $100 investment and her marginal tax rate is 28 percent, then the after-tax income she could have earned would equal $6.48 ($9.00 − $2.52). Thus, the opportunity cost of presently using cash to make the purchase would equal $106.48 ($100 + $6.48). If we compare the net opportunity cost of using cash ($106.48) with the net cost of financing the purchase ($118.00), we can see that even after taking into consideration the implicit cost of lost investment income, it is still cheaper for her to pay cash.

Assuming that she intends to make the purchase eventually, we can also observe that is definitely not worthwhile for her to delay the purchase. Given that the cost of the item will rise by $10 over the next year, and that her after-tax return on the invested cash is only $6.48, she can save $3.52 ($10.00 − $6.48) by purchasing with cash today.

AS A SOURCE OF EMERGENCY FUNDS Having easy and quick access to credit gives you funds that could be used in case of emergency if your available liquid assets were not adequate. Some people regard this feature as the single most important advantage of credit, since it allows them to hold a larger portion of their total investments in nonliquid assets, where yields have historically been higher. It would be a mistake, though, to rely upon credit too much or for too long a period of time. Borrowed funds must be repaid, meaning that eventually you must sell nonliquid assets and suffer potential losses if their prices are low when you sell them.

Disadvantages of Using Credit

After considering the reasons for using credit, you should also become aware of some of its disadvantages. The final decision to use credit—and how much to use—rests on a comparison of its advantages and disadvantages. The most important disadvantages are discussed in this section.

A TEMPTATION TO OVERSPEND As mentioned before, after you qualify for credit, you will probably be surprised at how willing lenders are to extend credit. Given these temptations, and without proper credit planning, you are in real danger of allowing the consumption component of your budget to get far out of hand. The only solution to this problem is to develop the discipline to stay within a planned budget, as we discussed in Chapter 4. Also, some people become so accustomed to using credit cards, they often forget purchases they made during a month. Consumption quite naturally becomes excessive, and the rude awakening arrives with the monthly statement. To guard against this form of overspending, some financial planners urge you to maintain a credit card expense journal, which is similar to the check stubs in a checking account. After each credit purchase, write down all pertinent information—payee, date, amount, reason for purchase, etc.—as you would on a check stub. Keep a weekly running total of credit card expenses and parenthetically deduct the end-of-week total from your checking account balance. You can then approximate what your cash balance will be after paying your monthly statement.

CREDIT COSTS The biggest cost associated with credit is the interest you pay, if your loan carries interest. At a minimum, you should know what the annual percentage rate (APR) is on the loan, how interest will be calculated, and what will be the total interest paid over the life of the loan. We'll cover these topics in detail later in this chapter. Occasionally there may be expenses directly connected with credit, such as an annual maintenance fee on your account. Indirect costs can be important, too. If your loan involves a credit card, you must be concerned about its safety: If it is lost or stolen, it can be used by someone else, with you paying the bill. The **Truth in Lending Act (TILA)** limits your loss to $50 per account, but this amount could be substantial if you lost five or six cards. You will also have the aggravation of notifying creditors and taking other steps to be protected under the law. Another indirect cost is the time it takes to review creditors' monthly statements for accuracy and then to write and mail your checks. Many people are not concerned with these indirect costs, but they may be important to you.

Truth in Lending Act (TILA): Sets rules regulating credit market. It also sets limits on your credit-related financial responsibilities.

LESS FLEXIBILITY WITH FUTURE BUDGETS The more we spend in one period, deferring payment until a later one, the less flexible is our future budget. In effect, we increase the fixed-expense component of the future budget. By itself, this practice isn't necessarily bad; but it sometimes happens that items purchased

Box 7.1
Simplifying Personal Finance

A Credit Card Register

If you update the register each time you write a check, your check register should indicate just how much you have in your checking account. Unless you or the bank make a mistake, you are not likely to be surprised by your monthly checking account statement. The same people, however, that keep excellent check registers are often surprised by the outstanding balance on their charge account, because they fail to keep similar information on their credit card use.

The first sign of credit card misuse is an unexpectedly large credit card balance. If you use "plastic money" often, you are likely to forget just how much you have charged. You might keep the receipts in your wallet with the good intention of periodically totaling your charges, but somehow that gets put off until the credit card statement arrives. By then it is too late: You have already overspent your budget.

You may have heard of food diets in which you are required to keep a running list of everything you eat. If each little snack is added to the list, you may eventually come to the realization that all those little snacks add up to one big eating spree. The same should hold true for a credit diet. If you maintain a running tally of your credit charges, you must inevitably confront your own excesses and reduce your overspending. You can do this by creating a credit card register that you update just like you would a check register.

Credit card companies, which have an interest in seeing you run up your outstanding balance, do not supply a credit card register. However, you can create your own out of an unused check register by using the accompanying illustration as a guide. Each time you charge a purchase, receive a credit for returned merchandise, or make a monthly payment, enter the transaction in the register and update the outstanding balance. If you get in the habit of making entries with each use of the account, you will eliminate the unexpected by knowing just how much you owe at any time.

Date	Description	Credit for Returns and Payments	Amount of Charge	Balance
				$74.20
1/2/92	Marshalls—sweater		$56.19	130.29
1/6/92	Sonoco—gas and milk		18.75	149.14
1/8/92	K mart—return of defective garden hose	$11.08		138.06
1/9/92	Lotus Blossom— dinner with the Williams		48.96	187.02

with credit fail to satisfy us as we thought they might at the time we purchased them. Holiday gifts usually come to mind as examples here. In these cases, we are left with the bills to pay, along with the temptation to buy new items to satisfy current consumption demands. This situation puts a strain on your budget.

How to Get Credit

Having decided you want credit, the next step is to apply for it. You can apply in person or by mail, but in either case, you probably will be asked to complete an application form that asks for personal and financial information. It is important to know what a lender looks for in a credit applicant, and what steps you can take to begin a credit record. If you are a woman, you may face special problems in this effort.

WHAT THE LENDER LOOKS FOR   Put simply, the only concern of the lender is your ability to repay the loan along with any related expenses. To assess this

185

ability, lenders often look at the three Cs of credit—your *character*, *capital*, and *capacity*. Character has to do with how you have handled yourself in previous financial dealings. Do you have checking and savings accounts and use them regularly? Do you use them properly, or are there frequent overdrafts? Have you used credit properly before by repaying your debts on a timely basis? These are some of the questions lenders frequently ask to judge creditworthiness. Capital refers to your financial strength, usually measured by net worth, a topic discussed in Chapter 3. Capacity means your ability to repay debt out of your future income. Here the lender looks not only at the amount of such income but also at future commitments that might restrict it.

Lenders may apply rules of thumb before granting a loan. For example, only consumers with monthly mortgage loan payments less than 25 percent of income and total loan payments less than 30 percent of income may be deemed credit-worthy. Others may use a more specific evaluation technique to weigh important factors in the credit-granting decision and arrive at a numeric guide to whether or not credit should be made available to you. The scoring system will be based upon the lender's bad-loan experience. Factors that are likely to weigh in your favor include home ownership, residential and job stability, education, and income. The use of other factors such as age, sex, and marital status has been abolished by antidiscrimination laws.

Regardless of the system lenders use to evaluate your credit application, the **Equal Credit Opportunity Act (ECOA)** insists that fairness be applied. You cannot be discriminated against because of race, color, age, sex, marital status, or related other factors. This does not mean that someone is automatically given a loan because of one or several of these characteristics; what it does mean is that lenders may not *deny* him or her a loan because of any one of them. ECOA also insures that lenders do not use such factors in credit-scoring formulas. Age may be requested, but if you are 62 or older, you must be given at least as many points as someone under 62. Finally, you are entitled by ECOA to receive a response from a creditor within 30 days after your application indicating if your request has been approved or denied. If denied, the response must be in writing, and it must either explain the reasons for the denial or indicate your right to an explanation. If you have had a loan request denied, by all means determine why. Knowing the reason will help you to remedy a situation that might prevent your access to credit in the future. If the lender's reasons do not seem justified and you feel you have been discriminated against, cite the law to the lender. If the loan is still denied, you should contact a federal enforcement agency for assistance or consider legal action against the lender.

BEGINNING A CREDIT RECORD Being aware of the factors lenders look at to assess your credit worthiness helps you improve your score and your chances of receiving credit. There are some practical things you can do.

- Open both checking and savings accounts (if you don't already have them) and, of course, use them properly. This means no "bounced checks" and a history of regular deposits to the savings account.
- Open a retail charge account with a local store or major oil company. These accounts are often easier to obtain than other loans. Then use the

---

Equal Credit Opportunity Act (ECOA): Ensures that you cannot be denied credit because of your race, color, age, sex, or marital status.

card and make sure you are prompt in remitting the monthly balance due. In this way you will begin to build a credit history.

- If you qualify for a small installment loan, take it even if the funds are not needed immediately. Repaying such a loan promptly each month helps establish a good credit record. If you don't need the funds, invest them in a short-term account and use the interest earned to offset interest on the loan.
- If you have recently moved, write for a summary of any credit record kept by a credit bureau in your former town. It will be helpful in establishing credit in your new town.
- Have a telephone installed; this item often appears as a factor in credit-rating formulas.

You may face special problems in getting credit if you are a woman, so you should take additional steps:

- Always use your own name in applying for credit. If you are Nancy Brown, who marries Edward Hall, you should use *Nancy Hall* or *Nancy Brown Hall* as your legal name, if you choose to use your husband's last name. You are not required to do so, however, and you can continue to use your maiden name. But definitely do not use a social title such as *Mrs. Edward Hall*. Not only could other women have this name, but also, any credit information under it goes to your husband's credit file and does not benefit you individually.
- Make sure all credit information is reported under your name as well as your husband's. While ECOA guarantees this for all joint accounts opened after June 1, 1977, it does not cover accounts opened prior to that date. The credit history of such an account may be in your husband's name only.
- If you are recently married, you should inform creditors accordingly and indicate that you wish to maintain your own credit record.

Credit history: A record of credit previously granted you. It should also indicate how responsible you were in handling that credit.

Once you begin using credit, you will establish a **credit history**. Many lenders do not maintain their own credit-investigating facilities, but instead use such services provided by major credit bureaus. In all likelihood, one or more of these bureaus will keep your credit history.

THE ROLE OF THE CREDIT BUREAU The United States has approximately 2,000 credit bureaus which function as clearinghouses for information about borrowers' credit histories. The bureaus in your area can be found in the Yellow Pages under such headings as "Credit" or "Credit Reporting Agencies." These bureaus are connected to five major firms by way of a computer hookup, so if you wish to make a credit card purchase in California, the seller can check your credit history even if you have never used your card outside of New York. The largest of these firms, TRW Credit Data, maintains over 90 million credit files. It is sometimes believed the credit bureau decides whether or not you receive credit, but this is not true. A credit bureau only stores information about how you have handled credit in the past and about any legal actions against you that might

Box 7.2
What's New in Personal Finance

National Credit Reporting Agency Charged with Sloppy Practices

Attorney generals in six states have charged TRW Inc., the credit-reporting giant, with repeatedly filling consumers' files with errors and illegally selling sensitive data to junkmailers. They specifically charge TRW with using sloppy procedures that create errors in consumer credit files; inadequately investigating consumer complaints about inaccuracies; allowing errors to recur in consumer files; and illegally selling consumer data to junkmailers.

Some of the states are asking for a court order forcing TRW to supply credit reports speedily, take steps to make sure errors don't recur, and investigate complaints about errors beyond merely asking a store or bank to reiterate its original data.

The state agencies have received numerous complaints about TRW. An example of a consumer whose complaint helped spur the lawsuits is Ricardo Alexander, a New York oral surgeon. He said his mortgage application was held up for months because his file contained derogatory data from several sources. TRW, he claims, told him to take up the mistakes with each business that supplied the credit data.

"You're guilty until proven innocent," said Dr. Alexander. "If you can get that screwed up with Ricardo Alexander, what the heck can happen to you if you're John Smith?"

A TRW official argued that the company can't be held solely accountable for errors and delays. Sometimes the bank or store that supplied the contested data is slow to respond. Furthermore, when you take into consideration the volume of credit reports they sell, there are not a large number of inaccuracies.

Attorneys for the state don't agree. They claim that in response to a consumer complaint, TRW simply asks the source of the data to verify what it reported. One suit charges that in every instance TRW accepts the creditor's version and does not request more specific information on the disputed data. The suit also claims that TRW has not developed procedures to keep previously eliminated erroneous data from creeping back into a consumer's file. This requires consumers to continually monitor their files to make sure the deleted information does not reappear.

The company response is that their data base would not be very accurate if they took the consumers' word in such disputes. In addition, consumers have the right to include a 100-word statement of their side of a dispute. Consumer groups have called this a hollow gesture because creditors may gloss over that statement, or make credit decisions using computer software that doesn't incorporate it.

SOURCE: Adapted from Michael W. Miller, "Six States Sue TRW over Credit-Reporting Practices," *The Wall Street Journal*, July 10, 1991, pp. B1, B2. Reprinted by permission of *The Wall Street Journal*, © 1991 Dow Jones & Company, Inc. All Rights Reserved Worldwide.

Credit report: A credit history record provided by a credit bureau to a prospective lender.

impair your financial strength in the future. As part of their review of your credit application, lenders may buy from the credit bureau a **credit report** about you. They use this report in their decision to extend you credit, although it is not the only factor they consider, and a good credit record doesn't automatically guarantee that credit will be given.

Fair Credit Reporting Act of 1971: Sets down your rights to a fair and accurate credit report and establishes procedures for correcting an inaccurate report.

IF YOU ARE DENIED CREDIT The **Fair Credit Reporting Act of 1971** entitles you to a fair and accurate credit report. If you have been denied credit, insurance, or employment because of your credit report, you have the right to obtain a free copy of your report within 30 days of denial. If the facts are correct but you feel they do not present your side of the story fairly, you may submit your own statement to be included in your file. You have a right to have information on a bankruptcy that is more than ten years old and other adverse information that is more than seven years old removed from your report. For an unsubstantiated or incorrect entry, you may insist that all those who have requested a credit report within the past six months be notified of that fact.

A credit report can determine whether or not you get that next job. Since 1988 most businesses have been prohibited from using lie-detector tests to screen applicants. Their response to this prohibition has been to rely more heavily on credit checks. Companies are required to notify you if you were rejected because of a poor credit rating. Some companies, however, have failed to follow this rule, so it is a good idea to check your credit report before you begin a job search.

You can review your credit report even if you are just curious about it. You will pay a fee of about $15, but it might be worth it to make sure that it is free of errors. For a larger fee, some credit reporting services will provide you with unlimited access to your credit report and notification whenever someone requests a copy of your file.

If you have trouble handling credit, you may consider credit counseling, discussed later in this chapter. However, be wary of credit repair clinics that claim they can reestablish your good credit for an exorbitant fee. They can accomplish no more than you can by contacting the credit bureau directly.

Secured credit card: A credit card secured by funds held at the bank issuing the card. Useful for those who are establishing credit or who are trying to overcome a poor credit history.

A **secured credit card** can be helpful if you are trying to reestablish a good credit record. The card is secured by funds that you have on deposit at the bank, assuring the bank repayment for your purchases. Consequently, banks that might not consider issuing you a typical credit card will have no problem granting you a secured credit card. For a small fee, a list of secured card issuers can be obtained from Bankcard Holders of America.

Sales Credit

Sales credit: Any credit arising from the sale of merchandise or services.

Sales credit arises from the sale of merchandise or services. Traditionally, most of this credit was offered by merchants, such as department stores, major oil companies, automobile dealerships, and furniture and appliance dealers, in an effort to expand their sales. While they are still important in supplying such credit, the major bank credit cards—Visa and MasterCard—have also become important sources. Sales credit is often symbolized by a credit card that is used to make service or merchandise transactions, although many of these cards can now be used for financial transactions as well, such as making a cash loan.

Kinds of Accounts

Open-end account: A credit agreement that establishes an ongoing line of credit covering future purchases. One agreement may cover a multitude of purchases.

Closed-end account: A credit agreement covering a single purchase with a set repayment schedule.

Regular charge account: A credit account with a merchant in which complete payment at the end of the billing cycle usually avoids all interest charges.

You can obtain sales credit in three different forms: first, as a regular (or 30-day) account; second, as a revolving account; and third, as a retail installment account. The first two are called open-end credit accounts; they are discussed below. The third is referred to as a closed-end account, and it is discussed in a later section. When you establish an **open-end account,** you will sign an agreement that covers all credit purchases and cash advances made in the account. This one agreement is binding as long as the account is open. In contrast, a **closed-end account** requires a separate retail installment contract for each purchase, but these are usually for large amounts and longer periods of time.

REGULAR CHARGE ACCOUNT People who use a **regular charge account** are typically those who view credit as a shopping convenience. Your purchase transactions for a month are accumulated and sent to you at the end of the month. You agree with the terms of this account by paying the total amount billed within

10 to 30 days after the billing date, and you avoid interest by so doing. Interest can be charged for late payment, however.

REVOLVING ACCOUNT   A **revolving credit account** allows you to make purchases up to a credit limit that is usually determined by your credit record and net worth. If you then pay the full amount due at the end of the month, you are using the account as a regular account. Often, though, you will make a partial payment, the amount of which depends upon how much credit you have used and the interest charged on the account. As the balance is reduced by payments, you may again make purchases up to the limit, so the account may never actually be paid off. Interest is charged each month on the unpaid balance. Your monthly payments are presumed to cover interest first and cover principal only if the payment exceeds the interest. The Truth in Lending Act requires the creditor to inform you each month as to the interest rate applicable that month, the applicable rate expressed as an annual percentage rate (APR), and the method used to determine the balance upon which the monthly rate is applied. Along with telling you how monthly interest will be charged, a revolving credit agreement will also include information about:

- the time available to pay your balance due without being charged interest;
- the minimum amount you must pay each month, and what happens if you don't pay it; and
- permission you give the creditor to investigate your credit history.

You will receive a monthly statement for each credit account you have. An example of such a statement is shown in Figure 7.2, where the period covered is the month of July 1990. This statement is patterned after one used by a major bank card, but it is typical of most monthly statements. Notice that the borrower made three purchases during the month and one payment; there were no credits for returned merchandise. The lender charged interest of $4.32 for the month, based on the monthly rate of 1.65 percent (which is an annual percentage rate of 19.80 percent). The sum of this interest and purchases was $92.61 ($4.32 + $88.29). Subtracting the $20.00 payment made during the month gives the net change during the month of $72.61; this amount is then added to the $215.00 beginning-of-the-month balance to arrive at the end-of-the-month balance of

FIGURE 7.2

A monthly statement for a revolving credit account.

Reference Number	Date	Description of Transaction		Amounts (Credit indicated by -)
69453987	7/05	K Mart 7549	Centerville, OH	$ 38.15
42874906	7/10	Payment		20.00-
69426933	7/12	Days Inns 033M	McDonough, GA	32.50
75539521	7/20	Mendelsons Retail	Dayton, OH	17.64

FINANCE CHARGE	Computed on an Average Daily Balance of	MONTHLY PERIODIC RATE	ANNUAL PERCENTAGE RATE	Payment Due Date	Statement Closing Date
$ 4.32	$ 261.83	1.65%	19.80%	8/15/90	7/31/90

Previous Balance	Payments	Credit Transactions	Debit Transactions	FINANCE CHARGE	New Balance
$ 215.00	$ 20.00	$ -0-	$ 88.29	$ 4.32	$ 287.61

Credit Limit: $1,000
Available Credit: $ 712.39
Minimum Monthly Payment: $ 20.00

$287.61. This amount or the minimum monthly payment of $20.00 must be paid by August 15, 1990. Also, notice that the borrower has a **credit limit** (the most that can be borrowed) of $1,000, and there is $712.39 ($1,000 − $287.61) of credit available at the beginning of August.

We mentioned above that it might be the borrower's intent to use a revolving account as a somewhat permanent form of credit. Before doing that, a person should consider other sources of credit that might be less expensive. In the preceding example, the APR was a rather high 19.80 percent. In July 1990, many consumer installment loans were being made at somewhat lower rates than this, and other loans, such as margin account loans or second mortgage loans, were substantially lower. Generally, revolving credit is expensive credit if it is used on a permanent basis, although there may be exceptions during periods when interest rates are rising rapidly and lenders are not adjusting their rates to match. That situation occurred during the late 1970s but is less likely to happen again because lenders have far greater flexibility in adjusting rates. Moreover, most lenders now use an average daily balance method for determining interest. This method takes each day's activities into account, which—as we'll see in the next section—eliminates any advantage in the time lag between your purchase and when interest is charged.

DETERMINING INTEREST ON A REVOLVING ACCOUNT   Interest on a revolving charge account is determined by applying the monthly rate to the balance in the account. It seems simple enough, except that there are various ways of determining what this balance is. The three most commonly used methods are the previous balance method, the adjusted balance method, and the average daily balance method. Using data from Figure 7.2, each of these methods is illustrated in Table 7.2.

The **previous balance method** is the simplest of the three. The rate is applied to the balance at the end of the previous month. As you see in Table 7.2, this means you multiply the rate, 1.65 percent, by the previous balance, $215.00, to arrive at the month's interest of $3.55. This method works to your advantage if you have considerable charges in the current month.

The **adjusted balance method** is more favorable than the previous balance method. The adjusted balance is equal to the previous balance less any payments or returns you made during the current billing cycle. Thus, in Table 7.2, the adjusted balance is simply $215 less the credit payment of $20. Applying 1.65 percent to $195 determines a finance charge of $3.22.

There are two variations to the **average daily balance method,** one includes purchases for the current billing cycle, the other does not. The *average daily balance method including current purchases* gives the most correct balance for applying interest. In this procedure, you weight a balance for the number of days it is outstanding. In the example, the beginning balance of $215.00 was applicable only for the four days, 7/1 through 7/4. Thereafter, other balances were appropriate for varying numbers of days. By weighting each balance for the number of outstanding days, you arrive at the total weighted balance of $8,116.73, which is then divided by 31 to arrive at the $261.83 average daily balance. This figure multiplied by 1.65 percent gives the interest amount of $4.32.

The other variation is the *average daily balance method excluding current purchases*. Again an average daily balance is computed. However, in this variation of

Credit limit: You may have outstanding charges up to this amount. Charges in excess of the credit limit may result in a penalty.

Previous balance method: The interest rate is applied to the outstanding balance at the end of the previous billing period.

Adjusted balance method: The interest rate is applied to the previous balance less any payments or returns made during the current billing cycle.

Average daily balance method: The interest rate is applied to the average outstanding balance over the billing cycle.

191

Consumer Credit

TABLE 7.2 · Three Different Methods for Computing Interest on a Revolving Credit Account (Based on data from Figure 7.2)

I. Previous Balance Method

Interest is charged on the previous balance

$$1.65\% \times \$215.00 = \boxed{\$3.55}$$

II. Adjusted Balance Method

Interest is charged on the previous balance less any current credits

$$1.65\% \times (\$215.00 - \$20.00) = \boxed{\$3.22}$$

III(a). Average Daily Balance Method (including current purchases)

Interest is charged on the updated balance considering the day a charge or credit takes place

Period	(a) No. of Days	(b) Balance	(c) (a) × (b)
7/1–7/4	4	$215.00 + $ -0- = 215.00	$ 860.00
7/5–7/9	5	215.00 + 38.15 = 253.15	1,265.75
7/10–7/11	2	253.15 − 20.00 = 233.15	466.30
7/12–7/19	8	233.15 + 32.50 = 265.65	2,125.20
7/20–7/31	12	265.65 + 17.64 = 283.29	3,399.48
	31		$8,116.73

$$\text{Average daily balance} = \frac{\$8,116.73}{31} = \$261.83$$

$$1.65\% \times \$261.83 = \boxed{\$4.32}$$

III(b). Average Daily Balance Method (excluding current purchases)

Interest is charged on the updated balance considering the day a current payment is made but ignoring current purchases or returns

Period	(a) No. of Days	(b) Balance	(c) (a) × (b)
7/1–7/9	10	$215	$2,150.00
7/10–7/31	21	$215.00 − $20.00 = 195	4,095.00
			$6,245.00

$$\text{Average daily balance} = \$6,245.00/31 = \$201.45$$

$$1.65\% \times \$201.45 = \boxed{\$3.32}$$

---

the average daily balance method the finance charge is less because new purchases are not included in the daily balance. As indicated in Table 7.2, the finance charge is only $3.32 when new purchases are excluded.

Lenders traditionally provide a **grace period** of 25 days during which interest on the loan balance is forgiven. This usually applies only when you have fully paid off the previous month's balance. The grace period normally lasts between the statement closing date and the payment due date. Recently, some lenders have eliminated the grace period, while others have offered their customers a choice between credit accounts with or without a grace period. Finance charges on the account with the grace period are based on a higher annual percentage rate, making it less desirable for someone who does not regularly pay off the entire amount due.

Grace period: Period in which interest charges are forgiven on the condition that the outstanding balance is fully repaid.

Spending,
Borrowing,
and Saving

For each revolving account you have, you should determine how the monthly balance is calculated and verify the monthly statement to make sure it is correct. Of course, you aren't likely to go through all the calculations for the average daily balance method, and it may not be necessary that you do. A quick glance between this month and last month should indicate if the number is approximately correct. A last piece of fairly obvious advice is to use those accounts that determine the monthly balance to your best advantage.

Major Issuers of Credit Cards

"Plastic money" is indeed an appropriate name for what we use to purchase many goods and services. Over 100 million Americans use credit cards regularly, and each user has about 5.2 cards. Of the number of cards issued, retail store cards are in first place. Over one-half of all families hold at least one retail store card. Most retail store cards are charge cards issued in conjunction with a regular charge account. Next in number of cardholders are bank credit cards. Table 7.3 indicates that over one-half of all households have at least one bank credit card. The major names of issuers include Visa, Mastercard, Discover, and Optima.

Bank credit cards: Credit cards, such as MasterCard and Visa, which are issued by banks.

BANK CREDIT CARDS The **bank credit cards**—MasterCard and Visa—are by far the largest suppliers of consumer installment credit. When you use one of these cards, you are actually borrowing from a bank, perhaps a local one, or you may have a card issued by one of the major banks, such as Chase Manhattan. We illustrated and discussed a typical credit card account earlier, which showed how the card is used to make purchases. But bank cards can also be used to make financial transactions. For example, you may be able to get cash advances from money machines with your card, and in some places you can use it to buy securities, such as stocks or bonds. Quite often issuers of these cards will offer other attractions, such as discounts on special purchases or a small percentage rebate on total purchases. The most recent promotional gimmick is to offer purchase protection on defective, stolen, or lost merchandise that had been purchased with a charge card. This protection, however, is secondary to that provided under the product's warranty or that provided by your homeowner's insurance policy. A worksheet, like that in Figure 7.3, can be used to compare the costs and benefits of various cards.

TABLE 7.3 ▪ Bank Credit Cards

Type of Credit Account	Percent of Households
All credit categories	74.9
Bank credit card	55.8
Mortgage	37.2
Motor vehicle	33.8
Home equity	10.6
Other	13.8

SOURCE: Gregory E. Elliehausen and John D. Wolken, "Banking Markets and the Use of Financial Services by Households," *Federal Reserve Bulletin* (March, 1992), p. 169.

Consumer Credit

CARD ISSUER:		
Cost Comparison		
Charge	Description	Cost
Annual membership fee[a]	Typically about $25 for bank credit cards, and higher for travel and entertainment cards.	
Annual percentage rate[a]	One-twelfth of the annual rate is applied to the outstanding balance to determine the monthly finance charge. If an introductory rate is offered, the regular rate should also be disclosed. The APR on cash advances is likely to be higher than the APR on credit purchases. Some issuers also practice *tier pricing*, whereby the APR is higher on balances above a certain amount.	
Variable rate information[a]	If the interest rate is variable, the disclosure will indicate the index or formula and the spread or margin that determine the APR. If there is a cap or a floor on the APR, this should also be indicated.	
Grace period[a]	Period within which the credit extended must be repaid in order to avoid finance charges will be indicated. If the card issuer does not provide a grace period, that fact must be disclosed.	
Balance computation method[a]	Method used to compute the balance upon which finance charges will be based.	
Minimum finance fee[a]	Minimum fee applied whenever there is a finance charge.	
Transaction fee[a]	Fee applied to each purchase.	
Cash advance fee[b]	Fee imposed for an extension of credit in the form of cash.	
Late payment fee[b]	Fee imposed for late payment of minimum monthly payment.	
Over-the-limit	Fee imposed for exceeding the credit limit.	
Replacement fee[c]	Fee for replacing a lost credit card.	
Return check charge	Fee for a check returned because of insufficient funds.	
Copy charge[c]	Fee for receiving a photostatic copy of receipt on sales or cash advance.	
Fees for optional services[c]	May include such things as credit life insurance, disability insurance, unemployment insurance, and credit card registration. See the benefits section below for a description of some of these benefits.	

FIGURE 7.3

Worksheet for credit card comparison.

Spending,
Borrowing,
and Saving

BENEFIT COMPARISON		
Benefit	**Description**	**Value**
Credit limit	If your credit balance exceeds this amount, you will be charged an over-the-line fee.	
Credit life insurance	Pays off the outstanding balance up to some set limit at the time of death.	
Total disability insurance	May pay off your account balance or make minimum monthly payments if you become totally disabled.	
Unemployment insurance	If you are involuntarily terminated from your employment, this may cover your minimum monthly payment during the period of unemployment.	
Rebates and discounts	Some cards offer a small percentage rebate on all credit purchases. Others offer discounts on special purchases such as airline tickets.	
Purchase price protection	If you charge something and then see the same product advertised elsewhere at a lower price within a specified time period, your account will be credited with the difference. This may be difficult to document and inconvenient to collect. In addition, there may be a limit on refunds.	
Accident insurance	Small amounts of coverage for accidental injuries.	
Rental car collision insurance	This may already be provided under your personal auto insurance.	
Merchandise warranty protection	The period of warranty may be extended by the card issuer.	
Credit card registry	Service that arranges for cancellation and replacement of credit cards in the even of loss	
Merchandise loss protection	Replaces the cost of lost or stolen items that were charged up to a specified limit. Insurance lasts for only a specified period after purchase, and may be secondary to protection under other insurance policies.	

[a]Information must be disclosed in a prominent table.

[b]Information must be disclosed somewhere on the application form.

[c]Information need be provided only upon request.

FIGURE 7.3

Continued.

Travel and entertainment (T&E) cards: Credit cards issued by finance companies catering to businesspeople and travelers.

TRAVEL AND ENTERTAINMENT CARDS Traditionally, **travel and entertainment (T&E) cards,** such as American Express, have catered to travelers—usually businesspeople—who frequently buy goods and services away from their hometowns. The cards are used to pay for hotel and motel accommodations, to buy airline tickets, and to pay restaurant bills. However, the T&E cards are expanding their services. The usual annual fee of about $50 for a T&E card is much higher than that of a bank credit card, and it is questionable whether it is worth it, since bank credit cards are so universally acceptable.

OTHER CARDS   We mentioned above that many retail establishments issue their own credit cards. In addition to Sears, you may have a Penney's card, or one issued by a local store that is part of a national company, such as Federated Department Stores. These stores generally prefer that you use their card rather than a bank card (many will not accept bank cards), since consumer credit is often a profitable part of their business.

For some people, the card used most frequently is their oil company card. While these are usually used on a 30-day basis with no interest charge, they can also be used on a revolving basis for major purchases of tires, batteries, or service work. At some stations, credit card users pay a higher price for gas than cash customers. Is it worth it? At a four-cent differential and an average price of $1.00 a gallon, and assuming you can defer payment for 30 days, the implicit interest rate is 4 percent per month and about 48 percent a year ($4 \times 12 = 48$)—a very expensive form of credit. You would be better off getting a cash advance on your bank credit card and buying your gas with cash.

CREDIT CARDS CONTRASTED WITH DEBIT CARDS   A credit card should not be confused with a debit card even though they may look identical. For example, the MasterCard II—a **debit card**—is a perfect clone of the MasterCard credit card. It is unfortunate that they look alike, because they are quite different in terms of their impact on your cash flow and on the protection you have under federal law. You can use a debit card at an automated teller machine or point-of-sale terminal. (Such terminals are located at numerous retail outlets and allow you to make transactions such as paying the retailer or obtaining cash.) Whenever you use the card, your bank deposit is reduced immediately, as illustrated in Figure 7.4. By contrast, a credit card transaction puts you in debt to the bank, which you reduce later by paying your monthly statement. A debit card is actually a form of checking account, which is how you should view it when considering its use. Make sure you know whether you're using a credit card or a debit card. The difference is important, because whenever you use a debit card, your bank balance is immediately reduced.

With a credit card, you are protected by the Fair Credit Billing Act, but a debit card comes under the Electronic Funds Transfer Act, where your protections are quite different. Your position is a much weaker one with respect to defective merchandise, poor service, or billing errors. And unlike with a stolen card, your losses can far exceed the $50 limit under the Truth in Lending Act. They can go to $500 if you fail to notify the financial institution within two business days after learning of the theft. Moreover, if you wait until 60 days or more after a bank statement has been mailed, your losses may be unlimited. Given a choice between using a debit or credit card, it is hard to see why you shouldn't always choose the latter.

SELECTING A CREDIT CARD   Many people who are good credit risks find their mailboxes overflowing with solicitations from credit card companies. Their major problem is not in getting credit, but rather in selecting the best credit from among the numerous offers. In order to make comparison shopping easier, and also to eliminate potentially misleading sales practices, Congress passed the Fair Credit and Charge Card Disclosure Act in 1988. The act empowered the Federal Reserve Board to set down rules governing the information that credit card com-

Debit card: Unlike a credit card, the price of a purchase is deducted immediately from your bank deposit.

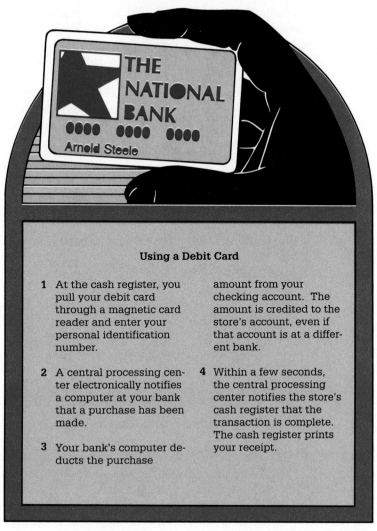

Using a Debit Card

1. At the cash register, you pull your debit card through a magnetic card reader and enter your personal identification number.

2. A central processing center electronically notifies a computer at your bank that a purchase has been made.

3. Your bank's computer deducts the purchase amount from your checking account. The amount is credited to the store's account, even if that account is at a different bank.

4. Within a few seconds, the central processing center notifies the store's cash register that the transaction is complete. The cash register prints your receipt.

FIGURE 7.4

Using a debit card.

panies must furnish potential consumers. The rules enacted under this law have provided for more detailed and uniform disclosure of rates and other cost information in applications and solicitations to open credit and charge card accounts.

The cost of credit can vary significantly among issuers and over time in response to changing conditions in credit markets. In addition to interest charges, the cost of using a credit card will include maintenance fees and other specialized charges. Many of these costs are described in the credit card comparison worksheet in Figure 7.3. Information on most of the items listed is typically disclosed prominently on the application form.

The benefit section of the worksheet in Figure 7.3 indicates the many types of services that card issuers have provided in an effort to attract customers. The value of many of these items is rather small. You would be wise to select from among offers of credit cards based upon an assessment of the relative costs itemized in the first section of the worksheet.

The best credit card for you will depend upon your credit practices. If you intend to pay off the entire balance each month, a card with a grace period and a low annual membership fee would be favored. Given the high cost of finance charges on credit cards and the relatively lower cost of credit from other sources, this is probably the best strategy for most people. However, if you do intend to incur finance charges on your credit card, then you may be better off by paying a higher annual membership fee in exchange for a lower APR. For example, if your average outstanding balance is $1,000, then a 1 percent reduction in the APR would save you $10 a year. Therefore, if the annual membership fee on this card is no more than $10 above the fee on a card with a higher APR, it could be your best choice.

Protection Against Credit Card Fraud

We mentioned previously that the Truth in Lending Act limits your losses from unauthorized uses of your credit cards to $50 per card; but, if your purse or wallet is stolen and if it contains a number of cards, your loss can be more than trivial. So it pays to be careful with them, and the following are suggestions that can help in this effort.

- Destroy old bills, receipts, and carbons, because these have your credit card number imprinted on them. Also destroy all credit cards you do not use.
- Watch clerks carefully while they are using your card to make sure they do not run impressions on other sales checks. Of course, ask the clerk to return your card immediately after it has been used.
- Make sure the sales check you sign is completed correctly, including the addition of separate line items; then, save your receipts, compare them to your monthly bill, and report any discrepancy immediately.
- Be extra careful in giving your number over the phone unless you initiated the phone call and want to charge the purchase. Any calls purporting to be "conducting a credit card survey" should be completely avoided. If a caller claims to be with the credit card company and is attempting to correct an error with another account that is somehow related to yours (you both have the same names, for example), ask for his or her name and number and offer to call back after you confirm the authenticity of the inquiry. It's a good bet the caller is a fraud.

If your cards are stolen or lost, contact each issuer immediately. This means keeping a list of addresses and phone numbers in a convenient and safe place; but remember, accidents such as these often happen on vacation, and your list will not do much good if it is at home. Getting ready for a vacation is hectic enough, but try to remember the list and don't store it in your wallet or purse, because that is what is usually lost or stolen.

Correcting Credit Mistakes

Despite you or the credit issuer being careful, mistakes do occur. It is important for your sake that they are corrected immediately, not only to save money if it's an overcharge but to protect your good credit rating. Both the Truth in Lending

Act and the Fair Credit Billing Act give you considerable legal protection against credit mistakes. Since it is very important that you understand some of these protections, they are discussed at length in the next three sections. This material is adapted from the *Consumer Handbook to Credit Protection Laws*, published by the Board of Directors of the Federal Reserve System.

BILLING ERRORS   The law defines a billing error as any charge:

- For something you didn't buy or for a purchase made by someone not authorized to use your account
- That is not properly identified on your bill or is for an amount different from the actual purchase price or was entered on a date different from the purchase date
- For something that you did not accept on delivery or that was not delivered according to agreement

Billing errors also include:

- Errors in arithmetic
- Failure to reflect a payment or other credit to your account
- Failure to mail the statement to your current address, provided you notified the creditor of an address change at least 20 days before the end of the billing period
- A questionable item, or an item for which you need additional information

If you think your bill is wrong, or you want more information about it, follow these steps:

1. Notify the creditor *in writing* within 60 days after the bill was mailed. Be sure to write to the address the creditor lists for billing inquiries, and tell the creditor: your name and account number; that you believe the bill contains an error and *why* you believe it is wrong; and the suspected amount of the error or the item you want explained.
2. Pay all parts of the bill that are not in dispute. But, while waiting for an answer, you do not have to pay the amount in question (the "disputed amount") or any minimum payments or finance charges that apply to it.
   The creditor must acknowledge your letter within 30 days, unless your bill can be corrected sooner. Within two billing periods—but in no case longer than 90 days—either your account must be corrected or you must be told why the creditor believes the bill is correct.
   If the creditor made a mistake, you do not pay any finance charges on the disputed amount. Your account must be corrected, and you must be sent an explanation of any amount you still owe.
   If no error is found, the creditor must promptly send you an explanation of the reasons for that determination and a statement of what you owe, which may include any finance charges that have accumulated and any minimum payments you missed while you were questioning the bill.

You then have the time usually given on your type of account to pay any balance.

3. If you still are not satisfied, you should notify the creditor within the time allowed to pay your bill.

A creditor may not threaten your credit rating while you're resolving a billing dispute. Once you have written about a possible error, a creditor is prohibited from giving out information to other creditors or credit bureaus that would damage your credit reputation. And, until your complaint is answered, the creditor also may not take any action to collect the disputed amount.

After the creditor has explained the bill, you may be reported as delinquent on the amount in dispute, and the creditor may take action to collect if you do not pay in the time allowed. Even so, you can still disagree in writing. Then the creditor must report that you have challenged your bill and give you the name and address of each person who has received information about your account. When the matter is settled, the creditor must report the outcome to each person who has received information. Remember that you may also place your own side of the story in your credit record.

DEFECTIVE GOODS OR SERVICES   You may withhold the remaining payment on any damaged or shoddy goods or poor-quality services purchased with a credit card, as long as you have made a real attempt to solve the problem with the merchant. Your withholding of payments results in what is called a **chargeback,** whereby the card issuer charges the disputed amount back to the merchant. At this point the merchant can dispute the chargeback. The card issuer must then decide whether to reissue the bill to you or proceed against the merchant for repayment.

Chargeback: A disputed amount charged back to the merchant by the credit card company.

This right to withhold payment may be limited if the card was a bank or a travel and entertainment card, or any card *not* issued by the store where you made your purchase. In such cases, the sale must have totaled more than $50, and must have taken place in your home state or within 100 miles of your home address.

PROMPT CREDIT PAYMENTS AND REFUNDS FOR CREDIT BALANCES   If you can avoid finance charges on your account within a certain period of time, it is obviously important that you get your bills, and get credit for paying them, promptly. Check your statements to make sure your creditor follows these rules:

Prompt Billing.   Look at the date on the postmark. If your account is one on which no finance charge is added before a certain due date, then creditors must mail their statements at least 14 days before payment is due.

Prompt Crediting.   Look at the payment date entered on the statement. Creditors must credit payments on the day they arrive, as long as you pay according to payment instructions.

Stores often give you a credit on your bill instead of cash when you return a purchase. If this results in a credit balance on your account, a store must make a refund in cash, at your request.

Cash Credit

Cash credit: Credit
extended in the form of
cash.

Cash credit simply means borrowing money; as we have seen, sales credit involves borrowing in connection with buying something. The distinction is a tenuous one since, in most cases, cash borrowed is also used to make purchases. The major distinction between sales and cash credit is the way you repay the debt. Cash credit is repaid either with a single payment at the end of a period of time, or by a series of uniform payments called installments. You might remember that earlier we said a form of sales credit is the retail installment account. This account is virtually identical to an installment cash loan, which is why it is explained now rather than before.

The Contract

Retail installment contract:
A contract between a
borrower and lender
establishing periodic
repayment of the amount
borrowed.

Promissory note: A
contract binding a
borrower to future
repayment of the amount
borrowed.

Security agreement:
Establishes the creditor's
security interest in the
good for which the credit
was extended.

The agreement between you and a person selling an item is called a **retail installment contract.** If you purchase the item by obtaining a cash loan from a bank, savings and loan, consumer finance company, or credit union, the agreement is called a **promissory note.** Although promissory notes can be unsecured—and in fact, many are—their use in consumer credit is almost always on a secured basis, with the purchased item serving as collateral. The retail installment contract is always on a secured basis. The creditor obtains a security interest in the property with the **security agreement,** which is a separate instrument.

INFORMATION THAT MUST BE PROVIDED   The Truth in Lending Act requires that each credit contract gives you the following information:

1. The amount financed
2. The total number of payments, the amount of each payment, and due dates
3. Finance charges expressed both as a dollar amount and as an annual percentage rate
4. The date when finance charges begin, if that date is different from the transaction date
5. An itemized list of all charges not included as part of the finance charge
6. The charges for late payments or default
7. A description of security held by the creditor
8. How finance charge refunds are determined in the case of prepayments
9. A description of prepayment penalties, if any

Creditors are also required to supply the following additional information when merchandise is purchased on time:

1. A description of the merchandise
2. The cash price
3. The deferred payment price
4. The down payment, including any trade-in

How Interest Charges Are Determined

Although the Truth in Lending Act requires lenders to state in writing the interest you must pay on a loan—both in dollars and as an annual percentage rate

(APR)—it is still important that you know how these calculations are made. Three approaches are in general use: the simple interest method, the discount method, and the add-on method. These are explained below, along with several techniques you can use to approximate the true APR on a loan.

SIMPLE INTEREST METHOD   Under the **simple interest method,** the interest payment is computed by applying a percentage rate to the outstanding loan balance during each payment period. This is the usual method for calculating a finance change on a revolving credit account like that discussed earlier. It is also used by many banks and credit unions for computing the interest due on automobile installment loans and home mortgages.

A loan of $1,000 to be paid off in 12 equal monthly installments of $88.85 is illustrated in Figure 7.5. Using the simple interest method, the monthly finance charge in column 3 is equal to the outstanding balance in column 1 times the monthly interest charge of 1 percent. The excess of the monthly payment in column 2 over the finance charge in column 3 serves to reduce the outstanding balance. You should notice that as the loan is repaid, the finance charge in column 3 declines. You should also notice that, given the equal monthly installments and the declining monthly finance charge, a larger portion of each subsequent monthly installment is devoted to loan repayment. Thus, the loan is paid off more rapidly toward the end of the monthly payments.

DISCOUNT METHOD   Under the **discount method,** the lender deducts the interest to be paid on the loan from the credit extended to you at the beginning of the loan. Therefore, the face amount of the loan will exceed the amount you want to finance. To finance a purchase of $1,000, you have to borrow more than $1,000. On a one-year loan, your total payments are determined by the following formula:

$$\text{Total payments on discount loan} = \frac{\text{amount finance}}{1 - (\text{discount rate} \times t)}$$

$$\$1,136.36 = \frac{\$1,000}{1 - (0.12 \times 1)}$$

where t is the term of the loan in years. Thus, to finance a $1,000 purchase for one year, at a discount rate of 12 percent you must repay $1,136.36. If this were a 12-month installment loan, you would owe $94.72 ($1,136.36/12) per month. The true interest rate on this discount installment loan would be much higher that 12 percent, because you would not have the full use of $1,000 during the entire year. As indicated in the cost comparison in Figure 7.6, the simple interest rate on an identical loan with monthly installments of $94.72 would be 24.28 percent, about twice the discount rate.

ADD-ON METHOD   The add-on method is by far the most widely used method for determining finance charges on consumer loans. Under the **add-on method,** the lender adds the interest to the value of the purchase you are financing to determine your total payments using the following formula:

$$\text{Total payments on add-on loan} = \text{amount financed} \times (1 + (\text{add-on rate} \times t)$$

$$\$1{,}120 = \$1{,}000 \times [1 + (0.12 \times 1)]$$

If the add-on rate is 12 percent per year and you intend to borrow $1,000 for one year, the interest charge of $120($1,000 $\times$ 0.12 $\times$ t (the term of the loan in years)) is added to the original principle of $1,000 to determine total repayments of $1,120 ($1,000 + $120). The monthly payments would equal $93.33 ($1,120/12). You should notice that an add-on rate of 12 percent is more costly than a similar loan with a simple interest rate of 12 percent. The monthly payments of $88.85 on the simple-interest loan are $4.48 less per month than the $93.33 monthly payment for a comparable add-on loan.

As with the discount loan, the true interest rate on an add-on loan is far greater than the add-on rate of 12 percent. Again, you are being charged as if you had the full use of $1,000 for the entire year. However, you have the use of a full $1,000 only for the first month. Since you repay principal with each payment, the total amount borrowed declines with each payment. In the current example, an add-on rate of 12 percent would entail the same monthly payments as a simple interest rate of 21.46 percent.

Month	Outstanding Balance (1)	Monthly Payment (2)	Monthly Finance Charge (3)	Monthly Loan Repayment (4)
1	$1,000.00	$ 88.85	$10.00	$ 78.85
2	921.15	88.85	9.21	79.85
3	841.51	88.85	8.42	80.43
4	761.08	88.85	7.61	81.24
5	679.84	88.85	6.80	82.05
6	597.79	88.85	5.98	82.87
7	514.92	88.85	5.15	83.70
8	431.22	88.85	4.31	84.54
9	346.68	88.85	3.47	85.38
10	261.30	88.85	2.61	86.24
11	175.07	88.85	1.75	87.10
12	87.97	88.85	0.88	87.97
Totals		$1,066.19	$66.19	$1,000.00

Method	Contract Rate	APR	Monthly Payment	Total Interest Paid
Simple interest	12%	12.00%	$88.85	$ 66.19
Discount interest	12%	24.28%	94.72	136.36
Add-on interest	12%	21.46%	93.33	120.00

ANNUAL PERCENTAGE RATE   Regardless of how the lender determines the interest charge, the government requires that the lender provide the borrower with the information on the true interest rate, or what is officially terms the annual percentage rate. The **annual percentage rate (APR)** is the ratio of the finance charge to the average amount of credit extended to you over the life of the contract, expressed as a percentage rate per year. Since the simple interest charge is also based upon the amount of credit extended in each period, the annual simple interest rate and the APR are the same.

Unfortunately, there is nothing simple about calculating the APR on installment loans. The actuarial method is the most accurate method for calculating the APR. It entails the use of either complicated formulas, annuity tables, or a financial calculator. Two simpler but less accurate approaches to calculating the APR are illustrated in Table 7.4 for the add-on example discussed previously. As you can see, the constant-ratio method is less complicated, but always overstates the true rate. The *n*-ratio method results in a rate very close to the true APR of 21.46 percent.

The APR is the rate you should use to judge the relative cost of credit. As indicated in Figure 7.6, identical contract rates can result in widely different interest payments and annual percentage rates. If you are comparing loans for identical amounts of credit and identical maturities, the loan with the lower APR will also have the lower finance charge.

AREAS OF SPECIAL CONCERN   In addition to recognizing how the finance charges are computed, it is important that you read the entire credit agreement carefully and understand each of the several clauses that may be included in the contract. The areas discussed in the following paragraphs should receive special consideration.

Prepayment and the Rule of 78.   Credit agreements will include a statement indicating how interest is to be calculated if you decide to repay the loan at any earlier date than scheduled. Agreements that utilize the add-on method for computing installment payments usually determine your interest refund by the so-called **rule of 78.** An example will show how this rule works to the lender's advantage. Suppose, as before, you have a $1,000 add-on loan for one year that carries total interest of $120. If you repaid the loan as scheduled you would make 12 monthly payments of $93.33 for total payments of $1,120.

Suppose that after making three payments you receive an unexpected amount of cash and you are considering using that cash to pay off your loan. How much interest will you save? You might guess $90, reasoning that interest is charged uniformly each month, in which case you would save 9/12 of the total (9/12 of $120 = $90). Good guess, but wrong. The rule of 78 allows lenders to earn interest at the quicker pace indicated by column 6 in Figure 7.7.

Under the rule of 78, the monthly interest earned by the lender is determined by the monthly interest factor in column 4. If we multiply the monthly interest factor by the total interest due on the scheduled loan, we can calculate the interest earned in each month in column 5. In Figure 7.7 the monthly interest factor

TABLE 7.4 · Two
Methods for Estimating
APR

APR = annual percentage rate $\\$ M = number of payment periods in one year $\\$ N = number of scheduled payments $\\$ C = dollar cost of credit $\\$ P = value of purchase financed	

Example: A $1,000 loan with add-on finance charges of $120 to be repaid in 12 monthly payments of $93.33.

Constant-Ratio Method	N-Ratio Method
$APR = \dfrac{2MC}{P(N + 1)}$	$APR = \dfrac{M(95N + 9)C}{12N(N + 1)(4P + C)}$
$= \dfrac{2 \times 12 \times 120}{1,000(12 + 1)}$	$= \dfrac{12 \times [(95 \times 12) + 9] \times 120}{12 \times 12 \times 13 \times (4,000 + 120)}$
$= \dfrac{2,880}{13,000}$	$= \dfrac{1,654,560}{7,712,640}$
$= 22.15\%$	$= 21.45\%$

for the third month is $^{10}/_{78}$. Therefore, the interest earned by the lender in the third month is $15.38 [($^{10}/_{78}$) × $120].

To determine the monthly interest factor we first add up the digits for the total number of payments on the loan. This is equal to the sum of the payment numbers in column 1 of Figure 7.7 ($1 + 2 + \cdots + 12 = 78$). For a one-year loan with monthly payments, the digits sum to 78. The sum of the digits (SD) for a loan of any number of years can be determined with the following formula:

$$SD = N\left(\frac{N + 1}{2}\right)$$

where N is equal to the number of months. For example, the sum of digits for a four-year loan is 1,176 [$48 \times (^{49}/_{2}) = 48 \times 24.5 = 1,176$].

The sum of the digits is the value in the denominator of the fraction in column 4 of Figure 7.7. To obtain the value in the numerator of the monthly interest factor we list the digits for the payments in reverse descending order. In reverse descending order the digits for the first payment would be 12, the second 11, and so on. Consequently, the interest earned by the lender in the first month equals $^{12}/_{78}$ of $120 ($18.46), and the interest earned in the second month equals $^{11}/_{78}$ of $120 ($16.92). To find the total interest earned by the lender through any payment month, as illustrated in column 6, we add up the monthly interest earned by the lender through the time of the loan payoff. For example, the total interest earned through month 3 is $50.77 ($18.46 + 16.92 + 15.38).

Loan payoff: The amount needed to eliminate your loan indebtedness during the term of the loan.

To calculate the **loan payoff** (the amount needed to eliminate the loan) at any point in time, you start with the original amount of the loan, excluding the add-on charge. To this amount you then add the interest the lender is entitled to receive, and subtract all payments you have made. In the current example, the loan payoff immediately following the third payment of $770.77 can be calculated as follows:

Original loan principle, excluding add-on interest:		$1,000.00
Interest owed lender: (total interest factor × add-on interest = $^{33}/_{78}$ × $120)		50.77
		$1,050.77
Less payments made to date: (3 × $99.33)		280.00
Loan payoff:		$770.77

You should always know your interest savings prior to a prepayment decision. If you do not prepay the loan, you have the opportunity of investing those funds elsewhere. It is optimal to repay the loan only if the interest savings on the loan exceed the value of your lost opportunities. The interest you would save by early repayment of the loan is listed in column 7 of Figure 7.7. It is equal to the add-on interest charge less the interest earned by the lender through the given point in time. In the current example, with repayment at the end of month 3, the interest saved is $69.34 ($120 − $50.77).

Of course, if you choose to pay off the loan, you will be giving up the opportunity of using those funds elsewhere. When the after-tax earnings on the alternative use of these funds exceeds the $69.23 in interest savings, you are better off not repaying the loan. For example, suppose you could invest these funds at an annual after-tax rate of 8 percent or 0.67 percent per month. We can estimate the return from the alternative use of these funds by first adding the cost of a monthly payment to the amount of the loan payoff and dividing the sum by 2. This approximates the average amount you would have in the investment ac-

FIGURE 7.7

A 12-month installment loan with an annual add-on interest rate of 12 percent. Initial amount refinanced = $1,000.

(1) Monthly Payment Number	(2) Monthly Payment	(3) Total Payments	(4) Monthly Interest Factor	(5) Monthly Interest Earned ($120 × Col. 4)	(6) Total Interest Earned	(7) Interest Refund ($120 − Col. 6)
1	$ 93.33	$ 93.33	12/78	$ 18.46	$ 18.46	$101.54
2	93.33	186.67	11/78	16.92	35.38	84.62
3	93.33	280.00	10/78	15.38	50.77	69.23
4	93.33	373.33	9/78	13.85	64.62	55.38
5	93.33	466.67	8/78	12.31	76.92	43.08
6	93.33	560.00	7/78	10.77	87.69	32.31
7	93.33	653.33	6/78	9.23	96.92	23.08
8	93.33	746.67	5/78	7.69	104.62	15.38
9	93.33	840.00	4/78	6.15	110.77	9.23
10	93.33	933.33	3/78	4.62	115.38	4.62
11	93.33	1,026.67	2/78	3.08	118.46	1.54
12	93.33	1,120.00	1/78	1.54	120.00	0.00
Totals 78	$1,120.00		1	$120.00		

Spending,
Borrowing,
and Saving

count over the remaining term of the loan (nine months), assuming you placed the required payoff amount of $770.78 in the fund and withdrew from it to make each monthly payment. This average balance is then multiplied by the rate of return earned over the investment period. In the current example the calculations are as follows:

$$\frac{\text{Loan payoff} + \text{monthly payment}}{2} = \text{average balance}$$

$$\frac{\$770.78 + 93.33}{2} = \$432.06$$

$$\text{Average balance} \times \frac{\text{after-tax}}{\text{monthly rate}} \times \text{months} = \text{return on investment}$$

$$\$432.06 \times 0.67\% \times 9 = \$26.05$$

Therefore, if we choose not to pay off the loan, we could earn $26.05 in additional investment income. However, this is less than the $69.23 we could save in interest charges. In this example, the best choice is early loan repayment.

The Acceleration Clause.   If you miss just one payment on a loan, the **acceleration clause** makes the entire unpaid balance due immediately. If you can't pay this entire amount, you stand a chance of having the loan collateral repossessed. Repossession is guided by state law, but it usually means the lender is free to sell the item for its best market price. From this amount are deducted any expenses connected with the sale, and the difference is applied to the credit balance. If it is greater, the lender remits the difference to the borrower; if it is less, the borrower is still required to pay the difference. Your main concern here is the price the lender receives in selling the repossessed item. Under forced sale conditions, it could be very low, and you bear the loss. Lenders do not usually apply the acceleration clause immediately, preferring instead to rely upon penalties for late payments, but it is not a factor to take casually.

The Add-on Clause.   Suppose you purchase some kitchen appliances from an appliance dealer and finance the deal with an installment loan for one year. Six months later you return to the same dealer and purchase a television set and tape recorder as part of an add-on to your earlier agreement. Eight months after that purchase, financial problems set in and you stop making payments on the loan. With an **add-on clause,** the dealer can repossess all the appliances he or she sold you, even though your total payments may have been more than enough to have paid for the earlier purchase. Fortunately, courts seldom enforce this clause.

The Balloon Payment.   The **balloon payment** is usually the last installment payment, and it is for an amount much greater than the other monthly payments. The problem with the balloon is that borrowers may not prepare sufficiently to make the payment, and so may require new financing when it is due or may have the item repossessed. Balloon clauses sometimes were used in the past as a means of defrauding borrowers, and this abuse led some states to make them illegal.

Acceleration clause: A late payment entitles the lender to demand that the entire unpaid balance be paid immediately.

Add-on clause: Allows the lender to repossess all goods financed under the agreement in the event of a missed payment.

Balloon payment: An amount larger than other periodic payments which is due as the last installment payment.

Consumer
Credit

Obtaining Credit and Resolving Credit Problems

Once you understand how credit works, the next step is to find a lender. After you are successful in arranging credit, the final step is to use it properly to avoid credit problems. Unfortunately, even the most financially prudent people can face these problems, and you should know how to deal with them.

Sources of Credit

There are many suppliers of credit, ranging from commercial banks at the top of a list to friends and relatives at the bottom. The discussion that follows will not attempt to explain detailed features of each but will focus instead on their most important characteristics. Comparative shopping is important in the credit market. We are in an era of volatile interest rates, and while it is true that similar lenders tend to charge about the same rates for similar loans, differences can exist. And don't underestimate the importance of saving 1 or 2 percent on the loan. For example, a 48-month installment loan for $5,000 will cost about $250 more at 16 percent than at 14 percent.

BANKING INSTITUTIONS Commercial banks, savings and loan associations, and credit unions all compete for your consumer credit dollar with similar offers. In addition to credit cards, these institutions generally provide revolving credit at lower interest rates in the form of overdraft protection credit lines, unsecured personal credit lines, and home equity credit lines.

Overdraft protection credit line: Credit is automatically extended to cover excess withdrawals from a checking account.

The financial institution where you have a checking account may offer your an **overdraft protection credit line.** If you write a check for an amount that exceeds the funds available, the bank automatically extends you a loan to cover the excess amount up to some predetermined credit limit. In addition to providing you with a convenient source of credit, the overdraft protection credit line has the advantage of saving you the embarrassment and cost of a bounced check.

Unsecured personal credit line: An unsecured credit line upon which you can withdraw cash.

An **unsecured personal credit line** is separate from your checking account. You must apply for it by submitting a loan application. After you are approved for an unsecured personal credit line, you access the credit line by writing specially issued checks or utilizing a special credit card. Each month you receive a statement indicated the amount you owe, the amount of credit still available, your finance charges, and your minimum monthly payment.

Home equity loan: A loan secured by the ownership in your home in the form of a second mortgage.

With a **home equity loan,** your credit is secured by your ownership in your home. Banks typically let you borrow up to 75 to 80 percent of the equity in your home. Home equity loans come in two forms, closed-end credit or open-end credit. With an *open-end home equity line of credit*, you can borrow up to a predetermined credit limit on a revolving charge account. A *closed-end home equity loan* is the same as a second mortgage on your home. You borrow a fixed amount for a set period of time.

Home equity loans have become extremely popular because interest charges on home equity loans up to $100,000 may be taken as an itemized deduction on federal income tax returns. Interest payments on all other consumer loans are presently nondeductible. Moreover, home equity loans are typically available at much lower interest rates than other consumer loans. In addition, loan repayment may be stretched out over many years, producing small monthly payments. On the negative side, home equity loans may entice some consumers into making long-term payments on purchases that provide short-lived satisfaction.

Early Redemption of a Certificate of Deposit: An Alternative Source of Funds

Certificates of deposit at banking institutions often represent an attractive short-term investment; they are essentially riskless when federally insured, and they often pay rates of return exceeding those on savings and money market accounts. The downside, of course, is that in a credit crunch you may find that you need to redeem a certificate of deposit before it has matured. When this occurs, most banks will levy a six-month interest penalty upon early withdrawal. This can amount to a significant dollar loss. For example, on a $10,000 CD at an APR of 8 percent, the interest penalty would equal $400.

The same bank that issued the CD may offer you a better alternative. Many banks will provide you with a personal loan secured by the CD. The APR on the CD-secured personal loan is often dependent on the rate you are earning on the CD. Some banks extend such secured loans at an interest rate 2 percentage points above the rate on the CD. If the rate you are earning on the certificate of deposit is 8 percent, then the rate on the personal loan would be 10 percent. The net interest rate on the loan principal after deducting interest income on the CD would equal only 2 percent.

In the present example, the interest penalty for early redemption on a $10,000 certificate is $400. The annual net interest charge on a $10,000 loan secured by the CD would equal $200 per year ($1,000 in interest paid minus $800 in interest earned). If the CD matures in the next two years, or if other funding becomes available within that time frame, then net interest charges on a loan would be less than the interest penalty on early redemption, making the loan the better alternative. The consideration of taxes can slightly complicate this analysis. Interest earned is taxable, and interest penalties are tax deductible.

CONSUMER FINANCE COMPANIES   There are two types of consumer finance companies: those that offer specialized loans, such as GMAC on General Motors automobiles, and those that offer general-purpose loans, both secured and unsecured. The specialized lenders are very dominant forces within their particular areas, and they usually offer interest rates at or below bank rates. Sometimes they are substantially below bank rates when they are part of auto dealers' sales promotion programs. Of course, the question then is whether you are getting the best price on the item purchased. Try to bring financing into the discussion as a separate topic after the price has been agreed upon. The objective is to get the best price *and* the best financing.

The general-purpose consumer finance companies are more willing to loan to first-time borrowers and to make loans on unsecured terms. Their administrative costs tend to be higher because they make many small loans, and their delinquency costs are also higher because of the poorer quality of the loans they make. As a result of these factors, you can expect their interest rates to be higher on these kinds of loans, but they may be competitive with higher-quality loans.

OTHER SOURCES   Some sources are not typical lenders to consumers but are nevertheless important. You can borrow on your ordinary life insurance policy up to its loan value, usually at a rate that could be far lower than any other available rate if the policy is older than, say, ten years. These loans are exceptionally easy to make, requiring you to do nothing more than write a letter. And you never have to repay them, but, of course, if you die your beneficiaries will receive only the face value of the policy less the amount of the loan outstanding. Insurance companies very often emphasize this fact to persuade you not to borrow in the first place or to repay any outstanding loans. Actually, a loan on your life insurance policy offers no greater hardship to your heirs than any other loan outstanding at your death. They all must be repaid, and it makes no sense to single one out and argue that it should be repaid before the others.

If you own stocks or bonds, you should consider using them as collateral for a loan. A bank will accept securities as collateral, or you can open a margin account with a stock brokerage firm. In either case, you can usually borrow up to 50 percent of the market value of the securities pledged. The interest rate on such a loan will probably be one to two points above the prime rate (the rate a bank charges its most creditworthy customer). This arrangement can be risky in a volatile market. Should the market price of the stocks fall, you may get a call for additional collateral. If you fail to provide the requested funds, the broker may force the sale of your stocks at a market low.

If you are really desperate and have something of value, consider a pawnshop. Pawnbrokers are willing to make loans on practically any item they feel can be resold if you fail to reclaim it after a specified period of time, usually 60 to 90 days. You will be able to borrow only a fraction of the item's market value and can expect to pay the very highest interest rates allowed. While they are bad places to borrow, they can be good places to buy if you are willing to take some risks on product quality and service.

As a last (or maybe first) resort, friends and relatives might extend credit to you. Before taking this alternative, bear in mind that credit misunderstandings have ended many friendships. The best advice if you do borrow (or lend) is to put the arrangement in writing, complete with all pertinent details that are found on other credit contracts. A "pay-me-back-when-you-can" loan is bad for both the borrower and the lender, because neither then knows how to budget for the loan. Also, remember that if either borrower or lender dies, heirs will be left to resolve the loan. While you may know and trust each other, your heirs may not.

A Credit Management Strategy

If your financial life is just beginning, you may be satisfied to simply get credit wherever you can. That situation doesn't last long, however, and as your assets and income grow, so does your access to credit. Now your problem is to use credit discriminatingly, and you will be better able to do so if you have an overall approach—that is, a strategy—for managing credit. Credit management is similar in many respects to cash management, discussed in the previous chapter. There, the objective was to maximize the return on short-term investments while achieving a reasonable degree of liquidity. Here, the objective is to minimize the cost of credit while simultaneously achieving both the target amount needed and a reasonable level of shopping convenience. Since we differ in how much credit we want and in our attitude toward convenience, our strategies for managing credit will also differ. But the following guidelines apply in most cases.

1. Use as much of the grace period as you can, and do not pay bills until the last allowable day. You can thus keep your money in an interest-earning account longer than if you pay bills with cash.

2. Do not have revolving charge accounts, or if you have one, use it as a 30-day account. We mentioned previously that most often this is expensive credit, and it should be used only if other credit is unavailable.

3. Take a broad view toward credit; that is, do not think in terms of borrowing here to buy this or borrowing there to buy that, but think instead of a total borrowing requirement. Then, search for the cheapest sources of credit to meet this requirement. For example, you might take a home equity mortgage on your home and with it buy a car, send your kid to summer camp, and enjoy a vacation. The interest on this loan could be far less than an installment loan on the car and personal loans for the other two activities—and no riskier.

4. Be careful of variable-rate loans if you think that interest rates may rise. The initial interest rate on a variable-rate loan is lower than on a fixed-rate loan. The variable rate, however, is indexed to other market rates of interest and automatically rises as they do. Without a cap on how high the rate may rise, you may wind up making much higher monthly payments than you expected. Under all circumstances you should try to avoid getting into a vicious credit cycle. This occurs when the interest payments on the debt become a burden, forcing you to search for other sources of credit just to repay the previous debt. Keeping track of your personal debt ratios can help you avoid this trap.

Resolving Credit Problems

The easiest way to resolve a credit problem is not to let it begin in the first place. This means limiting your credit to an amount your income can support. Credit counselors often feel this limit is about 20 percent of your take-home pay for consumer credit, not including your home mortgage. The 20 percent is applied in two ways: First, your monthly credit payments should not exceed 20 percent of your monthly take-home pay; and second, your total consumer credit should not exceed 20 percent of your total take-home pay for the year. If you exceed either one of these limits, you are courting financial danger. You can keep credit within the 20 percent limit by always figuring the impact of any new credit arrangement on your budget *before* you make a loan. If it does not fit in the budget then, it won't fit later, either.

Despite all precautions, you may still run into credit problems. If you do, the first step is to seek outside help. If that fails, you may have to consider bankruptcy. Also, the law entitles you to protection from lender harassment while you are having credit difficulties, or at any time, for that matter.

CREDIT COUNSELING You cannot resolve a credit problem by avoiding lenders. As a first step you should explain the nature of your problem to them and try to get their cooperation while you attempt to remedy the situation. Most lenders prefer being repaid in full, even if extra time is needed, rather than forcing you into bankruptcy, where they may collect only a fraction of their loans. Recognizing their common interest in helping troubled borrowers, many lenders support the activities of **credit counseling** services, over 200 of which are sponsored by

Credit counseling: Helps consumers with credit problems by rescheduling loans and eliminating negative behaviors.

the National Foundation for Consumer Credit. These counseling centers provide two levels of service. First, they work with the borrower to help him or her develop a reasonable plan for repaying debts. This plan often includes a budget. Second, if this budget indicates that income will not be sufficient to meet both living expenses and the existing debt repayment load, the counselor will work out a new plan between the borrower and lenders, with a new repayment schedule. The borrower then gives the counselor a certain percentage of each week's income, and this in turn is given to the lenders. This service is essentially free to borrowers, regardless of their income, as are other counseling services. If you have a credit problem, contact the Better Business Bureau or the Chamber of Commerce in your town, and inquire about credit counseling assistance. By all means, though, avoid any private credit counselor who supposedly specializes in working out your credit problems. The fee for this service can be as high as 35 percent of your total debt.

Action Plan for the Steeles Credit Card Balances

Background   The Steeles had every intention of paying their credit card balance each month. However, given unexpected medical and auto bills, their monthly income in some months has fallen behind their monthly cash outflow. They dealt with these intermittent cash crunches by making the minimum payment on their credit card and letting the outstanding balance grow.

The Problem   The Steeles currently have an outstanding credit card balance of $1,720. With a 19 percent APR, their monthly finance charge is now up to $27.23. Moreover, future purchases may push them over the credit card limit of $3,000, in which case they would have to pay an overlimit fee of $10. They would like to reduce their credit card balances, but are not sure how best to go about it.

The Plan   The Steeles should immediately pay off the outstanding balance on the credit card. The monthly finance fee of $27.23 may not sound like a lot of money, but it adds up to $326.76 a year. Credit cards typically represent high-cost credit. The Steeles can eliminate their credit card debt either by substituting lower-cost credit or by utilizing some of their liquid assets. They are likely to save money either way. The worst strategy is to do nothing and simply make the minimum payment on the outstanding debt.

In the future, the Steeles should try to improve their budgeting by estimating medical and auto expenses more generously. Unfortunately, there will always be some unexpected expenses. The family's liquid assets held as an emergency fund can be used to cover such unanticipated and unusual needs. By avoiding expensive debt that drains future income and managing the cost of debt more effectively, the Steeles will avoid a major financial planning pitfall.

The Rationale   If the Steeles decide to substitute lower-cost debt, there are numerous choices open to them. Obvious sources for families like the Steeles

Spending,
Borrowing,
and Saving

BANKRUPTCY   Over one-half million Americans file bankruptcy each year. Many people continue to regard bankruptcy as a calamity to be avoided at any cost. Others view it as an easy way to avoid all the bills that result from an enjoyable buying binge. Regardless of your viewpoint, bankruptcy is a serious step, and you should seek credit counseling before taking it. We cannot cover the whole scope of the bankruptcy act in this introductory text, but you should know certain general facts.

You can file for bankruptcy under either Chapter 7 of the bankruptcy code, called a straight bankruptcy, or under Chapter 13 of the bankruptcy code, called a wage earner plan. In most instances, neither can be used to avoid payments for alimony, child support, or taxes.

Over 70 percent of personal bankruptcies are filed under Chapter 7 as **straight bankruptcies**. This discharges all of your debts and thus provides you a fresh start. A straight bankruptcy may require you to sell off most of your assets. However,

Straight bankruptcy: A Chapter 7 bankruptcy in which most assets are sold off, most debts are discharged, and a fresh start is provided.

include home equity loans, insurance loans, loans on retirement accounts, margin loans on stocks, and checking account overdrafts.

They could even consider utilizing the 42-month CD that is about to mature. If they turn in the CD before maturity, their bank will levy a six-month interest penalty. However, they can avoid this penalty by using the CD as collateral for a personal loan. The bank that issued the CD will offer them such a loan at two points above the rate paid on the CD. On an 8 percent CD the bank will charge a 10 percent APR, a rate significantly below that charged on the credit card.

Using liquid assets to pay off the credit card debt is also a wise choice when the interest you save is more than the interest you lose on your depleted assets. When undertaking this analysis, you must remember that interest charges on consumer debt are paid out of after-tax dollars, whereas investments generate dollars on which taxes are due. Therefore, the best use of your funds will depend on a comparison of the after-tax interest rate on your debt and the before-tax interest rate on your investments. Given the interest rate on consumer debt, the following formula can be used to find the equivalent before-tax rate:

$$\text{Equivalent before tax interest rate} = \frac{\text{Interest rate on consumer debt}}{1 - \text{marginal tax rate}}$$

$$26.39\% = \frac{19\%}{1 - 0.28}$$

The marginal tax rate is the fractional amount of any additional dollar of income that must be paid in taxes. In the Steeles' 28 percent marginal tax bracket, they would have to achieve a before-tax return of 26.39 percent in order to earn an after-tax return of 19 percent. If you also take the potential overlimit charge into account, the necessary before-tax rate would be even greater. Since they are not earning this high a return on any of their investments, using savings to reduce their credit card debt is a cost-saving choice.

you are not left a complete pauper, and in most cases few assets are actually sold. Under federal exemptions, which may be more or less generous than state laws permit, you may keep from creditors $7,500 of equity in your home and about $3,000 in other specific assets. These exemptions are for each individual, and therefore double for a married couple.

If you have been through a straight bankruptcy, you cannot file again for another six years, and the record of the bankruptcy remains on your credit report for ten years. During this period it may be difficult for you to get credit or enter into normal everyday contracts such as rental agreements or purchase contracts. It may even hurt your employment prospects if potential employers access your credit records.

Under a Chapter 13 filing, the court creates a **wage earner plan.** This is a court-approved and -administered repayment schedule for employed persons with regular income. This allows debtors to retain their property and to repay all or part of their obligations over a three- to five-year period with protection from creditors. It will remain on your credit report for seven years. On the plus side, it indicates that by filing under Chapter 13 rather than Chapter 7, you made a sincere attempt to repay your debts.

To stem the rising tide of bankruptcies, significant changes were made on the bankruptcy laws in 1984. First, petitioners must now list their current income and expenses, and judges can dismiss petitions that, in their view, represent ''substantial abuses'' of the system. However, since the law does not spell out what abuses are, this has not been vigorously applied. Second, not all debts may be discharged in a Chapter 7 filing. Income taxes, child support payments, debts incurred in anticipation of bankruptcy, and damage awards to accident victims may all survive bankruptcy proceedings.

Fair Debt Collection Practices Act: Limits the tactics that creditors may employ in attempting to collect overdue loans.

PROTECTION FROM LENDER HARASSMENT   The **Fair Debt Collection Practices Act,** passed on March 20, 1978, entitles borrowers to be treated fairly by debt collectors. You are entitled to a written notice from the debt collector describing your debt in detail and what to do if you feel you do not owe the debt. You then have 30 days to send a letter to the debt collector denying the debt. The debt collector cannot continue collection efforts until you receive a written verification of the debt. Among other things, the debt collector cannot use abusive language, threaten you, harass you at work, or attempt to collect the bill through trickery. Finally, you can keep a debt collector from communicating with you by providing written notification that all contacts must cease.

A Summary of Federal Credit Legislation

We have alluded to most of the federal legislation in consumer credit as we discussed the various topics in this chapter. However, it is helpful at the end to have a summary of this legislation and, more importantly, to show the governing agencies that can assist you with a credit problem. Table 7.5 presents this summary. Along this line, you should also see the *Helpful Reading* section at the end of this chapter for publications that thoroughly explain your rights under these laws. Many of these publications are free.

TABLE 7.5 · U.S. Credit Legislation

ACT (Date Effective)	Major Provisions	Governing Agencies
Truth in Lending (July 1, 1969)	■ Provides specific cost disclosure requirements for the annual percentage rate and the finance charge as a dollar amount ■ Requires disclosure of other loan terms and conditions ■ Regulates the advertising of credit terms ■ Provides the right to cancel a contract when certain real estate is used as security	The following federal agencies are responsible for enforcing all of these Acts. The agency to contact for information or in case of a complaint depends on the particular creditor involved.
(January 25, 1971)	■ Prohibits credit card issuers from sending unrequested cards ■ Limits a cardholder's liability for unauthorized use of a card to $50	Store or business:
(October 1, 1982)	■ Requires disclosures for closed-end credit (installment credit) be written in plain English and appear apart from all other information ■ Allows credit customer to request an itemization of the amount financed, if the creditor does not automatically provide it	■ If a retail store, department store, consumer finance company, gasoline credit card, travel and entertainment card, or a state-chartered credit union is involved, contact one of the FTC regional offices, or Federal Trade Commission, (name of the Act), Washington, DC 20580.
Fair Credit Reporting Act (April 24, 1971)	■ Requires disclosure to consumers of the name and address of any consumer reporting agency which supplied reports used to deny credit, insurance or employment ■ Gives a consumer the right to know what is in his file, have incorrect information reinvestigated and removed, and include his version of a disputed item in the file ■ Requires credit reporting agencies to send the consumer's version of a disputed item to certain businesses or creditors ■ Sets forth identification requirements for consumers wishing to inspect their files ■ Requires that consumers be notified when an investigative report is being made ■ Limits the time certain information can be kept in a credit file	If a bank is involved, contact one of the following: ■ If it is a nationally chartered bank, contact: Comptroller of the Currency, Consumer Affairs Division, Washington, DC 20219. ■ If it is a state-chartered bank and a member of the Federal Reserve System, contact: Board of Governors of the Federal Reserve System, Division of Consumer Affairs, Washington, DC 20551. ■ If it is a state-chartered bank and is insured by the Federal Deposit Insurance Corporation, but is *not* a member of the Federal Reserve System, contact: Federal Deposit Insurance Corporation, Office of Bank Consumer Affairs, Washington, DC 20429.
Fair Credit Billing Act (October 28, 1975)	■ Establishes procedures for consumers and creditors to follow when billing errors occur on periodic statements for revolving credit accounts ■ Requires creditors to send a statement setting forth these procedures to consumers periodically ■ Allows consumers to withhold payment for faulty or defective goods or services (within certain limitations) when purchased with a credit card ■ Requires creditor to promptly credit customers' accounts and to return overpayments if requested	■ If a federally chartered or federally insured (FSLIC) savings and loan association is involved, contact: Federal Home Loan Bank Board, Washington, DC 20552. ■ If a federally chartered credit union is involved, contact: National Credit Union Administration, Division of Consumer Affairs, Washington, DC 20456.
Equal Credit Opportunity Act (October 28, 1975)	■ Prohibits credit discrimination based on sex and marital status ■ Prohibits creditors from requiring women to reapply for credit upon a change in marital status ■ Requires creditors to inform applicants of acceptance or rejection of their credit application within 30 days of receiving a completed application ■ Requires creditors to provide a written statement of the reasons for adverse action	On a state level, contact: ■ The Attorney General's Office ■ State Banking Department
(March 23, 1977)	■ Prohibits credit discrimination based on race, national origin, religion, age, or the receipt of public assistance	
(June 1, 1977)	■ Requires creditors to report information on an account to credit bureaus in the names of both husband and wife if both use the account and both are liable for it	

TABLE 7.5 · U.S. Credit Legislation

ACT (Date Effective)	Major Provisions	Governing Agencies
Fair Debt Collection Practices Act (March 20, 1978)	■ Prohibits abusive, deceptive, and unfair practices by debt collectors ■ Establishes procedures for debt collectors contacting a credit user ■ Restricts debt collector contacts with a third party ■ Specifies that payment for several debts be applied as the consumer wishes and that no monies be applied to a debt in dispute	
Home Equity Loan Consumer Protection Act (June 7, 1989)	■ Requires creditors to provide consumers with extensive information on open-end credit plans secured by the consumer's dwelling, and imposes substantive limitations on these plans ■ Information must be provided at time of application on payment terms, fees imposed under the plan, and for variable rate loans, information about the index and a 15-year history of the changes in the index ■ Limits the type of index that can be used for variable rate plans ■ Limits the creditor's rights to terminate a plan and accelerate repayment of any outstanding balance	
Fair Credit and Charge Card Disclosure Act (April 3, 1989)	■ Requires credit and charge card issuers to provide disclosures to consumers in solicitations and applications ■ Renewal notices including credit disclosures must be provided before fees are imposed to renew credit and charge card accounts	

SOURCE: Adapted from Money Management Institute, *Managing Your Credit*, 1986, pp. 36, 37, with update by authors.

Summary

Most people use credit every day, but effective use requires both planning and management. You must balance credit's advantages and disadvantages in deciding whether or not to use it, and you may have to take special steps to begin a credit record. Once you begin using credit, a credit bureau will maintain your credit history and will send credit reports to all lenders to whom you apply for credit. You have the right to review your credit history and should do so periodically to insure its accuracy.

Sales credit is supplied by merchants, banks, and other institutions in the form of charge accounts and installment contracts, while cash credit refers to money borrowed rather than borrowing as a result of a purchase. Major sources of credit in the United States are banking institutions, consumer finance companies, and credit unions. Other sources are ordinary life insurance policies, margin accounts with stockbrokerage firms, pawnshops, and friends and relatives. In using all these sources, it is wise to have a credit management strategy. Despite prudence and caution, credit problems can still arise. If they do, a first step is to seek the assistance of a credit counselor; a final step is filing bankruptcy. You are given certain legal protections against lender harassment during periods when repaying debts is difficult.

Key Terms

acceleration clause (p. 207)

add-on clause (p. 207)

add-on method (p. 202)

adjusted balance method (p. 191)

annual percentage rate (APR) (p. 204)

average daily balance method (p. 191)

balloon payment (p. 207)

bank credit cards (p. 193)

cash credit (p. 201)

chargeback (p. 200)

closed-end account
(p. 189)

credit counseling (p. 211)

credit history (p. 187)

credit limit (p. 191)

credit report (p. 188)

debit card (p. 196)

discount method (p. 202)

Equal Credit Opportunity
Act (ECOA) (p. 186)

Fair Credit Reporting Act
of 1971 (p. 188)

Fair Debt Collection
Practices Act (p. 214)

home equity loan (p. 208)

grace period (p. 192)

loan payoff (p. 205)

open-end account (p. 189)

overdraft protection credit
line (p. 208)

previous balance method
(p. 191)

promissory note (p. 201)

regular charge account
(p. 189)

retail installment contract
(p. 201)

revolving credit account
(p. 190)

rule of 78 (p. 204)

sales credit (p. 189)

secured credit card
(p. 189)

security agreement
(p. 201)

service credit (p. 180)

simple interest method
(p. 202)

straight bankruptcy
(p. 213)

travel and entertainment
(T&E) cards (p. 195)

Truth in Lending Act
(TILA) (p. 184)

unsecured personal credit
line (p. 208)

wage earner plan (p. 214)

Problems and Review Questions

1 Explain how credit serves as: (*a*) a shopping convenience; (*b*) a means to increase total consumption benefits; (*c*) a hedge against inflation; and (*d*) a source of emergency funds. What are several disadvantages of credit?

2 Describe the three C's of credit and why lenders feel they are important in evaluating a loan request. Then list five steps you can take to begin a credit record; list three extra steps that might be necessary if you are a woman.

3 What function does the credit bureau perform in the lender's evaluation of your credit application?

4 Shirley Szczesniak uses her credit card to purchase gasoline each month. She drives her car a lot and buys about 100 gallons a month. She has been paying about $.90 a gallon lately but notices that if she paid with cash, she could save three cents a gallon. Would you advise Shirley to use cash or continue using her card? Explain.

5 Is a credit card about the same thing as a debit card? Explain.

6 List steps you can take to protect yourself against credit card fraud.

7 Suppose you review your monthly statement of credit card activities and discover you have been charged for an item you didn't buy. Explain in detail what you should do.

8 Describe the information a lender must provide you on a credit contract. Why should you be particularly concerned about the following items: (*a*) the rule of 78, (*b*) the acceleration clause, (*c*) the add-on clause, and (*d*) a balloon payment?

9 Explain several steps you can take to avoid credit problems.

10 If a good friend of yours has had serious financial misfortunes lately and is unable to meet her debt payments, what advice would you give? Be sure to include the topic of bankruptcy, since she has heard that it eliminates all your credit problems. In your discussion, distinguish between straight bankruptcy and a wage earner plan.

11 Indicate the actions you should take if you are denied credit or employment because of an unfavorable credit report.

Consumer
Credit

12 Which method for determining the outstanding balance on a revolving credit account is likely to determine the lowest outstanding balance? Which method is likely to determine the highest outstanding balance?

13 Under what circumstances would you decide to obtain a credit card with a lower APR but a higher annual maintenance fee?

14 Suppose you were deciding whether or not to prepay a loan. Discuss the important facts that must be taken into consideration in order to make the least-cost decision.

15 Explain why home equity loans have become an important source of consumer credit.

Case 7.1
Should the Caseys Use Credit?

Mike and Helen Casey are a young couple, married about four years. They have no debts other than the usual monthly bills such as gas and electricity, the telephone, and newspapers. Both Mike and Helen work, and their combined incomes are quite good. Their approach to personal financial management has been to avoid all consumer credit, which they felt was the safest way to stay within their budget. However, they are beginning to wonder if this is really the correct approach. For one thing, all their friends have a number of credit cards they use frequently, and they also appear to make most of their major purchases with installment credit. For another, using cash all the time is often inconvenient, particularly when they are away from home and merchants are reluctant to accept their personal checks.

The Caseys are considering using credit extensively. To start, they think they might open regular charge accounts with local stores where they shop regularly. By doing so, they probably would put about $300 a month on this credit and be able to defer payment for an average of 30 days. Second, they would like to buy some furniture and major appliances in the upcoming year that will cost $4,000. They had initially vetoed this idea, preferring instead to wait until the following year, when Helen expects to receive a distribution from her deceased grandmother's estate. Now they are not so sure this is a good idea, because they believe that by waiting one year, they may have to pay 8 percent more for the same items. If they wish to buy now, they can obtain a personal cash loan for one year at 15 percent simple interest.

Questions

1 Would you advise the Caseys to open the regular accounts where they intend to spend $300 a month? Explain if they will save (or earn) any money by doing so.

2 If the Caseys are in a 28 percent tax bracket, do you think they should buy now, using the personal cash loan, or should they wait one year?

3 Assume the Caseys have $4,000 in an investment fund (earning 9 percent interest), which they could use without impairing their liquidity position. Explain whether you think they should buy now instead of waiting; and if they buy now, should they use the cash loan, or withdraw the funds from their savings account?

Case 7.2
Evaluating Nancy Tai's Revolving Account

Nancy Tai has recently opened a revolving charge account with MasterCard. Her credit limit is $1,000, but she has not charged that much since opening the account. Nancy hasn't had the time to review her monthly statements promptly as she should, but over the upcoming weekend she plans to catch up on her work.

In reviewing October's statement she notices that her beginning balance was $600 and that she made a $200 payment on November 10. She also charged purchases of $80 on November 5, $100 on November 15, and $50 on November 30. She can't tell how much interest she paid in November because she spilled a watercolor paint on that portion of the statement. She does remember, though, seeing the letters APR and the number 16 percent. Also, reading the back of her statement indicates interest was charged using the average daily balance method, including current purchases, which considers the day of a charge or credit.

Questions

1 Assuming a 30-day period in November, calculate November's interest. Also, calculate the interest she would have paid with: (a) the previous balance method; (b) the adjusted balance method.
2 Going back in time to when Nancy was just about to open her account, and assuming she could choose among credit sources that offered the different monthly balance determinations, and assuming further that Nancy would increase her outstanding balance over time, which credit source would you recommend? Explain.
3 In talking with Nancy, you have learned that she can also get credit through her credit union. An advertisement from the union shows that Nancy could take a personal cash loan at 14 percent on a discount basis or an installment loan at 12 percent add-on. Each is a one-year loan. Would you advise Nancy to use one of these to pay off her November 30 balance with MasterCard? (Assume the 14 and 12 percents are not APRs.) Nancy doesn't believe she will have enough funds to reduce the November balance until the end of next October.

Helpful Reading

Canner, Glenn B., Wayne C. Cook, and Nellie D. Middleton. "Payment of Household Debts," *Federal Reserve Bulletin*, April 1991, pp. 218–229.

DeMong, R. F., and J. H. Lindgren, Jr. "Home Equity Lending: Trends and Analysis," *Journal of Retail Banking*, Vol. 10, No. 4 (Winter 1990), pp. 41–44.

Federal Deposit Insurance Corporation, Office of Consumer Affairs. *Fair Credit Reporting Act: Your Rights.*

Federal Trade Commission, Bureau of Consumer Protection. *Credit Cards: Auto Repair Protection.*

Federal Trade Commission, Bureau of Consumer Protection. *Fair Debt Collection.*

Kowalewski, K. J. "Recent Changes in Consumer Bankruptcy Laws," *Economic Commentary*, Federal Reserve Bank of Cleveland, February 1, 1985.

Luckett, Charles. "Personal Bankruptcies," *Federal Reserve Bulletin*, September 1988, pp. 591–603.

Federal Reserve Publications

Copies of the following pamphlets are available upon request from Publications Services, Division of Support Services, Board of Governors of the Federal Reserve System, Washington, DC 20551.

What Truth in Lending Means to You

If You Borrow to Buy Stock

How to File a Consumer Credit Complaint

The Equal Credit Opportunity Act and . . . Age

The Equal Credit Opportunity Act and . . . Women

The Equal Credit Opportunity Act and . . . Doctors, Lawyers, Small Retailers

The Equal Credit Opportunity Act and . . . Credit Rights in Housing

Fair Credit Billing

Truth in Leasing

If You Use a Credit Card

Alice in Debitland: Consumer Protections and the Electronic Fund Transfer Act

Consumer Handbook to Credit Protection Laws

Helpful Contacts

Bankcard Holders of America, 460 Spring Park Place, Suite 1000, Herndon, VA 22070. Information of secured credit cards for a small fee. Mediates disputes between members and creditors.

National Foundation of Consumer Credit. Call 800–388–2227 for a member consumer credit counseling office near you.

Chapter 8

Consumer Durables: Satisfying Your Continuing Needs

Objectives

1 To estimate the replacement cost for consumer durables
2 To evaluate trade-offs between purchase price and cost of operations
3 To describe the characteristics of warranties
4 To obtain information on new and used car prices
5 To calculate the cost of owning and operating an automobile
6 To explain the complaint process for correcting auto defects
7 To state your rights under lemon laws

Alabama's highest court has upheld a jury award of damages for "mental anguish" in a lemon law case involving a Volkswagen Scirocco. This is believed to be the first such award in a breach of warranty case involving an automobile. Usually, only damages for "loss of value" to the vehicle are allowed. But of even greater importance is the potential for broad application of the ruling because the Alabama lemon law is part of the Uniform Commercial Code, accepted in 49 states.

The decision by Supreme Court Justice Gorman Houston resulted from an appeal by Volkswagen of America Inc. against a jury verdict in favor of Edwin O. Dillard, the owner of the Scirocco.

Dillard was awarded $7,000 in damages for loss of value to the vehicle and $8,000 "compensatory damages for mental anguish." The sole issue in VW's appeal was awarding damages for mental anguish in a lemon law case. There was no dispute over the facts of the case.

In July 1988, Dillard bought a new 1987 VW Scirocco. His records show 21 repair attempts during the first year and a half. Court records describe the primary problem as an erratic "hesitation, stalling, jerking," so Dillard had to exercise extra caution in entering traffic. Sometimes, the car "died" and had to be pushed. Sometimes, the exhaust was so dense that changing lanes was an adventure. Dillard said he had "near misses" that frightened and worried him.

Houston noted that state Supreme Court has traditionally recognized an exception to the general rule that damages for mental anguish cannot be awarded in ordinary breach of contract cases. That exception is "where the contractual duty or obligation is so coupled with matters of mental concern or solicitude with the feelings of the party to whom the duty is owed, that a breach of that duty will necessarily or reasonably result in mental anguish or suffering."

In the VW case, the court said the breach of warranty had caused Dillard "to suffer anxiety, embarrassment, anger, fear, frustration, disappointment and worry (not to mention the undisputed facts that the automobile has not been reliable or dependable and has not provided him with safe transportation)."

Consumer durables: Consumer goods that provide benefits that extend over a period of at least one year.

In this chapter we will examine those major family purchases called **consumer durables,** which may be strictly defined as goods that provide consumer benefits over a period of at least one year. The possession of such goods makes possible our high standard of living. However, owning consumer durables can also result in the unfortunate consequences described above.

Consumer Durables and the Household Budget

Table 8.1 shows personal consumer expenditures for the ownership and operation of consumer durables. Purchases of consumer durables compose about 14 percent of all consumer expenditures, consisting primarily of expenditures on the purchase of motor vehicles, and of furniture and household equipment. The cost of operating motor vehicles adds an additional 9 percent of consumer expenditures. Therefore, the average family spends about 23 percent of its total budget on either the ownership or operation of these goods. Because this category of goods represents a significant share of household expenditures, consumer durables deserve special consideration in our examination of personal finance.

Budgeting Considerations

Consumer durables create special budgeting problems. Expenditures on these items are typically not uniform over time. Without adequate planning, repair or

TABLE 8.1 · Average Annual Expenditures by Urban Consumer Units, 1991 Dollars

Item	Expenditure		Percent of Total Expenditure
Household expenditures		$29,824	100.0%
Household furnishings and appliances:			
Housefurnishings and equipment	$1,267		4.2%
Television, radios, and sound equipment	471		1.6%
Total		1,739	5.8%
Cost of owning and operating motor vehicles:			
Purchase	2,455		8.2%
Finance charges	345		1.2%
Insurance	562		1.9%
Gasoline and motor oil	1,023		3.4%
Maintenance and repair	562		1.9%
Rental, licenses, and other charges	196		0.7%
Total		5,143	17.2%
Total expenditures on household consumer durables and automobiles		$ 6,882	23.1%

SOURCE: U.S. Department of Labor, *Consumer Expenditure Survey, 1987*, Bulletin 2354, June 1990, Updated to 1991 prices by the authors.

replacement is likely to be an unexpected event that creates havoc with the household budget. In addition, replacement cost tends to be inadequately anticipated. Since most of us purchase a car or a refrigerator only once every few years, we don't keep track of changing prices. *Sticker shock* results when we realize how much we must now spend for replacement. An associated effect is called **savings illusion.** As our savings accumulate, we feel wealthier. But when the time comes to replace a major purchase, we find out that we are not really any better off. All we actually have been doing is accumulating funds to replace those consumer goods that have worn out.

Savings illusion: The failure to take recent price increases into account, thus creating an overestimate of our real wealth.

Another unique characteristic of a consumer durable is that it gives rise to multiple entries on the household budget. A product that is purchased with savings is listed as an expense at the time of purchase. If it is financed through borrowing, however, it will create inflexible future expenses until the loan is repaid. The continuing outflow required for maintenance and operations must also be budgeted. These future expenses will most likely show up in separate household accounts for maintenance, utilities, and fuels.

To prepare the master budget properly, we must estimate the cost of maintenance and operations. This estimate usually can be based upon the previous year's total with an adjustment for inflation. Of course, when you purchase a new product, you must either guess at these figures or rely on data supplied by the manufacturer or the government. These data will be discussed later in the chapter.

Replacement Cost

The cost of replacing a consumer durable can be financed either through accumulated savings or through borrowing. The previous chapter described how to decide whether to borrow or to use savings. If using your own savings appears the wiser alternative, estimating future replacement costs will help eliminate savings illusion.

Replacement cost: The cost of replacing new for old.

To estimate **replacement cost,** you will need three pieces of information: the expected date of replacement, the expected rate of inflation, and the present cost of replacement. Figure 8.1 contains service-life estimates for several major home appliances. By subtracting the age of your current appliances from these estimates, you can arrive at your expected time before replacement. For items that are not on this list, you will have to base your estimate upon the products' current working condition. In any case, these are only averages. If you take special care of your goods, the realized service life may be longer.

A slightly different method may be used for estimating replacement cost on your auto. Because most of us do not hold a car until it must necessarily be replaced, start with your own typical holding period. If you are replacing a used car, you will also need to know the trade-in value n that car to estimate net replacement cost, which is the purchase price of the new car minus the trade-in value of the old car. Table 8.2 contains estimates of the price of a used car as a percentage of the price of a similar model new car. The percentages were calculated by the Federal Highway Association based upon data supplied by the National Automobile Dealers Association (N.A.D.A.) for representative American-made cars. Multiplying the appropriate percentage by the expected value of a similar new car will provide an approximate trade-in value. This only a very rough estimate. If you would like to find out how your particular make or model is likely to hold its value, you might look at how similar makes and models in

FIGURE 8.1

Service-life estimates for major home appliances. (Source: Marilyn Doss Ruffin, "Consumer Appliance Decisions: Using Energy Labels," *Family Economics Review*, Summer 1978, p. 12.)

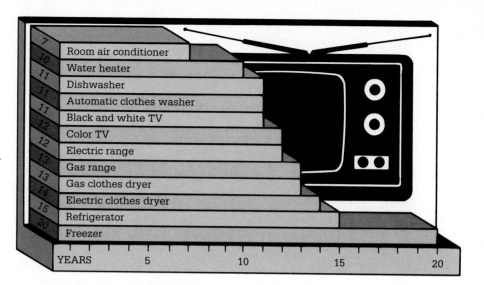

previous years have declined in price. You can look that information up in the *N.A.D.A. Official Used Car Guide*, available in most libraries.

The expected price of future purchases should be based upon present market prices plus an inflation adjustment for the time between now and the date of replacement. In order to arrive at an inflation adjustment factor, you will have to assume a future rate of inflation. If you have no reason to assume otherwise, base your forecast on the inflation rate for the last year. This figure is widely published in newspapers and magazines. Given this information and Appendix Table A.1, you can find the inflation adjustment factor. Multiplying the present price by the inflation adjustment factor will provide you with the estimated future expense.

Suppose you expect that over the next four years the annual rate of inflation will average 5 percent. If you locate the intersection of the 5 percent column and the row for period 4 in Appendix Table A.1, you will find the number 1.2155. This is the inflation adjustment factor. At a 5 percent annual rate of inflation,

TABLE 8.2 · The Market Price of a Used Car as a Percentage of the Market Price of a Similar New Car

Age at End of Year, in Years	Size				
	Large	Intermediate	Compact	Subcompact	Van
0	100%	100%	100%	100%	100%
1	75%	77%	82%	87%	69%
2	60%	63%	69%	75%	55%
3	46%	52%	58%	63%	44%
4	37%	42%	49%	54%	38%
5	29%	34%	41%	45%	32%
6	22%	25%	34%	37%	27%
7	16%	18%	28%	29%	22%
8	10%	13%	22%	21%	17%
9	5%	8%	16%	14%	12%
10	3%	4%	11%	8%	8%
11	1%	2%	5%	3%	4%
12	0%	0%	0%	0%	0%

SOURCE: Adapted from Federal Highway Administration, *Cost of Owning and Operating Automobiles and Vans 1984*, U.S. Department of Transportation, 1986.

what costs $10 today will cost about $12.16 four years from now. This can be calculated as follows:

$$\text{Present price} \times \text{inflation adjustment factor} = \text{future price}$$
$$\$10 \times 1.2155 = \$12.16$$

Replacement Costs for the Steeles

The Steeles purchased a newly constructed home in 1986. With this home came most of the major home appliances they are now using. Because these appliances are all the same age, the Steeles worry that they might have to replace several of them at once. In order to fully anticipate these expenses, they have carried out the worksheet calculations in Table 8.3. The appliances are listed in order of remaining service life. Where possible, this is based on the data in Figure 8.1. Their own estimate on the riding mower is that it will last about three more years. Next to remaining service life is the present cost of a replacement, including installation cost. The Steeles found these prices in local newspaper advertisements. Arnold and Sharon plan to upgrade the quality of several appliances and therefore have listed the prices of more expensive models rather than models comparable to the ones they are now using. The inflation factor is based upon an assumed rate of 5 percent. This factor multiplied by the present replacement cost presents the Steeles with their expected expenses in the last column of Table 8.3.

Inspection of this worksheet provides the Steeles with the knowledge that during the next three years, they are likely to incur over $3,000 in replacement costs for the color TV and the riding mower. If they are lucky, and these items last beyond their expected service life, those expenses may be postponed. However, postponing replacement increases the probability of many things going wrong at once, since it is expected that other goods will also need replacement in subsequent years. If the Steeles update the worksheet when they undertake their yearly budget, they will be forewarned of this possibility. They may then ensure that their savings provide enough liquidity to meet their expected cash needs.

The eventual replacement of the family cars should also be analyzed. The Steeles have been paying for their cars through trade-ins and borrowing. In about two years they expect to trade the Honda for a similar new small car. The worksheet in Table 8.4 contains their calculations. They figure it would cost them about $17,000 to purchase a similar compact car now. If inflation is expected to average 5 percent over the next two years, the inflation factor is 1.1025. Thus,

TABLE 8.3 · The Steeles' Worksheet for Major Home Appliance Replacement Costs

Appliance	Years to Replacement	Present Cost	Inflation Factor (5%)	Expected Future Cost
Color TV	2	$ 700	1.10	$ 770
Riding mower	3	2,000	1.16	2,315
Water heater	4	400	1.22	488
Dishwasher	5	550	1.28	702
Clothes washer	5	380	1.28	486
Electric range	6	650	1.34	871
Clothes dryer	8	280	1.48	414
Refrigerator	9	800	1.55	1,240

Spending,
Borrowing,
and Saving

TABLE 8.4 · The
Steeles' Worksheet for
Automobile
Replacement Cost

CAR: HONDA		
Item	Description	Amount
1	Present cost of replacement car	$17,000
2	Present age of used car	3 years
3	Years to replacement	2 years
4	Age of used car at replacement (item 2 + item 3)	5 years
5	Estimated annual rate of inflation	5%
6	Inflation adjustment factor (see item 3, item 5, and Appendix Table A.1)	1.1025
7	Expected future cost (item 1 × item 6)	$18,742.50
8	Percentage depreciation on used car (item 4 and Table 8.2)	41%
9	Trade-in value of used car (item 7 × item 8)	$7,684.43
10	Net replacement cost (item 7−item 9)	$11,058.07

the expected price of a similar new car at that time will be $17,000 × 1.1025 = $18,743. Using the depreciation schedule for compact cars in Table 8.2, a five-year-old compact car should trade in for about 41 percent of $18,743, or $7,684. Thus, the difference of $11,058 is the estimated net replacement cost to be covered by a down payment and an auto loan. If the Steeles had planned to trade up to a more expensive car, they would have separately estimated this price and then subtracted the $7,684 to estimate the potential cash outlay.

You should note that these techniques are used only for estimating future prices. When the time actually comes to trade in and purchase a new car, you should consult the pricing guides mentioned later in this chapter.

Selecting Major Home Appliances

An efficient selection process must include gathering and evaluating information. Information can be gained from talking to friends, visiting retail outlets, and reading such consumer-oriented magazines as *Consumer Reports* and *Consumer Research*. The gathering of this information may require some time, effort, and money.

The results of a Federal Trade Commission study on shopping behavior indicate that the average consumer visits about two stores, and typically compares about three brands, before purchasing a major home appliance. Over half the buyers make a purchase after five days of shopping. Whether this behavior is optimal is difficult to determine. Obviously, shopping should continue as long as additional search costs, including the cost of your time and the cost of transportation, are lower than the additional benefits generated by the search, measured in terms of lower prices or better quality.

The following pieces of information are essential for making an informed decision:

1 Prices of various brands at different stores

2 Available optional features

3 The product service record and service availability

4 The cost of operation and maintenance

5 Warranty coverage

227

It is unlikely that one purchase will appear superior in all five categories. Therefore, an accurate assessment of the trade-offs will play an important part in the selection process.

Prices and Options

When shopping, be sure to look at the total price. If you are planning to have the appliance delivered and installed, charges for these services as well as any finance charges should all be considered part of the good's total price. In addition, ask the salesperson whether any of the items in which you are interested will be on sale in the near future, and whether or not the store might do better than the listed price. Some large chain stores are known for providing advance information on upcoming sales, or for refunding part of the original purchase price if you buy the item immediately preceding the official sale period. Other smaller owner-managed stores are known for providing discounts only when requested.

When making comparisons between brands and within brands, you are likely to confront an array of prices and options. You will have to judge whether the optional feature is worth the added cost. On such items as microwave ovens and videotape recorders, *Consumer Reports* has found that most brands and most models accomplish the basic task for which they were built equally well. Cost differences are centered primarily on optional features, such as electronic memory and pause control. If you plan to use these features often, they may be worth the price. Usually, however, the novelty wears off and they end up as useless but expensive trim on the basic appliance. Those options that really do prove convenient or that provide for added safety are often suggested in the product survey articles in *Consumer Reports* and *Consumer Research*. These articles are also a good source of information on product quality and durability.

The Product Service Record and Service Availability

The results of product surveys conducted by the consumer magazines should help you judge relative performance. Of particular help are frequency-of-repair statistics collected by *Consumer Reports* in an annual survey of its readers. These results can be collected only on goods purchased in previous years, so they are somewhat dated. However, they may still prove useful in judging the problems you are likely to encounter with a general class of goods or the products of a specific manufacturer.

You can generally expect products with complicated mechanical parts, such as washing machines, to require more service than other, largely nonmechanical items, such as ovens. For such service-intensive products, both the service record and the availability of service are worth checking. Does the store that sold you the item provide customer support at a reasonable price? How will problems covered by a warranty be serviced? Are there manufacturer-authorized repair services in the immediate area? The prospect of qualified and convenient service may sometimes be worth a higher purchase price.

Costs of Operation and Maintenance

Your estimate of maintenance costs may be based upon suggested service intervals in the owner's manual and independent information on the product's service record. Be very wary of claims on cost savings made by manufacturers: They have often fallen short of the truth. Since 1978 the Federal Trade Commission has been examining products that claim to save energy under the Energy Policy and Conservation Act. Unfortunately, there are many products, and resources for enforcement are limited. The FTC has made significant progress however, in promulgating energy cost disclosure rules for major home appliances. Since May 1980, the manufacturers of seven appliance categories (refrigerators and refrigerator-freezers, freezers, dishwashers, water heaters, room air conditioners, clothes washers, and furnaces) must affix labels to their products indicating energy consumption under standard Department of Energy tests.

EnergyGuide: A federally mandated sticker indicating an appliance's energy usage.

A sample **EnergyGuide** label is shown in Figure 8.2. In large print is the expected yearly cost based upon an average national cost of energy and the needs of a typical household. Also indicated is the range of energy costs for comparable models. If you know the actual cost of energy in your area, you can find a more accurate estimate on the bottom half of the label.

If all appliances had identical prices and qualities, the best buy would be the appliance with the lowest cost of operation. However, the more energy-efficient appliances usually cost more to purchase. Consequently, you may find that you are better off financially by selecting a less energy-efficient appliance. Before you can decide which appliance is the best buy, you must first gauge the present worth of a reduction in the cost of operation.

The costs listed on the EnergyGuide are based upon current energy prices. As energy prices increase, so will the savings generated by a lower energy usage. For example, suppose you are considering two appliances, one with a cost of operation of $200 per year and the other with a cost of operation of $150 per year. If energy prices double, costs of operation are now $400 per year and $300 per year, respectively. You should notice that the savings from the lower cost rating have also doubled, going from $50 per year to $100 per year. Suppose, however, that instead of spending more for an energy-efficient appliance, you purchase a less expensive, less efficient model and place the savings on purchase price in the bank. The amount in the bank will also increase over time as interest is earned and compounded.

This discussion implies that the value of a reduction in the cost of operation will depend on both the expected after-tax return on your financial investments and the expected rate of inflation in energy prices. As your expected return on investments increases relative to the expected inflation in energy prices, a reduction in the published cost of operation becomes less valuable. Table 8.5 lists the present value of a $1 reduction in the cost of operation, as shown on the Ener-

TABLE 8.5 · The Present Value of $1 Reduction in the Published Cost of Operation

Interest Rate–Energy Inflation Rate Differential	Service Life in Years						
	5	7	10	12	15	17	20
5%	4.30	5.80	7.70	8.90	10.40	11.30	12.50
3%	4.60	6.20	8.50	10.00	11.90	13.20	14.90
1%	4.90	6.70	9.50	11.30	13.90	15.60	18.00
0%	5.00	7.00	10.00	12.00	15.00	17.00	20.00
−1%	5.20	7.30	10.60	12.80	16.30	18.60	22.30
−3%	5.50	7.90	11.90	14.70	19.30	22.60	28.00
−5%	5.80	8.60	13.40	17.00	23.20	27.80	35.80

Consumer
Durables

**Refrigerator-Freezer
Capacity: 23 Cubic Feet**

(Name of Corporation)
Model(s) AH503, AH504, AH507
Type of Defrost: Full Automatic

ENERGYGUIDE

Estimates on the scale are based
on a national average electric
rate of 4.97¢ per kilowatt hour.

Only models with 22.5 to 24.4
cubic feet are compared
in the scale.

$91

Model with
lowest
energy cost
$68

Model with
highest
energy cost
$132

THIS ▼ MODEL
Estimated yearly energy cost

Your cost will vary depending on your local energy rate and how you use the product. This energy cost is based on U.S. Government standard tests.

How much will this model cost you to run yearly?

Yearly cost

Estimated yearly $ cost shown below

Cost per kilowatt hour		
	2¢	$36
	4¢	$73
	6¢	$109
	8¢	$146
	10¢	$182
	12¢	$218

Ask your salesperson or local utility for the energy rate (cost per kilowatt hour) in your area.

Important Removal of this label before consumer purchase is a violation of federal law (42 U.S.C. 6302)

(Part No. 371026)

FIGURE 8.2

Sample EnergyGuide.

Spending,
Borrowing,
and Saving

gyGuide label, for a combination of service lives and interest rate–energy inflation rate differentials. Combinations not shown may be approximated by averaging the closest values. The differential is calculated by subtracting the expected annual rate of inflation in energy prices from the expected annual after-tax interest return on your financial investments.

Suppose you are considering an appliance with a service life of about ten years. You expect to earn an 8 percent after-tax annual return on your money over this period, and you expect energy prices to rise at a 5 percent annual rate over the same period. Under this 3 percent differential, the value to you of a $1 reduction in the published annual cost of operation is worth about $8.50. This means that, given two appliances, identical in all respects except for a $1 difference in the annual cost of operation, you should prefer the more energy-efficient model so long as it does not cost more than an additional $8.50.

Unless you believe we are headed for another energy crisis, you probably should use a positive 3 percent interest rate–energy inflation rate differential. Over the long run, a prudent investor should probably be able to earn 3 percent more than the rate of inflation. Even given this optimistic assumption concerning energy costs, reading the energy label may still have important advantages. Figure 8.2 indicates that comparable refrigerators have costs of operation that range from $68 to $132, a yearly cost difference of $64. Given a 15-year service life for refrigerators and an interest rate–energy inflation rate differential of 3 percent, each $1 reduction in cost of operations is worth $11.90. All other things being equal, the most efficient model is worth $761.60 ($11.90 × 64) more than the least efficient model. Since it is unlikely that the price spread between these two appliances is this large, you can certainly benefit by reading the energy label and calculating the value of the reduction in the cost of operation.

Warranties

Most consumers do not bother to read warranties. This is unfortunate, because the terms of a warranty can often provide sufficient reasons for selecting one product over another. **Warranty** and **guarantee** have the same meaning. They represent the seller's assumption of responsibility for the quality, character, or suitability of the goods sold. In a world of imperfect information, the buyer cannot know everything about the product being purchased. Therefore, the consumer requires some protection in the event the product does not perform as expected. It is the warranty that provides the needed protection.

Warranty or guarantee: The seller's assumption of responsibility for the quality, character, or suitability of goods sold.

"As is": The seller bears absolutely no responsibility for the quality or performance of the good.

Implied warranty: A warranty created by the operation of the law when no express warranty exists.

EXPRESS AND IMPLIED WARRANTIES   All products, except those sold **"as is,"** carry implied warranties. An implied warranty is imposed upon the seller by the operation of the law. In other words, the law sets down certain requirements that the seller must live up to. The **implied warranty** will consist of a warranty of merchantability and a warranty of fitness for purpose. *Merchantability* means that the buyer has the right to expect that the good is generally of the same quality as similar goods in its class, and that it does what it was built to do. A buyer has the right to expect that a washing machine washes clothes. *Fitness of purpose* means that if the buyer is relying on the seller to select a good for a particular purpose, and the seller has reason to know of that purpose, the good should prove suitable. For example, if the seller knows that the buyer wants a washing machine to wash

231

rugs, then the machine should be able to handle difficult tasks such as cleaning heavy rugs.

Not all products carry an **express warranty.** An express warranty is contractual in nature; that is, it depends upon the written or oral agreement between the buyer and seller. An express warranty need not be in writing, nor is it even necessary for the seller to intend to guarantee the item for an express warranty to exist. Statements of fact and promises expressed by the sales agent or manufac-turer either at the time of the sale or in previous advertisements can form the basis for an express warranty. However, you must carefully distinguish state-ments of fact from what is called **puffery.** This is typical sales talk meant to persuade the customer by overly praising the good. Statements such as, "This is a good buy," are mere puffery and do not carry an express warranty.

The **Magnuson-Moss Warranty Act of 1975,** regulates express written war-ranties. Before passage of this act, many written warranties contained clauses that relieved the seller of an implied warranty. In many of these situations, consumers would have been better off without an express warranty. One of the purposes of this act was to make such clauses ineffective by prohibiting written warranties from limiting the implied warranty to a shorter period than that covered by the written warranty. However, the seller can still avoid an implied warranty by selling the product "as is."

FULL AND LIMITED WARRANTIES   Another purpose of the Warranty Act was to set down requirements for full and limited warranties. It is now necessary that all written warranties be labeled either *limited* or *full.*

Express warranty: An oral or written agreement between buyer and seller concerning the character or performance of the good.

Puffery: Persuasive sales talk overly praising the good.

Magnuson-Moss Warranty Act of 1975: Federal law regulating the conditions and limitations contained in express warranties.

The **full warranty** label means that consumers are entitled to full remedies for a specified period of time. They may even request a replacement or refund if the warrantor has been given a reasonable number of attempts to fix the product and has been unsuccessful. This provision is termed **lemon protection,** and it is included only in full warranties. The *full* label also means that, during the period specified, consumers will not be charged for parts or labor, or associated transportation and travel. In addition, a full warranty cannot disclaim or limit the duration of implied warranties, be limited to the original owner, require a registration card to provide the date of purchase, or impose an unreasonable requirement as a condition of warranty coverage. Any warranty that does not meet these standards must be labeled a **limited warranty.**

Many products will carry both limited and full warranties. For example, the first year of ownership may be covered by a full warranty, with coverage reduced to a limited warranty in subsequent years. It is also possible that some components of the appliance will be covered by a full warranty, while others will have limited coverage or none. Many consumers mistakenly believe that the term *full* means that all parts are warrantied.

SHOULD YOU PURCHASE A SERVICE CONTRACT?   Whenever you purchase a major home appliance or a car, the salesperson will usually try to sell you a **service contract,** or what is also called an **extended warranty.** This is because service contracts have proven highly profitable for sellers, and not so profitable for buyers. Unless you are particularly hard on the products you use, the expected cost of repairs is typically much less than the cost of the service contract. For example, an MIT study for the National Science Foundation revealed that the cost of a service contract for a color TV set was almost 10 times the expected cost of repairs, and for a refrigerator it was about 16 times the expected cost of repairs.

A service contract is, in effect, the same as an insurance policy. You are insuring yourself against repairs on your consumer durables. The manufacturer or retailer is betting that the equipment won't break down, and you are betting that it will. In later chapters we will be discussing some of the basic principles of insurance protection. One such principle is that you should concentrate on insuring yourself against major financial calamities and bear any small risks yourself. The breakdown of the washing machine or the need for a valve job may seem major at the time it happens, but it is really minor relative to other financial losses you may suffer.

Selecting an Automobile

Except for a home, your car is probably the largest single purchase you will make. Therefore, it is appropriate for you to put some time and effort into this decision. To make the correct choice you will have to accurately assess your own needs, evaluate market alternatives, and consider financing options. Having all relevant information written down will prove helpful in making your final decision. Consumers can obtain a useful worksheet, along with background information, in *The Car Book*, available from the U.S. Department of Transportation, National Highway Traffic Safety Administration, Washington, DC 20590. Completing the

---

Full warranty: During a specified time period, purchases are entitled to full protection, including lemon protection and all repair-related costs.

Lemon protection: If the merchandise cannot be repaired after a reasonable number of attempts, the customer can elect to receive either a replacement or a refund.

Limited warranty: Any express warranty that does not meet all of the necessary conditions for a full warranty.

Service contract or extended warranty: For an initial fee, the seller agrees to repair the merchandise, either without charge or at a set charge, for a period beyond the initial warranty.

worksheet will force you both to confront your real needs and to identify important points of comparison.

The consumer magazines' coverage of automobiles is similar to that of home appliances. Reading the articles can help you identify those makes and models that are either best buys or especially trouble prone. Particularly helpful are the results of the *Consumer Reports* reader survey, in which consumers are asked to indicate their own experiences.

Pricing Information

The current practices accompanying automobile sales seem to have evolved from the horse trading of the past. A car is one of the few purchases we make that still involve haggling over price. In such market encounters the person with the best information will usually have the advantage. If you don't do some comparative shopping, you give the seller this advantage.

Sticker price: The manufacturer's suggested retail price for a car, usually listed on a window sticker.

Invoice price: The price the manufacturer charges the retailer for a car.

NEW CARS The manufacturer's suggested retail price is called the **sticker price.** This figure typically includes the base price for the standard car with dealer preparation, the prices for any optional features, and a destination charge for transporting the car to the dealer. The dealer rarely gets this price for a new car.

The most important piece of information you can have when bargaining with the dealer is the **invoice price.** This is the price the manufacturer charges the dealer for the car. Many car guides list invoice costs or provide a formula for estimating the invoice cost. Each year the April issue of *Consumer Reports* reviews that year's models. In addition, for a small fee *Consumer Reports* will send you a computer printout listing the invoice cost for the car and the options you have selected. *Car Facts*, supplied free of charge through many credit unions, also provides information on prices, safety records, and gas mileage. To use estimates of dealer cost provided by consumer groups, it is suggested that you first ask the salesperson for the minimum markup over invoice that is acceptable to the dealership. If this markup is favorable relative to other dealers you have visited, add it to their indicated invoice cost and make a firm offer. Don't waiver from your initial offer. If your money doesn't talk, be ready to walk.

When you purchase a new car, the salesperson is also likely to offer you an extended warranty for an additional charge. For the same reasons stated previously, it is usually not a good buy. Moreover, to a considerable degree the extended warranty may cover repairs already provided for under the regular warranty. A four-year, 48,000-mile extended warranty on a car that has a manufacturer's three-year, 36,000-mile regular warranty only extends coverage by one year and 12,000 miles. The limited additional coverage, however, has not deterred dealers from charging exorbitant prices. The New York attorney general's office found that over half the consumers in that state who purchased extended warranties were charged more than the manufacturer's suggested retail price.

USED CARS If you are considering buying, selling, or trading in a used car, the two most commonly used sources of pricing information are the *National Automobile Dealers Association Official Used Car Guide* and the *Kelley Blue Book Market Report*. These are on hand at most libraries and at banks where car loans are

Use a Car-Buying Service

If you are one of those persons who hates to haggle over price, or you are just too busy to roam from dealer to dealer searching for the best price, you may be interested in using a car-buying service to help you purchase your next car. It is a solution that may save you both time and money.

When Daniel Titus searched for a good deal on a new Toyota four-wheel-drive pickup truck, the best price he could find was $14,700. He then used a car-buying service run by AAA South Central New England. The club sent Mr. Titus to a dealer who sold him an identical truck for $13,100.

Under the Rhode Island program, participating dealers agree to sell cars to AAA members for between 3 and 6 percent over the dealer's invoice. Similar programs are run by 17 other AAA organizations. The Rhode Island organization had originally intended to charge a $75 fee for the service, but because of problems with state regulations it dropped the fee and offered the program as a free service to all 300,000 members.

Participating dealers benefit because of additional sales and because prenegotiated sales take less time and effort. Buyers benefit because they don't have to dicker with dealers over price. A AAA official says that a skilled negotiator might be able to bargain a better price, but "ours is a fair price for a fair product."

"Whenever I had to buy a new car, I hated it," says Elizabeth Hunter. This time, however, she claims her purchase, arranged through the AAA program, was a "truly enjoyable experience."

SOURCE: Adapted from Neal Templin, "Auto Club Finds Agency's Ruling Less Than AAA," *The Wall Street Journal*, April 12, 1991, pp. B1, B2. Reprinted by permission of *The Wall Street Journal*, © 1991 Dow Jones & Company, Inc. All Rights Reserved Worldwide.

made. They contain the average trade-in or wholesale price and the retail price for many different makes of used cars. Also included are estimated prices for optional equipment.

Your best buy is typically a two- to three-year-old used car. This is because the annual percentage depreciation in price is greatest over the first few years. Before selecting a model, you should consult the *Consumer Reports* readers' survey on frequency of repair records also published in the April issue. Obviously, try to avoid makes and models that are not on their recommended list.

If you are looking to purchase a used car from a dealer, a large sticker called the "Buyers Guide" should be posted in the window of each car. This will indicate whether the car is covered by a warranty, and if it is, what the warranty includes. About one-half of used cars are sold "as is," meaning there is no warranty. When you purchase a car "as is," you are fully responsible for any needed repairs. For those cars that are sold with a warranty, the previous discussion on warranties applies. If the car is still covered by an unexpired manufacturer's warranty, then the manufacturer is responsible for fulfilling the terms of this warranty, not the dealer who sold you the car. If you have any questions concerning warranty coverage, be sure to ask the dealer to explain the terms of the contract. Also be sure that all the dealer's promises are included in the written warranty.

Rebates and Dealer-Supplied Financing

Manufacturer's rebates and low-interest dealer financing are widely used advertising gimmicks. Once in the showroom, the consumer often finds that these items are being offered in place of the typical dealer discount. The true cost of the car may be unchanged or even greater.

A Federal Trade Commission investigation of promotions for dealer financing turned up numerous examples of unethical and possible illegal activities. In some cases consumers were offered the low rate on only a few cars and only if they made an unusually large down payment. In other cases the typical cash discount was unavailable and the car was loaded with high-cost options. The latest promotional strategy is to apply the low advertised rate only on loans of unusually short duration.

Under some circumstances, however, dealer financing may be a real bargain, particularly if the dealer has arranged a low-cost line of credit through the manufacturer or the local bank. Therefore, it may be worth your time to comparison shop and undertake the illustrated calculations on the worksheet in Table 8.6. For example, suppose you are offered the choice between either below-market financing or a discounted purchase price. Purchase option 1 in Table 8.6 consists of a $12,000 purchase price with 10 percent down, and the remaining balance financed at a below-market annual percentage rate of 5 percent over three years. Under purchase option 2, you receive a $1,000 discount on the price of the car, but you must supply your own financing. Which is the best deal?

The easiest way to determine the best option is first to search out alternative financing with an identical down payment and identical term. In this example, loans requiring a $1,200 down payment and 36 months to repay are compared. Given a discount of $1,000 on option 2, the purchase price would be reduced from $12,000 to $11,000. Consequently, as Table 8.6 indicates, if you placed $1,200 down (slightly over 10 percent) under purchase option 2, you would have to borrow $9,800.

Suppose that after calling local banks, savings and loan associations, and credit unions, you discover that the best rate on private financing with this down payment and term is at a 10 percent annual percentage rate. Your monthly payments under this alternative would equal $316.22 [The monthly payment can be calculated using Table 8.7: 9.8 (thousands) × $32.27 = $316.25.] This is slightly less than the monthly payment of $323.68 [10.8 (thousands) × $29.97 = $323.68] under purchase option 1.

The total cost of the car will equal the sum of the down payment and the monthly payments. Your monthly payments are less when you borrow $9,800 at 10 percent than when you borrow $10,800 at 5 percent. Therefore, given identical down payments, the best buy is the car with the lower purchase price and higher loan rate in this example. Under the preferred option 2, you save $7.43 per month, a total of $267.48 over the life of the loan.

A word of caution: Sometimes a lender will offer a loan at an attractive interest rate and then tack on to the monthly payment a charge for credit life insurance.

TABLE 8.6 · Worksheet on Comparative Auto Financing

	Purchase Option 1	Purchase Option 2
Price	$12,000.00	$11,000.00
Less: Down payment	1,200.00	1,200.00
Equals: Balance due	$10,800.00	$9,800.00
Interest rate (annual)	5.00%	10.00%
Monthly payment	$323.68	$316.25
Multiplied by: Term (months)	36	36
Total monthly payments	$11,652.68	$11,383.86
Plus: Down payment	1,200.00	1,200.00
Equals: Total cost	$12,852.68	$12,583.86

Spending, Borrowing, and Saving

TABLE 8.7 · Monthly
Payments on Each
$1,000 Borrowed

Annual Percentage Rate	Term of Loan (Months)			
	24	36	48	60
3%	$42.98	$29.08	$22.13	$17.97
4%	43.42	29.52	22.58	18.42
5%	43.87	29.97	23.03	18.87
6%	44.32	30.42	23.49	19.33
7%	44.77	30.88	23.95	19.80
8%	45.23	31.34	24.41	20.28
9%	45.68	31.80	24.89	20.76
10%	46.14	32.27	25.36	21.25
11%	46.61	32.74	25.85	21.74
12%	47.07	33.21	26.33	22.24
13%	47.54	33.69	26.83	22.75

Credit life insurance: Pays off the remaining loan balance upon one's death.

This insurance will pay off the remaining principal on the loan in the event of your death. In many states it is illegal to require that the borrower accept the **credit life insurance.** It is often unnecessary, high-cost insurance, the purpose of which is actually to increase the interest return to the lender. If credit life is being forced upon you, be sure to compare loans according to total monthly payments, including the credit life premium.

The Costs of Owning and Operating an Automobile

When deciding whether to purchase a car, and when planning your household finances, you will need information on the cost of ownership and operation. Runzheimer International, a management consulting firm, specializes in the collection of data on travel and living costs. Their estimates for the cost of owning and operating a representative compact, standard, and large-size car are given in Figure 8.3. For the owner who purchases a new car and trades it in after four years and 60,000 miles, the cost of owning and operating an automobile is a significant expense. As indicated in Figure 8.3, the owner of a 1991 Ford Taurus would incur over $20,000 in automobile expenses in the four-year period. For budgeting purposes, these expenses may be separated into the fixed cost of ownership and the variable cost of operation.

The Cost of Ownership

Cost of ownership: Fixed costs that do not vary with usage.

Ownership costs are fixed; that is, they do not vary with usage. No matter how much or how little you use the car, these expenses will remain relatively constant. Each of the following is considered a **cost of ownership:** auto insurance; license, registration, taxes; depreciation; and finance charges.

INSURANCE   The cost of insurance will depend upon the amount and type of coverage. Insurance will be discussed in detail in Chapter 12. Briefly, comprehensive insurance covers you against theft and fire. Collision insurance pays for damage to your car from an accident, regardless of who is at fault. Deductibles on each of these coverages indicate that the insurance company reimburses only losses that exceed this amount.

237

YOUR DRIVING COSTS			
4 year/60,000 mile cycle	**1991** **Ford Escort LX** **4-cyl. (114 CID)** **4-door hatchback**	**1991** **Ford Taurus L** **6-cyl. (182 CID)** **4-door sedan**	**1991** **Chevrolet Caprice** **8-cyl. (305 CID)** **4-door sedan**	**Average Cost**

DETAILS OF CAR COSTS

Operating Costs	**Cost per Mile**	**Cost per Mile**	**Cost per Mile**	**Cost per Mile**
Gasoline and oil	5.3 cents	6.7 cents	7.7 cents	6.6 cents
Maintenance	2.0 cents	2.2 cents	2.4 cents	2.2 cents
Tires	.8 cents	.9 cents	1.0 cents	.9 cents
	8.1 cents	9.8 cents	11.1 cents	9.7 cents
Ownership Costs	**Cost per Year**	**Cost per Year**	**Cost per Year**	**Cost per Year**
Comprehensive insurance ($100 deductible)	$ 93	$ 115	$ 115	$ 108
Collision insurance ($250 deductible)	225	258	258	247
Property damage and liability ($100,000, $300,000, $50,000)	353	353	353	353
License, registration, taxes	140	169	194	168
Depreciation	2,101	2,543	2,867	2,504
Finance charge (20% down; loan @ 12.0%/4 yrs.)	614	779	904	766
	$3,526	$4,217	$4,691	$4,146
	(or $9.66 per day)	(or $11.55 per day)	(or $12.85 per day)	(or $11.36 per day)
Depreciation for excess mileage per 1,000 miles over 15,000 miles annually	$106	$120	$123	$116

COST PER MILE

Based on the above figures, the motorist driving 15,000 miles a year would pay:

15,000 miles	@8.1¢	$1,215	@9.8¢	$1,470	@11.1¢	$1,665	@9.7¢	$1,455
*365 days	@$9.66	3,526	@$11.55	4,216	@$12.85	4,690	@$11.36	4,146
		$4,741		$5,686		$6,355		$5,601
Cost per Mile		**31.6 cents**		**37.9 cents**		**42.4 cents**		**37.3 cents**

The same person driving 20,000 miles a year would pay:

20,000 miles	@8.1¢	$1,620	@9.8¢	$1,960	@11.1¢	$2,200	@9.7¢	$1,940
*365 days	@$9.66	3,526	@$11.55	4,216	@$12.85	4,690	@$11.36	4,146
Added depreciation per 1,000 over 15,000 miles	@$106	530	@$120	600	@$123	615	@$116	580
		$5,676		$6,776		$7,505		$6,666
COST PER MILE		**28.4 cents**		**33.9 cents**		**37.5 cents**		**33.3 cents**

The same person driving 10,000 miles a year would pay:

10,000 miles	@8.1¢	$ 810	@9.8¢	$ 980	@11.1¢	$1,110	@9.7¢	$ 970
**365 days	@$7.60	2,773	@$9.27	3,384	@$12.19	4,449	@$9.68	3,535
		$3,583		$4,364		$5,559		$4,505
Cost per mile		**35.8 cents**		**43.6 cents**		**55.6 cents**		**45.0 cents**

*Ownership costs based on a four-year/60,000-mile retention cycle.

**Ownership costs based on a six-year/60,000-mile retention cycle.

FIGURE 8.3

Estimating driving costs. (Source: Runzheimer International. This data is presented with permission from Runzheimer International, the Rochester Wisconsin-based management consulting firm.)

Spending,
Borrowing,
and Saving

Property damage and liability insurance protects you from the cost of the harm you may cause to others. The Runzheimer cost estimate of this coverage is based upon a policy with limits of $100,000/$300,000/$50,000. The first number sets a limit on the financial responsibility of the insurer for harm to any single individual, the second number limits the insurer's liability for all individuals in a single accident, and the last number sets the liability limit on property damage.

LICENSE, REGISTRATION, TAXES   The state in which you live will impose these fees. Each state has its own formula for determining the cost of a license. This can vary depending upon the vehicle's weight and type, and your intended use of the motor vehicle.

With the purchase of a car you should receive a **certificate of title.** This authenticates your ownership of the car, and should be kept in a safe place. Never leave it in the car, since the car may be stolen. Another important document is the **certificate of registration,** which indicates that the vehicle has been properly registered with your state motor vehicle department. This document should remain in your car.

DEPRECIATION   **Depreciation** is the reduction in the market value of the vehicle due to passage of time, mechanical and physical condition, and number of miles driven. While depreciation does vary with usage, it is dependent primarily upon time, and, therefore, can be considered a fixed cost for any given year.

Depreciation is the greatest single cost over the four-year holding period. However, as an annual expense it declines steadily throughout the years of ownership. Table 8.2 indicated that a new large-size car will decline to 75 percent of its initial value at the end of the first year, and to 60 percent of its initial value by the end of the second year. In the first year, 25 percent of the new-car value is lost, but in the second year, only 15 percent of the new-car value is lost.

Your average annual depreciation will depend upon the age of your car and your holding period. If you purchased a new car each year for $10,000 and traded in the old car each year for $7,500, your average annual depreciation would be $2,500. Alternatively, if you purchased a new car every other year for $10,000 and traded in the two-year-old car for $6,000, the depreciation over the two-year period would be $4,000. After the total depreciation is divided by 2, the length of the holding period, the average annual depreciation is $2,000. The difference between average annual depreciation of $2,500 and average annual depreciation of $2,000 represents a yearly savings of $500. This is the dollar advantage of having a two-year holding period rather than a one-year holding period. The longer you hold the car, the smaller is your average annual cost of depreciation.

FINANCE CHARGES   The finance charges in Figure 8.3 assume that each car is purchased with a 20 percent down payment and financed with a four-year loan at an annual percentage rate (APR) of 12 percent. Over the four-year period, total finance charges will range from $2,456 for the compact car to $3,616 for the large car. If you purchase the car out of savings, you can eliminate these explicit finance charges; however, you give up the interest income you could have earned on those savings. This lost interest would also represent a cost of ownership. Consequently, whether or not you intend to finance the purchase with borrowed

Certificate of title: Legal evidence of your ownership of a motor vehicle.

Certificate of registration: A document indicating that your car is properly registered with the state motor vehicle department.

Depreciation: The reduction in the market value of a motor vehicle due to passage of time, mechanical and physical condition, and number of miles driven.

funds, you should consider the Runzheimer estimate of finance charges as a real cost of ownership.

OTHER COSTS OF OWNERSHIP   Any additional fixed costs that are incurred because of car ownership should also be considered. For example, if you rent a garage to house your car, the rental payments should be included in the cost of ownership. On the other hand, if you would normally live in a home with a garage, whether or not you own a car, then your additional or marginal cost of storage would be zero.

The cost of accessories may also be included. These may consist of such things as extra wheels for snow tires, radios, and trailer hitches. Items that have an effect on mechanical operation can be included under the maintenance component of operating expenses.

The Cost of Operation

Cost of operation: Variable costs that are directly related to usage.

Costs that are related directly to usage are called *variable costs*. The **cost of operation** includes all variable costs. Figure 8.3 lists the variable cost per mile for each component of operating cost.

GASOLINE AND OIL   After the cost of depreciation, this is likely to be your next largest vehicle expense. Fuel costs in Figure 8.3 are based upon an average price of $1.369. Your costs should be based upon your regional cost of fuel and your car's fuel economy. Driving 15,000 miles per year, the data in Figure 8.3 indicates that drivers of compact cars would spend about $360 less on gasoline and oil than drivers of larger cars.

MAINTENANCE AND TIRES   The owner's manual or your local mechanic should be able to recommend a maintenance schedule based upon the miles you typically drive. Maintenance and tires are not generally covered under an automobile warranty and therefore should be included in the household budget. For older cars on which the warranty has expired, unscheduled repairs and parts replacement should also be given consideration when estimating expenditures.

OTHER OPERATING COSTS   Metered curb parking, fees charged for parking lots, and toll charges for highways, tunnels, and bridges may all represent additional operating costs. In an urban environment these costs should not be overlooked; they can represent a significant cost of commuting.

The Total Cost of Ownership and Operation

By adding together the fixed cost of ownership and the variable cost of operation, you can calculate the total cost of the family car. For the mid-size car driven 15,000 miles per year, total annual cost of $5,686 would consist of $4,216 in ownership cost and $1,470 in operating cost. As in this example, the cost of ownership generally represents a larger portion of total auto expenditures than the cost of operation.

On a per-mile basis, the total cost per mile of the mid-size car driven 15,000 miles per year is 37.9 cents. This consists of 9.8 cents per mile in operating costs and 28.1 cents per mile in ownership costs. At this level of usage, ownership cost represent almost 75 percent of your auto-related transportation expenses. However, if the car is driven an additional mile, the variable cost of operations will increase by about 9.8 cents, while the fixed cost of ownership will remain relatively stable. This means that as the car is used more often, the relative importance of ownership cost will decline. It can be seen in Figure 8.3 that, at 20,000 miles per year, the cost of ownership including depreciation declines to about 71 percent.

The Mass Transit Alternative

In highly congested New York City, about 44 percent of the work force uses public transportation to get to work. In less densely populated Indianapolis, only about 3 percent of the work force uses public transportation. This difference can be explained in terms of relative availability, relative cost, and relative convenience of mass transit in each of these cities. If you have a mass transit alternative in your city, you should compare the relative costs of using a private auto versus public transit.

Sunk cost: A cost that has already been incurred, and therefore cannot be changed.

Marginal cost: Additional or incremental cost that will be incurred.

When judging the relative merits of public transit, you should first decide whether its use would permit you to do without owning and operating a motor vehicle. If so, you may weigh the cost of public transit against the total cost of ownership and operation. However, if you find you need the car anyway, then you should weigh the cost of public transit only against the cost of vehicle operation. This is because the cost of ownership is a **sunk cost:** It is something you have to pay whether or not you use the car. Therefore, if you own the car and want to know whether to drive it an additional mile or to use public transit to go the same mile, you should consider only the **marginal,** or additional, **cost** you will incur. In most circumstances the least costly alternative will depend upon the necessity of car ownership.

Using the data from Figure 8.3 for the mid-size car driven 15,000 miles, you should notice that the total cost per mile is 37.9 cents. However, the variable or marginal cost of an additional mile driven is only 11 cents, consisting of operating cost per mile of 9.8 cents per mile and depreciation for excess mileage over 15,000 miles per year of 1.2 cents per mile. In this example, if you use your car only for commuting, you might consider selling your car and using mass transit when the cost per mile on the mass transit system is less than 37.9 cents. Of course, this assumes that the added inconvenience of using the mass transit system does not offset any cost savings.

On the other hand, if you would normally maintain a car even if you used mass transit for commuting, then the only relevant cost in your decision making is the marginal cost of using the car for commuting. In this case, you would consider using mass transit only if the cost per mile fell below 11 cents. Since most people do want to own a car for other purposes, this explains why it is so difficult for mass transit to replace the auto.

The Leasing Alternative

If you find that you do need a car, but the need exists only for an occasional trip, you might consider an occasional rental as a practical alternative to ownership. By renting you avoid the high fixed cost of ownership, an exorbitant expense for a car that is seldom used.

If you need a car for longer periods of time but wish to hold down the high initial cost of ownership, you might consider leasing. Your current expenses and your periodic payments will be less than if you purchased the same car on credit. When you lease a vehicle, you are only paying rent for the car's long-term use. Your payments are determined primarily by the difference between the initial price of the car and the resale value of the car at the termination of the lease. If you finance a purchase, on the other hand, you are building equity as you pay off the loan principal. When you complete your car loan payments, you own the car. If you sell the car before all the loan payments are completed, you will receive any amount in excess of the loan balance.

There are two types of leasing contracts: closed-end and open-end. Both are covered by regulations specified in the **Consumer Leasing Act of 1977.** This act requires the leasing company (the lessor) to disclose in writing specific information about a consumer lease before you (the lessee) sign the lease agreement.

Consumer Leasing Act of 1977: A federal statute regulating leases on consumer goods.

The Closed-End Lease

The **closed-end lease** is also sometimes called the *net* or *walkaway* lease. You make fixed periodic payments based upon your estimated usage. When your lease expires, you simply return the car and pay a surcharge for mileage in excess of your estimate. Unless you have seriously damaged the vehicle, given it more than normal wear, or driven it more miles than the lease permits, you are not responsible for the value of the vehicle at the end of the lease term. Because the lessor is taking the risk as to what the value of the car will be when you return it, your lease payments generally will be higher than they would be under an open-end lease.

Closed-end lease: Your costs are determined at the time you lease the car. Under most circumstances, you are not responsible for the value of the car at the end of the lease.

The Open-End Lease

The **open-end lease** also has fixed periodic payments; however, the total cost remains unknown until the end of the leasing period. This is because the periodic payments are based upon the estimated resale value on the returned car, sometimes called the estimated *residual value.*

When you return the vehicle, the lessor will appraise it and compare the appraised value with the residual value stated in the lease. Under the Consumer Leasing Act, you have the right, at your expense, to obtain an independent appraisal by someone agreed to by both you and the lessor. If you get an independent appraisal, you and the lessor are bound by it.

If the appraised value of the car is the same as, or greater than, the residual value specified in the lease disclosure, you owe nothing. (Your contract will determine whether you get a refund for any excess value. You can ask the lessor to include the right to a refund in your contract.) Alternatively, if the appraisal indicates the vehicle is worth less than the specified amount, you may have to pay all or a portion of the difference. This cost is often called an *end-of-lease payment.*

You may be able to bargain for lower periodic payments if you agree to have a higher residual value put on the vehicle. Of course, setting a higher residual value increases your risk of having to make a large payment at the end of the lease. To

Open-end lease: The total cost of the lease is unknown until the end of the lease, when the estimated resale value of the car is determined.

242

ensure that consumers will not unknowingly enter into agreements with exorbitant end-of-lease payments, the Consumer Leasing Act requires that under most circumstances the end-of-lease payment can be no more than three times the average monthly payment on the lease. However, higher payments can be collected if you agreed to pay a greater amount, there was unreasonable wear or excessive use, or the lessor wins a lawsuit seeking a higher amount.

A Lease–Buy Comparison

Figure 8.4 contains a worksheet for comparing the cost of leasing versus purchasing a car on credit. The calculations are based upon a new car costing $17,000 plus tax. All of the costs associated with owning and operating a car are not shown on the worksheet. It is assumed that the costs of operations, maintenance, repairs, insurance, and registration are the same whether you purchase or lease. Therefore, these costs are irrelevant to the lease–purchase decision. Only costs that affect the decision are relevant costs.

The initial costs associated with leasing a car may include a security deposit, the first and last periodic payments, and a so-called capitalized cost reduction. Only the last item is considered a relevant initial cost. This is because the security deposit will be returned when the lease terminates, and the first and last payments are to be included under continuing relevant costs.

A capitalized cost reduction is, in effect, an advanced payment on the lease. It may or may not be required by the lessor. If you trade in a car you own, the capitalized cost reduction may be set equal to the value of the trade. The more you pay down initially, the lower your periodic payments will be. However, if you make a high initial payment in order to reduce your periodic payments, you lose one important advantage of leasing—the lower initial cost. In the worksheet example, it is assumed that initial decision-relevant costs include a 20 percent down payment and a 6 percent sales tax.

Continuing relevant payments will consist of periodic payments on the lease, and auto loan payments on the purchase. In the example, it is assumed that a four-year lease is being considered, for which periodic payments would total $13,920. The purchase option assumes an initial loan of $13,600 (equal to the difference between the purchase price of $17,000 and the down payment of $3,400). If this were financed over four years at an annual percentage rate of 12 percent, monthly loan payments would total $17,190.72 over the term of the loan.

Final costs at the termination of the lease may include an excess mileage charge, and miscellaneous items such as a disposition charge or a fee for excessive wear. Most leases have a mileage cap of 15,000 miles per year. The fee for each additional mile over the mileage cap can vary widely. Closed-end leases may reflect excessive wear on the car in either the excess mileage fee or in an adjustment for an overestimated residual value in the car.

The single final cost on the purchase side of the worksheet consists of the amount needed to pay off any remaining balance on the auto loan. This will be reduced, however, by the estimated resale value on the vehicle at the end of the holding period. At the end of the purchase alternative the consumer has a car worth $8,600, whereas at the end of the lease alternative the consumer owns nothing.

LEASING			PURCHASING	
Relevant Explicit Initial Costs				
Capitalized cost reduction	$ 0.00		Sales tax	$ 1,020.00
Miscellaneous costs	0.00		Down payment	3,400.00
			Miscellaneous costs	0.00
Total explicit initial costs	$ 0.00		Total explicit initial costs	$ 4,420.00
Relevant Explicit Continuing Costs				
Monthly lease payment	$ 290.00		Monthly loan payment	$ 358.14
× Months:	48		× Months	48
Total explicit continuing costs	$13,920.00		Total explicit continuing costs	$ 17,190.72
Relevant Explicit Final Costs				
Excessive mileage charge	$ 1,200.00		Loan payoff, if applicable	$ 0.00
Excessive wear and tear	0.00		Less estimated residual value	−8,600.00
Adjustment for overestimated residual value	0.00			
Miscellaneous items	0.00			
Total explicit final costs	$ 1,200.00		Total explicit final costs	$ −8,600.00
Relevant Implicit Costs				
Relevant explicit initial costs	$ 0.00		Relevant explicit initial costs	$ 4,420.00
Security deposit	290.00		× After-tax interest rate	.08
Lease prepayments	290.00		Annual implicit costs	$ 353.60
Total initial cash outflow	$ 580.00		× Terms of loan (years)	4
× After-tax interest rate	.08			
Annual implicit costs	$ 46.40			
× Terms of lease (years)	4			
Total implicit costs	$ 185.60		Total implicit costs	$ 1,414.40
Total Relevant Costs				
Explicit initial costs	$ 0.00		Explicit initial costs	$ 4,420.00
Explicit continuing costs	13,920.00		Explicit continuing costs	17,190.72
Explicit final costs	1,200.00		Explicit final costs	−8,600.00
Total explicit costs	$15,120.00		Total explicit costs	$ 13,010.72
Total implicit costs	185.60		Total implicit costs	1,414.40
Total relevant costs	$15,305.60		Total relevant costs	$ 14,425.12

FIGURE 8.4

Worksheet for the lease–buy decision.

In the last section of the lease-buy worksheet, relevant explicit costs are totaled for each of the options. If you consider just explicit costs, the purchase option looks much more attractive. However, remember that if you decide to purchase the car, your initial costs are far greater. Those funds that were used to make the initial payment on the purchase of the car could have been invested and earned you income. Therefore, you must also take into account the opportunity cost of your initial expenditures in the section of the worksheet entitled "relevant implicit cost."

To calculate the implicit cost of each option, you must first total up your initial cash outlay. For the lease alternative this will include your initial relevant expenses plus any lease prepayments or security deposit. Even though the security deposit and lease prepayments are either returned to you in the future or offset future obligations, you have still lost the income these funds could have generated over the term of the lease. If your initial cash outlay for the leasing alternative is $580 and you could have earned an annual after-tax return of 8 percent on these funds, then the total implicit cost is $185.50 ($580 × 0.08 × 4). For the purchase the total implicit cost is $1,414.40. It is larger than under the leasing alternative because it requires a much larger explicit initial cost.

When deciding on an open-end lease, it is suggested that unless you have good reasons for doing otherwise, you should set the estimated resale value on the purchase alternative equal to the estimated residual value in the lease. When figured this way, a downside error in the estimated residual value will wash out and not affect the correct decision. For example, suppose the residual value is $100 less than estimated. The resulting $100 end-of-lease payment will increase the relevant cost of leasing by $100. However, this also means that the trade-in value under the purchase alternative would be $100 less than expected, thus increasing the cost of the purchase alternative by $100. Since the cost of each alternative increases by the same amount, an error in the estimated residual value should not affect your choice.

This worksheet assumes you will hold the car for the entire term of the contract. However, the Consumers Bankers Association reports that about 30 percent of auto leases are terminated early. In addition to simply desiring a new car, early termination can be triggered by theft or accident. Regardless of the reason for termination, you may be responsible for depreciation in the market value of the car and for additional special charges upon breaking the lease. Be sure you understand just how much you will owe if you decide to return the vehicle before the scheduled expiration of the lease.

What If You Bought a Lemon?

Your chance of purchasing a new car with serious problems is about one in 800. Your chance of purchasing a car with at least a few defects is apparently much higher. Most of the complaints in the first year should be covered by the new-car warranty. To ensure that they are corrected, you should be prepared to deal with new-car defects and know how to seek remedial action.

The suggested procedure is to discuss the problem with the dealer first, allowing the firm an adequate opportunity to repair the defect. If the dealer is unwilling to honor the warranty or is taking an unreasonable amount of time to correct the problem, you should then contact the manufacturer. At the auto company, the person you should contact first is often called the *zone representative* or the *area service manager*. If you still do not receive satisfaction, your next step is to contact the consumer representative at the company's headquarters. If neither the dealer nor the manufacturer responds to your request, you may consider going to small claims court, entering arbitration, or hiring an attorney.

Whichever alternative you choose, be prepared to supply adequate records on all your attempts at repair or replacement. Accordingly, be sure you receive a repair slip each time you return the car for service. The receipt should be legible and should contain an accurate statement of your complaint, the date of service, and the attempted repairs. If the dealer suggests you do not need a repair slip because the car is under warranty, insist on your right to receive one. Also, retain copies of all relevant correspondence, and a diary recording each related conversation, including the date, the name of the person you discussed your problem with, and a summary of what was said.

Secret Warranties

Warranties were examined previously in the section on major home appliances. Everything stated there holds true for automotive warranties as well. One additional item, however, commonly known as the **secret warranty,** seems to be unique to the automotive industry. It takes effect after the written warranty has

Secret warranty or policy adjustment: An understanding between manufacturers and retailers that certain defects will be repaired at no cost only when confronted with strong consumer complaints.

Action Plan for the Steeles: The Energy-Saving Decision

Background The Steeles have been shopping for two room air conditioners, one for the family room and one for the master bedroom. Both rooms are the same size and will therefore require air conditioners of identical cooling capacity. They expect to leave the one in the family room on permanently during the summer months. The other air conditioner, in the master bedroom, will be used only during hot summer nights.

The Problem After reading *Consumer Reports* and visiting several appliance stores, they have concluded that the FrigiKing and the Cool-Save are both best buys in their respective energy classes. With identical cooling capacity and identical warranties, the FrigiKing costs $299, and the Cool-Save costs $699. However, according to the EnergyGuide, the more expensive Cool-Save uses only about 47 percent of the energy required to run the FrigiKing. The Steeles would like to know whether the expected energy savings are worth the additional cost. Which air conditioners should they buy?

The Plan Given that both appliances are identical except for purchase price and energy consumption, the purchase decision for the Steeles should depend upon these facts in addition to their planned usage.

Based upon energy consumption data and the local cost of electricity, the annual cost of operation can be calculated for assumed hours of use. The accompanying table lists these costs for both the FrigiKing and the Cool-Save. As can be seen, the annual savings attributable to the energy-efficient Cool-Save increase with planned usage.

The present value of a $1 reduction in the cost of operation can be found in Table 8.5. Assuming a seven-year service life and a 3 percent interest rate–energy inflation rate differential, the present value of a $1 reduction in the cost of operation is $6.20. Multiplying 6.2 times the annual cost savings provides an estimate of the present value of the savings in operational costs generated by the Cool-Save.

Spending,
Borrowing,
and Saving

expired. Under a secret warranty, the manufacturer repairs certain defects only when customers complain. Other, more docile customers are not told about this policy and are unfairly charged for repairs.

The industry prefers the term **policy adjustment** to *secret warranty*. Given the way the auto industry treats customers, it is a good idea to complain whenever you think your problem results from faulty workmanship or design. You should ask the zone representative whether policy adjustments have been made on similar problems, and whether a policy adjustment would cover your current defect. The Center for Auto Safety collects information on policy adjustments. They may be able to supply you with information on how a manufacturer has previously dealt with similar defects.

Arbitration

In *mediation*, an attempt is made to have the parties to the dispute reach their own agreement. Most consumer protection agencies, such as the Better Business

	Hours of Use				
	250	500	750	1,000	2,000
Annual cost of operations					
FrigiKing	$ 34	$ 68	$102	$136	$272
Cool-Save	16	32	48	63	127
Annual savings	18	36	54	73	145
Present value of $1 reduction in cost of operations	× 6.2	× 6.2	× 6.2	× 6.2	× 6.2
Present value of future cost savings	$111.60	$223.20	$334.80	$452.60	$899.00

The purchase price of the Cool-Save is $300 more than that of the FrigiKing. Therefore, the present value of the future energy savings must be greater than $300 to make the Cool-Save the better buy. With 500 or fewer annual hours of usage, the present value of the savings in operational costs is less than $300. Therefore, in this range of usage the FrigiKing is the better buy. However, at 750 hours of usage, the present value of the savings in operational costs exceeds $300, making the Cool-Save the better choice. Somewhere between 500 hours and 750 hours the value of the energy savings is just equal to the difference in purchase price.

It appears that the optimal purchase plan consists of purchasing the Cool-Save for the family room and the FrigiKing for the bedroom. The heavy usage in the family room warrants the higher purchase price of the Cool-Save. Alternatively, the air conditioner in the master bedroom will not be used often. If planned usage in this room is 500 hours or less, the Steeles would do better to purchase the cheaper FrigiKing. Given the limited usage in the master bedroom, the amount they save up front will easily cover the higher future cost of operations.

Arbitration: A process for settling disputes in which an impartial third party mediates and suggests a binding or nonbinding remedy.

Bureau, will first attempt to resolve the disagreement through mediation. If that doesn't work, arbitration may be entered into.

Arbitration is a process for settling disputes in which an impartial third party listens to arguments made by both sides and suggests a remedy that may be binding or nonbinding. In consumer-related disputes, the Federal Trade Commission sets down rules to ensure that the arbitration procedure is, in fact, impartial.

If you have a problem with a new car and do not receive satisfaction from the dealer or the manufacturer's representative, or you are dissatisfied with repairs made on a used car, your next step is to consider arbitration. A listing of the major arbitration programs is given in Table 8.8.

Entering arbitration has two significant advantages over using the court system: The process is relatively speedy, and there is no cost to the individual. However, there are also some disadvantages. The arbitrators need not be lawyers or knowledgeable mechanics. Thus, they may not fully understand your problem or your rights as a consumer. Furthermore, they will not award punitive damages, or compensatory damages related to such incidentals as lost wages or medical bills resulting from a defective car. Without your own lawyer, you may not know whether you would be entitled to such payments in the regular court system. In addition, by entering arbitration you may be accepting a potential decision that is legally binding.

You should realize that your chances of coming out of arbitration with a better offer than that provided by the dealer or manufacturer's representative are only about 50–50. Citing the large domestic automakers, *Business Week* reports that "GM's Pensa notes that 55 percent of the arbitrators either award the customer nothing or agree with the zone's last offer. Ford pegs that figure at 60 percent, while Chrysler reports that 42 percent of the awards made by its boards are adverse to the consumer."

TABLE 8.8 · Arbitration Programs

BBB Autoline
General Motors, AMC, Audi, Honda, Jeep, Nissan, Peugeot, Porsche, Renault, SAAB, and Volkswagen.
Federal guidelines require that Autoline settle dispute within 40 days of when it has the necessary data.
Details available on Autoline from local BBB.
Call (800) 955-5100.
American Automobile Association
Handles Toyota and Hyundai cases.
Call (800) 331–4331 for Toyota customers.
Call (800) 222–3717 for Hyundai customers.
Autocap (Automotive Consumer Action Program)
Administered through National Automobile Dealers Association, handles 15 makers of imports.
Call (703) 821–7144.
Chrysler and Ford have their own boards for handling complaints:
Chrysler Motors Customer Relations
(800) 922–1997.
Ford Consumer Appeals Board
(313) 337–6950 inside Maine.
(800) 241–8450 outside Maine.
State-run arbitration boards
Many states have arbitration boards that help enforce the lemon laws. State-run boards exist in Connecticut, Florida, Hawaii, Maine, Massachusetts, New York, New Jersey, Texas, Vermont, Washington, and the District of Columbia. Contact your state consumer-protection office for information.

Lemon Laws

All states, except Arkansas and South Dakota, have lemon laws to protect buyers. Generally, lemon laws declare that if a car dealer does not repair substantial defects covered by the new-car warranty within a reasonable period of time, the owner may be entitled to a comparable new car or a refund. A reasonable time is usually defined as four trips to the repair shop for the same problem or a total of 30 days in the repair shop. If the manufacturer or dealer does not supply a new car, the customer may go to court after attempting to arbitrate the matter.

The *Lemon Book*, available through the Center for Auto Safety, explains your rights and remedies and gives a breakdown of lemon laws by state. If your state does not have a lemon law, you can still go to court to enforce performance of express and implied warranties under the Magnuson-Moss Warranty Act, discussed earlier in this chapter.

Summary

Consumer durables provide long-term benefits, while committing us to long-term operational costs and creating the need for long-range planning. Such planning will involve the following questions. What is the future replacement cost likely to be? How much savings in operational costs can various models provide? How much protection do warranties afford? What fixed and variable costs are involved? In this chapter we have examined how each of these questions will affect the purchasing and budgeting of both major home appliances and the family auto.

Key Terms

arbitration (p. 248)

"as is" (p. 231)

certificate of title (p. 239)

certificate of registration (p. 239)

closed-end lease (p. 242)

consumer durables (p. 222)

Consumer Leasing Act of 1977 (p. 242)

cost of operation (p. 240)

cost of ownership (p. 237)

credit life insurance (p. 237)

depreciation (p. 239)

EnergyGuide (p. 229)

express warranty (p. 232)

extended warranty (p. 233)

full warranty (p. 233)

guarantee (p. 231)

implied warranty (p. 231)

invoice price (p. 234)

lemon protection (p. 233)

limited warranty (p. 233)

Magnuson-Moss Warranty Act of 1975 (p. 232)

marginal cost (p. 241)

open-end lease (p. 242)

policy adjustment (p. 247)

puffery (p. 232)

replacement cost (p. 224)

savings illusion (p. 223)

secret warranty (p. 246)

service contract (p. 233)

sticker price (p. 234)

sunk cost (p. 241)

warranty (p. 231)

Problems and Review Questions

1 What special characteristics and budgeting problems do consumer durables present?

2 Suppose it costs you $300 to replace your washing machine at today's prices. If you expect prices to increase by 10 percent over each of the next two years, about how much will it cost you two years from now?

3 Using the depreciation schedule in Table 8.2, and assuming zero inflation, estimate the trade-in value of a $10,000 compact car over each of the next 12 years. Now repeat your calculation, but instead assume a 5 percent yearly inflation rate.

4 Where can you find information on a product's service record and operational costs?

5 When shopping for a water heater, you find a $100 difference in purchase price between the most energy-efficient model and the standard model. How should you go about deciding whether the energy-efficient model is worth the extra cost?

6 What is the difference between an express and an implied warranty?

7 Does an item sold "as is" carry an implied warranty?

8 What requirements must a warranty satisfy before it can be labeled *full*? How do these differ for a limited warranty?

9 You purchase a stereo system from a local department store on the basis of the salesperson's assurance that this system is a "good buy." You later find out that it wasn't such a good buy. The same product is being sold elsewhere at a much lower price. Does the salesperson's statement constitute an express warranty? What action do you now take?

10 Suppose you purchase the stereo system and later find that it plays at only one speed. You also find that nobody manufactures records to be played at that speed. The product was not sold "as is," but you forgot to ask if there was a written warranty. What can you do?

11 What is the greatest cost associated with owning and operating a car?

12 How do you distinguish an ownership cost from an operating cost?

13 You commute 20 miles each day in your own car, and the estimated operational cost per mile is 15 cents. If you used the mass transit system, the same trip would cost you $2. Should you leave your car at home and ride the public transport?

14 Your new station wagon has 14,000 miles on the odometer. The new-car warranty expired at the 12,000-mile mark. Yesterday, while driving the car to school, the rear axle broke. The dealer tells you it will cost over $1,000 to have the problem fixed because the warranty has expired. What do you do?

15 Explain secret warranties and lemon protection.

Case 8.1
Ann Barnard Considers Alternative Holding Periods

Ann Barnard typically buys a new car and trades in the old one every five years. Because new cars are so expensive, she has recently been considering a change in her buying habits. She would like to know how much she might save in depreciation costs if instead she purchased a year-old car every four years.

Questions

1 Using a new-car price of $20,000 and the depreciation schedule for an intermediate-size car in Table 8.2, calculate the annual cost of depreciation given her present buying habits. Now calculate the annual cost of depreciation under the proposed change. What is the annual cost savings? What is the cost savings over the five-year holding period?

2 What other factors should Ann Barnard consider before she changes her buying behavior?

Spending,
Borrowing,
and Saving

The Reeds just purchased an intermediate-size new car for $13,000. They plan to trade in this car for a similar new car in five years. The Reeds estimate that inflation should average about 5 percent per year over the next five years.

Questions

1   Given that inflation averages 5 percent per year over the next five years, what will a similar new car cost five years from now?
2   Under this inflation assumption, what will be the trade-in value on their current car at that time?
3   The Reeds plan to purchase a new car in five years by trading in the then-old car and making up the difference in cash. What is the expected size of the cash payment five years from now?

Helpful Reading

Consumer Reports. "Who Needs an Extended Warranty?" January 1991, pp. 21–22.

Council of Better Business Bureaus. *How BBB Auto Line Works.* Alternative Dispute Resolution, Arlington, VA, 1989.

Dahringer, Lee D., and Denise R. Johnson. "Lemon Laws: Intent, Experience and a Pro-Consumer Model. *Journal of Consumer Affairs,* Summer 1988, pp. 158–170.

Gillis, Jack. *The Car Book* and *The Used Car Book.* Harper Perennial (annual edition).

United States Office of Consumer Affairs. *Consumer's Resource Handbook.* Single copies available by writing: Handbook, Consumer Information Center, Pueblo, CO 81009.

Helpful Contacts

American Automobile Association
(See your local directory.)

Better Business Bureau
(See your local directory.)

Center for Auto Safety
2001 S Street, NW, Suite 410, Washington, DC 20009
Clearinghouse for automotive complaints.

National Highway Traffic Safety Administration
Auto Safety Hotline, NEF-11 HL, 400 Seventh St., SW
Washington, DC 20590 (telephone 1–800–424–9393)
Keeps information on manufacturers' recalls and can provide printout of complaints on a particular make and model.

Public Reference, Federal Trade Commission, Washington, DC 20580
    Series of pamphlets on consumer issues:
    A Consumer Guide to Vehicle Leasing
    Facts for Consumers: Auto Service Contracts
    Facts for Consumers: New Car Buying Guide
    Facts for Consumers: Buying a Used Car
    How to Write a Wrong: Complain Effectively and Get Results

Chapter 9

Housing:
The Cost of Shelter

Objectives

1 To determine how much you can afford to spend on housing
2 To describe the several types of home ownership
3 To explain the real estate transaction from appraisal to closing
4 To understand the many kinds of home mortgages
5 To estimate whether it is financially more attractive to buy or rent
6 To know how to handle a potential foreclosure

The most prized piece of real estate is a single-family home on its own lot with a lawn. This was and still is the American Dream. A survey undertaken by the Market Opinion Research Corporation showed that, next to having a job, home ownership and health care were the most important concerns of the American public.

Other surveys have found that the average first-time home buyer is about 30 years of age, and that the buyer moving up to a larger home is approximately 8 years older. At the end of the 1970s, the leading edge of the baby boom entered the home-buying market, significantly increasing the demand for housing. Given this aging wave of baby boomers and the currently more favorable financial conditions, it is not surprising that the demand now appears to be shifting to larger and more expensive homes. Alternatively, with the shrinking 25-to-34 age population, buying a starter home may not be as difficult as it was in previous decades.

Housing Affordability Index: Published by the National Association of Realtors, it is related directly to the ability of a median-income family to purchase a median-priced home.

The National Association of Realtors publishes the **Housing Affordability Index** presented in Figure 9.1. When the median family income is enough to qualify for a conventional loan on an existing median-priced home, the index assumes a value of 100. When the index rises, more families find it easier to purchase and finance the typical home. For example, when the index rises to 110, those earning about 90 percent of the median family income will now qualify for a loan on a median-priced home.

During the 1970s and the beginning of the 1980s, housing became less affordable because of increases in both the cost of a home and the cost of finance. Consumer prices were rising rapidly, but housing prices were rising faster, creating substantial gains for those who were wise (or lucky) enough to purchase a home at the beginning of the 1970s. Along with rising inflation came rising interest rates, as shown in Figure 9.2. Those who were fortunate enough to beat high prices and high interest rates by purchasing a home in the early 1970s made a very wise investment.

The boom in the housing market ended in 1979 when home mortgage rates began to soar. With the exceptionally high cost of finance, homes became so

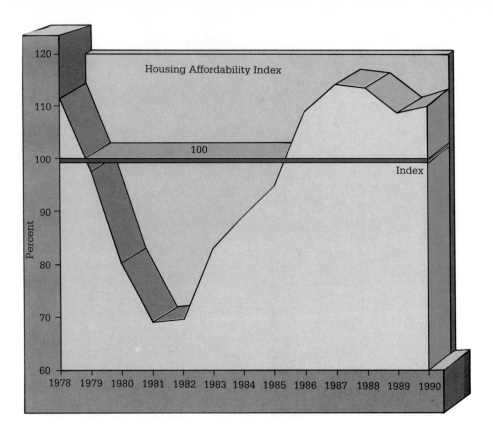

Housing Affordability Index

100

Index

Percent

120 —
110 —
100 —
90 —
80 —
70 —
60 —

1978 1979 1980 1981 1982 1983 1984 1985 1986 1987 1988 1989 1990

FIGURE 9.1

The Housing Affordability Index. (Source: National Association of Realtors®, *Monthly Report: Existing Home Sales, June 1991.*)

much less affordable that housing prices finally began to fall behind the rapid rise in the general price level. After a severe recession that seemed to hit the housing industry the hardest, mortgage rates turned downward in 1982. Since then housing has again become more affordable, recently fluctuating around an affordability index of 110.

It is unlikely, however, that housing will again be as good an investment as it was during the 1970s. Financial markets have changed substantially since that decade. If inflation increases, it is likely that financial markets will react more swiftly and with larger interest rate adjustments than they have in the past. Banks and savings and loan associations no longer have a captive source of funds that can be channeled into low-cost finance for the housing industry. The removal of ceilings on interest rates that depositors can earn, the creation of money market accounts, and the ability of lending institutions to offer adjustable rate loans have largely eliminated previous sources of cheap financing. This doesn't mean that buying a home may not still be a wise decision. It does mean that to benefit in the future you will have to consider carefully the housing market, the relative value of your potential home, and the real cost of financing before you purchase.

The housing data in Figure 9.3 indicate the need for caution in the housing market. The real price of housing, after adjustment for changes in the price level, actually declined slightly during the 1980s. Individual markets were even more

Spending, Borrowing, and Saving

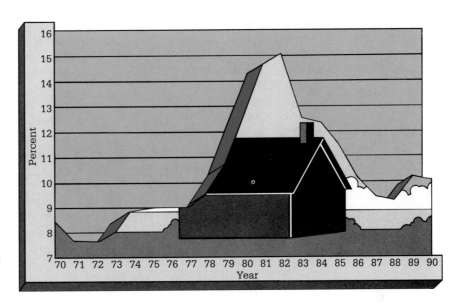

FIGURE 9.2

Effective rate on conventional home mortgages. (Source: *Economic Report of the President, 1991*, Table B-71, p. 368.)

risky, because some fared better and worse than this national average. As recent experience suggests, and many forecasters predict, housing should now be desired for the services it produces and not as the get-rich investment it once was.

Rent or Buy?

You have little choice in the matter: You need shelter. However, the ways in which you may satisfy that need are practically unlimited. Like most decisions, this one must take into account your preferred life-style and your financial constraints. You can decide on a rental that places minimal demands on your time or finances. You can purchase a single-family home, thus taking on all the responsibilities of maintenance and of carrying a home mortgage. Or you may prefer to

FIGURE 9.3

Average sales price of the kinds of new one-family houses sold in 1987. (Source: Current Construction Reports, Price Index of New One-Family Houses Sold, Fourth Quarter 1990.)

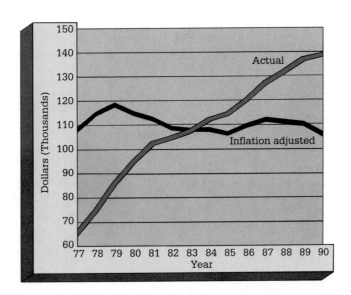

Housing: The Cost of Shelter

purchase a condominium or a cooperative, with characteristics falling somewhere between those of a rental unit and those of a single-family home. Obviously, your choice will, and should, depend on what makes your feel most comfortable. All we can do is point out the various advantages and disadvantages concerning your choice of shelter.

Figure 9.4 outlines some of the life-style considerations surrounding the choice. The following discussion will be concerned with the financial considerations. We do not mean to imply that the financial decision is the most important one. The financial decision is an objective one that we can help you analyze. Your preferred living arrangement is a personal choice.

To find out whether you are a candidate for home ownership, you should first estimate how much you can afford. Given this information, you can then examine housing within your price range. Once you understand what the market has to offer, you can decide whether it is financially more advantageous to buy or rent.

Determining What You Can Afford

The general rule of thumb for determining how much you can afford either to rent or purchase is that you spend no more than 25 percent of your after-tax income on housing expenses. For buyers, this usually implies a home purchase

FIGURE 9.4

Rent versus buy: personal considerations.

RENTING	BUYING
Life-Style Choices	
Landlord may place restrictions on pets, guests, and children. There also may be restrictions on how you may redecorate your rental unit.	For condos and co-ops, similar restrictions may exist in the bylaws. The single-family home provides the most freedom in choice of life-style. You need only abide by city zoning ordinances.
Privacy	
You may be bothered by both other tenants and the landlord. The landlord will have rights to inspect the premises and to show the unit to prospective tenants.	You can have as much or as little privacy as you want, depending on the type of home ownership you choose.
Maintenance	
Maintenance costs will be included in your rental payments. With a responsible landlord you will be free of maintenance concerns. With an irresponsible landlord your only remedy may be to move.	You alone are responsible. You must budget for maintenance expenses, and be prepared to do it yourself, or hire a capable person.
Mobility	
At the end of the leasing period you simply pack up and leave. If you must move before the lease is up for renewal, you usually can negotiate a mutually agreeable termination.	Selling costs may be considerable, including sales commissions and fixing-up expenses. You are at the mercy of the marketplace. If home demand is down, you must either accept a lower price or incur carrying costs until the market improves.
Financial Risk	
The only risk you face is the possible loss of your personal property in the rental unit. This risk can be covered by renter's insurance.	Your home is also an investment. You can insure it against natural disasters and most other risks. However, you cannot insure against a forced sale at below market price resulting from the loss of your job.

price of about two and one-half times after-tax income. Unfortunately, this is only a rule of thumb; the actual guidelines used by lending institutions can be a lot more complicated.

The Federal Home Loan Mortgage Corporation (popularly called Freddie Mac) recommends that your monthly housing expenses not exceed 28 percent of gross monthly income. Furthermore, it suggests that your total monthly debt payments, including housing expenses, not exceed 33 to 36 percent of your gross monthly income. Most lenders will attempt to abide by these ratios. However, you may find a few who are willing to surpass the recommended ratios if you have proven yourself creditworthy.

A worksheet incorporating the housing expense and repayment test set down by Freddie Mac is contained in Figure 9.5. You begin by entering your annual and monthly gross income on lines 1 and 2. This includes all before-tax income from normal and regular sources.

FIGURE 9.5

How much house can you afford?

		Sample Data	Your Data
1.	Annual gross income	$35,000	_____
2.	Monthly gross income (divide line 1 by 12)	$2,917	_____
Housing Expense Test			
3.	Housing expense-to-income ratio	×0.28	× _____
4.	Allowable housing expenditure (multiply line 2 by line 3)	$817	_____
5.	Estimated nonmortgage housing expenses	200	_____
6.	Affordable monthly mortgage payment under housing expense test (subtract line 5 from line 4)	$617	_____
Debt Repayment Test			
7.	Debt repayment-to-income ratio	0.36	× _____
8.	Allowable debt payment (multiply line 2 by line 7)	$1,050	_____
9.	Monthly installment debt and alimony	$120	_____
10.	Total nonmortgage expense and installment debt repayment (add line 5 and line 9)	$320	_____
11.	Affordable monthly mortgage payment under debt repayment test (subtract line 10 from line 8)	$730	_____
Your Affordable Home Purchase			
12.	Affordable monthly mortgage (enter the lesser value on line 11 and line 6)	$617	_____
13.	Monthly payment per $1,000 mortgage (see Table 9.1)	9.52	_____
14.	Your affordable mortgage (divide line 12 by line 13 and multiply by $1,000)	$64,786	_____
15.	Fractional amount borrowed	0.80	_____
16.	Your affordable home purchase (divide line 14 by line 15)	$80,982	_____

Housing: The
Cost of
Shelter

Next, multiply the allowable housing expense ratio on line 3 by your monthly gross income on line 2, and enter the result on line 4. This indicates the total amount you may devote to housing expenses. A maximum housing expense-to-income ratio of .28 is used in the example.

Line 5 includes all your nonmortgage housing expenses. These will consist of mortgage insurance premiums, property insurance, real estate taxes, and, when applicable, homeowners association or condominium maintenance fees. Subtracting nonmortgage housing expenses from line 4 indicates your affordable monthly mortgage payment under the housing expenses test.

The debt repayment test is used to ensure that other claims on your paycheck do not interfere with your ability to meet your mortgage payment. An allowable debt-to-income ratio of .36 is used in the example. If you plan to place 10 percent or less down on the purchase price, use the lower limit of .33. On line 9 include all installment debt with more than ten payments remaining, in addition to any other regular claims on your income, such as alimony payments. Adding in nonmortgage expenses and subtracting the total from the allowable debt payment on line 8 provides your affordable monthly mortgage payment under the debt repayment test.

You must satisfy both the home expense and debt repayment test, therefore your affordable monthly mortgage will be the equal to the lower of the values on line 6 and line 11. The next step is to determine how much you can borrow, given your ability to cover the monthly mortgage payments on line 12. To estimate this, you first need to know the current initial interest rates on home mortgages. You will find that interest rates differ by lending institution, type of mortgage, and size of down payment. However, after a few calls to local financial institutions, you should have some idea what the going market rate is. You then can use this rate to find your monthly payment per $1,000 of mortgage loan in Table 9.1. Enter this value on line 13. In the example, it is assumed that the annual interest rate on an expected 30-year loan with a 20 percent down payment is 11 percent. This produces the monthly payment per $1,000 of $9.52 on line 13. Divide line 12 by line 13, and then multiply the result by $1,000 to obtain an estimate of your affordable mortgage on line 14.

The home purchase price will be equal to the amount borrowed plus the down payment. Given a 20 percent down payment, the mortgage will equal 80 percent of the selling price, and the affordable home purchase price is $80,982 shown on line 16.

Types of Housing

Current data on the housing market can be found in Figure 9.6. Since World War II the U.S. Congress has pursued a policy of fostering home ownership through subsidies and tax breaks. That policy has largely succeeded, as demonstrated by the increase in owner-occupied housing. In 1940, only about 44 percent of housing units were owner occupied. This percentage rose to a high of 65.6 percent in 1980, but has since slipped to 63.9 percent of housing in 1989.

The 1980s exhibited the first decade-long reduction in the home ownership rate since the 1930s. Largely responsible for this decline were those in the less-than-35-years-old age group. A larger percentage of these young adults have

TABLE 9.1 · Monthly Payment per $1,000 of Mortgage Loan

Contract Interest Rate (%)	Duration of Loan (Years)					
	5	10	15	20	25	30
16	$24.32	$16.75	$14.69	$13.91	$13.59	$13.45
15	23.79	16.13	14.00	13.17	12.81	12.64
14	23.27	15.53	13.31	12.44	12.04	11.85
13½	23.01	15.23	12.98	12.07	11.66	11.45
13	22.75	14.93	12.65	11.72	11.28	11.06
12½	22.50	14.64	12.33	11.36	10.90	10.67
12	22.24	14.35	12.00	11.01	10.53	10.29
11½	21.99	14.06	11.68	10.66	10.16	9.90
11	21.74	13.78	11.37	10.32	9.80	9.52
10½	21.49	13.49	11.05	9.98	9.44	9.15
10	21.25	13.22	10.75	9.65	9.09	8.78
9½	21.00	12.94	10.44	9.32	8.74	8.41
9	20.76	12.67	10.14	9.00	8.39	8.05
8	20.28	12.13	9.56	8.36	7.72	7.34
7	19.80	11.61	8.99	7.75	7.07	6.65
6	19.33	11.10	8.44	7.16	6.44	6.00
5	18.87	10.61	7.91	6.60	5.85	5.37

lately decided to rent rather than buy. Since housing affordability generally increased during the 1980s, this change in behavior cannot be explained by financial factors. The Bureau of the Census suggests that the decline in home ownership is most likely due to changing life-styles. Nonmarried-couple households increased during the 1980s, and such nonfamily households are less likely to own homes than traditional married-couple families.

As you might expect, the home ownership rate for specific groups of households can diverge widely from this overall percentage. Home ownership varies directly with age, income, and net worth. Under age 35, only 39 percent of households own the home they are living in. By age 55 to 64, ownership has risen to 80 percent. Household income and net worth both increase with age, so that housing becomes both more affordable and more tax advantageous, because of federal income tax deductions for mortgage interest and property taxes. Over 88 percent of households with annual incomes exceeding $48,000 own their residences, and in those households with net worth of over $100,000 home ownership is at a high of 95 percent.

The data suggest that the typical household starts out in a rental unit. With an increase in income and the accumulation of the necessary down payment, families tend to purchase their first home when the head of the household is around age 30. And when they do purchase, the overwhelming choice is the traditional single-family home. Your household, however, need not be typical. Choose the types of housing and the type of occupancy that best fits your life-style and financial plan. To do that you must first familiarize yourself with the available types of housing and then analyze the financial benefits of buying versus renting.

APARTMENT HOUSING   Although any style of living unit can be rented, it is usually the apartment we think of first. The census data indicate a movement

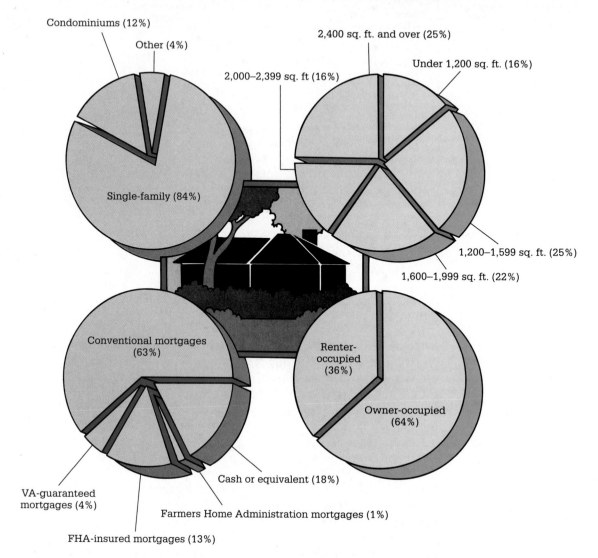

New Home Buyers Purchasing Each Type

Condominiums (12%)

Other (4%)

Single-family (84%)

Floor Area of New Single-family Homes

2,400 sq. ft. and over (25%)

Under 1,200 sq. ft. (16%)

2,000–2,399 sq. ft (16%)

1,200–1,599 sq. ft. (25%)

1,600–1,999 sq. ft. (22%)

Conventional mortgages (63%)

Renter-occupied (36%)

Owner-occupied (64%)

VA-guaranteed mortgages (4%)

Cash or equivalent (18%)

Farmers Home Administration mortgages (1%)

FHA-insured mortgages (13%)

Financing of New Single-family Homes

Percent of Housing Units Occupied

FIGURE 9.6

The housing market, 1988. (Source: U.S. Department of Commerce, Bureau of the Census, *Statistical Abstract of the United States: 1990.*)

toward building larger apartment complexes that offer attractive amenities such as swimming pools, tennis courts, and clubhouses. Outside of a cooperative or condo, such amenities would be difficult for the average homeowner to afford.

For mobile individuals demanding minimal responsibilities and an environment in which social relationships are nurtured, a large apartment complex may be desirable. This group seems to be the one to which new apartment construction is designed to appeal.

CONDOMINIUM HOUSING Condominium housing can offer the extras of apartment living along with the rewards of home ownership. However, strictly defined, **condominium** does not refer to a particular type of housing. It stands for a unique type of ownership where part of the property is individually owned and part is owned in common with other members of the condominium complex. You own your living unit and have a shared interest in other areas of the condominium site, such as recreational and maintenance areas. This means you will be responsible not only for the financing and upkeep of your individual unit, but you will also be assessed charges for the financing and upkeep of the common areas. Before you purchase, you should fully understand what these charges are and how they will be determined in the future.

As an owner, you are a member of the condominium association and will be able to vote for directors in whom most of the governing powers will be vested. Condominiums are created by the laws of the state where they are located. The laws provide a legal framework for the operations of the directors and for the conditions and restrictions imposed on a property. Although this framework will differ from state to state, in all states you have a right to receive copies of the basic documents in which the legal and economic bases of the condominium are set out. This information will be contained in the declaration, bylaws, operating budget, and management agreement for the condominium.

A comprehensive list of the questions you should ask and the facts you should consider are contained in an informative booklet entitled *Questions About Condominiums: What to Ask Before You Buy*, published by the U.S. Department of Housing and Urban Development, Washington, DC 20410. In brief, you should have information on the following points:

1. What property is owned in common? Some of the facilities that appear to be owned by the condominium complex may actually be leased. If they are leased, find out how the rental charges are determined. With no limit on the rental charges, exorbitant monthly assessments are possible.

2. How are the maintenance charges for the common areas allocated among the owners? The costs may simply be divided equally among the owners, or allocated according to some formula based on living space or purchase price. How this is determined will affect the market value of your living unit and your future monthly assessment.

3. Who governs the condominium association, and how are the members elected? Information on the individuals serving on the board of directors for the condominium association can often prove useful. For example, a board composed entirely of retirees is unlikely to favor enhancing the playground facilities.

4. What are the policy-making powers of the directors of the association? Do these powers unduly restrict the rights of owners, or can they be used in the future to do so? On the other hand, do they lack sufficient powers to handle negligent owners?

5. What was the previous operating budget for the association, and what does the prospective operating budget look like? Has required maintenance been postponed, and are these charges likely to become due in the future?

Condominium: A form of ownership in which there is an individual ownership interest in the living unit, but a shared ownership unit in the common areas.

261

Housing: The Cost of Shelter

6. What percentage of the units are currently rented? You may encounter restrictions on mortgage financing if fewer than 60 percent of the units are owner occupied.

COOPERATIVE HOUSING   As in a condominium, several owners share an undivided interest in cooperative housing. However, a **cooperative** has a corporate form. Instead of purchasing the individual living unit, you purchase stock in the corporation and then lease the living unit from the corporation. The corporation owns the living units and carries the mortgage on them. Its expenses are covered by the rents set in the lease agreements. As a stockholder, you can vote for the board of directors. One major problem associated with cooperatives is that you must receive the consent of the board of directors before you can transfer your stock and lease.

SINGLE-FAMILY HOUSING   The dominant form of shelter, single-family housing makes up over 67 percent of all living units, and 87 percent of all home purchases.

Single-family homes can be found to fit almost every need, if not every price range. The typical new home will contain almost 1,800 square feet in two stories and a slab, with three bedrooms, two baths, and a garage. If you can't find one that satisfies you, you can always consider having one built.

When you purchase a single-family home, you take on all the responsibilities of finance and maintenance that go with it. You are your own landlord and maintenance person, and must budget your money and time accordingly. When something needs to be fixed, you must be ready to do it yourself or have the funds to hire someone else.

MULTIFAMILY HOUSING   If you are considering purchasing a multifamily dwelling, you are looking for an investment that also satisfies your own need for shelter. The financial considerations concerning investment in real estate are not covered in this chapter. It is suggested that you read the sections in this chapter on real estate transactions and mortgage financing, and then turn to Chapter 16 for a discussion on investing in tangibles.

MOBILE HOMES   Over 90 percent of mobile homes are not very mobile. They travel only from the manufacturer to the dealer and finally to a housing site, where they usually remain permanently affixed. For this reason, the industry prefers the term *manufactured home*. Because the homes are constructed at the factory, the cost per square foot of living space is considerably less than for on-site construction.

The mobile home may be placed on a solitary plot or within a mobile home park. Parks often have common recreational areas and offer many of the conveniences of large apartment complexes. Typically, mobile home parks rent sites using long-term lease agreements. However, there are a few condominium mobile home developments, where you purchase the site and then pay a monthly maintenance fee to cover the cost of the common areas.

The construction of new mobile homes must satisfy safety requirements specified in the National Mobile Home Construction Act and must display a permanent label stating so. This label does not certify that the home will be approved for government-insured financing provided by the Department of Housing and Urban Development.

Because the market price of mobile homes has typically depreciated with age, financing has been a problem. Mobile homes are usually financed with a 20 percent down payment, a personal property loan of 10 to 15 years duration, and an interest rate a few percentage points above that on conventional home mortgages. For those who qualify, federally insured mortgages for longer durations and with lower down payments are available through the Federal Housing Administration (FHA) and the Veterans Administration (VA).

A Cost Comparison

When you purchase a home, you are undertaking a sizable investment of your own money. The financial question is, Would you be better off renting and investing your funds elsewhere? The answer will depend upon expected future housing prices, the expected return on financial investments, the length of time you expect to stay in one location, and the expected tax advantage from home ownership.

Several immediate and long-term tax advantages are associated with buying a home. If you itemize deductions—and you probably should if you have a home mortgage—both the state and local taxes you pay on the property and the interest you pay on the mortgage may be deductible from your adjusted gross income when you calculate your federal taxable income. This means that if you are in the 28 percent marginal tax bracket, each dollar you pay in property taxes and interest saves you 28 cents in federal income taxes. Naturally, the higher your marginal tax rate, the greater is the income tax advantage. As a renter, you may find these items included in the price of the rent, but you as a renter cannot take them as a deduction on your income tax return. It is true that the landlord can deduct these expenses, and this tax advantage to the landlord may be reflected in a lower rental price, but don't plan on it. Rental prices in most areas are set by supply and demand. During periods when rental units are scarce, it is unlikely that any of the landlord's tax advantage will show up in favorable rental prices.

Federal tax law changes enacted in 1986 and 1987 placed a few restrictions on the deduction of home mortgage interest. Mortgage interest is now fully deductible only on first and second homes, if total home mortgages do not exceed $1 million. In addition, for all interest on a second mortgage, such as a home equity loan, to be deductible, total mortgages must be both less than the market value of the home and less than $100,000 plus the cost of improvements and your remaining acquisition indebtedness.

For example, suppose you originally borrowed $90,000 when you purchased your current home, and the remaining loan balance is $60,000. Furthermore, you have spent $10,000 on home improvements. In this case, interest payments on first and second mortgages totaling $170,000 ($100,000 + $60,000 of remaining acquisition indebtedness + $10,000 of home improvements) would be fully deductible so long as the current market value of the home were at least $170,000.

Home ownership provides more than the immediate tax benefit. Special tax treatment accorded capital gains provides an additional long-term tax advantage. If you sell a home for more than you paid for it, you can defer paying taxes on the gain if you purchase another home within a two-year period. To qualify for the

Housing: The
Cost of
Shelter

Box 9.1
Simplifying Personal Finance

Keeping Track of Your Housing Capital Gains

You have a capital gain whenever you sell something for more than it cost you. The IRS is interested in your capital gains because it collects taxes on such gains at the same rate as on your other earnings. In order to make sure it doesn't miss any of those taxes, it requires the settlement agent at the closing on the home to report the details of the transaction to the IRS on a Form 1099B.

Congress has attempted to encourage home ownership by providing for special tax treatment. Paying taxes on your home ownership capital gains can be delayed as long as you purchase another home of equal or greater value within two years of selling the previous one, and file a Form 2119 with your personal income tax return. Additional favorable treatment includes a one-time tax exclusion on $125,000 of your gains if you are over 55 and cannot delay the taxes due by purchasing another home. Given these tax breaks, it is important to keep adequate records to ensure that you are not paying too much or too little in taxes.

For each home that you have owned, you should permanently retain records on:

- All documents relating to the financial circumstances of the purchase and sale of the home
- All costs incurred in preparing the home for sale and selling the home
- Form 2119
- The cost of all home improvements

The retention of these records will simplify the task of substantiating your cost basis and qualifying for your capital gains exemption.

Your capital gain is equal to the net sales price (selling price minus selling expenses) less the cost of the home and the cost of any improvements you have made on the home. While home owners usually do retain adequate records on the purchase and sale of a home, they often neglect to keep track of their home improvement costs. In order to reduce your potential capital gain, such improvements must consist of expenses other than for normal maintenance and repair. In addition, your expenses must be adequately documented. It is not the responsibility of the IRS to prove that you didn't make the improvements; rather, it is your responsibility to prove that you did. To substantiate these expenses, you should maintain a file labeled "home improvements," and simply place copies of any receipts or bills for home improvement expenditures along with a short explanation of what was done whenever these improvements occur.

When the tax on your capital gains is no longer delayed by the purchase of another home, you will have to pay taxes on all of your accumulated gains. In effect, you will have to total up the capital gains on each of the several homes you may have owned. The home owners capital gain exclusion of $125,000 may sound like a lot of money, but 20 or 30 years from now it may be worth a lot less. Above that exclusion, each dollar of documented home improvement costs will make you very glad that you have kept a file labeled "home improvements."

tax deferral you must file IRS Form 2119, *Sale or Exchange of Principal Residence*, to indicate the details of the sale and purchase. As an added bonus, after you reach 55, you need not pay taxes on $125,000 of these accumulated gains.

Finally, there is a hidden tax advantage that is often overlooked. Suppose you could rent your present home for $500 a month; this is the market worth of the shelter, which you are receiving. This value is part of the return from the investment in the home and may be thought of as an implicit rent paid to and received by yourself. However, payments to yourself are not considered income for tax purposes. Thus, the implicit rental income accompanying home ownership remains tax free.

Figure 9.7 shows a worksheet for comparing the relative costs of buying and renting a home. The worksheet contains entries for a one-year comparison and a five-year comparison. Both periods are considered because it is most likely that the best choice depends on the length of time spent at one location. The sample

Givens: Home: $100,000 Purchase Price
7% annual inflation

Mortgage: $80,000 loan
11% annual interest on outstanding balance with $20,000 down payment
monthly payment $761.86 for 30 years

Rent: $900 per month plus utilities

Marginal Tax Rate: 28%

ONE-YEAR COMPARISON

	Buying		Renting	
	Sample Estimates	Your Estimates	Sample Estimates	Your Estimates
Gross gain				
Appreciation	$ 7,000	_____		
Interest earned after taxes paid			$ 1,296	_____
Expenses				
Mortgage interest after taxes saved	6,323	_____		
Property taxes after taxes saved	1,235	_____		
Fuel and utilities	1,800	_____	1,800	_____
Insurance	300	_____	150	_____
Rent			10,800	_____
Repair and maintenance	1,000	_____		
Closing costs after taxes saved	2,000	_____		
Sales commission	6,420			
Total expenses	$19,078	_____	$12,750	_____
Net gain or loss (gross gain − total expenses)	(12,078)	_____	(11,454)	_____

Net savings from renting = $624

FIVE-YEAR COMPARISON

	Buying		Renting	
	Sample Estimates	Your Estimates	Sample Estimates	Your Estimates
Gross gain				
Appreciation	$40,255	_____		
Interest earned after taxes paid			$ 7,376	_____
Expenses				
Mortgage interest after taxes saved	31,279	_____		
Property taxes after taxes saved	7,101	_____		
Fuel and utilities	10,351	_____	10,351	_____
Insurance	1,725	_____	863	_____
Rent			62,108	_____
Repair and maintenance	5,751	_____		
Closing costs after taxes saved	2,000	_____		
Sales commission	8,415			
Total expenses	66,622	_____	73,322	_____
Net gain or loss (Gross gain − total expenses)	(26,367)	_____	(65,946)	_____

Net savings from buying = $39,579

FIGURE 9.7

Buy versus rent: cost comparison.

Housing: The
Cost of
Shelter

data are based upon a home that could be purchased for $100,000 or rented for $900 per month plus utilities. If purchased, it is assumed the buyer would place $20,000 down and borrow $80,000, to be paid back over 30 years at an annual percentage rate of 11 percent. It is also assumed that all prices, including the market price of the home, will rise at 7 percent a year.

The gross gain from buying is equal to the appreciation in the market value of the house. Looking first at the one-year comparison, the assumed appreciation rate of 7 percent is equal to $7,000 on the $100,000 house. This is not reduced by taxes, since it is assumed the gain can be postponed until age 55, at which time it is tax free. Of course, this assumption probably commits you to purchasing another house when this one is sold.

The gross gain from renting is based on the assumption that if you did not buy, the $20,000 would remain in an investment fund paying an annual interest rate of 9 percent. This investment would provide interest income of $1,800 before taxes. However, with an assumed marginal tax rate of 28 percent, interest earned after taxes is $1,296 = $1,800 × (1 − 0.28).

The related expenses of home ownership and renting are listed next. Mortgage interest payments can be taken from an amortization schedule prepared by your lender. This schedule will specify your yearly repayments on the loan and your yearly interest payments (for an example, see Table 9.2). On the present loan, mortgage interest payments for the first year are $8,782. Assuming you itemize deductions, the actual interest expense after taxes is $6,323 = $8,782 × (1 − 0.28). Similar tax adjustment should be made for property taxes and points, the prepaid interest component of closing costs.

All of the other expenses, except for the sales commission, are self-explanatory. The sales commission has been set equal to 6 percent of the expected market value of the home at the end of the holding period. Given an initial cost of $100,000, a one-year holding period, and an expected increase in value of 7 percent, the sales commission will be $6,420. Since this expense is postponed until the home is sold, it is an often-overlooked cost of home ownership.

The five-year comparison employs the same basic assumptions as the one-year comparison. The annual interest rate is 11 percent, and all prices, including fuel, insurance, maintenance, taxes, and rent, are assumed to rise at a 7 percent annual rate.

Such analyses, including this example, commonly show that renting appears the better alternative over the short run, whereas ownership is cheaper over the long run. The high turnover cost of buying and selling a home makes renting the better short-term choice. On the other hand, the inflation protection of home ownership makes it the optimal long-term choice.

The Real Estate Transaction

A home is most likely the largest single purchase you will make. Because it is so costly, and because few of us buy and sell homes often enough to become experts on the subject, you should seek the advice of experienced professionals. You may want to rely on an appraiser, a home inspector, a real estate agent, and an attorney.

The Appraisal

As a buyer or a seller, you need information on market price. Housing prices depend on a myriad of factors, the principal ones being size, construction, age,

TABLE 9.2 · Amortization Schedule

Year	Interest	Principal Repayment	Ending Principal Outstanding
1	$8,782.20	$ 360.10	$79,639.90
2	8,740.53	401.77	79,238.13
3	8,694.04	448.26	78,789.86
4	8,642.17	500.14	78,289.73
5	8,584.29	558.01	77,731.72
6	8,519.72	622.58	77,109.13
7	8,447.68	694.63	76,414.50
8	8,367.29	775.01	75,639.49
9	8,277.61	864.69	74,774.80
10	8,177.55	964.75	73,810.04
11	8,065.91	1,076.40	72,733.65
12	7,941.35	1,200.95	71,532.70
13	7,802.38	1,339.93	70,192.77
14	7,647.32	1,494.98	68,697.79
15	7,474.32	1,667.98	67,029.81
16	7,281.31	1,861.00	65,168.81
17	7,065.96	2,076.35	63,092.46
18	6,825.68	2,316.62	60,775.84
19	6,557.61	2,584.70	58,191.14
20	6,258.51	2,883.80	55,307.34
21	5,924.80	3,217.51	52,089.84
22	5,552.47	3,589.83	48,500.00
23	5,137.06	4,005.24	44,494.76
24	4,673.58	4,468.73	40,026.04
25	4,156.46	4,985.84	35,040.19
26	3,579.51	5,562.80	29,477.40
27	2,935.79	6,206.52	23,270.88
28	2,217.58	6,924.73	16,346.15
29	1,416.25	7,726.05	8,620.10
30	522.20	8,620.10	0.00

Amount borrowed: $80,000.00
Contract rate: 11.00%
Term (years):   30
Monthly payment: 761.86

and location. The last factor is often overlooked by first-time home buyers. There may be a wide spread in the selling price of identical houses in two different locations. Remember, you are really buying more than a home. You are buying into a neighborhood, a score of community services, and a school system. Only someone very familiar with the local housing market may be able to appraise all these and other relevant factors.

Professional appraisers may be located in the Yellow Pages under *Real Estate Appraisers*. Look for the listing American Institute of Real Estate Appraisers, National Society of Real Estate Appraisers, or Society of Real Estate Appraisers. Each organization certifies expert appraisers. If there are none listed in your area, contact a lender of home mortgages. Because they also require an appraisal, they should be able to provide you with a list of competent appraisers. In all cases, ask for credentials and references.

If you are a buyer, the mortgage lender will conduct an appraisal, but you should not rely on this procedure to determine the market value of your potential home. The lender's interest and yours are not the same. The lender wants to determine if the value of the house exceeds the amount borrowed by some safety margin. An independent appraisal may be necessary, because, as a buyer or a seller, you need to know that you are paying or receiving the market value.

The Real Estate Agent

Unless you as a buyer have a special agreement with the real estate agent, the agent will be representing the seller. You should keep this in mind. Many people fall into a comfortable relationship with the agent who is showing them homes, and in the course of casual conversation reveal too much about what they are willing to pay. Because the agent's interest must be with the seller, this information may be later used to undermine the buyer's negotiating position.

As a seller you can choose to use a real estate agent or not. Only about 15 percent of all house sales are made without an agent. However, with an agent's commission at about 6 to 7 percent of the sale price, selling the home yourself can appear to be an attractive alternative. To make the best decision, you must think in terms of earning the commission, rather than saving it. You will have to take on the work of advertising and showing the home, and dealing directly with potential buyers. This work can be both time consuming and, for some people, emotionally draining.

Before selecting a real estate agent to buy or sell a home, talk to several home owners and discover their personal experiences. First, ask for an overall assessment of the agent's performance. Then ask them whether their agent had many listings or was mainly showing homes listed by other real estate agencies. An agent with few listings may be in the real estate business only part time, and thus may not provide the publicity or attention you need. Ask home owners whether they felt pressured by the agent to sell their homes at low prices or buy homes they disliked. The decision to buy or sell is an important and complicated one. Even without an aggressive real estate agent, you will be under enormous pressure. Finally, ask what percentage of the sale price the agent took as a commission on the sale. This is a negotiable item. Many times an agent will agree to a reduction in the percentage charged in order to get a new listing or to see a sale completed. Remember, however, the smaller the commission, the smaller is the agent's incentive to devote time to the selling of your home.

If you are selling a home, you should have several agents appraise its value. Ask for documentation on the sale price of similar homes in the same neighborhood and the highest price at which each agent would be willing to list your home. Do not necessarily go with the agent willing to list your home at the highest price. Some unscrupulous agents may agree to list your home at a noncompetitive price just to get the listing. Their hope is to eventually get the homeowner to lower the listing price after it becomes obvious that there are no buyers in this price range. If you had an independent appraisal before contacting the real estate agents, you now should be in a good position to judge the honesty and knowledge of the agents with whom you are dealing.

Some real estate agencies will offer special inducements in an effort to get your home listing. These may turn out to be less valuable than first appearances would suggest. For example, some agencies will agree to buy your home if it cannot be sold by a specified time. Unfortunately, the price at which they are willing to purchase the home may be substantially below the price at which they are listing it. In addition, you may be still charged a commission, even though the home was purchased by the real estate agency at a low market price. Finally, the agreement may bind you to purchase a new home through this same agency, which will, of course, collect a commission on that transaction.

Be sure that the agent you choose to sell your home is a member of the Multiple Listing Service (MLS). This will provide information on your home to all other real estate agencies in your area who are also members of the MLS. All members of the MLS will have an interest in selling your home, because they will have a fee-splitting arrangement.

After you have selected a particular agent, you will be asked to sign a **listing agreement.** This is a contract between you and the real estate agent. It provides the agent with authority to act as your salesperson in return for a commission on the sale of the home. Important items on the contract will consist of the listing price, the commission, a description of the property, any terms and conditions for sale, duration of the listing, and exclusivity of the listing. The last item will determine whether you have the right to retain other sales agents during the term of the listing agreement.

There are three basic types of listing arrangements: the exclusive right to sell, the exclusive agency, and the open agreement. The **exclusive right to sell** entitles the agent to a commission regardless of who sells the property. Under an **exclusive agency agreement,** the seller agrees to retain one agent, but the agent collects the commission only if it is sold with the help of the agent. If you locate a buyer yourself, you don't pay a commission. In both of the above agreements the agent can co-broker the property, offering to split the commission with any other agent who can help find a buyer. With an **open agreement** the agent receives a commission only if he or she discovers a buyer. If you or another agent sells the home, you don't owe a commission to the agent who listed your home under an open agreement.

Beware of clauses that automatically extend the listing period, prohibit recording (public notice) of the listing agreement, or contain a net listing agreement. Each of these can result in serious problems for the seller. Automatic extensions beyond the typical 90-day period reduce the agent's incentive to sell your home in a timely manner. Public notice may be required if the contract is misrepresented. A **net listing agreement** provides the seller with a predetermined amount of money from the sale of the property. The real estate agent receives the difference between the sale price and the amount promised the seller.

The Home Inspection

Instead of depending upon a warranty as insurance against defects, get information on potential problems before you purchase. A thorough inspection by a qualified housing inspector should uncover problem areas that would otherwise go unnoticed. A home inspection will cost you between $125 and $250. For this amount, you should receive a written report stating the condition of the home and its component systems.

Listing agreement: A contract between the seller and the real estate agent providing the agent with authority to represent the seller in return for a commission on the sale.

Exclusive right to sell: Entitles the agent to a commission no matter who sells the property.

Exclusive agency agreement: The agent has an exclusive right to broker the property, but may agree to share the commission with other agents. If you locate the buyer yourself, you don't pay a commission.

Open agreement: Any agent can broker your home. The commission goes to the agent who locates a buyer. If you sell your home, you don't pay a commission.

Net listing agreement: Provides the seller with a predetermined amount of money from the sale of a property. The real estate agent receives the difference between the sale price and the amount promised the seller.

The American Society of Home Inspectors trains and certifies qualified individuals. They may be found in the Yellow Pages under *Building Inspection Services, Inspection Bureaus, Engineers,* or *Real Estate Inspectors.* Since most of the ASHI membership is in the East, you may not be able to find one in your area. In any case, be sure the inspector you hire has nothing to gain from your purchasing the home. The inspector should not, for example, run a remodeling firm or depend upon a real estate agency for support. Ask for the names of previous customers and insist on being present during the home inspection. The person you hire should be able to answer all questions you may have during the inspection.

The Purchase Contract

The offer to purchase a home is made on a document entitled *Contract to Purchase, Purchase Agreement,* or *Deposit Receipt.* When both the buyer and the seller have agreed to all the conditions in the purchase contract, it becomes a binding agreement that creates rights and obligations for both parties. For this reason, you should consult an attorney before you sign. Most real estate transactions are closed, however, without the aid of an attorney. Unfortunately, too many people consult an attorney only when they want to get out of a disagreeable contract. Such remedial action can be very costly.

You and your attorney should carefully examine the purchase contract to make sure it contains the following:

1. The purchase price, the down payment, and the type of financing. When buying a new home, beware of an "escalator" clause that would permit the builder to increase the price because of future cost increases.
2. Anticipated closing costs and prepaid items, and who will pay them.
3. A description of the property, and a list of all items being sold with the house. For new construction, plans and specifications should be included, and you should carefully review these with your architect and home inspector.
4. A statement as to who is responsible for the property from the date of the contract to the date it is conveyed to you.
5. The amount of the deposit, and the conditions under which the buyer or the seller might void the contract. For example, failure to buy or sell another house, inadequate financing, an unsatisfactory inspection report, or failure to obtain marketable title may all be good reasons for voiding the purchase contract.
6. A stated date after which the offer lapses if not accepted.

The process leading to the sale of a home begins with the buyer making an offer to purchase, with a signed purchase contract and a commitment of earnest money. The seller may then accept the offer, reject the offer, or make a counteroffer by altering some or all of the terms on the purchase contract. Likewise, the buyer may then accept the counteroffer, reject it, or make another counteroffer. This continues until both sides either terminate negotiations or agree upon a sale.

Spending, Borrowing, and Saving

Prudent cash and credit management is absolutely necessary as you plan for a successful future. Interest rates, liquidity, easy withdrawal, long term growth, and type of financial institution are factors that will make an impact on your decisions.

Consumer durables provide long-term benefits, while committing us to long-term operational costs and creating the need for long-range planning.

Effective use of credit requires both planning and management.

Before you buy a home, you should estimate the purchase price you can afford, examine housing in this price range, and calculate the risks and benefits of this decision.

Protecting
What You
Have

Another important element of
smart financial planning is
protecting your assets. Insurance
allows you to manage the risk
of major financial catastrophe:
life insurance protects your
dependents; property and
liability insurance protects your
assets; and health and disability
insurance protects your earning
capacity.

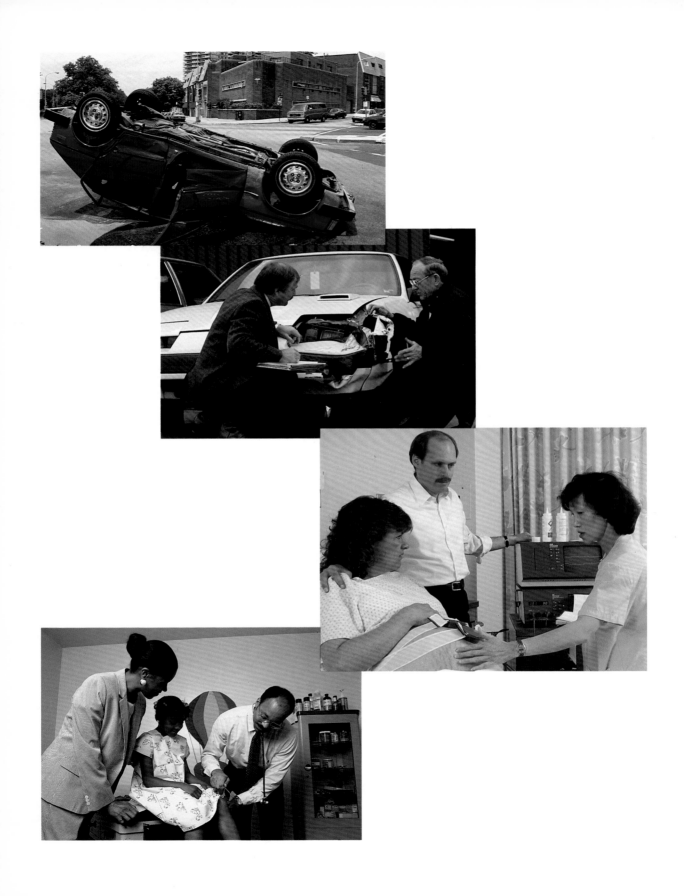

The buyer's deposit of **earnest money** demonstrates that the offer is made in good faith. If the offer to purchase is not accepted or lapses, the earnest money should be returned to the buyer. If the seller accepts the offer to purchase, a third party—either a broker, a title company, or an escrow agent—will hold the money in a trust account until the sale is closed or the contract is broken. If the buyer fails to purchase the home as indicated in the contract, the seller can keep the earnest money. Of course, if the seller breaks the contract, the deposit is returned to the buyer. If the sale goes through, the deposit is applied to the buyer's down payment on the purchase.

Title Search

The **deed** is a written document that transfers title, or ownership, to the buyer. However, the deed does not show who else might have rights to the property. In the **title search,** an attorney examines the public records to determine if others may have enforceable claims on the property. At the completion of the search, the attorney will render an opinion as to whether **marketable title** exists. A marketable title is free of all claims from other parties.

The mortgage lender will conduct a title search. However, the fact that you are granted a loan does not necessarily mean the title is free of all defects. A loan may be still granted if the lender feels assured that the full value of the loan can be repaid in spite of minor defects in the title. In addition, if the search is deficient, you may have no claim against the attorney. The attorney is financially responsible only to the client. If the lender ordered the search, the lender is the client and not you. For this reason you should have an independent examination or purchase title insurance.

The mortgage lender will require that you purchase **title insurance.** This insures the bank, not you, against a defective title. To protect your interest in the title, you can obtain owner's title insurance. You will save money by purchasing this coverage at the same time you buy the lender's policy. As with all insurance, coverage can vary. You should read the insurance contract carefully to be sure it covers all defects in title, both in and out of the public record.

Closing

The meeting at which the purchase and the mortgage are finalized is called the **closing.** The seller receives payment. The buyer undertakes the mortgage and receives the deed. By mutual agreement between the buyer and the seller, actual possession of the property may take place not at this time but at some later date. Whoever closes the sale is required to report the terms of the sale to the IRS in order to ensure compliance with tax law. Costs due at this time are called **closing** or **settlement costs.** A sample list of these costs is given in Figure 9.8. Some documents you might encounter at closing are listed in Figure 9.9.

BROKER'S COMMISSION   The seller typically pays the broker's commission on the sale of the home. It currently runs about 6 or 7 percent of the sales price, but the exact percentage is negotiable.

FIGURE 9.8

The high cost of closing. (Source: Timothy R. Dougherty, "Real Estate: I Owe What!?," *Newsday*, September 14, 1991, p. 36.)

Mortgage broker's estimate of closing costs for the purchase of a $178,500 house in Suffolk County, New York. In this example, closing costs plus a typical down payment of 20 percent or $35,700 would mean a total cash outlay of $47,582.

Item	Expense
Credit report	$ 70
Lender's title policy	658
Owner's title policy	441
Recording fees	70
Appraisal fee	250
Bank points and bank origination fee	3,250
Bank attorney fee	650
Tax service fee	65
New York state mortgage tax	950
Borrower's attorney fee	750
Insurance policy, one year	500
Fire insurance impounds, two months	80
Tax impounds, estimated, eight months	3,133
Termite inspection	70
Survey, if needed	350
Application fee	220
Lender's underwriting fee	150
Lender's processing fee	150
Messenger fee	75
Total estimated cost	$11,882

LENDER'S CHARGES   The buyer generally pays lender's charges. They include the lender's costs of processing the loan, plus any related costs such as property appraisal and inspection.

Points: Prepaid interest; one point is equal to 1 percent of the amount borrowed.

Points, also called *discount points,* may be included. This is a finance charge, rather than a charge for loan processing. One discount point is equal to 1 percent of the amount borrowed. On an $80,000 mortgage, for example, 1½ discount points are equal to $1,200. This has the effect of reducing the actual amount you are borrowing by the dollar value of the points, from $80,000 to $78,800. You still, however, owe the bank an unpaid balance of $80,000. Consequently, paying points raises the annual percentage rate (APR) on the loan above the **contract rate,** the rate applied to the unpaid balance in order to calculate your mortgage payments. This is because the APR calculates repayments as a percentage of $78,800 (amount borrowed), whereas, the contract rate calculates repayments as a percentage of $80,000 (amount owed).

Contract rate: The interest rate applied to the unpaid balance on the home mortgage.

PREPAIDS   If the loan is closed before the last day of the month, the lender will want the borrower to prepay the balance of that month's interest. The lender may also require the borrower to prepay mortgage and hazard insurance, typically about two months' premiums. Property tax payments will be prorated and charged to the buyer and seller as applicable.

You'll wish you knew more about real estate law when you start wading through the dizzying number of legal papers at closing. You'll also find yourself signing your name over and over again, sometimes on six copies of the same document. Here's a rundown on the paper chase.

Warranty Deed   This document officially transfers title to the buyer. The seller, not the purchaser, signs it and thereby warrants that the title is free of defects that might come to light after closing. Generally, the closing agent will then have the deed recorded at the local courthouse and send you a copy.

In some states a different type of deed, such as a bargain and sale deed, security deed, grant deed or special warranty deed, is used in lieu of a general warranty deed to transfer title.

Quitclaim Deed   This is a device often used to clear up problems with the title. The seller, or anyone with a potential claim against the property, signs it, thereby releasing any rights he or she might have. A seller conveys a quitclaim deed not to guarantee the title against claims but merely to give the buyer whatever interest in the property the seller may have.

Mortgage or Deed of Trust   The basic purpose of both documents is to secure the loan. When a debt is secured by a *mortgage,* the borrower signs a document that gives the lender a lien on the property.

When a debt is secured by a *deed of trust,* the buyer conveys title to a third party who holds it until the note is paid in full. The lender does not receive title but only the right to request that the property be sold should the borrower default. Both documents should be recorded.

Promissory Note   (also called mortgage note). This establishes the borrower's contract with the lender to repay the loan. It sets forth the terms under which the money is to be repaid and indicates whether the note is secured by a mortgage or deed of trust.

Owner's Affidavit   The seller swears in this document that there are no unpaid liens, assessments or other encumbrances against the house. The affidavit protects the purchaser, lender and title company. If the seller is lying, he or she can be sued for damages.

Purchaser's Affidavit   Sometimes the buyer is required by the lender to swear that there are no existing or pending suits, judgments or liens against him or her. If the buyer is lying, that is sufficient grounds for foreclosure.

Uniform Settlement Statement   This is the final version of the itemized account described in Figure 9.8, specifying who pays what transaction costs to whom. Both the buyer's and seller's signatures may be requested.

Other Documents   Papers you may also encounter during the closing include a termite inspection report, survey, title policy, truth-in-lending statement and various liability releases.

FIGURE 9.9

The house closing.

RESERVES   The borrower may be required to set up and periodically fund a reserve account, called an *escrow account.* This account ensures that future property taxes and insurance premiums will be paid.

TITLE CHARGES   The costs of the title search, title insurance, and document preparation are included in title charges. The seller often buys a policy for the buyer, and the buyer purchases one for the lender. A single premium paid at this time will keep the policy in force until the house is again sold.

GOVERNMENT CHARGES   There may be various state and local charges on the transfer and on the recording of the transfer. These charges are usually modest, but in some states they can run as high as 1 percent of the sale price.

OTHER CHARGES   The expenses of any inspections and surveys are also included in the closing costs. What prepurchase inspections are undertaken and who pays for them are negotiable items that should be included in the purchase contract.

Home Owners Warranty

Homes, like other goods, will be covered by implied warranties set down in state law. The nation's largest warranty program is run by the **Home Owners Warranty Corp. (HOW)**, which is tied to the National Association of Home Builders. Since its founding in 1974, it has issued over 2 million home warranties. Two more recent and smaller national programs include Home Buyers Warranty and Residential Warranty Corp. There are also a few regional firms providing home owner warranties.

The builder typically pays a one-time premium of between $2.20 and $5.00 per $1,000 of the sale price. The buyer receives a ten-year warranty covering a list of defects that decrease in number as the home ages. During the first year almost all defects in workmanship and materials are covered. During the second year the list of guaranteed items is substantially reduced, while in the remaining eight years only major structural defects are covered.

Under the HOW program, the home owner is first asked to request covered repairs from the builder. If the builder does not respond appropriately, HOW will attempt to remedy the situation through informal mediation, and then through formal arbitration. If it is decided that the defect is covered under the HOW program and the builder still does not make the needed repairs, HOW will cover the cost of the repairs minus a specified deductible. For failing to honor the warranty, the builder may be expelled from the HOW program.

Although HOW paid out about $68 million in claims during its first ten years of operation, *Consumer Reports* remains critical of this program. With unresponsive builders, the complaint procedure can be lengthy. In addition, the builder who created the problem is the one who is supposed to fix it. And finally, expulsion from the HOW program seems too mild a remedy, since the incompetent builder can still build non–HOW-covered homes.

Financing the Purchase

You can shop around for a home mortgage at a variety of financial institutions, including commercial banks, mutual savings banks, mortgage companies, and savings and loan associations. Today's mortgage market is highly competitive. You are likely to find the same lender offering both fixed and adjustable rate loans, in addition to offering several ways in which each of these loans may be structured. You should ask the loan officer to explain each of the loan options and discuss how each might fit your own financial situation. The decision is an important one. A typical mortgage will commit you to interest payments that, over the life of the loan, can equal as much as three times the original amount borrowed.

The larger your down payment, the lower the interest rate, and the longer the term of the loan, the smaller is the monthly mortgage payment. The typical home buyer makes a 20 percent down payment on a 30-year-mortgage. However, with mortgage insurance you may obtain a home mortgage with as little as 5 percent down.

Through various government agencies, home loan disclosure requirements are specified and enforced. Generally, you must receive information on all of the items discussed in this section on home mortgages. Furthermore, you should receive this information before you apply for the loan or pay a loan origination fee.

The annual percentage rate (APR), explained in Chapter 7 on consumer credit, is the most important disclosure. It takes into account the interest rate and other credit charges, such as mortgage insurance, points, and loan origination fees, into a uniform measure of cost. Unfortunately, the published APR on adjustable rate loans must be based upon the initial interest rate. Since the future interest rate on the loan may differ from the initial interest rate, the APR in the mortgage contract will not likely reflect the interest costs you will actually incur. Therefore, on adjustable rate loans the lender is also required to describe the circumstances that will lead to rate changes, and to give an example of the payment changes that can occur. For such loans, the circumstances under which rates may change are as important to know as the APR.

Realistically, it is impossible to present every repayment scenario for many adjustable rate loans. While loan officers will ordinarily try to be helpful, time constraints may prohibit them from providing you with a complete examination of the loan being offered. Therefore, some previous knowledge of mortgage instruments may greatly aid you in the search for a home mortgage. The mortgage comparison checklist in Figure 9.10 should prove helpful when reviewing the characteristics of the available mortgages. A graphic summary of various mortgage options is contained in Figure 9.11.

FIGURE 9.10

Mortgage comparison checklist.

Lender
 Loan type (fixed or adjustable) _____
 Annual percentage rate _____
 Duration (years) _____
 Percentage down payment _____
 Application fee _____
 Points _____
 Title insurance _____
 Prepayment penalty _____
 Other closing fees _____
 Mortgage insurance _____
 Initial interest rate _____
 Initial monthly mortgage payment _____
 Balloon payment _____

Additional Information on Adjustable Rate Loans
 Interest adjustment index _____
 Adjustment period _____
 Periodic rate cap _____
 Aggregate rate cap _____
 Periodic payment cap _____
 Negative amortization (Y/N) _____
 Adjustable duration (Y/N) _____

Additional Information for GEM and GDM Loans
 Mortgage payment schedule: Year 1 _____
                              Year 2 _____
                              etc. _____

Fixed Rate Mortgage

Traditionally, both interest rate and monthly payments are fixed for the life of the loan.

Adjustable Rate Mortgage

If there are no payment or rate caps, interest rate and monthly payments fluctuate according to an index.

Adjustable Rate Mortgage/Rate Cap

With a rate cap, even if the index rises, increases in the rate and monthly payment are limited.

Adjustable Rate Mortgage/Payment Cap

If the index increases, so does the interest rate. However, monthly payment charges are limited (although the total amount owed may increase).

Graduated Payment Mortgage

Interest rate usually fixed; payments rise gradually for first few years, then level off for duration of loan.

Growing Equity Mortgage

Interest rate usually fixed; but payments may rise according to agreed-upon schedule or an index. Increases are applied to principal, shortening term of loan.

Balloon Mortgage

Interest rate usually fixed; payments are also fixed but may apply only to interest. After short term, a final payment of principal is due.

Years from the date loan was granted

☐ Monthly payment

■ Interest rate

FIGURE 9.11

Mortgage formats. (Source: Federal Trade Commission, *The Mortgage Money Guide*, 1989.)

Fixed Rate Mortgages

Fixed rate mortgages:
Home mortgages on which the interest rate and monthly payment remain constant over the life of the loan.

Principal: The remaining balance on the amount borrowed.

Amortize: To satisfy an obligation by periodic payments of interest and principal.

Fixed rate mortgages have an interest rate and monthly payments that remain constant over the life of the loan. For example, if you borrowed $80,000 at 11 percent for 30 years, you would have level monthly payments of $761.86 over the entire 30-year-period. Part of each monthly payment will go to the repayment of **principal**—the amount owed—and part will go toward payment of interest on the principal.

When you repay a loan by periodic payments, you are said to **amortize** your debt. Table 9.2 contains an amortization schedule for a fixed rate loan. During the first years of the loan, most of the mortgage payment will go toward paying interest on the principal. As the amount owed declines, a larger percentage of the mortgage payment will go toward paying off the principal. Near the end of the loan period, almost the entire mortgage payment will serve to reduce the outstanding principal.

Adjustable Rate Mortgages

Adjustable rate loans:
Home mortgages on which the interest rate is periodically adjusted over the term of the loan.

The distinguishing feature of **adjustable rate loans** is that the interest rate on the loan is not fixed over the entire life of the loan. This feature is about the only

276

common characteristic of adjustable rate loans; there are almost as many types of them as there are homes. To add to the confusion, they come under various names—such as variable and flexible rate loans.

During the late 1970s, lending institutions began to experiment with offerings of adjustable rate loans. The movement away from fixed rate loans was prompted by the erratic nature of interest rates and inflation rates during the period. Because financial markets have been so changeable, lending institutions have become reluctant to lock themselves into fixed rate mortgages. Banks must pay current market rates of interest to obtain the funds they are lending out. If these rates move above the rates of return on fixed rate mortgages, the institutions will incur losses because they will be paying more to attract funds than those same funds are earning. Adjustable rate mortgages enable the lending institution to reduce or eliminate that risk. The institution should be able to offset at least partially the higher cost of funds with a higher return on its outstanding mortgages.

Although adjustable rate mortgages reduce the risk to lending institutions, they increase the risk to borrowers. An upward movement in interest rates means that the borrower will now have to pay additional dollars of interest on the remaining loan balance. To compensate the borrower for this future risk, adjustable rate mortgages carry an initial interest rate below the rate offered on a standard fixed rate mortgage. The difference between the initial rate on fixed and variable loans can vary widely as credit market conditions change. Over the past few years the differential has fluctuated around 2 percentage points.

The Federal Trade Commission suggests you examine all of the following when shopping for an adjustable rate mortgage:

- The initial interest rate
- How often the rate may change
- How much the rate may change
- The initial monthly payments
- How often payments may change
- How much payments may change
- The mortgage term
- How often the term may change
- The index to which rate, payment, or term changes are tied
- The limits, if any, on negative amortization

INTEREST RATE ADJUSTMENT PERIOD AND THE ADJUSTMENT INDEX   The interest rate on the remaining loan balance may be changed after a specified period. The period between one rate change and the next is known as the **interest rate adjustment period.** The majority of adjustable rate loans have an adjustment period of one year. The change in the rate is tied to the change in an **interest rate adjustment index** that tends to mirror the general movement in interest rates throughout the economy. The most common indexes are listed below.

Interest rate adjustment period: The time between potential adjustments in the interest rate applied to the outstanding loan balance.

Interest rate adjustment index: The index to which changes in the mortgage interest rate are related.

- National Average FHLB Mortgage Contract Rate
- National Average Cost of Funds to FSLIC-Insured Associations

Housing: The
Cost of
Shelter

- Regional Average Cost of Funds to FSLIC-Insured Associations
- Six-month U.S. Treasury Rate
- Five-year U.S. Treasury Rate
- Three-year U.S. Treasury Rate
- One-year U.S. Treasury Rate
- Three-month U.S. Treasury Rate

Financial analysts tend to favor the use of the National Average FHLB Mortgage Contract Rate as an interest rate index, because it seems to be less volatile than the other indexes.

To determine the contract interest rate on the outstanding mortgage balance, lenders add a few percentage points, called the **margin,** to the index rate.

Margin: The amount added to the index rate in order to calculate the interest rate on the mortgage contract.

$$\text{Index rate} + \text{margin} = \text{contract interest rate}$$

For example, suppose an index rate such as the National Average FHLB Mortgage Contract Rate were 11 percent at the time of adjustment, and the margin were 2 percentage points. The contract rate applied to the outstanding loan balance would be 13 percent. The amount of the margin differs from one lender to the other, but it is usually constant over the life of the loan.

Teaser rate: An abnormally low initial interest rate meant to attract borrowers.

A few lenders offer what have become known in the industry as **teaser rates,** which are a promotional gimmick. Over some initial period a reduced margin is used to calculate the adjustable rate. When this period ends, a higher margin is used to compute the rate over the remaining term of the loan. This produces an upward adjustment in the flexible rate independent of any change in the interest rate adjustment index.

RATE CAP Some loans may have rate caps that limit the movement in your interest rate. These typically limit increases, but may also limit decreases, in the rate. A **periodic rate cap** limits changes during any one adjustment period. Suppose you had a 1½ percent periodic cap, and the underlying index rate rose by 2 percent. The adjustable rate applied to the outstanding loan balance would be limited to a 1½ percent increase during this adjustment period. However, the unused half percent may be applied during the next adjustment period.

Periodic rate cap: Limits the movement on changes in the interest rate during any one interest rate adjustment period.

Aggregate rate cap: Limits the total change in the interest rate over the entire term of the loan.

An **aggregate rate cap** limits changes over the entire life of the loan. If you had a 5 percent aggregate cap on your mortgage rate, then no matter how high the financial index rose, a mortgage with an initial rate of 12 percent could never go above 17 percent. By federal law, all adjustable rate mortgages must have a lifetime ceiling on the contract rate. There is no federal limit on how high the cap may be, although most states do set limits.

Payment cap: Limits changes in the monthly mortgage payment.

PAYMENT CAP A **payment cap** limits changes in your monthly loan payments. Under a payment cap, it is possible for the interest rate on your adjustable rate loan to increase while your monthly payments either remain unchanged or do not increase as much as required by the interest rate adjustment.

Don't assume you don't have to pay the higher interest, however. For example, suppose you take out a 30-year, $80,000 mortgage at an initial interest rate of 11 percent and an annual adjustment period. At the 11 percent rate your initial monthly payments are $761.86. If, at the end of the first year, the interest rate rises to 13 percent, the monthly payments would ordinarily increase to $883.55. However, if the yearly adjustment under the payment cap is less than $121.69 = ($883.55 − $761.86), then the monthly payments will not increase to the level required to completely discharge the loan in the remaining 29 years. The difference between your monthly payment under the cap and the required payment may be made up in one of several ways. The term of the loan can be lengthened beyond the initial 30-year agreement. Alternatively, the term might remain unchanged, but the lending institution might require an additional lump-sum payment at the time the mortgage is to be paid up. Still another method is for future monthly payments to be increased. The lending institution should specify in the mortgage contract the method it plans to use.

In the current example, the amount outstanding on the mortgage at the end of the first year will be $79,639.90. At an annual percentage rate of 13 percent, interest payments alone amount to $862.76 per month. If the payment cap keeps the monthly payment from rising beyond $862.76, **negative amortization** will result. This term simply means that instead of your debt getting smaller over time, it will get larger. You will owe the lending institution more at the end of the year than you did at the beginning. Obviously, this situation can create problems for both you and the lending institution. For this reason, only about 4 percent of mortgage contracts permit negative amortization. In all other cases, the payment cap cannot hold monthly payments to less than the interest owed on the outstanding loan balance.

> **Negative amortization:** The resulting increase in the amount owed when the monthly payment is less than the interest due on the previous balance.

CONVERTIBLE FEATURES   Lenders have recently been promoting **convertible mortgages.** These are adjustable rate mortgages that can be converted into fixed rate mortgages during a specified time period, usually between the thirteenth and sixtieth months of the loan. The fixed rate will be determined by rules set down in the mortgage contract. If you elect to make the conversion, the lender will charge a fee that, most likely, will be equal to either a stated dollar amount or a percentage of the outstanding loan balance.

The rate on the fixed rate loan may depend on the value of the interest adjustment index at the date of the conversion. If you believe that interest rates will decline, then a convertible mortgage would allow you to get the benefits of an adjustable rate loan today and the expected benefit of a lower rate on a fixed rate loan at a future date.

You should be careful not to place too much value on the conversion feature. Adjustable rate loans rarely carry penalties for paying off a loan before it is due. Therefore, even with an ordinary adjustable rate loan, you always have the choice of paying it off and refinancing with a fixed rate loan. If you refinance, however, you will be charged closing costs and points on the new loan. The real value of the conversion feature is, consequently, the difference between the conversion fee and traditional refinancing charges.

> **Convertible mortgage:** An adjustable rate mortgage contract that permits the borrower to convert to a fixed rate contract at some point during the term of the loan.

Specialized Mortgage Formats and Creative Financing

Most borrowers will end up with either a basic fixed rate or adjustable rate mortgage. During times of tight credit and high interest rates, however, both lenders and borrowers have demonstrated an increasing willingness to experi-

Box 9.2
What's New in Personal Finance

New Mortgage Format:
Price-Level-Adjusted
Mortgages

The Department of Housing and Urban Development has devised a new home mortgage format called the price-level-adjusted mortgage (PLAM) that should make housing more affordable for moderate- to low-income families. The mortgages come with low initial monthly payments, about one-half the monthly payment on other types of mortgages. The low initial monthly payments lowers the housing expense-to-household income ratio, allowing more families to qualify for a home mortgage.

The catch is that your mortgage payments on a PLAM are likely to increase over the term of the mortgage, because the size of the monthly payment and the outstanding loan balance is adjusted for changes in the Consumer Price Index. For example, if a 30-year fixed rate mortgage had an interest rate of 11 percent, a PLAM might have a much lower contract rate of 4 percent. On a $100,000 mortgage the initial monthly payment on the fixed rate loan would be $952.32; whereas the PLAM would have an initial monthly payment of only $477.42. The monthly payments on the fixed rate mortgage would remain the same over the life of the loan. Alternatively, if the annual rate of inflation were 5 percent, the outstanding loan balance and the monthly payments on the PLAMS would be adjusted upward each year by 5 percent.

The payments on this mortgage can be found in the accompanying table. In the thirtieth year, the PLAM would require monthly payments of almost $2,000. This sounds like a hefty burden. But assuming that money wages also rose at the inflation rate, then the payments at the end of the mortgage would represent no greater hardship than the much smaller payments in year 1. Of course, there is no assurance that the money wages of a particular worker will keep pace with the rate of inflation. Therefore, PLAMs do entail more risk for the borrower than traditional fixed rate mortgages.

When compared with adjustable rate mortgages, however, they have the surprising benefit of actually having less variability from year to year. It is very possible for the rate on an adjustable rate mortgage to rise from 8 to 10 percent in one year, increasing the mortgage payment on a 30-year-mortgage by almost 20 percent. A PLAM would increase by 20 percent in a single year only if the annual inflation rate hit 20 percent, a very unlikely occurrence.

A worrisome characteristic of PLAMs is that the outstanding loan balance will grow, rather than decline, in the initial years of the mortgage, resulting in negative amortization. In the present example, the loan balance rises from $100,000 in the first year to $134,180 in the sixteenth year before finally beginning to diminish. After adjustment for inflation, however, the real value of the outstanding balance is actually declining. Moreover, if the home's market value is also rising at the rate of inflation, the real and dollar equity in the home is also increasing. Soft markets, unfortunately, may cause home prices to rise at less than the general rate of inflation, creating difficulties for those who must sell in the early years.

In order to assess the relative cost of a PLAM, you must compare the real rate of interest. On fixed and adjustable rate loans the real interest rate is the difference between the expected interest rate on the out-

Payment and Balance Adjustments on a $100,000 PLAM over a 30-Year Term Assuming a 4% Interest Rate and 5% Continuous Inflation

Year	Total Monthly Payments	Loan Balance at Beginning of the Year
1	$5,729	$100,000
2	6,015	103,151
3	6,316	106,288
4	6,632	109,394
5	6,964	112,451
6	7,312	115,436
7	7,677	118,327
8	8,061	121,094
9	8,464	123,708
10	8,888	126,133
11	9,332	128,331
12	9,799	130,257
13	10,288	131,863
14	10,803	133,094
15	11,343	133,889
16	11,910	134,180
17	12,506	133,891
18	13,131	132,939
19	13,787	131,230
20	14,477	128,660
21	15,201	125,115
22	15,961	120,466
23	16,759	114,573
24	17,597	107,280
25	18,477	98,414
26	19,400	87,785
27	20,370	75,182
28	21,389	60,372
29	22,458	43,098
30	23,581	23,078

SOURCE: U.S. League of Savings and Loan Associations.

standing balance (the contract rate) and the expected rate of inflation. It is the benefit the lender receives after adjustment for inflation. Since the PLAM is already adjusted for inflation, the real rate and the contract rate on the PLAM are the same.

If the contract rate on the fixed rate mortgage is 11 percent and the expected rate of inflation is 5 percent, then the expected real rate of interest on this mortgage is 6 percent. Given a 4 percent contract rate on a comparable PLAM, only you can decide if the lower rate is worth the unique risk.

You might think that the interest deduction on a PLAM is less favorable than on a traditional mortgage because the contract rate is so much lower. However, the IRS has decided that the inflation rate adjustment should be included in your interest deduction. The rules for calculating the exact annual interest deduction are complicated. But essentially, the IRS bases your interest deduction on the real rate (contract rate) plus the rate of inflation, making the deduction similar to that on non-PLAM mortgages.

Creative financing: Unique mortgage formats provided by sellers in order to satisfy the special needs of a buyer.

ment with new financial instruments. Some of these less common mortgage formats are provided by financial institutions. In other arrangements, termed **creative financing,** the seller of the home provides some or all of the financing. Details of these innovative forms of home financing are shown in Table 9.3.

Reading the Fine Print

In addition to understanding the economic characteristics of the loan, you must also understand the legal ramifications. This means reading the fine print and carefully examining each clause.

Acceleration clause: Allows the lender to require immediate repayment of the loan if the borrower misses a scheduled payment.

The **acceleration clause** will allow the lender to speed up the rate at which the loan comes due if you miss a payment. Be sure you understand how and when this clause becomes operative. Also, be wary of an acceleration clause that then permits the lender to foreclose on the loan "without notice."

Due-on-sale clause: Requires immediate repayment of outstanding balance when the mortgaged property is sold.

A **due-on-sale clause** requires immediate repayment of the loan when the property changes hands. Such clauses are common and have been enforced by the courts.

Prepayment penalty: A penalty on early repayment of the loan for reasons other than the sale of the home.

The prepayment clause indicates how early payment on the loan will be handled. The loan contract could impose a **prepayment penalty** if you repay the loan early for reasons other than the sale of the home. This clause is generally not permitted on adjustable rate loans.

Escrow account: Funds held by the lender to ensure payment of housing-related insurance and taxes.

On some loans, the lending institution adds to the monthly mortgage payment an amount to cover home insurance or property taxes. The lender accumulates these funds in what is called an **escrow account.** When the insurance or property taxes become due, the lender will pay these bills out of the funds in the escrow account. By doing so, the lender ensures that these obligations are being met.

An escrow account is required when the mortgage is insured by the Federal Housing Administration or the Veterans Administration, or when the loan is for 90 percent or more of the value of the house. In all other situations, the need for an escrow account is negotiable between the borrower and lender.

If possible, you should avoid setting up an escrow account. In most places the lending institution will pay no interest on the funds held. In the 12 states where lenders are required by law to pay interest on escrow accounts, the rate paid is typically less than the rate on a passbook savings account. You can do better by holding these funds in your ordinary savings account and paying your taxes and

TABLE 9.3 ▪ The Essentials of Creative Mortgage Financing

Type	Description	Considerations
Fixed rate mortgage	Fixed interest rate, usually long-term; equal monthly payments of principal and interest until debt is paid in full.	Offers stability and long-term tax advantages; limited availability. Interest rates may be higher than other types of financing. New fixed rates are rarely assumable.
Adjustable rate mortgage	Interest rate changes are based on a financial index, resulting in possible changes in your monthly payments, loan terms, and/or principal. Some plans have rate or payment caps.	Readily available. Starting interest rate is slightly below market, but payments can increase sharply and frequently if index increases. Payment caps prevent wide fluctuations in payments but may cause negative amortization. Rate caps, limit amount total debt can expand.
Renegotiable rate mortgage (rollover)	Interest rate and monthly payments are constant for several years; changes possible thereafter. Long-term mortgage.	Less frequent changes in interest rate offer some stability.
Balloon mortgage	Monthly payments based on fixed interest rate; usually short-term; payments may cover interest only with principal due in full at term end.	Offers low monthly payments but possibly no equity until loan is fully paid. When due, loan must be paid off or refinanced. Refinancing poses high risk if rates climb.
Graduated payment mortgage	Lower monthly payments rise gradually (usually over 5-10 years), then level off for duration of term. With flexible interest rate, additional payment changes possible if index changes.	Easier to qualify for. Buyer's income must be able to keep pace with scheduled payment increases. With a flexible rate, payment increases beyond the graduated payments can result in additional negative amortization.
Shared appreciation mortgage	Below-market interest rate and lower monthly payments, in exchange for a share of profits when property is sold or on a specified date. Many variations.	If home appreciates greatly, total cost of loan jumps. If home fails to appreciate, projected increase in value may still be due, requiring refinancing at possibly higher rates.
Assumable mortgage	Buyer takes over seller's original, below-market-rate mortgage.	Lowers monthly payments. May be prohibited if "due on sale" clause is in original mortgage. Not permitted on most new fixed rate mortgages.
Seller take-back	Seller provides all or part of financing with a first or second mortgage.	May offer a below-market interest rate; may have a balloon payment requiring full payment in a few years or refinancing at market rates, which could sharply increase debt.

insurance directly. If you have an escrow account, you should contact the lending institution to see if it can be closed.

Insured Mortgages

Conventional financing: Financing that is neither government insured nor guaranteed.

The term **conventional financing** is used for mortgages that are neither government insured nor guaranteed. Conventional mortgages may have private mortgage insurance on high-risk loans to protect the lender in the event you default on the loan. Where such mortgage protection is needed, however, it is normally arranged through either the Federal Housing Administration (FHA) or the Veterans Administration (VA). These programs make nonconventional mortgages available to individuals who might otherwise be considered poor credit risks.

TABLE 9.3 • Continued

Type	Description	Considerations
Wraparound	Seller keeps original low rate mortgage. Buyer makes payments to seller who forwards a portion to the lender holding original mortgage. Offers lower effective interest rate on total transaction.	Lender may call in old mortgage and require higher rate. If buyer defaults, seller must take legal action to collect debt.
Growing equity mortgage (rapid payoff mortgage)	Fixed interest rate but monthly payments may vary according to agreed-upon schedule or index.	Permits rapid payoff of debt because payment increases reduce principal. Buyer's income must be able to keep up with payment increases.
Land contract	Seller retains original mortgage. No transfer of title until loan is fully paid. Equal monthly payments based on below-market interest rate with unpaid principal due at loan end.	May offer no equity until loan is fully paid. Buyer has few protections if conflict arises during loan.
Buy-down	Developer (or third party) provides an interest subsidy which lowers monthly payments during the first few years of the loan. Can have fixed or flexible interest rate.	Offers a break from higher payments during early years. Enables buyer with lower income to qualify. With adjustable rate mortgage, payments may jump substantially at end of subsidy. Developer may increase selling price.
Rent with option	Renter pays "option fee" for right to purchase property at specified time and agreed-upon price. Rent may or may not be applied to sales price.	Enables renter to buy time to obtain down payment and decide whether to purchase. Locks in price during inflationary times. Failure to take option means loss of option fee and rental payments.
Reverse annuity mortgage (equity conversion)	Borrower owns mortgage-free property and needs income. Lender makes monthly payments to borrower, using property as collateral.	Can provide home owners with needed cash. At end of term, borrower must have money available to avoid selling property or refinancing.
Zero rate and low rate mortgage	Appears to be completely or almost interest free. Large down payment and one-time finance charge, then loan is repaid in fixed monthly payments over short term.	Permits quick ownership. May not lower total cost (because of possibly increased sales price). Doesn't offer long-term tax deductions.

SOURCE: Federal Trade Commission, *The Mortgage Money Guide.*

FEDERAL HOUSING ADMINISTRATION (FHA) FHA mortgages are not government loans. **FHA mortgage insurance** protects the lender against loss on the mortgage, thereby permitting the lender to offer more liberal credit terms to families who could not otherwise afford a home.

FHA mortgage insurance: Federally backed insurance protecting lenders against nonrepayment of mortgage.

The FHA insures mortgages when both property and borrower meet certain standards. Information on current requirements can be found by contacting the FHA or lenders that provide FHA-insured loans. If you are eligible, you may borrow up to a government-set maximum with a relatively low down payment of no more than 5 percent of the purchase price. Prior to 1984, the government also set a ceiling on the interest rates that could be charged on FHA-insured loans. This ceiling was often below competitive market rates of interest on conventional financing. Lenders made up for the low interest rate on FHA-insured loans by changing additional discount points to be paid by the seller. The government in its wisdom has since decided that it really can't set prices in private markets without causing serious disruptions. Each lender is free to charge whatever it

Box 9.3
Saving Money

Biweekly Mortgages

Most mortgages require that you repay the loan in monthly installments. You may have the choice, however, of obtaining a biweekly mortgage, on which you make a repayment once every two weeks. If you decide on a biweekly mortgage, you will end up making 26 biweekly payments during the year. When the biweekly payment is set equal to one-half the monthly payment, the total annual value of the biweekly payments will equal 13 monthly payments instead of the traditional 12.

With the extra monthly payment you will reduce the term of the mortgage and eliminate a good chunk of your future interest payments. In the accompanying table it can be seen that the higher the interest rate on the loan, the more interest you save and, therefore, the earlier you pay off

the loan. On a 30-year, $100,000 mortgage with an annual contract rate of 8 percent, a biweekly loan with a periodic payment of one-half the monthly mortgage payment would pay off after about 23 years; at a 12 percent rate it would pay off after only about 19 years. The corresponding interest savings range from $46,227 to $115,719. At first glance, a biweekly mortgage looks like an excellent idea.

You should remember, however, that your interest expense is less because you are paying off the mortgage at a faster rate. By using these dollars to pay off your mortgage at an earlier date, you give up the option of

either investing these funds elsewhere or using them to pay off higher-cost debt. The optimal strategy will depend upon which alternative provides the greatest after-tax savings or return.

Surprisingly, you don't need a biweekly mortgage to pay off your loan balance at a faster rate. Most traditional mortgage contracts allow you to make partial prepayments of principal at your discretion, thus providing you with greater flexibility than a similar biweekly loan. You probably already have the choice of making or not making a thirteenth monthly payment.

Annual Contract Rate (%)	Monthly Payment*	Biweekly Payment	Term of Biweekly Mortgage (Years)	Total Interest on Monthly Mortgage	Total Interest on Biweekly Mortgage	Total Interest Saved
12	$1,028.61	$514.31	19.04	$270,301	$154,582	$115,719
10	877.57	438.79	20.96	215,926	139,138	76,788
8	733.76	366.88	22.85	164,155	117,928	46,227

*Monthly payments on a 30-year $100,000 mortgage.

perceives to be a competitive market rate of interest. The insurance is paid for by adding one-half percentage point to the interest charged on the mortgage balance.

VETERANS ADMINISTRATION (VA) All veterans and current members of the Armed Services are entitled to loan guarantees through the Veterans Administration. The stated purpose of the program is to help veterans finance the purchase of reasonably priced homes at favorable rates of interest. The guarantee encourages lenders to make bigger loans with a smaller down payment than they otherwise could, because the government guarantees repayment of up to 60 percent of the loan, up to a legislatively set maximum. However, the VA requires that borrowers have a debt repayment-to-income ratio of 41 percent or less.

The Veterans Administration still sets an interest rate ceiling on VA-insured loans. When the ceiling is below rates on conventional loans, you can expect lenders to add on discount points to make up for the difference.

PRIVATE MORTGAGE INSURANCE If you obtain a conventional mortgage with less than a 20 percent down payment, you will probably be required to purchase **private mortgage insurance.** This insures the lender for the difference between the 20 percent usually required and the lower down payment. The up-front premium is about 1 percent of the mortgage amount. There is also an annual charge of about 0.4 percent that is added to the monthly mortgage payment. Annual premiums should be discontinued when your equity in the home reaches 20 percent of the home's market value. However, lenders are slow to remove this charge, therefore, you should request that the insurance be eliminated when you have accumulated the required equity in the home.

Private mortgage insurance: Privately backed insurance protecting lenders against nonpayment of mortgage.

Refinancing

If you took out a mortgage at a high interest rate, and rates have since come down, you should consider the possibility of refinancing the loan. Your first step is to contact your current lender concerning refinancing. If you have been a good customer, the lender may be willing to reduce some of the up-front costs associated with refinancing. Your up-front expenses will consist of a possible prepayment penalty on the old loan, and points and origination costs on the new loan. Your future savings will consist of lower monthly mortgage payments. To determine whether or not you should refinance, you must estimate your payback period, that is, the length of time required for your future savings to cover your up-front expenses. With the average family moving once every seven years, you most likely should not refinance if the payback period is longer than seven years.

Because loans may be written in so many ways, the proposed new loan is likely to differ by more than just the interest rate. You must also weigh these additional factors into your decision to refinance. For example, you may be considering giving up a high fixed rate mortgage for a currently low adjustable rate mortgage. This exchange may be profitable if rates stay low. Whether such an exchange is attractive to you depends upon how much risk you are willing to accept.

Figure 9.12 (on page 288) contains a worksheet for calculating the approximate payback period. To calculate your monthly savings at the lower interest rate, the new monthly payment should be based upon the outstanding loan balance and the remaining term on the old loan. Given a refinancing cost of $2,300 and savings on monthly mortgage payments of $55.20, the reduction in mortgage payments would pay for the cost of refinancing in three years and six months. This is only an approximate payback period, because it does not consider the differential tax treatment for mortgage interest and closing costs, or the different rates at which low- and high-interest mortgages pay back principal.

You should recognize that the tax treatment of points differs for refinancing. On the initial home mortgage the IRS has decided you can deduct all points representing prepaid interest in the year the loan is taken out. For refinancing, however, the deduction must be spread out over the term of the mortgage. In the current example, you would have an annual itemized deduction of $60 = $1,200 ÷ 20 years. Of course, if you sell the home before the mortgage is paid off, any remaining nonitemized points may be deduced in the year of the sale.

Housing: The Cost of Shelter

What If You Can't Meet Your Mortgage Payments?

Foreclosure: A legal process that terminates your rights to a mortgaged property and forces its sale.

The unexpected can happen. You can lose your job, or your business can enter troubled times. Whenever the possibility exists that you may be unable to meet your future mortgage payments, your first step is to contact the lending institutions. If you do not meet your scheduled payments, the lender probably has the right to demand immediate payment on the remaining loan balance. Failure to meet this demand may result in **foreclosure**. This legal process terminates your rights to the property and forces its sale. You receive any excess of the sale price over the amount needed to discharge the loan. Of course, because of the immediacy surrounding the sale, the price may be relatively low, leaving you with little

Action Plan for the Steeles: Refinancing

Background   In 1986 the Steeles purchased their present home. They financed the purchase with a $160,000, 30-year, adjustable rate mortgage from First Federal Savings and Loan. The mortgage has an annual interest adjustment cap of 1 percent, and an aggregate interest rate cap of 16 percent. Annual adjustments on the anniversary of the closing date are based on the most recently published value of the National Average FHLB Mortgage Contract rate. The mortgage is assumable, and there are no prepayment penalties.

The Problem   The Steeles recently received notice from First Federal that the adjustable rate on their home mortgage will equal 8 percent over the next year. Accompanying this notice was an offer to exchange their adjustable rate for a fixed rate on the remaining balance and term of their current mortgage. For a renegotiation fee of $500 they could exchange their adjustable rate of 8 percent for a nonassumable fixed rate of 9 percent. They wonder whether they should accept First Federal's offer. If interest rates rise again, their payments on the adjustable might skyrocket. On the other hand, Arnold feels that he might be transferred in another year or two, in which case they would have to sell their current home.

The Plan   The first thing the Steeles should do is to contact other lenders to make sure this is the best available offer. Assuming that it is, they might then consider what might happen under different assumptions.

Under the worst-case scenario, inflation could increase, pushing the change in the interest rate on the adjustable mortgage to its limit. The accompanying table indicates what would happen given upper-limit adjustments in the interest rate. The remaining unpaid balance on their home mortgage is about $154,000; at 9 and 8 percent rates of interest, this would mean a monthly payment of $1,307 and $1,236, respectively. In the first year the adjustable rate mortgage would save the Steeles $103 per month. In the third year the monthly payment on the adjustable rate mortgage would rise above the monthly payment on the fixed rate mortgage. But even at the end of the third year, there would still be a slight overall total benefit of $96 from having selected the adjustable rate mortgage.

or nothing in return. Fortunately, this process involves costs and risks for the lending institution, so that you may both benefit by avoiding foreclosure. This is why you should contact the lending institution before you actually have to miss payments. It is possible that, through a renegotiation of the loan, the monthly payments can be reduced. This reduction can be accomplished by stretching out the term of the loan, postponing repayment of principal, or even negative amortization. If you are experiencing a temporary setback in earnings, the lender may provide you with a supportable schedule of payments until you resume your previous financial status. If your problems are more permanent, you may have to

Year	Fixed Rate Mortgage		Adjustable Rate Mortgage		Difference	
	Rate	Monthly Payment	Rate	Monthly Payment	Monthly	Annual
First	9%	$1,307	8%	$1,204	$103	$1,236
Second	9%	1,307	9%	1,304	3	36
Third	9%	1,307	10%	1,405	−98	−1,176
					Total	$96

Only in the unlikely event that the adjustable rate again rose by the maximum amount in each of these years would the fixed rate mortgage begin to appear more favorable by the beginning of the fourth year. With less than maximum upward adjustments on the adjustable rate mortgage, the fixed rate mortgage looks like an expensive alternative. If interest rates remain flat over the next three years, the fixed rate mortgage will cost the Steeles $3,708 more in monthly payments. The Steeles will have to ask themselves whether the elimination of future interest rate risk and the accompanying uncertainty in mortgage payments is worth this potential cost.

Obviously, this is a very difficult and important decision. The wrong interest rate assumption could commit them to paying thousands of additional dollars should they remain in the present home. Unfortunately, no one can perfectly forecast interest rate movements. Anyone who could would become a millionaire overnight through speculation in financial markets.

Given the strong possibility that the Steeles might move within the next few years, keeping their present adjustable rate mortgage is probably the preferred alternative. Only under the worst-case inflation scenario does the fixed mortgage look better by the fourth year.

Another factor they should consider is that the fixed rate is nonassumable, while the adjustable rate is assumable. If inflation does pick up, the government could tighten credit markets in an effort to control inflation. An assumable mortgage with a small margin can help them sell a home in a tight credit market.

	Sample Estimates	Your Estimates
Current Loan		
Outstanding balance	$80,000	_____
Remaining term	20 years	_____
Interest rate	12%	_____
Monthly payment	$880.80	_____
Refinancing		
Initial balance	$80,000	_____
Term	20 years	_____
Interest rate	11%	_____
Monthly payment	$825.60	_____
Closing costs	1,100	_____
Points (1½%)	1,200	_____
1. Old monthly payment	$880.80	_____
2. New monthly payment	−825.60	_____
3. Monthly savings (subtract line 2 from line 1)	$55.20	_____
4. Refinancing costs— closing plus points	$2,300.00	_____
5. Approximate pay-back period, in months (divide line 4 by line 3)	41.7	_____

FIGURE 9.12

Refinancing worksheet: Calculating the approximate payback period.

consider selling the house and buying down or moving into a rental unit. The loan renegotiation may permit you the time you need to sell the house on your own and avoid a forced sale at a depressed price.

When your lending institution appears uncompromising, you may still be entitled to some special help if you have a federally insured FHA or VA loan. To find out if you qualify, you should contact, respectively, the U.S. Department of Housing or the Veterans Administration. These agencies can provide free homeowner counseling, and under the Home Mortgage Assignment Program, reduce or suspend mortgage payments for unemployed workers for a period up to three years. The one requirement is that you can show that you kept up with the mortgage payments while you were working.

If a potential foreclosure seems likely, you should consult an attorney. Under the bankruptcy code you may be able to force the lending institution to accept a proposed repayment plan, or at least delay the forced sale until you can sell the property at a favorable price.

Summary

Choosing a place to live is a major financial decision requiring a well-defined strategy. You should estimate the purchase price you can afford, examine housing in this price range, and then calculate the relative gain or loss associated with the buy-rent decision. If you decide that purchasing a home is the better alternative, seek help from professionals, including an appraiser, a home inspector, a real estate agent, and an attorney specializing in real estate. To finance the purchase, you can select from among numerous mortgage formats, including both fixed and adjustable rate loans with a variety of payment options. The discussion in this chapter should provide guidance in that selection.

Key Terms

acceleration clause (p. 281)

adjustable mortgage loan (p. 276)

aggregate rate cap (p. 278)

amortize (p. 276)

closing (p. 271)

closing costs (p. 271)

condominium (p. 261)

contract rate (p. 272)

conventional financing (p. 282)

convertible mortgage (p. 279)

cooperative (p. 262)

creative financing (p. 281)

deed (p. 271)

due-on-sale clause (p. 281)

earnest money (p. 271)

escrow account (p. 281)

exclusive agency agreement (p. 269)

exclusive right to sell (p. 269)

FHA mortgage insurance (p. 283)

fixed rate mortgage (p. 276)

foreclosure (p. 286)

Housing Affordability Index (p. 253)

Home Owners Warranty Corp. (HOW) (p. 274)

interest rate adjustment index (p. 277)

interest rate adjustment period (p. 277)

listing agreement (p. 269)

marketable title (p. 271)

margin (p. 276)

negative amortization (p. 279)

net listing agreement (p. 269)

open agreement (p. 269)

payment cap (p. 278)

periodic rate cap (p. 278)

points (p. 272)

prepayment penalty (p. 281)

principal (p. 276)

private mortgage insurance (p. 285)

settlement costs (p. 271)

title insurance (p. 271)

teaser rate (p. 278)

title search (p. 271)

Problems and Review Questions

1 Why was real estate such a good investment during the 1970s? Are these conditions likely to repeat themselves?

2 If your income after taxes is $28,000 per year, and you expect to pay about $100 per month on utilities, about how much can you afford to spend on monthly rental payments?

3 Given an affordable monthly mortgage payment of $650, and a mortgage interest rate of 14 percent on a 30-year loan, what is the size of the affordable mortgage? Given this affordable mortgage, and a 12 percent down payment, what is the affordable purchase price?

4 Explain whether the term *condominium* refers to a type of housing, a type of ownership, or both. How does a cooperative differ from a condominium?

5 Suppose you had $6,000 in mortgage interest payments during the year, and you were in the 28 percent marginal tax bracket. What is the real cost of the mortgage interest payments after tax considerations? Suppose you had $6,000 in rental payments during the year, and you were in the 33 percent marginal tax bracket. What is the real cost of the rental payments after tax considerations?

6 Suppose housing prices rise at a 10 percent annual rate over the next five years. If a house now costs $100,000, how much will it bring after five years and the payment of a 6 percent sales commission?

7 What are the tax advantages attached to home ownership, and under what conditions will long-term capital gains on the sale of a residence be tax free?

8 What occurs at *closing*? Give three items that would be included in closing costs.

9 A lender is offering an 11 percent fixed rate mortgage, requiring a down payment equal to 20 percent of the home's purchase price. The lender estimates that clos-

ing costs should be equal to $500 plus 4 points. How much will closing costs be on a $120,000 home?

10 What are the relative advantages of fixed and adjustable rate loans?

11 What are some important characteristics of adjustable rate loans that you should examine carefully?

12 An adjustable rate mortgage has a yearly interest rate adjustment cap of 1 percent. If the indexed rate moves up by 1½ percent in the first year, and ½ percent in the second year, how much can the interest rate on the remaining loan balance move up after the first year, and after the second year?

13 Suppose you expect your income to increase significantly over the next few years. You would like to purchase a home that more closely fits your future income status, rather than your present circumstances, thereby avoiding relocation expenses in a few years. What types of mortgages might be of interest to you?

14 You are thinking of retiring in about 15 years. You would like to purchase a home now but would like to have it paid off before retirement. You plan to live on reduced income during retirement, so the tax deductions on mortgage interest would not be significant at that time. What types of mortgages might be of interest to you?

15 What does the term *conventional financing* mean? What government programs exist for nonconventional financing?

16 Whom does private mortgage insurance protect, and why is it sometimes required?

17 Name two government organizations that can help you obtain a home mortgage with a relatively small down payment.

18 What is a PLAM, and how is it affected by the rate of inflation?

19 What is the distinguishing feature of a convertible home mortgage?

20 What is foreclosure, and how might you avoid an impending foreclosure?

Case 9.1
How Much House Can Kim and Dan Bergholt Afford?

Kim and Dan are both government workers. They are considering purchasing a townhouse in the Washington, DC, area for about $280,000. They estimate monthly expenses for utilities at $220, maintenance at $100, property taxes at $280, and home insurance payments at $50. Their only debt consists of car loans requiring a monthly payment of $350.

Kim's gross income is $45,000 per year and Dan's is $38,000 per year. They have saved about $60,000 in a money market fund on which they earned $5,840 last year. They plan to use most of this for a 20 percent down payment and closing costs. A lender is offering 30-year variable rate loans with an initial interest rate of 8 percent given a 20 percent down payment, and closing costs equal to $800 plus 3 points.

Before making a purchase offer and applying for this loan, they would like to have some idea whether or not they might qualify.

Questions
1 Estimate the affordable mortgage and the affordable purchase price for the Berholts.
2 Suppose they do qualify; what other factors might they consider before purchasing and taking out a home mortgage?
3 What future changes might present problems for the Bergholts?

The real estate agent tells the Bergholts that if they don't care to purchase, they might consider renting. The rental option would cost $1,400 per month plus utilities estimated at $220 and renter's insurance of $25 per month.

The Bergholts believe that neither of them is likely to be transferred to another location within the next five years. After that, Dan perceives that he might move out of government service into the private sector. Assuming they remain in the same place for the next five years, the Berholts would like to know if it is better to buy or rent the townhouse. They expect that the price of housing and rents will rise at an annual rate of 7 percent over the next five years, the same rate they expect to earn on the money market fund. All other prices, including utilities, maintenance, and taxes are expected to increase at a 4 percent annual rate. After federal, state, and local taxes, they get to keep only 55 percent of a marginal dollar of earnings.

Questions

1 Given the information in this and the previous case, estimate whether it is financially more attractive for the Bergholts to rent or purchase the townhouse over a five-year holding period. (Assuming the initial interest rate of 8 percent, interest payments over the five-year period would equal $87,574.)
2 Suppose it turns out that they have to relocate after one year. Which is the preferred alternative after one year? (Interest payments over the first year would equal $17,852.)

Helpful Reading

Board of Governors of the Federal Reserve System. *A Consumer's Guide to Mortgage Lock-ins.*

Board of Governors of the Federal Reserve System. *A Consumer's Guide to Mortgage Refinancings.*

Board of Governors of the Federal Reserve System. *Home Mortgages: Understanding the Process and Your Rights.*

U.S. Department of Housing and Urban Development. *Avoiding Mortgage Default.*

U.S. Department of Housing and Urban Development. *Guide to Single Family Home Mortgage Insurance.*

U.S. Department of Housing and Urban Development. *Home Buyer's Vocabulary.*

U.S. Department of Housing and Urban Development. *Wise Rental Practices.*

U.S. Department of Commerce, Bureau of the Census. *Characteristics of New Housing: 1990.* Current Construction Reports, June 1991.

U.S. Department of Commerce, Bureau of the Census. *Homeownership Trends in the 1980's,* Series H-121, No. 2, December 1990.

U.S. Department of Commerce, Bureau of the Census. *Housing Vacancies and Homeownership, Annual Statistics: 1990,* Current Housing Reports.

U.S. Department of Commerce, Bureau of the Census. *Who Can Afford to Buy a House?* Current Housing Reports, H121/91-1, May 1991.

Helpful Contacts

Division of Consumer Affairs, Board of Governors of the Federal Reserve System 20th and C Streets, NW, Washington, DC 20551 (telephone 202–452–3946). For complaints dealing with financial institutions.

HSH Associates
1200 Route 23, Butler, NJ 07405
For a small fee, they provide information on mortgage rates in your area; or if it you already have a loan, an ARM Check Kit to guide you through recalculation of your adjustable rate mortgage.

Office of Fair Housing and Equal Opportunity
U.S. Department of Housing and Urban Development
Room 5204, Washington, DC 20410 (telephone: 1–800–424–8590).
For housing discrimination complaints.

Protecting What You Have

Before you go forth to make your millions, you should ensure that nothing can deprive you or your family of the basic necessities of shelter and support. In the first chapter of this text, we discussed a building-block approach to success, in which you first create a solid foundation upon which you can build subsequent successes. One of the stones in that foundation is adequate insurance protection. Without it, later financial successes may unexpectedly crumble, leaving you or your family with nothing but debt. In Part Three you will learn how insurance can protect you against many of life's common financial disasters.

Insurance is one area in which a wrong purchase is very easy to make. The objectives are complicated, the terminology is confusing, and the sales agent may not be working in your best interest. Moreover, if you buy without adequate forethought, your mistake will become apparent only after it is too late. What good does it do to realize you purchased the wrong kind or amount of insurance *after* the auto accident, *after* the home fire, or *after* the disabling illness?

Insurance is purchased for many reasons. However, the basic and most important purpose of insurance is to protect you against *major* financial catastrophe. No matter what kind of insurance you're examining—be it life, health, or property—you should keep this primary objective in mind. With this, and a good understanding of the chapters that follow, you should be able to select the amount and type of insurance protection you and your family really need.

Part 3

Chapter 10

Life Insurance: Protecting Your Dependents

Objectives

1   To know how to estimate the maintenance requirement for dependent survivors
2   To calculate your life insurance protection needs
3   To understand the important provisions in a life insurance policy
4   To describe the major kinds of life insurance
5   To judge the relative merits of different insurance plans
6   To learn how to make cost comparisons on life insurance plans
7   To be able to choose the type and amount of protection that is best for you

Chicago, Ill.—John Cramer and Henry Block were alike in many ways. They were both 29 years old when they died in similar New Year's Eve collisions. Both were careful drivers who did not drink and drive. But there was no way either could avoid a head-on collision as a drunken driver swerved left of center. John and Henry also each had a $100,000 life insurance policy, but this is where the similarities end. John was single with no dependents. He had purchased a variable life policy because it had been advertised as a tax-advantageous saving program. He named his parents as beneficiaries, never expecting that they would receive the proceeds.

He knew his parents had adequately prepared for their retirement years and were not depending on his support. To them the $100,000 now represents a sad reminder of their loss. By using it to fund a scholarship in their son's name, they hope to turn the money into a positive remembrance.

Henry wasn't searching for an investment. The policy he purchased was meant to provide for the future needs of his family. After the birth of their first son, David, he and his wife, Carol, decided that a $100,000 renewable term life insurance policy on Henry was necessary for their family's financial security. Since then they

hadn't given their life insurance needs much thought, even after the birth of two additional children, Hank and Sarah.

Carol now wonders about the children's financial future; $100,000 doesn't seem as much as it did when they purchased the policy. She remembers joking about how wealthy she would be if something happened to Henry. She also remembers discussing how they planned to send all three children to college. With determination and hard work, she still expects to achieve their shared hopes. But she can't help thinking how much easier it would now be if they had just increased Henry's insurance.

Life insurance is a topic that most people would rather not discuss. Anything that questions our own mortality is almost always distasteful. In addition, we confront a special language we don't understand, and costs that are difficult to compare. Moreover, we are sometimes subjected to high-pressure sales tactics from aggressive life insurance agents. It would be very nice if the whole problem of life insurance would just go away. Unfortunately, avoidance is often not the best policy.

The life insurance decision requires a considerable amount of effort. You must first examine the reasons why you might need life insurance. If you feel you do need insurance, you must then decide upon the appropriate kind and amount of insurance protection. This means gathering information on the life insurance market. Life insurance policies differ widely in both cost and coverage, and you can easily misunderstand what is being offered to you. Finally, you must be able to conduct a cost comparison so as to satisfy your insurance needs at the lowest possible cost. Most people do not devote this much effort to the life insurance decision. This is the reason for the industry adage, Life insurance is sold, not bought.

This is unfortunate, because a more positive attitude can produce substantial rewards. Life insurance is an integral part of a well-thought-out financial plan. It can provide your dependents with security against possible financial hardship resulting from your premature death. Without life insurance these contingencies must be covered by your present savings. If you first had to accumulate substantial savings before providing this security, you might be overly cautious in your career decisions and your financial investments.

297

Effort taken in the life insurance decision can give you substantial cost savings, in addition to peace of mind. The Federal Trade Commission has estimated that billions of dollars have been lost by holding life insurance policies that paid below-market rates of return and by prematurely terminating policies with high surrender charges. With a little knowledge, you can avoid these pitfalls.

Fundamental Insurance Concepts

Life insurance is only part of a bag of tools you can use to manage financial risk. To understand how this tool and others, such as health, disability, and property insurance, can best be applied, you must first know a few basic concepts in insurance and risk management. Given this foundation in the principles of insurance, the information provided in this and the next two chapters should help you avoid many of the major financial catastrophes that can occur.

Risk

It is impossible, and probably not even desirable, to eliminate all risk from your life. Every day brings you unexpected pleasures and unforeseen disappointments. Without them, life would be bland and unexciting. That new job can be rewarding or frustrating. The new car can provide hours of enjoyment or hours in the shop. Everything you do involves some risk.

You willingly undertake certain risks because they provide the possibility of financial gain. In the stock and bond markets you accept **speculative risks** in the hope that you will receive a compensating return on your investments. Speculative risk exists when both gain and loss are possible.

Speculative risk: Exists when there is the opportunity for both gain and loss.

There are some risks, however, that you certainly could do without. These risks provide only the opportunity for loss, with no possibility of gain. Examples include the risk that your home might burn to the ground or that your car might go off the road. Each represents a potential financial drain on your resources and is said to contain pure risk. **Pure risk** exists when only loss is possible and the loss is the result of accidental circumstances. You may undertake certain precautions to reduce these risks, such as keeping a fire extinguisher in your home and driving only in good weather. However, individual action may not be enough to significantly reduce pure risk. In some circumstances, group action in the marketplace may be necessary. It is pure risk we seek to protect against when we purchase insurance.

Pure risk: Exists when only loss is possible and the loss is the result of accidental circumstances.

POOLING OF RISK All market insurance involves a pooling of risk. For each of us individually, the future is highly uncertain. However, when we combine many individuals, functioning under similar circumstances, future events affecting the group as a whole become highly predictable. It is difficult to forecast with any certainty whether you will have an auto accident on a given weekend. However, it is not too difficult to predict how many accidents will take place nationally on that weekend. This ability to forecast with great certainty the likelihood of events for large numbers of individuals allows us to join together and pool our risks.

If we can estimate total losses suffered by a given group of individuals, then we know the necessary amount of financial reserves that will reimburse these same individuals for their expected losses. When group members share the cost of this reserve, by each member paying what is termed a *premium*, they share the group's losses. Each member is committed to paying a certain premium but is also freed from the possibility of a larger financial loss. The premium represents the cost of the risk transfer.

The premium should be based upon the average loss experience for the group as a whole. When using past loss experience to project future losses, insurance companies must be wary of adverse selection. **Adverse selection** is the tendency for those with higher than average risk to desire insurance coverage. If, over time, those at high risk either purchase insurance or continue coverage to a greater extent than those at low risk, then average losses must rise. The insurance company will then find that the premiums it has collected do not adequately cover the losses it had insured. If the insurance company is unable to meet its obligations, it is insolvent. This may result in widespread financial loss and great hardship for many policy holders who had paid premiums for nonexisting protection. It is hard to think of a greater tragedy than to have suffered a loss, only to find that the insurance protection you were depending on is not there.

Underwriting is the process of selecting and classifying risk exposure. The person who does this is called an *underwriter*. It is the underwriter's responsibility to guard against adverse selection by denying coverage to those who are at greater risk than that of the insured group. This can lead to negative publicity for the insurers, who are often accused of being heartless because they deny coverage to those who most need it. In doing this, however, the underwriter is protecting not only the interest of the insurance company. The underwriter is also guaranteeing the continued protection of the many policy holders who are relying on this company to be there in time of need.

Obviously, if everyone in the group suffered a loss at the same time, the reserves could not cover all the losses. Consequently, we cannot successfully insure ourselves against risks that affect the group as a whole; we can only insure against risks that are personal in nature. For this reason, private market insurance does not cover losses resulting from wars, nuclear accidents, or floods. Where such insurance does exist, it is viable only when backed by a government with the power to levy taxes and print money.

In the marketplace, the insurance company manages the reserve pool of funds. In doing so, it incurs some transaction costs and some financial risks. The company must receive adequate compensation for processing and policing the many claims, and for assuming the risk that the pooled reserves may not be adequate to meet all of the claims. Consequently, insurance companies will receive more in premiums than they pay out in claims. This doesn't mean that insurance is a bad deal. It does mean there is an expected cost attached to using the market place. Therefore, you should decide whether the transfer of risk is worth the additional cost before purchasing insurance.

INSURABLE INTEREST In order to have an **insurable interest,** you must be related to the insured event in such a way that if the event occurs, you will incur a financial loss. Without this requirement, you would be **gambling,** not purchasing insurance. For example, I cannot purchase insurance against loss of the space shuttle. I have no financial interest in the enterprise. If it were lost, I would not suffer any financial harm. An agreement whereby I would receive payment if the shuttle were unsuccessful would be a gamble rather than an insurance contract.

Adverse selection: The tendency for those with higher than average risk to seek or continue insurance coverage.

Underwriting: The process of selecting and classifying risk exposure so that an insurance company may decide which applications for insurance it will accept.

Insurable interest: An interest in which you may experience financial loss and an interest for which you can purchase insurance protection.

Gambling: Wagering on a risky event in which you have no insurable interest.

However, companies having payloads aboard the shuttle can and do enter into insurance contracts dependent on the shuttle's success. The financial loss these companies would suffer if the shuttle mission were unsuccessful represents an insurable interest.

INDEMNIFICATION   Another way in which insurance differs from gambling is that payment under an insurance contract should not exceed the value of the loss. At most, insurance is meant to provide **indemnification;** that is, a return to your financial status before the loss. You should not receive a net financial gain when an insurance policy pays off. For this reason, you should not insure an article for more than it is worth. Over insurance is a waste of money, because an insurance company will not pay out more than the market worth of the loss.

Of course, no fair market value can be placed on a human life. Consequently, the amount of life insurance we can take out on ourselves and our relatives is practically unlimited. The concept of indemnification, however, is important when we take out life insurance on our business associates. In business relationships, the amount of life insurance must be limited by the amount of financial harm.

Risk Management

Risk management consists of identifying, evaluating, and determining how to handle your risks. Your health, property, and ability to generate income are constantly at risk from numerous sources. You need to enumerate these risks and then determine how threatening each is to you and to your family's financial survival. You must then choose the best method or combination of methods for dealing with each of your risk exposures. There are four basic techniques for managing risk: risk reduction, risk avoidance, risk transfer, and risk retention.

RISK REDUCTION   You engage in **risk reduction** when you lower the probability of a loss by taking preventive action. Examples of personal risk reduction include the use of car bumpers, football helmets, seat belts, and smoke and burglar alarms. Each reduces the probability of major property damage, the probability of loss of life, or both.

RISK AVOIDANCE   **Risk avoidance** involves reducing or eliminating the probability of a loss by avoiding the cause of the loss. If you avoid smoking and the heavy use of alcohol, you avoid severe risks to your health.

Risk avoidance is termed a conservative strategy because it calls for a change in our behavior. Sometimes, the cost of changing our behavior is just too high for us to accept. You could avoid the risk of flying by not flying, but this would limit both your business career and your vacation alternatives. Furthermore, you must be careful that the avoidance of one risk does not increase another. By not flying, you may be accepting greater risks by driving.

RISK RETENTION   When the cost of eliminating the risk far exceeds the benefits of eliminating the risk, your best decision may be **risk retention.** This can be true for both major losses and minor losses. For example, it would be prohibitively

Indemnification: The restoration of the financial state that existed before you incurred a loss.

Risk management: The process of identifying, evaluating, and deciding how to deal with risk.

Risk reduction: Reducing the probability of loss through preventive action.

Risk avoidance: Reducing or eliminating risk through behavior modification.

Risk retention: Accepting risk as the least costly, best course of action.

**Protecting
What You
Have**

expensive—if not impossible—to insure your property against loss to war or insurrection. Consequently, you must assume the risk.

You can insure against the cost of appliance repairs with a service contract. The expected cost of repairs, however, is typically much less than the cost of the service contract. In addition, when the appliance does need repairs, it is usually a minor inconvenience rather than a major financial catastrophe. Your optimal strategy is to retain small risks, but transfer the large ones.

Risk transfer: Eliminating the possibility of probabilistic loss through the purchase of insurance.

RISK TRANSFER   By purchasing an insurance contract, you engage in **risk transfer.** With life, health, auto, and home owner's insurance the associated risks of major financial loss are transferred from you and your family to the insurer. Transferring risk is an important tool for eliminating major risks that cannot be feasibly disposed of through risk reduction or avoidance. No matter how moderate and healthful your life-style may be, there is still the possibility of a disabling sickness or premature death. The resulting expense and loss of income could lead to drastic changes for both you and your family. For protection against risks such as this, transferring risk through market purchase insurance is the best risk management strategy.

Estimating Your Life Insurance Needs

The two most important reasons for buying life insurance are that it can serve as a convenient means of saving, and it can provide financial security for dependents. You must judge its performance as a form of savings against all alternative methods. However, there is no substitute for the death protection it provides. You may *want* to use life insurance as a savings vehicle, but you *need* it for the insurance protection. Therefore, we will first examine ways in which you may estimate your own need for life insurance protection.

A study by the American Council on Life Insurance found that among 14 percent of households with children, neither parent was covered by life insurance. In the other 84 percent the average amount of coverage, including both group and individual insurance, was only a little over $100,000. Although this may sound like a significant amount of death protection, many of these families are probably inadequately protected.

Young adults are often sold life insurance when they graduate from college. Like Henry in the opening story, they later tend not to review the adequacy of their coverage. The paradoxical result is that those who don't need protection have too much, and those who really need the protection have too little. To avoid this situation, it is probably a good idea for you to sit down and calculate your life insurance needs at least once every three years. You should also recalculate whenever the family undergoes a significant change, such as the birth of a child or the purchase of a home.

The needs of the survivors may be many and varied. Funds will be necessary for death-related expenses. In addition, the survivors may require continuing financial support and funds for specialized needs such as educational expenses. The dollars to cover all of these expenses must come either from the liquidation of your family's present net assets or from your life insurance proceeds. After you decide what assets might be used to support your survivors, any needs in excess of this amount must either remain unsatisfied or be covered by life insurance. The accompanying worksheets and text will help you judge your life insurance protection needs and the adequacy of your present coverage.

The Clean-Up Fund

Expenses that are related directly to the death and that must be paid for at the time of death may be budgeted for in the **clean-up fund.** This fund should also include any liabilities that would be convenient or preferable to liquidate at this time. The typical items included in a clean-up fund are listed on the sample worksheet in Figure 10.1.

FUNERAL AND BURIAL COSTS The price of a funeral and burial can vary widely, depending on your style of departure. A standard funeral and burial cost between $3,000 and $5,000. However, you can hold this expense down to about $1,000, if you decide on an inexpensive cremation.

ESTATE TAXES Both the state and the federal government may collect taxes on the death estate. These are discussed in Chapter 18 on estate planning.

Under federal estate tax laws, an unlimited amount may be transferred to your spouse tax free. If you have a substantial estate—over $600,000—and a nonspousal estate transfer, you will have to estimate your tax liability at this point. This is particularly important if you own a business. Covering the tax liabilities will allow your beneficiaries to avoid a forced sale in a possibly depressed market.

PROBATE COSTS The lawyer who wrote your will can probably estimate the probate costs associated with the validation of your will and the distribution of your estate. As a second-best estimate, you may calculate probate costs at 4 percent of the value of the assets distributed through the probate process. For example, you would incur about $3,200 on an estate with $80,000 in assets. These assets should not include life insurance proceeds, since life insurance payouts to beneficiaries other than the estate avoid probate.

UNINSURED MEDICAL COSTS Your estimate of uninsured medical costs will depend upon the quality of your health insurance coverage (see Chapter 11). You can generally count on the cost of your medical care at death exceeding deductibles on your medical insurance policy. Therefore, you should enter any deductibles as an uninsured medical cost. In addition, you might enter another $500 to $1,000 for expenses that are medically related but not covered by medical insurance. Consequently, if you had a $300 deductible on your medical insurance, you might conservatively enter $1,300 for uninsured medical costs.

OUTSTANDING LOANS DUE The amount you enter under *outstanding loans due* will be equal to the value of the loans you would like to see paid off at the time of your death. Generally, it is a good idea to include any consumer-type loans you may have. These are probably at high rates of interest and will represent an unnecessary burden on your dependents. If you had $1,000 payable on your charge cards and a $5,000 auto loan, you might enter $6,000 for outstanding loans due.

FIGURE 10.1

Clean-up fund
worksheet.

	Sample Entries	Your Entries
1. Funeral and burial costs	$3,500	_____
2. Estate taxes	-0-	_____
3. Probate costs	3,200	_____
4. Uninsured medical costs	1,300	_____
5. Outstanding loans due	6,000	_____
Total clean-up fund	14,000	_____

The outstanding balance on a home mortgage may or may not be included in the clean-up fund. The payments on any loan that is not included in the clean-up fund must be covered under the family maintenance fund.

The Family Maintenance Fund

Family maintenance fund: Funding for the ongoing support of dependent family members.

The most important of your insurance protection needs is the **family maintenance fund.** It will insure the viability of the dependent family unit. The size of the fund will reflect the level of living you would like to see maintained. You probably want to budget an amount at least large enough to eliminate the need for major financial adjustments. On the other hand, you probably don't want to budget an amount that makes you worth more to your family dead than alive.

THE MULTIPLE-OF-SALARY APPROACH Because your family's living needs will depend upon the levels of their needs and prices in the future, estimation can be extremely difficult. In an effort to simplify the process, life insurance planners have devised tables indicating your income maintenance needs as a multiple of your gross earnings. This information is published by major banks and life insurance companies. The calculations in these tables are usually based upon the following assumptions:

1. The family requires 75 percent of its previous after-tax income to maintain its standard of living.
2. There is a surviving spouse with two children.
3. The support will continue until the insured reaches age 65.
4. The dependents are eligible for Social Security benefits.

Table 10.1 contains salary multiples based on these assumptions. It is published by The Principal Financial Group. According to these estimates, a worker at age 35 with gross annual income of $40,000 would need 11 times the gross income of $40,000, or $440,000, in the family maintenance fund. This multiple is found by locating the row with the closest gross income and the column with the closest age to that of the insured.

303

TABLE
10.1 · Insurance
Requirements to
Replace 75% of
Earnings After Taxes to
Insured's Age 65 (as a
multiple of gross
annual pay)*

Gross Annual Pay	25	30	35	40	45	50	55
$ 20,000	14	13	12	10	9	7	6
30,000	14	13	12	10	9	7	5
40,000	13	12	11	10	9	7	5
60,000	12	12	11	9	8	6	5
80,000	12	11	10	9	8	6	4
100,000	11	10	9	8	7	5	4
150,000	10	10	9	8	7	5	4
200,000	9	9	8	7	6	5	5

*After-tax income varies among individuals. Factors such as investment rate of return, inflation rate, and individual debt, needs, goals, and retirement benefits should be determined on a personal basis.

SOURCE: The Principal Financial Group.

THE NEEDS APPROACH   If you desire a more exact method of determining your maintenance fund, you can try the needs approach. In over half the families in the United States, both the husband and the wife work outside the home. In these families the surviving spouse may or may not be able to provide partial income maintenance at the death of the insured. Under such circumstances, the 75 percent income replacement typically assumed in a multiple-of-salary chart may tend to under- or overestimate the required amount of insurance protection. If, for this or any other reason, the assumptions employed in a multiple-of-salary chart do not fit your own situation, you may have to employ a more complicated needs approach in calculating your family maintenance requirements. The following steps and the worksheet in Figure 10.2 will lead you through the computations.

FIGURE 10.2

Family maintenance fund: needs approach.

		Sample Entries		Your Entries
Step 1.	Monthly survivors' expenses		$ 4,000	
Step 2.	Monthly survivors' take-home pay	$ 670		
Step 3.	Monthly survivors' benefits	1,840		
	Total contribution by survivors		−2,510	
Step 4.	Monthly maintenance requirement		$ 1,490	
Step 5.	Calculate size of maintenance fund		× 12	
	(a) Annual requirement		$ 17,880	
	(b) Multiply by number of years until the youngest child is independent		× 10	
	Family maintenance fund		$178,800	

Step 1: Calculate the monthly expenses for the dependent family unit. If you keep a family budget, you can estimate the monthly living expenses for the surviving family members based upon these data. Be sure to include all items that are jointly consumed and exclude only those items that are independently consumed by the insured. For example, the home must still be heated and maintained, but the family may no longer need that second car.

If you have not kept track of your monthly expenses, or you find it difficult to identify marginal expenses for the insured, you might rely on data based upon average family budgets. Various studies tend to support the percentage of income consumed by the head of household presented in Figure 10.3. To estimate the

FIGURE 10.3

Family head's consumption expenditure as percentage of family income.

.30 — Two adults

.26 — Two adults, one minor dependent child

.22 — Two adults, two minor dependent children

.20 — Two adults, three minor dependent children

.18 — Two adults, four minor dependent children

amount spent for the exclusive support of the insured, multiply total family take-home pay by the appropriate percentage. If you subtract the resulting amount from the family's take-home pay, you are left with the approximate expenditures necessary to provide for the continued support of the surviving members in a typical household.

The entries in Figure 10.2 assume combined take-home pay of $5,000 per month and a family with three dependent children. Consumption by one of the adult family members in a three-child family would be equal to .20 × $5,000, or $1,000 per month. Therefore, the dependent family would require $4,000 per month in maintenance expenditure.

After you have arrived at monthly living expenses based upon current expenditures, you may want to add in any additional expenditures the family might incur with the death of the insured. This may include additional homemaking expenses and lost fringe benefits. For example, many workers receive family medical insurance as a fringe benefit, but this coverage may lapse at their death. In this situation, the monthly cost of medical insurance should be added to living expenses in order to assure the family's continued protection.

Step 2: Calculate total monthly survivors' take-home pay. You will have to estimate the amount the surviving family members can contribute to their own support. After the death of the insured, survivors may find new sources of income. On the other hand, the additional homemaking responsibilities placed on the surviving spouse may reduce that person's ability to participate in the labor market. The example in Figure 10.2 assumes the surviving spouse will bring home part-time earnings of $670 per month.

Step 3: Calculate total monthly survivors' benefits. If your job is covered by Social Security, each of your children is eligible for monthly benefits until age 18. In addition, the surviving parent may be eligible for parental benefits until the youngest child reaches age 16. The surviving parent then enters a blackout period during which benefits are discontinued. However, when the surviving parent reaches age 60, benefits may again be paid out under a widow(er)'s pension. Your local Social Security office may project your benefits. If not, you can either turn to Appendix B, "The Social Security System," for help in calculating your benefits or enter one of the following ballpark estimates.

Estimates of Monthly Social Security Benefits for Dependent Survivors

	Average Annual Social Security-Covered Earnings				
	Less than $10,000	$10,000–$15,000	$15,000–$25,000	$25,000–$35,00	$35,000 and over
One surviving child	$360	$ 470	$ 570	$ 740	$ 870
Parent and one child	720	940	1,140	1,480	1,740
Maximum family benefit (parent and two or more children)	730	1,120	1,390	1,720	2,030

Include benefits for each of the surviving children in your calculation as long as the total is less than the maximum amount the family is permitted to receive. Do not include Social Security benefits for the surviving spouse if he or she plans to earn more than $7,080 per year. At earnings above this, spousal benefits are sharply reduced.

If you have a private insurance plan that provides monthly survivor benefits, you will want to add this to any Social Security benefits to arrive at total survivors' benefits. For example, if Social Security provided $1,740 per month and a private pension plan provided $100 per month, then total monthly benefits would be $1,840.

Employer-sponsored retirement plans will often provide some type of benefit for the survivor's spouse. In fact, when retirement annuities are provided employees, both preretirement and postretirement spousal survivorship benefits are in most instances required under the Retirement Equity Act of 1984. These benefits are mandatory and can only be withdrawn with the consent of the non-employee spouse. For those who die after retirement, the surviving spouse must receive a monthly benefit equal to at least one-half the amount they had received jointly. If the employee dies before retirement, but after rights to a retirement annuity have been earned, the surviving spouse must receive a reduced annuity from either the date of the employee's death or the date of the earliest possible retirement, whichever is later.

Step 4: Calculate the monthly maintenance requirement.   The monthly maintenance requirement is equal to the difference between the expenditure needs of the dependent family unit and the support provided by potential income and benefits. To calculate this amount, add survivors' take-home pay in step 2, and survivors' total benefits in step 3, and subtract the sum from total monthly expenses in step 1. For the sample data, the monthly maintenance requirement is $1,490.

This requirement may change over time. However, some of the changes may offset each other; for example, Social Security benefits are reduced as children become self-supporting. Thus, your estimate of a monthly maintenance requirement for the present age structure of your family may hold up reasonably well until the youngest child reaches age 16. If the surviving spouse does not expect to become self-supporting after the youngest child reaches age 16, you may want to calculate a separate monthly maintenance requirement for the surviving spouse over the years that Social Security benefits are blacked out.

Step 5: Calculate the size of the maintenance fund.   The monthly maintenance requirements must be paid out of the maintenance fund. In estimating the appropriate size of the maintenance fund, you should consider two important facts: one, with inflation, monthly expenses will rise over time; and two, the maintenance fund will be invested and will earn an interest return. If you sum up the maintenance requirements over the years of dependency, you will have arrived at the necessary size of the maintenance fund under a very special assumption, i.e., the after-tax interest return on the maintenance fund is just equal to the rate of inflation. A few years ago this assumption may have been unwarranted. However, with banking deregulation, even unsophisticated investors are likely to be able to protect their savings against inflation.

Specialized Funds

You might consider setting up various specialized funds to meet temporary needs that are not covered by the maintenance fund. Special funds for emergencies, education, and retirement are definitely worth thinking about, and are listed on the specialized fund worksheet in Figure 10.4.

AN EMERGENCY FUND   You may want to be fairly generous in estimating the size of your emergency fund, since emergencies might be more difficult to handle in a single-parent household. A good rule of thumb is three to six months of the survivor's expenses included in Figure 10.2. If most of these expenses are guaranteed by survivors' benefits, a multiple of 3 should be sufficient.

AN EDUCATIONAL FUND   College students over 18 years of age are no longer entitled to survivors' benefits under Social Security. Therefore, if you plan to provide a college education for your children, you should consider the need for an educational fund. Tuition and fees, room and board, books and supplies, transportation, and personal expenses for a resident student are now about $7,000 per year at public institutions. (Cost data on other types of institutions can be found in Chapter 2.) Thus, a four-year college education can cost about $28,000.

A RETIREMENT FUND   If you think that pension benefits from private plans and Social Security might not provide enough support for the surviving spouse, you might want to set an additional amount aside in a retirement fund to eliminate this deficiency. If you multiply the annual deficiency in support times 20 years, you will have a decent estimate of the amount needed in the retirement fund, assuming retirement at age 65.

FIGURE 10.4

Specialized fund worksheet.

	Sample Entries		Your Entries
Emergency fund		$12,000	
Educational fund			
Cost per child	$28,000		
Number of children	× 3		×
		$ 84,000	
Retirement fund			
Annual requirement	$ 3,000		
Multiply by 20 years	× 20		× 20
		$ 60,000	
Other funds		-0-	
Total specialized fund		$156,000	

The Insurance Protection Gap

Once you have estimated the total needs of the dependent family—consisting of the clean-up fund, the maintenance fund, and specialized funds—the next task is to determine how these needs will be met. Figure 10.5 contains a worksheet for calculating the insurance protection gap.

You should examine three basic sources of funding:

1. *Financial investments.* These should be counted at present market value after taxes. You should include your personal portfolio, plus any lump-sum distributions from retirement plans that pay out upon death.
2. *Tangible goods.* You may have some items the family will no longer require. These should be valued at their market price after taxes and selling costs.
3. *Life insurance.* The face amount of your present policies, minus outstanding loans on those policies, is available for future support. You should also include any group coverage you have at work, plus the $250 death benefit under Social Security.

Funding needs less funding sources represents your survivors' unfunded needs. You obviously will have to provide sufficient insurance protection for your survivors' unfunded needs. However, covering only their unfunded needs may not protect your survivors adequately from immediate financial hardship. Your survi-

FIGURE 10.5

Worksheet: the life insurance gap.

	Sample Entries		Your Entries
Funding Needs			
1. Clean-up fund	$ 14,000		
2. Family maintenance fund	178,800		
3. Specialized fund	156,000		
Total funding needs		$348,800	
Less Funding Sources			
1. Financial investments	$ 56,000		
2. Tangible goods	10,000		
3. Life insurance			
(a) Group insurance	$ 50,000		
(b) Individual insurance	-0-		
(c) Social Security	250		$250
Total sources		($116,250)	( )
Unfunded Needs		$232,550	
Unfunded Estate Liquidity		-0-	
Life Insurance Protection Gap		$232,550	

vors may be hard-pressed to convert the funding sources into cash in order to meet immediate death-related expenses such as estate taxes. For this reason, you should check your funding needs and sources in Figure 10.5 to ensure that your liquid resources—those readily convertible into cash—are sufficient to cover the clean-up fund, which should include all immediate death-related expenses. The deficiency in liquid resources should be entered under unfunded estate liquidity.

Your survivors' unfunded needs plus their unfunded estate liquidity equals your **life insurance protection gap.** If a gap exists on your own worksheet, it is time to start considering additional life insurance coverage.

The Special Language of Life Insurance Policies

A life insurance policy is a contract between you and the insurance company. As with all contracts, you should read it carefully and understand it fully before you sign. This may require some tenacity on your part, since many companies provide sample policies only with great reluctance. Furthermore, to understand the agreement you must first master the special language of the life insurance industry. However, the efforts are worth the trouble. Purchasing the wrong kind of insurance or the wrong type of policy can prove costly.

The Basic Policy

In return for amounts paid to the insurance company while you are living, the life insurance agreement obligates the company to pay out a stated amount at the time of your death. Although policies differ widely in language and coverage, this basic agreement should contain some common terminology.

FACE AMOUNT   The dollar amount stated on the face of the policy is the **face amount.** In the absence of special provisions or additions, the face amount minus any outstanding loans on the policy is the amount paid out at death. Special provisions, such as an accidental death clause which increases the payout when death is due to accident circumstances, may affect the actual payout at death.

LIVES COVERED   Most policies are taken out on the life of one person and are called **single life policies.** There are, however, policies with more complicated coverage. A **joint life policy** covers more than one person. With this policy coverage, the face amount is paid out at the first death. This may be important to a family that desires to replace the income lost at the death of either the husband or the wife. In this case, a $100,000 joint life policy can be considerably less expensive than a single life policy of $100,000 on the husband and a single life policy of $100,000 on the wife.

A **survivorship joint life** policy operates in the reverse manner. It pays out on the death of the last individual in the group. This policy is particularly useful in estate planning, when taxes must be paid at the death of the surviving spouse.

PREMIUM   The periodic payment made to the insurance company is called the **premium.** Depending on the particular policy, this payment may be made on an annual, semiannual, monthly, or even weekly basis. A service charge is usually added for premiums that are paid other than annually.

DIVIDEND Insurance may be purchased from either mutual insurance companies or stock insurance companies. Typically, the mutual insurance companies issue participating policies, and the stock insurance companies issue **nonparticipating insurance.** A few stock companies do write policies with limited participation, however.

Participating insurance gets its name from the fact that policy holders participate in the earnings and mortality experience of the insurer. If the mutual insurance company pays out less in claims than it expected, the policy holders participate in this good fortune by receiving back the surplus funds in the form of what is called a **dividend.** This dividend is considered a partial return of your initial premium and is therefore nontaxable.

If the company had only unexpected gains, participating insurance would be a great buy. However, policy holders may participate in both unexpected gains and losses. Mutual insurance companies tend to charge higher premiums than stock insurance companies in order to create a fund to cover any unexpected costs. Should these costs occur, dividends need not be paid out. A dividend payment is not guaranteed, and payments will fluctuate with the earnings experience of the mutual insurance company.

CASH AND SURRENDER VALUE The **cash value** of a life insurance policy is equal to the savings accumulated during the existence of the policy contract. Not all insurance policies have a cash value; only those that allocate a part of each year's premium to savings do. In many insurance policies the insured may borrow against the policy's cash value at an interest rate either specified in the policy or set periodically by the insurance company. Closely related to the policy's cash value is its **surrender value.** This is the amount returned to the policy holder when coverage is terminated. Typically, the surrender value of the policy is equal to the cash value plus surrender dividends, minus outstanding loans and surrender charges.

BENEFICIARY The person or instrument (e.g., a trust fund) that receives the proceeds of the policy when you die is the **beneficiary.** You may specify a primary beneficiary and a contingent beneficiary. The **contingent beneficiary,** also termed the *secondary beneficiary*, receives the proceeds if the primary beneficiary dies before you do. You may also specify more than one person as either a primary or a contingent beneficiary. For example, suppose Arnold Steele takes out a policy naming his wife, Sharon, as primary beneficiary, and their two children, Nancy and John, as contingent beneficiaries. If Sharon dies before Arnold, the children, or more likely a trust fund for the children, will receive the insurance proceeds.

Special Provisions

The worth of a life insurance policy will depend upon more than just the policy's face amount or cash value. It will also be influenced by the various specialized provisions contained in the policy and the addition of any options, also called **riders,** to the insurance contract. The features you are most likely to encounter are described in Figure 10.6. Some of these provisions are determined by state law, and others can be added by the insured.

Nonparticipating insurance: Future net premiums are not dependent upon the earnings and mortality experience of the insurer.

Participating insurance: Policyholders participate in the earnings and mortality experience of the insurer through dividend adjustments.

Dividend: A partial return of premium dependent upon the earnings of the insurer.

Cash value: An amount equal to the savings accumulated during the existence of the policy contract.

Surrender value: The amount returned to the policyholder when coverage is terminated.

Beneficiary: The individual who receives the proceeds from the life insurance policy.

Contingent beneficiary: The one who receives the proceeds if the primary beneficiary dies first.

Rider: A specialized provision meant to modify or extend coverage in an insurance contract.

PROVISION	DESCRIPTION
Accidental death benefit	This option provides that, if the death of the insured is accidental, the death benefit will be some multiple of the face amount of the policy. If it doubles the face amount, it is sometimes known as a *double indemnity* provision.
Convertibility	You can exchange one kind of insurance for another without a medical examination. For example, your term insurance policy might be convertible to a specified amount of whole life at each age.
Cost-of-living adjustment	Automatically increases both the face amount of the policy and the premium. You have the right to reject this inflation-adjusted coverage, but if you do so, you may forfeit your right to all future cost-of-living adjustments in the face value of the policy.
Disability waiver of premium	If you become disabled, this rider requires the insurance company to take over premium payments on the policy. It usually takes effect six months after the beginning of the disability period.
Grace period	If you stop making payments and the cash value of your policy is depleted, coverage must cease, but not until the specified grace period ends. This period is usually 31 days.
Guaranteed insurability	Allows you to increase the face amount of the policy, by stated amounts and at specified dates, without a medical examination. A worthwhile option for those who expect a future increase in insurance protection needs.
Incontestability	Prohibits the insurance company, after some period of time, from challenging your unintentional mistakes and omissions on the insurance application.
Nonforfeiture clause	This clause ensures that you will not lose the cash value of your policy if you cease making payments. The cash value may be disposed of in one of three ways: You may receive it in cash, you may use it to extend premium payments on the life insurance coverage, or you may use it to purchase a reduced amount of single-premium life insurance.
Renewability	Allows you to renew your coverage without a medical examination. However, your premiums for subsequent periods may be higher.
Settlement option	This provision determines how the face amount of the policy will be paid out. The choice of settlement option can also be left to the beneficiary.

FIGURE 10.6

Special provisions of life insurance policies.

Kinds of Insurance Protection

Life insurance can be grouped into two basic categories: term and cash value. Most policies can be easily classified under one of these headings. A few, however, such as universal life, discussed later in this chapter, have the characteristics of both term insurance and cash value insurance.

Term Insurance

Term insurance: Has no cash value buildup; provides only death protection.

Term insurance provides only death protection. A term policy does not build up a cash value. If the insured discontinues premium payments, the coverage simply lapses after a specified grace period. Life insurance agents sometimes attempt to discourage people from purchasing term insurance by suggesting that if they survive the period of coverage, they have in effect paid for nothing, since the policy has no residual value. This is not true. They have paid for and received a reduction in the financial risks associated with the possibility of dying. Such risk reduction is not costless, nor is it valueless.

As we will see, there are many kinds of term insurance. Some are sold under the name term insurance and others are not. In addition, some policies that are sold under the *term* label are not true term policies. The distinguishing feature of a term policy is that it does not have a savings component. Under a true term policy, the entire premium pays for death protection. Therefore, term provides the greatest amount of death protection for each premium dollar.

Because of tax advantages extended to employer-provided term life insurance, this is the type of group life insurance that is typically furnished to employees. The Bureau of Labor Statistics reports that 92 percent of all employees in medium and large-size firms receive term life protection. The face amount of the employer-supplied insurance is on average equal to about one-and-a-half times the employee's annual salary. This coverage is particularly attractive to older workers. Current law prohibits employers from providing such workers with less insurance protection than younger workers, even though the cost of a given face amount of term protection may be much greater for this group.

RENEWABLE TERM   A **renewable term** policy covers the insured for a fixed period of time. The time period may be one, five, or ten years, or until a specific age, such as 65. Not all term is renewable, and even renewable policies may prohibit renewal after a certain age. With renewable term the insured may usually renew the policy without a medical examination. However, each time the policy is renewed, the premium is increased to reflect the greater mortality risk associated with age. Since the premium covers only death protection, young individuals at low mortality risk can purchase large amounts of term protection at minimal cost. After the age of 65, term protection can become prohibitively expensive.

Premiums on a yearly renewable term policy providing a $25,000 death benefit are illustrated in Figure 10.7. The premium is $65 for the first year and increases each year until age 75, when coverage is terminated. The dark blocks in Figure 10.8 indicate premiums on a five-year renewable term policy with a level $25,000 death benefit. The premium is $95 for each of the first five years. For each subsequent period of renewal, the yearly premium is increased.

> **Renewable term:** Term insurance that may be periodically renewed over some defined term without a medical examination.

FIGURE 10.7

Death benefit and premium for a yearly renewable term policy.

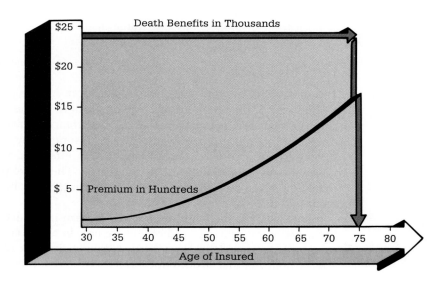

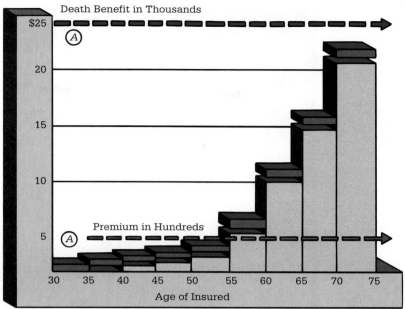

FIGURE 10.8

Death benefit and premium for a level renewable-convertible term policy.

The two dotted lines A illustrate a conversion to ordinary life at age 35. Both the death benefit and higher premium remain level for life. Bars represent annual premiums on the 5-year renewable term policy.

Decreasing term: A term policy with level premiums but decreasing death protection.

Group mortgage life: A policy designed to pay off the remaining balance on the mortgage at death.

Deposit term insurance: Returns a lump-sum amount at the end of the term of protection; not true term insurance.

DECREASING TERM **Decreasing term** is usually packaged as a one-year renewable policy. Its premium remains constant over time. The increased risk of mortality is reflected in a declining amount of death protection, so your insurance coverage automatically decreases as you age.

A decreasing term plan with an initial $25,000 death benefit is depicted in Figure 10.9. Over the 25-year period, the annual premium is equal to $80. However, the death benefit is steadily reduced until it reaches zero at age 55.

GROUP MORTGAGE LIFE A form of decreasing term insurance, **group mortgage life** is designed to pay off the remaining balance on a mortgage. The death benefit declines as the remaining balance on the mortgage falls. As with traditional decreasing term insurance, the premium remains level over the term of the mortgage. The face amount at any time may not exactly equal the remaining balance, so if you die, the beneficiary will receive an amount only approximately equal to the remaining balance.

Group mortgage life is sold through the bank that holds your mortgage. The bank collects a commission from the insurance company for functioning as a sales agent. The bank also benefits in another way: It is the beneficiary on the insurance policy. This arrangement insures that the mortgage is paid off at your death. Your family will have no say in how the proceeds are spent. If you have a low-interest mortgage, paying it off may not be the wisest use of insurance proceeds.

DEPOSIT TERM What has been advertised as **deposit term insurance** is not true term insurance, because it has a savings component. With a typical deposit term

315

Life Insurance

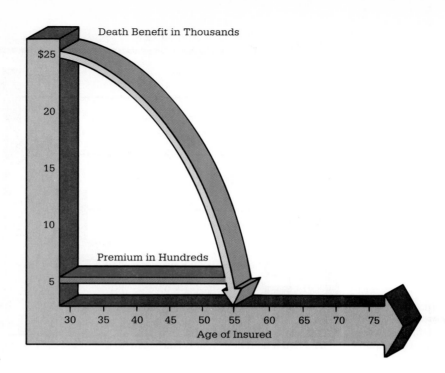

Death Benefit in Thousands

$25

20

15

10

Premium in Hundreds

5

30 35 40 45 50 55 60 65 70 75

Age of Insured

FIGURE 10.9

Death benefit and
premium for a yearly
decreasing term policy.

policy, you are supposedly purchasing something similar to 10- or 15-year renewable term. Each year you pay a term premium on the policy. However, during the
first year of coverage you pay an extra premium, which is the deposit. At the end
of the coverage period you may get back an amount equal to double the extra
premium paid during the first year. This represents the saving component. In
reality, however, the deposit you made in the first year may be going to pay the
sales commission received by the agent. The insurance company is able to pay
you back a lump sum amount after ten years, because over the ten years you have
paid a higher-than-standard premium on the term protection. When these excessive premiums are taken into account, the rate of return on the first year's deposit
is much less than it at first appears. Also, if you terminate the policy before a
specified number of years, you may lose the deposit. Most insurance analysts
have been highly critical of deposit term and suggest you avoid purchasing this
type of policy.

Cash Value Insurance

Cash value insurance:
Insurance that provides
both death protection and
cash value buildup.

Cash value insurance functions both as death protection and as a savings vehicle.
Part of each year's premium goes to pay for death protection, and part goes into
savings that is accumulated in the cash value of the policy. For an insured beginning coverage at age 25, about 70 percent of the premiums in the initial years will
go into the savings element. Over the first 20 years, 40 to 50 percent of the
premium will accumulate as savings. If the insured terminates coverage, the accumulated savings may be received in a lump-sum payment.

The actual amount of death protection provided is equal to the difference between the policy's face value and its cash value. The amount of death protection will decline over time as the cash value of the policy approaches the face amount of the policy.

One characteristic that often attracts people to cash value policies is that the insured may borrow from the insurance company an amount equal to the cash value at an attractive rate of interest. If the insured should die while owing money on the policy, the amount paid to beneficiaries will be reduced by the amount of the loan.

Whole life, or straight or ordinary life: Cash value insurance with level lifetime payments.

WHOLE LIFE   With **whole life,** also called **straight** or **ordinary life,** premium payments are level over the lifetime of the insured. The lower broken line in Figure 10.8 indicates the yearly premium on a $25,000 death benefit whole life policy taken out at age 35. Between the ages of 35 and 55, the yearly premium on the whole life policy is more than the yearly premium on the comparable term policy. However, after age 55 the term premiums are greater. Whole life's larger premiums in the early years build up cash value and reduce the need for death protection in the later years. In addition, they help pay for the increased risk of mortality in the later years.

The cash value of this policy will increase slowly in the early years and more rapidly later on. Around age 100, the cash value of the policy equals the face amount, and the policy is said to be paid off. The rise in the cash value of the policy is predetermined, and the insured is often presented with a schedule indicating what the cash value of the policy will be in each year.

Limited payment life: Cash value insurance with level premiums over a limited number of years that provides insurance protection over an entire lifetime.

LIMITED PAYMENT LIFE   Under a **limited payment life** policy, premium payments remain level up to a certain age, usually 65, and then cease. However, the insurance protection remains effective over the entire life span. This protection is accomplished by charging higher premiums than on a comparable straight life policy over the payment years in order to provide a more rapid buildup in cash value. The insurance company then uses part of the interest earned on the cash value to provide continued protection after premium payments terminate.

Endowment life: Rapid buildup of cash value, with payoff of face value after a set number of years.

ENDOWMENT LIFE   An **endowment life** policy pays off its face value after a set number of years, thus providing rapid cash value buildup with death protection. With recent changes in the tax law, the cash value buildup on most traditional endowment policies no longer qualifies for tax deferral. Consequently, such policies are rarely sold any more.

Modified whole life: Level premiums with varying death protection tied to life-cycle needs.

MODIFIED WHOLE LIFE   Most families require less insurance protection in later years. **Modified whole life** attempts to fit the needs of the family throughout the life cycle by automatically reducing the death benefit as the insured ages. As in a whole life policy, the premium payments remain level for life. However, premium payments on a modified life plan will be lower than those on a whole life policy providing identical protection in the early years.

A modified life plan for a 30-year-old male, providing a level $25,000 death benefit until age 60, is illustrated in Figure 10.10. After age 60, the death benefit drops to $17,500 and remains level for life. The annual premium payments are $280 for life.

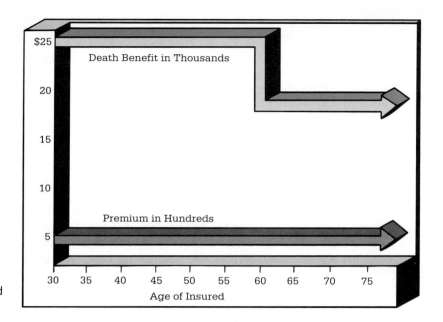

$25

Death Benefit in Thousands

20

15

10

5

Premium in Hundreds

30   35   40   45   50   55   60   65   70   75

Age of Insured

Adjustable life: The face amount of this policy may be adjusted by specified amounts at defined time intervals.

ADJUSTABLE LIFE   Under an **adjustable life** plan, both the premium payments and the face amount of the policy are adjustable. The insured is allowed to change coverage as need varies and to change premium payments as income varies. The basic idea seems to be a good one, but this plan has some characteristics you should be wary of.

The face amount of the policy may be increased only by specified amounts at specified time intervals. Unless the policy contains a guaranteed insurability rider, you may have to take another medical exam when you desire to increase the face amount. In addition, a sales charge may be built in to pay the insurance agent a second commission when you increase the insurance coverage. With the added sales charge and the medical exam, increasing the face amount of an adjustable life policy may cost about as much as taking out a new whole life policy.

The premiums are adjusted by allowing the insured to move between term protection and cash value protection. When the insured's income increases, higher premiums can be paid in order to build up cash value. During periods of financial distress, premiums can be cut by opting for lower-cost term protection. The implicit assumption is that when you can afford it, you should purchase cash value insurance. As we will later see, this assumption may be unwarranted.

UNIVERSAL LIFE   Universal life was first sold in 1981. Today, premiums on universal life policies are about 26 percent of all new premium payments. This tremendous growth in market share was offset by a reduction in whole life insurance and, more recently, term insurance.

Universal life: Permits flexible premium payments, affecting the size of the cash buildup.

Unlike traditional whole life, **universal life** permits flexible premium payments, affecting the size of the cash buildup. The premium payment on universal life is often called a contribution and, within certain limits, is voluntary. Out of this contribution the insurance company deducts a charge for term insurance protection and the cost of management. The remainder is deposited in an in-

Borrowing Your Cash Value

The cash value on your life insurance can represent a convenient source of liquidity. In most cases, you can promptly tap the cash value with a policy loan. Since the loan is 100 percent collateralized by the policy's cash value, there is no need for a credit check or other financial inquiries that can delay a typical bank loan.

To your advantage, policy loans need never be repaid, and policy loan rates are often substantially below those on other consumer financing. On the negative side, loans will reduce the death benefits, which is probably the primary reason you purchased life insurance in the first place. Moreover, since most of the begin-

ning premiums go to pay sales commissions, there may not be much cash value to borrow against unless the policy has been in effect for a number of years.

When deciding on a policy loan, you should be sure to look at the true opportunity cost of borrowing, which may exceed the policy loan rate. The cash value on your life insurance will earn interest and grow over time. However, if you borrow against the policy, the cash value is used as collateral for the loan. Because the loan may be made at an interest rate that is below what the insurance company can earn on its invested assets, this may reduce the rate earned on the policy's cash value. This practice is called "direct recognition."

For example, suppose you have a universal life policy currently earning 11 percent on cash value, on which you may obtain a policy loan for 8 percent. If you decide to borrow against the policy, the insurance com-

pany may reduce the rate earned on the collateralized portion of the cash value to only 5 percent, thus forcing you to give up an additional 6 percent return on the cash value. The true opportunity cost of borrowing is, therefore, equal to 14 percent, the policy loan rate of 8 percent plus the reduced interest rate on the cash value of 6 percent.

When deciding whether to borrow in order to invest your funds elsewhere or when deciding whether to borrow here or elsewhere, the true opportunity cost of 14 percent, and not the policy loan rate of 8 percent, is the starting point for comparison purposes. Tax considerations, of course, can make comparative valuations much more complicated. Interest earned on the cash value is tax deferred until the policy is surrendered. If the policy is never surrendered, income taxes need never be paid on the death benefits.

terest-bearing account. The interest earned either is determined periodically by the insurance company or is tied to an agreed-upon index.

You receive periodic reports on a universal life policy indicating the cost of the term protection, the management expenses, and the earned return on cash value. This provides a significant advantage over traditional whole life, where you may have no idea how much you are really paying for death protection or how much you are really earning on the policy's cash value. Given the more detailed information on a universal life policy, you are in a better position to judge the relative merits of purchasing term insurance separately and investing the difference.

Those who have compared universal life with traditional whole life have concluded that universal life does generally provide a better return on the invested cash value. Indeed, the primary reason for consumer interest in universal life has been the high advertised rate on the investment account. However, there are additional attractions. Within limits set by the company and the government, the insured may borrow against the accumulated cash value. Furthermore, most universal life policies allow the insured to increase the death protection, although another medical examination may be required.

Variable life: Permits selective investment of cash value in a market portfolio that determines the cash value in the policy.

VARIABLE LIFE   In many ways, **variable life** is similar to universal life. Like universal life, it has a term insurance component and an investment component. A minimum death benefit is guaranteed by the term insurance, while the cash value buildup and additional death benefit protection depend on the performance of selected market portfolios of stocks, bonds, or money market funds. You may be permitted to decide how the cash value will be allocated among the available portfolios and when funds should be switched between portfolios.

If your market portfolio does poorly, the cash value buildup will be less than with either whole or universal life. The speculative risk associated with variable life reduces its ability to secure the financial future of your survivors. Variable life should be compared with other tax-advantageous investments and only secondarily looked upon as death benefit protection. The government recognizes its speculative characteristics by requiring that only registered security dealers be permitted to sell this policy. As on universal life policies, management fees and early withdrawal penalties should be examined closely.

Variable life has not experienced the phenomenal growth of universal life. Its lackluster performance may be due partly to the restrictions on who may sell the policy and partly to the fact that variable life provides less flexibility than universal life. With variable life policies, annual premiums are fixed by the insurer. Regardless of how the market may look, you must contribute to at least one of the policy's portfolios to keep the policy in force. In contrast, universal life permits you to vary the amount you contribute each year and even to skip payments when there is sufficient cash value to cover the cost of insurance protection.

Variable universal life: Combines the flexible premiums of universal life with the investment selection of variable life.

VARIABLE UNIVERSAL LIFE **Variable universal life** is also sold under various other names, such as universal life II. It combines the flexible premiums permitted under universal life with the investment selection permitted by variable life. Depending on your outlook, you can say it blends the best or the worst of each. By allowing both contributions and investments to vary, it becomes a more flexible speculative investment. However, like a traditional variable life policy, if your cash value falls far enough, you may be required to contribute additional funds or lose your family's insurance protection. Furthermore, a forced payout of cash value will require the immediate payment of all deferred tax. This may present a severe hardship for those who have borrowed against the policy's cash value. After repaying those loans, they may have nothing left with which to pay the tax bill.

Selecting the Right Policy

In the past, the life insurance industry has not been noted for price competition. A Federal Trade Commission study indicated that high-cost policies often competed successfully with low-cost policies. Apparently, consumers have had difficulty comparing relative costs. Traditional whole life policies have been particularly difficult to compare, because insurance companies have not supplied information on the rate of return for the savings component. Also, life insurance agents have been known to misrepresent the actual cost of the policy. The agent would add up the premiums paid over the 20-year period and subtract from this amount the dividends received and the cash value at the end of the 20 years. The result would often be negative, erroneously indicating to the buyer that the insurance did not "cost" anything. Of course, this calculation ignores the time value of money. Had the consumer been depositing the net premiums into an account paying a competitive market rate of interest over the same period, the total amount in the account at the end of 20 years would have been much greater than the cash value of the policy at that time. The difference between the value in this imaginary account and the cash value of the policy at the end of the 20-year period represents the real cost of the life insurance policy.

The Interest-Adjusted Net Cost Index

Interest-adjusted net cost index: A useful industry-provided index for comparing the relative cost of similar life insurance policies.

Recently, with the prodding of government and consumer groups, the life insurance industry has begun to supply reliable data for cost comparisons. The National Association of Insurance Companies has suggested the use of 10-year and 20-year **interest-adjusted net cost indexes,** sometimes called surrender indexes, for valuing life insurance policies. The method for calculating this index is illustrated in Figure 10.11. As you can see from the illustration, the computations are quite complex. Fortunately, you are not required to estimate this index number when making cost comparisons; it should be supplied by the insurance company. All you really need to know is that the higher the interest-adjusted net cost index,

FIGURE 10.11

How to calculate the interest-adjusted net cost index.

Policy: Participating whole life
Face Amount: $25,000
Premium Rate per $1,000 of Face Amount: $21.82
Issue Age: 35

Year	Premium	Dividend	Net Payment	Accumulated Net Payments at 5%	Cash Value
1	$545.50	-0-	$545.50	$ 572.78	-0-
2	545.50	-0-	545.50	1,174.19	$ 54.99
3	545.50	$35.25	510.25	1,768.66	687.11
4	545.50	40.50	505.00	2,387.34	1,319.37
5	545.50	45.75	499.75	3,031.45	1,990.56
6	545.50	51.00	494.50	3,701.20	2,661.75
7	545.50	56.25	489.25	4,399.97	3,332.94
8	545.50	61.50	484.00	5,128.17	4,004.13
9	545.50	66.75	478.75	5,887.26	4,717.80
10	545.50	74.25	471.25	6,676.44	5,431.53

Net Cost: The net payment each year is equal to the premium minus the dividend. If the net payments are deposited in an account with a 5% return, at the end of 10 years the accumulated value of the net payments will equal $6,676.44. The cash value on this policy is equal to $5,431.53 at the end of 10 years. The net cost is equal to the difference:

$$\text{Net cost} = (\$6,676.44 - \$5,431.53) = \$1,244.91$$

Interest-Adjusted Net Cost Index: To find the index value we must work backward. If we made level annual deposits into an interest-earning savings fund, and if the dollar amount in this savings fund at the end of 10 years were just equal to the net cost of the policy, then the level annual deposit would equal the index value we are searching for.

For example, suppose you deposited $1 in a savings account at 5% interest compounded annually. By the end of 10 years, you would have $13.21 in the account. If you divide the net cost by 13.21, you find the value of annual deposits that would provide a fund equal to the net cost.

$$\text{Interest-adjusted net cost index per \$25,000 of face amount} = \frac{1,244.91}{13.21} = 94.24$$

$$\text{Interest-adjusted net cost index per \$1,000 of face amount} = \frac{94.24}{25} = 3.77$$

the greater is the cost for a given dollar amount of insurance protection. A word to the wise: If the insurance company is unwilling to supply you with the value for this index, don't buy the policy. They are probably trying to hide the fact that this is a high-cost policy.

You must be careful not to use the index for comparing the relative cost of dissimilar policies. Most important, don't use the index to compare the cost of term insurance to cash value insurance. The cash value insurance will always appear cheaper if you do. The reason for this is simple. The interest-adjusted net cost index measures the cost of a given face amount of life insurance and not a given amount of death protection. If you purchase a term policy with a $10,000 face amount, you are receiving a full $10,000 of death protection over the period of coverage. On the other hand, when you purchase a $10,000 cash value policy the amount of death protection is equal to the face amount of the policy less the policy's cash value. Thus, the death protection declines as the cash value builds. Over time, the cash value insurance provides less pure insurance protection than a term policy with an identical face value. Therefore, per $1,000 of face value, the term policy will likely have a higher interest-adjusted net cost index.

The interest-adjusted net cost index also has another shortcoming. As the illustration in Figure 10.11 indicates, the index is based upon an assumed rate of return on savings of 5 percent. When market rates are above this amount, the net cost index will not perfectly reflect the relative value of two dissimilar policies. It will tend to understate the relative cost of policies that have higher current premiums but lower future premiums and higher future dividends.

You should recognize that life insurance will differ in cost because of policy riders. The riders attached to a contract play an important role in determining the worth of the policy to you, and should be weighed carefully when making comparisons. The first step is to make sure you are not comparing apples and oranges. The second step is to take a close look at the apples. The same company may sell a high-commission and a low-commission version of the same policy with identical riders. At times, unethical insurance agents have pointed to an independent survey indicating that their company's product was rated favorably, while forgetting to tell the prospective buyer that the rated policy was different from the higher-cost policy being offered.

Once you have decided what type of protection you want, there are rate-screening services that claim to help you find a low-cost policy. The three most often cited in the press are Insurance Information, Inc., Insurance Quote, and Select Quote. Each can be contacted through an 800 number. Insurance Information provides you with a survey of policies for a fee. The other two services do not charge for information, but they do represent insurers and they will offer to sell you a policy.

The Insurance Company

Over the past few years the insured public has been as much concerned over the health of their insurance company as they have been with their own. A *Wall Street Journal*/NBC News survey found that 46 percent of those polled believed U.S. insurers were "just somewhat sound" or "not at all sound." Moreover, about 8 percent of those surveyed have either changed companies or cashed in their policies because of these worries. The bankruptcies of a few large and several small insurers have stimulated these concerns. While most who were insured by those companies will eventually get most of their funds back, in the interim they will not be able to get at their assets or receive the high returns they had anticipated.

Providing the consumer with help on this matter are firms that rate the financial soundness of an insurance company. The three most important rating agencies are A. M. Best Co., Moody's Investors Service, Inc., and Standard & Poor's Corp. Publications by these services can be found at most university and public libraries.

You should check the rating of the insurance company before you buy a policy. If you have cash value insurance, you should continue to monitor the financial health of the company for as long as you hold the policy. The top solvency rating given by each of these firms is shown in Figure 10.12. There has been much bickering among company representatives as to which firm does the best job of rating the insurance companies. Because ratings often differ by rating agency, it is a good idea to monitor all three services.

Recent insurer failures have been blamed on three principal reasons: one, competition among insurers to attract customers by offering products with a high return; two, investment in high-yield but risky instruments such as junk bonds and real estate in order to pay high returns to customers; and three, "runs" by insureds to withdraw funds when it appears that the insurer may be in financial trouble.

Unfortunately, monitoring the rating agencies may not provide complete protection. Some insurers have received very high ratings for financial soundness just before they failed. This may be especially so if there is a run by insureds to withdraw their cash values. Even a perfectly solid company, which could meet all of its obligations over a longer period of time, may be forced into insolvency today if all the insureds demand their cash back at the same time. In response to this threat, A. M. Best Co. now claims to have revised its rating analysis to take this "run on the bank" potential into account.

FIGURE 10.12

Top insurance industry ratings.

Company	Rating	Comment
A.M. Best Company	A+ (Superior)	"Assigned to those companies which in our opinion have achieved the highest possible ratings when compared to the norms of the life/health insurance industry. A+ (Superior) rated insurers ability to meet their respective policy holder and other contractual obligations."
Moody's Investors Service	Aaa	"Insurance companies which are rated Aaa are judged to be of the best quality. Their policy obligations carry the smallest degree of credit risk. While the financial strength of these companies is likely to change, such changes as can be visualized are most unlikely to impair their fundamentally strong position.
Standard & Poor's Insurance Rating Services	AAA	"Insurers rated AAA offer superior financial security on both an absolute and relative basis. They possess the highest safety and have an overwhelming capacity to meet policyholder obligations."

The general feeling among industry analysts is that the industry is basically sound, and that policy holders should be wary of insurance agents who exaggerate the difficulties faced by some insurers. This may be merely an unjustified attempt to generate a sale. However, if your insurance company is down-rated, you should consider the associated benefits and costs of changing insurers. This is not an easy decision. If you surrender your policy, you may incur substantial surrender penalties and tax liabilities. The tax liabilities can be eliminated or deferred if you decide to switch your investment earnings into another policy and fill out a "1035 exchange form" with the new company. But there may be no way of avoiding additional high first-year commissions and another medical exam to prove insurability on a new policy. One intermediate step between doing nothing and switching insurers is to take out a policy loan. By borrowing against the policy instead of surrendering it, you at least enhance your own liquidity while avoiding surrender charges and protecting death benefits. If the company fails, you have gotten part of your money out; and if it recovers, you can always repay the loan.

Term or Cash Value Insurance?

Term insurance provides the greatest amount of insurance protection for each premium dollar. This fact may be extremely important to young families with dependent children that need large amounts of insurance protection but cannot afford the higher premiums on a cash value policy. The major drawback associated with term protection is that it is either impossible to get or extremely expensive in old age. But then, few people need insurance protection in their later years. For those who do, one possible solution is to purchase term insurance that is convertible to whole life. Then, if you later perceive a need for insurance protection in your retirement years, you may convert the term protection to whole life.

As stated previously, group term insurance is often provided at your place of employment. Under many group plans, you can purchase additional supplemental term insurance from the group provider at reasonable rates without a physical. Don't assume, however, that group supplemental term is necessarily a best buy. For young, healthy individuals, *The Wall Street Journal* found several cases in which individually purchased term insurance cost much less.

Cash value insurance will accumulate savings which may be later borrowed against or withdrawn. This savings feature is often stressed in sales promotions. First, it is promoted as a method of forced savings for retirement. By paying the premiums when due, you are assured of saving a certain amount each period. But who needs to be forced? Any time we are forced to do something, it means we don't have the right to make a decision. Efficient personal finance requires decisions and not force. Second, cash value insurance is promoted as a can't-lose proposition. If you die, you have the insurance protection; if you live, you have the savings. Unfortunately, the savings have often accumulated at unattractive rates of interest. For many years Consumers Union has suggested that individuals would be better off purchasing lower-cost term and investing the difference. One such plan is illustrated in Table 10.2. Suppose you used the net payments (premiums − dividends) for the policy in Figure 10.11 to purchase term insurance in-

Box 10.3
Saving Money

Low-Commission Policies Reduce Costs

"Till death do us part." That's what a lot of people think when they buy life insurance.

More often than not, however, it doesn't work out that way: By the end of year five over half of all policyholders have called it quits. And that can be expensive, because divorcing the typical cash-value insurance policy in the early years often means giving up most or all of the money you've put into the policy.

One option is to buy term insurance that's renewed annually. But if you know you want permanent protection combined with tax-deferred savings, there is another alternative: "low-load," or low-commission, insurance.

Surprisingly, many buyers of full-commission life insurance aren't aware that they are paying commissions at all. "Because they aren't writing a separate check for the commissions, they think they aren't paying any," says Elliot S. Lipson, an insurance consultant with Horizon Financial Advisors in Atlanta.

Typically, however, 100% to 150% of the first year's premium for a traditional full-commission insurance policy goes toward distribution costs and paying commissions for the agent and the insurer. So if you walk away in the early years, the cash value available to take with you is typically zip.

With low-load policies, however, there aren't any sales commissions for agents, and distribution costs are a third or less of typical agent-sold products. Because the products are sold directly to consumers—without high overhead costs—firms are able to offer the less-expensive product. So if you cash in such policies in early years, you get back most of the money you put into them. (See a typical comparison of surrender values in the accompanying table.)

Individuals shopping for insurance usually don't hear about low-load insurance products from agents. To find one, people often need to contact companies directly. The Individual Investor's Guide to Low-Load Insurance Products, available from International Publishing Corp. in Chicago (312–943–7354), includes lists of companies that sell low-load insurance and annuities.

Cash Surrender Values on a Low-Load and Full-Commission Policy from Ameritas Life Insurance Corp. Illustrations are for a 50-year-old nonsmoking man paying a $7,500 annual premium for a universal life policy with a $500,000 death benefit.

End of Year	Low-Load Policy	Full-Commission Policy
1	$ 7,022	–0–
2	14,188	$ 1,815
3	21,415	8,945
4	28,755	16,422
5	36,358	24,276
10	85,235	70,258
15	158,302	127,637
20	265,255	199,489

SOURCE: Excerpted from Ellen E. Schultz, "Take Low-Load Road to Higher Pay-Out," *The Wall Street Journal*, September 9, 1991, pp. C1, C9. Reprinted by permission of *The Wall Street Journal*, © 1991 Dow Jones & Company, Inc. All Rights Reserved Worldwide.

stead, and then deposited the difference in a savings account. You would have $25,000 worth of death protection if the face amount of the term policy plus the amount in the savings account averaged $25,000 over each year. This is the way payments are allocated in Table 10.2. Assuming the side savings fund earned a 5 percent annual return after taxes, the amount in the side savings fund would equal $5,677.44 after ten years. This compares favorably with the cash value of $5,431.53 at the end of ten years on the whole life plan in Figure 10.11. Obviously, at after-tax rates of 5 percent or above on the side savings account, purchasing term and investing the difference are optimal. However, should rates fall below 5 percent, the whole life policy may be the better buy.

TABLE 10.2 · Buying Term and Investing the Difference at 5% After Taxes

Year	Term Rate per $1,000	Term Expenditure*	Annual Deposit	Term Protection†	End of Year Side Savings
1	$2.57	$63.12	$482.38	$24,517.62	$ 506.50
2	2.75	65.93	479.57	24,013.93	1,035.37
3	3.00	70.62	439.63	23,525.00	1,548.75
4	3.15	72.60	432.40	23,018.85	2,080.21
5	3.31	74.37	425.38	22,494.41	2,630.87
6	3.51	77.16	417.34	21,951.79	3,200.62
7	3.79	81.08	408.17	21,391.22	3,789.22
8	4.05	84.22	399.78	20,811.00	4,398.45
9	4.35	88.13	390.62	20,210.93	5,028.53
10	4.75	92.69	378.56	19,592.92	5,677.44

*The term expenditure plus the annual deposit equal the net payment in Figure 10.11.

†The term projection plus the amount in the side savings fund will equal about $25,000 each year.

Consumers apparently followed the suggestion of Consumers Union during the 1970s by increasingly purchasing term rather than cash value insurance. Even during the 1980s, new premiums on term policies continued to increase relative to those on whole life insurance. However, as Figure 10.13 indicates, when compared with premiums on all types of cash value policies, terms share of all new premiums declined in the 1980s. This decline resulted from the introduction of universal life and variable life. These policies captured a significant percentage of the cash value market because they do exactly what the critics suggest. They combine term and a side savings account in one convenient package. Another reason is that the advertised interest and returns on the savings component have been relatively attractive.

However, there are several things you should realize before you jump at the rates being advertised on universal life policies. The quality of the coverage will depend upon both the cost of the underlying term insurance and the return on the cash value. If you are paying for expensive term coverage, a high return on the cash value may be no bargain. The insurance company will subtract from each premium the cost of insurance protection and a sales commission; what is left goes to build cash value. If you consider the sales commission on the savings component, your actual return may be much less than the advertised rates. Commissions on universal life policies vary from 5 percent to 90 percent of the first year's premium. In addition, there may be sales charges on premiums in subsequent years.

Two other things are worth considering before purchasing a universal life policy. The rate the company guarantees to pay in future years may be much less than the current rate. Future rates will not necessarily be lowered to the guaranteed rate, but the company may have the option to do so. In addition, if you decide to surrender the policy for its cash value, there may be severe penalties. You may have to forfeit some of those previous interest earnings.

Weighing the Tax Advantage of Cash Value Insurance

A major selling point for cash value insurance has been the supposed tax advantage for individuals in high tax brackets. The interest earned on the policy's cash

FIGURE 10.13

Market share of annualized new premiums on life insurance policies. (Source: Life Insurance Marketing and Research Association.)

	1981	1982	1983	1984	1985	1986	1987	1988	1989	1990
Universal life	2%	9%	18%	30%	38%	35%	27%	26%	27%	26%
Variable life	1	2	2	3	3	3	3	1	1	1
Variable universal	—	—	—	—	1	3	7	7	6	6
Term	19	18	15	12	11	12	12	13	13	13
Whole life	78	71	65	55	47	47	51	53	53	54
	100%	100%	100%	100%	100%	100%	100%	100%	100%	100%

value avoids taxes at the time it is credited to the savings component. A 9 percent tax-sheltered yield on the cash value is equivalent to a 12.5 percent taxable yield for someone in the 28 percent marginal tax bracket. However, if you decide to surrender the policy, you will have to pay tax on the interest earnings at that time. One alternative is to borrow against the cash value instead of surrendering the policy. But, again, you may run into problems. Both the company and the government can limit the amount you may be permitted to borrow.

For those interested in maximizing the tax advantage of cash value insurance **single-premium whole life** offers the best alternative. With a single premium and, in effect, the tax-free returns earned on that premium, you prepay all of the future premiums on a whole life policy. Furthermore, the policy has a significant cash value against which you may borrow. Unfortunately, cash value insurance shelters only the interest earnings; it does not shelter the income used to pay the premiums. If you are not already at your contribution limits on savings vehicles that shelter both income and return, you shouldn't consider buying cash value insurance for the tax advantage. A tax-deductible Individual Retirement Account (IRA) will earn tax-free interest and may reduce your current taxable income. This topic is discussed further in Chapter 17.

Single-premium whole life: Maximizes the tax advantages of cash value insurance by prepaying all future premiums with a single present payment.

Participating Versus Nonparticipating Insurance

Historically, policy holders with participating insurance have done better than those with nonparticipating insurance. The major reason for this was the unexpectedly high interest rates during the late 1970s and early 1980s. Those with participating insurance received some of the benefits of the higher interest rates because mutual insurance companies passed on part of the higher return on their investment portfolios as dividends to policy holders. On the other hand, those with nonparticipating insurance often had cash values accumulating at a historically low rate set at the time coverage was initiated. In an effort to compete, stock insurance companies have been offering policies with a type of participation. Universal life and variable life are two such policies, because the policy holder participates in current market returns.

There is no assurance that policy holders with participating insurance will continue to do better in the future. In fact, during a period of unexpectedly low interest rates, nonparticipating insurance could outperform the other. Little

Background Arnold earns a gross annual income of $60,000 as a chemist. Sharon, working part time as an accountant, grosses about $15,000 per year. They have two dependent children: Nancy, age 9, and John, age 7. They do not intend to have any more children. When John reaches age 16, Sharon plans to work full time. This additional income will help the family finance a college education for both Nancy and John.

Only Arnold has life insurance. His coverage consists of a term policy with a face amount of $50,000 and a straight, nonparticipating cash value policy with a face amount of $50,000. The term policy is part of the group protection provided by his employer. The straight life policy was purchased when he graduated from college. It now has a cash value of about $4,000, of which he has borrowed $2,000. The guaranteed insurability rider on this policy allows him to purchase an additional $25,000 of protection at age 37, his present age.

The Problem The Steeles want to know whether they might need additional life insurance protection. Should they need additional protection, they would like to know how they might go about providing it. Arnold could take advantage of the guaranteed insurability rider on the straight life policy and up the face amount to $75,000. However, he has been attracted to the advertisements for universal life policies and wonders if he is passing up a good thing by not purchasing such a policy.

The Plan The Steeles should first calculate their life insurance protection needs following the procedure outlined in this chapter. In estimating the family maintenance fund they should avoid the multiple-of-salary approach, since this may overstate the insurance needs for a two-income family. They definitely must estimate Arnold's insurance needs, because he is the primary market worker. However, they may also consider insurance protection for Sharon. Her death would reduce family income and no doubt increase homemaking expenses. Even more important is the fact that they seem to be relying on her return to full-time employment to help finance college educations. Should she die, the family might not have a sufficient college fund.

When they calculate Arnold's protection needs, they are likely to find a significant life insurance protection gap. A family with two dependent children will need, in most circumstances, more than $100,000 of protection for the primary market worker. Also, it does not seem likely the $25,000 guaranteed insurability rider will close that gap. Arnold is probably going to need large amounts of additional death protection over the next 14 years, until John graduates from college. Both Arnold and Sharon can most inexpensively finance these needs with term protection.

Since Arnold and Sharon are not currently taking full advantage of retirement accounts that can shelter both income and interest returns from taxes, they shouldn't be considering additional cash value insurance. Instead, they can either add term protection to their existing coverage or convert completely to term insurance.

Arnold's straight life policy should be surrendered only after careful consideration of all factors. There may be severe penalties on the early withdrawal of cash value. If so, it may be worthwhile to hold on to the policy a little longer to avoid the penalties. In addition, a new policy may be loaded with sales commissions, making it an unattractive alternative. Unfortunately, Arnold's straight life policy was taken out when interest rates were much lower and premiums higher. The same nonparticipating policy written today would carry a lower premium. One solution to this problem is for Arnold to contact the insurance company to find out what alternatives they might be willing to offer him. It is possible that they will lower the premiums in order to be more competitive. They may also allow him to convert to term or universal insurance without penalties and sales commissions. The insurance company is not likely to provide these options unless Arnold asks.

With regard to the guaranteed insurability rider, he should realize that he has already paid for this right in his previous premiums. If he is in poor health, he should definitely exercise this option. However, if he is in good health, he should weigh the cost of adding a $25,000 face amount to this policy against the cost of obtaining additional coverage elsewhere.

Whether or not they surrender the straight life policy, the family will probably need additional term protection on both Arnold and Sharon. They should shop around for this additional coverage and purchase the policy, all other things equal, with the lowest interest-adjusted net cost index. In searching for low-cost protection, Arnold should contact the group insurer where he works. He might find that he can increase the face amount on the group policy at a moderate cost. In addition, both Arnold and Sharon should inspect group plans offered by professional and fraternal organizations of which they are members. Such organizations often sponsor group insurance plans at attractive rates.

When dealing with life insurance agents, the Steeles should seek out those agents that are Chartered Life Underwriters (CLU). This designation indicates that the agent has both the experience and knowledge necessary to adequately explain the product. It also provides some assurance the agent has made life insurance his or her primary career and is likely to still be around if they later need additional help.

guidance can be offered in this selection except to suggest that if you want certain payments, opt for the nonparticipating policy. If, on the other hand, your budgeting is flexible enough, and you are willing to participate in the earnings experience of the industry, then purchase the participating insurance.

Summary

Life insurance is a key element in a well-formulated personal financial plan. Its primary purpose is to provide a financial safety net for dependent family members at the premature death of the insured. To make sure this safety net is adequate, the death protection needs of the potential survivors must be estimated. If there is an insurance protection gap, it can be closed with additional life insurance. The life insurance can consist of either cash value insurance or term insurance. Each category includes many different kinds of policies. Each policy has a unique variation in premium payment, or death protection, or cash value buildup. The discussion in the chapter should help you evaluate each and choose wisely.

Key Terms

adjustable life (p. 318)

adverse selection (p. 299)

beneficiary (p. 311)

cash value (p. 311)

cash value insurance (p. 316)

clean-up fund (p. 302)

contingent beneficiary (p. 311)

decreasing term (p. 315)

deposit term insurance (p. 315)

dividend (p. 311)

endowment life (p. 317)

face amount (p. 310)

family maintenance fund (p. 303)

gambling (p. 299)

group mortgage life (p. 315)

indemnification (p. 300)

insurable interest (p. 299)

interest-adjusted net cost index (p. 321)

joint life policy (p. 310)

life insurance protection gap (p. 310)

limited payment life (p. 317)

modified whole life (p. 317)

nonparticipating insurance (p. 311)

ordinary life (p. 317)

participating insurance (p. 311)

premium (p. 310)

pure risk (p. 298)

renewable term (p. 314)

rider (p. 311)

risk avoidance (p. 300)

risk management (p. 300)

risk reduction (p. 300)

risk retention (p. 300)

risk transfer (p. 300)

single life policy (p. 310)

single-premium whole life (p. 327)

speculative risk (p. 298)

straight life (p. 310)

surrender value (p. 311)

survivorship joint life (p. 310)

term insurance (p. 313)

underwriting (p. 299)

universal life (p. 318)

variable life (p. 319)

variable universal life (p. 320)

whole life (p. 317)

Problems and Review Questions

1 Explain the primary reason for having insurance. For what other reasons might people hold life insurance?

2 What three funding categories are used to estimate life insurance needs? Explain the purpose of each.

3 Why would a two-income family more accurately estimate the family maintenance fund with the needs approach? Discuss other family characteristics that would cause one to prefer the needs approach over the multiple-of-salary approach.

4   What types of family assets might be used to satisfy death protection funding requirements?

5   What is the difference between joint life and survivorship joint life?

6   One life insurance expert suggests that people should never buy participating life insurance, because the purpose of life insurance is to reduce risk, not increase it. Discuss.

7   Renewability and guaranteed insurability are not the same. Explain the difference.

8   If a young family expects that its life insurance needs will increase in the near future, what policy options might they find desirable?

9   What is the distinguishing characteristic of term insurance? Why isn't deposit term true term insurance?

10 What kinds of insurance might offer the best protection against unexpected inflation? Explain why.

11 Suppose you wanted to leave your dependents with enough funds to pay off the home mortgage. Under what conditions would you prefer decreasing term insurance over group mortgage life, and vice versa?

12 If you perceive a need for insurance protection in your retirement years, might you prefer whole life over term life today? Why? Can you think of situations in which you might need insurance protection in your later years?

13 Suppose you took out a universal life insurance policy that charges a 20 percent sales commission on each dollar paid into the policy and pays a 10 percent annual return on the policy's cash value. What is the actual percentage return at the end of one year on each premium dollar placed in the savings component?

14 How does universal life differ from variable life? Which one entails greater risk?

15 How is the interest-adjusted net cost index calculated? Why shouldn't the net cost index be used to compare cash value insurance with term insurance?

**Case 10.1
The Wright
Family
Maintenance
Fund**

Sue and Tom Wright are both assistant professors at the local university. They each take home about $25,000 per year after taxes. Sue is 37 years of age, and Tom is 35. Their two children, Mike and Karen, are 13 and 11.

Were either one to die, they estimate that the remaining family members would need about 75 percent of the present combined take-home pay to retain their current standard of living while the children are still dependent. This does not include an extra $50 per month in child-care expenses that would be required in a single-parent household. They estimate that Social Security benefits would total about $1,000 per month in child support.

Both Tom and Sue are knowledgeable investors. In the past, average after-tax returns on their investment portfolio have equaled or exceeded the rate of inflation.

Questions

1   Were Sue Wright to die today, how much would the Wrights need in the family maintenance fund? Explain the reasons behind your calculations.

2   Suppose the Wrights found that both Tom and Sue had a life insurance protection gap of $50,000. How might they go about searching for protection to close that gap?

Case 10.2
Costing a Cash Value Policy

David Lombard is considering the purchase of a $10,000 face amount, nonparticipating, whole life policy. The life insurance agent tells David that the $10,000 insurance protection really won't cost him anything. The annual premiums on the policy are $500, and at the end of ten years the cash value on the policy will be $5,000. Therefore, David can get back all of his premium payments at the end of the ten years.

David decides to make some calculations on his own. He figures that if he deposited $500 annually in a savings account that had a 5 percent annual return after taxes, he would have $6,603.39 after ten years. He wonders if the insurance policy is really the great deal the agent says it is.

Questions

1 Calculate the ten-year net cost for this policy.
2 Calculate the ten-year adjusted net cost index on the $10,000 face amount, and per $1,000 of face amount.
3 If David wants to know whether or not he is really getting a good deal, what should he do at this point?

Helpful Reading

"A.M. Best Introduces New Index to Evaluate Small Insurers." *Best's Review—Life-Health Insurance Edition*, March 1990, pp. 17, 104.

American Council of Life Insurance. *Life Insurance Fact Book* (Annual).

Asinof, Lynn. "Group Life Insurance Often Costs More." *The Wall Street Journal*, September 3, 1991, pp. C1, C19.

Bellet, Adam Z. "Employer-Sponsored Life Insurance: A New Look." *Monthly Labor Review*, October 1989, pp. 112–115.

Belshy, Gary. "Don't Gamble with Your Life Insurance." *Money*, July 1991, p. 116.

Mabie, Robert. "20-Year Dividend Comparisons; Life Insurance Companies." *Best's Review—Life-Health Insurance Edition*, July 1990, p. 64.

Nelson, Stephen L. "Use Your PC to Explore Life Insurance Options." *PC-Computing*, February 1991, p. 264.

Ort, David E. "Survivor Income Benefits Provided by Employers." *Monthly Labor Review*, June 1991, pp. 13–18.

Simons, Margaret, and Cynthia Thompson. "Life Insurance Benefits for Retireds." *Monthly Labor Review*, September 1990, p. 17.

Synder, Arthur, "Ratings—There Is a Difference." *Best's Review—Life-Health Insurance Edition*, October 1991, p. 12, 14, 16.

Helpful Contacts

National Insurance Consumer Organization
121 North Payne Street, Alexandria, VA 22314
Provides guidance on selection of insurance policies. Publishes comparable rates of return for different policies.

Health Care and Disability Insurance: Protecting Your Earning Capacity

Objectives

1 To describe the separate components of basic health-care coverage
2 To discuss the need for major medical insurance
3 To list the important providers and insurers of health care
4 To compare and evaluate health-care insurance plans
5 To list sources of disability income
6 To estimate your disability insurance needs

As the Krause family unfortunately knows, adequate health care may mean more than just purchasing health insurance. The financial soundness of the health insurer must also be taken into consideration. Serious illness and injury is difficult to deal with, even without the stress that medical bills and lost income can create. Appropriate health and disability insurance can at least reduce the increasingly heavy financial burden. From 1979 to 1989, prices in the health-care industry increased at almost twice the rate of increase in other consumer goods. To protect their workers from these rising costs, employers now spend over $3,000 per worker on health-care insurance.

The Bureau of the Census reports that more than 240 million Americans, or 87 percent of all Americans, have some type of private or public health insurance coverage. Unfortunately, that leaves over 30 million without any health insurance protection. Most of the private coverage, about 82 percent, is group coverage related to the past or current employment of a family member. Because health insurance coverage is primarily work related, young adults aged 16 to 24, who are more likely than other age groups to be unemployed, are also more likely to be without health insurance protection. Young adults make up only 14 percent of the population, yet they represent over 24 percent of those without any private or public health-care insurance. Equally important is the fact that many young adults experience a break in coverage. Over one-half of those with coverage were without health insurance for at least one month during the last year.

Many of those with insurance are inadequately covered because they have the wrong kind or amount of protection, either incorrectly believing that current protection is sufficient, or simply not giving the subject the attention it deserves. Adequate protection includes reimbursement for major medical expenses through health-care insurance and compensation for lost income through disability income insurance. The U.S. Congress estimates that 2.4 million American families experience catastrophic health-care costs in excess of $3,000 that insurance does not pay.

Protection against loss of income due to illness or injury is even less adequate than health-care coverage (see Figure 11.1). Only 45 percent of the work force has private long-term disability income insurance. Apparently, most people feel either that the chances of becoming disabled are too small to require protection, or that government programs will prove sufficient. As we will see, both assumptions are incorrect.

Health-Care Insurance

As stated previously, the overwhelming majority of those with private health insurance obtained it through a group insurance plan offered at the workplace. For several reasons, this insurance is often a very attractive deal. First, because of lower administrative costs and because of lower health risks than exist for the population as a whole, insurance companies will on average charge lower premiums for employer-sponsored health insurance. Second, almost one-half of these plans are entirely paid for by the employer, with most of the rest requiring minimal employee contributions. Finally, you and your family are probably eligible regardless of your physical condition.

You might think that most of us have little need to consider health insurance. You simply accept what the employer is offering. This assumption is incorrect. Today, many companies will offer their employees a choice among two or more health-care plans with differing employee premiums and differing schedules of benefits. And in families where both the husband and wife are employed outside the home, these choices are greatly compounded. Not only must each compare the plans offered by their individual employers, they must also consider whether it is better for them to join their respective group plans separately or to participate in only one, listing the spouse as a dependent. No doubt the company personnel officer will help you compare and contrast the available options, but

FIGURE 11.1

Percent of full-time employees participating in employee medical benefits program, 1989. (Source: U.S. Department of Labor, *Employee Benefits in Medium and Large Firms, 1989*, Bulletin 2363, June 1990, p. 4.)

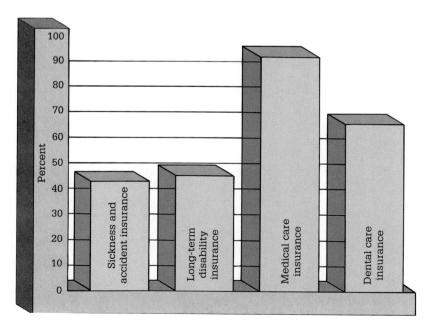

Health Care and Disability Insurance

the final decision on what is best for you and your family must be yours. Furthermore, you alone can determine the adequacy of your group coverage and select a supplemental individual or family nongroup policy if you find a serious gap in your health-care protection.

Types of Coverage

Unlike auto and home owners' policies examined in the next chapter, there are no standard formats for health-care policies. This means that most plans will not provide an explanation of coverage that is broken down into the discrete components discussed below. However, after you read the policies closely and discuss them with insurers' representatives, you should be able to reorganize the benefits provided into a more comparable format.

Most policies include **comprehensive health insurance** coverage providing both basic health-care benefits and major medical protection. Figure 11.2 contains a worksheet that was used to compare comprehensive benefits offered by a typical fee-for-service plan, such as might be offered by Blue Cross/Blue Shield, and a local health maintenance organization (HMO). This or a similarly styled worksheet can prove extremely helpful when comparing many-faceted health-care insurance plans.

BASIC HEALTH-CARE COVERAGE Three components—hospital insurance, surgical insurance, and medical insurance—make up **basic health-care insurance.** Each can be purchased separately, but they are usually combined and sold as a basic health-care package.

Hospital insurance will help pay for room and board, and other medically related expenses while in the hospital. It can take the form of indemnity coverage, expense coverage, or service benefit coverage. *Indemnity insurance* provides for specific dollar payments made directly to you for each day you are in the hospital, regardless of your actual expenses. *Expense insurance* provides for cash reimbursement either to you or to the provider of health care, based upon expenses actually incurred. *Service benefit* insurance guarantees the provision of certain medical services and makes payments only to the provider of health care.

Hospital **indemnity insurance** typically ranks as least preferable. This is the type of hospital insurance most often sold on television and in newspapers. Although receiving $100 to $150 a day for each day you are in the hospital may sound attractive, it is not likely to cover even your room and board. In addition, many of these policies do not begin payments until you have been in the hospital a set number of days. With the average hospital stay a little over seven days at an average charge of about $4,000, don't plan on collecting much from an indemnity policy that commences payments after the fifth day.

More adequate benefits are generally provided by **hospital expense insurance,** which pays for room and board up to a set daily maximum. In 1990 the average charge for a semiprivate room was $297 per day. To determine current costs in your area, you need only contact a local hospital. A good policy should cover most, if not all, of this expense. In addition, hospital expense insurance should pay for other hospital-related expenses, such as laboratory procedures, surgical materials, and X rays, typically stating payments for these items as a percentage

Comprehensive health insurance: Provides both basic health-care benefits and major medical protection.

Basic health-care insurance: Consists of hospital, surgical, and medical coverage.

Hospital insurance: Provides coverage for room and board, and other medically related expenses while in the hospital.

Indemnity insurance: Provides a specified dollar benefit regardless of actual cost.

Hospital expense insurance: Pays actual cost up to a daily maximum.

	Fee-for-Service Plan Coverage	HMO Plan Coverage
Basic Health Care		
Hospital stay	Semiprivate rate for 120 days per confinement; covers illness, injury, psychiatric cure, and alcohol/chemical dependency (excess covered under major medical provision)	Unlimited days paid in full for illness and injury 20% co-insurance and maximum 30 days per year for psychiatric care and alcohol/chemical dependency
Diagnostic X rays and lab	UCR (usual, customary, and reasonable) charge	Paid in full
Emergency services	In area: Hospital charges paid in full, doctors' fees at UCR, ambulance not covered Out of area: same as in area	In area: $15 co-payment, ambulance paid in full Out of area: UCR charge
Physician Services		
Surgery	UCR charge	Paid in full
Hospital visits	UCR charge	Paid in full
Office visits	Not covered with exception of 50% UCR for psychiatric care Major medical coverage	$10 co-payment for psychiatric care and 20% co-insurance for alcohol/chemical dependency
Home visits	Major medical coverage	$10 co-payment
Maternity care	Same as for illness and injury	Paid in full
Prescription drugs	Major medical coverage	$3 co-payment per prescription
Major Medical		
Lifetime max./person	$250,000	Unlimited
Deductible/yr./person	$100	None
Deductible/yr./family	$300	None
Coinsurance/yr./person	20% co-insurance $2,000 maximum expense	20% co-insurance where indicated
Supplemental Benefits		
Accident dental services	Major medical coverage	Paid in full
Adult periodic exam	Not covered	Paid in full
Blood	Major medical after first two pints	Paid in full
Complete hearing exam	Not covered	Paid in full
Immunization and preventive injections	Not covered	Paid in full
Pediatric routine	Not covered	Paid in full
Physical therapy	Major medical coverage	20% co-insurance
Private-duty nursing	Major medical coverage	Paid in full
Routine dental services	Not covered	Not covered
Routine eye exam	Not covered	$15 co-payment
Skilled nursing facility	Not covered	Paid in full with prior approval

FIGURE 11.2

Plan comparison worksheet.

of the maximum payment for room and board. This is not a trivial supplemental benefit. On average, such items can double the cost of a hospital stay. However, if unique tests and procedures are involved, the total hospital bill could easily run four times the amount actually paid for room and board.

Health Care
and Disability
Insurance

Service benefit coverage is the preferred approach to reimbursement. This type is provided by Blue Cross and many HMOs. For qualified and participating hospitals, full reimbursement for covered services is made directly to the health-care provider, so long as the charges are less than the specified policy limit defined in dollar terms or days of stay. With service benefit insurance you don't have to constantly keep track of hospital costs in order to ensure adequate coverage. The one drawback is that you may have to stay in a qualifying hospital to receive 100 percent reimbursement.

Surgical insurance should cover the fees of the operating surgeon and the anesthesiologist. (For the surgical costs of selected operations, see Table 11.1.) An expense-type policy might provide a list of covered operations along with the maximum amount to be paid for each. A preferred policy, such as one offered by Blue Shield, agrees to pay all surgical costs, as long as these are **usual, customary, and reasonable (UCR)** for your geographic area. If you have a policy with this provision, be sure to find out whether your physician will accept this amount as payment in full. If the doctor will not, find out how much extra he or she is planning to charge you. Don't be embarrassed to discuss fees. If you are going to be charged more than UCR, it is the physician who is making money an issue, not you.

Medical insurance provides payments for general nonsurgical physician care at the office or in the hospital. Average fees for office visits are also shown in Table 11.1. Traditional insurance has used an indemnity approach, paying you so much

TABLE 11.1 • Sample Charges for Medical Services

First office visits:	
Family practice	$ 34
General practice	35
Nonsurgical specialists	50
Surgical specialists	55
Office revisits:	
Family practice	28
General practice	28
Nonsurgical specialists	33
Surgical specialists	34
Surgical procedures:	
Appendectomy	801
Breast augmentation (bilateral)	2,397
Cholecystectomy	1,029
Complete rhinoplasty	2,500
Complete obstetrical care	1,569
Coronary artery bypass with three autogenous grafts	4,834
Diagnostic knee arthoscopy	708
Dilation and curettage	450
Implant pacemaker	1,500
Hospital expenses:	
Daily charge for semiprivate room	297
Average cost to hospital per day	586
Average cost to hospital per stay (7.2 days)	4,207
Maternity care:	
Hospital charges	2,842
Physicians' fees	1,492
Total	4,334

SOURCES: Medical Economics, October 2, 1989, published by Medical Economics Company, Inc., Oradell, NJ 07649. Fees for office visits are based upon a regional average. Other data are from the Health Insurance Association of America, *Source Book of Health Insurance Data, 1990.*

for each visit. Because you are likely to go to a doctor during the year, as indicated in Table 11.2, such insurance is relatively expensive. It has proven efficient, however, as one component of a comprehensive health-care plan offered by a health maintenance organization (HMO). Under an HMO, office visits may be fully covered, or you may be required to make a small co-payment. A **co-payment** is a dollar fee covering less than the full cost of the service. Its purpose is to limit unnecessary use.

MAJOR MEDICAL COVERAGE   The one component of health-care insurance you should not do without is **major medical insurance,** because it eliminates the greatest risk to your financial health. Basic health-care coverage may not pay all of your health-care expenses, either because particular services are not covered or because you have exceeded the limits on coverage. Major medical is the backup you need when catastrophic illness strikes. If, after reimbursement under basic health-care insurance, your health-care expenses exceed a stated deductible, major medical will pick up part of the overage. Most policies have a **co-insurance** clause under which the insurer pays 80 percent of the overage and you pay the other 20 percent. The better policies put a dollar limit, perhaps $2,000, on your out-of-pocket expenses. The illustration in Figure 11.3 is based on the major medical provisions for the fee-for-service policy in Figure 11.2. In this example, health-care costs total $9,200, of which basic health coverage pays $4,900, leaving a total overage of $4,300. After a deductible of $100 and a co-insurance payment of $840, your total out-of-pocket expenses would be $940. According to the terms of this policy, the amount you pay normally cannot exceed $2,000 per year.

EXTENDED HEALTH-CARE COVERAGE   With recent attempts by government, hospitals, and insurers to reduce the average hospital stay, nursing or rehabilitative care at home or in a skilled nursing facility is becoming increasingly important. Where coverage for such services does exist, it applies only to services absolutely required by the illness or injury. Most nursing homes are not skilled nursing facilities, and insurers will not typically pay for care that is primarily personal or custodial.

DENTAL INSURANCE   **Dental insurance** is a nice fringe benefit if it is included in your group plan and paid by your employer. One of the fastest-growing forms of insurance, dental insurance is similar to other kinds of health insurance. Many plans require a deductible, have maximum reimbursement limits, or have co-payments. One major difference is that dental insurance covers the cost of preventive care, usually paying all of the fees for routine checkups and cleanings, 20 percent or more of the cost of fillings and other dental treatment, and 50 percent

TABLE 11.2 ▪
Number of Yearly
Physician and Dental
Visits per Person in the
United States

Type of Visit	Age					
	Under 6	6–16	17–24	25–44	45–64	65 and Older
Physician Visits	6.7	3.3	4.4	4.8	6.4	8.9
Dental Visits	.7	2.4	1.7	2.0	2.2	2.1

SOURCE: Bureau of the Census, *Statistical Abstract of the United States, 1990,* p. 103.

Health Care
and Disability
Insurance

FIGURE 11.3

	Cost	Basic Health Payment	Overage
Hospital bill	$5,200	$3,000	$2,200
Physician services (office visits)	840	—	840
Surgical services	2,400	1,900	500
Prescription drugs	760	—	760
Totals	$9,200	$4,900	$4,300
		Minus individual deductible	− 100
			$4,200
			× .20
		Co-insurance	$ 840

You pay the lesser of the deductible ($100) plus the co-insurance ($840) or $2,000.

FIGURE 11.3

Sample illustration of major medical coverage.

or so of the cost of orthodontia, bridges, and crowns. If your dental insurance is not part of your overall health insurance plan, it may not be cost-effective to buy the insurance on your own. Data on visits and charges can be found in Tables 11.1 and 11.2. You should be able to plan for these expenses in your yearly budget. Expensive dental surgery to correct birth deformities or injuries is in most cases already covered under the surgical expense component of the basic health-care package.

SPECIFIC DISEASE AND ACCIDENT INSURANCE Widely sold through the media, specific disease insurance is one policy you should definitely not purchase. Not only is it likely to be a poor bargain, it also makes no financial sense. Why would you want a policy that covers you if you have cancer but pays nothing if you have a heart attack? You need broader coverage that pays out no matter what the cause of illness. Companies offering such policies are playing on our fears of a dreaded disease.

Although accident insurance is often sold by reputable major insurers, the reasons against purchasing it are much the same as those for not purchasing specific disease insurance. The purpose of health-care insurance is to reduce your financial risks. Gambling on the cause of future illnesses and injuries does not serve that purpose.

Important Provisions

No matter what type of health-care coverage you may have, certain provisions will indicate the quality of your insurance coverage. Generally, those with shorter waiting periods, fewer exclusions, and higher policy limits offer better protection.

Long-Term-Care Insurance

Several life insurance companies have recently introduced insurance policies designed to cover the cost of long-term health care. Medicare and most traditional health insurance limit nursing home care to a fixed number of days in a skilled-care facility. However, many elderly Americans enter a nursing home, not because they need specialized medical care, but rather because they simply can no longer care for themselves. The Health Insurance Association of America reports that 22 percent of those age 85 or older are in nursing homes, and that 2 out of 5 people over age 65 are likely to spend some time in one. At an average annual cost of $30,000, this type of noninsured custodial care could rapidly deplete the family estate.

By covering the cost of custodial care when it can be demonstrated that you can no longer care for yourself, long-term-care insurance can close the gap in traditional health insurance coverage. However, as economists are fond of saying, "There's no such thing as a free lunch." The Health Insurance Association of America indicates that a policy paying $80 per day of nursing home expenses, with a 20-day deductible, costs about $480 a year for the average 50-year-old. The annual premium increases to $1,135 per year for a 65-year-old, and $3,840 per year for a 79-year-old. The Families USA Foundation, and A. M. Best Co. estimate that such premiums are simply not affordable for 85 percent of Americans beyond age 65. Moreover, an inflation rider that adjusts the daily benefit for future price increases would raise those annual premiums to $660, $1,400, and $4,200, respectively.

Many who do purchase long-term-care policies apparently have second thoughts about those high premiums after a few years. A congressional subcommittee reports that between 1986 and 1989 more than 30 percent of long-term-care policies lapsed. Since the policies have no buildup of cash value, those individuals paid thousands of dollars for benefits that will never be received.

Even those committed to the long-term payment of premiums may also be disappointed. There have been press reports that a number of individuals have not received the benefits that were anticipated. Some mistakingly thought their policies covered custodial care, whereas the contracts covered only more restrictive skilled or intermediate care. In other cases, insureds were denied benefits because they did not reveal preexisting medical conditions on ambiguous application forms. Other insureds were denied payments because they did not satisfy all benefit requirements. For example, some policies cover your nursing home expenses only if they are preceded by a three-day hospital stay. Under this requirement, about half of the people presently in nursing homes would be denied benefits.

Confronted by these seemingly unfair practices, the National Association of Insurance Commissioners is working up acceptable standards for long-term-care policies. Among the standards they are currently considering are the following:

- Common measures of value for cost comparison

- Definitions of terms so that all policies have the same meaning

- Inflation protection

- Prohibition of any requirement that insureds must receive skilled nursing care or hospitalization before custodial care is covered

- Required medical examinations of insureds that would eliminate postclaim denial of benefits.

WAITING PERIOD UNDER PREEXISTING CONDITIONS CLAUSE All individual policies and some group policies will contain a **preexisting conditions clause,** which excludes from coverage certain types of injuries and illnesses that began before the policy was issued. These conditions may later be covered after a specified **waiting period.**

Be sure you understand how you and your family might be affected by this clause. It is a common means of denying payment. You may be better off keeping a less-than-satisfactory policy rather than waiting the necessary time before you are fully covered under a new policy. Also, beware of policies that do not waive the preexisting conditions clause after a given period of time.

Preexisting conditions clause: Excludes from coverage certain medical conditions that existed before the policy was initiated.

Waiting period: Preexisting conditions may be covered after this period of time.

Guaranteed renewability:
Guarantees coverage up to
a specified age upon
payment of premiums,
although future premiums
may increase.

GUARANTEED RENEWABILITY   Unless you are purchasing temporary coverage to bridge a gap between group insurance policies, you should consider purchasing insurance that is guaranteed renewable until age 65. **Guaranteed renewability** means that no matter what your health, your coverage will continue so long as you pay the premiums. The company does, however, retain the right to increase rates for a given class of insureds.

POLICY LIMITS   The maximum amount the insurance company will pay out is particularly important on the major medical portion of your coverage. The limit may hold for each benefit period, usually a calendar year, over a lifetime, or for each illness or accident. Never purchase a policy with a limit of less than $250,000 on hospitalization payments for a given illness or accident per benefit period, or less than a lifetime maximum of $500,000. The likelihood of huge medical expenses, although small, does exist.

WAIVER OF PREMIUM   This clause waives your premium payment should you be unable to work because of illness or injury. If your health insurance policy does not contain this provision, you must plan for these payments under your disability income protection.

EXCLUSIONS   Some injuries and illnesses will not be covered even when there is no medical history of them. For example, intentionally self-inflicted injuries, injuries covered by workers' compensation, mental illness, or injuries resulting from war or military service are typically excluded. Such elective procedures as cosmetic surgery and dental treatment may be covered only if the condition being treated results from birth defects or accidental injuries.

Some policies will cover maternity expenses, and others will exclude them. Although a maternity plan may be helpful if you are planning an addition to your family, it is not necessary financial protection. After all, you should be able to budget adequately for these expenses over at least a nine-month period. Of much greater importance is how your policy handles the costs of childbirth complications and the costs of treating birth defects. Families capable of bearing children should have insurance that covers all costs of complications and costs of the newborn. Not having this coverage leaves you open to substantial and unnecessary risk. In the United States, 8.3 percent of infants weigh less than 5½ pounds at birth. While most of these infants may be normal except for size, many hospitals require that each spends some time in an intensive-care unit. The specialized care provided in such units can leave you with a substantial hospital bill. If your policy covers dependents only from age 14 days on, you will not be covered for these current and future expenses. Most states have responded to this situation by requiring that all policies covering dependents begin protection at birth. However, policies excluding newborns are still sold in states that do not have this requirement. If you are of child-bearing age, avoid these policies.

Insurers and Providers

Both the government and the private sector supply health-care insurance. The federal government, through the Medicare programs, is the primary provider of insurance for those 65 and over. The private sector provides supplemental insurance to those in this age group, and the entire insurance program for the rest of the population. **Blue Cross/Blue Shield,** a nonprofit health-care insurer, is the nation's largest private insurer. Next are the commercial insurers, basically companies specializing in life and health insurance. Health maintenance organizations (HMOs), the most recent entrants into the health insurance market, occupy the smallest share. However, with the backing of major companies, such as Blue Cross/Blue Shield, which is also the nation's largest operator of HMOs, their market share is growing rapidly.

BLUE CROSS/BLUE SHIELD   Blue Cross and Blue Shield work in conjunction with each other to supply both hospital and medical insurance. Blue Cross is largely sponsored and controlled by hospitals and provides hospital insurance using the service benefit approach. Blue Shield, typically under the control of local medical societies, supplies medical and surgical coverage.

About 90 percent of Blue Shield's benefit expenditures go directly for physicians' services. The traditional insurance sold by Blue Shield pays for specified medical procedures and uses a usual, customary, and reasonable (UCR) fee-reimbursement policy. This policy is based upon fees charged in your local area and is typically set at a level that would provide complete reimbursement for bills submitted by most physicians. In other words, if your physician bills you for more than the UCR, the majority of patients in your area have been charged less for the same service. Your physician may require a supplemental fee agreement under which you will pay any excess charges not paid by Blue Shield, but in the event you are billed for excess amounts, refer the bill back to Blue Shield for negotiation.

Because the Blues are exempt from taxation as nonprofit organizations, and because of the economic benefits they derive from their huge size, they can usually provide comprehensive benefits at lower cost than other traditional insurers.

COMMERCIAL INSURERS   As used in the health-care industry, the term **commercial insurer** stands for any private company that is not associated with Blue Cross/Blue Shield. A commercial insurer may be either a not-for-profit or a for-profit corporation. These companies control a little over 40 percent of the health-care insurance market.

Without a standard format for health-care policies, and given the willingness of many of these companies to tailor their policies to meet the specific needs of groups and individuals, general statements regarding the quality and types of plans offered by commercial insurers is impossible. Among their ranks are some highly reputable companies willing to experiment with novel group benefits, including routine dental coverage and alcohol abuse treatment. On the other hand, you will find companies selling dread disease or indemnity policies that pay out little of what is collected in premiums. If you understand the basics of health-care insurance discussed in this chapter and you compare the policies of various insurers, you should be able to steer clear of the hucksters to find some attractive insurance alternatives in the commercial market.

HMOs   A **health maintenance organization (HMO)** differs from the other insurers because it is not only the provider of insurance but also the provider of the

Fee-for-service health insurance: The insured selects a provider of medical care and is then reimbursed for covered medical expenses.

health care. The HMO premium represents a prepayment for future medical services, which are then provided as needed at little or no out-of-pocket cost. With traditional **fee-for-service health insurance,** you seek out a provider of medical care and are then reimbursed for covered medical expenses. The amount of reimbursement may be based upon a usual, customary, and reasonable rate, or it may be set at some fixed amount. You may be responsible for amounts over and above these set rates.

The Health Maintenance Act of 1973 specified stringent requirements for federally qualified HMOs. In brief, they must provide an extensive list of comprehensive benefits, guarantee open enrollment periods for specific times during the year, and purchase insolvency insurance to protect policy holders in the event the HMO cannot meet its debts. In return, the law relieved the industry from many state laws limiting the formation of HMOs and provided that most employers must offer an HMO alternative when available.

Membership has grown rapidly to over 30 million members in about 600 HMOs and now includes about 17 percent of workers having employer-sponsored health plans. The reason more workers are not members probably is the higher employee contribution required under an HMO plan. Although they are more expensive, HMOs also tend to be more comprehensive. They typically stress preventive health care by paying for periodic physical examinations and other routine office visits with lower deductibles and co-insurance payments than fee-for-service insurance. In addition, many plans also cover such items as dental services, prescription drugs, and extended nursing care. (See Table 11.3.)

There are two basic types of HMOs: the group-staff arrangement and the individual practice arrangement. The **group-staff HMO** provides services at one or more locations with salaried physicians. The **individual practice arrangement (IPA)** contracts with private physicians who maintain their own offices and then pays them on a fee-for-service schedule. Individuals then choose from among the participating physicians for their needed medical services. IPAs generally offer a greater choice of physicians and more conveniently located medical services. Although slightly more costly than group-staff HMOs, IPAs have proven popular. Over the last few years membership in IPAs has grown much more rapidly than in group-staff HMOs.

Group-staff HMO: Delivers health services at one or more facilities through groups of physicians working on a salaried or contractual basis.

Individual practice arrangement (IPA) HMO: Physicians maintain their own offices and then are reimbursed by the HMO for services performed.

If all other factors are equal, your choice between a traditional insurer and an HMO should be based on a comparison of your estimated savings on the direct cost of medical services versus the higher monthly premium. The HMO will often prove the better choice for families with more and younger children, because their direct expenses for routine office visits are likely to be higher under a traditional insurer.

Open-ended enrollment plan: An HMO plan in which members may use providers outside the HMO but incur additional cost in the form of a deductible or co-insurance payment.

Recently, some HMOs have begun to offer an **open-ended enrollment plan.** Under an open-ended plan, you may select non-HMO providers if you are willing to incur additional costs in the form of higher deductibles and co-insurances. This provides a health-care alternative for those who find that they are dissatisfied with the HMOs choice of providers.

Preferred provider organization (PPO): Selectively offered health-care services providing care to insureds at a lower out-of-pocket cost.

PPOS   Virtually nonexistent in the mid-1980s, **preferred provider organizations (PPOs)** currently enroll over 10 percent of the participants in employer-sponsored plans. A PPO is only a provider, not an insurer. It works either directly with an employer or through the employer's insurer to provide medical services at less

TABLE 11.3 · Percent of Full-Time Medical-Care Participants, by Coverage for Selected Categories of Medical Care, Medium and Large Establishments, 1989

Category	HMO Plans		Fee-for-Service Plans	
	Care Provided	Covered in Full	Care Provided	Covered in Full
Hospital room and board	100	92	100	5
Hospital miscellaneous*	100	92	100	5
Extended-care facility†	93	32	80	2
Home health care	99	86	72	7
Hospice care	30	26	46	5
Inpatient surgery	100	98	100	20
Outpatient surgery§	100	97	100	26
Physician visits:				
In hospital	100	99	100	8
Office	100	44	98	2
Diagnostic X ray and laboratory	100	98	100	15
Private-duty nursing	93	89	87	1
Mental health care:				
In hospital	95	8	99	2
Outpatient	100	1	93	(a)
Alcohol abuse care:				
Inpatient detoxification	99	55	97	3
Inpatient rehabilitation	55	10	68	1
Outpatient	59	7	57	(a)
Drug abuse care:				
Inpatient detoxification	99	55	96	3
Inpatient rehabilitation	53	10	63	1
Outpatient	57	7	53	(a)
Prescription drug, nonhospital	90	9	98	2

SOURCE: Thomas P. Burke and Rita S. Jain, "Trends in Employer-Provided Health Care Benefits," *Monthly Labor Review*, February 1991, p. 25.

*Services provided during a hospital confinement.

†Some plans provide care in an extended service facility only to a patient who was previously hospitalized and is recovering without the need of the extensive care provided by a general hospital.

§Charges incurred in the outpatient department of a hospital and outside of the hospital.

[a]Less than 0.5 percent.

Note: Because of rounding, sums of individual items may not equal totals.

than customary rates to the company's employees. Those who choose a PPO option may still be able to utilize non-PPO services at increased cost. For example, under one company plan, families using PPO services have no medical bills, while those using non-PPO physicians pay the first $150 to $300 of charges and 20 percent of all medical bills up to $2,300. PPOs have not been around long enough to adequately assess the type of health care being offered. Where tried, however, they have proven popular.

MEDICARE AND MEDICAID Medicaid is neither an insurer nor a provider of health care. It is a joint federal–state effort to cover the medical expenses of the indigent. Unless you find yourself in this group, you will not have contact with Medicaid services. The coverage and quality of the services offered differ from state to state. Information can be obtained at your state's welfare office.

In one way or another, **Medicare** concerns us all. We either have a relative who is affected by the program or we will eventually consider enrolling ourselves. A federal health insurance program for those 65 or older, or those with chronic kidney failure or certain other disabilities, it consists of two parts: Part A is hospi-

Medicaid: A joint federal–state sponsored program covering medical expenses for the indigent.

Medicare: A federal health insurance program for those age 65 or older, or those with certain sicknesses or disabilities.

tal insurance and Part B is medical insurance. Coverage under each part is outlined in Figure 11.4. The hospital insurance is financed through the Social Security taxes you pay while you work. The medical insurance is voluntary and is partly paid by premiums from those who choose to participate. These programs are administered through the Social Security Administration. You should contact a local office for information and applications.

Workers' compensation: State programs providing health and disability income coverage for work-related illnesses and injuries.

WORKERS' COMPENSATION All states have **workers' compensation** programs that help pay for medical expenses and lost income resulting from work-related illnesses or injuries. However, not all workers are covered, nor is coverage required in all states. You should ask your employer whether or not you are covered. If you are, the type and amount of benefits you may receive are set down in state laws. Your personnel office or the state compensation office can provide you with a schedule of potential benefits.

FIGURE 11.4

Coverage under Medicare Part A and Part B. (Source: U.S. Department of Health and Human Services, *Guide to Health Insurance for People on Medicare.* Updated for 1991 coverage.)

MEDICARE HOSPITAL INSURANCE BENEFITS (PART A)			
	For Covered Services Each Benefit Period		
Service	**Benefit**	**Medicare Pays**	**You Pay**
Hospitalization: Semiprivate room and board, general nursing, and miscellaneous hospital services and supplies. Includes meals, special care units, drugs, lab tests, diagnostic X rays, medical supplies, operating and recovery room, anesthesia, and rehabilitation services.	First 60 days	All but $628	$628
	61st to 90th day	All but $157 a day	$157 a day
	*91st to 150th day	All but $314 a day	$314 a day
	Beyond 150 days	Nothing	All costs
	A *benefit period* begins on the first day you receive service as an inpatient in a hospital and ends after you have been out of the hospital or skilled nursing facility for 60 days in a row.		
Posthospital skilled nursing facility care: In a facility approved by Medicare. You must have been in a hospital for at least 3 days and enter the facility within 30 days after hospital discharge.	First 20 days	100% of approved amount	Nothing
	Additional 80 days	All but $78.50	$78.50
	Beyond 100 days	Nothing	All costs
	Medicare and private insurance will not pay for most nursing home care. You pay for custodial care and most care in a nursing home.		
Home health care	Unlimited as medically necessary	Full cost	Nothing
Hospice care: Available to terminally ill.	Unlimited as medically necessary	All but costs of outpatient drugs and inpatient respite care	Limited cost sharing for outpatient drugs and inpatient respite care
Blood	Blood	All but first 3 pints	For first 3 pints
*Sixty reserve days may be used only once in a lifetime; days used are not renewable.			

Selecting Health-Care Insurance

For many people, health insurance selection is tied to employment selection. They simply refuse to accept a job unless the employer provides adequate health-care protection. On the other hand, because of the tie-in between employment and health insurance, a few individuals in ill health may be deterred from looking for a job. They fear that employers, concerned about rising medical costs, may be reluctant to hire them. The Americans with Disabilities Act of 1990 provides some help to these prospective workers by setting down hiring restrictions on businesses that employ more than 15 people. Basically, an employer cannot deny a person a job because that individual's medical condition may cause increased insurance claims or higher insurance premiums. Preexisting conditions, however, can be excluded from coverage as long as these same exclusions are applied to all other workers.

Health insurance is a significant fringe benefit provided to most full-time workers. About 92 percent of full-time employees in medium and large-size firms receive such employment-related health-care benefits. Health-care selection for these covered employees may entail no more than choosing among a list of employer-provided options. Unfortunately, employee coverage drops to only

FIGURE 11.4

Continued.

MEDICAL INSURANCE BENEFITS (PART B)			
	For Covered Services Each Calendar Year		
Service	Benefit	Medicare Pays	You Pay
Medical expense: Physician's services, inpatient and outpatient medical services and supplies, physical and speech therapy, ambulance, etc.	Medicare pays for medical services in or out of the hospital. Some insurance policies pay less (or nothing) for hospital outpatient medical services or services in a doctor's office.	80% of approved amount (after $100 deductible)	$100 deductible* plus 20% of balance of approved amount (plus any charge above approved amount)**
Home health care	Unlimited as medically necessary	Full cost	Nothing
Outpatient hospital treatment	Unlimited as medically necessary	80% of approved amount (after $100 deductible)	Subject to deductible plus 20% of balance of approved amount
Blood	Blood	80% of approved amount (after first 3 pints and $100 deductible)	For first 3 pints plus 20% of balance of approved amount after $100 deductible

*Once you have had $100 of expense for covered services in a calendar year, the Part B deductible does not apply to any further covered services you receive in that year.

**YOU PAY FOR charges higher than the amount approved by Medicare unless the doctor or supplier agrees to accept Medicare's approved amount as the total charge for services rendered.

82 percent in smaller firms with less than 100 employees, and is virtually nonexistent for part-timers. Those who are not covered will face the difficult task of searching for and paying for appropriate individual coverage. Some helpful hints that might guide that journey are given in Figure 11.5.

GROUP COVERAGE   Group coverage is generally less expensive than individual insurance. If you are one of the few who cannot take part in a group plan at work, look into group policies offered through fraternal and professional organizations. But be careful. Some insurers advertise their policies as part of a group plan but provide none of the expected cost savings. When the identifiable group is not likely to be in any better health than the population as a whole, there is little reason to believe the policy is a good buy. For example, if the group policy is sold

FIGURE 11.5

Shopping for health insurance.

HINTS ON SHOPPING FOR PRIVATE HEALTH INSURANCE

Shop Carefully Before You Buy   Policies differ widely as to coverage and cost, and companies differ as to service. Contact different companies and compare the policies carefully before you buy. If an agent won't help you, don't buy from that agent.

Don't Buy More Policies Than You Need   Duplicate coverage is costly and not necessary. A single comprehensive policy is better than several policies with overlapping or duplicate coverages. For comprehensive coverage, consider continuing the group coverage you have at work; joining an HMO; buying a catastrophic or major medical policy or buying a Medicare Supplement policy.

Check for Preexisting-Condition Exclusions   Many policies exclude coverage for preexisting health conditions.
   Don't be misled by the phrase, "no medical examination required." If you have had a health problem, the insurer might not cover you for expenses connected with that problem.

Beware of Replacing Existing Coverage   Be suspicious of a suggestion that you give up your policy and buy a replacement. Often the new policy will impose waiting periods or will have exclusions or

waiting periods for preexisting conditions your current policy covers.
   On the other hand, don't keep inadequate policies simply because you have had them a long time. You don't get credit with a company just because you've paid many years for a policy.

Be Aware of Maximum Benefits   Most policies have some type of limit on benefits which may be expressed in terms of dollars payable or the number of days for which payment will be made.

Check Your Right to Renew   Beware of policies that let the company refuse to renew your policy on an individual basis. These policies provide the least permanent coverage.
   Most policies cannot be canceled by the company unless all policies of that type are canceled in the state. Therefore, these policies cannot be canceled because of claims or disputes. Some policies are guaranteed renewable for life. Policies that can be renewed automatically offer added protection.

Policies to Supplement Medicare Are Neither Sold nor Serviced by State or Federal Government   State Insurance Departments approve policies sold by insurance companies but approval only means the company and policy meet

requirements of state law. Do not believe statements that insurance to supplement Medicare is a government-sponsored program. If anyone tells you that he or she is from the government and later tries to sell you an insurance policy, report that person to your State Insurance Department. This type of representation is a violation of federal law.

Know with Whom You're Dealing   A company must meet certain qualifications to do business in your state. This is for your protection. Agents also must be licensed by your state and must carry proof of licensing showing their name and the company they represent. If the agent cannot show such proof, do not buy from that person. A business card is not a license.

Keep Agents' and/or Companies' Names, Addresses and Telephone Numbers   Write down the agents' and/or companies' names, addresses and telephone numbers; or ask for a business card.

Take Your Time   Do not let a short-term enrollment period high-pressure you. Professional salespeople will not rush you. If you question whether a program is worthy, ask the salesperson to explain it to a friend or relative whose judgment you respect. Allow yourself time to think through your decision.

**Protecting
What You
Have**

"exclusively" to "any American of any age who ever served in any of the Armed Forces anywhere in the world," you probably can do better elsewhere.

Previously, workers who lost their jobs were also likely to lose their health insurance protection. To remedy this doubly disastrous situation, Congress now requires employers with 20 or more workers to provide terminating employees with continued health-care coverage. This must be made available to those ex-workers who cannot obtain either alternative group insurance or Medicare coverage. The employer may charge you for the insurance, but in most instances the cost to you cannot be more than 102 percent of group insurance rates.

Mandated continuation periods are listed in Figure 11.6. When the continuation period ends, the group coverage must be convertible to an individual policy. Although the individual policy can have a higher price and provide fewer benefits, it still may be wise for you to exercise your conversion rights. An entirely new policy would exclude preexisting conditions and require a waiting period before full coverage began. The continuation and conversion of previous health insurance coverage can be used to eliminate any gaps in coverage due to a change in employment or marital status.

Family members also have a right to request a continuation of benefits for three years with the right of conversion thereafter. The circumstances under which benefits would be continued include death of the covered worker, separation or divorce from the covered spouse, or loss of dependent status by a child of an insured parent. If you are a young worker without coverage in your new job, continuing coverage under a parent's group plan is a good idea. As stated previously, it is this age group that is least likely to have adequate health insurance protection.

INDIVIDUAL COVERAGE   Most group insurance plans offer expensive comprehensive health coverage that includes basic health and major medical benefits. Individual policies cost 30 to 40 percent more, with a comprehensive family policy costing over $3,000 a year. You can hold down this expense by purchasing only major medical coverage with large deductibles and making out-of-pocket payments for your basic health needs. Increasing the deductible from $100 to $1,000 can cut your premiums by 40 to 50 percent. If you set aside an emergency

FIGURE 11.6

Continuation period for group health insurance.

Qualifying Events	Beneficiary	Term of Coverage
Termination Reduced hours	Employee Spouse Dependent child	18 months (For individuals who qualify for Social Security disability benefits, special rules extend coverage an additional 11 months)
Employee entitled to Medicare Divorce or legal separation Death of covered employee	Spouse Dependent child	36 months
Loss of "dependent child" status	Dependent child	36 months

Box 11.2
Saving Money

A Flexible Spending Account for Medical Expenditures

Employer-provided flexible spending accounts generally permit you to allocate a portion of your salary for this purpose. Sometimes employers match employee contributions or contribute a fixed amount. If tax qualified, the salary dollars paid into this account are tax-exempt. These dollars may then be used to pay for expenses that would be deductible from personal income taxes under IRS guidelines.

One popular use of flexible spending accounts is to pay for the deductibles and co-insurance on health insurance plans. The money placed in the flexible spending account can be used to pay the difference between the employee's medical expenses and the amount paid for by the company's health plan. Normally, you would have to earn $138.89 in taxable income to pay for a $100 deductible if you were in the 28 percent marginal tax bracket and your total medical expenses for the year did not exceed 7.5 percent of your family's gross income. Using tax-exempt dollars through a flexible spending account would result in a savings of $38.89, regardless of your proportional medical expenses.

As employers increase deductibles and co-insurance payments in order to hold down the increasing cost of medical insurance, the tax savings provided by flexible spending accounts becomes greater. There is, however, one significant drawback. At the end of the year, any unused funds you have allocated to this account are forfeited. You either use it or lose it.

For those engaging in personal financial planning, this should not be a serious problem. If you review previous budgets and your upcoming medical needs in the pro forma budget, you should be in a good position to estimate your flexible account needs conservatively and obtain the maximum tax advantage.

fund, you can use those resources to self-insure against unexpected basic health costs. Meanwhile, the major medical insurance provides you with the backup protection you need in case of catastrophic illness or injury.

MAJOR MEDICAL COVERAGE   When comparing and evaluating health plans, the first thing you should look at is the major medical coverage. Seriously consider only those that provide adequate major medical protection. Although the basic health coverage will affect your day-to-day expenditure, it is the major medical coverage that pays out in time of greatest need. If the employer's health-care plan has a maximum limit on reimbursement of less than $250,000 per illness or per lifetime, you should consider supplementing your employer's coverage with privately purchased major medical insurance.

Most employers have recognized the importance of adequate major medical protection. A 1989 survey of group policies in medium and large firms found that 89 percent of the participants had major medical protection. For most, the maximum benefits payable were quite good. Of those with major medical coverage, 78 percent either had no maximum or lifetime policy limits of $500,000 or more. In addition, two-thirds of the policies limited out-of-pocket expenses to $1,500, and the most common deductible was a low $100. Only 3 percent had severely inadequate maximum benefits of less than $100,000.

HMO VERSUS TRADITIONAL INSURANCE   Assuming that adequate major medical protection exists, you might then turn to analyzing the basic health benefits. Unless the plan is being offered for the first time, the experiences of your co-workers should prove relevant. Try to find other workers with families having similar characteristics to your own and who are living in an area close to

Managed care: A health program that manages the services you receive in an attempt to provide adequate care while containing costs.

your home. This is particularly important if you are evaluating a managed-care plan, such as an HMO or PPO. **Managed care** is the current term applied to a health insurance plan that attempts to put together a coherent network of providers. Your primary-care physician usually serves as the gateway or gatekeeper to this network. It is the gatekeeper's job to guide you through the network so as to ensure that you receive appropriate medical care in the most efficient and inexpensive way. This will limit your choice of physicians and hospitals. Therefore, when considering a managed-care plan, you must analyze both the quality of coverage and the quality and location of the covered services. If you travel a lot or you have children living at school, be sure you understand how you will be reimbursed for medical expenses incurred outside the local area network.

An HMO is likely to cover more basic health-care benefits than a fee-for-service plan. It can do this because it charges a slightly higher premium and is more successful at holding down hospital and diagnostic costs. To find out whether the added expense is worth it, simply add up your family's out-of-pocket medical expenses for each of the last few years. If the HMO would have covered these expenses, and they exceed the additional annual premium on the HMO, then it might be the preferred plan for your family. Generally, the larger and the younger the family, the more attractive the basic health coverage of an HMO will appear.

If your family has been reluctant to seek medical care when needed because of the necessary out-of-pocket expenses under traditional insurance, the first-dollar coverage provided by many HMOs may be very attractive. In this situation the benefit-cost analysis based on previous expenses would be irrelevant. You might instead base your decision on the average number of office visits in Table 11.2. For example, a family with both parents and two children might average 19.1 office visits per year. At $29 a visit, an HMO that provided office coverage would be worth about $554 more than a plan that did not.

Some advocates of HMOs have suggested that they are better than traditional insurers because they concentrate on preventive rather than curative medicine. Because the physician has a financial interest in seeing you remain healthy, you supposedly receive better preventive care and therefore remain healthier. It is a nice idea, but there just aren't enough data yet to test whether it is true or false. What we do know is that participants in HMOs have fewer severe illnesses and spend fewer days in the hospital. But your family's health will not necessarily improve just because you join an HMO. Remember that HMOs are relatively new and therefore must attract members who are presently covered by other plans. Those who are currently in ill health are likely to remain with their previous insurer, because of exclusions for preexisting conditions and because of a required waiting period before full coverage begins. Therefore, the new insurer is likely to start off with a group of individuals that are in better-than-average health.

Unfortunately, the financial trade-off is the easiest part of your decision analysis. Your family's attitude toward medical care is likely to be a more important deciding factor. A Rand Corporation study found that patient dissatisfaction was higher for HMOs. If you like being pampered, you might think twice about joining an HMO. Because the doctor receives incentives for containing costs, you might find your hospital stay is shorter than those of patients with traditional coverage. The 1980 census reported the annualized hospital rate per 1,000 individuals at an average of 438 days for HMOs, 725 days for Blue Cross/Blue Shield, and 1,631 days for the population as a whole, including those on Medicare and Medicaid. There is no evidence that a shortened hospital stay is detrimental to your health, but neither is there any evidence that HMO members have shorter stays because they get better faster.

The differences in medical care will be most noticeable if you join an HMO with an individual practice arrangement (IPA). A participating physician may be treating both patients with traditional insurance and those with HMO insurance. However, the fee the doctor receives for the HMO member is likely to be less than the amount collectible from those with traditional insurance. This might cause your physician to favor the higher-paying clients, especially during peak periods of demand.

THE INSURANCE COMPANY   Be sure to investigate the financial soundness of the medical insurer. As the plight of the Krause family, highlighted at the beginning of this chapter, illustrates, a bankrupt insurer could leave you financially ruined. Moreover, their story may not be that uncommon. In 1991 Blue Cross and Blue Shield of West Virginia collapsed and left $50 million of medical bills unpaid. Many doctors and hospitals are now trying to collect those bills from patients. In addition, *The Wall Street Journal* reports that five of the 73 Blue Cross/Blue Shield plans do not meet minimum funding standards established by regulators.

In many states commercial insurers are covered by a state guarantee fund that protects policy holders if an insurer gets into financial trouble. Technically, however, Blue Cross/Blue Shield companies are not viewed as insurance companies and, thus, are not covered by the guarantee funds in most states.

HMOs that are federally qualified by the Health Care Financing Administration must carry insurance to cover the unpaid bills of patients in the event they become insolvent. They are also required to include clauses in all contracts with doctors and patients prohibiting them from collecting directly from patients. Nevertheless, you still may suffer if preexisting conditions prevent you from obtaining insurance elsewhere.

A. M. Best and the other rating agencies mentioned in the previous chapter can be used to check out the financial stability of the commercial insurers. Physicians in your area should be able to provide some insight on the financial soundness of local and regional insurers such as HMOs and the Blues. Be wary of companies that have been stretching out the payment of physician's fees or hospital expenses. This can indicate impending financial problems.

MEDICARE AND MEDIGAP INSURANCE   Both Medicare hospital and medical insurance are a good buy at the time you become eligible. Medicare will, however, leave some serious gaps in your health-care coverage. You can consider closing them with a private supplemental health insurance policy. As Figure 11.4 shows, Medicare does require substantial deductibles and co-insurance payments. In the event of catastrophic illness, these payments could deplete the investment portfolio generating your retirement income.

Medigap insurance: Private insurance meant to partially or totally cover those health-care expenses that are not reimbursed by Medicare.

Medigap insurance is designed to fill this gap between Medicare covered and Medicare noncovered expenses. A medigap policy that places a realistic limit on deductibles and co-insurance payments is an excellent choice. Furthermore, if

**Protecting
What You
Have**

you purchase a medigap policy within six months of turning age 65 and enrolling in Medicare Part B, federal law now states that you cannot be turned down or charged extra because of your health status or medical condition. And once you have coverage, a medigap policy may not be canceled or a renewal refused because of your ill health.

Under directions from the U.S. Congress, the National Association of Insurance Commissioners (NIAC) has developed ten standardized policies. Medigap insurers can promote only those policies as supplemental medicare insurance; all must sell at least a basic policy (expected to cost from $300 to $400 per year) that addresses the following gaps in Medicare benefits:

- Either all or none of the Medicare Part A inpatient hospital deductible
- The Part A hospital co-insurance for days 61–150
- The Part A co-insurance amount for each of Medicare's 60 nonrenewable lifetime hospital inpatient reserve days used
- The reasonable cost of the first three pints of blood or equivalent quantities of paced red blood cells per calendar year unless replaced in accordance with federal regulations
- The Part B co-insurance amount after the policy holder pays the $100 annual deductible

Medigap policies do not cover procedures that Medicare would consider unnecessary, nor do they cover custodial nursing care. Furthermore, federal and state permission to sell medigap insurance does not mean that the policies are reasonably priced or that the insurer is financially sound. Therefore, be sure to shop around.

Disability Income Protection

Only those workers with dependents need life insurance, but every worker needs disability income protection. Young workers often purchase life insurance while ignoring the much greater risk of disability. This is especially unfortunate because your chances of suffering a serious disability are surprisingly high. The Social Security Administration estimates that a 20-year-old has over a 20 percent probability of experiencing an insured disability before reaching age 65 (see Figure 11.7). Since the requirements for an insured disability are rather strict, it is likely that many more individuals will experience a significant earnings loss at some point in their work life. In fact, over one-fifth of 55- to 64-year-olds state that they have a work disability that limits the kind or amount of work they do.

Long-term disability insurance that bridges at least part of the gap between when short-term benefits end and retirement begins is provided to almost one-half the work force in firms with over 100 employees. In smaller establishments only about one-fifth of employees are similarly covered. Those without long-term disability protection must rely entirely on Social Security benefits, or a declining bank account. Furthermore, few will be able to collect the Social Security benefits they may be depending on. The rules are quite strict. You must be able to prove the disability is total and will last for at least one year or terminate in death. Nothing is paid out for partial disability unless it is preceded by a period of total disability. And if you do qualify, benefit checks do not begin until at least six months after you become disabled.

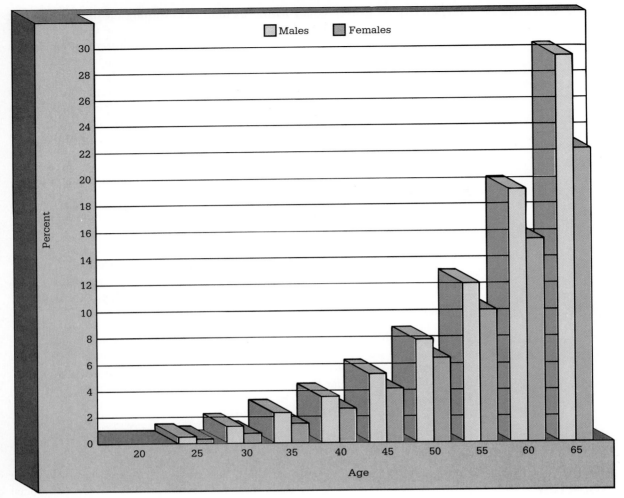

FIGURE 11.7

Probability of Social Security insured disability from age 20 to given age. (Source: U.S. Department of Health and Human Services, A death and disability life table for the 1966 birth.)

Sources of Disability Income

In the event you become disabled, you will probably have to rely on a variety of sources for support. Listed below are some common means of support used by the disabled during periods of reduced market income.

Accident insurance: Pays a set dollar amount in the event of physical dismemberment.

ACCIDENT INSURANCE   Also called *dismemberment insurance*, **accident insurance** pays the insured a set dollar amount for the loss of life, limb, or sight. It pays nothing when the physical loss is caused by an illness rather than an accident. Furthermore, the amount paid is unrelated to your actual income loss. Its major selling point is its low price. One company charges $2 a month for $150,000 of accident life, with smaller payments for dismemberment. The price is low because your chances of collecting are small.

DISABILITY INCOME INSURANCE As with health-care insurance, the cheapest **disability income insurance** is obtained through group coverage sponsored by employers. Group benefits are usually integrated with Social Security payments and workers' compensation to provide a level of benefits dependent upon current wages. This usually does not exceed 60 percent of salary.

Individual disability income policies usually provide a set dollar amount of coverage. Premiums may be stated in terms of each $100 of monthly disability benefits purchased. Various endorsements and riders are available to tailor the policy to individual needs. For example, the amount of benefits may be dependent upon whether or not you qualify for Social Security disability benefits.

Both short-term and long-term disability income plans are available. Short-term coverage usually begins immediately after an accident but has a short waiting period for disabilities resulting from sickness. Benefit payments may then continue for six months, or at most, two years. Long-term disability income insurance typically has a longer waiting period, but benefits will continue for either a stated number of years or until age 65.

The conditions for receiving disability payments are generally more stringent under long-term disability insurance and may even change with the duration of the disability. For example, you may be considered disabled over the first two to five years if you cannot perform the duties of your own occupation. Payments after this period, however, will continue only if you are unable to engage in any occupation for which you are reasonably fitted by education, training, or experience.

PENSION PLANS Instead of purchasing separate group disability insurance, some employers will incorporate a disability option into the existing pension plan. If you are disabled before normal retirement age, you may be able to receive an immediate pension under a disability clause in the pension plan. The method for calculating monthly benefits may or may not differ from that used for normal retirement. However, even at reduced benefit levels, this alternative may be desirable.

Also look for a waiver of contributions clause. Under this option the employer will continue to contribute to your pension plan for as long as you are disabled. Thus, at normal retirement age you could collect the full retirement pension even though you had not worked up until normal retirement age.

SOCIAL SECURITY To be considered disabled under the Social Security law, you must have a physical condition that prevents you from doing any substantial gainful work, and that is expected to last 12 months or is expected to result in death. In 1991, if you could earn over $500 a month in gross wages, after deductions for medical services and equipment required because of your impairment, you were considered capable of substantial gainful employment. Obviously, these requirements rule out Social Security payments for all but the severely and, apparently, permanently handicapped. Because you and your family could suffer a severe reduction in income and still be ineligible for disability income from

Social Security, you will likely have a need for private disability income insurance.

To receive this disability income protection, you must have accumulated a sufficient number of work credits in recent employment. The precise requirements and method for calculating the monthly benefit are explained in Appendix B on Social Security.

WORKERS' COMPENSATION If the disabling injury or illness is work-related, you may also be entitled to disability benefits under your state's workers' compensation statutes. These laws hold employers strictly liable for injuries in the workplace. This means that the employer is responsible, regardless of who is at fault. In return for assuming strict liability, compensation paid by employers is limited to mandated amounts. The benefits vary from state to state and are generally set equal to a given percentage of the average weekly wage within the state.

Specific types of injuries, such as loss of an arm, may come under the state's definition of permanent partial disabilities. For such injuries, the worker may receive a lump-sum payment or weekly payments for a limited time.

Many states also provide maintenance and benefits for workers undergoing rehabilitation. Workers' compensation or related programs may handle this coverage. Again, specifics can be provided at your state's workers' compensation office.

WAIVER OF PREMIUM OR PAYMENT CLAUSES Life and health insurance policies should be examined for clauses that waive future premium payments in the event of disability. If you have mortgage life insurance on your home, or credit life insurance on a car loan, be sure also to examine these for a disability clause.

Insurance Clauses Affecting Disability Benefits

The quality of your disability insurance protection will depend upon more than just the promised monthly benefits. It will be determined largely by the duration and conditions under which the benefits will be paid.

DEFINITION OF DISABILITY How disabled must you be before you can collect benefits? The answer depends on the exact wording in the insurance contract. A policy that considers you disabled if you cannot perform the main duties of your regular occupation is better than one that considers you disabled if you are unable to engage in any occupation for which you are reasonably suited by education and experience. For example, a surgeon suffering the loss of a hand would be considered disabled under the first definition, but not necessarily under the second, if he or she could practice some other medical specialty. Obviously, both of these are better than a policy that considers you disabled only when you cannot engage in any type of paid work.

Most policies provide for some compensation in case of partial disability. Some definitions of partial disability are related to income loss, while others are defined in terms of the physical handicap. In many policies, however, you must experience a period of total disability before you collect partial benefits. The level of partial benefits may be equal to a set percentage of total disability benefits or geared to the income loss created by the partial disability. For example, if you earned $2,000 a month before the disability and now earn $500 a month, you have suffered a 75 percent reduction in income. If the maximum monthly benefit under the insurance policy is $1,000, you will receive a partial benefit equal to 75 percent of the $1,000 maximum monthly benefit. In this situation, partial disability benefits are $750 per month.

ELIMINATION OR WAITING PERIOD   The time between the onset of the disability and the beginning of disability payments is the **disability elimination** or **waiting period.** The longer the elimination period, the less likely you are to collect, and therefore, the lower your premium.

Disability elimination or waiting period: The time between the onset of the disability and the beginning of disability benefits.

A good method of holding down your insurance costs is to opt for the longest elimination period you feel comfortable with. An emergency fund of highly liquid assets would permit you to continue to meet your financial obligations during this time. This is a highly rewarding strategy. Increasing the waiting period from 7 days to 60 days can reduce premiums by more than 50 percent; from 7 days to a year reduces them by more than 65 percent.

Be sure you understand how the policy handles intermittent disabilities. If you are disabled and then return to work after recuperating, must you again go through a waiting period if you have a relapse? Most policies don't require another elimination period if you are disabled by the same cause within six months after returning to work.

BENEFIT PERIOD   Depending on the policy, benefit payments may last one, five, ten years, or until age 65. Your greatest financial risk is a lifetime disability. The best risk-reduction strategy is to opt for the policy with the longer **benefit period,** and to hold down your premiums by choosing a longer elimination period. If this strategy proves too expensive, policies with shorter benefit periods may be used to protect income during a readjustment period or during the financially demanding child-rearing years.

Benefit period: The duration of disability benefits.

COORDINATION OF BENEFITS CLAUSE   Many policies use a **coordination of benefits clause** to state the maximum disability income you may receive from all insurance sources, both public and private. The maximum is usually stated as a percentage of your current income. Without this limit, you might be able to earn more by owning multiple policies and not working.

Coordination of benefits clause: Ensures that disability benefits received from all sources are not greater than either some defined amount or a maximum percentage of previous earnings.

SOCIAL INSURANCE SUBSTITUTE   The **social insurance substitute** may be included as a rider or as part of the basic policy. In the event you are disabled but still do not satisfy the strict requirements for Social Security benefits, or are not covered by Workers' Compensation, this provision will replace those benefits with private insurance payments. This is a highly desirable provision because it eliminates an important source of uncertainty regarding your total disability payments, thus permitting you to estimate more accurately potential disability income.

Social insurance substitute: Provision of private disability income benefits in the event that social insurance benefits are not forthcoming.

PROVISION FOR REHABILITATION   Some policies explicitly provide for the continuation of benefits while you are in a rehabilitation program. This provision ensures that your benefits will not be terminated if you enter a work-related program. Some policies even state that tuition and equipment expenses for such

357

Health Care and Disability Insurance

programs will be covered. If you are disabled, and your policy does not contain this provision, you should check with the insurance company anyway. They may be more than willing to cover these expenses. After all, they have an incentive in seeing you return to gainful employment.

RENEWABILITY   The disability policy should be renewable without evidence of insurability; however, renewability provisions do vary.

The most unfavorable provision is found in policies that are **class cancellable.** This means the insurance company has the right to cancel an entire class of policies. For example, it can cancel all policies written before a specific date or within a specific state. If you are in poor health, this action can leave you in the position of finding expensive alternative coverage.

Next best are policies that are guaranteed renewable. These cannot be cancelled as long as you pay your premiums; however, the premiums can increase. Better yet are policies that are *guaranteed renewable and noncancellable.* Such a provision gives you the right to renew your policy at the same premium.

Class cancellable: The insurer can cancel policies for an entire class of insureds.

Action Plan for Steeles Selecting a Group Plan

Background   Arnold's employer offers a choice of health-care insurance plans, including a local HMO operated under an IPA, and traditional fee-for-service insurance. Principal coverage under each health-care plan is outlined in Figure 11.2.

Over the last few years, the Steeles have been members of the HMO. They have been generally satisfied with the service, although in a few instances they had to go out of their way to find a specialist who was a participating physician. Except for a small co-payment on prescription drugs, the comprehensive benefits offered by the HMO have eliminated almost all of their out-of-pocket expenses. This saving has more than paid for any locational inconvenience in the delivery of medical services.

The Problem   Previously, both health-care plans have been fully paid for by the employer. However, the HMO has recently increased its membership fee substantially. In an effort to get workers to sign up for the less expensive fee-for-service plan, the company is now offering a $20-a-month cash payment to families that choose this insurance alternative.

Arnold and Sharon reviewed the family's use of health-care services for the previous year and estimated that only $180 would have been left uncovered by the fee-for-service plan. The proposed annual cash payment of $240 thus appears to be the better alternative. The Steeles must decide within the month whether they will switch insurance. If they do nothing, they will be automatically reenrolled in the HMO.

The Plan   The Steeles should begin their comparison with an examination of major medical benefits. The fee-for-service plan certainly provides adequate protection for most families, with a policy limit of $250,000 and 20 percent coinsurance up to a $2,000 out-of-pocket maximum. However, the HMO provides

Protecting
What You
Have

INFLATION PROTECTION   A policy written to cover a certain percentage of your salary will provide some inflation protection. That is, as your salary increases, your insurance protection will increase correspondingly. If you are instead purchasing insurance that provides fixed-dollar payments, an *option to purchase* rider should be considered. It permits you to purchase additional protection in the future without evidence of insurability.

Ensuring that you have the appropriate level of protection at the beginning of the disability provides only partial protection against inflation. If your dollar benefits are unchanged during the period of disability, then inflation will erode the real worth of these payments. Social Security benefit payments are normally adjusted for increases in the cost of living, so that at least a portion of your disability payments may receive inflation protection. However, some disability policies provide for a dollar-for-dollar reduction in benefits to offset increases in Social Security payments, thus leaving your total compensation from Social Security and private disability insurance unchanged. A policy that establishes the company's dollar payments at the beginning of the disability, and that does not

for unlimited covered expenses without co-insurance payments for all injuries and most illnesses. Given these provisions, the HMO provides superior protection in the event of catastrophic illness or injury.

The Steeles should be especially aware of the major medical provision, since Arnold has above-average health risks as a chemist. He is covered by Workers' Compensation for job-related illnesses and injuries. But he handles many hazardous chemicals each day, and it may be difficult to prove that an illness was caused by any one of these products. Thus, there is a chance that, should he become ill, he will be denied benefits under Workers' Compensation.

The HMO also provides superior basic health coverage, paying for office visits, prescription drugs with a small co-payment, and all surgical fees. Where the fee-for-service plan does cover physician fees, it pays the UCR charge, which may leave the Steeles with some uncovered expenses.

If the decision were based solely on the benefits provided, the HMO would be the better choice. But is it worth the extra cost? Their estimated $180 in uncovered expenses would have to come out of after-tax dollars. Only uninsured medical expenses exceeding 7.5 percent of adjusted gross income are tax deductible. Considering the Steeles' combined income, they would be unlikely to have deductible medical expenses under either insurance plan. In a 28 percent marginal tax bracket, they would have needed about $250 in taxable income to pay for the estimated uncovered expenses. This is more than the $240 taxable cash benefit offered by the employer. Thus, with both benefits greater and costs less, the Steeles would seem to be better served by the HMO.

One last point: Had the analysis indicated that a switch appeared favorable, the Steeles would also have to examine the preexisting conditions clause in the fee-for-service plan. It may be better to remain with less favorable coverage than to be uninsured because of a preexisting condition.

Having a Living Will

Breakthroughs in medical science now make it possible to extend life far beyond what we had previously thought likely only a few decades ago. But advances in the extension of life do not always go hand in hand with improvements in the quality of life. For those who worry about being kept alive in a vegetative state with little or no chance of recovery, the "living will" can be the answer.

A living will is really not a will at all. It is a medical directive indicating the type of life support you are willing or unwilling to receive in the event you are unconscious or in a coma and unable to speak for yourself. In most states it is a legal document and, therefore, the state you live in may specify the precise form it must take.

In order for a living will to be effective, it must state your wishes precisely, so that your intent is clear. The Harvard Medical School's Health Letter, called the Medical Directive, distributes a living will that lists 12 standard medical procedures and treatments. For each you can make your wishes very clear by indicating the type of life-prolonging treatment you are willing to accept. (For a small fee, copies can be obtained by contacting Harvard Health-Medical Directive, P.O. Box 380, Boston, MA 02116.)

The Patient Self-Determination Act of 1991 requires that all institutions receiving Medicare or Medicaid funds inform patients upon admission of their right to sign an "advance directive." This includes a living will in which you have the right to refuse life-sustaining treatment, and a health-care power of attorney in which you appoint someone to make health-care decisions for you if you are unable to. You don't have to sign an advance directive, but if you do, a record of it should be kept in your medical file.

The time to make these decisions, however, is not upon entry into a health-care facility. By that point you may be incapacitated and your family may be in crisis. It is better to plan for such emergencies well in advance, when both your health care and financial concerns can be combined into a fully integrated plan. In addition to a living will and a health-care power of attorney, this plan should include a last will and testament and a durable power of attorney. Similar to the health-care power of attorney, the durable power of attorney enables a designated guardian to manage your financial and legal matters if you are unable to. After all, who is going to cash your checks and pay your bills when you cannot? If you fail to specify your choice in advance, the court may appoint someone who is not of your own choosing.

You should review these documents periodically to ensure that they still conform with your wishes. As you get older or your family situation changes, the kind of medical care you desire may also change. You can then revise or revoke old documents so as to conform to your changing desires.

permit future reductions in these payments, is preferred. Better yet is one with a cost-of-living rider that automatically adjusts dollar payments during the disability period for increases in the Consumer Price Index.

Determining Disability Income Insurance Requirements

Your disability income requirements will depend on the duration and severity of the disability. For disabilities lasting six months or less, you may have to rely on sick leave, short-term group disability benefits provided by an employer, or workers' compensation if the disability is work-related. Lacking those, an emergency fund equal to six months' wages can provide the needed support through this interim period. For disabilities lasting longer than six months, you will have to consider your income needs until, typically, age 65, when retirement benefits begin. A good rule of thumb is that you should plan to replace about 60 to 70 percent of your lost gross income. This figure is based on the assumptions that some of your disability benefits will be nontaxable, and that you will no longer incur work-related expenses. (Employer-provided benefits will be largely taxed, but privately purchased disability benefits will be tax-free.) In any case, you may find it difficult to replace a larger percentage of your income through private insurance, since most insurers do not want to provide an incentive for not working.

Starting with your income replacement requirements on line 1 of Figure 11.8, you can then reduce this amount by your current sources of disability income. Include income benefits from existing group and individual policies. Be sure to examine your pension plan for an early retirement option in case of disability, and list this income source on line 4. The estimated Social Security payments on line 5 can be supplied by an insurance agent or calculated using the Social Security appendix to this text. Don't include potential payments from workers' compensation. You want to have adequate coverage whether or not the disability is work related.

If you just want a rough estimate of what Social Security disability benefits would be, you can use the estimates in Table 11.4. The basic disability benefit would be received by the disabled worker. In addition, you can assume that mothers caring for dependent children under age 16 and earning no more than $500 a month would additionally receive 50 percent of the basic monthly disability benefit. Children under 18 years of age would also get 50 percent of the basic benefit. In all cases, however, you should assume that total payments to the disabled worker, dependent children, and caring mother do not exceed the maximum family benefit contained in Table 11.4.

	Average Annual Social Security, Covered Wages				
	Less than $10,000	$10,000 to 15,000	$15,000 to 25,000	$25,000 to 35,000	$35,000 and over
Worker alone	$500	$630	$ 760	$ 970	$1,070
Worker, spouse, and one child (family maximum)	740	940	1,140	1,450	1,610

Your total integrated benefits are listed on line 6. This is not necessarily equal to the sum of lines 2 to 5. You must examine each of your policies for coordination of benefits clauses and social insurance substitute riders. Participation limits set down in these sections of the disability policies may limit your total integrated benefits to less than the summed total of lines 2 to 5.

If you subtract your total integrated benefits from your total income replacement requirements on line 1, you will have determined your need for additional income insurance protection on line 7. You may be able to satisfy this need through additional individual or group insurance. If you do purchase additional insurance, make sure its benefits will not be offset by a reduction in prospective payments under your present policies.

FIGURE 11.8

Estimating your disability insurance needs.

DISABILITY INSURANCE

1. Income replacement requirements (60%–70% of gross income lost) _____
2. Group insurance benefits _____
3. Individual insurance benefits _____
4. Early retirement benefits _____
5. Social Security benefits _____
6. Total integrated benefits (_____)
7. Additional disability income insurance needed _____

Summary

Protection against the financial consequences of illness and injury is provided by health-care insurance and disability insurance. Health-care insurance is meant to cover the cost of medical treatment. It consists of basic health-care coverage and major medical coverage. Many workers choose from among group plans, including both traditional insurance and health maintenance organizations, offered by their employers. Disability insurance is meant to replace a portion of income lost due to illness or injury. It is provided publicly through Social Security and workers' compensation programs, and privately by insurance companies. A good financial plan should include protection against all the major financial consequences of a serious illness or injury.

Key Terms

accident insurance (p. 354)

basic health-care insurance (p. 336)

benefit period (p. 357)

Blue Cross/Blue Shield (p. 343)

class cancellable (p. 358)

co-insurance (p. 339)

commercial insurer (p. 343)

comprehensive health insurance (p. 336)

coordination of benefits clause (p. 357)

co-payment (p. 339)

dental insurance (p. 339)

disability income insurance (p. 355)

disability elimination period (p. 357)

fee-for-service health insurance (p. 344)

group-staff HMO (p. 344)

guaranteed renewability (p. 342)

health maintenance organization (HMO) (p. 343)

hospital expense insurance (p. 336)

hospital insurance (p. 336)

indemnity insurance (p. 336)

individual practice arrangement (IPA) HMO (p. 344)

managed care (p. 351)

major medical insurance (p. 339)

Medicaid (p. 345)

medical insurance (p. 338)

Medicare (p. 345)

medigap insurance (p. 352)

open-ended enrollment plan (p. 344)

preferred provider organization (PPO) (p. 344)

preexisting conditions clause (p. 341)

service benefit coverage (p. 338)

social insurance substitute (p. 357)

surgical insurance (p. 338)

usual, customary, and reasonable (UCR) (p. 338)

waiting period (disability) (p. 357)

waiting period (health care) (p. 341)

workers' compensation (p. 346)

1   What kinds of insurance provide protection against the financial consequences of illness and injury?

2   Discuss the three forms of reimbursement undertaken by hospital insurance policies. Which is the preferred coverage? Explain why.

3   What is the difference between medical insurance and major medical insurance? Which is more important? Why?

4   Suppose you have $5,000 of health-care expenses that are not covered by your basic health insurance. You have a major medical policy with a $500 deductible and 20 percent co-insurance. What are your out-of-pocket expenses?

5   What is the nation's largest insurer of health care? Which branch of this organization supplies the hospital insurance?

6   For certain procedures, Blue Shield agrees to pay the physician a UCR fee. How is this fee determined? What should you do if you are charged in excess of this amount?

7   How does an HMO differ from traditional insurance provided by Blue Cross/Blue Shield and most commercial insurers? How would you go about comparing the relative benefits of purchasing traditional insurance or joining an HMO?

8   How does an HMO differ from a PPO?

9   Name the two government programs that provide health-care benefits. Which one is run entirely by the federal government?

10   Why should group coverage cost less than individual coverage?

11   A family with two adults and three children under 17 is considering purchasing medical insurance to cover doctors' fees for office visits. Estimate the expected value of this protection. Why is this health-care insurance necessary or not necessary?

12   How does Social Security define "substantial gainful employment"? Explain how definitions of disability contained in private insurance policies can determine the quality of the insurance protection.

13   It is impossible to purchase disability insurance covering 100 percent of lost income. Why?

14   What part does the elimination period play when planning for adequate disability income protection?

15   Discuss some disability income protection strategies that can help you cope with the erosion of benefits due to inflation.

16   What type of nursing home care is traditionally not reimbursed under health insurance plans?

17   What is the purpose of a living will?

18   What should comprehensive health insurance cover?

19   How can an employer sponsored flexible spending plan help save you tax dollars?

20   What is meant by managed care?

The Hurleys have narrowed their choice of disability insurance for Mr. Hurley down to two policies. They both cost the same and are identical except for those differences outlined below. They are guaranteed renewable, and have an elimination period of 15 days.

	Policy 1	Policy 2
Monthly benefit	$500	$300
Benefit period	10 years	To age 65
Maximum replacement from all sources	Lesser of $2,000 a month, or 60% of income	60% of income

Mr. Hurley is currently 35 years of age with two children. Over the next ten years his child-rearing responsibilities should end. His current job pays $30,000 a year and is covered by Social Security. He calculates potential family disability benefits from Social Security at about $900 a month while the children are still at home. He is currently in line for an upper-level management position. Should he get it, his salary would increase substantially.

Questions

1 From the Hurleys' point of view, discuss the relative merits of each policy. Which would you recommend?
2 Which policy provides the better inflation protection? Why?
3 Do these policies provide adequate income replacement for the Hurleys?
4 Suppose the Hurleys must limit the amount spent on disability insurance to the cost of these policies. Are there any changes in coverage that might lower their risk without increasing their premiums? Explain.

Walter and Ella have decided that the time has come for them to consider expanding the family unit. In preparation, they examined their health-care insurance for maternity coverage. The policy was written by a commercial insurer and is identical to the fee-for-service plan in Figure 11.2. As stated, benefits for maternity care are the same as for illness or injury. Their insurance agent informs them that for an extra $100 a year in premiums, they can purchase first-dollar coverage on all maternity-related expenses. This would include prenatal and postnatal office visits for Ella.

Questions

1 Is the $100 maternity care endorsement worth the cost? Without this endorsement, how much is a typical pregnancy likely to cost the Sisaks?
2 What other provisions should the Sisaks look for? What coverage is essential at childbirth?

Committee on Labor and Human Resources. *The Health Care Crisis: A Report to the American People.* U.S. Government Printing Office, Washington, DC, 1990.

Health Insurance Association of America. *Source Book of Health Insurance Data* (annual). HIAA, Washington, DC.

U.S. Department of Commerce. *Health Insurance Coverage 1986–88.* Current Population Reports, Series P-70, No. 17. U.S. Government Printing Office, Washington, DC, 1990.

U.S. Department of Labor. *Employee Benefits Survey: An MLR Reader*, Bulletin 2362. U.S. Government Printing Office, Washington, DC, 1990.

U.S. Department of Labor. *Employee Benefits in Medium and Large Firms, 1989*, Bulletin 236. U.S. Government Printing Office, Washington, DC, 1990.

U.S. Department of Labor. *Health Benefits Under the Consolidated Omnibus Budget Reconciliation Act*. U.S. Government Printing Office, Washington, DC, 1991.

Helpful Contacts

Society for the Right to Die
250 West 57th Street, New York, NY 10107
Provides information and forms on living wills in 41 states and the District of Columbia.

United Seniors Health Cooperative
1331 H St. N.W., Suite 500, Washington, DC 20005 (telephone 202–393–6222).
Provides information on new open-enrollment provisions for medigap policies.

Chapter

12

Objectives

1 To understand the basic components of the homeowners' and auto insurance packages

2 To list and explain the standard formats for homeowners' insurance policies

3 To learn how to evaluate your auto and home insurance needs

4 To be able to find and fill any gaps in your homeowners' and auto coverage

5 To know how to handle insurance claims for the home and auto efficiently

6 To calculate your deductible casualty loss

When Everything Disappears in a Cloud

Great, muscular clouds of battleship gray, their bottoms tinged in black, boiled overhead. They rolled across the plains and over the town ominously, but they were a common springtime sight in north Texas, and the people were used to them. Nevertheless, by nightfall, Wichita Falls, a town of 97,000 souls that lies about 30 miles south of the Oklahoma line, would be hit by a disaster that would leave 45 dead and hundreds injured. And 20,000 people would lose their homes. Men, women, and children would be unable to sleep that evening and for many nights to come because of trauma and emotional aftershocks.

Louise Covington arrived at her small frame home in the suburb of Faith Village and started fixing dinner. While she worked, Mrs. Covington was half-listening to the police band on the kitchen radio. Shortly before 6 P.M., a dispatcher's voice suddenly broke the monotone of routine messages. "We got two, maybe three, funnels over the Certain Teed," the dispatcher declared. Mrs. Covington dropped her mixing spoon.

The Certain Teed building supply outlet was just a few blocks behind her house.

Running into the back yard, the woman stared up in horror. Two wide, curling black ropes were undulating like huge snakes up into the clouds. Suddenly, they converged and formed a monstrous, roaring funnel that filled the sky. As buildings under the tornado's half-mile base began exploding and disappearing, Louise Covington ran back inside to open windows and unplug the television. Following a prescribed drill known to every north Texan, her husband, Shorty, hurried into the bathroom and lay down. Their teenage son, Tifton, followed, clutching the family's frantic little dog in his arms. Before joining the family, Louise Covington glanced outside one last time. A refrigerator was cartwheeling down the street, and a neighbor's roof was coming apart. Slamming the hallway doors shut, she hurried into the bathroom.

By the time the vortex arrived, the Covingtons were laying with their heads next to the bathtub. The force of the tornado threw Louise against the tub, stunning her. When she opened her eyes again a few seconds later, the house was still being battered. She could see the bathroom ceiling slamming up and down. "Shorty!" she yelled, rising. "We've got to go into the hall! The bathroom's fixing to go!" But their son, Tifton, sat motionless with shock, the little dog still in his arms. Louise picked up both boy and dog, lugging them into the hall. But just as she laid them down, the tornado sucked out the windows of the adjacent bedroom and the bedroom door blew inward. Horrified, not believing what she was seeing, Louise watched as the struggling dog was pulled out of the boy's arms, sucked across the bedroom, out the top of the window, and up into the dark sky. Summoning all her strength, she pulled the bedroom door shut and lay down again in the hallway.

SOURCE: Excerpted from Nancy Golonka, "How to Protect What's Yours," Acropolis Books Ltd. and the Insurance Information Institute, 1983.

The Covingtons eventually found the dog, physically unharmed, huddling in a garage around the corner. Luckily, they all escaped injury, but much of what they owned was destroyed during the tornado's brief existence. Money cannot replace Grandma's special china, or photos of the children; but it can help restore many of the material possessions needed for everyday survival.

The first time many people read their insurance policies closely is after a catastrophe like the one in Texas. Some will be surprised to find their homeowners' insurance covered more than they expected, while others will find the payout less than adequate. Insurance adjusters will descend on the scene to provide quick reimbursement of losses. Because of different policies or different coverage, owners of similar homes will find the adjusters making widely divergent settlement offers. No doubt, some will feel cheated, but most likely none will be. With a little forethought and financial planning, you might be one of the luckier ones.

In this chapter we will examine both homeowners' and auto insurance. Each is a package of component policies covering a myriad of disasters at home or on the road. Both can provide nonoverlapping protection against property loss and personal liability. **Property loss insurance** reimburses you for damage to your property due to accidental or natural circumstances, or due to the negligence of others or yourself. By **negligence** we mean the failure to exercise the care expected of a prudent person. **Personal liability insurance** provides protection from claims against you resulting from the financial harm your negligence may cause others.

The homeowners' insurance package usually provides better protection, at a lower cost, than the sum of its parts. Over the years, homeowners' policies have evolved into a few standard formats that seem to serve adequately the needs of the typical homeowner or renter. In order to fully understand the differences among homeowners' policies, it is first necessary to review some standard insurance terminology and the basic elements of a homeowners' policy.

The Terminology of Homeowners' Policies

You will find that most homeowners' policies are written in a clear and straightforward style. In fact, if you can't understand your policy and your insurance agent can't provide an adequate explanation of your coverage, you may have sufficient reason for finding another insurer. However, even the best-written policies contain some points that require an explanation to help you fully realize what you have purchased and how you are protected.

ALL RISKS VERSUS NAMED PERILS INSURANCE The policy should indicate whether you have **all risks coverage** or **named perils coverage.** The type need not remain the same throughout the policy. You may find that some items come under all risks insurance and others come under named perils insurance. All risks protection doesn't necessarily cover you against all risks. It does protect you against all risks that are not specifically excluded in the policy. Named perils insurance is just what the term implies: It covers only risks that are specifically stated in the policy. Therefore, with all risks protection you should see a list of circumstances not covered, while under named perils you should see a list of circumstances that will be covered.

The difference is important, because each places differing obligations on the insurer and the insured. Under all risks coverage, the insurance company is responsible for showing that your loss was not due to one of the specific exemptions stated in the policy. Alternatively, under named perils coverage, it is your responsibility to demonstrate that your loss was due to one of the named perils.

REPLACEMENT COST VERSUS ACTUAL CASH VALUE The policy should indicate whether you will be reimbursed for losses at replacement cost or actual cash value. When the insurance company agrees to pay **replacement cost** on damaged goods, you receive the amount needed to replace new for old, with no deduction for depreciation. For example, if the roof on your home is destroyed, the insurance company will pay for the construction of a new roof, regardless of the age of the old one.

Property loss insurance: Reimburses you for damage to your property due to accidental or natural circumstances, or due to the negligence of others or yourself.

Negligence: The failure to exercise due care, the care expected of a prudent person.

Homeowners' Insurance

Personal liability insurance: Protects you against claims resulting from the financial harm your negligence may cause others.

All risks coverage: Insurance covers all risks that are not specifically excluded in the policy.

Named perils coverage: Insurance covers only risks that are specifically named.

Replacement cost: The amount needed to replace new for old, with no deduction for depreciation.

368

Protecting What You Have

All Risk and Concurrent Causation

The difference between all risks and named perils homeowners' coverage has proven very important for property owners in California. Jack Garvey had an all risks homeowners' policy in 1978, when an earthquake separated a two-story addition from his house, leaving a gap of several inches. One of the specific exclusions in his policy was damage resulting from an earth movement. Nevertheless, Mr. Garvey requested reimbursement. The insurance company refused payment, and they went to trial.

Garvey's lawyer claimed coverage under the "doctrine of concurrent causation." It states that whenever a loss results from a combination of two causes, one excluded and the other not, the loss is covered. With an all risks policy, if one of the concurrent factors is not specifically excluded, then the loss is most likely covered. Earth movement wasn't covered by Mr. Garvey's policy, but negligent construction was. The jury awarded him $47,000 in compensatory damages and $1 million in punitive damages, because the insurance company was unable to prove that all of the circumstances responsible for Mr. Garvey's loss were specifically excluded.

In light of this and other similar court interpretations extending the reach of all risk coverage, insurance companies have rewritten their policies in an effort to limit recovery under the doctrine of concurrent causation. The new policies avoid using the term *all risks* and instead now cover "risks of direct physical loss unless the loss is excluded."

The Garvey case finally arrived at the chambers of the California Supreme Court in 1989. In a ruling that pleased the insurance industry, the decision of the trial court was set aside. The court decided that a loss is not necessarily insured just because a covered peril exists somewhere in the chain of causation. If this were so, it would be almost impossible for an insurance company to exclude any loss, thus forcing many consumers to purchase more insurance than they might desire. The Supreme Court mandated that the trial court must first determine the primary cause of the loss. In the case of the Garveys, if the primary cause of the loss was negligent construction, then they are covered. On the other hand, if the primary cause was the earthquake, then they are not.

Actual cash value: Market value, which is equal to replacement cost minus depreciation.

Actual cash value is equal to replacement cost minus depreciation. If the typical roof lasts 20 years and yours is destroyed in the tenth year, under actual cash value reimbursement you would receive only 50 percent of the funds needed to replace the roof. This could place you in a very unfortunate position if you did not have the additional funds needed to repair the structural damage to the home. Without a roof over your head, you would need to rent some place to live. In addition, you would still be responsible for the mortgage payments on the home. Failure to pay could wipe out a good portion of your remaining equity in the home. For this reason, most homeowners' policies provide for reimbursement at replacement cost for structural damage and reimbursement at actual cash value for the contents. Moreover, additional living expenses while the structure is being repaired may be partially or totally reimbursed.

Co-insurance: Requires the homeowner to become a co-insurer when the home is insured for less than 80 percent of its replacement value.

REPLACEMENT COST PROVISION Homeowners' policies contain a provision that requires the homeowner to provide **co-insurance** when the dwelling unit is insured for less than 80 percent of replacement value. Replacement value is the cost of rebuilding the home from the foundation up. It should be approximately equal to the price of a similar new home minus the cost of the lot and foundation.

The following example shows how a co-insurance clause works. Suppose the replacement value of your home is $100,000. If your insurance coverage on the dwelling is at least $80,000, the insurer would pay the full cost of repairing

369

covered damages to the dwelling, up to the face amount of the policy. However, if your protection is for less than $80,000, you would receive less than full replacement cost. You would, in effect, become a co-insurer by having to pay the difference when repairing the structure.

Let's look at a specific example. Suppose a fire in the kitchen causes structural damage that would cost you $10,000 to repair. If you carry $50,000 of insurance on a home with $100,000 replacement value, you would fall below the 80 percent requirement. In this situation the amount you would receive from the insurance company would be calculated under the following formula:

$$\frac{\text{Amount of dwelling protection}}{80\% \times \text{replacement cost of dwelling}} \times \frac{\text{cost of damage at}}{\text{replacement cost}} = \text{insurance payout}$$

$$\frac{\$50,000}{80\% \times \$100,000} \times \$10,000 = \$6,250$$

The payout is reduced by the ratio of your actual protection to the 80 percent requirement. Thus, you would receive only $6,250.

There is one important exception to the above analysis. If the actual cash value of the loss is greater than the $6,250 calculated under the co-insurance formula, then the insurer would reimburse at actual cash value up to the policy limits. For example, if the actual cash value of structural damage to the kitchen, equal to replacement cost minus depreciation, is estimated at $8,000, you would receive $8,000 rather than $6,250. Notice that this reimbursement is still less than $10,000 replacement cost, the amount received by a comparable fully insured homeowner.

Co-insurance may seem like a scheme designed to cheat homeowners, but it actually serves a very good purpose. Most losses are for much less than the replacement value of the home. Without the co-insurance clause, some homeowners might be tempted to reduce insurance costs by carrying less than full coverage on the home, leaving them with inadequate coverage in the case of total destruction.

INFLATION GUARD ENDORSEMENT   With rises in the general price level, the cost of replacing your home should also increase. This means that unless you periodically increase the face amount of dwelling protection, your coverage will eventually fall below 80 percent of the replacement cost of the home. To protect against this, you can include an **inflation guard endorsement** that periodically increases the face amount of dwelling protection. The increase may either be set at an agreed-upon percentage or tied to an index of construction costs.

Be careful, because the inflation guard endorsement does not necessarily mean that you have the right amount of coverage. Even with the endorsement, it is still your responsibility to make sure that there is neither too much nor too little dwelling protection.

DEDUCTIBLE CLAUSE   A deductible clause limits payments to damages that exceed a given dollar loss. For example, a $100 deductible means that payments will be made only for damages exceeding $100, and then the amount of the payout will be reduced by $100. Under a $100 deductible, you would receive $400 back on a $500 loss. By including a deductible, the insurer eliminates the

Inflation guard endorsement: Periodically increases the face amount of dwelling protection to reflect rising market prices.

cost of handling many small claims. This saving can be passed on to the home-owner through lower insurance rates. Including deductibles in your policy is an excellent way of holding down your insurance costs.

Some policies contain a disappearing deductible. For example, the insurer might agree to pay 111 percent of the excess of any loss over $50, up to losses of $500. If you suffer a loss of $150, the insurer will pay you 111 percent of $100, or $111. If your loss is $500 or more, you will receive complete reimbursement.

MORTGAGE CLAUSE You will discover in the **mortgage clause** that payments for damages to the dwelling and surrounding structures are made to the mortga-gee, if the mortgagee is named in the policy. The mortgagee is the lender, not you. The lender may hold the money to pay for repairs or to pay off the loan if the house is not rebuilt.

OTHER INSURANCE AND THE APPORTIONMENT CLAUSE If you have more than one insurance policy, you will find that each will pay only for damages up to their proportionate share of coverage. The **apportionment clause** makes it impos-sible for you to collect more than 100 percent of your losses by having multiple policies.

Because of the significant cost advantage of having all your homeowners' pro-tection under one policy, you are not likely to want dual coverage. This clause is important, however, when you have additional coverage on a business conducted in the home. In this situation it may be unclear whether a particular loss is to be covered under your homeowners' insurance or your business insurance. Whoever pays, the apportionment clause makes sure you will not collect more than 100 percent of the value of the loss.

SUBROGATION CLAUSE Most insurance policies, both homeowners' and auto, contain a **subrogation clause** that places your right to sue for recovery after the insurer's. If the insurer pays you for a loss, it can then seek to recover its payments from the party who caused the harm. You are entitled to sue for and collect only amounts that exceed those you have received from the insurer. Likewise, the insurer cannot sue for or collect more than you were paid under the insurance coverage.

Property Coverage

Homeowners' policies contain two sections: Section I on property coverage and Section II on liability protection. The first section includes a discussion of your coverage for losses to the dwelling unit and your personal belongings. It states the method for determining reimbursement and the types of losses covered. Subsec-tions A, B, C, and D in Section I are organized by type of property loss and typically begin with a discussion of coverage on the dwelling.

COVERAGE A—DWELLING PROTECTION **Dwelling protection** generally pro-tects you against damage to the structure resulting from fire, lightning, civil com-motion, smoke, hail, vehicle damage, aircraft damage, riot, and explosion. Unless the dwelling has been unoccupied for the previous 30 days, you may also be covered for damage resulting from vandalism and malicious mischief. Loss from earthquake, flood, nuclear accident, and war will be specifically excluded.

Mortgage clause: Insurance payments for structural damage are made to the mortgage holder.

Apportionment clause: Apportions financial responsibility among multiple insurers so that the insured cannot collect more than 100 percent of the loss.

Subrogation clause: Places your right to sue after the insurer's.

Dwelling protection: Protects against structural damage to the home.

371

Property and
Liability
Insurance

The face amount of your dwelling protection is the most important number in the homeowners' policy. As stated previously, to avoid co-insurance payments, it should be set at or above 80 percent of the cost of rebuilding. The amount of dwelling protection is also important because most of your other property loss limits will be stated as a percentage of the amount of insurance carried on the dwelling.

COVERAGE B—APPURTENANT STRUCTURES Structures other than the dwelling unit are called **appurtenant structures.** They include the garage, the storage shed, and even the mailbox. These will usually be covered for losses up to 10 percent of the amount on the dwelling unit.

COVERAGE C—CONTENTS The loss of **unscheduled personal property**—items that are not specifically listed in the policy—from theft or damage at the home will generally be covered for about 50 percent of the dwelling coverage. This coverage is not as generous as it sounds. First, reimbursement is usually set at actual cash value, and second, there are much lower limits on specific valuables. Typical examples of coverage limits are $200 on money, coins, and numismatic property, and $1,000 on boats and boating equipment resulting from any loss. For loss of theft the limits are $1,000 on jewelry, watches, and fur; $2,500 on silverware, goldware, and pewterware; and $2,000 on guns. If your valuables exceed these limits, you can take out additional insurance coverage by attaching a personal property floater to your homeowners' policy.

One aspect of a homeowners' policy that most people overlook is the protection it provides away from home. If you read this subsection, you will likely find that your personal property away from home is covered for at least 10 percent of the value of the personal property on the premises.

COVERAGE D—LOSS OF USE This often-unnoticed subsection on additional living expenses can prove extremely helpful in event of serious loss. If a covered loss leaves your home uninhabitable, it will pay for the additional expenses necessary to retain your normal living standards. The limit on this might be expressed as 10 to 20 percent of dwelling protection prorated for the amount of time spent out of the house, or as a stated period of time over which additional expenses will be paid.

TOTALING UP THE COVERAGE It is unlikely that a single catastrophe would permit you to collect up to each of the previously stated limits. However, if such a disaster did occur, the total reimbursement could be considerably greater than the face amount of the homeowners' policy. On a policy with a face amount of $100,000 in dwelling protection, the maximum payout is as follows:

Dwelling	$100,000
Appurtenant structures (10%)	10,000
Unscheduled property on premises (50%)	50,000
Unscheduled property off premises (5%)	5,000
Additional living expenses (20%)	20,000
Total coverage	$185,000

In addition, you might also receive payment for the following incidentals.

Theft of Items from Cars. Surprisingly, your homeowners' policy provides an incentive for locking your car. Property taken from your car is covered only if there are signs of forced entry.

Credit Card and Check Forgery. Assuming you promptly notify the credit card company when you lose your card, you may be covered up to $1,000 against misuse of that card. Moreover, in addition to reimbursement for losses suffered through credit card or check forgery, the insurance company may also defend you in any suit demanding payment under these circumstances.

Debris Removal. The insurance company may pay the cost of removing property damaged under a covered loss.

Emergency Removal. If your property is damaged while you are removing it from the premises in order to avoid a covered peril, you may still be reimbursed. For example, suppose your roof is damaged by a covered loss, and you temporarily move your belongings to a storage garage to avoid damage to your personal property while the roof is being repaired. If, in the interim, the storage garage burns down and you lose your belongings, they will be covered the same as if they had been at your home.

Fire Department Charges. If your fire department charges for a service call, the insurance company will probably pay up to $250 of service charges.

Necessary Repairs After Loss. You have an obligation to protect your property from further damage after a loss. Reasonable expenses for temporary repairs, such as boarding up a broken window until it can be replaced, will probably be compensated.

Trees, Shrubs, Plants, and Lawns. When the covered loss causes damage to your landscaping, you may be reimbursed for up to 5 percent of the dwelling protection.

EXCLUSIONS ON PROPERTY LOSS COVERAGE The following classes of property are specifically excluded from contents coverage, either because they are nonpersonal in character or because they are more appropriately covered by other types of policies:

1. Articles described separately in a personal articles floater, or insured elsewhere
2. Animals, birds, or fish
3. Motorized land vehicles and electronic communication and sound devices attached to them
4. Aircraft and parts
5. Property of roomers, boarders, and tenants
6. Property in an apartment regularly rented to others
7. Property rented or held for rental to others
8. Business records
9. Credit cards and fund transfer cards, except as provided under additional coverages

Property and
Liability
Insurance

Liability Coverage

Liability coverage, explained in Section II of the homeowners' policy, protects you and your family from the financial harm your negligence causes others. The three components to this protection consist of personal liability insurance, medical payments insurance, and insurance against physical damage to the property of others.

COVERAGE E—PERSONAL LIABILITY The insurer will pay, up to the limits of protection, all legally obligated expenses for bodily injury or property damage, assuming you did not intentionally inflict them. In addition, the insurer will also pay defense and settlement costs if it decides to fight the payment in court. However, once the insurance company has paid up to the policy limits, it is no longer legally responsible for further damage payments or for the legal defense.

The standard limit under this section is $100,000. This is not much protection when your actions result in serious physical harm. For example, if you are sued for $150,000 and your liability coverage is for $100,000, the insurer might decide to pay $100,000 to the injured party, leaving you with the cost of defending against a potential $50,000 award.

COVERAGE F—MEDICAL PAYMENTS COVERAGE Minor injuries that occur on your property are covered by medical payments insurance, regardless of who is at fault. Off your premises it pays for minor injuries that are caused by you. It doesn't pay the medical bills for you or your family, only the medical bills of others.

Most policies limit payments to a relatively small amount, $500 to $1,000 per person. While this is not major dollar protection, it nevertheless serves a useful purpose by providing the means and incentive for timely medical treatment. This protects both you and the insurer. Immediate inspection and documentation of the injury may prevent the filing of larger claims resulting from exaggeration or delayed medical action.

DAMAGE TO THE PROPERTY OF OTHERS Similar to medical payments coverage, property liability insurance pays for minor property damage, regardless of who is at fault. The limits are $250 to $500 per occurrence.

EXCLUSIONS ON LIABILITY COVERAGE The homeowners' policy doesn't cover slander or libel, nor does it protect you against business-related liabilities. Professional practices need special malpractice insurance, and this need is generally recognized. Where problems occur, they usually have to do with defining a business. For example, if you take on an occasional baby-sitting job, you may or may not be covered under your homeowners' policy. However, if you regularly take in the neighbor's children for a fee, you probably will not be covered. If there is any question that your activities might constitute a business, you should check with your insurance agent.

If your child works part time delivering papers or mowing lawns, be sure your policy covers these activities. Most homeowners' policies will state that the busi-

Box 12.2
Simplifying Personal Finance

Protecting Your Valuables at School

Computers, jewelry, and television sets are among the valuable items that millions of college students have taken back to school with them.

But what happens if these possessions are stolen?

Most students' personal belongings are insured by their parents' homeowners' insurance policies, says Barbara Taylor, consumer consultant for the Insurance Information Institute, a New York-based industry group.

Some items, however, may require special coverage, she adds. Homeowners' policies usually cover property away from home, up to a limit of 10 percent of the contents (furniture and clothing, etc.) coverage. For example, if the parents' house is insured for $100,000, the contents coverage typically would be $50,000 and the coverage for property moved to a college dorm would be $5,000.

"Talk with your agent," advises Taylor, "if you'll be moving such high-ticket items as jewelry or watches worth more than $1,000. Since coverage for theft of these items may be limited, consider an inexpensive 'personal articles floater' to get full coverage."

Anyone taking a computer to college also should check with the family's insurance agent, she suggests. Policies usually cover home computers, but you may need a "rider," or special coverage, to protect the computer on campus.

If the student is moving to an off-campus apartment, however, the off-premises homeowners' coverage may not apply, says Taylor. Some insurance companies require a separate renter's policy since they consider the student no longer a part of the household.

Renter's policies are inexpensive. They cost about $125 a year and provide "plenty" of property and liability protection.

Education is also beneficial when it comes to protecting valuables. Many schools offer crime awareness seminars that give students preventive measures as well as information on what to do in case something gets stolen.

Finally, students shouldn't overlook protecting personal items such as books, leather jackets, and expensive bags. While these items can't exactly be insured, students can avoid leaving them unattended in such public places as the student snack bar and the library. "[Students] think they are only going to be gone for a few seconds, and then when they return, their things are gone," says Gary Rus, crime prevention officer at USC in Los Angeles, California.

Rus suggests students put their name and the security department's phone number on the inside of books and jackets. "That way if somebody finds it, we'll be able to get on it right away," he says.

Following are some tips to college students for protecting their property in a dormitory room or apartment:

- Don't go anywhere without locking your door.

- Engrave identification numbers on TVs, stereos, and computers. Marked items help police identify recovered property.

- Don't store money or blank checks in obvious places such as desk drawers.

- Don't leave jewelry on top of the bureau.

- Buy a smoke detector if your room doesn't have one.

- Don't prop open outside doors if you are expecting visitors. Offer to meet them outside at a certain time, instead of endangering yourself and your roommates.

SOURCE: Cliff Smith, "Protecting Your School Valuables," Gannet News Service, September 17, 1991.

ness exclusion does not apply to occasional and part-time business activities of an insured person who is under 21 years of age.

Generally, your liability coverage will not extend to accidents in your automobile or aircraft. It will cover boating accidents on boats having less than a stated horsepower and less than a given length. For these exclusions you will need specialized insurance.

Policy Format

The present homeowners' policy took its standard form in the 1950s. Today there are established formats into which almost all policies can be categorized. The coverage under each is outlined in Figure 12.1.

Basic Format (HO-1) provides the least coverage, insuring against the 11 most common perils on a named peril basis. Only a few of these policies are sold, because most homeowners correctly demand more adequate protection.

Broad Form (HO-2) also provides named perils coverage for both dwelling and personal property. However, it is broader than HO-1, including seven additional named perils. It is the second most popular homeowners' insurance package.

Special Form (HO-3) is now the most widely purchased form and is highly recommended for most homeowners. It provides all risks coverage on the dwelling and named perils coverage on the personal property. The typical excepted perils on the all risks coverage are flood, earthquake, war, and nuclear accident.

Contents Broad Form (HO-4) is for renters. The dwelling is not covered because it is the landlord's responsibility. Coverage on personal property is for the same named perils as under HO-2. There is also additional living expense coverage equal to 20 percent of the limit on personal property, and protection on tenant improvements to the property equal to 10 percent of the personal property coverage.

Comprehensive Form (HO-5) provides all risks coverage on both the dwelling and personal property. It differs from HO-3 in that HO-3 includes only named perils coverage for personal property. The Comprehensive Form has the most protection and is the most expensive of all policies. In place of HO-5, some insurance companies provide HO-3 with Comprehensive Endorsement HO-15.

Condominium Form (HO-6) is similar to renters' form HO-4. Like the landlord, the condominium association usually provides insurance for the building and other structures. This may not cover, however, the condominium owners' additions and improvements to the dwelling unit. Therefore, the Condominium Form covers the owners' interest in additions to the dwelling unit at replacement cost up to a set limit. Furthermore, additional living expenses are paid for up to 40 percent of the coverage on personal property, instead of 20 percent. The policy also provides for endorsements in the event the owner is assessed for property or liability losses not covered under the association's insurance.

Older Home Form (HO-8) is for homes with actual cash value substantially below their replacement cost. For many older homes, the cost of replacement may be many times current actual cash value. All other forms require dwelling protection at 80 percent of replacement cost in order to avoid problems under the co-insurance clause. This would require owners of certain older homes to carry exorbitant amounts of dwelling protection. In addition, the insurance companies would have to charge high rates, because whenever the potential payout on the policy is substantially above actual cash value, there is a tremendous incentive for arson.

With Older Home insurance, the dwelling is insured for its market value. With the potential for arson reduced, owners of older homes can obtain reasonably priced insurance. The ideas is to be able to return the dwelling to a serviceable condition, but not necessarily with materials of like kind and quality.

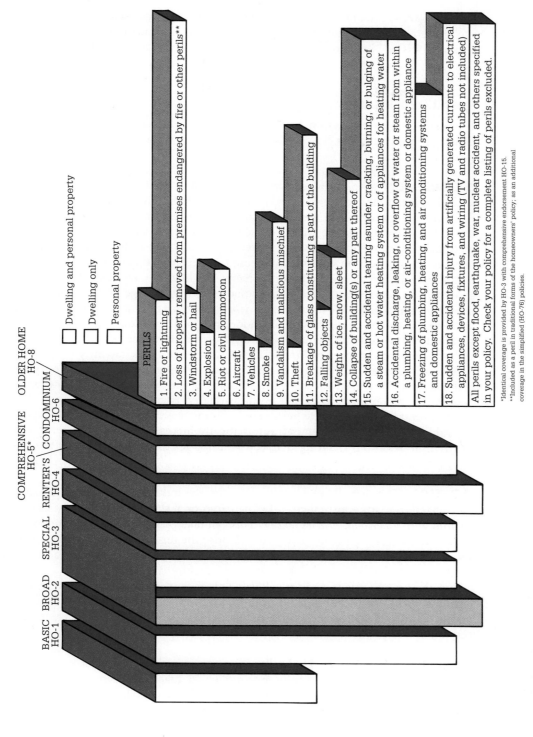

FIGURE 12.1

Perils against which properties are insured under the various homeowners' policies.
(Source: Nancy Golonka, *How to Protest What's Yours*, Insurance Information Institute, 1983, p. 293.)

Property and Liability Insurance

Comprehensive Endorsement Form (HO-15) This provision extends the coverage offered under HO-3 by providing all risks coverage on contents. In combination with HO-3, it provides the same coverage as HO-5.

Specialized Insurance

To close a gap in protection from either a standard exclusion or an insurance liability limit, you might consider some of the following additions to your homeowners' policy.

Endorsement: An amendment to the basic policy extending or changing the type of insurance coverage.

ENDORSEMENT An **endorsement** is a paragraph that amends the original policy. It is added to make the standard policy more closely fit your individual needs. For example, coverage on personal property is often stated as a percentage of dwelling protection. If the standard policy states that personal property is covered up to 50 percent of dwelling protection, and you feel that your belongings need greater protection, you may increase the percentage with an endorsement.

Endorsements may also be used to change the kind of coverage. Most policies agree to pay actual cash value on personal property damage. With an endorsement for "replacement cost coverage," you could change that. The perils insured against may also be changed with an endorsement. As previously mentioned, the standard policy excludes damage resulting from earthquakes. At additional cost, an endorsement can provide financial protection from this calamity.

A small business in your home might also be covered by business pursuits endorsement. However, for anything substantial you will need a separate business insurance policy to cover all business-related risks.

Of interest to most homeowners is an "inflation guard" endorsement. As housing values rise, this endorsement automatically increases your coverage. It is a worthwhile addition, ensuring that you will not get caught short under the co-insurance clause.

Floater: Schedules property for specific coverage.

FLOATERS The term **floater** is left over from the industry's early days, when it specialized in marine insurance. Like the cargo on a ship, your valuables can be insured with a *personal articles floater*. This can take the form of a separate policy or an endorsement to the original policy. Under the unscheduled property coverage, fairly low limits are set on payments for damaged or stolen valuables. If you need coverage beyond these limits, you can acquire it with a floater.

In a floater, the property is *scheduled*. This means it is described in terms of type and quality, and its value is supported by a report from a professional appraiser or bill of sale. Personal articles floaters usually cover all risks with no deductible.

Umbrella coverage: Provides catastrophic protection that begins where basic coverage ends.

AN UMBRELLA POLICY **Umbrella coverage** is written over an underlying homeowners' policy and a family auto policy. It takes over when the liability limits on these policies are reached. For example, if your homeowners' policy covers liability losses up to $100,000, an umbrella policy can protect you from losses in excess of $100,000, up to $1 million or more.

An umbrella policy is often written on a "following form" basis, meaning it will follow the form of the underlying coverage on which it was written. Consequently, you will be insured for the same perils as in the underlying policy. Some umbrella policies, however, will provide for extended perils coverage along with increased limits.

National Flood Insurance Program: A federal program that insures homeowners located in flood plains against flood damage.

FLOOD INSURANCE   Because flood damage is an excluded peril under homeowners' policies, you will have to rely on the federal government's **National Flood Insurance Program** for protection. If you are thinking of buying a home in a potential flood area, you should check to see whether you can obtain this insurance before you purchase. The government reports that people living in areas subject to flooding are about 26 times more likely to be flooded than to have their homes burn.

The community must participate in the program before individual homeowners are able to purchase government flood insurance through local insurance agents. Community participation is a two-stage process. In the first stage you can buy only limited amounts of insurance. In the second stage the amount of protection is more liberal. Owners of property in a flood zone who have a federally guaranteed home mortgage are required to carry flood insurance in a participating community. Many lenders fail to advise property owners about this requirement. To find out what the situation is in your area, check with the insurance agent for your homeowners' policy. The federally backed policies are provided through most property and casualty insurers.

Selecting Homeowners' Insurance

Now that you understand the basics of homeowners' coverage, you should be able to compare policies and select an insurer using the following steps:

STEP 1   You can start the selection process by first determining what and how much insurance you need. An insurance agent will help you determine replacement cost based upon type of construction and building costs in your locality. You can arrive at a similar cost figure yourself by calling the local builders' association for current construction costs per square foot and then multiplying this number by your square footage. However, if your home is nonstandard or has a potential market price of over $200,000, you might want a more reliable estimate of replacement cost. For this you should hire a professional appraiser. Two organizations providing competent appraisers are the American Institute of Real Estate Appraisers and the Society of Real Estate Appraisers.

STEP 2   Decide on the type of coverage and the required additions to that coverage. For most owners of single-family homes, Special Form HO-3 is probably the most appropriate. However, those with unique older homes, or with especially valuable personal property, should respectively consider HO-8 and HO-15.

Your analysis of required additional coverage can begin with an inventory of your personal property. Review the sample limits in the section on unscheduled property coverage. If it appears that you own valuables exceeding those limits, you will need an appraisal of current actual cash value in order to take out a scheduled property floater. Next, review the discussion of specialized insurance, and make a list of what endorsements or special coverage you feel are necessary.

STEP 3 Contact an agent from a major insurer. Explain to the agent how much insurance you think you need, what format you find most desirable, and what additions you think are necessary. No doubt the agent will have some recommended changes or additions. You should consider these and accept the ones you believe are worthwhile. Finally, get a price on the total package, including endorsements and floaters.

You don't want to purchase the policy at this point. Market studies have found significant differences in the cost of similar policies. It is recommended you talk to at least two other insurers, and get a price on the same policy you discussed with the first agent. This shouldn't be too difficult. As stated previously, homeowners' policies are fairly standard, so an HO-3 from one company will be almost identical to an HO-3 from another company.

STEP 4 The last step before purchasing is to check out the insurance company and the insurance agent. You want the company to be there when you need help, and you want to be justly paid when you have a covered loss. The financial condition of the insurer can be checked out in *Best Key's Rating Guide on Property and Casualty Insurers*, available in most public libraries. This guide summarizes each insurer's financial stability with a simple letter grade. Preferably, you should go with a company having an A or A+ rating, avoiding any company with less than a straight A rating. You are purchasing insurance to lower your risks; you don't want to gamble on the insurer's continued existence.

Checking out how well a company deals with its clients is a more difficult task. You should consider the experience of any friends who have applied for reimbursement on covered losses within the last few years. In addition, you should contact your state's insurance commission to see if they have any information on the companies in which you are interested. In some states the insurance commission will supply you with the number of customer complaints by company.

Some companies sell their policies through company employees called **direct writers.** Other companies use **independent agents,** who work on commission and sell policies for two or more companies. If you buy from an independent agent, this individual will handle your claim. A company with direct writers will have a separate claims department. Obviously, the character and reliability of the particular agent who sells you the policy are more important when you are dealing with an independent. Therefore, check out the independent with the Better Business Bureau and with previous clients.

Companies that use direct writers save on selling costs, a saving that can be passed on to you in lower premiums. In addition, survey results from *Consumer Reports* indicate that consumer satisfaction was not appreciably different for companies using direct writers and companies using independent agents. This suggests you might do better purchasing through a direct writer. However, these surveys test satisfaction, and not expectations. Consumers using independent agents may have expected and received better service. If you value personalized service and have found an independent agent who is considerate of your needs, he or she may be worth a few dollars more in premiums.

STEP 5 After you purchase the policy, be sure to conduct an annual review of your insurance needs, updating your dwelling protection and acquiring new ap-

Direct writer: An insurance agent who is an employee of an insurance company and who works exclusively for that company.

Independent agent: An insurance agent who works on commission for two or more insurance companies.

praisals as market prices change. If the insurance company needlessly increases your rates, try comparison shopping again.

Making Sure You Collect on a Loss

Having adequate insurance coverage is not enough to ensure that you will receive appropriate compensation in the event of property loss. Policy holders with identical losses and identical coverage may receive different levels of reimbursement simply because each approaches the claim process differently. Making good on a claim requires documentation, notification, and evaluation.

DOCUMENTATION   The first step in filing a claim should be taken before the loss occurs. The loss must be documented. Of course, doing so is a lot easier while you still have your property in good condition.

When you apply for scheduled property coverage with a floater, you will be required to document the property's actual cash value. Be sure to update the appraisals whenever market prices change, including both upward and downward movements. During periods of rising prices, an outdated appraisal will provide you with less-than-adequate insurance coverage. Alternatively, during falling prices, you may be paying for too much protection. The insurer is unlikely to pay more than replacement cost; therefore, too much insurance is a waste of money. It is also a good idea to photograph your valuables, with closeups of any identifying characteristics, such as trademarks, copyrights, and signatures.

On unscheduled property coverage, evidence of worth need be supplied only after the loss. You are entirely responsible for documenting and describing your loss to the insurance company. To do this, you should keep an inventory of your belongings, including a description of each item that indicates all identifying marks, the original purchase price, and the date of purchase. For the more expensive items you should include a copy of the bill of sale in your records. While taking inventory, you should check for items that might exceed the recovery limits on your homeowners' policy. Consider scheduling these goods with a floater. Take photos of every room in your house, or better yet, make a videotape tour of your home. Now take all of this documentation and store it in a safe place away from the home. If your house burns down, you don't want this destroyed with it.

NOTIFICATION   When a property loss occurs, you should first contact the relevant civil authority, then take whatever steps are needed to protect your property from further damage. Your failure to notify the police or a credit card company in the event of theft may invalidate your coverage. Next, contact your insurer. Your agent should be able to inform you immediately whether you are covered, in addition to supplying information on what you should do next. Insurance agents are used to dealing with tragedies. At a time like this, the support they can provide in seeking alternative shelter or assistance with repairs and debris removal can be invaluable.

Next, before anything is repaired or removed, be sure you have fully documented the loss. Take photos of the damage. If you followed the previous advice, you will now have a set of before-and-after snapshots. Also, request copies of any police or fire reports on the damage, and get the names and addresses of any witnesses to the mishap.

EVALUATION   If the insurer feels your claim may be covered, an adjuster will be sent to verify the claim and determine the amount of loss. You should supply the adjuster with copies of all the evidence of loss you have collected. Under most circumstances, a settlement offer will be made promptly. Don't be too hasty to accept. The insurance company's objective in making a prompt settlement offer is probably honorable and good business practice. They believe that the client needs immediate help and will judge the company by how quickly the representatives respond to that need. But it may be a while before you fully realize all that you have lost. Take the time to review your inventory of damaged items and to search out the replacement cost on these goods. Because actual cash value is equal to replacement cost minus depreciation, the current market price of a similar good will play an important part in determining the insurance payout under either replacement cost reimbursement or actual cash value reimbursement.

Let the adjuster make the first settlement offer, and request an explanation of how the amount was determined. If you feel the offer is too low or you are denied payment on what you believe is a covered loss, you may state your case to the adjuster and ask that the settlement offer be reconsidered. If you still can't agree, you can demand that the settlement be submitted to arbitration. However, this is not costless. You and the insurer will be required to split the cost of the arbitrators' fees. Obviously, you should demand this only if the prospective benefits from arbitration exceed your share of the cost.

One less costly but potentially less effective action is to write your state's insurance commission. They are not likely to take action on an individual complaint. But if yours is one of many, the state commission may decide to look into the problem.

You may be able to deduct any unreimbursed casualty losses on your personal income tax return. Only sizable losses, however, are likely to lead to any significant tax savings. The rules for reducing your taxable income by the amount of the loss are quite strict. First, you can only reduce your taxable income by the amount by which the loss exceeds 10 percent of your adjusted gross income. Second, the loss must be assessed at market value and not replacement cost.

Automobile Insurance

Automobile insurance is meant to protect you against three risks: (1) bodily harm and property damage to others from negligent operation of the vehicle; (2) personal injury to you, your family, and guests riding in your car; and (3) damage or loss of your car due to fire, theft, or collision. Of the three, the first has the potential for the greatest financial loss.

Who Needs Auto Insurance Coverage?

The simple answer is that if you drive a car, you do. Your chances of being involved in a serious, fatal accident are less than 1 percent (see Figure 12.2). However, you have about a 75 percent chance of being in some kind of car

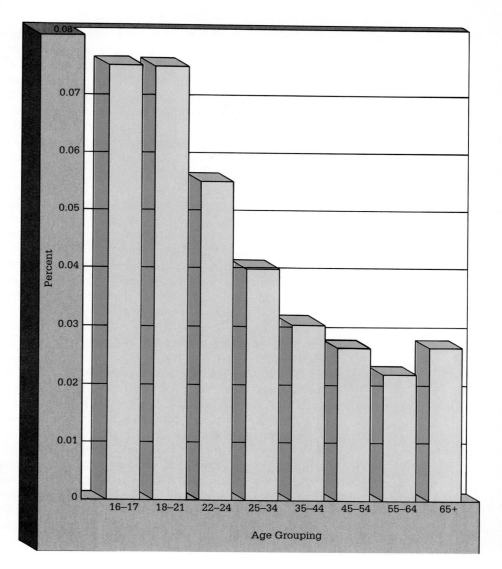

FIGURE 12.2

Probability of a licensed
driver being involved in
a fatal accident.
(Source: *Statistical
Abstract of the United
States, 1990*, Table
1041, p. 608.)

accident over the next five years, and if you are an unmarried male driver under
age 25, the odds are even higher. In most states, liability insurance is mandatory.
However, regardless of state requirements, it is just downright foolish to take a
car on the road without adequate coverage. One accident can result in hundreds
of thousands of dollars in claims against you and your estate.

Coverage Under the Family Auto Policy

The standard policy covers you and other family members living with you. It also
protects others when driving one of your covered cars, and you and your family
when driving someone else's auto.

The **Family Auto Policy** and the more recently introduced **Personal Auto Policy** follow a standard format used by most insurers. Policy comparisons are fairly easy, because coverage is usually divided into identical parts listed in the same order. However, auto policies tend to be written in stilted language and are difficult to read. If your policy contains the terms *first party*, *second party*, and *third party*, just remember that the first party is you and the second party is the insurer. If you collide with another car, the driver of that car becomes the third party. Claims by you or your passengers are first-party claims. Those by the driver or passengers in the other vehicle are third-party claims.

PART A—LIABILITY

The most important component of your auto insurance is liability coverage. It operates much the same as liability coverage under the homeowners' policy, except that it applies only to damages resulting from an auto accident.

The Family Auto Policy has a **split liability limit.** If your policy has one, you will see the liability limits presented in the following format: 100/300/10. The first number indicates the maximum amount the insurer will pay for bodily injury to a single person. The second number is the maximum amount the insurer will pay for all injuries sustained in a single accident, and the last is the insurer's liability limit for property damage in a given accident. For example, suppose there were two riders in the other car. One sustained $210,000 in bodily injury and the other $80,000 in bodily injury. The insurer would reimburse the first rider for $100,000 and the second rider for the full $80,000 sought, since total payments are under the $300,000 limit for a single accident. In addition, the insurer would pay for damage to the other vehicle up to $10,000. You would be responsible for the excess liability, which would include $110,000 to the first rider and any property damage exceeding $10,000.

The Personal Auto Policy has a **single liability limit.** This means the insurer will pay up to this limit for each accident, regardless of how this amount may be divided among the injured and for property damage. When the single liability limit on one policy is the same as the limit per accident on a split liability policy, the single liability limit provides the better coverage. In the previous example, a single liability limit of $300,000 would have left you with little or no excess liability.

You may find that the limits on your policy will depend upon which state you happen to be driving in. Where state laws require higher limits than those shown on your policy, the state requirements should apply. However, you may be required to pay the insurer the difference between your liability limits and the amount the company pays out under a given state's liability laws.

In addition to damages up to your policy limits, the insurer will also cover the cost of defending you in a lawsuit. This coverage will include such supplementary costs as legal and defense fees, premiums on appeal bonds, and the cost of bail bonds up to about $250. When in court, you may receive payments for up to about $50 a day in lost earnings. However, you can collect these payments only so long as the insurer has not paid out damages up to the liability limits. Once the company has reached that point, perhaps through an out-of-court settlement with the injured party, then further legal costs are all yours.

Don't try to skimp on this area of auto coverage. Many states require you to have at least 10/20/5. This level is much too low to serve as a standard for your own needs. Middle-income families should have at least 100/300/25, or preferably 300/500/25. You will find that a relatively small percentage increase in your annual premium can substantially increase the liability limits. Those in an upper-income bracket are especially vulnerable to lawsuits and should consider an umbrella policy raising liability protection on both the homeowners' and auto policy to $1 million or more.

A liability limit of $300,000 may sound like a lot of protection. It actually isn't. The damages suffered by a severely injured person who is unable to work can easily exceed this figure. You might suggest you don't need this much insurance because you don't have $300,000 in assets to protect. But the higher your protection, the less likely it is that you will have any excess liability above your insurance coverage. Moreover, court awards can be based on more than just your present assets; they can also be based upon your future earning potential. With inadequate liability coverage, you could be forced to sell everything you own and to make continuing payments out of your future income.

PART B—MEDICAL PAYMENTS   Injuries to you, your family, and guests riding in your car are insured under **medical payments coverage,** regardless of who is at fault. The coverage also applies when you or your family are riding in other vehicles, or when one of your family members is hit by a car while walking. The typical limits on payments are low, between $500 to $5,000 per person. It is not meant to take the place of a good health insurance plan. In fact, if you have good health insurance, you should consider holding limits in this part to a minimum. The only situation your health insurance does not cover is injury to a guest rider. However, your liability insurance, or that of the other driver, may cover the guest's injuries.

Some companies will include death and disability insurance under the medical payments section. A special life insurance or disability policy would take care of these contingencies with broader coverage than would a policy that covers only auto accidents.

Medical payments coverage: Covers minor medical expenses for those riding in your car during an accident.

PART C—UNINSURED MOTORISTS

Uninsured motorists coverage is worthwhile low-cost protection, about $11 per year for a policy with 25/50/10 limits. In most states, damage to your auto is not covered under uninsured motorists. It primarily covers bodily injury to you or your family members from either an uninsured driver or a hit-and-run driver. The coverage also applies when riding in other cars or walking. However, for the policy to pay off, the other driver must be at fault.

You may want to carry this protection even if your state requires auto liability insurance, since there is no way the state can ensure that every driver is financially responsible. The need for this coverage is apparent when you consider that over 15 percent of drivers do not carry auto insurance. However, some financial planners advise clients do without uninsured motorist coverage if they have adequate health and disability insurance.

In many areas you may purchase supplementary **underinsured motorists coverage.** This operates in the same manner as uninsured motorists, except that when the other motorist is insured for less than the damages, your policy pays for the difference up to specified limits.

PART D—DAMAGE TO YOUR AUTO

Part D consists of two separate components, collision and other than collision. **Collision coverage** pays for damage to your car in a collision, regardless of who is at fault. If the other driver is responsible for damages, your insurer will seek reimbursement, and refund the deductible if it is successful. **Other than collision coverage,** previously called comprehensive auto coverage, provides all risks coverage on your car. Specifically included are such perils as fire, theft, falling objects, windstorm, flood, earthquake, and collision with an animal. Both coverages carry deductibles, and under either, the insurer has the option of paying for repairs or paying you for the actual cash value of a similar auto.

Because the actual cash value on older cars is small, it is generally recommended that you not purchase property damage insurance on cars five years or older. The premiums do not justify the minimal benefits in case of loss. With newer cars, you can hold down your premiums by including higher deductibles. Again, the optimal strategy is to take on the small risks yourself and use the savings to transfer the big risks.

EXCLUSIONS

Most policies will exclude noninstalled sound and CB equipment from theft coverage. The chances of such accessories being stolen are just too high. You might consider covering these with a floater on your homeowners' policy.

A few other common exceptions are important to your personal liability coverage. Some are clear-cut, and others are not so obvious. If you think you might be subject to any of the following exclusions, you should discuss the matter with your insurance agent.

- You are not covered if the accident was intentional.
- You are not covered when you are driving someone else's car without permission.

- You are not covered when driving a car you own, if it is not listed on your policy. However, when you trade in a listed car for another, your old insurance will cover the new car for a 30-day grace period, during which the insurance company should be notified of the purchase.
- You are not covered when you are carrying passengers or property for a fee, except in the case of carpools.
- You are not covered under your family auto policy when driving a motorcycle.
- You are not covered if you are driving a car that is not yours but is made available to you on a "furnished and available" basis, such as a company car.
- You are not covered when driving a noninsured car of a live-in relative.
- You are not covered by the family auto policy when driving a rental car unless you are a "named insured." Both the individual whose name appears on the declaration page and the resident spouse are named insureds. The standard family auto policy covers the named insured when driving any "owned or nonowned automobile." Resident relatives are covered only when driving an "owned or nonowned private passenger automobile."

The Cost of Auto Insurance

A. M. Best Co. reports that in 1988 the average auto premium on a passenger vehicle was $518. This represented a significant increase in auto premiums over those paid in previous years. Using all other prices on consumer goods as a benchmark, we can state that between 1982 and 1988, auto insurance premiums increased at three times the rate of price increase on all other consumer items. No doubt a large part of the increase in premiums was due to the higher cost of claims. Recent changes in claims cost indexes published by A. M. Best Co. are illustrated in Figure 12.3.

ROLLBACKS Many states have responded to this situation be enacting programs designed to hold back the rising costs of premiums and claims. In California, voters in 1988 passed Proposition 103, which attempted to mandate a 20 percent reduction in insurance premiums. The California Supreme Court has since decided that a 20 percent rollback may be excessive and therefore limited rollbacks to the point where the insurance company would earn no more than a fair return on its investments. The regulators are now trying to decide just what is a fair return.

No-fault insurance: Allows policy holders to recover financial losses from their own insurer, regardless of who is at fault.

Verbal threshold: Injured individuals may sue for reimbursement for physical injuries that satisfy this definition.

Monetary threshold: Injured individuals may sue for medical expenses that exceed this amount.

NO-FAULT INSURANCE Other states have attempted to hold down the cost of insurance by introducing no-fault plans. A **no-fault insurance** plan is one that allows policy holders to recover financial losses from their own insurer, regardless of who is at fault. In return for receiving reimbursement from your own insurer, there may be restrictions placed upon your right to sue. You retain the right to sue only when your physical injuries are severe according to a **verbal threshold,** or your medical expenses exceed a **monetary threshold.** By eliminating the costly

Property and
Liability
Insurance

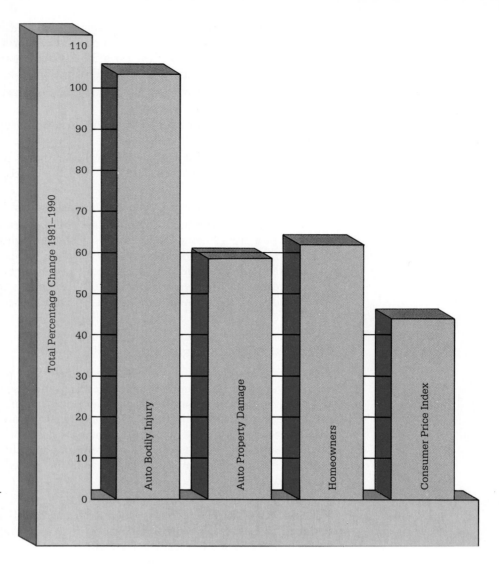

FIGURE 12.3

Percentage increase in
the cost of claims, 1981–
1990. (Source: *Best's
Review, Property &
Casualty Edition*, May
1991, p. 78.)

and timely determination of who is at fault in most accidents, no-fault insurance
is meant to provide lower insurance premiums.

No-fault insurance has not always worked as intended. Twenty-five states, the
District of Columbia, and Puerto Rico have now adopted no-fault laws. But in
only 14 of these states are there thresholds that limit the right to sue. Nonexisting
or low monetary thresholds, such as $400 in Connecticut, can result in wide-
spread first-party payments for small claims, and costly legal suits on all others.
New Jersey, a no-fault state, led the nation in auto premiums in 1989, with an
average premium of over $1,000 per car.

Nevada, Pennsylvania, and Georgia have all abandoned the no-fault experiment after drivers in those states experienced sharp increases in premiums. Insurance companies, however, continue to believe that no-fault insurance can be a
success if properly written. They are generally lobbying for changes in no-fault

Rental Car: A Collision Damage Waiver May Be Unnecessary

In most states, if you rent a car, the rental agent will attempt to sell you a collision damage waiver (CDW), also called a loss damage waiver. It looks like auto insurance, but it isn't. It is actually a waiver of the rental firm's right to charge you for damage to the rental car. Coverage under the waiver is typically excluded under a number of circumstances, such as reckless driving or use by other than the authorized driver. The cost for this limited protection can be very high, from $9 to $15 a day, which totals from $3,285 to $5,475 over a 365-day year.

If you don't purchase the collision damage waiver, you could be held liable for the full value of the rental car. Nevertheless, most people don't need this high-cost protection. The Insurance Information Institute reports that about 60 percent of auto insurance companies extend the collision coverage on your auto policy to rental cars. This extended coverage typically applies so long as you do not drive a rental car more than about one month out of the year. If you do plan to drive a rental car for a longer period, or your auto policy does not cover rental cars, you can purchase temporary short-term rental coverage from an auto insurance company at much less than the cost of a CDW.

The use of a credit card to rent a car can also eliminate the need for a collision damage waiver. Certain American Express, Master Cards, and Visa cards automatically provide collision protection when the rental is charged on their credit card. This coverage is secondary protection, covering any damage not paid for by your auto insurance company.

Car rental agents are not likely to inform you of this alternative protection. When Public Interest Research Groups surveyed 111 rental agencies, only nine agents suggested that they might be covered by their own auto insurance, while only five mentioned that similar coverage might be provided by a credit card.

Rental agencies are also likely to sell you two other types of protection you probably don't need, personal accident insurance (PAI) and personal effects coverage (PEC). PAI costs from $1.50 to $4.00 per day and insures against death and at least part of your medical expenses. If you have adequate life and health insurance, you don't need this additional protection. PEC at a daily average cost of $1.50 insures items in the car against theft or damage. This is in most cases already covered under your homeowners' policy.

The promotion of such high-cost, and in many cases unnecessary, protection has prodded governmental action. More than 20 states have passed laws that regulate the cost of the collision damage waiver, and in New York and Illinois they have been prohibited.

Rep. Cardiss Collins of Illinois has been leading the effort to get the U.S. Congress to adopt a similar ban. The legislation would make the rental car companies responsible for any damage over $100. For reckless driving and other specified situations, however, the renter may still be held liable for damage to the vehicle. Several rental car companies have lobbied against the bill, arguing that if it is adopted, future damage costs will drive them out of business. But not all rental companies are against the bill. In fact, several large companies favor a ban.

A spokesman for Hertz believes that collision damage waivers hurt the industry. Their use allows some companies to offer artificially low prices in advertisements because of the profits they make on CDWs. For example, a car rented for $89 a week had a CDW costing $13 a day. That is $2 a week more than you pay to rent the car.

Personal injury protection (PIP): Mandatory coverage in no-fault states that allows you to collect expenses for personal injury from your own insurer, regardless of fault.

laws to set verbal thresholds that restrict all but the severely injured from entering the courtroom. A study conducted by the Insurance Research Council found that states with a high threshold (Florida, Hawaii, Minnesota, and New York) were more successful in holding down increases in auto injury costs.

Although the required minimum amount of coverage varies, in all no-fault states you are required to carry **personal injury protection (PIP).** This permits you to recover medical and hospital expenses, lost wages, and other injury-related expenses up to your policy limits from your own insurer, regardless of fault. However, because lawsuits are still possible, in most of these same states you also must carry personal liability protection.

A sometimes confusing point is that in all but one state, Michigan, no-fault does not cover property damage. Consequently, you will be able to collect only for damage to your car if either you collect from the driver at fault or you collect under your collision insurance.

Factors Determining Cost

The cost of your insurance policy will depend upon your risk class. It is based upon factors over which you have some control, such as your driving record, and others over which you have no control, such as your age. If other drivers in your age group are accident prone, you are going to be charged more for insurance, independently of how good or bad a driver you happen to be. This may sound discriminatory, and in a sense it is. However, an efficient system of insurance requires the assignment of probabilities to groups of events. The insurance company must be able to discriminate, based upon past experience, between apparent high-risk groups and low-risk groups.

Individual auto insurance premiums are determined in a two-stage process. First, each state is divided into territories, and each territory is assigned a base rate dependent on risk factors and costs within that region. Next, the base rate is multiplied by a value that is based upon the risks associated with the personal characteristics of the insured. Your risk classification will taken into account each of the following factors: your age, sex, marital status, educational level, driving record, and even the kind of car you drive.

When discounts are offered (see Table 12.1), they are figured from the base rate, not from the individual auto insurance premium. A young male driver, for example, might receive a 10 percent discount for having taken driver education. If his base rate is $200 and his annual premium is $760, his discount would be $20, not $152.

DRIVING RECORD   One factor over which you definitely do have some control is your driving record. A chargeable accident (basically, one that is your fault) or a serious driving violation will increase your premiums by 40 percent or more. A history of such behavior can cause your rates to double and may result in a cancelling of your policy. You will then have to purchase very expensive insurance from a company specializing in high-risk drivers or from the *shared* market

TABLE 12.1 • Typical Discounts Offered by Auto Insurers

Discounts Offered for Cars with the Following Features	Discounts Offered for Insureds with the Following Characteristics
Anti-locking brake system Anti-theft devices Automatic seat belts or air bags High-level brake light	Away-at-school driver Car-pool driver Driver training Good driving record Good student record Mature driver Multi-car household Multi-policy household Non-smoking driver Retired driver

in your state. In this market, which is also called the *assigned risk* market, your policy is placed in a pool with those of other high-risk drivers. The insurance companies agree to jointly share the cost and risk of providing for the insurance needs of these drivers.

CAR MAKE AND MODEL It is obvious that a car requiring more expensive repairs will carry higher rates for property damage coverage than other vehicles. What is not so obvious is that certain cars will carry higher rates for liability coverage and collision because the chances of you, your passengers, and others being seriously injured in this particular car are greater.

The relative mix of age groups driving a particular car should affect that car's risk exposure. However, even after we consider that factor, some cars are just more accident prone than others. The insurance companies have responded by providing discounts for cars in low-risk groups and surcharges for cars in high-risk groups. The next time you think about buying a car, it is probably wise to check with your insurance agent to find out how your planned purchase ranks. The insurance saving on an alternate purchase might more than outweigh any saving on purchase price.

Before, At, and After the Accident

The odds are overwhelming that you will be involved in at least one auto accident. Accordingly, having the correct coverage and understanding what you should and should not do can prove extremely rewarding.

BEFORE THE ACCIDENT Adequate liability protection is a must. After reading the above discussion on the Family Auto Policy, you should have a good idea of the other coverages that are needed. Talk over your needs with an agent from one of the major auto insurers. To help in your comparison shopping, you might fill out a worksheet like that in Figure 12.4, listing the kind, amount, and cost of each coverage. Request those discounts listed in Table 12.1 that appear applicable and get price quotes from at least two other insurers.

You probably already realize that there can be significant cost differences for similar policies from different auto insurers. Therefore, comparison shopping should prove worthwhile and not much trouble. As with homeowners' insurance, most auto companies sell a standardized policy, making it easy to compare features and price. Moreover, it may be wise to shop for both homeowners' and auto insurance at the same time, since some companies provide a multiple-policy discount when both are purchased.

Checking with your state department of insurance can also prove helpful. It may be able to provide some background information on insurers in your state. A few states, such as Pennsylvania and Massachusetts, even publish pricing guides listing premiums charged by specific insurers.

AT THE ACCIDENT If you are driving a car involved in a collision, you must stop the vehicle immediately. Do not, however, leave it in a position that creates a traffic hazard and causes another accident. Give your name and address, and the registration number of the vehicle involved, to the other driver, any injured persons, and the arriving police officer. Obtain the names and addresses of all persons involved in the accident, and witnesses to the accident. Furthermore, get the name of the arriving policy officer, and obtain a copy of the officer's accident report. (See Figure 12.5.)

Make notes of the circumstances concerning the accident, including the position of the cars before and after the accident, traffic signs, road and weather condition, and road obstacles. Step off the skid points to measure them, and locate the point of collision. If you have a camera with you, photograph the damage and the accident scene.

Assist the investigating officer by providing all factual information when requested. Do not offer any opinion on the cause of the accident, or admit any guilt or blame. If others are injured, your first reaction may be to feel responsible. On calmer reflection, you might realize the fault was not yours. If you are arrested, ask to meet with your attorney before offering any explanation.

Action Plan for the Steeles Holding Down the Cost of Auto Insurance

Background The Steeles have received a renewal notice on their auto insurance. They were surprised to find that their auto premiums had increased substantially. An accompanying letter from the insurance agent assured them they were favored customers receiving both a good driver's discount and a multiple-car discount. Most of the increase was due to a rise in the cost of property damage coverage. This increase was deemed necessary after new data indicated that accidents and thefts had risen dramatically in their locality.

The coverages and premiums for next year are shown in the table.

Coverages and Limits of Liability	1991 Van	1989 Honda
Bodily injury and property damage ($100,000/$300,000/$50,000)	$316	$316
Uninsured and underinsured motorists ($100,000/$300,000)	70	70
Collision ($100 deductible)	290	300
Other than collision ($50 deductible)	110	120
Total premium by vehicle	$786	$806

The Problem The Steeles are not sure whether or not they should pay these premiums without first doing some comparison shopping. They also would like to know if they might be better off reducing either the breadth or limits of their auto coverage.

The Plan The Steeles should get insurance cost estimates from other companies. Given the wide range in auto premiums, comparison shopping is recommended

Do not make any payments, or accept any payments, at the scene of the accident. A settlement offer should be considered only after you have discussed the matter with your agent and, possibly, an attorney.

If there are serious injuries, your first obligation is to seek medical aid. You may make the injured person more comfortable, but do not move the injured in any way that might aggravate a serious injury. Even if the accident was not your fault, if your actions contribute to the other person's injuries, you may be liable. If you think that you or anyone in your car might be injured, be sure to seek treatment immediately. You will be reimbursed under your medical payments coverage.

AFTER THE ACCIDENT   Be sure to report the accident to your insurance agent as soon as possible, and to file any written reports required under your state's motor vehicle statutes. Most policies require that you notify the company within one day of the accident. If you fail to satisfy this requirement, the insurer can later refuse to honor any claim resulting from the accident.

when in doubt. Some companies specialize in insuring good drivers by providing these drivers with larger than usual discounts. With their good driving records, the Steeles should seek out a few of these companies. When comparison shopping, they should be sure they are getting prices on identical coverage. Therefore, they should first review the appropriateness of their present insurance.

The current liability limits are the lowest a family with their financial resources should have. They should consider raising these ceilings now. If not, they should definitely do so when Sharon takes on a full-time accounting position. If they want to save on auto insurance, they ought to consider changes in property damage coverage. It is probably too soon to drop these coverages on the Honda, but they should consider doing this in a year or two. They may now, however, decide on increasing the deductibles. Their present coverage, with deductibles of $100/$50, is costing $820. After checking with their agent, they will find that deductibles of $250/$100 will reduce the cost of this coverage to about $500.

The Steeles may have overlooked a gap in their present coverage. The trailer camper is not listed on their auto policy. Should the trailer be damaged in an accident or stolen, their auto insurance will not cover this loss. However, their liability protection will still apply. Should the trailer come loose and cause damage, they would be protected against the claims of others under their auto insurance. The Steeles' homeowners' policy specifically states that coverage on trailers is limited to $500. In addition, it does not cover theft when the trailer is away from the resident premises. For about $50 a year, the trailer could be covered for property damage on the auto policy. Given the relatively low market value of this item, $2,100, the Steeles will have to decide themselves whether they really need this additional protection.

FIGURE 12.4

Auto insurance
comparison worksheet.

Company _____

	Limits	Deductible	Annual Rate
Liability	_____		_____
Medical payments	_____		_____
Personal injury protection (no-fault states)	_____		_____
Uninsured motorists	_____		_____
Underinsured motorists	_____		_____
Collision		_____	_____
Other than collision		_____	_____
Total Cost			_____

Discounts (See Table 12.1)

Type	Percentage Discount	Dollar Discount
1. _____	_____	_____
2. _____	_____	_____
3. _____	_____	_____
etc. _____	_____	_____

Total Dollar Discounts   (_____)

Total Cost After Discounts   ══════════

FIGURE 12.5

Auto accident checklist.

AUTO ACCIDENT CHECKLIST

1. Stop the vehicle immediately and remain at the scene until a police officer arrives.
2. Give your name and address, those of the vehicle's owner, and the registration number of the vehicle to:
   (a) Any injured person
   (b) The owner, operator, or attendant of any damaged vehicle
   (c) Any police officer at the scene of the accident
3. Obtain the name and address of the driver of the other vehicle, all passengers, and witnesses.
4. Obtain license numbers of all vehicles involved.
5. Make notes of all significant circumstances surrounding the accident.
6. If there are serious injuries, make the injured person comfortable and phone for medical aid immediately. Under no circumstances should you move the injured person.
7. If you or any passenger in your car is injured, consult with your doctor immediately and encourage others to do so.
8. Obtain a copy of the police officer's accident report.
9. File all accident report forms required by the state or local government.
10. Report the accident to your insurance company as soon as possible.

Keep track of all your accident-related expenses, including medical payments, lost wages, and additional traveling costs. These are all collectible damages when the other driver is at fault. If you think these losses may be sizable, you should seek the advice of an attorney. You may find that, in addition to the economic damages, you may also be able to collect for pain and suffering.

In a suit for damages, the plaintiff's attorney usually recovers a contingency fee. A few lawyers may be willing to work on an hourly basis, however. The contingency fee is normally 30 percent of the awarded damages, but the exact percentage is negotiable. This pays only for the lawyer. Whether you use an hourly basis or a contingency fee, there will be added expenses for such things as expert witnesses. These additional expenses must be paid whether you win or lose the case. Be sure to request that the lawyer first seek your approval before incurring any of these extra costs.

If the accident was your fault and it appears the damages awarded may exceed the liability limits on your policy, the insurer should inform you of this likelihood. You must then independently hire an attorney to take over when the insurer's participation ends and to make sure the insurance company has operated in your best interests.

Summary

Homeowners' and auto insurance are your principal defenses against major risks to your property from damage and liability. Adequate protection is an essential component of every financial plan. Homeowners' and auto insurance are sold in standard formats covering the important needs of most insureds. Homeowners' insurance protects your dwelling and its contents from most common disasters. It also protects you from liability exposure that is not related to your business or auto. The auto insurance package protects you and your family from liability and property damage resulting from auto accidents.

Key Terms

actual cash value (p. 369)

all risks coverage (p. 368)

apportionment clause (p. 371)

appurtenant structures (p. 372)

co-insurance (p. 369)

collision coverage (p. 386)

direct writer (p. 380)

dwelling protection (p. 371)

endorsement (p. 378)

Family Auto Policy (p. 384)

floater (p. 378)

independent agent (p. 380)

inflation guard endorsement (p. 370)

liability coverage (p. 374)

medical payments coverage (p. 385)

monetary threshold (p. 387)

mortgage clause (p. 371)

named perils coverage (p. 368)

National Flood Insurance Program (p. 379)

negligence (p. 368)

no-fault insurance (p. 387)

other than collision coverage (p. 386)

Personal Auto Policy (p. 384)

personal injury protection (PIP) (p. 389)

personal liability insurance (p. 368)

property loss insurance (p. 368)

replacement cost (p. 368)

single liability limit (p. 384)

split liability limit (p. 384)

subrogation clause (p. 371)

umbrella coverage (p. 378)

underinsured motorists coverage (p. 386)

uninsured motorists coverage (p. 386)

unscheduled personal property (p. 372)

verbal threshold (p. 387)

1 Explain the difference between all risks insurance and named perils insurance. List three perils not ordinarily covered under the basic homeowners' policy.

2 Which cost is greater, replacement cost or actual cash value? Why?

3 What is the difference between unscheduled property and scheduled property? How is scheduled property insured?

4 Julie's employer provides her with a portable computer for use at home so she can finish a marketing report she has been working on. During a break-in at her home, the $2,000 machine is taken. Might she be covered under her homeowners' policy?

5 Larry recently started operating a mail-order business in the basement of his home. Unfortunately, a fire put an end to his dreams of success by destroying about $10,000 worth of goods that had been temporarily stored in his basement. Will his homeowners' policy cover the loss? Why or why not?

6 While on her newspaper route, Jane's daughter tosses a paper through a subscriber's front window, causing $300 in damages. Is Jane possibly covered by her homeowners' insurance?

7 List seven standard formats for homeowners' policies. Which policy best serves your own needs? Why?

8 Why is it important to insure your dwelling for at least 80 percent of its replacement cost? How does the co-insurance clause operate?

9 What is the most important component of your auto insurance coverage? Why?

10 Who is covered under the Family Auto Policy? List several situations in which this policy would not protect you from personal liability.

11 Ruth had stopped for breakfast during a long morning drive up to the ski slopes. While she was inside eating, someone broke into her car and made off with over $500 in ski equipment. What should she do? Under what policy might she be covered?

12 Last week Fred traded in his old junker for a new sports car. Not used to the fast response of a sports car, he accidentally drove it off a country road into a field, killing a cow. The car suffered extensive damage, and the farmer is demanding compensation for the dead cow. Fred had insurance on his old car. However, he hadn't yet gotten around to informing his insurer of the trade-in. Will his old policy still cover him?

13 While riding to school on her bicycle, Ruth was run off the road by a hit-and-run driver. Except for a broken arm that is healing nicely, she was unhurt. Under which insurance policy, and under what section of that insurance policy, might her parents apply for reimbursement of medical expenses?

14 While stopped for a red light on Main Street, Ralph's car was hit from behind by a negligent driver. Because he was in a state with no-fault insurance, and since nobody was injured, he didn't think it was necessary to get the other driver's name and license number. Under what section of his auto policy is he covered?

15 Name several factors insurers consider when setting auto insurance rates. How might you hold down your auto insurance costs?

16 Why do auto insurers prefer a high monetary threshold?

17 Where would a homeowner obtain flood insurance?

18 Peter is away at college and drives the family car only when he comes home on special occasions. How might Peter's family hold down the cost of their auto insurance?

19 Why is it wise to review your auto policy before you rent a car?

20 Why is uninsured motorists coverage sold in states that have laws requiring compulsory auto insurance?

It was around midnight when the smoke alarm woke Peter and Barbara Page. The fire had started in the attached garage and was already flaming when the fire department arrived. By the time it was put out, the Pages' home had sustained damages that would take $20,000 to repair. In addition, their Honda, with a market value of $8,000, was totally destroyed.

When the Pages purchased their home, they took out a homeowners' policy with $60,000 worth of dwelling protection. Since then they have received several letters from the insurance company suggesting they increase the dwelling coverage. For one reason or another they just never got around to responding. Now the insurer tells them that because their coverage was for less than 80 percent of the home's replacement value, as determined by the replacement cost provision, the insurance company probably will not pay the full cost of repairs. To avoid co-insurance payments, they should have been carrying at least $90,000 in dwelling protection.

Questions

1   Given the position of the insurance company, what is the smallest reimbursement the Pages can expect?
2   Is there any chance they can collect for the destroyed auto? How much and from whom?
3   Suppose the Pages disagree with the insurer's cost estimates. What course of action should they follow?

Bob Brown was recently involved in a minor auto accident. His car was hit from behind, and he in turn slammed into the car in front of him. He would like someone to explain his coverage and show him where in his auto policy each of his losses might be covered. Help him out by doing that for each of the following items.

1   The cost of a medical checkup for his passenger, Ruth
2   The front and rear damage to his car
3   The damage to the car in front of him
4   The damage to the car behind him
5   The total amount of liability protection for bodily harm and property damage

Helpful Reading

All-Industry Research Advisory Council (now the Industry Research Council). "Compensation for Automobile Injuries in the United States."

Best's Review: Property/Casualty Insurance Edition. A. M. Best Co. (monthly).

Taylor, Barbara, and Lynn Brenner. How to Get Your Money's Worth in Home and Auto Insurance (New York: McGraw-Hill, 1991).

Helpful Contacts

Insurance Information Institute
110 William Street, New York, NY 10038
Offers numerous publications on property and casualty insurance. Will answer insurance questions on hotline (1–800–942–4242).

Investing
for
the Future

The next four chapters deal with investments. They explain different investment alternatives, discuss investment strategies, and describe important aspects of the investment process. Above all, they continuously alert you to the trade-off between the return you can expect from an investment and the degree of risk you must take to earn it. According to many financial advisers, failure to understand this trade-off is the single most important reason investors lose with their investments—and these losses are often catastrophic in relation to the investors' net worths. To succeed as an investor, you need an understanding of investment risk, and realistic expectations of investment return.

Along with considering investment risk and return, you must also ask whether or not you should be investing in the first place. Of course, the answer depends on how broadly we define *investment*. If it includes assets held for liquidity or to accommodate your life-style, the answer is you should be investing immediately and constantly. On the other hand, if we follow a more narrow definition and include only those assets we hold for the specific purpose of increasing our net worths, then investment should come *only after* we have provided for adequate liquidity and have enough insurance to protect us against unexpected losses.

A key to successful investing is to understand *why* you are investing. Is it to provide for retirement? Educate your children? Buy a new car three years in the future? Or are you simply looking for a way to lower your income taxes? Your answers to these questions help determine the type of investment vehicles you should choose. This notion of linking specific investments to specific savings goals was introduced in Chapter 3 in the discussion of planned savings. Throughout Part Four, we will continue to stress the importance of having clearly defined investment objectives.

Part 4

Investment Basics: Understanding Risk and Return

Objectives

1 To understand why investment goals are important in shaping an investment program and determining your investment needs

2 To identify the basic investment alternatives

3 To understand the nature of risk and its various sources, and the relationship of risk to investment return

4 To see how a portfolio of diversified investments reduces risk, and how to manage remaining risk using the beta concept

5 To be able to determine what return on a security would justify the risk undertaken by investing in it

6 To begin thinking in investment terms with respect to gathering financial and economic information, selecting a broker, opening an account, and executing orders

If at First (or Second) You Don't Succeed. . . .

Some amateurs who manage their own portfolios achieve results that many a pro would envy. A notable example is Francis LaBrecque, 37, whose portfolio today exceeds $600,000. When he was 18, LaBrecque took the $500 he had saved and put the entire roll into American International Travel Service, where his mother worked as a clerk in the bookkeeping department. At first AITS climbed in value, and for a few giddy weeks it looked as though he had tripled his investment. But then the company got into trouble. Eventually it sank out of sight. LaBrecque still has the worthless certificates. He regards them as reminders of two basic mistakes he made: failing to sell once he had made a decent profit, and selecting stocks on emotion rather than research.

Nowadays $500 is small change to LaBrecque: He pocketed some $5 million in 1984 when he sold an auto parts supply company he had founded. But at the time, the AITS flier wiped him out, and he went back to doing what he then did best: fixing up junked automobiles in and around Hyde Park, the blue-collar Boston neighborhood where he was raised.

During those years, LaBrecque remained "fascinated by Wall Street and the stock market," he says. "I figured that there had to be a system, something that would give you a 50% chance or better of winning." Back in 1971 he had plunged into the market again, this time with $15,000. Once again he fell on his face. Stocks he invested in first rose in value, offering him profits he failed to take, and then collapsed. For example, he bought 100 shares of Eastern Air Lines at about $20 and watched it soar to $32 and then tumble to $13. By 1978 LaBrecque's $15,000 had shriveled to $6,000.

Refusing to give up, LaBrecque turned to reading all he could about investing. At the end of 1976 he started over. He liquidated his shrunken $6,000 portfolio, consisting of "junk spread all over the place," he says, and put a new system to work. He had the idea that he could beat the market by applying a straight 20% rule to all his investments. If a stock he owned went up by that amount, he would sell it and take his profit. If it dropped 20%, he would sell and swallow his loss.

The system worked, but only just. From 1976 through 1979, he made an average of $3,000 a year. "For all the work I was putting in, brokers' fees, and so on, I really wasn't making anywhere near what I should have." He went back to reading: books, newsletters, newspapers, magazines. He became a fan of *Value Line*. This time around he learned about margining and options, both potentially perilous if the market goes the wrong way.

Often betting the right way, he began to make what he calls "real money." Along with his system, he credits his broker, Richard Whelan of Merrill Lynch in Boston. At the time he sold his company, the portfolio was worth about $220,000. He has since built it up to more than $600,000 and has taken out some expensive toys along the way—among them a further addition to his automotive collection, a $60,000 Ferrari.

LaBrecque describes himself as "semiretired" these days, but he packs in a lot of activities. He enrolled in Northeastern University's business school in 1981, getting an MBA in 1982, and the past summer he taught entrepreneurship to an MBA class at the school. ("He's fantastic. You can tell he's done it all himself," says one student.)

For all his successes in the stock market, LaBrecque is hardly a blind booster of Wall Street. Amateur investors, he says, are all too often "suckers waiting to be taken." He believes investing should be taught in college. He goes so far as to suggest that would-be investors should be licensed before they are allowed to put their money at risk, just as people must be licensed to drive a car.

SOURCE: Excerpted from Colin Leinster, "Six Who Won in the Market," *Fortune 1987 Investor's Guide*, pp. 72–74. © 1987 Time, Inc. All rights reserved.

Francis LaBrecque is an amazing man—dynamic entrepreneur, respected teacher, and successful investor. His investment success, though, did not come easily, and he might even admit that luck had something to do with it. He obviously was willing to take risks—an important part of investing—and he worked hard at developing an investment approach. Understanding investment risk and relating it to expected investment return is the key to being a successful investor over the long run. It is also the main theme of this chapter.

Goals and Investment Alternatives

Our investment goals differ. If you are a young person starting a career, you may want to achieve a goal different from that of people preparing for retirement. You are concerned with building an estate; they are concerned with preserving what they have. You may be willing to sacrifice current income; they might depend upon it to meet living expenses. Obviously, an investment that's good for you may be totally inappropriate for them. Before starting an investment program, define your goals as clearly as you can, then indicate specifically how an individual investment relates to these goals. Goal definition is made easier when you understand yourself better, that is, when you are aware of your investment needs. Then you can look at the basic investment alternatives.

What Are Your Needs?

Surprisingly, perhaps, earning a return on an investment is not the only need many people try to satisfy from investing. The pleasure associated with many investments derives from your using them (your home) or simply owning them (your antiques). Also, if you are looking for a dollar return, this goal has to be further defined to state whether you want more now or more later, that is, a current versus a future return. And people are quite different in their tax situations and attitudes toward risks.

Action Plan for the Steeles Stock Portfolio Management

Background   In late December 1992, the Steeles had invested $22,800 in common stocks—$6,800 in a mutual fund and $16,000 in five different companies. They found the mutual fund on their own, while the stocks were recommended to them by their stockbroker. Arnold and Sharon told the broker that they wanted safe stocks which offered a yield (current return) about the same as they might earn on one-year certificates of deposit. Earning this amount would leave them no worse off than if they invested in CDs; if the stock prices appreciated, they would be in a better position.

The Problem   The Steeles' stock investments (shown in the accompanying table) are earmarked for retirement. If they perform well, Arnie may retire at an earlier age. The key to success is selecting stocks that fit well with the Steeles' objective. Equally important is achieving a high degree of safety—the Steeles do not wish to invest in highly speculative situations.

The Plan   Sell 100 shares of InChemCo, the 50 shares of Dow Chemical, and the 100 shares of Cincinnati Gas and Electric. This will provide $8,400 that should be invested in the Fidelity Fund, or possibly another fund that places even greater emphasis upon growth; for example, the Magellan Fund. There will be a $400 net capital gain, which will involve about $120 in taxes. Commissions will be about $100.

Rationale for the Plan   While the Steeles' portfolio includes high-quality stocks, it has a number of serious weaknesses. First, too much (26 percent) is invested in InChemCo (Arnie's employer). The company has a stock purchase plan, which is

TANGIBLE AND INTANGIBLE INVESTMENTS The first major classification of investments is based on whether an asset is tangible or intangible. Tangible assets, also called hard assets, are anything you can (but don't necessarily) use or enjoy while owning them. Houses, antiques, gold coins or bullion, diamonds and other precious stones, land, and even certain automobiles are examples of **tangible investments.** Some people might object to referring to some of these as investments, since your main reason for buying them is not to earn a return, but that's not an important distinction. Anything that has the potential to increase in value over time is an investment, regardless of its other characteristics. If you can sleep on it, drive it, and enjoy looking at it, all the better. If fact, many Americans have found over the years that their most profitable investments were the tangible ones, particularly their homes. During most of the 1970s, you would have done much better owning the average home than the average common stock. Another factor important to some people is the greater personal control they have with tangible investments. If you invest in an apartment complex, for example, you can decide what the rents will be or how much upkeep to provide. If you invest in an apartment complex indirectly, say, through a limited partnership or a corporation, someone else makes those decisions for you. If you like to control things, you have a mental disposition for tangible investments.

   Intangible investments, also called financial or paper assets, are actually claims to tangible assets or the earnings those assets produce. For example, a share of

appealing since shares can be purchased at a discount; however, this does not justify a continual holding, and 100 shares should be sold.

Second, combining Dow Chemical with InChemCo places too much emphasis upon the chemical industry. The Dow shares should also be sold.

Third, while the Steeles' investment approach seems sensible, actually it does not fit well with their long-range goal. In effect they are investing in high-yield stocks rather than high-growth stocks. Not only is this approach contrary to their objective, it means they must pay income taxes on dividends received. It would be much better to invest in stocks that offer higher future returns as opposed to higher yields. Since finding good growth stocks is difficult and since the Steeles have minimal investment skills, a mutual fund is more appropriate than individual stocks. The Steeles have sizable gains in Xerox and Ameritech, so selling them is not advised since it would result in unwanted taxable capital gains.

The Steeles' Stock Portfolio

Stock	Number of Shares	Current Price	Total Value	Amount Invested	Expected Yield
Fidelity Fund	400	$17.00	$ 6,800	$ 3,000	3.2%
InChemCo	200	30.00	6,000	3,800	2.0
Dow Chemical	50	50.00	2,500	3,000	5.2
Cin. Gas & Elec.	100	29.00	2,900	3,100	8.6
Xerox	50	48.00	2,400	1,500	6.3
Ameritech	40	55.00	2,200	1,800	5.1
			$22,800	$16,200	

common stock is a claim against the issuing corporation's assets and an entitlement to any dividend or other distributions the corporation might make.

CURRENT VERSUS FUTURE RETURN   Some investments offer a return the moment you invest in them—a savings account, for example. Others pay a return less frequently. Most bonds pay interest twice a year, and most stocks that pay dividends usually do so four times a year. Dividends, interest, or any other type of asset income you receive on a regular basis during a year is called a **current return.** Many people prefer owning investments that offer current return, since it supplements their other income. Retirees, for example, often depend upon current investment income to meet living expenses.

Some investments, however, offer no current return whatsoever. Your only return comes about if you can sell the investment to someone else (or have it redeemed by the issuer) at a price greater than what you paid for it. Since this exchange takes place in the future, it is called a **future return,** or simply a capital gain. The common stocks of many growth companies have never paid dividends and probably will not for some time in the future. Investors buying these stocks realize that their only return will be from price appreciation over time. These kinds of investments appeal to investors who do not want or need current return but instead are investing to achieve future goals. The Steeles fall into this category (see the accompanying action plan).

Some investments offer both current and future return. For example, if you buy a share of IBM common stock for, say, $100, you will receive a yearly dividend of around $4.80, giving you a 4.8 percent current return on your investment. Obviously, you would be looking for a better return than this in buying IBM, and you would hope to get it through price appreciation. Your target might be 10 percent a year. An investment's **total return** is the sum of its current and future return, and in the IBM example, this would be 14.8 percent. Before making an investment, then, you should decide what proportion of total return you want as current return and what proportion as future return.

YOUR INCOME TAX SITUATION   After reading Chapter 5, you know the importance of income taxes in overall financial planning. As you move into higher tax brackets, you have a greater incentive to choose investments that avoid or defer taxes. For example, interest on municipal bonds is not subject to federal income tax, but interest on a U.S. Treasury bond is. Suppose for a $1,000 investment you could earn $80 a year in the municipal bond or $100 in the Treasury bond. Which do you prefer? With no taxes to consider, your answer should be out in an instant—the Treasury bond. But suppose you are in a 28 percent tax bracket; now your choice is less clear. The Treasury bond would yield $72 after taxes, but the municipal bond would yield $80, clearly making it a better pick.

YOUR ATTITUDE TOWARD RISK   Your attitude toward risk will also shape your investment horizons. Some of us are by nature **risk averters.** We feel extremely uncomfortable in risky situations and prefer to avoid them or at least expect adequate compensation for undertaking them. Going back to the choice between the two bonds above, it could be that an investor in a 28 percent tax bracket would still prefer the Treasury bond to the municipal, not on the basis of after-tax return, but simply because it is a less risky investment. He reasons that an issuing

Current return: Dividends, interest, or other types of asset income received on a regular basis.

Future return: A return expected in the future resulting from the potential sale of an asset that has appreciated in value.

Total return: Sum of current return and future return.

Risk averters: Investors who prefer to avoid risk or at least expect adequate compensation for undertaking risky investments.

municipality has a far greater chance of defaulting on its interest or redemption obligation than does the U.S. Treasury, and to him, the after-tax greater return is not worth the added risk.

Just as there are risk averters, there are also **risk seekers**—but these aren't foolish people. Risk seekers also expect additional return for undertaking risky investments, although they don't demand as much as risk averters. To them, a marginally better return of 1 percent might be enough to buy the municipal bond. Both risk-seeking and risk-averting approaches can be satisfied in investment markets. In fact, investor differences help make these markets function as smoothly as they do.

Risk seekers: Investors who will undertake risky investments for less compensation than that demanded by risk averters.

Basic Investment Alternatives

There are many different kinds of investments, and Table 13.1 summarizes their return and risk characteristics by five different categories. The rankings assigned to each (A++ is the best and F− the worst) reflect your authors' opinions. Your instructor might have different rankings. Reaching a ranking everyone agrees with is impossible; for one thing, it depends upon the period of time you use to measure risk or return, and for another, the techniques one uses to measure each can differ. Table 13.1 simply provides a rough idea of these two characteristics. Also, the ranking is for a typical investment within the class, but there are many variations within each class. For example, a typical common stock is riskier than a typical corporate bond, but not every common stock is riskier than every corporate bond. A share of AT&T common stock might be far less risky than a bond issued by Fly-by-Night Airlines. A detailed discussion of each of these kinds of investments is presented in the next three chapters, but a brief overview of all is a helpful start.

INVESTMENTS HELD FOR LIQUIDITY   Chapter 6 explained investments that satisfy your liquidity needs. Remember from that discussion that there are degrees of liquidity, ranging from checking and savings accounts that are almost perfectly liquid to certificates of deposit that have penalties for early withdrawal. Also, while we give these investments a return rank of only a C, bear in mind that they frequently have done far better than some of the other investments with higher ranks, particularly during high-inflation periods.

SECURITIES WITH LONG OR NO MATURITIES   By maturity, we mean the length of time you must wait before the issuer agrees to redeem the security. Corporate and government bonds, which represent creditorship claims—that is, the issuer borrows money from you and promises to repay it in the future—have maturities ranging from one to over 30 years. Common stock and most preferred stock, which represent ownership claims—that is, you are a part owner of the business—have no maturities. The issuing corporations never redeem them, and the only way you can recover your cost is by selling them to someone else. Of course, there is no guarantee you will sell at the same price you paid for them; you might get more, you might get less. When we say in Table 13.1 that there is no appreciation with bonds and preferred stock, we mean that such appreciation is not what investors *expect* from these securities *when they are issued*, since the

TABLE 13.1 • Investment Alternatives

Investment	Dividends, Interest, Rents (Current Return)	Potential Price Appreciation (Future Return)*	Rank† Total Return	Rank† Total Risk
I Investments held primarily for liquidity: savings accounts, money market deposit accounts and mutual funds, U.S. Series EE and HH bonds, and certificates of deposit	Yes	No	C	A+
II Securities with long or no maturities)				
Bonds and notes:				
U.S. Treasury issues	Yes	No	C+	A
Municipal and state government issues	Yes	No	B−	A−
Corporate issues	Yes	No	B	A−
Preferred stock	Yes	No	B−	B+
Common stock	Some	Yes	A−	B−
III Pooling arrangements				
Mutual funds:				
Income funds	Yes	No	B	A
Growth funds	Some	Yes	A	C
Balanced funds	Yes	Yes	B+	B
Investment trusts	Yes	Yes	B+	B
Limited partnerships	Some	Yes	B	C−
IV Contractual claims				
Warrants and rights	No	Yes	A+	D
Put and call options	No	Yes	A+	D
Commodity and financial futures	No	Yes	A++	F−
V Tangible assets				
Real estate:				
Personal residence	No	Yes	A	A
Others	Maybe	Usually	B+	D
Gold and other metals	No	Yes	B+	D
Jewelry and collectibles	No	Yes	A−	F

*This does not consider price appreciation that is embedded in the investment, such as that sold on a discount basis; e.g., U.S. Treasury bills, U.S. Series EE bonds, and zero-coupon bonds. Nor does it include cyclical price variation arising from interest rate changes.

†Rank is based upon a typical investment, but there are many variations within each class.

interest or dividends they pay are fixed, and cannot grow. However, their prices do fluctuate with respect to changes in interest rates overall. Therefore, it is possible to have capital gains—or capital losses—with them.

Because of price volatility, bonds, preferred stocks, and common stocks are all considered risky, but common stocks are the riskiest of the three, and all can be very risky during unsettled economic times. None of these are suitable investments if there is a possibility you may need to sell them to raise cash. They are more appropriate for long-term investment.

Box 13.1
What's New in Personal Finance

"Do Small Investors Have a Chance?"

The answer to the question just posed in an emphatic *yes*. In this age of insider information, computerized investment strategy, and megabuck trading, you might think the small investor ought to call it quits and look for a comfortable mutual fund. Although many have taken that route, an equal number—if not more—have hung in there and are doing quite well, thank you.

Evidence of the small investor's success is usually hard to come by, but one indication is the performance of investment clubs who are affiliated with the NAIC (National Association of Investment Clubs). As the graph shows, in relation to the overall market, the clubs' performance has been quite good for the period indicated: they beat the market in 10 of the 15 years—a performance many professional money managers did not achieve.

Why are the clubs, and the small investors who are their members, successful? There probably are a number of reasons, but the most important seem to be that they do considerable research before investing in specific securities, and they then hold them for the long run,

which avoids frequent trading and high commissions. Moreover, they often act on instincts or plain common sense. For example, a club in a rural Ohio community, called the Farmerette Investment Club, has been remarkably successful by sticking to companies with products and services its members know well. Not surprisingly, you find Bob Evans Restaurants (an Ohio-based company) and Ralston Purina (a company serving the agricultural industry) in the club's portfolio.

So, if you are investing $200 instead of $200,000, you can take heart that investment ante is less important than investment skill and hard work. As usual, doing your homework often leads to the higher grade.

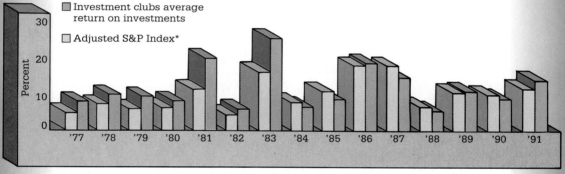

*Adjusted to include dividends as well as appreciation

Performance of investment clubs. (Source: National Association of Investment Clubs, Royal Oak, MI.

POOLING ARRANGEMENTS A pooling arrangement allows you to achieve greater diversification for your investment dollar than if you attempt to buy individual securities. For example, one share of a mutual fund gives an ownership interest in perhaps as many as 100 different common stocks. Pooling arrangements also provide professional investment management. Not only do you reduce risk through diversification, you might also improve your return.

CONTRACTUAL CLAIMS A contractual claim gives you a legal right or obligation to buy or sell something at a given price within a given period of time.

Warrants and rights are issued by corporations, and they usually entitle you to buy a certain number of shares of the issuing corporation's common stock. Put and call options are similar to warrants and rights except that they are issued (written) by individuals. A *call* entitles buyers to buy, and a *put* entitles them to sell, shares of a corporation's common stock. People who buy options pay a price for them, since they are actually privileges, not obligations. If you buy an option entitling you to buy, say, 100 shares of General Motors stock at $60 a share, you are not forced to make the purchase; and if GM's stock price fell below $60, you would choose not to. So, the most you can lose is what you paid to buy the option.

Commodity and financial futures are like options, but they differ in one important aspect. Rather than being a privilege to buy or sell something, they are an obligation to do so. If you enter into a futures contract on, say, 5,000 bushels of corn at a price of $3.00 per bushel, you are obligated to comply with that agreement regardless of what happens to the price of corn. Even if it falls to $2.00 a bushel, you must buy it at $3.00; thus, your losses with futures contracts are not limited as they are with options. Your potential future return with options and futures is extremely high—but so are your losses, and that is why we rank them highest in risk.

TANGIBLE ASSETS   Only a few of the many tangible assets are listed in Table 13.1. We have singled out the personal residence from other real estate because it has been such a good investment for so many people. Perhaps our risk assessment is too favorable, but in many cases the prices of homes have not been as volatile as prices of common stocks or even U.S. Treasury bonds. Other real estate, particularly raw land, is another story.

The demand for gold, other metals, and jewelry and collectibles is highly erratic over time. All these kinds of investments are exceptionally risky. With some, such as collectibles, you need specialized knowledge to compete in their markets.

Risk and Return

Your review of the data in Table 13.1 should reveal that, generally, as the risk of an investment increases, so does its expected total return. There are some exceptions to this pattern, but they are usually explained by the federal income tax law. For example, we show a personal residence as having less risk and a better return than common stock primarily because of the tax advantages associated with home ownership. If these were taken away, the return would certainly fall, and the risk might increase. This positive direct relationship between risk and return can be called the **iron law of risk and return,** and it serves as a good forewarning: If you are seeking high returns, be prepared to undertake high risks.

Iron law of risk and return: The strong positive correlation between higher investment return and greater risk.

What Is Risk?

Risk: Often thought of as a possibility of loss; but a better definition is variability of return.

You probably have an intuitive understanding of **risk** as the possibility of losing some or all of your investment. Games of chance are considered very risky because you can lose your entire bet. Most stocks and bonds are risky because their prices might decline after you buy them, and some may even go into bankruptcy, costing you practically your entire investment. This is the dismal side of risk, but there is also a bright side. You wouldn't invest in a risky venture unless you anticipated a high return. Therefore, an evaluation of risk must consider these high returns as well as losses, and it is actually better to view risk as a range of possible returns—positive and negative. The greater this range, the greater an investment's risk. This concept is illustrated in Figure 13.1, which shows three hypothetical $1,000 investments. Investment A is a deposit in a savings account promising to pay 10 percent interest for the upcoming year. Assuming the deposit is FDIC insured, you are virtually certain of getting back $1,100 at the end of the year and earning a return of $100. Investment B is a U.S. Treasury bond that pays interest of $120. If you bought the bond for $1,000 and sold it for the same amount a year later, you would get back $1,120. But this result is not assured. Suppose instead that the bond's price could go up or down by $50 during the year. In the first case, your total return would be $170 ($120 + $50), while in the second it would be $70 ($120 − $50). Investment C is a speculative common stock that pays no dividends. Your only return is through price appreciation. If its price increased by 30 percent over the year, you would make $300 on your $1,000 investment. If the price decreased by 10 percent, you would lose $100.

A is a risk-free investment since it has no range; i.e., it has only one outcome. C is the riskiest investment since it has the widest range of possible returns ($400). B has some risk, since its range of returns is $100. Estimating the range of possible returns provides a good approximation of risk, and it is often used for that purpose.

FIGURE 13.1

Range of possible returns for three $1,000 investments: A, B, and C.

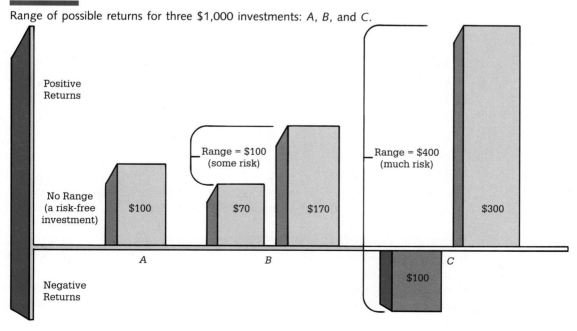

Investment Basics

Sources of Risk

What factors make an investment risky, that is, widen its range of possible returns? The various sources of risk can be placed into two groups: those associated with changing conditions of the overall economy, and those related to changing conditions of the issuers of the securities.

CHANGING ECONOMIC CONDITIONS   Practically every investment's return is influenced by changes in economic conditions. First, many investments have **inflation risk,** which means their returns may not keep pace with the rate of inflation. Any investment that pays a fixed number of dollars of return is subject to inflation risk because the purchasing power of your fixed return declines during inflation. Most government and corporate bonds fall in this group, explaining why investment advisers suggest not buying them if you expect inflation to increase.

Second, many investments are subject to **business cycle risk.** Economic growth seldom takes place in an even-keel manner. Usually, there is a period of rapid expansion followed by a period of recession. The profits of most businesses tend to follow these cycles, and so do the prices of their common stocks. The prices of real estate and other tangible assets also move in step with the economy, and their returns are similarly influenced by it.

Closely related to both inflation risk and business cycle risk is **interest rate risk.** This risk has to do with the relationship between the price of a fixed-return security that has already been issued and returns available on newly issued, similar securities. For example, suppose you bought a government bond for $1,000 that paid $100 a year in interest, a yield of 10 percent. What would happen, though, if a month later, because of tightened credit conditions, the government began issuing new bonds that yielded 12 percent? The bond you bought would still yield only 10 percent, but if you tried to sell it, nobody would be willing to give you $1,000 for it, since they could just as easily buy newly issued bonds paying $120 interest on $1,000. The buyer would expect the same percentage return on yours as he or she could get with any other bond of that type, so you would have to sell yours at a loss. At a price of $833, for example, your bond would also have a current yield of 12 percent, as calculated below:

$$0.12 = \frac{\$100}{\$833}$$

Thus, you would lose $167 ($1,000 − $833) by holding the bond during a period of rising interest rates. Interest rate risk has become increasingly important in recent years because interest rates have been so volatile.

CHANGING CONDITIONS OF THE ISSUER   Even in very good economic times, some firms go bankrupt; and in bad times, many do. You may buy the stock of a promising growth company anticipating a high return over time but then find that, because of poor management, the firm does not do well. In addition to this **management risk,** other sources of risk have to do with the issuer's condition. First, the company's line of business presents certain risks, usually called **business risk.** Making personal computers in the 1980s was inherently riskier than selling

Inflation risk: The risk that an investment's return may fall short of the inflation rate.

Business cycle risk: Fluctuations in an investment's return resulting from fluctuations in the business cycle.

Interest rate risk: The risk that the price of a fixed-return asset will decline if interest rates rise.

Management risk: Poor earnings performance of a firm associated with poor management.

Business risk: Risk associated with a company's product or service lines.

consumer perishables such as food. (Osborne Computer—an eventual bankrupt—was riskier than General Mills.) Another source of risk has to do with the way a company raises capital. Firms that borrow heavily are inherently riskier than those that issue mostly common stock. During periods of economic stress, the firm with a large amount of interest due its bondholders will be more vulnerable to bankruptcy than a firm without such payments. This risk is often called **financial risk,** and corporate financial managers attempt to minimize its impact, considering the firm's need for expansion capital.

RISK AND TIME It is often felt that investment risk is influenced by the passage of time, and there are two perspectives on the issue. First, the greater the time before an investment's return is expected, the riskier the investment—all things considered. The rationale is simple: We never know what the future holds, and the further we extend our projections, the more likely they are to be wrong. This implies greater variation in returns with long-term, rather than short-term, investments.

The second perspective, though, is somewhat different. Here, we ask the question, Are we more likely to achieve an investment goal by holding an asset for a shorter or a longer period of time? Of course, the answer depends very much upon the type of asset held. Consider a risky one, such as common stocks. Suppose we learn (as we soon shall) that common stocks have shown an average yearly return of about 12 percent over the past 60 years or so. We would like to invest in them and hope to earn the average yearly rate in the future. Are we more likely to achieve this goal by holding stocks for one week, one year, or ten years? You probably guessed the last choice—and you are right. The longer the investment horizon, the greater the odds of earning the annual rate. This is why we realize that holding stocks for short periods of time is risky. This message was driven home very forcefully by "Black Monday"—October 19, 1987—when the stock market fell about 23 percent. The prospect of losing 23 percent of your portfolio in *one* day is indeed evidence of considerable risk. But, if you invested on October 18 and continue to hold the stocks in the future, the 12 percent annual return may still be realized—eventually.

How Much Return Do You Need?

Having looked at risk, let us turn our attention to return. Suppose you are willing to undertake risk. How much return should you realistically expect to receive for doing so? The answer to that question for a specific investment is called the investment's **required rate of return.** It is important to understand that all investments are influenced by expected inflation. Investors are interested in real—rather than nominal—rates of return. A **real rate of return** takes inflation into consideration, while a nominal rate of return does not. If a given investment offers a nominal 10 percent annual rate of return, its real rate is only 4 percent if annual inflation over its life is expected to be 6 percent. Thus, it is always advisable to express historical rates of return in real terms, or at least have both inflation rates and nominal rates handy. If you can get 10 percent on an investment today while your parents could get only 4 percent on the same kind of investment 20 years ago, the probable explanation is higher expected rates of inflation today, which has nothing to do with the investment itself.

Financial risk: Risk associated with the use of considerable debt in a company's financing arrangement.

Required rate of return: A realistic estimate of the minimum return an investment must offer to be attractive, given its degree of risk.

Real rate of return: Inflation-adjusted nominal return.

411

OVER SIX DECADES OF EVIDENCE Financial analysts have been examining rates of return for some time. The results of one such study are summarized in Table 13.2. The first part of the table shows how much $1,000 would have increased if it had been invested in the four kinds of securities indicated. (Also shown is the CPI.) It is presumed that all interest or dividend earnings were reinvested in the security as they became available. The common stocks are a broad index of such stocks called the Standard and Poor 500 Stock Index; this index is a comprehensive measurement of stock prices of the largest and most important corporations in the United States. The years shown in the table were selected to illustrate the risks inherent in the various securities. As you can see, although you would have done considerably better in common stocks over the 65-year period, the road was quite bumpy along the way. Your $1,000 in 1925 was up to $2,204 in 1928, but if you held on until 1932, you were down to $789. Meanwhile, you would have done almost twice as well in either long-term government or corporate bonds. Notice the reversal in common stocks from 1936 to 1937 and from 1972 to 1974; you can lose a considerable amount of money in common stocks in a rather short period of time.

Returns and Inflation. Looking at rates of return provides additional insights on the alternative investments. First, notice that Treasury bills and inflation were fairly close over the entire period. Assuming this relationship will continue, if you invest in one of the most liquid and safest of securities—Treasury bills—you can expect to earn a return slightly higher than the inflation rate. Going into other securities should provide a greater real return. The historical average with common stocks was 8.9 percent (12.1 − 3.2); with government and corporate bonds, it was 1.7 (4.9 − 3.2) and 2.3 (5.5 − 3.2) percent, respectively.

TABLE 13.2 ▪ Returns from Four Investments and Changes in the Consumer Price Index (Selected Years)

	Selected Years	Common Stocks	Long-Term Government Bonds	Long-Term Corporate Bonds	U.S. Treasury Bills	Consumer Price Index
Year-end values of $1,000 invested in each	1925	$ 1,000	$1,000	$ 1,000	$1,000	$1,000
	1928	2,204	1,175	1,186	1,099	955
	1932	789	1,407	1,439	1,204	730
	1936	2,367	1,746	2,116	1,213	780
	1937	1,538	1,750	2,174	1,217	804
	1945	3,965	2,513	2,930	1,233	1,015
	1955	18,561	2,868	3,527	1,381	1,497
	1965	53,008	3,460	4,552	1,823	1,777
	1972	84,956	4,136	5,760	2,577	2,371
	1974	53,311	4,268	5,647	2,976	2,894
	1978	89,592	5,342	7,807	3,728	3,778
	1983	198,744	7,294	10,862	6,317	5,652
	1986	330,668	13,720	19,833	7,934	6,166
	1990	517,499	17,993	27,177	10,429	7,464
Rates of return:						
Average annual, 1926–1986		12.1%	4.9%	5.5%	3.7%	3.2%
Highest return, single year		+54% (1933)	+40% (1982)	+44% (1982)	+15% (1981)	+18% (1946)
Lowest return, single year		−43% (1931)	−9% (1967)	−9% (1969)	0% (1938)	−10% (1932)
Range		97%	49%	53%	15%	28%

SOURCE: *Stocks, Bonds, Bills, and Inflation: 1991 Yearbook*™. © Ibbotson Associates, Inc., Chicago.

Risk Premium. The difference between an investment's required return and the return on Treasury bills is often called the investment's **risk premium.** In other words, the bill rate is considered a risk-free rate of return; you can earn this without taking any risks. Any investment with risk must offer a return greater than this risk-free rate. Otherwise, you would not invest in it. For example, the risk premium on common stocks is 8.4 percent (12.1 − 3.7). You might notice the relative risk of each investment by looking at the range of returns between the highest and the lowest. This range goes from 97 percent for common stocks (the highest) to 15 percent for Treasury bills (the lowest).

MORE EVIDENCE AND MORE INVESTMENTS   Extending our horizons to include other investments provides additional information about return performance. Table 13.3 shows compounded annual rates of return and rankings for 14 different investments from 1971 to 1991 (June 1 to June 1). Over the entire period, Old Master paintings were your best bet (these also were the best for five years), and four of the first five ranks go to tangible assets. Inflation during this period most likely explains the superior performance of tangible assets, but notice what happened over the ten-year period, when inflation fears cooled; stocks and bonds ranked 1 and 3, respectively. What you probably learn from Table 13.3 is that it is often to your advantage to be widely diversified across a spectrum of assets.

The Rewards of Diversification

The advice, "Don't put all your eggs in one basket," is particularly applicable in the area of investments. By holding a **portfolio,** which is simply a group of assets held at the same time, certain risks can be avoided. In the short run, you might be lucky and do very well with one or two investments; but eventually luck reverses itself, and profits turn to losses. Unquestionably, an important part of a sound investment program is adequate **diversification.** Below, we explain diversification and show how it applies to investing in common stocks. However, diversification is important in all investments, and the broad topic of portfolio management is covered in Chapter 15.

**TABLE 13.3 ·
Compounded Annual
Rates of Return (%) on
Various Investment
Categories: 1971–1991
(June 1 to June 1)**

Category	20 Years		10 Years		5 Years		1 Year	
	Rate	Rank	Rate	Rank	Rate	Rank	Rate	Rank
Old Master paintings	12.3	1	15.8	2	23.4	1	6.5	5
Common stocks	11.6	2	16.0	1	13.3	3	11.8	3
Chinese ceramics	11.6	2	8.1	5	15.1	2	3.6	8
Gold	11.5	4	−2.9	11	1.0	12	−0.7	12
Diamonds	10.5	5	6.4	6	10.2	4	0.0	11
U.S. stamps	10.0	6	−0.7	10	−2.4	13	−7.7	13
Bonds	9.4	7	15.2	3	9.7	5	13.2	2
Oil	8.9	8	−5.9	12	8.5	6	20.7	1
3-month Treasury bills	8.6	9	8.8	4	7.0	7	7.1	4
Housing prices	7.3	10	4.4	7	4.6	9	4.7	6
U.S. farmland	6.3	11	−1.8	11	1.3	11	2.1	9
Consumer Price Index	6.3	11	4.3	8	4.5	10	4.7	6
Silver	5.0	13	−9.3	14	−4.8	14	−18.9	14
Foreign exchange	4.5	14	3.6	9	5.4	8	0.2	10

SOURCE: Salomon Brothers.

Eliminating Random Risk

When you hold a limited number of assets, you open yourself to all the risk factors discussed above; that is, you are taking on risks associated with the overall economy as well as those associated with individual firms. A portfolio eliminates these latter risks. If you like the personal computer industry and put all your "apples" into Apple Computer, you rise or fall with this one stock. By putting half your money into Apple and the other half into, say, Tandem, you divide the risks associated with these two firms. If Apple fails in market acceptance, Tandem might prosper. Of course, both might prosper or both might fail, but the probabilities are greater for one prospering or failing.

Studies have shown what happens to risk as you increase the number of securities in a portfolio. A fairly typical outcome is shown in Figure 13.2. This is a hypothetical, randomly constructed portfolio with individual securities drawn by chance from the S&P 500 stock index. What do you find interesting in the figure?

First, notice the extent to which risk can be reduced by holding only a few securities in a portfolio. With only five, you can cut your risk almost in half. After 15, you have virtually eliminated all the risk that can be eliminated, which is called **random risk.** Second, no matter how much you diversify, you cannot eliminate all risk, and that which remains is called **market risk.** In other words, even if you owned all the stocks in the S&P 500, you still could expect price movements up and down (risk) over time.

Managing Market Risk

Since you cannot eliminate market risk, the next best step is to manage it. By managing risk, we simply mean that you receive sufficient return over time to compensate you for undertaking it. A general but very, very important first rule is: *If you invest in securities as risky as the overall market, you should receive a risk premium equal to that of the overall market.* Recall our discussion earlier about risk premiums, and how the overall market has averaged about an 8.4 percent risk premium over a long period of time. Now we put that information to use. Suppose you are contemplating investing in the overall market (either by drawing 15 securities randomly or by buying a mutual fund that approximates the market). What is your required return for one year? Step 1: Determine what the rate will be on risk-free, one-year U.S. Treasury securities. Step 2: Add the risk premium and you have your answer. For example, if the U.S. Treasury securities rate is 6 percent, the required market return is 14.4 percent (6 + 8.4). Although simple, it is nevertheless a sound approach for estimating a required return. Assuming you invest, are you guaranteed the 14.4 percent return? Of course not. It could be much higher or much lower, as we saw in Table 13.2.

A second, and equally important, rule in investment risk management is: *If you invest in securities more or less risky than the overall market, you should expect a risk premium greater or less than the overall market premium in direct proportion to the greater or lesser risk taken.* Common sense tells us we should receive a higher return if we take greater risks, but, unfortunately, it doesn't tell us *how much* higher. More sophisticated—but not difficult to understand—techniques are needed to answer this question.

Random risk: Risk associated with any single asset; it can be reduced by holding the asset in a portfolio.

Market risk: Risk associated with unpredictable movements of the overall market; it cannot be reduced by a portfolio.

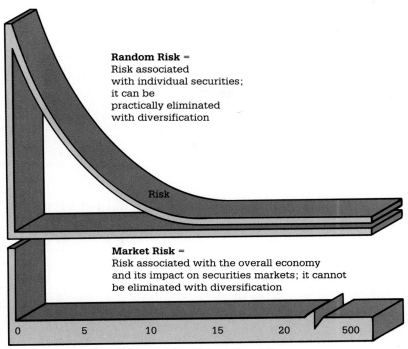

Random Risk =
Risk associated
with individual securities;
it can be
practically eliminated
with diversification

Risk

Market Risk =
Risk associated with the overall economy
and its impact on securities markets; it cannot
be eliminated with diversification

| 0 | 5 | 10 | 15 | 20 | 500 |

Number of Securities in Portfolio

FIGURE 13.2

Risk reduction in relation to the number of securities (randomly selected) in the S&P 500 stock index.

Beta: A statistic that measures the responsiveness of an asset's return in relation to changes in the overall market return.

ESTIMATING A STOCK'S RISK   The first step now is to determine the risk of an individual security in relation to the overall market. This is done with a statistical figure called **beta**. A security's beta measures the responsiveness of its return over time to that of the overall market. For example, if Apple Computer's beta is +1.5, it means that if the stock market goes up 10 percent, Apple's common stock goes up 15 percent; if the market goes down 10 percent, Apple goes down 15 percent. A beta value indicates relative risk, with higher betas meaning greater risk. Table 13.4 summarizes ranges of beta values and their meanings, and Table 13.5 shows examples of betas of companies that might be familiar to you.

Betas are not difficult to calculate, although the method involves a type of statistical analysis that may not be familiar to you. Fortunately, betas are available from a number of sources, such as the one cited in Table 13.5.

ESTIMATING A STOCK'S REQUIRED RETURN   After determining a security's beta value, you can then estimate its required return. Considerable historical evidence shows that stock returns over time are related to their beta values; specifically, risk premiums are shown to be directly proportional to beta values. The following equation expresses this relationship:

Stock risk premium (%) = stock's beta value × market risk premium (%)

If a stock has a beta of +1.5, its risk premium should be 12.6%:

$$12.6\% = 1.5 \times 8.4\%$$

TABLE 13.4 · What
Beta Values Mean

Range of Beta Values for a Security	What It Means
Less than zero; that is, a negative beta	The security's price moves in the opposite direction from the market; very few securities have negative betas over extended periods of time.
Zero	The security's return is independent of the market; this could be a risk-free U.S. Treasury security, where return is guaranteed regardless of the market's performance.
Zero to +1.0	The security's price moves in the same direction as the market but not as much; securities with betas less than 1.0 are considered conservative investments.
Equal to +1.0	The security has the same risk as the market; if you bought all beta 1.0 stocks, your portfolio's return and risk would be the same as if you bought the overall market.
Greater than +1.0	The security's price moves in the same direction as the market but by a greater percentage amount; buying these securities increases your risk relative to the market.

TABLE 13.5 · Beta Values for Various Companies

Company	Major Business	Beta Value
Atlantic Richfield	Oil refinery	0.85
Consolidated Edison	Public utility	0.75
Dayton Power and Light	Public utility	0.70
Deltona Corporation	Land development	0.95
Federal Express	Overnight mail delivery	1.10
Liz Claiborne	Apparel manufacturer	1.55
MCI	Communications	1.15
Merck	Pharmaceuticals	0.95
Merrill Lynch	Stock brokerage	1.20
Mid South Corporation	Railroad	0.20
Paine Webber Group	Stock brokerage	1.65

SOURCE: *Value Line Investment Survey Summary and Index*, April 13, 1990, published by Value Line, Inc., 711 3rd Avenue, New York, N.Y. 10017. Copyright © 1990 by Value Line Publishing, Inc.; used by permission.

The total required return on a stock consists of the risk premium plus the expected return on risk-free Treasury securities. If this latter rate is 6 percent, the stock's total required return is 18.6 percent (6 + 12.6). The diagram in Figure 13.3, which incorporates the figures we have just used, is a convenient way to express and summarize the important relationship between required return and risk.

THE IMPORTANCE OF THE RISK-FREE RATE OF RETURN   Before leaving risk and return, you should understand the important role played by the rate of return on U.S. Treasury securities. All required rates of return depend upon it, and if it changes, so will these rates. For example, if this rate went up to 11 percent, all other rates would similarly increase by 5 percent; the market return will now be 19.4 percent, and a 1.5 beta security will be 23.6 percent. The market risk premium, of course, is an estimate, and it might change if investors become more or less enthusiastic about potential profits in the market. However, for someone investing on a long-term basis, it is not unrealistic to look upon the premium as being relatively constant. A current "ballpark" figure often used is 8 percent.

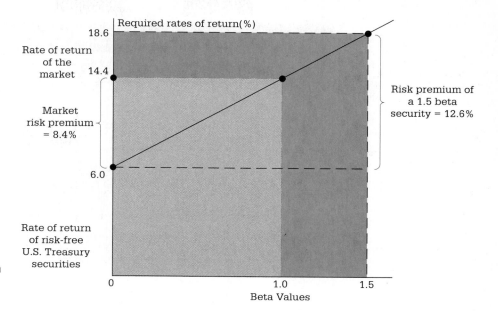

Required rates of return(%)

Rate of return
of the
market

Market
risk premium
= 8.4%

Risk premium of
a 1.5 beta
security = 12.6%

Rate of return
of risk-free
U.S. Treasury
securities

Beta Values

FIGURE 13.3

Required rates of return
in relation to beta
values.

Thinking Investments

If you have little background in the area, investing seems a very complicated business. In some ways it is, but in many ways it is not. Like any subject unfamiliar to us, it overwhelms us at the beginning, but our confidence grows once we gain an understanding of its terms and basic processes. After you finish the next three chapters, you will have a sound background to make your own investment decisions. The next step is to keep in touch with the securities markets.

Getting Information

Good investment decisions require good research, and good research requires information. There is no shortage of information on investments, and your biggest problem is usually deciding what's useful and what isn't. To begin with, most daily newspapers have a financial section that reports stock and bond prices along with other statistical data. You also will usually find stories about local businesses here. These can be exceptionally important, because many companies that become successful start as small businesses somewhere. Don't overlook the opportunities you have to become acquainted with firms in your area and to follow their progress closely. While you may not get "inside" information on these firms, the information you can get might give you a slight edge over investors outside the area.

After local newspapers, it's a good idea to start reading a national newspaper that's geared primarily toward business—*The Wall Street Journal*. This excellent publication provides thorough, up-to-the-minute reporting on all aspects of business and finance. Most serious investors eventually subscribe to the *Journal* and read it religiously.

Each issue of *The Wall Street Journal* shows the Dow Jones stock averages. The most widely watched barometer of overall stock performance is the Dow Jones Industrial 30, shown in Figure 13.4. When someone explains how the market did

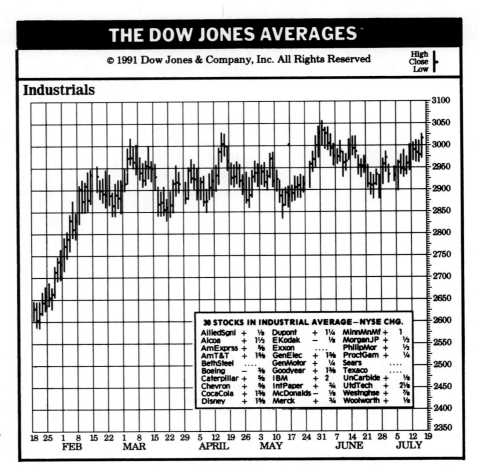

FIGURE 13.4

The Dow Jones Industrial Average. (Source: *The Wall Street Journal*, July 9, 1991. Reprinted by permission of *The Wall Street Journal*, © 1991 Dow Jones & Company, Inc. All Rights Reserved Worldwide.

yesterday, he or she is probably referring to this average. Since it includes only 30 stocks, it is a far narrower indicator than the Standard and Poor 500 stock index, which was used earlier in this chapter in the discussions of returns over time and determining a market risk premium. Actually, these series move closely together, and watching one is sufficient.

A sister publication to the *Journal* is *Barron's*, published weekly and directed exclusively toward investments. *Barron's* contains considerable statistical data and features columns and stories about different firms. In addition to newspapers, a number of magazines contain investment information. *Forbes* and *Fortune* are exclusively investment oriented, while *Money*, *Changing Times*, and *Consumer Reports* cover a wider range of personal finance topics. All are excellent magazines, but the latter three are more appropriate for the beginning investor. Moreover, their other articles are exceptionally useful.

In addition to getting information about investing, it is a good idea to keep up with business and economic news in general. The weekly magazines, such as *Business Week*, *Newsweek*, and *U.S. News and World Report*, are very helpful in this effort.

If you like to hear as well as see investment advice, you should tune in *Wall Street Week*, one of the most popular of all the Public Broadcasting System's shows. Its host, Louis Rukeyser, and his panelists and weekly guest show a human side to investments that is often lost in all the numbers and formulas. But, if it's numbers and formulas that you like, then watch CNBC on cable or the *Nightly Business Report* on PBS.

As your knowledge of investments increases, you might consider taking investment courses and seminars at local universities. Here you will learn the academics' views of the field, which is often a more tempered and cautious one than those found in the outside world. Also, many stock brokerage firms periodically offer seminars on a wide range of investment topics. These are usually free, and the speakers or seminar leaders are often well-qualified individuals with a great deal of investment experience. Obviously, the firm sponsoring the seminar wants you as a customer, so don't expect a totally unbiased view. Do expect a great deal of promotion for the investments under discussion. Make sure they are suitable for your investment goals regardless of how great they appear.

Investment Advisory Services

There are thousands of individuals registered with the Securities Exchange Commission (the SEC, a federal government agency). These people have licenses to offer (for a fee, usually) investment advice. But don't assume their government licenses guarantee good advice. Some of it is, but much of it isn't; or at least, it's no better than what you can find free at the library.

LIBRARY SOURCES Most libraries contain three excellent investment services: *Moody's*, *Standard and Poor's*, and *Value Line*. Of course, you can also subscribe to each and have it delivered to your home, but they are relatively expensive. Among other things, each offers a manual containing financial data for several thousand companies and a weekly newsletter that reports on economic trends and specific industries and companies. Each also recommends stocks to purchase or avoid. To become familiar with all their publications, you should visit your local or school library and ask the reference librarian to show them to you. Certainly, if you are doing any research on an individual company's securities or on an industry, start with one of these publications.

ADVISORY SERVICES YOU PAY FOR When you read *Barron's* for the first time, you probably will be surprised at the number of advertisements by investment advisers appearing there. These advisers usually offer a weekly or monthly newsletter. Some also offer "hotline" connections that allow you to call for their up-to-the-minute advice, or they might call you if there is an important change in their opinions. You pay handsomely for these services, and the logical question is, Are they worth it? It is difficult to answer this question. To begin with, you have to evaluate them on a risk-adjusted basis. Many tout that they beat the market, but it isn't clear they do so, after considering risk. They tend to do well in bull markets (an expression meaning rising prices), but not so well in bear (falling-price) markets. Moreover, some will have you buying and selling securities very frequently, which substantially increases commissions costs. After these are deducted from your gains, your net return might not be any better than if you simply put together a random portfolio and held it for the entire period. Finally, unless you have sufficient funds to offset their advisory fees—which can be as high as $500 a year—their cost is simply too high in relation to the amount you invest.

Do Things on Paper First

Suppose you have decided to start investing. Should you begin immediately? We don't think so. It is often a good idea to have a trial period where you make investments on paper. This is especially true if you plan to pick your own securities. This trial period, if you do it seriously, will familiarize you with the mechanics of investing and will give you first-hand experience with price volatility. Of course, you can always mimic a trial period by going back in time and selecting securities and then seeing how your selections would have fared, but this experience is often not the same as investing for future periods. Generally, we have some background on the general market or specific securities, which is bound to influence our investment decisions. (Most of us like to cheat by picking known winners!)

KEEP HONEST RECORDS   The whole experience will be useless if you fail to keep honest records. It's surprising how much we wish to avoid admitting—even to ourselves—the mistakes we make. If you pick a stock and its price goes down, then measure your loss as carefully as you might measure a price increase. If the stock or bond pays dividends or interest, note that too, along with the date it's received. In this dry run you should buy all the risky securities you might want to buy later. Include options and futures contracts in your portfolio if you are thinking of buying them. It is better to understand their enormous risks now rather than later, when it can cost you dearly.

EVALUATE YOUR PERFORMANCE   After a time, say, three months, you should designate a cutoff date and measure your performance for the period. A form, such as the one illustrated in Figure 13.5, is helpful in doing this.

As you see, the investor (Cindy Lipton) narrowed her investment choices to five common stocks. Cindy assumed she had about $5,000 to invest and planned investing about $1,000 in each security. When the quarter ended, she was somewhat surprised with the results and very glad she started investing with a dry run. As you see, she lost $206.57 for the quarter, and this figure doesn't include commissions she would incur if she actually wanted to sell out on August 31. Cindy was woefully underdiversified. Even though she bought five securities, three are in the computer industry—Apple, Tandem, and IBM.

Notice the relatively high total commissions in relation to the total amount invested: about 3.5 percent ($172/$4,983.75). While this wouldn't be too bad if Cindy planned to hold the portfolio for some time, it is very high if she were to turn it over every quarter. If she did, the commissions alone would probably consume all her gains.

NAME: _Cindy Lipton_

REPORTING PERIOD: _1/1/91 – 3/31/91 (13 weeks)_

Securities	(1) No. of Shares, Bonds, etc.	(2) Purchase Price per Unit	(3) Total (1) × (2)	(4) Commissions	(5) Total Invested (3) + (4)	(6) Closing Prices	(7) Total Closing Market Value (6) × (1)	(8) Gain or (Loss) (7) − (5)	(9) Dividends or Interest	(10) Total Gain or Loss (8) + (9)
1. Apple Computer	23 shares	$42.75	$983.25	$25.00	$1008.25	$49.00	$1127.00	$108.75		$108.75
2. Armco Steel	190 shares	5.25	997.50	35.00	1032.50	4.25	807.50	(225.00)		(225.00)
3. Tandem	60 shares	16.50	990.00	35.00	1025.00	16.00	960.00	(65.00)		(65.00)
4. Exxon	22 shares	45.50	1001.00	36.00	1037.00	49.50	1078.00	41.00	11.00	52.00
5. IBM	8 shares	105.00	840.00	31.00	871.00	98.00	784.00	(87.00)	9.68	(77.32)
6.										
7.										
8.										
9.										
10. Money Market Fund										
			$4811.75	$176.00	$4983.75		$4756.50	$(227.25)	$20.68	$(206.57)

Supplementary information:

A Interest on margin balance = $ ——— (amount borrowed × margin rate)

B Dividends on stock sold short = $ ———

Gain (Loss) This Period:

1 Dollar return = Column (10) − (A) − (B) = $ (206.57)

2 Rate of return = dollar return ÷ Column (5) = -0.0415 (4.2%)

3 Rate of return annualized = rate of return for the period × 52/N (N = number of weeks held) = -16.8%

FIGURE 13.5

A portfolio summary sheet.

Box 13.2
Saving Money

Periodic Investment Plans:
A Good Idea Gone Bad?

Some years ago, stock brokerage firms began offering periodic investment plans (PIPs), the idea of which was to help small investors establish a routine investment approach. You pick the stocks and tell the broker how much you wish to invest in them each period (say, every three months). That's it. Make out your check each quarter and watch your portfolio grow.

The idea is good, but it seems that over the years the brokers have increased commissions and fees to a point where you are probably better off investing in a mutual fund. One large brokerage house, for example, charges 4 percent on dividend reinvestments up to $100. Reinvestments above $100 are subject to diminishing rates that decline to 1.5 percent on amounts over $500. On top of these charges, you pay commissions on an initial investment and periodic reinvestments. These commissions range between 10 percent and 1.15 percent. And, of course, when you sell and begin withdrawing funds, there are additional commissions.

The accompanying table shows dollar accumulations with a PIP versus two no-load mutual funds. The first is assumed to have operating costs of 1 percent of assets—about average for all equity funds. The second is an index fund with an operating cost ratio of 0.25 percent of assets. Other assumptions in each case are: (1) a 12 percent total annual return consisting of a 4 percent dividend return and 8 percent price appreciation; (2) quarterly investments; and (3) withdrawal of funds after the years indicated.

The PIP does worse in every case, although the differences versus the average fund might not be described as enormous. However, that seems an appropriate description when the PIP is compared to the index fund. It also describes the differences between the average fund and the index fund—a point mutual fund investors should take to heart.

Of course, a PIP allows you to select your own investments. You might do better than a mutual fund; but then, you might do worse.

Plan	Accumulations		
	PIP	Avg. Fund	Index Fund
$1,000 initial investment plus $100 each quarter:			
10 years	$ 9,275	$ 9,930	$10,452
20 years	35,676	35,778	39,881
$100 initial investment plus $100 each quarter:			
10 years	6,570	7,325	7,650
20 years	27,077	28,238	31,156

Cindy's quarterly rate of return of −4.2 percent indicates that if her performance remained the same, she would lose 16.8 percent (about ⅙ of her original investment in one year. Needless to say, this loss is considerable and Cindy concluded that she needed more experience before investing on her own.

Selecting a Stockbroker

If you are still interested in investing after the dry run, the next step is selecting a stockbroker. The number of brokers available has grown since the industry was deregulated in 1974. In very recent years, even commercial banks and savings and loans have entered the stock brokerage business, and the chances are good that some of these institutions, along with traditional stockbrokers, are located in your community. The major distinction between stockbrokers is whether they are considered a full-service or a limited-service (usually called a discount broker) firm.

Full-service stockbroker: A stockbroker who provides a wide range of services, including research and advice, but generally charges high commissions.

FULL-SERVICE STOCKBROKERS As the name implies, a **full-service stock-broker** provides a wide range of investment products—usually any you can think of—along with recommendations from its research department on which securities to buy or sell. Full-service firms are the ones you are probably familiar with: Merrill Lynch ("a breed apart"), Prudential Bache ("rock solid—market wise"), and others, such as Dean-Witter (a division of Sears Financial Services).

The full-service broker is often involved in selling stocks of companies that have their first public offerings, and being one of their customers allows you to participate in these offerings. Sometimes these are profitable; other times they are not. But the greatest benefit a full-service broker can offer you is advice on selecting stocks and managing your portfolio. As we shall soon see, you pay for these services through substantially higher commissions. If you fail to use them, you are in effect wasting your money. Are their advice and management services worth the higher commissions? Again, this is a difficult question to answer for the same reasons cited earlier in evaluating professional investment advisers. Certainly, some people have done very well with their full-service brokers—Francis LaBrecque, who was cited in our chapter-opening vignette, for example—while others feel their broker's advice is no better than what they can get free from the library. You should know that a broker's sales representative (the person you probably call your "broker") is a salesperson first and an investment adviser second. This person may call you frequently to inquire about your investment needs. Of course, frequent calls can lead to frequently buying and selling, which in turn reduces your investment profits or adds to your losses. A conscientious full-service broker will discourage frequent transactions (called "churning the account") and will, instead, become familiar with your investment objectives and help you arrange a portfolio to achieve them.

Discount broker: A stockbroker who provides most services except research and advice, and offers low commissions.

DISCOUNT BROKERS The advent of the **discount broker** in the mid-1970s introduced important changes in the stock brokerage business. The discounter emphasizes only one thing—low commissions. And, as Table 13.6 shows, these can be substantially below commissions charged by full-service brokers, although they are less expensive on small trades. As you can see, brokers' commissions vary widely, and you should ask for a commission schedule before opening an account. You should see from Table 13.6 why small investors who trade frequently find it difficult to show any gains. With the ten-share transaction, even the lowest percentage of 5.1 means that if you bought and sold the ten shares only once in a year, you must show price appreciation of 10.2 percent simply to cover commissions. Very few investors are good enough to overcome this burden.

TABLE 13.6 · Illustrative Stock Brokerage Commissions: Common Stock Transactions

Transaction	Value of the Transaction	Commissions: Cost and Percentage of Value					
		Full-Service Broker		Well-Known Discounter		Smaller Discounter	
		$	%	$	%	$	%
10 shares @ $35	$ 350	18	5.1	35	10.0	25	7.1
200 shares @ $25	5,000	130	2.6	89	1.8	35	0.7
500 shares @ $18	9,000	225	2.5	107	1.2	58	0.6

SOURCE: Advertised rates and telephone inquiry.

ROUND LOTS AND ODD LOTS   The basic trading unit when placing orders is 100 shares. Orders for 100 shares, or multiples of 100 shares (e.g.; 300 shares) are called **round lots;** orders for a fraction of 100 shares are called **odd lots.** So, an order for 250 shares involves one round lot of 200 shares and an odd lot of 50 shares. Odd lots involve an added commission, which is usually quite small. However, you should determine the amount if you trade odd lots frequently.

STOCKBROKER INSURANCE   If you make your own investment decisions, there is virtually no reason why you should not use a discount broker, but one factor that needs to be considered is whether discount brokers are as safe as full-service brokers. Most are, since most carry insurance through **Securities Investor Protection Corporation (SIPC),** which insures accounts up to $500,000; and some brokers—full-service and discount—provide added protection. Surely, before selecting any firm, ask about SIPC and other coverages. But remember; SIPC doesn't insure you against losses if your broker fails; all it does is guarantee that any securities held by a broker will be returned eventually to you, or to another broker, in a liquidation process. That could take some time, though, and in the interim the prices of securities you own might fall drastically while your account is frozen.

Selecting a stockbroker is an important decision, but its importance is often distorted. Many first-time investors seem to believe that stockbrokers have "inside scoops" that are not available to others, and that the only way to profit in the market is through them. An honest broker should discourage that view. In fact, brokers could run into serious problems with the SEC if they attempted to profit—or assisted their clients in profiting—from inside (privileged) information.

Kinds of Accounts

Having picked a stockbroker, you should next open an account. This doesn't take much time. If you are married, it's a good idea to open a joint account, with each spouse having authority to initiate orders. Your account can be either a cash account or a margin account.

CASH ACCOUNT   A **cash account** is similar to a regular charge account used by many retailers, except you must pay for securities you purchase within five working days after the purchase is made. So, if you buy on Monday, you have until next Monday to come up with the cash, unless that Monday is a holiday, in which case the due date is Tuesday. The same time frame applies when you sell securities; that is, you must deliver shares sold within five working days. Some brokers will ask for an initial deposit before executing orders; others will not. If you wish, the broker can have your shares mailed to you, or you can choose to let the broker hold them. Holding your own shares prevents problems that might arise if the broker goes bankrupt or experiences other difficulties, but you must take steps to safeguard them, and a safe-deposit box is the only really safe place.

Actually, holding shares may not be possible in the future. Plans are currently in progress to do away with stock certificates, and your ownership interest would be shown only in so-called "book-entry" form.

Round lots: Orders for 100 shares or multiples of 100 shares.

Odd lots: Orders for less than 100 shares.

Securities Investor Protection Corporation (SIPC): A government agency that insures investor accounts with stockbrokers.

Cash account: A stock brokerage account similar to a regular charge account.

Margin account: A stock
brokerage account that
allows borrowing from a
stockbroker, using
securities as collateral.

Initial margin requirement:
An amount that must be
deposited when buying
securities on margin; the
current rate is 50 percent.

Maintenance margin
requirement: A minimum
equity required in an
account to continue using
a broker's loan.

Leverage: Using borrowed
funds, such as with a
margin account, to buy
securities.

MARGIN ACCOUNT

A **margin account** sounds mysterious to the uninformed. Actually, it is nothing more than a loan the broker makes to you using your securities as collateral to support the loan. Here's how it works:

Say you open a margin account by depositing $3,000. (All brokers require a minimum deposit for a margin account, and the Board of Governors of the Federal Reserve System requires an **initial margin requirement** of 50 percent of the value of securities purchased.) Then, you buy 100 shares of ABC stock at $50 a share. Thus, you bought $5,000 worth of stock, ignoring commissions, with a $3,000 deposit; obviously, the other $2,000 came from your broker. Now, what happens if the stock goes up or down in value? No problem, if it goes up. You can sell whenever you like and repay the $2,000 loan *plus interest* and pocket the difference. If it goes down, keep one simple fact in mind—the loss is all yours. You don't share it with the broker. So, if ABC goes down to $30 a share and you then sell, the broker still gets $2,000 *plus interest* and you still pocket the difference—$1,000 in this case. You lose $2,000, which is $20 ($50 − $30) a share times the 100 shares.

Perhaps the mystique surrounding margin trading is the possibility of getting a margin call (this means your broker calls and asks for more money) if the price of a security falls below a certain level, called the **maintenance margin requirement.** This requirement varies among firms but cannot be less than the minimum of 25 percent of the market value of your securities set by the Board of Governors of the Federal Reserve System. If a broker had, say, a 30 percent requirement, this means the security in our previous example could go no lower than $28.57 a share before you would get a margin call. The way you get the above number is as follows:

Step 1. Divide the broker's loan by 1.0 minus the maintenance margin requirement; that is, $2,000.00/1.0 − 0.3 = $2,000.00/0.7 = $2,857.14.

Step 2. Divide your answer by the number of shares held: $2,857.14 ÷ 100 = $28.57.

Since you still owe the broker $2,000, your equity in the account is $857.14 ($2,857.14 − $2,000.00). As a check on your math, your equity should be 30 percent of the market value of your securities. In this example, 30 percent of $2,857.14 is $857.14, so our math is correct.

Using a margin account magnifies your gains or losses, as would any loan you use to buy securities. In the previous example, if you had used your own funds, you could have purchased only 60 ($3,000/$50) rather than 100. Thus, if the price of the stock had gone up or down by $10, for example, your gain or loss would have been $600 rather than $1,000. A loan allows you to **leverage** your investment, which automatically increases the range of possible returns, which in turn is synonymous with more risk. Keep that in mind: leverage always increases risk.

Kinds of Positions

After you open an account with a broker, the next step is to begin trading. Brokers refer to this as opening a position, and there are two kinds you can take: a

Investment
Basics

long position, meaning you buy securities, and a **short position,** meaning you sell securities (that you don't own).

A long position is what you typically associate with investing: You buy, and then own, securities. A long position can be viewed as buying now and selling later. In contrast, with a short position you sell now and buy later. This seems confusing, and certainly more mysterious than a margin account. How can you possibly sell securities you don't own? The broker helps you accomplish this by lending the securities to you. Here's how it works:

Suppose you think KLM stock is overvalued at $40 a share and sure to go down in price over the next year. Your strategy is to sell 100 shares now at their high price and then buy them a year later after their price has fallen. You call the broker and tell him you wish to short-sell 100 shares of KLM. He will execute your order in exactly the same fashion as if you already owned the shares, and the buyer will receive 100 shares from your broker. Where did your broker get the shares? He probably borrowed them from other clients who own KLM shares and hold them in margin accounts. Is the broker adding risks to these clients by lending their shares? No, because the broker will insist that you deposit sufficient margin to cover potentially adverse price movements. In the above example, you would have to deposit at least 50 percent, or $2,000. You could deposit more if you wanted to, but it would be foolish to do so, since your deposit does not earn interest.

If you guessed correctly about KLM's price and it declines to $30 a share, you close out your short position by buying the stock and returning the borrowed shares to your broker. Your account was credited $4,000 when you sold them, and you need only $3,000 to buy them back. The $1,000 difference is your gain. If you deposited $2,000 to initiate the short sale, your account would now have $3,000 in it. If you guessed incorrectly about KLM and its price went up to $50 when you decided to close your position, you would lose $1,000 and your account would have only $1,000 left in it.

Is a short position any riskier than a long one? Probably so, because the long-run trend of stock prices has been upward, and you're betting against the trend with a short sale. Moreover, you lose all earnings potential on your margin deposit, and you also must pay any dividends declared on stocks sold short. If KLM declared a $1.00-per-share dividend while you were short, you would have to pay $100. (You probably are wondering if this means that two dividends are paid on the same stock—one by you and one by KLM. Yes, because the person who loaned the shares expects to receive a dividend, as does the person who bought them from you.)

Kinds of Orders

You place an order when you wish to buy or sell securities. Your order will be executed either on the floor of an organized exchange, such as the New York Stock Exchange, or between brokers in what is called the over-the-counter market. These will be explained in Chapter 15. You can place three kinds of orders: a market order, a limit order, and a stop order.

MARKET ORDER   A **market order** instructs your broker to buy or sell securities at the best possible price. At the time you make a transaction, the broker will give

Long position: A purchase of securities.

Short position: Sale of securities you don't own.

Market order: An order to buy or sell securities at the market price prevailing when the order is executed.

you an up-to-the-minute price of a security. For example, you might call wishing to buy 100 shares of Alcoa. The broker will use his quotation terminal to find the last price paid for a share of Alcoa; assume it was $50. If you then instruct the broker to buy or sell Alcoa "at the market," you are placing a market order. Are you guaranteed a price of $50? No, even though your order may be executed in less than two minutes, Alcoa's price could change during this time.

LIMIT ORDER   A **limit order** sets the price that you are willing to pay for a security. For example, if Alcoa's price is very volatile, you may fear that it could increase during the time it takes to execute a market order. If $50 a share is the top price you want to pay, you would use a limit order specifying that price. Limit orders remain in effect until they are either cancelled or executed. Some investors do not want limit orders to remain "alive," so they place day orders, which are limit orders that are automatically cancelled at the end of the day they are placed. Limit orders are not that important for actively traded issues such as Alcoa, since the large number of buyers and sellers usually keeps the stock's price from fluctuating widely within a short period of time. However, shares of less actively traded stocks are different. Perhaps as few as 200 or 300 shares trade each day, and substantial price changes are then possible. Limit orders are more appropriate here.

Limit order: An order to buy or sell securities at a specific price.

STOP ORDER   A **stop order** (often called a stop-loss order) is a market order that is triggered by the market price of a security. It is used to protect profits or limit losses. Suppose you bought Alcoa at $50 and its price subsequently increased to $80. You would have a nice profit but might not wish to sell, because Alcoa's price could go still higher. You could then place a stop-loss order on

Stop order: An order that is triggered by the market price of a security; often used to stop losses.

427

Investment Basics

Alcoa at a price of, say, $75. If its price continued to rise, the order would be meaningless; but if its price fell to $75 (the trigger), the stop-loss order would become a market order. Again, you would not be guaranteed a $75 price, but only the best price your broker could get, which might be higher or lower, as is the case with all market orders. Stop orders are used by investors who do not wish to watch their securities closely or make frequent selling or buying decisions. (Stop orders can also be used to buy securities.) Also, some investors use such orders because they feel they lack adequate discipline to make correct decisions during emotionally charged periods. As a security's price falls, you are often tempted not to sell because you convince yourself it's bound to increase again. Consequently, you sit and watch as the price falls—perhaps back to the original purchase price, eliminating your entire gain. With a stop order, you make the selling decision without the emotional atmosphere created by a falling price.

Summary

People have different investment goals because their investment needs are different. After you determine your own needs, you can evaluate basic investment alternatives, which range from perfectly safe bank deposits to extremely risky commodity futures contracts. Compare the expected risks and returns of each investment. There is an "iron law of risk and return" that states that higher expected rates of return are *always* associated with higher expected levels of risk. Historical data clearly show the relationship of greater risks associated with greater returns. In order to reduce risk, investors diversify their holdings by constructing a portfolio of different kinds of investments. Risk that remains after diversification is called market risk. Because it cannot be eliminated, it must be managed. One management technique is to find a beta value for a security and relate the security's required return to it.

You begin an investment program by getting information. When you are ready to invest, you must select a stockbroker, who can be a full-service or a discount broker. Once you have a broker, you must decide whether to open a cash or margin account, and then place orders to buy or sell securities. The three basic orders you can place are a market order, a limit order, and a stop order.

Key Terms

beta (p. 415)

business cycle risk (p. 410)

business risk (p. 410)

cash account (p. 424)

current return (p. 404)

discount broker (p. 423)

diversification (p. 413)

financial risk (p. 411)

full-service stockbroker (p. 423)

future return (p. 404)

inflation risk (p. 410)

initial margin requirement (p. 425)

intangible investments (p. 403)

interest rate risk (p. 410)

iron law of risk and return (p. 408)

leverage (p. 425)

limit order (p. 427)

long position (p. 426)

maintenance margin requirement (p. 425)

management risk (p. 410)

margin account (p. 425)

market order (p. 426)

market risk (p. 414)

odd lots (p. 424)

portfolio (p. 413)

random risk (p. 414)

real rate of return (p. 411)

required rate of return (p. 411)

risk (p. 408)

risk averters (p. 404)

risk premium (p. 413)

risk seekers (p. 405)

round lots (p. 424)

Securities Investor Protection Corporation (SIPC) (p. 424)

short position (p. 426)

stop order (p. 427)

tangible investments (p. 403)

total return (p. 404)

1 How do tangible and intangible investments differ, and what investor needs can be satisfied with tangible investments?

2 Identify or explain the following items: (a) current return, future return, and total return; (b) risk seeker versus risk averter; (c) iron law of risk and return; (d) nominal versus real rate of return; (e) full-service versus discount broker; and (f) market order, limit order, and stop order.

3 Drew Dugan is considering investing in one of three securities listed in the following table. Drew isn't familiar with return or risk and would like you to explain the data. Also, he would like your opinion on which security to invest in; he generally considers himself a risk-seeking individual.

	Securities		
	A	B	C
Highest expected return	50%	15%	30%
Lowest expected return	−30%	10%	−20%
Most likely return	20%	12%	22%

4 What sources of risk are associated with the overall economy; what sources are associated with individual issuers of securities? Explain two perspectives of the relationship of risk to time.

5 From 1925 through 1990, which intangible investments were the most and the least risky? Explain and provide evidence for your answer.

6 Referring to Table 13.2, indicate the best- and poorest-performing securities over the period 1965–1978. (*Hint:* calculate *percentage* increases.) What does your answer suggest about investment risk? Explain.

7 How many securities must you hold for adequate diversification? Does diversification eliminate all risk, or does some remain? Explain.

8 What is meant by managing risk, and how is the beta concept used in this effort?

9 Dan Stramm thinks if you invest in common stocks, you ought to get three times as much return as you would if you invest in Treasury bills. Do you agree with Dan? If not, explain how you would estimate a required return for common stocks.

10 List some sources of financial information and advisory services.

11 What steps should you take if you intend to have a trial period before actually investing?

12 Distinguish between a margin account and a cash account. What is meant by buying stocks on margin, and how much margin do you usually need to both open and maintain a margin account?

13 Allen Gold thought Exxon's common stock was far overpriced at $45 a share; therefore, he executed a short sale on 100 shares. How did his stockbroker assist in arranging this short sale, and how much profit (ignore commissions) will Al make if: (a) Exxon goes down to $40 a share, or (b) if it goes up to $50 a share? Does Al have to put up any money for this short sale? Would you recommend short selling as a routine practice over the long run? Explain.

14 Explain market, limit, and stop orders. In what situations would investors use stop orders? Explain.

Bart Parks is a bachelor, 33 years old, with a good income and a reasonable net worth. Bart has about $20,000 invested in individual common stocks, most of them recommended by his broker, Buzz Bushkin. He's done well with Bushkin over the years, and he is particularly pleased that Bushkin always gives him a list of several stocks to choose from, instead of just one. Bart has saved another $3,000 for the market, and he asked Bushkin for a new list, which appears below. Bushkin recommends Alpha Dynamics, but Bart is concerned with this selection because he has heard Alpha's latest product—an automatic envelope opener—has not met huge market acceptance.

Bart has turned to you for help, and in response you gathered data on expected returns and betas (shown below).

Securities	Current Price	Expected	Beta
Bushkin's alternatives:			
Alpha Dynamics	$10	30%	2.0
Beta Depressants	18	10%	0.3
Gamma Globulins	6	32%	3.1
U.S. Treasury bills	—	10%	0.0
A market mutual fund	16	18%	1.0

Bart doesn't consider himself either excessively risk averting or risk seeking, but he does expect a return commensurate with the degree of risk inherent in a security. Also, Bart's current holdings give him adequate diversification, so that need not concern him in selecting a stock now.

Questions

1 Explain if you agree or disagree with Bushkin's selection.
2 Should the information Bart has heard about Alpha's new product be a concern in his selection? Explain.
3 Assuming Bart takes Bushkin's advice, calculate the commission he'll pay and compare this to the commission he probably would pay to a discount broker.

Pat and Ed Delaney are a married couple with two children. Both have professional positions, and their joint income is over $70,000 a year. Their net worth is well over $100,000, and they have excellent liquidity with very little short-term debt.

The Delaneys want to start an investment program by investing in growth stocks. They believe their situation calls for the services of a full-service broker who will guide their selections. One of the brokers they interviewed urged them to open a margin account, since the amount they wanted to invest initially—$10,000—was not enough, in her opinion, to achieve adequate diversification. She put together a list of ten stocks and urged the Delaneys to invest $2,000 in each one.

Questions

1 Assuming the Delaneys would pay 12 percent a year on the broker's loan associated with the margin account, determine their net annual return (expressed as a percentage of the amount they invest) if their stocks paid a current dividend of 5 percent and increased in market value by 20 percent. Make a similar calculation assuming a current dividend of 5 percent and a decrease in market value of 20 percent. (Ignore commissions in both your calculations.) What advice do you have for the Delaneys about leverage?

2 Suppose the broker has a maintenance margin requirement of 30 percent. Ignoring dividends and commissions, how low could the market value of the Delaneys' holdings go before they would get a margin call? For simplicity in calculations, assume they bought 2,000 shares of only one stock at $10 a share.

3 What other advantage(s) might the Delaneys have with a margin account? Given their particular situation, do you recommend one for them? Explain.

Helpful Reading

Changing Times

Giese, William. *"Small Investors Can Make It Big."* November 1990, pp. 30–35.

_____. *"What to Do with a Chunk of Cash."* April 1991, pp. 35–38.

Schiffres, Manuel. *"Dow 6000: Why It's Closer Than You Think."* July 1991, pp. 30–35.

_____. *"Getting Started in Stocks."* July 1991, pp. 51–56.

Money

Edgerton, Jerry. *"Avoiding 10 Common Investing Myths."* January 1991, pp. 130–133.

Ellis, Junius. *"All-Pro Stockbrokers."* November 1990, pp. 152–164.

Simon, Ruth. *"Why Good Brokers Sell Bad Funds."* July 1991, pp. 94–99.

Sivy, Michael. *"How Investors Like You Can Stay Ahead."* November 1990, pp. 78–81.

The Wall Street Journal

Geyelin, Milo. *"Discount Broker Is Held Liable for Losses."* June 18, 1991, p. C1.

Kristol, Irving, *"How to Restructure Wall Street."* November 1, 1991, p. A14.

Newman, Anne. *"As Small Stocks Soar, So Do the Costs of Trading Them."* October 28, 1991, p. C1.

Power, William, and Michael Siconolfi. *"Stock Certificates Move a Step Closer to the Scrap Pile."* July 16, 1991, p. C1.

_____. *"Broker's Case Shows Justice Can Be Slow."* April 12, 1991, p. C1.

Helpful Contacts

U.S. Securities and Exchange Commission
Washington, DC 20549
A very useful publication is *What Every Investor Should Know.*
   Investor complaints: Office of Consumer Affairs (telephone 202–272–7440).
   Copies of filed documents: Public Reference Room (telephone 202–272–7450).
   Locator for other telephone numbers: 202–272–3100.

To obtain a background check on a securities dealer, including past and pending legal problems, contact your state's securities agency and request a report through the North American Securities Administrators Association's Central Registration Depository.

To find beta values for many companies, consult *Value Line Investment Survey*, available at many public and university libraries.

14

Stocks and Bonds: Your Most Common Investments

Objectives

1 To understand the nature of common stocks and common stockholder rights, and to know how to estimate the total return on common stock investment

2 To recognize the important strengths securities analysts look for in common stocks

3 To learn how to identify different investment opportunities in common stocks, and how to read stock quotations reported in financial and local newspapers

4 To understand the nature of corporate and government bonds and the different kinds of bonds issued

5 To know how to calculate the current yield and the yield to maturity on bonds, and how to read bond quotations in financial and local newspapers

6 To recognize and understand both default and interest rate risks in bonds

7 To understand the nature of preferred stock and how it compares to common stocks and bonds

Columbus, Ohio—When Phil Hallum and his wife Elaine bought their first house some time ago, one thing they got with it was a deep green, thick lawn—the kind you like to walk in barefooted on a summer evening. What Phil and Elaine didn't know was that this horticultural masterpiece resulted not from hard work or even prayer, but from the services of a company called ChemLawn (now a part of Ecolab, Inc.), which came out four times a year and sprayed its magic formula. Phil figured this service cost about two or three times as much as doing the job himself, but, what the heck, his time had to be worth something—particularly on a warm, spring Saturday when the golf course beckoned.

The Hallums were happy with ChemLawn, as were most of their neighbors, and their curiosity was more than casually aroused when, in one of the company's mailings, they read that it was going to go public by selling shares of common stock to it lawn-care customers. The price was $5 a share, low enough to encourage Phil and Elaine to tell management to put them in for 100 shares. Unfortunately, a lot of other ChemLawn users must have had the same idea, because the Hallums were able to buy only 60 shares when they became available.

While it was not your basic "sound investment approach rooted in strong fundamental analysis," this decision paid off well for the Hallums. Along with greening America, ChemLawn greened the bank accounts of those farsighted customers who preferred playing golf to spraying the lawn. First, ChemLawn split its shares 5 for 1, giving the Hallums 300 shares, then it split them 3 for 1, increasing their holdings to 900 shares. When Phil and Elaine finally sold out ten years later, the price of each share was $35.50. If you put that into your calculator and multiply it by 900, you come up with $31,950, which isn't too shabby for a $300 investment.

Apart from personal residences, the most favored investments of most Americans are common stocks issued by U.S. corporations, and bonds issued by both U.S. corporations and governments—federal, state, and local. You may not buy a bond or stock on your own, but there is a very good chance you will own them indirectly, either through a retirement or profit-sharing plan, or through some other pooling arrangement. Many people, though, do own stocks and bonds directly. It doesn't take an undue amount of your time, or make excessive demands upon your skills, to put together a portfolio of stocks and bonds than can provide you with a current return and/or reasonable growth in market value over time. Were the Hallums lucky? Sure, but they followed one good piece of investment advice: Invest in companies familiar to you. Their satisfaction with ChemLawn led them to believe many other people would also be satisfied as ChemLawn expanded. Their hunch proved to be correct.

Common Stock

Common stock: Shares that give you an ownership interest in a company.

Everybody likes to get in on the ground floor of an emerging growth company, as the Hallums did. To do this you must buy a company's **common stock.** While it is riskier than bonds or preferred stock, it gives you a stake in the company's future—for better or worse. It is safe to say that with few exceptions, you should buy common stock only when you are willing to risk that its future price will exceed its current price; if you don't think that will happen, then you should invest in something else. Essentially, most common stocks are for the future, but in varying degrees; some are completely growth oriented, others are far less so. We'll look at the total return you can expect from common stocks, along with the

433

Stocks and Bonds

different types available; but regardless of the kind you buy, your rights as a shareholder are the same. Let us now see what some of these rights are.

Shareholders' Rights

Suppose you were thinking of buying 100 shares of Mead Corporation (a paper and forest products company with other diversified interests) at $36 a share in mid-July 1991. Along with receiving a stock certificate evidencing your ownership, illustrated in Figure 14.1, you would have become one of about 23,000 people or institutions owning Mead common stock, and you would have an interest of 0.0000016 (100/63,000,000) in the company. Although your holding is a minuscule one, you are nevertheless an owner of Mead. And although you have far less power than someone owning a million shares, you have identical privileges. You have the right to vote for members of the board of directors or in other matters affecting the company; you have the right to maintain your proportionate interest in the company; and, you have the right to share in its distribution of earnings or assets.

FIGURE 14.1

A sample common stock of the Mead Corporation. (Courtesy of the Mead Corporation.)

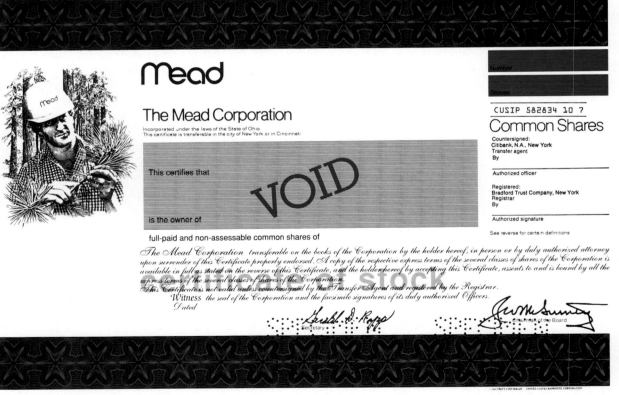

THE RIGHT TO VOTE In most cases your voting right gives you one vote for each share of common stock you own, although some stock is classified as non-voting. In contrast to voting in political elections, in a corporation you can assign your vote to someone else through a **proxy.** So, if you can't make the annual stockholders' meeting where voting takes place, you can return it with your signature, either giving or not giving authority to vote your shares. It is hard to get excited over a voting right if you own 0.0000016 of a company. However, if you and several friends are contemplating going into business and forming a corporation to do so, then be very careful about who owns how many shares and how these shares might be voted in controversial decisions. Hardly anything is more powerless than a minority interest in a corporation, even if that minority is 49 percent. Make sure in these situations to have an attorney's advice before the corporation is formed and shares are distributed.

THE PREEMPTIVE RIGHT Your right to maintain a proportionate interest in a company is called the **preemptive right.** If Mead wanted to sell 10 million more shares of common stock to raise capital, you would have the right to buy 16 (0.0000016 × 10,000,000) more shares. You probably guess the preemptive right is about as important as the voting right with most stocks you will buy. But again, you should see that it can be important in small, closely held corporations. It is possible to have a corporation organized in such a way that you give up your preemptive right, so again, it pays to be careful if you are about to get into such an arrangement.

THE RIGHT TO SHARE IN EARNINGS OR ASSET DISTRIBUTIONS Your obvious intent for investing in a company is to receive a return. With common stock you have the right to participate (in proportion to the number of shares you own) in any distribution of earnings or assets. This right is limited, however. For example, most states prohibit any distributions that would impair the firm's capital and subject its creditors (usually bondholders) to greater risk. In addition, if the corporation has any preferred stock outstanding, any current or past unpaid dividends must be paid on it before any distributions are made to common stockholders. This means as a common stockholder you come last in line, behind bondholders and preferred stockholders. You are said to have a **residual claim;** that is, you get what is left. Although this sounds dismal, actually, getting what is left is why you buy common stock in the first place. While bondholders and preferred stockholders have prior claims, the amounts they are entitled to are fixed each year; that is, regardless of how well (or poor) the company does, the amount they get is the same. In contrast, the amounts available to common stockholders vary in direct proportion to the company's profits. Figure 14.2 illustrates this relationship.

The hypothetical company has bonds outstanding requiring $5,000,000 a year in interest and preferred stock requiring $3,000,000 a year in dividends. This represents $8,000,000 of fixed obligations that must be paid before any earnings are available to common stockholders. If the corporation has a bad year and earnings are only $9,000,000, common stockholders' claims would be $1,000,000; but if the corporation has a good year and earnings are $19,000,000, the bondholders' and preferred stockholders' distributions would still total $8,000,000, but common stockholders' claims would now be $11,000,000. It

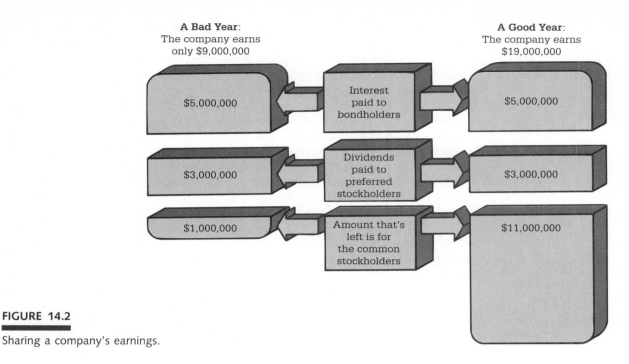

A Bad Year:
The company earns
only $9,000,000

A Good Year:
The company earns
$19,000,000

$5,000,000 — Interest paid to bondholders — $5,000,000

$3,000,000 — Dividends paid to preferred stockholders — $3,000,000

$1,000,000 — Amount that's left is for the common stockholders — $11,000,000

FIGURE 14.2

Sharing a company's earnings.

should be noted the corporation may not pay out all the common stockholders' claims in dividends. In fact, most companies retain a portion of the earnings and reinvest them in the business. For example, in the good year just described, perhaps $5,000,000 would be paid in dividends and $6,000,000 retained. In the bad year, it is possible that no dividends would be paid. However, many companies continue paying common stock dividends, even in very poor years. Mead, for example, had earnings of $2.26 a share in 1984 and paid a dividend of $0.53 per share. Although its earnings fell to $1.51 per share in 1985, it actually increased the dividend to $0.60 a share.

Total Expected Return from Common Stock

Expected return: A return, consisting of current return and future return, that an investor expects from an investment.

As mentioned in the previous chapter and earlier in this one, you buy most common stocks anticipating both a current return—that is, a cash dividend each year—and a future return in the form of price appreciation. An estimate of the total return a security will provide is its **expected return.** It is helpful to look at the total expected return, TR, as the sum of current return, CR, and future return, FR; that is,

$$TR = CR + FR$$

Current return can be expressed in ratio or percentage form. For example, if you expected to receive a $1.00 dividend on a share of Mead in 1991 (an amount estimated by one stock advisory service) and if you paid $36 a share, your expected current return would be 2.8 percent, calculated as follows:

$$CR\% = \frac{\$1.00}{\$36.00} = 0.028, \text{ or } 2.8\%$$

When expressed in percentage form, current return is also called current yield. With a current yield this low, it is doubtful anyone would have paid $36 a share for Mead when risk-free U.S. Treasury securities were yielding 6 percent at the time. Obviously, investors were buying Mead not just for current return but for returns expected in futures years.

Another type of dividend many corporations pay is called a **stock dividend.** With this kind of dividend, you don't receive cash; instead, you receive shares of the company's stock. For example, if you owned 100 shares of Mead and the company declared a 10 percent stock dividend, you would get an additional 10 shares. Are stock dividends attractive? Not really, because every stockholder gets a proportionate increase in shares. All you then have are more shares of stock but no more assets or greater earning potential for the company. As a result, the day a stock dividend is paid, the price of the stock goes down by the same percentage as the percentage increase in the number of shares. Instead of having 100 shares of Mead at, say, $36 a share, you would have 110 shares at $32.73 a share.

Closely related to a stock dividend is a **stock split.** Here, a company simply gives you and all other stockholders more shares of stock. Two-for-one splits are the most common, which means the number of shares you own doubles. (Mead accomplished a two-for-one stock split in May 1987.) Are stock splits by themselves desirable? No, for the same reasons stock dividends aren't. Granted, many companies that have done well, such as ChemLawn in this chapter's opening vignette, sometimes split their shares to lower the stock's price and broaden its market appeal. But it's not the split that adds value, it is the underlying strengths of the company.

EARNINGS AS A SOURCE OF DIVIDENDS　All dividends must come eventually from earnings. If a corporation's dividends exceed the sum of its current earnings and earnings it has accumulated in the past, then it is actually liquidating itself. It is relatively easy for potential investors to estimate a current dividend, because it is also relatively easy to estimate both a company's current earnings and the proportion of those earnings it is likely to distribute. Moreover, many companies indicate what the current dividend will be. But it is not so easy to estimate future earnings and future dividends. How much Mead will earn per share in 1993 or 1997 is not an easily answered question. Nor is it easy to know the company's future policy with respect to dividend distributions. Mead might undergo a complete change in the nature of its business, and this change might demand more cash, forcing Mead to cut the proportion of its earnings it pays in dividends.

EXPRESSING FUTURE DIVIDENDS IN THE TOTAL RETURN EQUATION
Bringing future dividends into the total return equation is done most easily by expressing them as a percentage return, and the most commonly used percentage is the company's expected *annual growth* in dividends in the future. So, if you thought Mead's dividends would grow at a 10 percent annual rate each year in the future, this is its future return percentage. Add this to the current return percentage to arrive at the total return percentage; that is,

$$TR\% = CR\% + FR\% = 2.8\% + 10\% = 12.8\%$$

It makes sense to include the dividend growth factor since a stock with a growing dividend should be worth more than one without growth. Moreover, the growth

The Importance of Regularity in Investing

Doing things on a regular basis is often thought to help in living the peaceful life. In investing, regularity not only provides a good night's sleep, it might increase your portfolio return. Regularity actually fits well with two investment strategies many advisers tout—dividend reinvestment plans and dollar cost averaging.

Dividend Reinvestment Plans

A dividend reinvestment plan allows shareholders of a company to use dividends they receive on their stocks to acquire additional shares. The big advantage is that you avoid paying commissions. Considering that commissions on small transactions often are as much as 5 percent of the transaction value, this savings should not be taken lightly. Over 1,000 companies now offer dividend reinvestment plans, so you shouldn't have trouble finding one in an industry that appeals to you. For information on offering companies listed on the New York Stock Exchange and the American Stock Exchange, see the December issue of Standard and Poor's *Quarterly Dividend Record,* available in many libraries. A more comprehensive source is the *Directory of Companies Offering Dividend Reinvestment Plans,* available (at a cost) from Evergreen Enterprises, P.O. Box 763, Laurel, Md. 20707-0763.

An added attraction to some plans occurs when the company offers a discount on shares purchased through dividend reinvestment. This seems almost too good to be true—indeed, it may be so in the future. At present, less than a dozen companies listed on the New York Stock Exchange offer discounts, and the number shrinks each year.

Dollar Cost Averaging

Dollar cost averaging is a system of buying securities by investing a *given sum of money* on a regular basis; for example, $100 each month. By not varying the investment amount, you automatically acquire more shares when prices are low and fewer shares when they are high. Why is this a big deal? Because many investors tend to follow their emotions, rather than their heads, when it comes to buying securities. Consequently, they are prone to invest more as prices rise and less, or nothing at all, when prices fall. Thus, the "regular" investor acquires more shares over time for a given amount invested because his or her average cost is lower.

Combining the Two

What's the connection between dividend reinvestment plans and dollar cost averaging? Simple: since most companies pay dividends on a regular basis, you dollar cost average while you reinvest. In short, you have the proverbial 1-2 punch at work. Clearly, neither method guarantees success, particularly if you limit investments to only one or several companies. But there is reasonably good evidence indicating that applying the method over a decent portfolio of companies and for a long period of time often leads to better earnings than do more sophisticated approaches.

factor allows you to make return comparisons among different stocks with different current return characteristics. For example, suppose another stock was available at $36 a share that was similar to Mead in risk but with a different dividend. Say it paid $2.00 a share—twice as much as Mead. Is it a better buy? Looking only at current return, you might say yes: Its current return percentage is 5.6, also twice Mead's. But if its expected growth rate was only 2 percent, then Mead would be the better choice because the other stock's total return would be only 7.6 percent (5.6 + 2.0). A comparison of future dividends with each stock, as shown in Figure 14.3, indicates that for about nine years after purchase, dividends are higher with the other stock, but then Mead takes the advantage and keeps it thereafter.

This illustration should also alert you to the very long time horizon many investors use in evaluating common stocks. The more you shorten this horizon, the more advantage you give to companies with good current dividends but poor growth prospects; conversely, the more you extend it, the more you favor growth

FIGURE 14.3

Future dividends with
Mead and another
company.

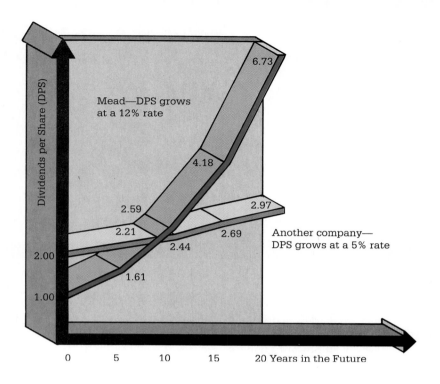

companies. After 20 years, Mead's dividend is over twice that of the other company.

COMPARING EXPECTED RETURN WITH REQUIRED RETURN Recalling our discussion of a required rate of return from the previous chapter, you should remember that it incorporates a risk factor for an individual security (its beta), along with a current risk-free rate of return. The required rate of return's purpose is to determine the minimum acceptable rate that will compensate you sufficiently for undertaking risks inherent in the security you plan to buy. We can now compare an estimate of a security's expected return to this required return to judge whether or not it should be purchased. The rule is to buy securities that have expected rates greater than their required rates, and not to buy (or sell) those in the reverse situation. Figure 14.4 summarizes the calculations necessary to determine each of these rates for Mead. As you see, its required rate was determined to be 4.4 percentage points higher than its expected rate, making Mead an unattractive purchase at that time (July 1991).

This leads to a final logical question: "Why were some investors clearly willing to pay $36 a share when the analysis indicates they shouldn't?" Several answers are possible: First, people may have quite different estimates of Mead's dividend growth. The 10 percent figure was an advisory service's estimate. But another financial analyst might disagree. It often happens that two people looking at the same data draw quite different conclusions about a company's future dividends as projected from its dividend history. Then, too, it could be argued that past dividends are poor guides to future dividends whenever a company is undergoing

439

Required Rate of Return		Expected Rate of Return	
1. Market risk premium	8.0%	1. Current market price of stock per share	$36.00
2. Mead's beta weight	1.40	2. Expected 1991 dividend	$ 1.00
3. Mead's risk premium = Line 1 × Line 2 = 8.0% × 1.40 =	11.2%	3. Current yield = Line 2 ÷ Line 1 = $0.65 ÷ 36 =	2.8%
4. Risk-free rate on U.S. Treasury securities =	6.0%	4. Expected annual growth in dividends	10.0%
5. Required rate of return = Line 3 + Line 4 =	17.2%	5. Expected rate of return = Line 3 + Line 4 =	12.8%

Difference equals 4.4%:
The decision is to not buy
Mead since its required rate
of return exceeds its expected
rate of return.

FIGURE 14.4

Comparing Mead's required rate of return to its expected rate of return, mid-July 1991.

important changes, such as Mead was in 1991. Now the analyst's job is even harder and potentially more at odds with somebody else's, since it is most difficult to determine the impact of these changes upon the company's future earnings.

A second explanation of the seemingly too-high price is that people can differ also in their assessment of risk (or the risk premium of 8 percent). Some investors might have seen less risk in Mead than its 1.4 beta weight indicates. Beta analysis is only one approach to measuring risk (although it is a very good one). Some investors might have used other approaches. And they might come to different conclusions about whether or not a stock should be purchased or sold.

What Securities Analysts Look for in Common Stocks

Securities analyst: A professional who evaluates investments.

Trying to find common stocks with expected returns greater than required returns is not an easy task. A professional who does this for a living is called a **securities analyst.** Almost all stock brokerage firms employ them, as do many other financial institutions, and there are thousands who are self-employed, selling their services for a fee. Each analyst attempts to develop his or her own approach for evaluating securities, but they are classified broadly as *fundamentalists* or *technicians*. Regardless of methods, the analyst's end product is usually a research report describing the company investigated, an opinion on the company's securities (whether they should be bought, held, or sold), and reasons for the opinion. A comprehensive research report prepared by Value Line on Mead Corporation appears in Figure 14.5. It is well beyond the scope of this introductory text to explain all the material contained on this one page and, furthermore, it would take some training in corporate accounting to really understand it. However, beginners can still make good use of the report. Notice in the upper left-hand corner Value Line's ratings on Mead as to timeliness and safety. With the

Investing for the Future

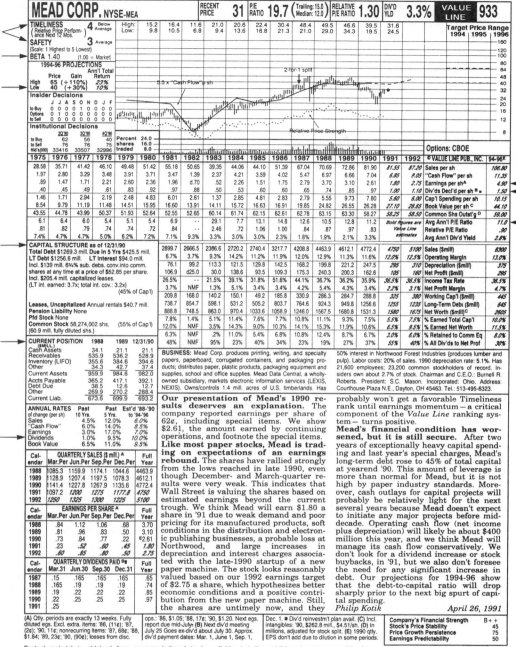

FIGURE 14.5

Value Line's research report on the Mead Corporation. (Source: *Value Line Investment Survey*, April 26, 1991, p. 933. © Value Line Investment Survey; used by permission of Value Line, Inc.)

former, Mead is assigned a 4 (which is considered below average), while it gets a 3 with the latter (average). The range is from 1 to 5, with lower numbers for better ratings and higher numbers for worse ratings. Also, the discussion about the company's current situation and its prospects for the future can be understood easily by the beginner.

STRONG FUNDAMENTALS The group of analysts called **fundamentalists** look for underlying strengths in the company. First, and perhaps most important, they look for *earnings potential*. Their key question is: How much can the company earn, per share of common stock, in the next year, the next two years, or even the next five years? Notice in the Value Line report, Mead's earnings for 1991 are estimated at $1.80 per share. Projecting to the 1994–1996 period, Value Line estimates the annual figure to be $4.90; obviously, they see Mead's earnings rebounding very sharply from the depressed figure of 1991.

Along with an **earnings-per-share (EPS)** figure, analysts usually provide an EPS multiplier—called the **price-earnings (P-E) ratio**—that relates EPS to the market price of the stock. For example, an analyst might feel that a company's stock, such as Mead's, should sell for 11.0 (Mead's 17-year average) times its current EPS. In 1991, then, Mead should have had a market price of $19.80 (11.0 × $1.80). Since Mead was selling at $36, the analyst would conclude the shares were overvalued and should not be purchased.

You probably notice that this valuation approach gives the same answer to the question of Mead's value as did the dividend approach discussed previously. This is not always the case, and differences of opinion are common in security analysis. There is considerable guesswork in any valuation approach, which leads to different estimates of value. That is why it is a good idea to get more than one opinion on a stock you are considering buying.

After earnings and dividends potential, securities analysts look for **balance sheet strength.** A business balance sheet does not differ greatly from the personal balance sheet discussed in Chapter 3. Just as it is important for an individual to have more assets than liabilities and to have enough liquidity, so is it for a business. Therefore, analysts often look at the net worth figure and at current assets and current liabilities, as the Value Line report shows in Figure 14.5. It also discusses the company's **capital structure,** which has to do with the way it raises long-term funds to sustain its activities. An analyst also looks for undervalued assets. In the personal balance sheet, assets are valued at market prices; but in the business balance sheet, assets are valued at their original costs to the company. For example, Mead might own forest land for which it paid $100 an acre years ago. If a precious resource, such as oil or some mineral, were subsequently discovered on the land, its market value could soar to over $1,000 per acre, but its value on Mead's balance sheet would remain at $100. Since the asset is undervalued, so might be the stock of the company owning it, making it an attractive purchase.

Analysis of the company's balance sheet should also reveal whether the company is maintaining and replacing its productive assets properly. A sudden substantial drop in maintenance expense, or depreciation charges taken each year that far exceed new equipment purchased, could mean the company is deteriorating in its capacity to produce output at low cost in the long run. Obviously, this doesn't bode well for long-run growth, nor does it justify a relatively high

Fundamentalist: A securities analyst who looks for underlying strengths in a company.

Earnings per share (EPS): Total earnings of a company divided by the number of shares of common stock outstanding.

Price-earnings (P-E) ratio: Market price of a stock divided by earnings per share.

Balance sheet strength: An attribute of a company showing sound assets, good liquidity, manageable debt, and other features.

Capital structure: The amount and kinds of long-term funds raised by a company.

current market price for the stock, regardless of the company's current earnings, which might be quite good. Balance sheet strength is just as important as earnings and dividends strengths, and its review should be an integral part of the analyst's report.

While fundamentalists will look in a variety of places to gather pertinent information about a company, they frequently begin their search by examining its annual financial report. This is usually a very long document covering many aspects of the company's recent and distant financial history. It will also include a discussion by management of what happened in the previous year and what can be expected in the upcoming year. If you have singled out a company for investment, by all means get a copy of its most recent financial report and read it thoroughly. An illustration of summary data for Mead, as presented in Mead's 1990 financial report, are shown in Figure 14.6.

TECHNICAL STRENGTH   Technical securities analysts, called **market technicians,** are less concerned with earnings, dividends, and balance sheet strength and are more concerned with interpreting a security's historical movements in price (or volume—that is, the number of shares traded). They look for patterns believed to be clues as to how a security's price will move in the future. There are probably as many different patterns as there are technical analysts interpreting them, but a fairly common one is shown in Figure 14.7.

The chart shows price movements of the stock of a hypothetical company over a two-year period. The trend is sideways, but notice the up-and-down movements along the way. Many analysts would draw the top and bottom zone lines, as we have done, and consider them meaningful. The bottom line is referred to as a **support line;** each time the price moved down to the support, buying enthusiasm increased and price rebounded. The top line is called a **resistance line,** and each time the price went up to it, selling enthusiasm increased and it fell. If price succeeds in breaking a resistance or support line, the technical analyst feels a major price movement might take place. For example, we show a breakout at the end that the analyst might interpret as a signal KFP's price will be in the 40 to 50 range in the near future. The bottom part of the graph shows the weekly volume of KFP shares traded. Volume is seen often as an indication of buying or selling enthusiasm. If a stock's price goes through a support or resistance line with very heavy volume, the movement is considered even more important. This was the case with KFP.

Along with analyzing price movements, many technical analysts look for other signs that might signal market strength or weakness. An often-watched barometer of the market is the **new highs-new lows index,** which shows the number of stocks making new price highs versus the number making new lows. *New* means within the past 12 months. If the ratio of new highs to new lows begins to increase gradually, this signals the market is gaining strength; the market is thought to be weak in the reverse situation.

Analysts use many other such indicators, but are any of them worth your time to study? And should you chart a stock's price and look for patterns in the chart? You are likely to get mixed answers to these questions. Academic researchers often say no. They have undertaken research to determine if technical analysts can indeed foretell major price movements and practically all of it shows they cannot. Or, at least technicians do no better—and often they do much worse—

Market technician: An analyst who evaluates companies by studying historical movements of their stock prices or volume of shares traded.

Support line: Technical indicator showing the lowest price range for a stock over some period of time.

Resistance line: Technical indicator showing the highest price range for a stock over some period of time.

New highs-new lows index: A technical indicator showing the number of stocks trading at 12-month highest prices relative to the number trading at 12-month lowest prices.

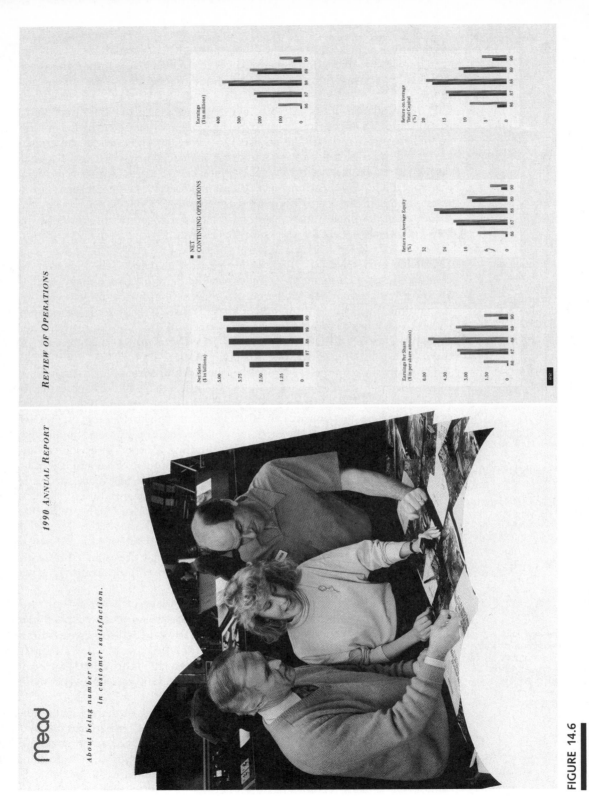

FIGURE 14.6

Mead's financial report. (Courtesy of the Mead Corporation.)

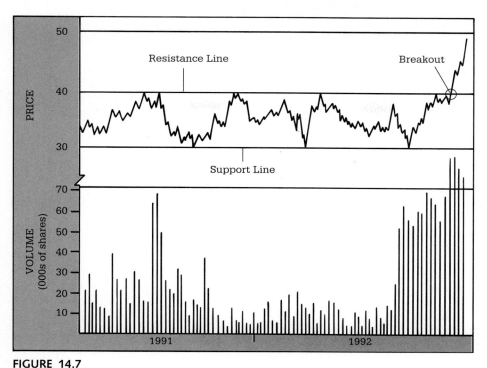

FIGURE 14.7

A stock chart for KFP Company.

than a simple buy-and-hold strategy of selecting securities randomly. Even when some analysts beat this simple approach, after you add in commissions you would pay in frequently buying and selling stocks, you are still worse off. Analysts who use these methods will, of course, defend their practice, and it should be noted that many stock brokerage firms employ technicians and rely heavily on the advice they give.

Opportunities in Common Stocks

Your opportunities to earn a return with common stocks are as varied as the many different kinds of corporations that issue them. You can buy very conservative stocks with low risk, or you can find those that are extremely risky. The total return you can expect over the long run should reflect your willingness to assume risk—the more you take, the higher your return. The following are the different kinds of stocks most investors buy.

Growth company: A company with expected earnings growth greater than the growth of the overall economy.

GROWTH COMPANIES The earnings and dividend-paying potential of a **growth company** is expected to grow at a rate faster than the growth rate of the overall economy. The price of its common stock should also grow rapidly in the future. Of course, there are all sorts of growth companies. IBM is one, Apple Computer is another. IBM represents less risk than Apple, because it has a long

445

Stocks and Bonds

history of achieving growth, and its chances of continuing to do so in the future are very good. Apple, on the other hand, is a relative newcomer, but it may have the more rapid growth. If you are interested in buying growth stocks, get as many recommendations as you can from brokers or other advisers, and narrow down the field to 10 or 15 companies that appeal to you. Also, don't overlook situations in your community or where you or your friends are employed. Remember how the Hallums got into ChemLawn? Opportunities such as this can happen again.

Income stocks: Stocks that pay high dividends in relation to their market prices.

INCOME STOCKS As their name suggests, **income stocks** pay high dividends in relation to their market prices and offer good current rates of return. However, they vary considerably in risk, so be sure to review this characteristic before investing. Sometimes, although a stock's current yield is high, there is a good chance the company will reduce its dividend and thereby reduce your yield. Mead cut its dividend from $0.88 a share in 1982 to a $0.50 a share in 1983. Dividend cuts happen regularly, so the key issue is whether or not the company can sustain its current dividend. Because of their capabilities for doing this, public utilities are often considered the best income stocks. In recent years their dividend yields have been in excess of 7 percent, and some also offer reasonable growth prospects. They are not without risks, though, as investors learned with public utilities which have not been permitted to use nuclear reactors.

BLUE CHIPS The popular expression **blue chip** really doesn't tell you much about a stock. It usually refers to low-risk stocks—those you can count on to deliver the dividend or growth you expected when you bought them. It also usually refers to what is called *high-capitalization stocks*, which means the issuing corporations are very large companies with many millions of shares outstanding. Being a blue chip doesn't guarantee success, however. The New York Central Railroad was the bluest of the blue in the 1920s and bankrupt in the 1960s.

Blue chip: A low-risk stock that reliably provides investors with the expected dividend or growth.

CYCLICAL STOCKS **Cyclical stocks** are more responsive to changes in the business cycle than are other stocks. Companies in the capital goods industries, such as Schlumberger (a manufacturer of oil-drilling equipment) experience far greater volatility in earnings than companies in the food business, such as General Foods. As a result, their stock prices also tend to be more volatile. When the world price of oil was over $42 a barrel and oil exploration was hectic, oil refiners and manufacturers of oil drilling equipment enjoyed a boom; but when the situation reversed in the early 1980s, many did very poorly. Schlumberger (also seen as a blue chip) saw its stock price fall from over $150 to under $40 a share in less than a year. Investors like to "play" cyclical stocks by buying them in recession periods and then selling out as the economy improves. Sounds easy, but it isn't, because it is almost impossible to know when the stock's price is at the bottom of its cycle. (It's easy to know after the cycle is over and it becomes history!) Surely, many people were buying Schlumberger at $75 a share, convinced it could go no lower and was a terrific buy at half its previous high.

Cyclical stocks: Stocks that are highly responsive to changes in the business cycle.

SPECIAL SITUATIONS While anything can be a **special situation,** the most common is when one company is expected to take over another. Almost always these takeovers result in a substantially higher price for the stock of the company taken over. For example, NCR's price was about $50 a share in 1990 when AT&T announced it would offer $80 a share. It went to over $90 a share when AT&T "sweetened" the terms of the merger. If an investor can get in on a takeover shortly before the event takes place, the profit opportunity is enormous. Naturally, the trick is to know if and when a takeover will occur. If you don't have inside information, you must rely upon opinions of so-called experts in identifying takeover situations. Very often these opinions are no better than random guesses. Other special situations could be undervalued assets (explained earlier), changes in key managers, favorable or unfavorable legal opinions, granting of a license or patent, a new and unexpected invention, and many others. All these events can change a company's financial outlook dramatically and its stock price accordingly.

Special situation: Any potentially profitable investment opportunity, but often referring to a possible takeover.

Stocks and Bonds

How to Read Stock Quotations

Considerable financial information about many companies is published every day in both hometown newspapers and the important financial newspapers, such as *The Wall Street Journal.* Unfortunately, some people cannot use this information because they have not learned how to read stock quotations. Actually, it's very simple once you understand the symbols. Figure 14.8 shows a typical day's quotations as they appear in the financial pages. Notice the inclusion of the dividend yield and price-earnings (P-E) ratio, explained earlier. Investors pay close attention to them, so they are reported along with price and volume data.

If you are interested in a stock traded in the over-the-counter market (also explained in the next chapter), you might also find it listed in the newspaper. However, less information is provided for these stocks, as shown in the following typical listing.

Name and Indicated Regular Dividend		Sales (100s)	Bid	Asked	Net Change
Velcro	.92	63	$19\frac{1}{4}$	$20\frac{1}{2}$	$+\frac{1}{2}$

The name of the company is Velcro, and its indicated regular dividend is $0.92 a share. The number 63 means 6,300 shares traded on the reported day. A bid price is the price you would get if you were selling the stock, while the asked price is what you would have to pay to buy the stock. There is always a spread between these two prices, and if you were actually thinking of buying and selling, you could try to get a better price. For example, instead of accepting the bid price of $19\frac{1}{4}$ to sell Velcro, you could offer to sell at a higher price, say, 20. If there are no offers to sell at $19\frac{1}{4}$, yours may be accepted. The net change refers to the increase or decrease in the asked price from the previous trading day. Velcro's asked price increased from 20 to $20\frac{1}{2}$. You should notice that even though the current yield is not reported for over-the-counter stocks, you can easily calculate it by dividing the indicated dividend by the asked price. (Velcro's was 4.5 percent: $0.92/$20.50 = 0.045, or 4.5%.)

Stock Options (Puts and Calls)

Call option: A right to buy a specified number of shares of a stock at a specified price within a specified period of time.

Rather than investing in stocks directly, some investors prefer an indirect approach using stock options. The most popular of these is a **call option,** which gives its owner the right to buy a specified number of shares of stock at a specified price (called the strike price) at any time before a specified date (called the option's maturity). There are standardized contracts for hundreds of individual stocks, and you can even buy them for stock indexes such as the Standard and Poor's 500. An example will illustrate how a call option works.

Suppose IBM is selling for $160 a share. You would like to buy 100 shares but feel $16,000 is too much to invest in IBM. You notice, though, that you could buy a call option on IBM that would allow you to buy 100 shares at $160 any time within the next six months (most options have maturities of nine months or less). The option costs $1,500, an amount within your means. Suppose IBM's

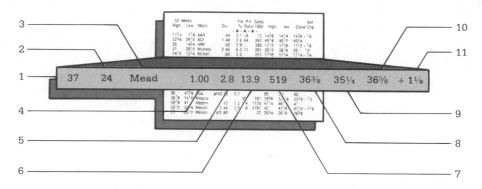

1. The highest price per share paid in the past year; prices are quoted in dollars and eighths of dollars, so a price of 10⅛ = $10.125 a share. Mead's highest price was $37.

2. The lowest price per share paid in the last year. Mead's lowest price was $24.

3. The company's name, which is usually abbreviated. For example, McKess is McKesson and Robbins, a pharmaceutical company.

4. The indicated regular dividend in the current year based upon what the company has paid in the last quarter or six months. Some companies also pay extra dividends in good earnings years, but these are not shown. Mead's regular dividend was estimated at $1.00 a share.

5. The current yield, which is found by dividing the current year regular dividend by the closing price of the stock. Mead's current yield is 2.8 percent.

6. The price-earnings ratio, which is the company's earnings over its last fiscal year divided into the closing price of the stock. Mead's ratio is 20.8.

7. The number of shares sold on that day, in hundreds. For example, 519 means 51,900 shares of Mead stock.

8. The highest price paid for the stock that day. Mead's was 36⅜ (36.375).

9. The lowest price paid for the stock that day. Mead's was 35¼ (35.25).

10. The last price paid that day. Mead's was 36⅜.

11. The difference between the closing price that day and the closing price of the previous day. For example, Mead's closing price on the previous day was 1⅛ ($1.125) lower than its closing price on the reported day.

FIGURE 14.8

How to read stock quotations.

price eventually goes to $200 a share; you then decide to exercise your option to buy 100 shares at $160, and your profit is $2,500 ($40 a share × 100 shares minus what you paid for the option—$1,500). In this case, the option was a good investment. But suppose IBM's price fell below $160 and remained there for the remaining life of the option. Now you would lose your entire $1,500. You probably notice that IBM must go to $175 before you break even. While possible, the odds of this happening over a period of just six months are not good. Options, then, offer very high profit opportunities but are extremely risky.

> Put option: Reverse of a call option—allows the holder to sell, rather than buy, shares.

A **put option** works exactly like a call option except it gives you the right to sell shares, rather than buy them. Investors frequently use put options to lock in prices of securities they own, which serves as a form of insurance to protect the value of their portfolio. Of course, you pay for put options too, and over time these payments will reduce the portfolio return substantially. Finally, several option contracts are available on bonds, but bond option trading is far less popular than stock options.

Warrants and Rights

Warrants, rights: Option-type securities issued by corporations.

Warrants and **rights** are other option-type securities. They are similar to call options, but there are important differences. First, they are issued by corporations—not individuals—in relation to corporate new financing. For example, a corporation may issue bonds with warrants attached that allow investors to buy shares of the company's common stock at a fixed price within some period of time. Genesco (an apparel and footwear firm) issued warrants several years ago that can be used to buy one share of its common stock at $8.00 a share until the warrants expire in late 1993. This format is fairly typical of many warrants and, as you see, they have considerably longer maturities than put and call options. Rights come into existence when a corporation attempts to sell common stock to existing stockholders by virtue of their preemptive rights (discussed earlier in this chapter). In contrast to warrants, rights are in existence for only short periods of time, such as a month, and they are not used frequently.

Warrants, though, are fairly widely used, and their popularity is increasing. The Genesco warrant had a closing price of about $1.00 in mid-1991, while the common stock closed at around $5.50 a share. Is the warrant a good deal at that price? It depends on your perspective. Remembering that the strike price is $8.00, you can see that if the common stock doesn't get to at least $9.00 a share before 1993, you will suffer losses if you bought the warrant for $1.00—and you will lose your entire investment in the warrant if Genesco's common stock fails to go over $8.00 a share.

Bonds

Perhaps the only bonds you are familiar with are U.S. Series EE bonds. You may have received some as presents at birthdays or graduations. Actually, these bonds are only a very small part of all the bonds outstanding in the United States, and their characteristics are somewhat different from the others'. Many corporations and all levels of government—state, local, and federal—issue bonds to raise financial capital. They have a twofold appeal to investors: They are usually safer than common stocks, and they generally have a higher current return.

Although more investors are now considering bonds than they did in the past, it is still unlikely you will own bonds directly. But there is a good chance you will own them indirectly through your retirement fund, or perhaps through a mutual fund specializing in bond investment. In either case, it is important to understand bonds as investment vehicles and to be able to decide if they are appropriate for you.

Characteristics of Bonds

Fixed return: A return of a specific dollar amount each year, characteristic of bonds and preferred stock.

Regardless of who issues them, bonds have many similar characteristics. The most important of these is the **fixed return**. In contrast to common stocks with their varying returns, the return from most bonds is known the moment you buy them—assuming you hold them to maturity and the issuers do not default on payments. Details of a bond issued by Dreyer's Grand Ice Cream are shown in Figure 14.9.

Face value: An amount for which a bond is redeemed at maturity.

FACE VALUE   The **face value** of a bond is the amount for which the issuer agrees to redeem the bond at its maturity. When a bond is issued, it has a set life; for example, a 25-year bond means the bond will not be redeemed by its issuer until

NEW ISSUE

$50,000,000

6½% CONVERTIBLE SUBORDINATED DEBENTURES DUE 2011

The Debentures are convertible into Common Stock of the Company at any time on or before May 25, 2011, unless previously redeemed, at a conversion price of $32 per share, subject to adjustment under certain conditions.

Price 100%

(Interest payable June 1 and December 1 in each year)

Copies of the Prospectus may be obtained in any State only from the undersigned as may lawfully offer these securities in such State.

HAMBRECHT & QUIST

INCORPORATED

June 2, 1986

FIGURE 14.9

Announcement of a convertible bond issue. (Courtesy of Hambrecht & Quist.)

---

25 years after the date it is issued. Dreyer's bonds had a 25-year life when they were issued in June 1986. In effect, bondholders lent money to the issuer and are not asking for repayment of the loan until 25 years later. This probably seems like a long time to you, and it is; but many bonds are issued with maturities this long and longer. However, many have shorter maturities, and issuers frequently stagger bond maturities to accommodate the many different needs of potential investors.

Practically all corporate bonds sold to the public have the same face value—$1,000—although some (mostly those issued by various governments) have higher face values. When a bond series is issued, the issuer attempts to adjust its interest rate so that it can be sold *at par*, which means it is sold at the face value. However, bonds issued in the past and currently traded on bond markets may have market prices completely different from their face values, since interest rates may have increased or decreased since their issuance.

SEMIANNUAL INTEREST PAYMENTS   Most bonds pay interest twice a year. The amount of interest you receive is stated on the bond and expressed as a percentage of par value. For example, a 12 percent bond pays $120 a year ($1,000 × 0.12) in interest, or $60 each six months. Dreyer's bond pays 6.5 percent interest, or $65 a year. This rate is often called the **coupon rate.** This term is a carry-over from the past, when most bonds were coupon bonds and you received interest by clipping coupons from the bond and presenting them to a bank for payment. Since all corporate bonds now are registered, rather than coupon bonds, the interest checks come directly to you, or to your broker if your certificates are held at a firm.

Coupon rate: Stated interest rate on a bond.

REDEMPTION AT MATURITY OR EARLIER   As just mentioned, the issuer agrees to redeem your bond at its maturity. However, many corporate bonds (and some government bonds) can be redeemed earlier at the discretion of the issuer. These **callable bonds** allow the issuer an earlier redemption, and such redemption usually takes place at a price above face value. For example, a bond may be callable at $1,100. Corporations attach calls to bonds to give them greater flexibility in future financing. It might be necessary to raise capital even in periods when interest rates are very high; therefore, a corporation might sell bonds yielding, say, 18 percent. Interest rates might then fall, and the corporation could sell similar bonds and pay interest of only 12 percent. Naturally, it would like to do this, and the call feature allows it to. It issues 12 percent bonds and uses the proceeds to redeem the 18 percent bonds. What's good for the corporation, though, isn't good for you. You may have thought that you would receive 18 percent for 20 years, but the bond is redeemed at the end of two years. That is why callable bonds yield more than noncallable bonds, and why you should look closely for a call feature on any bond you are considering buying. While some corporations do not exercise calls unless interest rates drop dramatically, many others will call as soon as it is even slightly profitable to do so. There is not enough information in Figure 14.9 to determine Dreyer's bonds' redemption characteristics.

Callable bonds: Bonds that can be redeemed before their maturities.

THE CONVERTIBLE FEATURE   A particularly attractive bond to potential common stock investors is the convertible bond. A **convertible bond** may be redeemed, but it may also be converted into shares of the issuing corporation's common stock. For example, MAPCO (an integrated energy company) has a convertible bond that allows you to exchange one bond for 22.22 shares of its common stock. The bond pays 10 percent annual interest on its face value. Suppose you paid $1,000 for this bond; is it a good investment? It could be, but much depends upon the price of MAPCO's common stock. Suppose the stock is selling for $40 a share; then the bond's value as common stock—its **conversion value**—is $889 ($40 × 22.22), which is less than the $1,000 you paid for it. And since you could get a 12 percent yield on Treasury bonds at the time you were getting 10 percent on the MAPCO bond, you might think it is a poor investment. But suppose MAPCO's common stock increases to $80 a share: Now the bond is worth at least $1,778 ($80 × 22.22). You should see from this example that convertible bonds are quite different from conventional bonds. They offer potentially higher returns by virtue of their conversion privilege, but they are also riskier. Also, it takes a specialized skill to determine the investment quality of convertibles, so it is a good idea to work with a professional if you are interested

Convertible bonds: Bonds that can be converted into shares of the issuer's common stock.

Conversion value: The value of a bond as determined by the value of the common stock into which the bond can be converted.

Investing for
the Future

in buying them. Value Line publishes a survey of convertibles and offers excellent advice on those it feels are attractively priced. As you see in Figure 14.9, Dreyer's bonds are also convertible. Given the conversion price of $32, this means each bond converts into 31.25 shares of common stock (31.25 = $1,000 ÷ $32).

Who Issues Bonds?

Bonds are a favorite financing medium for many corporations and governments. It might surprise you to know that corporations typically raise more money each year through the sale of bonds than through the sale of common and preferred stock, as Table 14.1 shows. Most corporate bonds are the conventional variety (sometimes called "plain vanilla") that pay interest twice a year and are redeemed at maturity. Along with convertible bonds just discussed, in recent years some corporations have added new features (called "new flavors") to enhance their appeal to investors. For example, several companies have issued bonds that convert into commodities. Sunshine Mining has a bond outstanding that converts into 50 ounces of silver, and Texas International has issued a bond that converts into 29 barrels of crude oil. The idea behind each of these is to give the investor both a current return (the Sunshine bond has an $8\frac{1}{2}$ percent coupon rate) and a hedge against inflation. Theoretically, if inflation increases, so should the prices

Commodity-backed bonds: Bonds that are convertible into certain commodities.

of silver and crude oil. Bonds of this type are called **commodity-backed bonds.** Another type of inflation-hedge bond has its rate tied to a variable interest rate, such as the Treasury bill rate. These are called **floating rate bonds,** and they have been issued mostly by commercial banks and other financial institutions. Also, a number of corporations have issued **zero-coupon bonds.** These bonds pay no semiannual interest; you earn your return by buying them at prices less than face value and receiving face value at redemption (they are identical in this respect to U.S. Series EE bonds). Their main appeal is that they lock in a known rate of return. You do not have to worry about what rates might be available in the future to reinvest semiannual interest payments, as you must do with a conventional bond. These bonds are ideally suited for IRA accounts but have certain tax disadvantages if you own them directly.

Floating rate bonds: Bonds with interest payments tied to interest rates on other securities, usually Treasury bills.

Zero-coupon bonds: Bonds that pay no semiannual interest; interest is earned by buying such bonds at prices below their face values.

Municipal bonds: Bonds issued by state and local governments.

Municipal bonds are issued by state or local governments to finance capital projects such as schools, hospitals, bridges, airports, and many others. A particularly attractive feature of the municipal bond is that the interest it pays is not subject to federal income taxes. If you are in a 28 percent tax bracket and a municipal bond is available with a 10 percent yield, you would have to earn 13.89 percent on an alternative investment to do as well. The following formula

TABLE 14.1 · New Security Issues of Corporations (in Billions of Dollars)

	1990	1989	1988
Common stocks	$19.4	$26.0	$35.9
Preferred stocks	4.0	6.2	6.5
Total stocks	$23.4	$32.2	$42.4
Bonds	235.0	318.8	353.1
Total new issues	$258.4	$351.0	$395.5

SOURCE: *Federal Reserve Bulletin,* June 1991, p. A-33.

Stocks and Bonds

converts the tax-free yield to an equivalent pretax yield so you can easily compare the two:

$$\text{Pretax yield equivalent} = \frac{\text{tax-exempt yield}}{1.0 - \text{your tax rate}}$$

For the preceding example, we have

$$0.1389 \ (\text{or } 13.89\%) = \frac{0.10}{1.0 - 0.28} = \frac{0.10}{0.72}$$

Treasury issues: Debt instruments issued by the U.S. Treasury.

Agency issues: Debt instruments issued by agencies of the federal government.

The federal government has two different kinds of debt securities. First are those issued by the U.S. Treasury, or **Treasury issues,** as part of the ongoing process of financing the national debt. The second type, **agency issues,** are those issued by government agencies, such as the Federal Housing Administration, the Government National Mortgage Association, the Farmers' Home Loan Administration, and others. There is a huge amount of federal debt outstanding, as Figure 14.10 shows. The primary appeal of federal debt is that it is considered free of default risk—you usually do not expect the federal government to repudiate its debt obligations. While Treasury issues are considered somewhat safer than agency issues in this respect, both can be viewed as virtually free from default risk; however, they are still subject to interest rate risk.

FIGURE 14.10

Federal debt outstanding March 31, 1991 (in billions of dollars). (Source: *Federal Reserve Bulletin,* June 1991, pp. A-29 and A-32.)

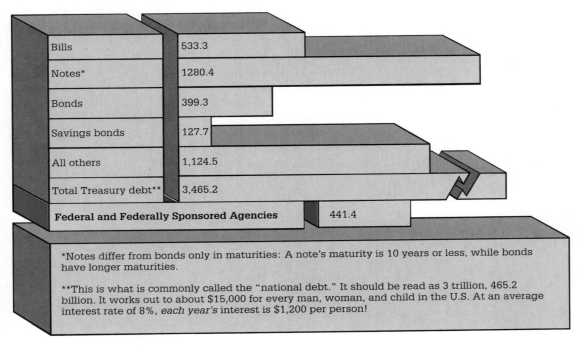

Bills	533.3
Notes*	1280.4
Bonds	399.3
Savings bonds	127.7
All others	1,124.5
Total Treasury debt**	3,465.2
Federal and Federally Sponsored Agencies	441.4

*Notes differ from bonds only in maturities: A note's maturity is 10 years or less, while bonds have longer maturities.

**This is what is commonly called the "national debt." It should be read as 3 trillion, 465.2 billion. It works out to about $15,000 for every man, woman, and child in the U.S. At an average interest rate of 8%, *each year's* interest is $1,200 per person!

Buy Treasuries Directly

Investors throughout the world consider U.S. Treasury-issued securities the bedrock of safety. Actually, from a safety perspective a Treasury security is the same as currency itself; the major difference is that one pays interest and the other does not. Despite their advantages, unfortunately, small investors seldom buy Treasuries, primarily because they are unaware of how easy it is.

That might change in the future, though, since buying Treasuries now can be done directly through the Treasury, eliminating the middleman and the usual buy/sell commissions. Over 1 million Americans are currently using the Treasury Direct program, and the number is growing rapidly.

It's simple to sign up: Get an application form from the nearest Federal Reserve Bank or one of its branches. Fill out the form, being careful to include your Social Security number and your bank's nine-digit "routing transit" number (call your bank if you aren't sure of the number).

Treasuries are sold at auctions, and you must be sure to submit the application before the auction day. Information about upcoming auctions will be available at the Federal Reserve bank. Your application is referred to as a "noncompetitive tender," which means that you agree to accept the average yield that arises from competitive bidding at the auction.

After the purchase you now have a Treasury Direct account. Interest paid on the securities each six months will be forwarded to your bank, as will the redemption of the securities at their maturity. What could be easier? Finally, a brief summary of Treasury securities is shown below.

Security Name	Maturity	Minimum Investment	Interest Information
U.S. Treasury bills	Up to 1 year	$10,000 (cashier's check)	Interest is earned via a discount from $10,000
U.S. Treasury notes	1–10 years	$1,000–$5,000 (personal check)	Interest is paid semiannually
U.S. Treasury bonds	10–30 years	$1,000 (personal check)	Interest is paid semiannually

Your Rights as a Bondholder

Bond indenture: Document accompanying a bond issue—a contract between the issuer and bondholders.

Just as stockholders have certain rights, so do bondholders. Bondholders' rights are described clearly in a document that accompanies each bond issue—the **bond indenture.** The indenture is actually a contract between the issuing institution and the bondholders. In some respects it is similar to a loan agreement you sign when you borrow from a bank. Since it is impossible for the issuer to have an individual contract with each bondholder, the indenture acts as a comprehensive contract covering all bondholders. To see that the issuer lives up to its agreements in the indenture, a trustee (which is usually a large commercial bank) is appointed to represent bondholders.

Protective covenants: Restrictions placed upon a bond issuer designed to strengthen the bondholders' position.

Mortgage bonds: Bonds secured by collateral.

Debentures: Bonds not secured by collateral.

Subordinated debentures: Bonds with claims given to other bond issues; these bonds offer poor recovery in a liquidation.

PROTECTIVE COVENANTS OF THE INDENTURE Because of the risk of bankruptcy, many bond indentures contain **protective covenants** (restrictions) to strengthen the bondholders' position. Perhaps the best protection is provided by **mortgage bonds,** which are secured by collateral. In the event of bankruptcy, the bondholders' interest is protected by the pledged property, which does not have to be shared with other creditors or stockholders. Bonds without supporting collateral are called **debentures,** and there are still other bonds that offer even less protection. These are called **subordinated debentures.** (Dreyer's bonds are this

455

type, as shown in Figure 14.9.) If you buy this kind of bond, your claim to assets in liquidation are subordinated to (meaning they come after) the claims of another issue. For example, a corporation might issue bonds in 1993. Its investors are very concerned that their position will be weakened if the corporation borrows again, since the new bondholder's claims would be equivalent to theirs. So they include in the indenture that any new bonds must be subordinated to their claim. Naturally, if the corporation needed more money in 1994 and issued more bonds, they would have to be subordinated debentures.

Along with the common restrictive covenants are many others that might be included in the indenture. For example, the issuer may be prohibited from paying dividends on common stock unless a certain level of earnings is reached, or salaries and other compensation of chief executives might be subjected to certain limits, or certain assets may not be sold without bondholder approval. Practically any restriction can be written into the indenture if bondholders believe it strengthens their position. Of course, the issuer balances all these against the interest it must pay on the bonds: the more stringent the restrictions, the less interest on the bonds. In effect, bondholders trade off income for protection.

SINKING FUNDS Another common protection is to have the issuer establish a **sinking fund,** which consists of reserving funds for the purpose of gradually retiring bonds before their maturity.

Sinking fund: A system for gradual retirement of a bond issue.

Expected Return from Bonds

If you buy a bond at its face value when it is issued and eventually redeem it at its face value, then your return would consist exclusively of the semiannual interest payments you would receive each year. The above situation may not happen, however. You may buy the bond for more or less than its face value, which leads to a capital loss or gain if you hold it to maturity. Or you may sell the bond before maturity, and the price you receive will probably be different—perhaps quite different—from your purchase price. Therefore, just as with common stocks, a bond's return may consist of both a current return and a future return. Each must be considered in evaluating investment performance.

CURRENT RETURN OR CURRENT YIELD The current return with a bond comes from the semiannual interest payments. This is often expressed in percentage form and called the **current yield.** To calculate the current yield, all you need to do is divide the annual interest by the current market price of the bond. Suppose you have a bond that pays $120 a year interest: If its current market price is $1,000, then its current yield is 12 percent ($120/$1,000). If its price is $800, its current yield would be 15 percent ($120/$800). The formula is

Current yield: A bond's annual interest divided by its market price.

$$\text{Current yield} = \frac{\$I}{\$P}$$

where

$$I = \text{annual interest}$$
$$P = \text{current market price}$$

Current yields for corporate bonds are published in each edition of *The Wall Street Journal* and in the financial sections of Sunday editions of some local newspapers.

YIELD TO MATURITY   In addition to current yield, bond investors often are interested in a bond's **yield to maturity,** which may differ from current yield. A yield to maturity is the return you would earn by buying a bond today and holding it until it is redeemed by the issuer. A precise calculation of yield to maturity requires the use of present value tables, but a close approximation is possible using the following formula:

$$\text{Yield to maturity} = \frac{\$I + (\$1,000 - \$P)/N}{(\$P + \$1,000)/2}$$

where

$$I = \text{annual interest}$$
$$P = \text{current market price}$$
$$N = \text{number of years remaining to maturity}$$

It is assumed the bond has a face value of $1,000. Let us return to the bond mentioned above and assume its market price is $800 and that it has ten years to maturity. Its yield to maturity is 15.6 percent, as calculated below:

$$\frac{\$120 + (\$1,000 - \$800)/10}{(\$800 + \$1,000)/2} = \frac{\$140}{\$900} = 0.156 \text{ or } 15.6\%$$

As you see, the bond's yield to maturity is slightly more than its current yield. Actually, if a bond has few years remaining to maturity, the current yield is a poor measurement of your actual rate of return. To see this, assume that the bond just described matures in one year. The numerator above would then be $320, and the denominator would still be $900; yield to maturity would be 35.6 percent ($320/$900), which is quite different from 15 percent.

   Yields to maturity are not published for corporate bonds in *The Wall Street Journal*, but they are published for U.S. Treasury securities. You may also find a listing of U.S. Treasury securities along with their yields to maturity in your local newspaper.

Risks of Bond Investment

Bonds have two main sources of risk: default risk and interest rate risk. Each is important and should be understood thoroughly.

DEFAULT RISK   **Default risk** has to do with probability of actually receiving the promised interest and redeeming the bond at face value. If the probabilities of both of these happening are high, the bond is considered low risk; if the probabilities are low, the bond is risky. As we have just seen, default risk depends in large measure on the protections provided in the indenture. All things considered, a subordinated debenture is much riskier than a mortgage bond. But default risk also depends upon the financial strength of the issuer. You probably would be safer with a Sears or DuPont subordinated debenture than a mortgage bond issued by Fly-by-Night Airlines using a dilapidated hangar or vintage airplane as collateral.

Very frankly, neither you nor we are sufficiently skilled to do our own bond safety analysis; it is far better to rely upon professional rating services. The major sources—Standard and Poor's and Moody's—are shown in Figure 14.11. Of course, you can expect bond yields to vary by each rating class, with the lowest yield on AAA-rated bonds.

It is important to know that municipal bonds are not free of default risk. This fact was brought home to investors in dramatic fashion in the early 1980s by the massive failure of bonds connected with the Washington Public Power Supply (WPPS, commonly pronounced *whoops*) in the Northwest. If you are thinking of investing in municipals, by all means seek adequate diversification and consult one of the ranking services before you invest.

FIGURE 14.11

What the bond ratings mean.

Standard and Poor's (S&P)	Moody's	Description
AAA	Aaa	The highest quality, carrying the smallest degree of investment risk and generally referred to as "gilt edge."
AA	Aa	Also of high quality, differing in only small degree from the highest rating in ability to repay the debt.
A	A	Possesses many favorable investment attributes and considered upper medium grade obligation; a strong capacity to pay interest and repay principal, but somewhat more susceptible to adverse effects of changes in circumstances and economic conditions.
BBB	Baa	A medium grade obligation; has adequate capacity to pay off debt, but adverse economic conditions or changing circumstances are more likely to lead to a weakened capacity to pay interest and repay principal. Moody's, in addition, considers the rating to have some speculative characteristics.
BB	Ba	The highest of the purely "speculative" ratings; protection of interest and principal payments is considered very moderate and not well safeguarded during both good and bad times over the future.
B	B	Generally lacking characteristics of the desirable investment; assurance of interest and principal payments over any long period may be small.
CCC	Caa	Considered in poor standing; elements of danger to payment of principal or interest may be present. Moody's includes some issues in default in this category, while S&P does not.
CC	Ca	Speculative in a high degree; having other marked shortcomings. Moody's also uses for some issues in default.
C	C	S&P reserves the rating for bonds that are not paying interest; Moody's denotes issues with extremely poor prospects of ever attaining any real investment standing.
D		S&P only; reserved for issues in default, with interest and-or principal payments in arrears.

INTEREST RATE RISK   After you purchase a bond, your investment will be subject to **interest rate risk.** This risk results from the fact that if credit conditions tighten or loosen after your purchase, interest rates in general will go up or go down. Along with these changes, the market price for your bond will also change. The primary factor determining how risky a bond is in relation to interest rate changes is its maturity; the longer the maturity, the greater the price volatility and risk. This is seen best through the use of an example.

Let us assume you are considering three different 12 percent bonds: One matures in one year, another in five years, and the third in 20 years. Assume further that each is currently selling for $1,000, meaning each has a yield to maturity of 12 percent. Now assume that after you purchase each one, yields to maturity on identical new bonds (1) increase to 15 percent, or (2) decrease to 9 percent. Let us see what would happen to the market prices of the three bonds. The new market prices were calculated using the formula just given for calculating yield to maturity. We just plugged in yields to maturity (15 percent, 9 percent), and solved for the respective *P*s. Table 14.2 shows the results. As you see, if yields to maturity rise to 15 percent, your loss is greatest with the 20-year bond and least with the one-year bond; but if interest rates fall, you enjoy the biggest gain with the 20-year bond and, again, the least with the one-year bond. It should be clear that your greatest exposure to risk is with long-maturity bonds.

Preferred Stock

Preferred stock: A hybrid security with characteristics of both common stock and bonds.

Preferred stock represents a third choice for investors. It is often called a hybrid security because it has characteristics of both common stock and bonds. It is unfortunate the word *preferred* is used to describe this type of security, for it suggests that in some way it must be superior to common stock. While preferred stock is certainly different from common stock, it isn't necessarily preferable.

Characteristics of Preferred Stock

Most of preferred stock's characteristics make it similar to bonds, except one: By law it is considered a form of equity ownership. Therefore, preferred stockholders rank behind bondholders in terms of asset distributions in the event of liquidation. If a corporation files bankruptcy, all its creditors' claims must be settled

TABLE 14.2 ·
Changes in Market
Prices of Three Bonds
in Response to
Changes in Interest
Rates

Yield to Maturity	Market Prices		
	1-Year Bond	5-Year Bond	20-Year Bond
9%	$1,029	$1,123	$1.316
12%	1,000	1,000	1,000
15%	961	891	760
Change in Yield to Maturity	Change in Market Prices		
Down by 3%	$+29	$+123	$+316
Up by 3%	−28	−109	−240

before any payments can be made to preferred stockholders. Figure 14.12 shows a preferred stock issued by the Mead Corporation.

DIVIDEND FEATURES   Like common stock, preferred stock is paid a dividend, not interest. However, the dividend is usually a fixed amount, and it is often expressed as a percentage of par value (which is usually $100), similar to how interest is paid on bonds. For example, an 8 percent preferred stock would mean that an $8-a-year dividend is paid on each share of stock. Even though a preferred stock has a par (or face) value of $100, its price in the marketplace could be quite different, depending again upon the overall level of interest rates. Some preferred stocks do not have par values; they simply state the dollar amount of dividend. Mead's preferred stock is this type; as you see in Figure 14.12, it pays $2.80 each year in dividends.

Preferred dividends can be **cumulative** or **noncumulative.** Cumulative means that if a dividend is not declared in one year, it accumulates and must be paid in a future year before any dividend can be paid on the common stock. With noncumulative stock, a missed dividend is lost forever. It is important to know that a

Cumulative, noncumulative: Feature of preferred stock indicating if nondeclared dividends will (cumulative) or will not (noncumulative) carry forward to future years.

FIGURE 14.12

A sample preferred stock of the Mead Corporation. (Courtesy of the Mead Corporation.)

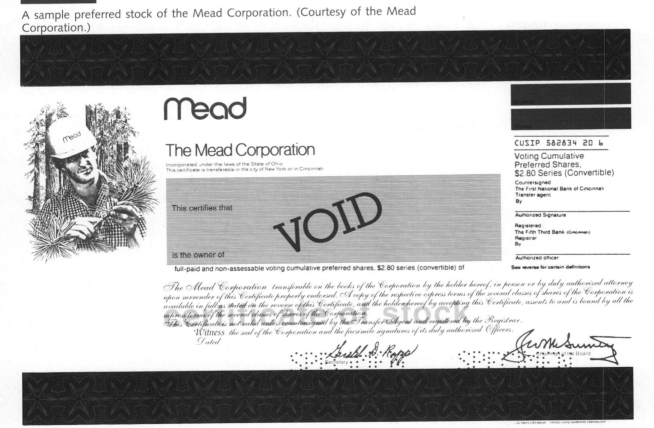

corporation is not required legally to pay preferred dividends. In contrast to bond interest, which becomes a legal liability of a corporation the moment it is due, preferred dividends are not liabilities until they are declared. You can find some preferred stocks with many years' dividends in arrears, and some speculators frequently buy these stocks, anticipating an improvement in the company's earnings and knowing that all the accumulated dividends must be paid before management can resume regular dividend payments on the common stock.

A few preferred stocks have **participating dividends,** which means that after common stockholders have received a stated dividend, any distribution above this amount must be shared with the preferred stockholders. This is an extremely attractive feature to attach to preferred stock. A corporation that does so usually has financial weaknesses and must offer this bonus to make its preferred stock salable. Mead's preferred stock is cumulative but not participating.

PREFERRED STOCKHOLDERS' RIGHTS   As mentioned previously, preferred stockholders do not enjoy the same legal protections as bondholders do. However, there are similarities. For example, preferred stock is also issued under an indenture agreement, and many of the same protective covenants are written into the indenture. Some indentures go so far as to give voting rights to preferred stockholders (which they almost never have) if the common stockholders fail to live up to the terms of the indenture or are unable to manage the business profitably. However, these restrictions are rare. You are better advised to think of preferred stock as a considerably weaker instrument than a bond with respect to your protections in bankruptcy.

THE CONVERTIBLE FEATURE   A growing number of new preferred stocks are convertible. Just as in the case of convertible bonds, **convertible preferred stock** converts into a given number of shares of the company's common stock. For example, Mead's preferred stock converts into 2.81 shares of its common stock. In recent years, the convertible feature has replaced the participating feature as a ''sweetener'' to help sell the preferred.

Expected Return from Preferred Stock

The expected return from nonconvertible preferred stock is calculated in the same way as the expected return on bonds. You receive a fixed annual dividend (usually paid quarterly), which is the current return, and you may have a future capital gain or loss if you sell the preferred for a price more or less than your purchase price. It must be noted, though, that most preferred stock does not have a maturity date when the corporation must redeem it. It is said to be issued in perpetuity. Therefore, you cannot calculate a yield to maturity, but you can calculate a current yield in the following way:

$$\text{Current yield} = \frac{\$D}{\$P}$$

where

D = annual dividend
P = market price of the preferred stock

A preferred stock paying $2 a year in dividends and having a market price of $18 would have a current yield of 11.11 percent ($2/$18). This is the same calculation we made to find a bond's current yield. Although the preferred stock may not have a redemption date, it may have a call option attached, allowing a corporation the right to call the shares if it wishes to.

If they are listed on the organized exchanges (Mead's isn't), preferred stocks are reported in the same sections as common stock in *The Wall Street Journal* or other newspapers. The symbol *pf* appears after the name of the company, designating the issue as preferred. While many companies have issued preferred stock (particularly public utilities), many more have not. This is so because they often view preferred stock as a poor substitute for bonds in raising capital, since bond interest can be deducted in figuring the corporation's income tax, but preferred dividends cannot be deducted. At tax rates most corporations pay, this amounts to a substantial difference in tax dollars.

Action Plan for the Steeles Investing for the Children's Education

Background   As a first step in financial planning, the Steeles have set forth specific investment goals. The most important is providing a college education for John and Nancy. College expenditures will begin in about ten years and Arnie and Sharon must start investing now, and continuously over the next ten years, to accumulate sufficient funds. The Steeles have estimated college expenses in nominal dollars (see Chapter 4), but now they must adjust these amounts to take into consideration the expected annual inflation rate for college expenses, which they estimate at 6 percent. The accompanying table indicates the inflation-adjusted amounts the Steeles must accumulate.

Year (from Now) Expenses Begin	Nominal Amount	Inflation-Considered Amount (6% Rate)
10	$12,000	$21,490
11	12,000	22,780
12	24,000	48,293
13	24,000	51,190
14	12,000	27,131
15	12,000	28,759
Total	$96,000	$199,643

The Problem   The Steeles must earn no less than 6 percent after taxes on their investments *each year* to accumulate the needed amounts. Their pretax rate of return must be 8.6 percent [(6%/(1 − 0.30)], assuming a marginal tax rate of 30 percent. While yield is very important if the Steeles are to stay within their savings budget, they regard safety as even more important.

The Plan   The Steeles should limit their investments to either U.S. Treasury bonds or highest-quality municipal bonds. When the Steeles were developing

Investment Quality of Preferred Stock

Another aspect of the tax law also makes preferred stock a less desirable investment from the individual investor's point of view. A provision in the tax law allows corporations to exclude from their taxable incomes up to 80 percent of dividends they receive from stocks of domestic corporations. For example, if General Motors Corporation received $1,000 in dividends from shares of IBM stock it owned, only $200 would be subject to GM's corporate income tax. This provision encourages corporations to invest in both common and preferred stocks, but particularly in the latter. As a result, current yields on preferred stocks are reduced relative to bonds, because corporate buying in the marketplace bids up the prices of preferred shares. This is why you usually find preferred yields less than long-term bond yields, even though they are riskier investments. While they may be attractive to a corporate investor, preferred stocks are not attractive to

their plan, yields on ten-year Treasuries and ten-year municipals ("munis") were around 8.5 and 6.3 percent, respectively. Each type of bond can be purchased in zero-coupon form with a maturity matched to the date funds are needed in the future. Since the after-tax yields of the munis and Treasuries were fairly close, the Steeles will select the Treasuries for the first-year investment. But this might change in the future if yield differences favor munis.

Specifically, they will buy "Treasury strips" with a ten-year maturity. Suppose the Steeles wanted to invest a sum now that would be sufficient to cover the $21,490 needed in ten years. Since each bond has a $1,000 redemption value, they would need to buy 21.49 bonds (round to 21). Ten-year strips were quoted at a price of $429 per bond. So the Steeles would have had to invest $9,009 (21 × $429) in year 1 to accumulate the needed $21,490 ten years later.

The Steeles can buy the strips directly or through a mutual fund (e.g., Benham Target Maturity Trust). They will use the Benham Trust to avoid commission, although their yield will be slightly less because of the fund's operating costs.

Rationale for the Plan   Zero-coupon bonds are the only investment that guarantees a future sum of money. If the Steeles selected interest-bearing bonds, they would face the problem of reinvesting the periodic interest payments. If these subsequent investments must be made at lower rates, their target accumulations will not be achieved.

If rates do decline in the future, the Steeles will have a problem if they continue investing in zero-coupon bonds. However, they have decided to stick with safety, which means they must revise their savings plans to reflect larger savings requirements; unless, of course, the annual inflation rate of college costs declines. Falling interest rates often accompany falling inflation rates, but there is no assurance that this correlation will continue in the future.

you. It is difficult to see why you should invest in them unless other sweeteners, such as convertibility, are attached to help sell them. Some corporations have begun issuing floating rate preferred stock similar to floating rate bonds discussed previously. But again, this feature has been added to appeal mostly to corporate investors looking for temporary investments of cash, and you as an individual can usually earn a higher yield in floating rate bonds.

Summary

Common stocks represent ownership interests in a company. As an owner, you have the right to vote, a preemptive right, and the right to share in earnings or asset distributions. The total expected return from common stock consists of a current return in the form of dividends and a potential future return in the form of a capital gain. To determine if a stock should be purchased, it is necessary to compare its expected total return with its required return: Only if expected return exceeds required return should it be purchased. Different companies represent different common stock investment opportunities: There are growth companies, income stocks, blue chips, cyclical stocks, and special situations. Put and call options give investors opportunities to sell or buy stocks at predetermined prices within a given period of time. Warrants and rights are similar to call options, except that they are issued by corporations, not individuals.

Bonds are issued by both corporations and governments. They offer a fixed return in the sense that their interest payments are fixed over their lives. Bonds are subject to two important sources of risk: default risk, which has to do with the issuer not making interest payments or redeeming the bonds; and interest rate risk, which means bond prices change in response to changes in credit conditions.

Preferred stock is often characterized as a hybrid between common stock and bonds. Although inferior, preferred stockholders' rights are similar to bondholders' rights. Preferred stock has certain income tax peculiarities that influence its yield, and these tend to make it unattractive to individual investors, relative to bonds.

Key Terms

agency issues (p. 454)

balance sheet strength (p. 442)

blue chip (p. 447)

bond indenture (p. 455)

call option (p. 448)

callable bonds (p. 452)

capital structure (p. 442)

commodity-backed bonds (p. 453)

common stock (p. 433)

conversion value (p. 452)

convertible bonds (p. 452)

convertible preferred stock (p. 461)

coupon rate (p. 452)

cumulative (p. 460)

current yield (p. 456)

cyclical stocks (p. 447)

debentures (p. 455)

default risk (p. 457)

earnings per share (EPS) (p. 442)

expected return (p. 436)

face value (p. 450)

fixed return (p. 450)

floating rate bonds (p. 453)

fundamentalist (p. 442)

growth company (p. 445)

income stocks (p. 446)

interest rate risk (p. 459)

market technician (p. 443)

mortgage bonds (p. 455)

municipal bonds (p. 453)

new highs-new lows index (p. 443)

noncumulative (p. 460)

participating dividends (p. 461)

preemptive right (p. 435)

preferred stock (p. 459)

price-earnings (P-E) ratio (p. 442)

protective covenants (p. 455)

Problems and Review Questions

1 Explain your rights and return potential as a common stockholder, bondholder, or preferred stockholder. Discuss whether one of these is better than the other two.

2 Suppose you and two friends are considering forming a corporation to produce and market computer software programs that each partner has written. Explain whether you think you should be concerned about voting rights and the preemptive right, assuming each shareholder receives 1,000 shares.

3 Magna Corporation has the following securities outstanding: 1,000,000 shares of common stock, 200,000 shares of $2.50 (annual dividend) preferred stock, and $10,000,000 of 15 percent bonds. Calculate earnings per share available to common stockholders if Magna earns: (a) $5,000,000; (b) $2,200,000; (c) $1,000,000.

4 Explain a stock dividend and further explain if you would prefer it to a cash dividend. What are stock splits, and how desirable are they?

5 Bartholomew Industries' common stock indicates a dividend of $2 a share next year, and its dividend has been growing at an annual rate of 15 percent. If its stock has a current market price of $40 a share, calculate your total expected return on the stock.

6 Bartholomew Industries' (see Question 5) common stock has an estimated beta of 2.2. Assuming you could earn 9 percent on U.S. Treasury securities and the market risk premium is 8 percent, should you buy the stock? Explain, using your answer from question 5 here.

7 Tartan Corporation has the following ten-year data:

Number of common shares outstanding	1,000,000
Average annual earnings	$2,635,000
Average market price of the common stock	$20/share

Securities analysts think Tartan will earn $5 million next year and have 1,200,000 common shares outstanding. What price do you expect for its common stock next year?

8 You heard the following news commentary on television last night: "Milt Davis, Morrel-Lunch's chief technical analyst, noted that IBM broke through its two-year resistance line and could be headed for the $170–$180 area." What do you think Milt is talking about? Explain.

9 The following listing appeared in the financial pages of a local newspaper; explain what it means.

52 weeks									Net
High	Low	Stock	Div	Yld.	P-E	High	Low	Close	Chg.
$17\frac{3}{4}$	$7\frac{1}{8}$	AAR	.44	3.1	18	$14\frac{1}{8}$	14	$14\frac{1}{8}$	$+\frac{1}{4}$

10 Briefly explain the following: (*a*) call option; (*b*) put option; (*c*) warrants; (*d*) rights. Are these risky investments? Explain.

11 What two features of bonds might make them more appealing than common stocks, and what kind of investor is likely to buy bonds?

12 Explain the following terms: (*a*) bond indenture; (*b*) coupon rate; (*c*) redemption; (*d*) callable bond; (*e*) convertible bond; (*f*) conversion value; (*g*) commodity-backed bond; (*h*) zero-coupon bond; (*i*) floating rate bond; (*j*) protective covenants; (*k*) mortgage bonds; (*l*) debentures; (*m*) subordinated debentures; (*n*) sinking fund.

13 You are thinking of buying NAD company's 8 percent bond. You can buy it for $900 and it matures in five years. Calculate and then compare the *current yield* and *yield to maturity* on this bond.

14 Instead of the NAD bond described in Question 13, suppose you could buy a five-year, 6 percent municipal bond selling at par. If you are in a 33 percent tax bracket, would you prefer this bond to NAD's, assuming they are of equal risk? Explain.

**Case 14.1
Ed Driessen's
Stock Pick**

Ed Driessen is in a management trainee program at Leyton and Leyton Company, a manufacturer of business forms and accounting systems. During his first month on the job (January 1993), Ed was assigned to the sales department to become familiar with its operations. In reviewing customer accounts, Ed happened to notice a substantial increase in orders from Antogen, Inc., a hospital supplies company with diverse interests in that area. Since most of these orders were for invoices, purchase orders, and other forms related to sales, Ed reasoned that Antogen might be on the verge of increasing its sales and profits rapidly. If this were to happen, its common stock might be a very good buy.

Before buying, however, Ed thought it would be a good idea to research the stock at the local library. One day during his lunch hour, he stopped there and gathered some data and made a photocopy of Antogen's price chart. (The data and the chart are shown at right.) Ed isn't quite sure how to use all this information, but a friend of his indicated that it shows fairly good performance and that Ed's investment should work out well for him. Ed is ready to buy the stock, but would first like your opinion. He is single and has good insurance coverage, and his position with Leyton and Leyton seems very secure and promising for the future.

Questions

1 Assume that at the time Ed asks your advice, the rate of return on U.S. Treasury securities is 9 percent and that a market risk premium of 8 percent seems appropriate. Using the 1983–1992 dividend growth rate, do you think Ed should buy the stock? Explain your answer. Suppose you use the dividend growth rate indicated for 1993 and 1994 instead of the 1983–1992 rate; what is your answer then? Which rate do you feel is the more appropriate? Explain.

2 Rather than using a dividend approach, suppose you prefer to judge a stock's value by looking at earnings per share (EPS). Based on the available data, does an earnings approach indicate the stock is a good buy? Explain your answer.

3 Does the stock's price chart help you in making a decision? Explain.

4 What do you think of Ed's hunch? Do you feel he has information that might not be available to investors in general? Does the information given suggest that other investors are not aware of Antogen's prospects for growth? Explain.

5 All things considered, do you think Ed should buy the stock? Defend your answer. (Assume Ed already has adequate diversification.)

DATA FOR ANTOGEN, INC.

Current market price per share: $50
Earnings per share (EPS):
    Average annual growth 1983–92: 10%
        1992 actual $3.60
        1993 estimated $4.30
        1994 estimated $5.20

Dividends per share:
    Average annual growth 1983–92: 10%
        1992 actual $1.00
        1993 estimated $1.20
        1994 estimated $1.44

Average price-earnings (P-E) ratio:
    1983–92 10
    1992   12
Current beta estimate: 1.5

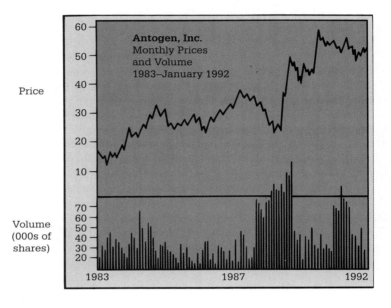

Case 14.2 The DuBays' Preference for Bonds

Nelson and Claire DuBay are in their early 50s. Their two children are both grown and living in their own households. Nelson and Claire have reasonably good positions, and their combined income in 1992 was over $75,000. Their net worth of about $150,000 is mostly in their house and furnishings, but they do have adequate liquid resources. The DuBays are concerned about retirement. Neither has a particularly good retirement plan, and their savings were depleted substantially by college costs for their children. However, they live on a rather modest budget and believe they can save about $10,000 a year for the next ten years or so. Nelson and Claire would both like to retire at age 62. Therefore, considering the reinvestment of earnings at even modest rates, such as 7 to 10 percent, they should have between $140,000 and $160,000 at retirement time. Of course, they would like to have much more than this, if that would be possible.

However, the DuBays are very concerned about risks associated with the investments they might make to achieve their objective. In discussing the situation with their stock-broker, Edith Klune, they conclude that common stocks simply have too much risk and possibly not enough return to achieve their goal in only ten years. Klune has suggested they limit their investments to corporate and government bonds. To help them, she prepared the accompanying list and suggested they purchase $2,000 of each bond each year, beginning January 1, 1993.

467

Issuer	Coupon Rate	Par Value	Year of Maturity	Current Market Price	S&P Rating
1. U.S. Treasury	9%	$1,000	2017	$1,200	—
2. BIM Corporation	7%	1,000	1997	900	AA
3. City of Oakland, California—General Revenue Bonds	7%	1,000	2007	1,000	BBB
4. Vaga Foods	14%	1,000	2002	1,100	B
5. AT&T	6%	1,000	2002	900	AAA

Questions

1 Assuming the DuBays are in a 28 percent tax bracket, and following Klune's advice, calculate the *current yield* and *yield to maturity* on each bond. Express the municipal bond's yields in pretax yield equivalent form.

2 Consider now the issue of price appreciation with the bonds, and explain how this might influence the DuBays' selection. For example, how does the U.S. Treasury bond compare to the AT&T bond in this respect? Since the DuBays do not apparently need high current return, which of the two do you recommend?

3 Discuss *interest rate risk* and *default risk* of the U.S. Treasury bond relative to the AT&T bond.

4 Do you agree with Klune's advice for the DuBays? Do you think default risk has been considered adequately? Explain.

Helpful Reading

Barron's

Slatter, John. "Stick with Quality: A Blue Chip Formula for Capital Gains." August 8, 1991, pp. 18–19.

Changing Times

Frailey, Fred W. "Stocks That Pay and Pay." October 1991, pp. 44–45.

Giese, William. "Investing Where Profits Go Up and Up." January 1991, pp. 53–56.

Kosnett, Jeff. "Will Muni Bonds Weather the Storm?" November 1991, pp. 73–76.

Schiffres, Manuel. "Cheap Thrills from Cheap Stocks." April 1991, pp. 49–52.

———. "Investing Where the Bargains Are." November 1990, pp. 37–42.

Money

Edgerton, Jerry. "Today's Best Way to Invest." December 1991, pp. 98–99.

Meyer, Marsha. "The Safest Bonds." November 1991, pp. 112–113.

The Wall Street Journal

Anders, George. "Picking the Winners in Initial Public Offerings." April 13, 1991, p. C1.

Donnelly, Barbara. "Riding High on the Small Stock Wave." April 15, 1991, p. C1.

Gottschalk, Earl C. "Proxy Statements Offer Juicy Tip-offs at Some Firms." April 17, 1991, p. C1.

Newman, Ann. "Sleuthing for Stocks Meant for Stardom." October 22, 1991, p. C1.

Helpful Contacts

Many investors use public or university libraries to access information about specific companies and industries. The advisory services listed below have numerous publications and are particularly useful data sources. Ask a reference librarian for the specific publications carried by the library. Since the publications are expensive, you should try library copies (before considering a purchase) to determine their value to you.

Moody's Investors Service, Inc.
99 Church Street, New York, NY 10007
Comprehensive information for bond and stock investments.

Standard and Poor's Corporation
825 Broadway, New York, NY 10004
Similar to Moody's; its *Monthly Stock Guide* covers over 5,000 firms. If you use a full-service broker, he or she might give you a copy.

Value Line Publishing, Inc.
711 Third Avenue, New York, NY 10017
Its *Investment Survey* is very popular because of its successful stock ranking system. It also has an excellent publication covering options, warrants, and convertibles. As noted in Chapter 13, it is also a good source for companies' beta values.

National Association of Securities Dealers
Finance Dept., 9513 Key West Avenue, Rockville, MD 20850
Ask for the *Nasdaq Fact Book and Company Directory* ($15), which provides address, phone number, stock symbol, and one-year price history for many smaller companies.

You can receive a company's annual report by contacting the company directly. Usually, reports are provided by the corporate treasurer's office.

Chapter 15

Portfolio Management: Do It Yourself or Leave It to Others?

Objectives

1 To understand what is meant by portfolio management and why monitoring a portfolio is important

2 To evaluate the factors involved in deciding whether you will make your own investment decisions, or invest in pooling arrangements where many of these are made for you

3 To recognize the many different kinds of mutual funds and the important services they offer

4 To be able to evaluate a mutual fund in terms of its expected return and risk and suitability to your investment goals

5 To identify other kinds of pooling arrangements: unit investment trusts and limited partnerships

6 To understand the broad aspects of securities markets, including industry regulation

Welcome to the Fast Foods of Investing

Baton Rouge—Phillip Piccard was the quintessential first-time investor. Fresh out of college, he began investing in common stocks, primarily at the urging of a friend who was an avid investor. His first trades were successful, convincing him that making money in the market was easy. The rest of the story is familiar: too much trading, too little diversification, and terribly poor selections put Phillip's losses at $1,000 by year's end. He had started with only $5,000, and if the situation didn't change, he faced losing all his savings within four years.

Over the year Phillip spent several hours a day "managing" his portfolio. At first, this had been more fun than work. But Phillip increasingly thought, What fun is it to lose $1,000 a year? Finally, he had enough. He sold everything he owned and transferred the money to a mutual fund (the Magellan Fund) that invested in growth companies. Although he didn't recoup his entire losses immediately, Phillip noted that the fund's return had been about 24 percent in the previous year. He figured that that was about 44 percentage points more than he had earned during that time—and investing in the fund would have required virtually no effort.

Welcome, Phillip, to the world of mutual funds, often called the "fast foods" of investing. May *your* return each year be 24 percent—but don't count on it. These funds will make your investment life easier, but there is still plenty to do. Is Magellan the best fund for your objectives? How good was a 24 percent return? (Other funds did much better in that year.) Finally, do you intend to hold Magellan through all market cycles, or would you rather switch your money into other mutual funds, and can you do that with Magellan?

Phillip Piccard still does his own investing. But rather than spending his time picking individual securities, he plans to invest in mutual funds, as do millions of other Americans. Phillip's problems haven't ended, though, as the vignette indicates. Perhaps his most important immediate task is to specify his investment objectives.

Investing without specific investment goals and objectives is usually emotional investing. If you fall into this approach, you probably will be buying on the basis of tips or hunches and selling for the same, or even less realistic, reasons. Don't expect much success with this approach, unless you are very lucky. As we explained in Chapter 13, you should begin your investment program by first asking: What are your investment goals? That is, what do you expect from your investments? After you determine your goals, the next important step is to construct an investment portfolio. The portfolio is the link between your investment goals and the specific investments you make to achieve them. As you construct the portfolio by determining component weights—what percent to stocks, to bonds, and so forth—you take the vital step of ranking your goals in importance.

This chapter begins with the important topic of portfolio management. It also includes a discussion of the pooling arrangements that are often necessary to achieve adequate diversification. Since the most important pooling arrangement is the mutual fund, it receives most of our attention. A discussion of securities markets concludes the chapter.

Portfolio Management

A portfolio is any combination of assets. If you own a house, some jewelry, and a savings account, you have a portfolio. A well-balanced portfolio includes tangible as well as intangible assets, although for many investors, their homes represent most of the tangible assets in their portfolios. Portfolio management has three main activities: the first is to determine the initial component weights and specific assets; the second is to monitor the portfolio over time and to evaluate its performance periodically; and the third is to make changes to the portfolio based upon performance evaluation or changing goals.

Setting up the Portfolio

Setting up a portfolio reflects a number of considerations, as Figure 15.1 indicates. For example, a midlife couple might wish to provide funds for their children's education. They would need to avoid loss of capital while trying to increase the portfolio value to achieve the future goal. Clearly, assets in the portfolio must be selected in relation to the investor's goals, so assets suitable for one investor may be completely inappropriate for another.

ESTIMATING PORTFOLIO RETURN AND RISK After you decide on your investment goals, you then select specific investments. As you do, it is a good idea to frame concrete ideas as to what returns are likely over the next year and what will be the portfolio's risk. Table 15.1 shows how a $5,000 portfolio might be constructed. The investor in this case is looking mostly for capital appreciation and expects to get it next year through a growth mutual fund, an individual company (Omni Enterprises), and a precious-metals mutual fund. She also is expecting to earn current income from her bond fund and money market mutual fund.

Portfolio risk is broadly estimated by examining the risks of the specific investments. As discussed in the two previous chapters, the beta weight can be used to approximate this risk for common stocks. The growth fund's beta of 1.2 tells the investor it will be about 20 percent riskier than the overall market, and Omni's beta of 2.5 indicates 2.5 times as much risk. Default risks for bonds are estimated with bond ratings; this investor's mutual fund invests only in bonds rated as

TABLE 15.1 • An Investment Portfolio

Investments	Amount Invested*	Risk	Market Values		Dividends/Interest	
			Expected Next Year	Realized at Year-End	Expected Next Year	Realized During the Year
I. Invested for capital appreciation (50%):						
A. Growth mutual fund	$1,400	Beta = 1.2	$1,570	$1,650	$ 28	$ 30
B. Omni Enterprises	1,100	Beta = 2.5	1,325	1,050	-0-	-0-
II. Invested for current income (40%):						
A. Money market mutual fund	1,000	Risk free	1,000	1,000	130	90
B. Speculative bond fund	1,000	Medium risk†	1,000	1,050	140	140
III. Invested for inflation protection (10%): Precious metals mutual fund	500	High risk	550	525	-0-	-0-
Totals	$5,000		$5,445	$5,275	$298	$260
Percentage return based on $5,000	—		8.9%	5.5%	6.0%	5.2%

*In a period-by-period evaluation, the amount invested should be the market values of the securities at the beginning of each period. For example, the amount invested in the next period will be $5,275, not $5,000. Using market prices rather than historical prices is more appropriate for making current decisions since it shows the opportunity cost of holding a security. Other than possible income-tax implications, the historical price that you paid for a security should be of no interest to you in managing your portfolio.

†Most of the bonds held by the fund are B-rated by Standard and Poor's and Moody's.

Investing for the Future

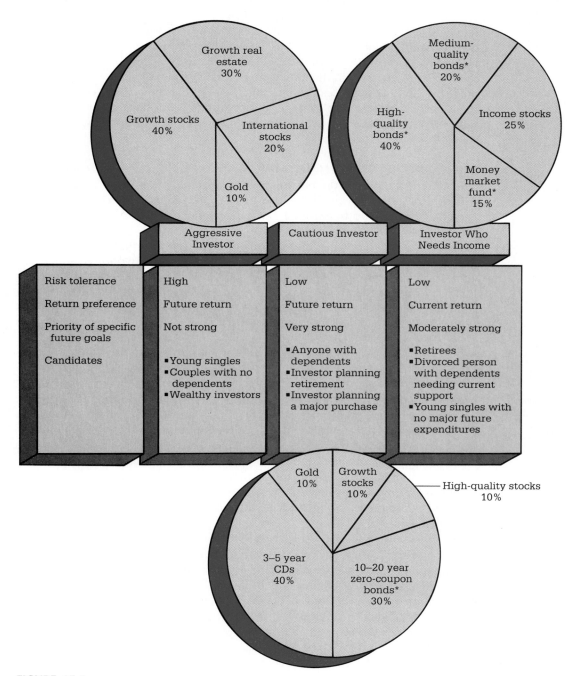

Aggressive Investor

Growth real estate 30%
Growth stocks 40%
International stocks 20%
Gold 10%

Cautious Investor

Investor Who Needs Income

Medium-quality bonds* 20%
High-quality bonds* 40%
Income stocks 25%
Money market fund* 15%

	Aggressive Investor	Cautious Investor	Investor Who Needs Income
Risk tolerance	High	Low	Low
Return preference	Future return	Future return	Current return
Priority of specific future goals	Not strong	Very strong	Moderately strong
Candidates	▪ Young singles ▪ Couples with no dependents ▪ Wealthy investors	▪ Anyone with dependents ▪ Investor planning retirement ▪ Investor planning a major purchase	▪ Retirees ▪ Divorced person with dependents needing current support ▪ Young singles with no major future expenditures

Gold 10%
Growth stocks 10%
High-quality stocks 10%
3–5 year CDs 40%
10–20 year zero-coupon bonds* 30%

FIGURE 15.1

Portfolios are designed to meet specific investment objectives. These differ, depending upon circumstances and the investor's risk tolerance. Three cases are shown. The asset weights in each portfolio were recommended by a financial planner. They should be considered as broad approximations, since more exact amounts would require detailed information about specific investors. Also, it is assumed the investor has suitable housing, sufficient funds to meet liquidity needs, and adequate life insurance.

speculative. She would not dare buy these bonds individually because adequate diversification would be impossible. The money market fund is considered risk-free, while the precious-metals fund will be as risky as holding the metals directly. The investment in the money market fund, it should be mentioned, is not made for liquidity purposes (assume that has already been considered). Rather, it is for current income. On balance, the investor's portfolio must be considered rather risky, with 80 percent of her funds invested in securities that can show considerable price volatility.

EXPRESSING RETURN QUANTITATIVELY You should have a clear idea of the return you expect from the portfolio in the upcoming year. Return can come in the form of interest or dividends and price appreciation. Interest and dividends shouldn't be too hard to estimate, but price appreciation usually is. Despite the difficulty, estimate a number. Do you expect the price to be up 5 percent, 10 percent, or what? If you can't form a quantitative expectation, how can you later evaluate performance? As you see from Table 15.1, our hypothetical investor expresses clearly the price appreciation and dividends and interest she expects in the upcoming year. She expects her overall portfolio to increase 8.9 percent ($445/$5,000) in value, and she expects to earn about 6.0 percent ($298/$5,000) in dividends and interest. Her expected total return, then, is 14.9 percent.

Monitoring the Portfolio

Monitoring the portfolio: Watching investments during the year and evaluating performance at year-end.

Monitoring the portfolio involves watching the individual investments during the year and evaluating performance at year's end. We will discuss portfolio changes in the next section, but for now let us assume that once we establish an investment period (such as the year), we don't change the portfolio unless there is a substantial change in one of the securities we own, or a significant change in the investment environment. Given this assumption, monitoring during the year simply means being on the alert for such changes. Obviously, if Omni Enterprises declared bankruptcy, the investor might wish to do something with the stock immediately.

What constitutes a significant change in the investment environment is not an easy question to answer. In recent years, the environment has been an extremely unstable one. If you overreact to changes, you will be buying and selling much too frequently for effective investment. Many financial advisers suggest that you frame an opinion on the future course of the economy and arrange your investments accordingly. Then stick with those investments until there are reasonably clear indications the economy has shifted direction. The planning period we are discussing does not have to be a calendar year; in fact, it doesn't even have to be a year. It could be a two- or three-year period, or longer.

CALCULATE THE PORTFOLIO RETURN Evaluating the portfolio at the end of the period requires two steps. First, get your investments' closing prices and the dividends and interest you received. With this information, determine your realized return. As Table 15.1 shows, the investor's actual return was less than she expected. Capital appreciation was 5.5 percent ($275/$5,000)—not 8.9 percent—and current return was 5.2 percent ($260/$5,000)—not 6.0 percent.

Total return was 10.7 percent versus an expected total return of 14.9 percent. What happened? The big disappointment was Omni Enterprises. Interest rates apparently fell during the year; we know this because the bond fund increased in value. However, the drop in interest rates was a mixed blessing since it led to a lower return on her money market fund. The advantages of a portfolio should be quite clear from this example. Poorer-than-expected performance in one security can be offset by better-than-expected performance in another. Naturally, it doesn't always work this way; all investment values could be down or up. Quite often, though, it does.

MAKE COMPARISONS   The second step in evaluation is to compare your portfolio's performance to that of other portfolios. While this procedure can be complicated, there are a few simple tests you can make. For example, compare your return to that available on risk-free investments such as certificates of deposit or money market accounts. Over an extended period of time, you should do better than these; if not, you have to ask yourself why you're taking the risks in your portfolio. A second simple test is to pick one or several mutual funds that seem similar to your portfolio, and then compare your performance to theirs. If you don't do as well, you should consider selling your securities and investing in one of the funds. Since our hypothetical investor is already invested in several mutual funds, it would be more appropriate for her to evaluate these funds directly. This topic is covered later in this chapter.

Changing the Portfolio

Changing the portfolio involves buying new assets or selling existing ones. Financial advisers agree that portfolio change is necessary as your goals change. Not all of them agree, however, that you should change investments in response to expected changes in the investment environment, as alluded to above.

Buy-and-hold strategy: A method of portfolio management that does not attempt to trade securities over economic cycles.

BUY-AND-HOLD STRATEGIES   As the name implies, a **buy-and-hold strategy** means you do not attempt to enhance your portfolio return by "trading with the investment cycle." People advocating the buy-and-hold approach argue that economic cycles cannot be forecasted. Since you can't forecast cycles, there is no way you can consistently benefit by trading in anticipation of them, and all you do is make your stockbroker wealthy by trying. Buy-and-hold advocates stress the importance of *carefully constructing* a well-diversified portfolio to begin with rather than continually *changing* one to improve performance.

The growing evidence that economic cycles cannot be forecasted certainly supports this view. Even the so-called experts have been consistently off their forecast targets, often by so much that any random forecasting device forecasted as well. If you like the idea of simply building and then holding a portfolio, there is no reason to be defensive about its simplicity.

Market timing: A method of portfolio management that changes a portfolio's composition in relation to expected market changes.

MARKET TIMING STRATEGIES   **Market timing** attempts to change a portfolio's composition in anticipation of expected changes in returns among different investments. Timing strategies range from the complex to some that are very simple. The complex strategies involve trading all kinds of investments (including options and futures), using short sales, and leveraging through margin accounts.

The simple ones usually involve going back and forth between a common stock mutual fund and a money market fund. The simpler versions are growing in popularity, and certain advisers now specialize in offering timing advice or in managing portfolios based upon their timing methods.

Since no evidence overwhelmingly supports even professional market timers, you should think twice before attempting your own timing techniques. If a formula appeals to you, our advice again is to try it on paper first and evaluate it critically. If it seems to work, then consider investing in a mutual fund family that allows you to switch among individual funds at little or no cost. (Fund switching will be explained later in this chapter.)

MARKET TIMING CAN INCREASE INVESTMENT RISK   You must realize, however, that market timing can increase investment risk. This is illustrated best with an example. Columns 2 and 3 in Table 15.2 show hypothetical returns available with U.S. Treasury bills and common stocks over four periods of time. If you had invested in bills at the beginning and held them, your average return would have been 9 percent. Similarly, if you had bought and held stocks, your average return would have been 15 percent. But what would have been your average return had you sold at the end of each period and reinvested in the other asset? The answer depends, of course, on how accurately you guessed which asset would give the better return. Column 4 in Table 15.2 assumes you always held the higher-yielding asset: that is, you guessed perfectly each period. With this clairvoyance your average return would have been the most possible—26 percent. Column 5, though, shows what would have happened had you forecasted perfectly incorrectly—a negative 2 percent return. If you were partially correct in your forecasts, the average return would have been somewhere between these extremes. Recalling that risk is associated with variation in returns, you should see why timing is riskier than buy and hold. Sure, there is a possibility of a greater average return over time, but there is also the possibility of a lower average return. And remember, the nature of risk is precisely this *greater variation* in expected return.

Should You Make Your Own Investments?

This section examines the issue of whether you should select investments and manage your portfolio or invest in pooling arrangements and let others make many of your investment decisions. The most important factor to consider is performance: Do you believe you can select securities that will perform as well as

TABLE 15.2 ·
Hypothetical Returns and Market Timing

(1) Period	(2) Return on U.S. Treasury Bills	(3) Return on Common Stocks	(4) Return If You Guess Correctly Each Period	(5) Return If You Guess Incorrectly Each Period
1	+10%	+40%	+ 40%	+10%
2	+ 8	−20	+ 8	−20
3	+12	+50	+ 50	+12
4	+ 6	−10	+ 6	−10
Total	+36%	+60%	+104%	− 8%
Average return	+ 9%	+15%	+ 26%	− 2%

those selected by professional managers? Historically, the small investor has not done as well as the pros, but recent studies seem to show their performances are not all that bad, either. The key to beating the pros apparently rests with successfully investing in the small companies the pros tend to overlook. We mentioned in the previous chapter that attractive investment opportunities can exist with small companies that might be familiar to you as an employee or a customer, or because their home office is in your community.

Of course, you need adequate diversification regardless of the specific securities you select. Investing in only one or two local companies could prove disastrous, but putting 10 or 20 percent of your funds in them with the rest invested in a mutual fund could give adequate diversification and a chance for good growth with the locals.

After considering the return issue, you must consider the relative costs of investing on your own versus investing in pooling arrangements. There are two kinds of costs to consider: stock brokerage commissions and your own time.

STOCK BROKERAGE COMMISSIONS AND DIVERSIFICATION We showed in Chapter 13 that it takes about 10 to 15 different securities to have an adequately diversified portfolio. Suppose we take the lower number and then ask how much commissions would cost relative to the amount available for investment.

Table 15.3 gives some insights to that question. If, for example, you have only $2,000 to invest, you must buy five shares of ten different stocks, assuming an average purchase price of $40 a share. Using the commission schedule of a limited-service broker, we arrive at a commission of $14.075 per transaction and $140.75 for ten transactions. This total is 7.04 percent of the amount invested. Is this high? Probably not, if you simply buy and hold your securities. But if you buy and sell frequently, these commissions will be almost impossible to overcome. If you buy and sell only once during a year, your total is 14.08 percent, which is about equal to the expected total profit in most years. Surely, if you are considering market timing, you need much more than a $2,000 investment!

As the amount you invest increases, your commissions as a percentage of the amount invested decline. With $40,000, you are finally buying round lots. But even here, the percentage is still 2.1, which is fairly high if you buy and sell frequently. It might be possible to reduce commissions by dealing with a deep discount broker, although any savings here usually means buying in round lots

TABLE 15.3 · Stock Brokerage Commissions in Relation to Amount Invested

	Amount Invested				
	$2,000	$4,000	$8,000	$16,000	$40,000
No. of shares of each stock	5	10	20	40	100
Value per transaction	$200	$400	$800	$1,600	$4,000
Commission per transaction	$ 14.075	$ 19.65	$ 30.80	$ 50.40	$ 82.00
Total commissions	$140.75	$196.50	$308.00	$ 504.00	$ 820.00
Total commissions as a percent of amount Invested	7.04%	4.9%	3.9%	3.2%	2.1%

ASSUMPTIONS: 1. Ten individual stocks purchased.
2. Average purchase price of $40 per share.
3. Full-service stockbroker.

and at a fairly high value per transaction. Before investing, then, make sure you get a fee schedule and then estimate your commission cost using the approach detailed in Table 15.3.

THE COST OF YOUR TIME   You must consider your investment of time if you manage your own portfolio. If you buy your own securities, count on putting quite a few hours each year into this activity. These hours may bring more pleasure than pain, if you enjoy the work, but at least recognize that it does take time.

Another factor to consider is your emotional temperament. Some people simply feel uncomfortable making investment decisions. In a sense, some of us are "sore losers" who are particularly bothered by the "wrong" decisions we make; that is, when we look back at alternatives that were available at the beginning of a period, we really regret not selecting the ones that eventually prove to be best. Your money market fund may have earned 15 percent last year, but stocks did 30 percent. Rather than being satisfied with a fairly good return, you feel bad because you didn't invest in stocks. If these feelings come easily to you, as they do to many of us, then pooling arrangements are for you. We will begin our discussion with mutual funds.

Mutual Funds

Mutual fund: A corporation that invests in securities issued by other corporations.

Net asset value (NAV): The net value of one mutual fund share determined by the net market value of the shares the fund owns.

A **mutual fund** is a corporation that invests its funds in securities issued by other corporations or governments. When you buy shares of a mutual fund, you are buying a proportionate interest in the fund's securities. As a simple example, if a fund owns 100 shares each of IBM, Xerox, and General Motors, and if you own 10 percent of the fund's outstanding shares, then you effectively own ten shares in each of those corporations. The value of a mutual fund share—called its **net asset value (NAV)**—depends upon the values of its underlying securities; in the above example, those are IBM, Xerox, and General Motors. Suppose that on a particular day, the market values below existed, then NAV is calculated as follows, assuming the fund has no liabilities:

(1)	IBM—$120/share × 100 shares	= $12,000
(2)	Xerox—$80/share × 100 shares	= 8,000
(3)	GM—$70/share × 100 shares	= 7,000
(4)	Value of the fund's portfolio	= $27,000
(5)	Number of shares outstanding in the fund =	1,000
(6)	Net asset value (NAV) per share = **(4)** divided by **(5)**	= $ 27

Owning 10 percent of the shares outstanding means you own 100 shares and the value of your investment is $2,700 ($27 × 100). Surely, the first bit of information you want when considering a mutual fund's shares is its NAV per share.

Characteristics of Mutual Funds

To many investors, the single biggest advantage of a mutual fund—after diversification—is its professional management. As mentioned previously, which securities to buy and when to buy and sell them are very difficult decisions—and time consuming if you take them seriously. By investing in a mutual fund, you transfer these problems to someone else, who may have better training to handle them. Mutual funds charge for these services, but the charges are quite minimal and usually worth it. Before looking more closely at mutual fund selection, you should first understand some characteristics of mutual funds.

Load fund: A mutual fund that charges commissions on share purchases.

No-load fund: A mutual fund with no purchase commissions.

LOAD VERSUS NO-LOAD FUNDS   A **load fund** is one that charges commissions on the shares you buy; a **no-load fund** does not charge commissions. In a load fund, the price you pay for a share is called the offer price, and it is higher than NAV, the difference being commission. In a no-load fund the price you pay is NAV. (We should point out that mutual funds typically have some liabilities outstanding at any point, and these are deducted from the funds' assets to arrive at *net* assets; however, these liabilities are inconsequential in comparison to assets.) Mutual funds' NAVs are reported in most newspapers, and some also show offer prices, as indicated in Figure 15.2. Notice that Trend Fund is a no-load fund, but the Blue Chip Fund has a load. The size of the load (or commission) varies among funds and is often expressed as a percentage of the offer price. As you see, Blue Chip had a load of $0.56 ($18.77 − $18.21), and expressing this as a percentage of its price gives 2.89 percent ($.56/$18.77). The figure is fairly common among load funds, although some are much higher.

FIGURE 15.2

Typical listing of mutual funds.

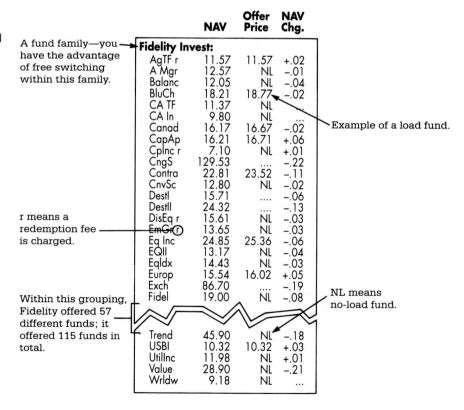

A fund family—you have the advantage of free switching within this family.

r means a redemption fee is charged.

Within this grouping, Fidelity offered 57 different funds; it offered 115 funds in total.

Example of a load fund.

NL means no-load fund.

	NAV	Offer Price	NAV Chg.
Fidelity Invest:			
AgTF r	11.57	11.57	+.02
A Mgr	12.57	NL	−.01
Balanc	12.05	NL	−.04
BluCh	18.21	18.77	−.02
CA TF	11.37	NL	...
CA In	9.80	NL	...
Canad	16.17	16.67	−.02
CapAp	16.21	16.71	+.06
CpInc r	7.10	NL	+.01
CngS	129.53	....	−.22
Contra	22.81	23.52	−.11
CnvSc	12.80	NL	−.02
DestI	15.71	....	−.06
DestII	24.32	....	−.13
DisEq r	15.61	NL	−.03
EmGr r	13.65	NL	−.03
Eq Inc	24.85	25.36	−.06
EQII	13.17	NL	−.04
Eqldx	14.43	NL	−.03
Europ	15.54	16.02	+.05
Exch	86.70	....	−.19
Fidel	19.00	NL	−.08
Trend	45.90	NL	−.18
USBI	10.32	10.32	+.03
UtilInc	11.98	NL	+.01
Value	28.90	NL	−.21
Wrldw	9.18	NL	...

Obviously, with commissions, you should be concerned with whether or not load funds outperform no-loads. On balance they do not. There have been spectacular performers on each side—but there also have been dreadful losers, and most studies show their average performances to be about the same, on a risk-adjusted basis. So why buy a load fund? There is no compelling reason to do so, unless you receive other advantages, such as investment advice. If you invest regularly, saving commissions gives you that much more money invested, and over the long run these extra amounts will produce a substantial addition to the value of your holdings.

In addition to the commission, or front-end load, some funds also have a redemption charge, or rear-end load. The Emerging Growth Fund illustrated in Figure 15.2 has a 1 percent redemption charge. The increasing popularity of funds, coupled with their apparent success, prompted many funds to begin front- and rear-end loads.

OPEN-END VERSUS CLOSED-END FUNDS An **open-end fund** issues shares at their NAV to anyone caring to buy them and, equally important, is also willing to redeem shares at their NAV. For example, if you held shares in any of Fidelity's funds, you could have sold them back to the funds at any time. You generally buy or sell shares directly from or to the fund, rather than through a stockbroker. Of approximately 3,000 total mutual funds in existence, about 2,700 are open-end funds, and their greater popularity is due in part to the assurance investors have

Open-end fund: A fund that issues or redeems shares at their NAVs.

in always being able to sell their shares at NAV. They are also widely advertised, and the load funds are promoted by sales representatives. If you want information about open-end funds, including a free directory giving addresses and phone numbers for practically all of them, write the Investment Company Institute, 1600 M Street, NW, Washington, DC 20036. The Institute's *Mutual Fund Fact Book* ($2.00) is also a good buy.

A **closed-end fund** is different in a number of respects. First, it has a relatively fixed number of shares outstanding. Second, you buy these shares as you would buy shares of any other corporation; that is, its shares are traded on organized exchanges or in the over-the-counter market. (These terms are explained later in this chapter.) This means you engage the services of a stockbroker in buying or selling them. Third, because the fund neither buys nor sells shares to the public, you must buy or sell them from or to another party, which further means you are not guaranteed their NAV, as either a seller or a buyer. Finally, these funds are seldom promoted, so chances are good you won't know much about them unless you do research on your own. However, quite a few closed-end funds are available with a variety of investment objectives, and Figure 15.3 shows just a few.

DISCOUNTS ON CLOSED-END FUNDS ENHANCE THEIR APPEAL A major point of interest about closed-end funds is the size of premium or discount, which is the difference between their market prices and their NAVs. As you see in Figure 15.3, some of the funds were selling at premiums while others were selling at discounts. More often than not, these funds sell at discounts, which enhances their investment appeal. For example, suppose you can buy Adams Express at an 8 percent discount. To keep things simple, suppose Adams Express

FIGURE 15.3

Typical partial listing of closed-end funds.

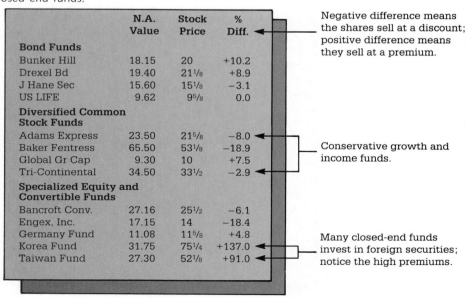

	N.A. Value	Stock Price	% Diff.
Bond Funds			
Bunker Hill	18.15	20	+10.2
Drexel Bd	19.40	21⅛	+8.9
J Hane Sec	15.60	15⅛	−3.1
US LIFE	9.62	9⅝	0.0
Diversified Common Stock Funds			
Adams Express	23.50	21⅝	−8.0
Baker Fentress	65.50	53⅛	−18.9
Global Gr Cap	9.30	10	+7.5
Tri-Continental	34.50	33½	−2.9
Specialized Equity and Convertible Funds			
Bancroft Conv.	27.16	25½	−6.1
Engex, Inc.	17.15	14	−18.4
Germany Fund	11.08	11⅝	+4.8
Korea Fund	31.75	75¼	+137.0
Taiwan Fund	27.30	52⅛	+91.0

Negative difference means the shares sell at a discount; positive difference means they sell at a premium.

Conservative growth and income funds.

Many closed-end funds invest in foreign securities; notice the high premiums.

held securities that offered a 10 percent current return. If you invested $100 in these securities directly, you would get $10 in dividends or interest. But you need to invest only $92 in Adams Express to get a $10 return. Rather than a 10 percent rate of return, your rate is 10.87 percent ($10/$92). This is a sizeable increase in return for no increase in intrinsic risk. You should realize, though, that the size of the discount varies over time, and it could increase after you invest. This means the market price of your shares declines relative to NAV, and if you then sell, you do so at a loss, or at a relatively smaller gain than would have been the case had the discount remained the same. If you are interested in closed-end mutual funds, you should do some research to determine their suitability for your particular situation. A good place to start is *Value Line Investment Survey*. It shows the portfolios these funds hold and beta values for each. Adams Express, for example, has a beta of about 0.92, while Tri-Continental's (the largest) is slightly higher—0.95. If you bought either of these, you achieved a broad market portfolio at an 8 or 3 percent discount.

THE FUND'S OBJECTIVES   It is obviously important to select a fund that is attempting to achieve the same investment goal you are. If you call or write a fund, you will be sent a **prospectus** and a **shareholder report**. The prospectus describes the fund in detail, and the shareholder report indicates how the fund has performed in the past and the securities it currently holds. Risks associated with investing in the fund are also discussed, and they should be read as thoroughly as material describing the fund's objective and its past performance.

Figure 15.4 indicates the more common fund objectives. As you see, there are a number from which to choose. While growth, income, and balanced funds are the most popular, many investors use the other funds also. **International funds** and **global funds** allow you to invest in foreign countries where returns have often been higher than in the United States. **Sector funds** make it possible to

Prospectus: A document describing a fund in considerable detail.

Shareholder report: A statement showing how a fund has performed in the past and the securities it currently owns.

International fund, global fund: A fund that invests in foreign securities.

Sector fund: A fund that invests in only one industry.

FIGURE 15.4

Types of mutual funds.

Type of Fund	Objective	Primary Investment Securities
Growth	Price appreciation over time	Common stocks
Income	High current return	Bonds, preferred stocks
Balanced	Moderate growth plus moderate current return	Bonds, preferred and common stocks
Money market	High liquidity plus higher current return than bank savings accounts	Money market securities
Maximum capital appreciation	Exploit opportunities to earn high returns	Varies, depending upon strategy
Sector	Invest in one industry	Common stocks
International	Earn returns in countries outside the U.S.	Common stocks
Global	Earn returns in both the U.S. and foreign countries	Common stocks
Index	Earn returns equal to a market index, such as the S&P 500	Common stocks or bonds; depends on the index

invest in one industry if you think that industry will do better than the overall economy. **Maximum capital appreciation funds** use a number of investment strategies in an effort to earn high returns. For example, some look for companies that might be acquired (at high prices) through takeovers. Some invest in distressed companies (even bankrupts) that are expected to recover.

A particularly interesting fund is an **index fund.** It invests in securities that comprise a market index, such as the S&P 500 stock index. Its sole objective is to earn the return the index earns. Beginning investors often feel they can do better than a simple index, which has no investment strategy or approach. In actuality, however, many investment professionals do not perform as well as an index. Studies indicate, for example, that fully two-thirds of equity mutual funds underperform the S&P 500 on a risk-adjusted basis.

A particularly popular fund is the **money market fund,** with far more money invested in them than in any other type. There are several reasons for this popularity. For one thing, these funds are known as dollar funds, which means you always buy or sell shares at $1.00 each. Actually, the fund is a form of checking account, allowing you to write checks against your balance in the account. You earn interest daily and can withdraw all funds credited to your account at any time. Withdrawals can be made by telephone or wire, but are more frequently made by checks. The usual minimum withdrawal is $500, but some accounts allow checks for any amount. The big appeal is the earnings on the account. In contrast to some checking accounts that pay no or low interest, these funds usually offer rates that are about the same as those earned on liquid money market instruments.

Important Mutual Fund Services

Along with a professionally managed and well-diversified portfolio, mutual funds offer other appealing features. Some of the more important services are described below.

REINVESTMENT PLANS   A **reinvestment plan** allows you to automatically reinvest the fund's dividends and capital gain distributions into additional shares of the fund. You choose the amount you wish to reinvest: It can be all or only a fraction of the total distributed. Many investors like to receive dividends in cash but prefer having capital gain distributions reinvested. When you fill out an application to buy shares, you indicate how you wish to handle reinvestment.

TRANSACTIONS BY TELEPHONE   Once you have completed an application, you can buy or sell shares by calling a toll-free telephone number. You can also arrange to have funds wired to your bank, which eliminates delays with checks in transit. If you sell shares and have the funds wired, they can be in your interest-earning bank account the next day.

FUND SWITCHING   **Fund switching** allows you to withdraw money from one fund to reinvest in another, so long as both funds are members of the same family (Fidelity, for example). If the fund is a no-load, this feature is particularly attractive for investors trying market-timing techniques. Generally, switches up to a

Maximum capital appreciation fund: A fund that uses a variety of strategies in an effort to earn high returns.

Index fund: A fund that attempts to match the return on a market index.

Money market fund: A fund that invests in money market instruments issued in large denominations.

Reinvestment plan: An option a fund investor can choose to have cash distributions used to acquire more fund shares.

Fund switching: An option allowing fund investors to switch among funds within a fund family.

483

Portfolio
Management

certain number can be made without charges; however, you will pay commissions on a load fund. Be sure to determine your fund's policy before you begin making switches.

ADAPTABILITY TO IRAS   Most mutual funds make attractive IRAs (the IRA is discussed in Chapters 5 and 17). This is so because of the wide range of investment objectives available and their relatively low administrative costs, which usually are less than $20 a year. To open an IRA, all you need to do is indicate your intent to the fund and you will be sent a simple document for your signature. This document, along with the completed application form to the fund, automatically makes your investment an IRA.

Selecting a Mutual Fund

Once you have defined clearly your investment objective, you will find many funds available for your choice. Picking one or two is a difficult task. You can get started by looking at a fund's historical performance and comparing it to its risk. Use a beta value (if one is available) in this effort. Other steps to take include reviewing the fund's current holdings, comparing its expenses in relation to its earnings or to the market value of its securities, and seeing how often it buys and sells securities (called the fund's portfolio turnover).

EVALUATE PERFORMANCE   A fund must indicate its past performance in its financial reports to shareholders. Figure 15.5 shows such a report for Fidelity Fund, a very large, open-end growth and income fund that is part of the Fidelity family. This report is typical of reports all mutual funds provide investors, although some will show the cumulative value of a given investment, such as $1,000. Actually, with a cumulative total return figure you can determine cumulative value. It is a useful concept and should be understood. You should also understand the average annual total return and how this return should be adjusted for risk.

Growth of a $1,000 Investment.   Since Fidelity does not indicate the growth of $1,000, we must calculate it. Fortunately, it is a simple calculation. For example, the cumulative total return for ten years is 255.34 percent for Fidelity. If you invested $1,000, held it for ten years, and reinvested all distributions in Fidelity as they were received, you would have earned $2,553.40 and the $1,000 would have grown to $3,553.40. You should see that a $1,000 investment in the S&P 500 would have grown to $3,681.15 at the end of ten years.

Average Annual Total Return (AATR).   The average annual total return (AATR) is a difficult calculation and cannot be solved accurately without time-value-of-money techniques. Fortunately, fund reports provide the values. Fidelity's 13.52 percent average annual total return for ten years is the rate you would have earned by investing $1,000 ten years ago and having that grow to $3,553.40 today. This is a good return but, as you see, the S&P 500 did better for one year, five years, and ten years. Using time-value-of-money techniques and a calculator, we determined the average annual total return for the S&P 500 for ten years to be 13.92 percent.

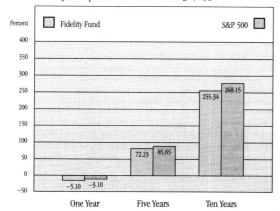

Performance Update

Cumulative Total Returns
for the period ended December 31, 1990

Percent — Fidelity Fund · S&P 500

	One Year	Five Years	Ten Years
Fidelity Fund	−5.10	72.23	255.34
S&P 500	−3.10	85.85	268.15

The charts show Fidelity Fund's total returns which include changes in share price, and reinvestment of dividends and capital gains. Figures for the S&P 500, an unmanaged index of common stock prices, include reinvestment of dividends. S&P 500 is a registered trademark of Standard & Poor's Corporation.

Top Ten Equity Holdings
as of December 31, 1990

International Business Machines Corp.
Baxter International, Inc.
Bristol-Myers Squibb Co.
UAL, Inc.
Bankers Trust New York Corp.
Lubrizol Corp.
Block (H&R), Inc.
U.S. West, Inc.
Coastal Corp. (The)
Sherwin-Williams Co.

Average Annual Total Returns
for the period ended December 31, 1990

One Year	Five Years	Ten Years
−5.10%	11.49%	13.52%

When you look at Fidelity Fund's ***average annual total returns,*** you should note that figures for more than one year assume a steady compounded rate of return and are not the Fund's year-by-year results, which fluctuated over the periods shown.

All performance numbers are historical; the Fund's share price and return will vary and you may have a gain or loss when you sell your shares.

FIGURE 15.5

Data from Fidelity's 1990 reports. (Source: Fidelity Fund Annual Report, December 31, 1990.)

The Reinvestment Assumption. A key input in determining both the average annual total return and the cumulative total return is the assumption of immediate reinvestment of fund distributions. To illustrate the situation, let's look at 1989 and 1990. While funds actually make quarterly distributions, we will assume that all distributions were made at mid-year and then reinvested at the average NAV for the year. We also assume that one share was owned at the beginning of each year. All the data used below were available in Fidelity's 1990 report.

		1989	1990
(1)	NAV, beginning of year	$15.42	$17.93
(2)	NAV, end of year	$17.93	$16.30
(3)	Average NAV = [(1) + (2)]/2	$16.68	$17.12
(4)	Distributions during the year	$ 1.85	$ 0.74
(5)	Shares acquired during the year = (4)/(3)	0.111	0.043
(6)	Shares owned at year end	1.111	1.043
(7)	Value of shares owned at year end = (2) × (6)	$19.92	$17.00
(8)	Change in value during the year = (7) − (1)	$ 4.50	−$ 0.93
(9)	Average annual total return = (8)/(1)	+29.2%	− 5.2%

Figure 15.5 shows the 1990 return as −5.1 percent instead of 5.2 percent. The slight difference arises from not using quarterly distributions.

The year-to-year changes in returns reveal the riskiness of investing in a fund. In Fidelity's case, going from a +29.2 percent return to a −5.2 percent return suggests quite a bit of risk. Risk is often incorporated into an analysis by determining a fund's beta value and using it to adjust the average annual total return (AATR), as shown below.

Risk-Adjusted Return. Professionals who evaluate mutual fund performance often make comparisons among funds using the risk-adjusted rate of return, RAROR. One very simple way to calculate this is shown below:

$$\text{RAROR} = \frac{\text{AATR}}{\text{fund's beta weight}} - \text{S\&P 500 return}$$

Fidelity Fund's beta was estimated at 1.05, which means it is a bit riskier than the overall market. Using Fidelity Fund's ten-year AATR and the S&P 500 ten-year AATR, we have

$$\text{Fidelity's RAROR} = \frac{13.52}{1.05} - 13.92 = 12.88 - 13.92 = -1.04\%$$

The −1.04 percent indicates the amount the Fidelity Fund underperformed the S&P 500. A positive number would indicate a good performance; and the larger the positive number, the better the performance. Of course, a negative number, such as Fidelity's, indicates poor performance.

Box 15.2
Saving Money

Focus on Loads and Annual Expenses

You have $1,000 to invest and are considering mutual funds. Two have come to your attention: Fund A has an 8.5 percent load and typically incurs operating expenses at 2 percent of net assets; Fund B is a no-load fund with an expense ratio of 0.25 percent. If each fund manager earns, say, 12 percent each year before expenses, how much better off are you with Fund B? Answers are below.

B's advantage is anything but trivial, but you probably think this example is stretched to make a point. It is somewhat, but not completely. There are funds with loads as high as 8.5 percent, and you certainly can find two funds with that much difference in expense ratios.

Saving money, then, is simple: First, ignore all load funds; second, select only those no-load funds with low operating expense ratios. But, as with all simple plans, there are a few hitches. First, by eliminating all load funds you cut out a few super performers, such as Fidelity's Magellan Fund—the best performer of all funds over the past 15 years. By re-

laxing the rule to exclude only high-load funds (loads over 5 percent), you keep most of the better performers, including Magellan.

Second, many load funds are sold by stockbrokers who also provide investment and portfolio management advice. Notice in the table that the load has far less importance with long holding periods. Paying $820 over 20 years may not be an excessive amount if the broker provides useful advice.

The table clearly shows that operating costs are the real villain in the long run. Indeed, some studies have shown that selecting funds with low cost ratios is the most consistent method of selecting funds that are likely to perform well in the future. One mutual fund family, Vanguard, emphasizes low costs, and its funds typically have the lowest ratios in the industry. Not surprisingly, its funds—particularly its index funds—are consistently among the better performers.

Years After Investment	Accumulations:		B's Advantage	Advantage Due to:	
	Fund A	Fund B		No Load	Low Costs
1	$1,007	$1,120	$ 113	$ 95	$ 18
10	2,373	3,106	733	265	468
20	6,156	9,646	3,490	820	2,670

REVIEW THE FUND'S CURRENT PORTFOLIO   At this point, you should look at each fund's current holdings. Space prevents a listing of all the securities held by Fidelity, but a summary shows the fund held stocks and bonds of over 170 different companies in 16 basic industry groupings. Fidelity was well diversified (Fidelity's top ten equity holdings are shown in Figure 15.5.)

EXAMINE EXPENSES AND PORTFOLIO TURNOVER   Managing a mutual fund involves certain administrative expenses. The greater these expenses, the fewer resources the fund has to invest or make shareholder distributions. These expenses are usually related to the size of the portfolio and the frequency of security purchases and sales. This frequency is measured by a turnover percentage. (For example, if a fund replaced 10 percent of its holdings with new holdings, its turnover would be 10 percent.) Table 15.4 shows Fidelity's data for three years: 1988 through 1990. It is important, by the way, to express expenses as percentages of investment income or average net assets because funds are quite different in size, and a large fund naturally has higher expenses than a small one. The ratio of expenses to average net assets for most equity funds is around 1.0 percent. Fidelity's ratios are well below this figure, indicating that management controls expenses rather well.

TABLE 15.4 · Fidelity
Fund Management
Expenses and Portfolio
Turnover

	1988	1989	1990
Ratio of expenses to:			
investment income	15.39%	14.10%	14.63%
average net assets	0.66	0.64	0.67
Portfolio turnover	259%	191%	175%

SOURCES: Fidelity Fund financial reports for 1990.

MUTUAL FUND RATINGS   You can get help in selecting mutual funds from a number of sources, including financial advisory services that charge fees. More readily available sources, though, include *Barron's*, *Money*, and *Forbes*. *Money* has a "Fund Watch" column appearing in each monthly issue. In addition, it ranks about 700 funds twice a year, reporting each fund's one-, five-, and ten-year performance along with a risk rating. It also gives each fund's address and phone number, making it easy for you to get information. *Forbes* has an annual report that gives one- and ten-year performances. An attractive feature of the *Forbes* report is that it measures performance in both up and down markets. For example, the 1990 *Forbes* ratings (see the September 3, 1990, issue) gave Fidelity Fund a B in up markets and a B in down markets. (The best rating is A+ and the worst is F.)

Other Pooling Arrangements

Mutual funds are not the only pooling arrangements. The most important of the others are unit investment trusts, limited partnerships, and investment clubs. Each is explained below.

Unit Investment Trusts

Unit investment trust: A pooling arrangement similar to an open-end fund; however, the investment portfolio is relatively fixed (unmanaged) over the fund's life.

A **unit investment trust** is similar in some respects to an open-end mutual fund, but there are important differences. A stock brokerage firm creates a trust by buying a portfolio of securities and holding them as trustee. The firm then sells claims to the portfolio (called units) to individual investors. In most cases you can sell your units back to the trust at their NAVs, which may be quite different—higher or lower—from their original cost to you. Basically, this is how an open-end mutual fund works. The big difference is that the original portfolio of securities remains intact until they are redeemed or the trust is dissolved. The trust is thus an unmanaged fund, reducing administrative expenses considerably; but you do pay a commission (usually 4 percent) to the trust originators.

Unit investment trusts were used extensively in the 1970s to capture higher interest rates on short-term securities that normally were unavailable to smaller investors because of their high minimum prices. The rise of the money market mutual fund took much of this market away, but trusts are still used for many long-term bonds. Figure 15.6 shows an advertisement for a municipal bond trust. Although information highlights are provided in the ad, you really need the prospectus to understand the details of the trust. An attractive feature of many trusts is the availability of monthly interest checks. Be careful, however, of any claim to

FIGURE 15.6

Advertisement for unit investment trusts invested in municipal bonds. (Courtesy of Clayton Brown and Associates, Inc.)

instant liquidity: Although the units are immediately redeemable, you may do so at a loss. In most analysts' view, this makes them illiquid.

Limited Partnerships

A **limited partnership** is a legal arrangement that combines features of a corporation and a general partnership. It is similar to a corporation in that most investors (called *limited partners*) are inactive in management of the business, preferring instead to turn over these responsibilities to a person called the *general partner*. It resembles a partnership in that profits or losses from the business are passed directly to the partners, rather than being profits or losses of the business itself. It is the federal income tax implications of this last feature that makes limited partnerships appealing. For example, suppose you invested $1,000 in a corporation and owned 10 percent of the shares. Suppose further that the business did poorly and showed a $20,000 net loss for the year. This corporate loss would have no personal income tax implication. In a limited partnership, however, you would take your share of the business loss on your individual tax return. In the above example, you could deduct $2,000 (10 percent of $20,000) in the year of the loss. If you were in a 28 percent tax bracket, you would have reduced your taxes by $560, and the IRS would have "underwritten" 56 percent of your investment. Limited partnerships are often called **tax shelters,** and you can see why; however, limited partnerships are also used even where tax advantages are not the most important goal.

LIQUIDITY WITH LIMITED PARTNERSHIPS   Unlike mutual funds and unit investment trusts, limited partnership interests cannot be sold in any readily available markets. If partnership interests are held by the public and if the promoter is a large stock brokerage firm, they might be able to find a buyer, but there is no guarantee. If the partnership is privately held, selling your interest may be extremely difficult. You might wait until the partnership is dissolved to recover your original investment plus any capital appreciation. Obviously, if liquidity is an important concern, then a limited partnership interest is not a suitable investment.

THE TAX SITUATION WITH LIMITED PARTNERSHIPS   The 1986 Tax Reform Act eliminated many of the tax advantages previously associated with limited partnerships. The act's loss limitation rules stipulate that any loss from a limited partnership can be used to offset gains from other limited partnerships, but any combined net loss cannot be used to offset other forms of income, such as earned income or portfolio income. (See Chapter 5 for a review of the loss limitation rules.) Since the act allowed special exemptions for the oil and gas industry, the limited partnership has remained an important entity for investors in this area; however, their importance in other industries has diminished appreciably.

Investment Clubs

For many people, an **investment club** is the ideal way to achieve diversification: It gives them an opportunity for fun and fellowship, along with a possibility of profit. In 1972 there were over 14,000 clubs affiliated with the National Association of Investment Clubs (NAIC), but that number sank along with the stock market in 1973 and 1974. By 1979, there were only about 3,600 clubs, but since then NAIC's membership has gone up dramatically as more people again have become interested in securities.

Investment clubs have many different objectives, ranging from investing in hard assets, such as gold and diamonds, to buying stable income stocks offering high dividend income. But for a club to be successful, members must share a common objective. You invest in a club by paying monthly dues, usually in the $25 range, which are then used to buy securities selected by the membership. Most clubs reinvest dividends and capital gains. Securities are often recommended for purchase by members given the task of researching a specific company or industry, and this is perhaps the most enjoyable part of being a member. You can expect divergent opinions and robust discussion in any club where members take their investments seriously. If you would like to join an investment club but don't know how, you can write the NAIC at Department B, 1515 E. Eleven Mile Road, Royal Oak, MI 48067.

Securities Markets

On a normal day about 150 million shares of stock are traded on the New York Stock Exchange. Assuming an average price of $40 a share means that about $6 billion worth of securities change hands on just this one exchange and just for common and preferred stocks and warrants. Add to this the combined total values of options, commodity futures, bonds, notes, and all short-term debt securities, and you begin to see the magnitude of the securities industry. Given its huge size and diversity, it is indeed a marvel that it functions at all, much less as smoothly as it does. We will explain some of the reasons why it does in the following sections.

Organized Exchanges

Organized exchange: A physical place where securities are traded.

Facilitating the exchange process is the **organized exchange,** which is usually understood as a physical place where buyers and sellers—or their representatives—face each other in making transactions. Each exchange has a floor that is arranged to trade specific securities at specific locations. Only members of an exchange are authorized to make trades, and only securities listed on the exchange are traded. A new member is admitted to an exchange by buying a seat from a current member. These are usually very expensive; for example, a seat on the New York Stock Exchange was sold for $1.1 million in 1987.

New York Stock Exchange (NYSE): Largest organized exchange in the world.

THE NEW YORK STOCK EXCHANGE   The **New York Stock Exchange (NYSE)** is the largest organized exchange in the world. Practically all the large corporations in America have their securities listed there. In total, over 1,500 firms are listed, with over 2,000 different stocks. To be listed on the NYSE, a business must meet certain requirements, such as having at least 2,000 stockholders owning 100 or more shares and a minimum of 1,100,000 shares of stock held by the public. Many firms appreciate having their securities listed on the NYSE, since it is often taken as a sign of financial strength and maturity. However, it certainly is no guarantee of success; many listed companies have gone into bankruptcy over the years. A section of the NYSE trading floor is dedicated to trading corporate bonds, and about 1,000 different bonds are traded there.

Trades are conducted on the floor of the NYSE between brokers representing buyers and sellers. They are facilitated by a specialist who has the responsibility of maintaining a continuous and orderly market in a given stock. Each broker attempts to get the best price for his or her customer. After a trade is completed, an employee of the exchange will record all the details of the transaction, which are then entered into the exchange's computer and transmitted to over 12,000 electronic display units throughout the world. If you are in a stockbroker's office,

Action Plan for the Steeles Selecting Mutual Funds

Background On December 31, 1992, the Steeles had $6,400 invested in Fidelity Fund, and they are considering increasing the investment by another $8,400 (see their action plan in Chapter 13). However, an analysis of Fidelity Fund has disappointed them. They have found that Fidelity did not perform as well as the overall stock market from 1981 through 1990.

The Problem The Steeles are considering switching from Fidelity to another fund. To aid them in making a decision, they decided to examine performances of other common stock funds over the same period. Such performances were available in the February 1991 issue of *Money* magazine. As a first screen, they selected those funds with ten-year cumulative total returns greater than 400 percent (see the accompanying table). Only six (out of 510 equity funds) qualified.

Arnie and Sharon were amazed at how much better these funds had done in comparison to the Fidelity Fund over ten years. But, in looking at performance over shorter periods, they noticed that performance varied considerably. For example, the Pacific A Fund did very poorly in 1990, and the CGM Fund did miserably over the three-year period.

This latter analysis prompted the Steeles to use another screen, this time looking for those funds that did better than the Vanguard S&P 500 Index Trust—a fund that attempts to match the performance of the S&P 500 stock index. This screen selected only ten funds.

The Plan Comparing the Fidelity Fund's performance with the ten in the second list did not indicate very inferior results. Indeed, if the loads charged by the load funds are taken into consideration in calculating returns, the Fidelity Fund's performance would be quite similar to several—Putnam and Nationwide, for instance.

The main point this simple review indicates is that the Steeles should consider diversifying among the better-performing funds rather than trying to find the *single best* fund. So they will call each fund and request a financial report and prospectus. Rather than investing $8,400 more in the Fidelity Fund, they will select at least two other funds from their list. They are leaning toward the no-load funds, including the Vanguard S&P 500 Index Trust.

you most likely will see such a unit and the constant stream of transactions taking place on the floor of the exchange.

American Stock Exchange (Amex): Another (smaller) organized exchange in New York City.

THE AMERICAN STOCK EXCHANGE   The **American Stock Exchange (Amex)** is very similar to the NYSE in terms of physical layout and trading details, but it has easier listing requirements. Often called the "junior board," the Amex is younger than the NYSE and has less prestige. A good number of its listed securities are from relatively unknown companies nationally, and a fairly large percentage are energy oriented. As you probably guess, on balance the volatility of Amex securi-

Rationale for the Plan   Most funds pursue an investment approach or strategy which may work well in some years but not so well in others. By diversifying among funds, the Steeles will reduce their overall risk while not necessarily reducing their long-run return.

Fund	Cumulative Total Return (CTR %)				Load (%)	Phone Number
	1 Year	3 Years	5 Years	10 Years		
Funds with ten-year CTRs of 400% or more:						
Fidelity Magellan	−4.5	57.8	97.2	588.0	3.00	800–544–8888
Merrill Lynch Pacific A	−9.2	36.5	176.4	577.5	6.50	800–637–3863
Phoenix Growth	6.1	44.6	91.7	420.4	6.90	800–243–4361
CGM Cap Development	1.1	19.3	77.6	412.2	NL	800–345–4048
Sequoia	−3.8	36.6	66.4	411.9	NL	212–245–4500
Fidelity Destiny I	−3.2	45.3	82.4	400.3	9.00	800–544–8888
Fidelity Fund	−5.1	44.1	72.3	255.9	NL	800–544–8888
Vanguard S&P 500 Index Trust	−3.2	47.6	82.5	253.7	NL	800–662–7447
Funds beating Vanguard's S&P 500 Index Trust in all four periods:						
AIM Weingarten	5.6	59.8	119.3	311.8	5.50	800–347–1919
Financial Industrial, Inc.	1.0	53.5	84.4	303.4	NL	800–525–8085
FPA Paramount	1.6	49.2	91.6	381.5	6.50	800–421–4374
IAI Regional	0.3	55.2	103.8	319.7	NL	612–371–2884
IDS New Dimensions	5.4	50.1	106.2	330.9	5.00	800–328–8300
Investment Co. of America	0.7	47.7	88.5	335.3	5.75	800–421–9900
Janus Fund	−0.7	69.3	96.3	331.4	NL	800–525–3713
Nationwide Fund	0.3	56.7	88.0	292.9	7.50	800–848–0920
New York Venture	−2.9	58.7	90.7	328.5	4.75	800–229–2279
Putnam Growth & Inc.	2.4	49.2	87.7	268.6	5.75	800–225–1581

SOURCE: *Money*, February 1991, various pages. © 1991, Time Inc. All rights reserved.

ties is higher than that of NYSE securities. The Amex also has a bond-trading area, and bond transactions on the Amex are conducted in the same way as those on the NYSE.

REGIONAL STOCK EXCHANGES   Along with the two major exchanges, there are 14 **regional stock exchanges,** such as the Cincinnati Stock Exchange and the Pacific Coast Stock Exchange. Regional exchanges list securities of companies within their geographic areas, but very often these securities also are traded on the NYSE or Amex. In this respect they are duplicates, and it is hard to justify their existence. Together, all the regional exchanges account for a little less than 10 percent of all trading on organized exchanges.

> Regional stock exchanges: Stock exchanges located in the United States but outside New York City.

ORGANIZED OPTIONS AND FUTURES EXCHANGES   Options are traded on five organized exchanges: the Chicago Board Options Exchange, the American Option Exchange (part of the Amex), the Philadelphia Option Exchange, the Pacific Coast Exchange, and the New York Stock Exchange. Options are traded in a manner similar to stock trading.

There are over a dozen organized commodity exchanges in the United States and Canada, and others throughout the world. Trading on commodity exchanges differs somewhat from trading on stock exchanges. It takes place by public outcry and through a complicated series of hand signals. You might have seen pictures of commodity trading and wondered how anything is ever accomplished in what appears to be bedlam. If you have an opportunity to visit any organized exchange—but particularly the commodity exchanges—don't pass it up; although free, they are sufficiently entertaining to be worth an admission charge.

Over-the-Counter Markets

Trading over the counter sounds like an illegal activity—but it's not. In fact, in terms of the number of different stocks traded, it is the largest securities market, surpassing the NYSE and Amex combined. In contrast to an organized exchange, the **over-the-counter (OTC) market** consists of a network of securities dealers who trade securities through an extensive communication system called **NASDAQ** (National Association of Securities Dealers Automated Quotations System). In addition to common and preferred stocks and warrants all government and many corporate bonds are traded in the OTC market. Any securities dealer can buy or sell through NASDAQ, and many stockbrokerage houses make a market in a given stock, which means they buy and sell securities for and from their own portfolio rather than acting as an agent of a customer. Most OTC stocks are of relatively small and unknown companies. Many of these eventually become large, prosperous businesses, and promoters of small companies often tout that tomorrow's IBMs are found today in the OTC market. Of course, that's true, but it is also true that many of tomorrow's bankrupts are found there. The point is, trading some OTC stocks is very risky. Don't be fooled into thinking that if it is an OTC company with an exotic name, it must be a big money maker in the future. Actually, where a security is traded should be the least important consideration in judging whether or not it is worth buying.

> Over-the-counter (OTC) market: Securities trading via electronic communications.
>
> NASDAQ: Name of the electronic communications system used in the OTC market.

Investing
for the
Future

After you have provided for adequate liquidity and enough insurance to protect against unexpected financial loss, you may choose to increase your net worth with investments. Keep in mind that there is always a tradeoff between the return you can expect from an investment and the degree of risk you must take to earn it.

Your investment alternatives
include purchasing stocks or
bonds, pooling your investment
into a mutual fund, trading
securities in an organized
exchange, or buying real estate
or other tangible assets that will
increase in value.

Planning for Your Long-Term Needs

Estate planning has two primary objectives: first, to transfer your assets at death according to your wishes; and second, to transfer those assets intact to those that are left behind.

When you retire, you will want to enjoy yourself and live comfortably which is why you should begin to plan for retirement immediately. Retirement planning involves an explicit consideration of present versus future needs, and an examination of how present resources may be allocated to serve future needs.

Binding Arbitration
Versus Litigation

On the advice of a registered representative of a large brokerage company, an elderly couple invests most of their life savings—about $30,000— in bonds issued by a now-defunct energy company. They lose everything and appeal to the broker for compensation on the grounds the representative put them in an unsuitable investment. The company declines to make restitution—now what? In a growing number of cases, the answer is binding arbitration.

Investors with gripes such as the elderly couple's, or those involving excessive trading (called "churning"), unauthorized transactions, or any other misconduct, can file a claim to have the dispute settled through binding arbitration. Claims are filed either with the National Association of Securities Dealers or with the New York Stock Exchange or American Stock Exchange. The process is quite simple and relatively inexpensive, with filing fees ranging from $15 to $1,000 (for disputes in excess of $500,000).

If a claim is less than $2,500, it is settled by one arbitrator who rules on the evidence provided by each side. Larger claims are heard by three to five-person panels in a formal hearing that is similar to a trial. Each side can be represented by an attorney, issue subpoenas, and cross-examine witnesses. If your claim goes to a hearing, expect to be on the "hot seat," with the opposing attorney trying to show that you were an intelligent investor, making your own investment decisions drawn from alternatives suggested by the representative. You, of course, must show that your losses were caused by the representative.

Establishing such evidence might be difficult if you do not keep accurate records of your communications with the rep. As usual, the best evidence is in written form; but you should keep a careful diary of verbal communications, such as tips or other forms of advice. Note the time and date and carefully record the nature of the conversation.

The alternative to arbitration is litigation. This route is very expensive, and it is usually not advised if a claim is less than $200,000 or so. The big advantage with litigation is that you can also go after punitive damages, which may not be allowed in arbitration. Actually, you might not have a choice in the matter. Most brokerage houses insist that you sign a customer's agreement form when you open an account. If you read it closely, you probably will find a clause that states that all disputes must be settled by binding arbitration. And, once you agree to arbitration, you cannot later seek litigation if the arbitrators bring in a judgment you dislike. So, if you don't care for that arrangement, read the agreement carefully and insist the binding arbitration clause be deleted before you sign. You can get more information on arbitration from the NASD (Two World Trade Center, New York, NY 10048) or the New York Stock Exchange (11 Wall Street, New York, NY 10006).

Regulation of the Securities Industry

Prior to the Securities Act of 1933, fraud in the securities industry was widespread. Worthless securities issued by companies existing only on paper were often promoted and sold to the public. Corporate financial reports were rare, and many companies refused to issue them on grounds they revealed proprietary information. Although fraud is far less a problem today, do not assume it is gone altogether. If you are offered an investment deal in a small company whose shares are not traded interstate, be particularly careful. Get all the information you can from your broker, and if that doesn't answer your questions, contact an appropriate government official.

Securities Act of 1933:
First major law regulating the securities industry; deals primarily with new security issues.

FEDERAL AND STATE LAWS The **Securities Act of 1933** aimed at regulating the issuing of new securities on an interstate basis. Among other things, it required that all new issues be registered with the Securities and Exchange Commission (SEC) and that prospectuses be provided to potential buyers. It also imposed

495

penalties—both fines and prison sentences—for false communications or false prospectuses. The **Exchange Act of 1934** dealt with trading of outstanding securities. It regulates the organized exchanges and the OTC market. It also established the SEC as the regulatory agency of the securities industry, and its main thrust was to eliminate price manipulation. Along with these federal laws, most states also have laws regulating securities trading within their geographical boundaries. The federal laws apply primarily to securities traded interstate; however, the SEC can be contacted for any suspected fraudulent activity in securities trading. (See the government section of your local phone directory.)

SELF-REGULATION In addition to federal and state regulation, the securities industry has its own internal regulatory process. Most of this is found in the National Association of Securities Dealers' Rules of Fair Practice, Code of Procedure, and Uniform Practice Code. These three documents cover a wide range of trading activities, specifying rules and appropriate conduct guidelines for NASD members.

An extremely important part of self-regulation is the process of **binding arbitration.** If you have a complaint against your broker for not handling a transaction properly, or for pressuring you to invest in securities totally inappropriate for your investment objectives, or for any suspected misconduct, you can appeal to any of the organized exchanges or the NASD for binding arbitration to resolve the problem.

Claims less than $2,500 are usually resolved quickly by one arbitrator, but claims above that amount involve more complicated procedures. As its name implies, decisions are final. When considered against the only alternative for seeking a resolution—hiring your own attorney and filing a suit—binding arbitration makes a great deal of sense, since it is much cheaper and faster.

Exchange Act of 1934: Most comprehensive law regulating securities industry; deals with all aspects of securities trading.	

Binding arbitration: A method of resolving disputes among stockbrokers and customers.

Summary

A portfolio is any combination of assets. In setting up a portfolio it is important to estimate its return and risk. To better evaluate portfolio performance, expected return should be expressed quantitatively. It is important to monitor a portfolio, which involves watching the portfolio during the current period for significant developments and evaluating performance at period end.

The decision to make your own investments or to invest in pooling arrangements should consider your ability to earn comparable investment returns and costs of investing. These costs include brokerage commissions and your own time. A pooling arrangement is used primarily to achieve diversification. The most popular pool is a mutual fund, which can be load or no-load, open- or closed-end. A unit investment trust is similar to an open-end mutual fund, except that it holds an unmanaged portfolio of securities. A limited partnership may be an attractive pooling arrangement because of its favorable federal income tax deductions. Investment clubs offer investors a more active role in a pooling arrangement and are usually a form of entertainment as well as an investment pool.

Considerable securities trading takes place on organized exchanges. Many other securities are traded in the over-the-counter market, which is simply a network of dealers who trade through a system called NASDAQ. The securities industry is regulated primarily through two pieces of legislation: the Securities Act of 1933 and the Exchange Act of 1934. In addition to federal legislation, most states have regulatory laws and commissions, and the industry has self-regulation through the National Association of Securities Dealers.

American Stock Exchange (Amex) (p. 493)

binding arbitration (p. 496)

buy-and-hold strategy (p. 475)

closed-end fund (p. 481)

Exchange Act of 1934 (p. 496)

fund switching (p. 483)

global fund (p. 482)

index fund (p. 483)

international fund (p. 482)

investment club (p. 490)

limited partnership (p. 490)

load fund (p. 479)

market timing (p. 475)

maximum capital appreciation fund (p. 483)

money market fund (p. 483)

monitoring the portfolio (p. 474)

mutual fund (p. 478)

NASDAQ (p. 494)

net asset value (NAV) (p. 478)

New York Stock Exchange (NYSE) (p. 491)

no-load fund (p. 479)

open-end fund (p. 480)

organized exchange (p. 491)

over-the-counter (OTC) market (p. 494)

prospectus (p. 482)

regional stock exchanges (p. 494)

reinvestment plan (p. 483)

sector fund (p. 482)

Securities Act of 1933 (p. 495)

shareholder report (p. 482)

tax shelters (p. 490)

unit investment trust (p. 488)

Problems and Review Questions

1 What is a portfolio, and why is it important to evaluate a portfolio's return and risk characteristics? How can you estimate its risk, and why is expressing expected return quantitatively helpful in portfolio evaluation?

2 Explain the steps in monitoring a portfolio, indicating how you can evaluate a portfolio's performance over a past period of time.

3 Explain market timing, contrasting it to a buy-and-hold strategy. Then illustrate how a simple timing approach that shifts investments between a common stock mutual fund and a money market mutual fund may be riskier than simply buying and holding these investments.

4 A friend of yours has $4,000 to invest. She intends to buy growth stocks when she thinks their prices are low and then resell them after their prices have increased. Assuming she wants reasonable diversification, what advice do you have for her? Explain.

5 What is a mutual fund? What is its NAV and how is it calculated? What are some important mutual fund services?

6 Kim Karnes is thinking of buying the three mutual funds listed below:

	NAV	Offer Price	Closing Price on NYSE
Alpha	10.50	N.L.	—
Beta	21.00	22.90	—
Gamma	30.75	—	$26.25

But Kim doesn't know what any of the above means. Help Kim by explaining the difference in the three funds.

7 You bought 100 shares of an open-end mutual fund one year ago at $10 a share. You received a $0.50-per-share distribution six months ago when the fund's NAV was $12.50 a share. If the fund's NAV at the end of the year was $12 a share, calculate your rate of return on the fund for the year.

8 In reference to the fund in Question 7, suppose you found out the fund's total administrative expenses were $200,000 and there were 500,000 shares to the

fund outstanding at year end. You also learn the fund's turnover was 125 percent, its beta was 1.2, and last year's rate of return on the S&P 500 Stock Index was 22 percent. Provide an evaluation of the fund.

9   Provide a brief explanation of the following, indicating their advantages and disadvantages: (a) a unit investment trust; (b) a limited partnership; (c) an investment club.

10   Compare an organized exchange to the over-the-counter market. What are the NYSE, Amex, and NASDAQ?

11   Briefly explain regulation in the securities industry, including a discussion of binding arbitration.

Case 15.1
Evaluating Cliff Swatner's Portfolio

Cliff Swatner is single, 33 years old, and owns a condominium in New York City worth $250,000. Cliff is an attorney and doing well financially. His income last year exceeded $90,000, and he has sufficient liquid assets to supplement his condominium and other tangible assets. Several years ago, Cliff began investing in stocks and bonds. He made his selections on the basis of articles he read describing good investment opportunities. Some have worked well for Cliff, but others have not. Cliff has never taken the time to evaluate his portfolio performance, but he intends to do so in the future. As a first step he has gathered the information below. Cliff has indicated that his investment goal is to increase his net worth.

Security	Date Purchased	Purchase Prices	Number of Securities Held at 1/1/92	Indicated 1992 Return per Unit	Market Prices 1/1/92	Market Prices 6/30/92
1. Anglow, Inc. (common)	6/30/88	$7.50/share	200	$1.00	$ 15	$ 13
2. Baxter Bakeries (12% bonds)	9/30/88	$1,050/bond	5	$120.00	$800	$825
3. Gear Company ($3.00 convertible preferred)	3/31/90	$30/share	100	$3.00	$ 60	$ 80
4. U.S. Treasury 10% bonds (2012 maturity)	6/30/89	$1,000/bond	4	$100.00	$1,100	$1,200
5. Zoom, Inc. (common)	6/3090	$22/share	300	$ .20	$ 24	$ 21

Questions

1   Assuming half of the interest and dividends indicated above were actually received in the first half of 1992, calculate the realized return—in dollars and annualized rate—for that period.

2   Based on January 1, 1992, prices, what is the expected current return on Cliff's portfolio for 1992? What is the expected return based on purchase prices? Which prices do you feel Cliff should use to evaluate his performance or to make decisions about holding or selling securities? Explain.

3   Suppose Cliff's investment goal is to have half of his portfolio in high-current-yield securities and the other half in growth stocks. Does his current portfolio achieve that goal? Explain.

4   Explain whether Cliff's portfolio is adequately diversified. If you feel it is not, explain what changes you would make. Also explain whether you feel Cliff needs more concrete goals to shape his investment portfolio.

Lorrie and Dave Byron are saving for their children's education. They estimate they will need about $10,000 a year for a six-year period beginning nine years from now. The Byrons have sufficient liquidity and will not need these investment funds until then. They have decided that mutual funds represent the best investment media for them, and they are currently trying to select one for their first investment of $3,000.

Lorrie is impressed with the Sun Income Fund, which invests mainly in fixed-income securities. Lorrie notes that it has a good history of making distributions and that its rate of return last year (1992) was 17.0 percent. Dave disagrees with Lorrie's selection; instead, he favors the Ambrux Capital Appreciation Fund. It invests heavily in the common stock of growth companies, and it distributes very little each year, preferring rather to reinvest capital gains. He argues that since they will not need distributions, it doesn't make sense to invest in a fund that features them. He also notes that Ambrux's rate of return last year was 33.4 percent, a much better performance than Sun's.

Lorrie agrees that growth might be a better investment goal than high current income, but she thinks it doesn't matter how much a fund distributes, since they will elect to have all distributions reinvested in the fund anyway. Her preference for the Sun Fund rests mostly with her feeling that it is less risky—and she thinks the beta values for each support this view.

Questions

1 Using the data below, calculate the rates of return for each fund for 1991 and 1992. Your figures for 1992 should agree with the values given in the case. Calculate the average rate of return for the two-year period for each fund.
2 Show how much their $3,000 investment would be worth as of December 31, 1992, assuming it was invested in one or the other fund. Assume distributions during the year were used to acquire additional shares at the average NAV for the year.
3 Assuming each fund is no-load and they are similar in other important respects, which do you recommend for the Byrons? Explain the reason(s) for your choice. Be sure to comment on the issue of distributions from the funds.
4 Explain whether you think it might be a good idea for the Byrons to divide their investments between the two funds.

	Sun Income Fund	Ambrux Capital Appreciation Fund
NAV:		
December 31, 1990	$16.50	$12.50
December 31, 1991	15.00	11.00
December 31, 1992	16.00	14.00
Distributions per share:		
1991	$ 3.00	$ 0.50
1992	1.50	0.60
Current beta value	0.60	1.20

Helpful Reading

Changing Times

Bodnar, Janet. *"Big Ideas for a Little $."* August 1991, pp. 28–32.

Davis, Kristin. *"Mutual Funds: How Much Did You Make?"* January 1991, pp. 65–66.

Schiffres, Manual. *"Investing: Great Ways to Go Global (3 International Portfolios)."* February 1991, pp. 37–40.

Wilcox, Melynda Dovel. *"Buy High, Buy Low, Sit Pretty (Dollar Cost Averaging)."* November 1990, pp. 77–78.

Money

Edgerton, Jerry. *"New Ways to Make the Most in Mutual Funds."* May 1991, pp. 138–154.

———. *"How to Make Money in Mutual Funds."* February 1991, pp. 106–114.

Simon, Ruth. *"Safe Ways to Make Money in Small Stocks."* April 1991, pp. 144–154.

———. *"Eight Little Funds That Could."* March 1991, pp. 134–138.

Updegrave, Walter. *"Double Your Money in Three Years."* August 1991, pp. 62–69.

The Wall Street Journal

Asinof, Lynn. *"Old Standby: The Investment Club Approach Finds a 'New' Popularity."* July 17, 1991, p. C1.

Clements, Jonathon. *"Taking the First Step in Picking Your Fund."* July 23, 1991, p. C1.

———. *"Selecting a Fund? Expenses Can Be Crucial."* July 24, 1991, p. C1.

Barron's

Eaton, Leslie. *"Pro's Picks: A Seasoned Observer's Advice on Funds to Buy."* April 8, 1991, pp. 31–34.

Helpful Contacts

National Association of Investment Clubs
1515 East 11 Mile Road, Royal Oak, MI 48067

Filing an arbitration claim:

National Association of Securities Dealers
Two World Trade Center, New York, NY 10048
(telephone 212–858–4400)

American Arbitration Association
140 West 51 Street, New York, NY
(telephone 212–484–4000)

New York Stock Exchange, 11 Wall Street, New York, NY 10005

American Stock Exchange, 86 Trinity Place, New York, NY 10006

U.S. Securities and Exchange Commission
Washington, DC 20549
(Office of Consumer Affairs: telephone 202–272–7440)

Investment Company Institute
1600 M Street, Washington, DC 20036
(telephone 202–293–7700)
The Institute has a number of useful free publications concerning mutual funds.

See the Action Plan for the Steeles in this chapter for the telephone numbers of various mutual funds.

140 West 51 Street, New York, NY
(telephone 212–484–4000)

To find beta values for many mutual funds, see Weisenberger's annual publication, *Investment Companies*, which is available at many public and university libraries.

Chapter 16

Investing in Tangibles: Real Estate and Other Real Assets

Objectives

1 To understand what is meant by an income-producing property and how one should be evaluated for investment purposes

2 To recognize why land investment is usually considered risky and suitable primarily for wealthy investors

3 To see why vacation homes can be good investments and how the federal income tax law affects their potential returns

4 To understand the differences between real estate investment trusts (REITS) and real estate limited partnerships, and to see how each serves as an indirect route to real estate investment

5 To identify different methods for holding gold or silver as investments

6 To appreciate the inherent risks in precious metals, gems, hobbies and collectibles, and commodity futures contracts

Cottage Industries—A New Growth Sector?

Erie, PA—A few years ago, Sue and Joe Jarmene were facing the prospect of becoming empty-nesters when their youngest son, Bob, entered college. Like many middle-aged couples, the Jarmenes would find adjusting to the new lifestyle difficult. For Joe, it meant more free evenings to enjoy together; for Sue, it meant too many daytime hours with little to do. Although there were employment opportunities available to Sue, they really didn't need additional income, and none of the jobs seemed to offer nonfinancial satisfaction.

In a word, Sue was bored, and to soften the boredom, she devoted more time to her hobby of creating knitted Christmas ornaments. After a few months, Sue had more ornaments than she could possibly use or give away, and it was either stop production or rent a warehouse. Fortunately, there was a third alternative, sug-gested by a friend, which was to rent a booth at an arts-and-crafts festival and sell the excess. The venture was an instant success, as were others that followed. Before she realized it, Sue was a part of America's new growth trend—the cottage industry; all she needed now was the cottage.

The Jarmenes decided to put the business on a full-time basis by buying an old house in a historic section of Erie that featured small shops, several good restaurants, and a variety of personal-service businesses. The house was moderately priced but in need of substantial improvements. All told, the investment was slightly over $80,000, although their down payment and other cash contributions were only $10,000. Mortgage payments, utilities, and other related expenses amounted to about $1,200 a month, a figure far above what Sue hoped to clear in sales. But by carrying other craft items on consignment from several of her friends, she was able to bring monthly cash inflows close to a break-even point.

Clearly, the Jarmenes weren't getting rich on their venture, but that wasn't their motive for starting it. Moreover, since the business was a hobby (in the view of the IRS), deductions were limited for tax purposes. Despite these drawbacks, the business eventually proved to be a financial success as the property increased in value. With a firm offer of $100,000 for the building, Sue and Joe were now considering accepting the offer and starting all over with a larger place down the street. Along with enjoying a craft, the Jarmenes had become successful real estate investors. Sue had a new complaint, though: Now there were too few hours in her day.

The Jarmenes' real estate venture worked out well for them; not only did it show a good dollar return, but it also provided an outlet for their craft activities. This "double-duty" feature, characteristic of many tangible assets, enhances their investment appeal considerably. Moreover, tangible assets have done well during inflationary periods, and since many investors expect inflation to be a continual problem throughout the 1990s, the demand for tangible assets should continue to be strong. Demand's path is seldom a smooth one, however, so you can expect sharp ups and downs along the way. Tangible assets are therefore risky, and sometimes you need specialized skills to manage them effectively. So, if you are thinking of investing in tangible assets, you must be willing to take risks and to work hard to achieve your investment goals.

Real Estate

The advantages of home ownership as an investment have been explained in Chapter 9 and will not be repeated here. Our concern in this chapter is with real estate that is not your principal residence. Such real estate includes income-producing properties, land, and vacation homes. We assume in this section that you would own and manage the property yourself. Pooling arrangements are examined in the next section.

Income-Producing Property

Income-producing property: A real estate investment that provides periodic rentals.

An **income-producing property** is one that provides periodic rentals. As the owner, you receive these rents each period (usually each month), and it is your responsibility to provide tenants all the services specified in the rental agreement. These services can range from virtually nothing—all you provide is the land—to practically everything, such as heat and air conditioning, painting and repairs, water and sewerage, and possibly other services. From gross rentals you must deduct costs of providing tenants' services; the difference is your **net operating income (NOI),** which is one source of return. Another is a gain if you happen to sell the property for more than you have invested in it; and a third source is any tax savings you might enjoy because of deductions allowed by the IRS.

Net operating income (NOI): A profit measurement—the difference between gross rentals and the costs of providing tenants' services.

ALTERNATIVES AVAILABLE   The three sources of return vary considerably depending upon the type of property you are considering. For example, an apartment unit in a deteriorated part of town may not show capital appreciation over time; in fact, its market value may decline. In order to be economically viable, this investment would have to show a high NOI or have special tax deductions. Alternatively, another property might show a poor NOI but be located in a growing part of town where property values are rising rapidly. In this case, you might accept the lower current return in favor of the higher expected future return. As you see, property investment is very much like common stock investment, where you also must decide between current or future return.

Another factor to consider is the property's physical condition, and there is usually a trade-off here too. While the real estate market is not perfect in the sense that property prices always reflect their true economic value, nevertheless, they are extremely efficient in this respect. This implies that the poorer the condition of a property, the lower its price. Such situations offer opportunities to first-time buyers without much cash: They can buy lower-priced properties and invest their own time and efforts to improve them. This is called using **"sweat equity"** as a replacement for financial equity, and it has helped many ambitious people launch successful endeavors in real estate. Naturally, you shouldn't think that every neglected property can be improved by sweat equity; in fact, many are so considerably overpriced, given their poor physical conditions, that they are better left alone. And it would be foolish to jump into this investment arena without proper training and, possibly, guidance from someone experienced in the area.

"Sweat equity": Use of your own labor to enhance a property's value.

Along this line, many real estate professionals will tell you to stick to properties familiar to you at the start and gradually undertake more ambitious projects as your knowledge and experience grow. This strategy applies particularly to finding potentially profitable properties and arranging suitable financing to buy them. We can't help you with finding properties, but our discussion of financing appears in Chapter 9, and the material that follows will show you how to calculate a return on property investment and how to evaluate it. And, by all means, do calculate a return for each property you are thinking of buying. It forces you to look critically at the economics of the investment and to avoid emotional factors that often are present in buying real estate.

Finally, after you buy a property, you must manage it professionally and in a businesslike manner. Prompt collection of rents and payment of bills are a must, and so is routine maintenance. All this takes time and effort that should be considered before investing. Contrary to what some realtors may tell you, there are very few properties that manage themselves.

MEASURING RETURN   Measuring the return from a real estate investment is somewhat involved—primarily due to income tax complexities—but the techniques are not difficult to understand. An example will help clarify them. In 1992, Arnold and Sharon Steele were considering a number of investment opportunities. One property particularly appealed to them. It was a duplex situated in a good neighborhood that was mostly residential, but with some service and retail businesses. It was not far from their home, making it convenient to manage. Property values in the neighborhood did not fluctuate much and had been increasing at about 5 percent a year. The duplex was in sound physical condition, featuring brick construction, and it had been improved within the past ten years by the addition of separate heating and air conditioning units for each apartment. Each tenant paid $400 a month rent and all utilities except water and sewerage. Lawn service and snow removal were provided by the owner.

The seller's asking price was $80,000, but she most likely would have accepted $75,000 from a buyer with financing in hand. Arnold and Sharon discussed the property with a loan officer from a savings and loan, who indicated that a $60,000, 12 percent (fixed rate), 30-year loan would be available to them. This means the Steeles needed a $15,000 down payment. Details of the loan appear in Table 16.1.

To evaluate this investment, Arnold and Sharon followed standard guidelines used by most realtors and property appraisers. These guidelines involve a series of steps.

Step 1.   Calculate the first year's net operating income (NOI) and cash flow before taxes. This is done in Figure 16.1. It is important to make these estimates of NOI as accurate as possible because subsequent years' NOIs are based on it. In the Steeles' case, insurance, property taxes, and sewer and water are obtained readily from existing records; but vacancy losses, advertising, licenses and permits, and repairs and maintenance are not so easily determined and require careful estimating. Even though tenants pay their own utilities, keeping the heating and air conditioning units in good shape is the Steeles' responsibility. In addition, they must allow for periodic painting as well as plumbing or electrical repairs.

TABLE 16.1 · Details of the Steeles' Mortgage Loan

Year	Total Payments	Annual Payoff		Loan Balance
		Interest	Principal	
1	$7,406	$7,188	$218	$59,782
2	7,406	7,161	245	59,537
3	7,406	7,130	276	59,261

Amount: $60,000.

Term: 30 years.

Monthly Payment: $617.17.

Rate: 12%; adjustable to a maximum of 16%.

		%	2				3		Comments
1	GROSS SCHEDULED RENTAL INCOME						9	600	$800 a month
2	Plus: Other Income							—	
3	TOTAL GROSS INCOME						9	600	
4	Less: Vacancy and Credit Losses							960	
5	GROSS OPERATING INCOME						8	640	
6	Less: Operating Expenses								
7	Accounting and Legal				—				
8	Advertising, Licenses, and Permits				60				should be adequate
9	Property Insurance				440				we're sure of this
10	Property Management				—				
11	Payroll—Resident Management				—				
12	Other				—				
13	Taxes—Workmen's Compensation				—				
14	Personal Property Taxes				—				
15	Real Estate Taxes				900				
16	Repairs and Maintenance				700				may not be enough
17	Services—Elevator				—				
18	Janitorial				—				
19	Lawn				—				
20	Pool				—				
21	Rubbish				—				
22	Other				—				
23	Supplies				—				
24	Utilities—Electricity				—				
25	Gas and Oil				—				
26	Sewer and Water				450				from seller's records
27	Telephone				—				
28	Other				—				
29	Miscellaneous				—				
30					—				
31	TOTAL OPERATING EXPENSES						2	550	
32	NET OPERATING INCOME						6	090	
33	Less: Total Annual Debt Service						7	406	
34	CASH FLOW BEFORE TAXES						(1	316)	looks bad!

FIGURE 16.1

Calculating the first year's net operating income (NOI) and cash flow before taxes.

The $700 allowance for these latter items should be adequate but may not be in the event of a major problem. If everything goes according to plan, the property will show a negative cash flow of $1,316 in the first year, which doesn't sound good. As you see in Figure 16.1, **cash flow before taxes** is simply NOI minus total annual debt service.

Step 2. Calculate cash flows before taxes for the remaining number of years the property will be held. In order to do this, two estimates are needed. First, you must estimate how much NOI will grow (or decline) over time, and second, you must determine how long the property will be held. Of course, each of these estimates is often difficult to make. The Steeles feel they will hold the property at least six years and maybe longer, but to simplify our calculations we assume they sell it after three years. As for growth in NOI, the Steeles feel a 5 percent annual rate is reasonable. Given these assumptions, the NOIs and before-tax cash flows can be calculated. They are shown in Table 16.2 and, as you see, the picture is still a bleak one.

Step 3. Determine the impact of income taxes. If a property shows a profit, it is, of course, taxable. Equally important, if the property shows a loss, it can offset other taxable income you might have and thereby reduce your income tax liability. (Offsets are subject to the loss limitation rules, explained in Chapter 5. To earn the maximum offset of $25,000, the taxpayer must be active in managing the property and have an adjusted gross income of less than $100,000. The Steeles meet each restriction.) Table 16.3 shows the income tax impacts for each of the three years. As you see, the property shows a loss in each year. Since these losses would reduce the Steeles' other taxable income, they have value, the amount of which depends upon the Steeles' marginal tax rate. Assuming a 28 percent marginal tax rate, the Steeles would reduce their tax liability each year by the amount shown in Table 16.3. You have probably noticed that the higher your marginal tax rate, the greater the value of a tax loss. Since many properties show losses—at least in their early years—you can understand why property investment is particularly appealing to investors in high tax brackets. For the same reason, it might not be profitable to low-bracket investors.

To understand **depreciation,** you need to know that it is an income tax deduction that allows you to recover the cost of an asset as it wears out over time. In the Steeles' case it is allowed on the building, but not on the land on which the building sits. Therefore, the Steeles must estimate the land's value and subtract it from the purchase price. Assuming the land's value is $10,000 and subtracting it from $75,000 gives $65,000, which is called the property's **depreciation basis.** Now, you can write off a portion of this basis each year using several allowable methods. We show the easiest, called straight line depreciation. You divide the basis by the number of years the IRS allows as its estimated life to arrive at an

TABLE 16.2 ·
Calculation of Cash Flow Before Taxes

	Year 1	Year 2	Year 3
NOI (expected to grow at 5% each year)	$ 6,090	$ 6,395	$ 6,714
Less debt service	(7,406)	(7,406)	(7,406)
Cash flow before taxes	$(1,316)	$(1,011)	$(692)

TABLE 16.3 ·
Calculation of Income
Tax Impacts

	Year 1	Year 2	Year 3
Cash flow before taxes, from Table 16.2	$(1,316)	$(1,011)	$(692)
Add principal payments, from Table 16.1*	218	245	276
Deduct depreciation	(2,364)	(2,364)	(2,364)
Taxable income (loss) from the property	$(3,462)	$(3,130)	$(2,780)
Steeles' marginal income tax rate	×0.28	×0.28	×0.28
Value of the taxable losses	$ 969	$ 876	$ 778

*Principal payments are not tax deductible; interest payments are, however.

annual depreciation expense. The 1986 tax law set this write-off period at 27.5 years (regardless of how long the building actually lasts); therefore, the Steeles will have a $2,364 ($65,000/27.5) deduction each year.

After-tax cash flow: A profit measurement— before tax cash flow adjusted for income tax flows, which can be positive if a property shows tax losses.

Step 4. Calculate the **after-tax cash flow.** Bringing together the before-tax cash flow from Table 16.2 with the value of the taxable losses from Table 16.3 gives us the after-tax cash flow in Table 16.4. As you see, the investment is looking better, and had your analysis stopped at Table 16.2, your evaluation of the property would have been far poorer than it is now. But is it a good investment? To answer this question we need additional steps.

Step 5. Estimate the property's resale value at the end of the holding period and calculate the after-tax amount of cash you would receive from selling it. These are also difficult figures to estimate, but let's assume the property's market value increases at the same rate as the increase in its NOI (a fairly common assumption), which was 5 percent a year. Then its value at the end of three years will be $86,822 ($75,000 × 1.05 × 1.05 × 1.05). But when it's sold, the Steeles probably will pay a realtor's commission of, say, $6,078 (this is a 7 percent commission, which is fairly common: $86,822 × 0.07 = $6,078). So, they will net $80,744 ($86,822 − $6,078) from the sale. However, the IRS will want a portion of their gain, and also a portion of the depreciation deductions they have taken. In IRS jargon, this latter item is called **recapture.** The taxes the Steeles will owe—$3,594—from sale of the property are calculated in Figure 16.2. Subtracting the $3,594 from the net proceeds from sale of the property—$80,744— leaves the Steeles with $77,150; and after they pay off their mortgage balance of $59,261 (see Table 16.1), they can pocket the difference of $17,889 ($77,150 − $59,261).

Recapture: A taxable gain resulting from the sale of an asset which has been depreciated.

Step 6. Estimate the annual rate of return. Using the cash flows in Table 16.4 along with the initial investment of $15,000 and the ending value of $17,889, we

TABLE 16.4 ·
Calculation of After-Tax
Cash Flow

	Year 1	Year 2	Year 3
Cash flow before taxes—Table 16.2	$(1,316)	$(1,011)	$(692)
Value of taxable losses—Table 16.3	969	876	778
After-tax cash flow	$(347)	$(135)	$ 86

FIGURE 16.2

Calculation of taxes due
from sale of the
property.

Net gain on the sale = $80,744 − $75,000 =	$ 5,744
Plus three years' depreciation = 3 × $2,364 =	7,092
Total	$12,836
Steeles' marginal income tax rate	× .28
Taxes due from the sale	$ 3,594

can calculate the precise rate of return with calculator or computer programs. Assuming neither is available, we can roughly estimate the rate following procedures shown in Figure 16.3. This figure is 0.0554, or about 5.5 percent.

How good (or bad!) is this rate of return? There are several factors to consider in answering this question. First, it is an after-tax return, and it should be compared with other returns on an after-tax basis. When the Steeles were considering this investment, the return on tax-free municipal bonds (with long maturities) was about 7.5 percent.

Step 7. Take risk into consideration. Measuring risk in property investment is exceptionally difficult. Surely, you have noticed that practically all of the gain

Action Plan for the Steeles Investing in a Rental Property

Background   The Steeles have read that real estate is an excellent investment, and they have located a rental duplex that requires a $15,000 down payment. Financing the down payment would require selling some of their stocks or mutual fund shares.

The Problem   Arnold and Sharon like the idea of managing a property. They have very basic household-repair skills, but they are not discouraged by the work commitment accompanying such an investment. They would enjoy upgrading the property through landscaping and painting and then keeping it in good shape.

The Plan   The property must offer no less than a 10 percent annual after-tax return to compensate the Steeles adequately for the risk they would assume with an additional $60,000 in mortgage debt. While Arnie and Sharon feel that a 5 percent appreciation factor is realistic, they recognize that even real estate prices do not always increase. Indeed, when they were looking at the property, prices locally and nationally had weakened and the real estate outlook was anything but excellent.

The Steeles' analysis (presented in this chapter) indicated a return of only 5.5 percent. They also did some "what if" analysis on their home computer and determined that if tenants' rents could be raised from $800 to $900 a month, everything else unchanged, the return would increase to about 11 percent. Equally important, annual cash flows are positive each year (see accompanying table), which means no adverse affect on the Steeles' budget. The Steeles felt that tenants would not resist a rent increase, since rents had not been raised for several

FIGURE 16.3

Estimating rate of
return on the
investment.

1.	Annual cash flows after taxes—Table 16.4:	
	Year 1	$(347)
	Year 2	(135)
	Year 3	86
2.	Net proceeds after taxes from sale of the property	17,889
3.	Total cash inflows	$ 17,493
4.	Initial investment	$ 15,000
5.	Ratio of total cash inflows to initial investment (line 3 divided by line 4)	1.1662
6.	Line 5 minus 1.0 = rate of return for three years	0.1662
7.	Average annual rate of return = line 6 divided by 3	0.0554

came from selling the property, and not from the annual cash flow. This situation was also experienced by the Jarmenes in the vignette at the beginning of this chapter; it is also characteristic of many—if not most—property deals. This means the rate of return is very sensitive to a few critical factors, which are the assumed future selling price of the property and the amount of the down payment. To illustrate the first factor, if you assume the selling price increases by 8

years and since the property would be improved in physical appearance. If their assumption is correct, the property return looks attractive.

It is impossible to tell the Steeles that they should or should not buy the duplex. They are aware of the risks and have prepared a good analysis. The decision now is theirs. Some financial planners, though, would urge a more cautious plan.

Rationale for the Plan Apart from the added risk associated with more debt, investing in the duplex creates an excessive reliance upon real estate in the Steeles' portfolio. At the end of 1992, real estate represented about 63 percent of the Steeles' total assets (see Chapter 3). If they acquire the duplex, the amount rises to 86 percent ($280,000/$325,540). Even if we look only at investment assets, real estate's share goes from 0 to 70 percent ($75,000/$107,800). Moreover, the Steeles are also considering buying a vacation condominium in three years—another real estate investment. The Steeles should do more "what if" planning, this time focusing on what could happen to their family if worst-case possibilities occurred. Suppose Sharon works fewer hours, or Arnold's raise is much smaller, or an apartment is vacant all year? The fixed mortgage obligations do not change, and the family must sacrifice other goals.

Duplex's Cash Flow Assuming $900 Monthly Rentals

	Year 1	Year 2	Year 3
NOI	$7,170	$7,529	$7,906
After-tax cash flow	431	682	945

509

Investing in
Tangibles

percent a year, instead of 5 percent, the rate of return jumps to about 15 percent. Now the investment looks fairly good in relation to municipal bonds. However, getting an 8 percent increase each year might be extremely difficult, and the annual increase could just as easily be 2 percent. The point is that this property is a very risky investment, and it should be recognized as such. The Steeles must make the best and most realistic estimates they can to evaluate the property, and they shouldn't fool themselves, or let a realtor fool them, with overly optimistic guesses of future prices.

LEVERAGE ALSO MAGNIFIES RATE OF RETURN AND RISK   Real estate investment often involves substantial amounts of borrowed funds. This provides leverage in exactly the same way as using a margin account to buy common stocks. Many of the popular get-rich-quick books focus on real estate investment where high rates of leverage are possible. In the Steeles' case, these promoters would argue the Steeles should offer a down payment of only $10,000 or even $5,000, borrowing the balance on a second mortgage arrangement or through a land contract. As you might guess, with a smaller down payment their rate of return increases, even after allowing for additional interest on the additional funds borrowed.

Leverage seems almost like magic—put in a little less and get out a little more. Of course, it isn't magic, and it works to your advantage only as long as property prices are increasing; but if they remain constant or decline, then leverage works against you. Many unfortunate real estate investors learned this lesson the hard way when real estate prices peaked in the early 1990s. Some lost every dollar they had invested, including in some cases a substantial amount of equity in their personal residences, which they used to start the credit pyramid. Don't be fooled by such schemes—they're all risky. Instead, take a realistic view of real estate as a possible addition to your portfolio. A property such as the one the Steeles examined will not make you rich no matter how much you leverage it; but it can be a decent investment, particularly if you don't mind dealing with tenants and doing the necessary maintenance to keep the property in shape.

Investing in Land

The advice to "buy land because they're not making any more of it" has appealed to many investors. Some have become very wealthy by holding a key piece of land in a rapidly developing community or in an area where major deposits of natural resources have been found. Apart from these sensational ventures, more modest—but certainly not poor—returns have been found in land investment. For example, referring to Table 13.3 in Chapter 13, you can see that farmland shows an average annual return of 6.3 percent for the 20-year period that ended on June 1, 1991; but Table 13.3 also shows its return was a negative 1.8 percent for the ten years that ended on that date.

The risks associated with land depend directly on the kind of land you buy. The price of farmland, for example, usually reflects the prices of crops that can be grown on it, and this explains why farmland did so well in the inflationary 1970s when commodity prices were rising. It also explains why its return fell in the 1980s when commodity prices fell. Commodity price volatility is likely in the future, so you can expect farmland prices to be volatile as well. Natural resource land, such as coal land in eastern Kentucky or West Virginia, also shows this pattern, but land held for residential or commercial development represents a different set of risks. Usually, such land is unproductive until development is finished, meaning there is no income from crop or mineral sales to help offset costs of holding the land. And these costs can be considerable, particularly during periods of high interest rates, or if the property's zoning leads to high property taxes. Moreover, the future value of such land is determined greatly by future population and business trends that are not easily predicted.

Most land investments are characterized by poor cash flows during their holding periods; poor tax-sheltering opportunities, since land is not depreciable; and a high future payoff when the land is finally developed or sold. All this adds up to considerable risk, which increases many times if you also cannot diversify. As a result, land investment is usually appropriate only for the very wealthy. Now that we have covered both land and income-producing properties, it is helpful to summarize investment characteristics of different types of each. This is done in Table 16.5. Before you invest in any property and regardless of whether you plan to own it directly or through a pooling arrangement, you should consider very carefully the characteristics shown in this table.

The Vacation Home

There was a time when only the very wealthy could consider owning a vacation home. Today, millions of Americans do. True, most of these people have incomes far in excess of the national average, but not all of them are "super rich." A number of factors explain the growing popularity of vacation homes. First, we have more leisure time and are looking for ways to enjoy it. Second, it is easier and more commonplace to rent a vacation home during periods when it is not used; in many instances, rental managers take care of all rental details and simply mail a check to the owner. Third, the federal income tax law might allow certain deductions that increase your after-tax income, making the vacation home more affordable. Finally, in some cases the vacation home has shown an excellent return on investment.

As you would probably expect, persons or families most interested in vacation homes are those in their middle ages who are planning retirement. Their goal is to have a place to enjoy occasionally during their remaining work years and then to serve as a principal residence in retirement. Popular areas for these people are the Sun Belt states, particularly Florida, Arizona, Georgia, and North and South Carolina. Surprisingly, even many young people are considering vacation homes. Retirement may be the last thing on their minds; instead, they are looking for current enjoyment and a good investment.

WHERE TO LOOK   Only you can judge what vacation area and kind of home appeal to you. If you like photographing alligators in the Louisiana swamps, you probably won't be happy in a condo at Cape Cod. But you should think twice before buying a vacation home in the swamps, particularly if you might want to sell it some day. While this is a stretched example, it should make the point that the market value of a vacation home depends very much upon its appeal to other

TABLE 16.5 • Characteristics of Property Types

	Agricultural and Underdeveloped Land	Predeveloped Land	New Apartments	Existing Apartments	Individual, Strip, Commercial, and Small Office Properties
Function	Agricultural, forest, and mineral production; recreation	Held for investment and speculation on successful development	Shelter, housing, amenities, and living environment	Shelter, housing, amenities, and living environment	Exchange goods, distribution centers; personal services; administration and management
Investment characteristics:					
Cash flow	Low (or negative)	Negative	Low to medium	Reasonable	Average to good
Tax shelter	Low	Low	High	Low to medium	Low to medium
Inflation hedge	Good	Good	Good	Good	Low
Operating risk	High	High	High	Average	Average to high
Liquidity	Relatively illiquid	Generally hard to sell	Generally good for smaller units	Generally good for smaller units	Low to average
Mortgage financing	Financing primarily by sellers and specialized government programs.	Financing almost exclusively available from seller; favorable financing terms reflected in higher selling price	70–80% conventional financing, with land lease possible for developer to "mortgage out"	70–80% financing available from conventional sources; seller often carries back secondary financing	70–80% conventional sources; seller may often provide secondary financing
Ownership characteristics:					
Owner's equity	Generally owned by user with increasing tendency to investment by institutional investors and partnerships	Owned primarily by individuals, partnerships, and large corporations	All types of owners, including many individuals and partnerships	All types of owners, including many individuals and partnerships	Smaller investors, individuals, small groups
Size	Can be bought in all sizes, but meaningful operating economies require substantial holdings	Can be of any size	All sizes; tend to be somewhat larger than existing apartments	All sizes; tend to be many small units available	Moderate
Management time required	Heavy; constant supervision required if in use	Low, although it is essential that important developments be monitored, but when disposition occurs, substantial management time could be required	Extensive for initial rent-up; average to heavy for ongoing operations	Average, except that "problems" can make excessive time demands	Average to high, particularly where leases are of shorter term
Management expertise required	Very high; timing of paramount importance	Moderate, although ability to interpret—and influence—political and economic trends is important	Average	Average	Average

TABLE 16.5 • Continued

	Agricultural and Underdeveloped Land	Predeveloped Land	New Apartments	Existing Apartments	Individual, Strip, Commercial, and Small Office Properties
Economies of size	With the trend to use of more advanced technology and larger capital-intensive equipment, large land holdings advantageous	Large acreage can represent substantial economies of scale	Substantial economies realized with larger units	Substantial economies realized with larger units	Low, unless multiple properties owned
Economic characteristics: Users	Farmers, ranchers, individuals, corporations	Large corporations, individual speculators	Families and individuals of moderate means or those who choose not to own a home (usually rents for more than an existing unit)	Families and individuals of moderate means or those who choose not to own a home	Households, small businesses, chain stores, white-collar workers
Term of use	Lifetime down to yearly leases	1–5 years	Year leases, condominiums, and cooperatives to lifetime	Month to month, some year leases, condominiums and cooperatives	1-year to long-term leases
Demand influences	Population levels, food and other consumption levels, technology, transportation systems	Population trends, general economic conditions, land-use controls, transportation systems, availability of money for development, government programs (new communities financing)	Population increases, family formation rates, social and economic changes, life-style modes, amenity packages offered	Population increases, family formation rates, social and economic changes	Population levels, transportation access and technology, parking, competition
Supply influences	Water availability, transportation access, removals due to development activity, fertility and soil conditions, scenic or other recreational possibilities	Land-use regulations, conversion to developed status, establishment of parks and natural preserves, regional growth patterns, density and sprawl trends, volume of land promotion activity	Removals from housing stock by demolition or condemnation, availability of money for new financing, land-use approval process, political environment, special government programs (FHA subsidized housing, housing allowances)	Removals from housing stock by demolition or condemnation, political environment, conversions to other use (condominiums), conversions from other uses (e.g., hotels); supply of new units	Land or lot availability, existence of commercial "strip," local government attitude toward transportation and strip development
Government controls	Crop subsidy programs, formal financing programs, land-use controls	Land-use controls, restrictions on marketing practices	Restrictions on condominiums, property tax assessment policies, financing availability (specialized government programs), land-use regulations	Restrictions on convertibility to condominiums, property tax assessment policies, financing availability (specialized government programs)	Zoning, building codes, willingness to supply services, traffic control

SOURCE: Adapted from Edmund Ficek, Thomas B. Henderson, and Ross H. Johnson, *Real Estate Principles and Practices*, 4th ed. (Columbus: Macmillan Publishing Company, 1987). pp. 492–493.

people. Locating in an area of strong demand improves the financial side of your investment by making renting much easier and by allowing the property's market value to keep in step with inflation. However, there is another aspect to the location issue: If you buy in an area that is already very popular, you usually pay a premium price for the home. Vacation home advisers often tell you to look instead for areas that are not current hot spots but have good growth prospects. It isn't easy determining today where tomorrow's vacation spots will be, but it may be worth a try.

In recent years the vacation home market has been hit very hard by the overall recession. In some areas, particularly in the Northeast and certain parts of Florida, prices have fallen as much as 40 percent. This sharp decline should indicate two factors of importance: First, this type of investment can be very risky; second, there may be some good values for potential investors.

WHAT KIND OF HOME TO BUY   After you find a location, the next question is what kind of home to buy. Buying one requiring frequent care and maintenance will cut into your vacation time. (Do you really want a weekend getaway that needs weekly lawn mowing and regular painting?) On the other hand, if you are used to living in a conventional home, you might feel very uncomfortable in a condo where you ride the elevator each time you go out. Also consider whether you intend to rent the place. If so, who will make the arrangements? If you own an isolated cabin in the woods, these are your responsibilities; but with a condo in a major development, all these services can be provided—for a fee, of course.

Because buying a vacation home is such a major purchase, you should take considerable time researching alternatives. Listing each important factor on paper along with an importance rating to family members is an excellent idea. Try to get a family consensus on location and type of dwelling. Then, you must see if it fits within the family budget. In this respect you should now be able to understand most of the cash flows related to the investment, with the possible exception of the federal income tax situation. As usual, it is extremely important and often makes the difference between buying and not buying.

FEDERAL INCOME TAX IMPLICATIONS   The tax law is complex in this area, and to make matters worse, it seems to change constantly. At present, the tax treatment depends upon how frequently you use the home personally and how frequently it is rented. There are three possible situations.

Situation 1.   You rent it for 14 days or less. In this case the IRS is not concerned with your property as an investment. This means you need not report any rental income, but you cannot take any expenses other than those you normally take as itemized deductions. For example, you cannot deduct operating expenses such as utility bills, depreciation, or maintenance costs; but you can deduct mortgage interest and property taxes if you file an itemized return.

Situation 2.   You use the property for 14 days or less (or not more than 10 percent of the total days it is rented, whichever is greater). In this situation, the property is treated like any other real estate investment, with one exception: A portion of mortgage interest—determined by the percentage of personal-use days to total-use days—cannot be deducted either as a business or personal itemized expense. It is again important to recognize that any business loss is subject to the loss limitation rules discussed previously and in Chapter 5. To deduct losses, you must be active in managing the property. Unfortunately, that is not the case with many vacation home complexes.

Situation 3.   You use the property 15 days or more (or for more than 10 percent of the total days it is rented, whichever is greater) and also rent it for 15 or more days. Now, the property is a combination of personal residence and business, and its tax treatment is similar to that of hobbies. In short, this means you cannot have a business loss for tax purposes. It sounds simple, but there is a complication having to do with the amount of total expenses you can deduct. The IRS insists that you allocate expenses on the basis of the property's use as a business and as a personal residence. An example is shown in Table 16.6. In this case the taxpayer used the property 15 days and rented it 30 days, for a total of 45 days. The personal percentage then is 1/3 (15/45) and the business percentage is 2/3 (30/45). All expenses are allocated on the basis of these percentages. Notice the loss of $200 resulting from the business cannot be used to offset other income.

Notice in particular how much tax difference one day can make. Had the taxpayer stayed one fewer day, he or she would have been in situation 2, and total deductions would have been $1,800 (the total net loss) less allocated personal mortgage interest. For purposes of an example, if we assume this amount is $200, the deduction would have been $1,600, which is far more than the $900 with situation 3. It is extremely important that you estimate as carefully as possible how often you will use and rent the vacation home so that you can evaluate the

TABLE 16.6 ·
Determining Federal
Income Tax Deductions
on a Vacation Home

	Allocations		
	Personal 1/3	Business 2/3	Total
Rentals	$ —	$ 3,000	$ 3,000
Less: Taxes and interest	(900)	(1,800)	(2,700)
Operating expenses	(400)	(800)	(1,200)
Depreciation	(300)	(600)	(900)
Net income (loss)	$(1,600)	$(200)	$(1,800)
Amount deductible for tax purposes	$ 900	-0-	$ 900

tax situation correctly before you buy a place; and it is just as important after a place is bought so that you can take full advantage of tax provisions. You need to review the law before you buy a place or, if you already own one, before you decide how to use it for the year. Also, keep in mind the test for days of personal use includes only those days you actually use the home. Days spent there fixing up or remodeling don't count in this test. Therefore, if one of the personal-use days in the above example was a "fix-up" day, it wouldn't have counted. As usual, you must keep good records to support the residency test, as well as all deductions you claim. Finally, you should realize the example illustrated in Table 16.6 is a fairly simple one that does not address all the possible complications that might arise.

Investing in Real Estate Through Pooling Arrangements

Even a modest investment in real estate requires a fairly large down payment. Most investors cannot achieve adequate diversification if they use such a large sum for only one investment. To overcome this problem, various pooling arrangements have developed, the most important being the **real estate investment trust** (usually called a **REIT**) and the real estate limited partnership. Each of these is examined below.

Real Estate Investment Trusts (REITs)

Real estate investment trust (REIT): A pooling arrangement (similar to a closed-end mutual fund) that invests in real estate and real estate mortgages.

A REIT is a type of closed-end investment company similar to closed-end mutual funds explained in the previous chapter. To be considered an investment company for tax purposes, the REIT must derive 70 percent of its income from real estate and distribute no less than 90 percent of its income as cash dividends. Many REITs are publicly held, which means their shares are traded on organized exchanges or in the over-the-counter market. In effect, you buy or sell their shares as you would the shares of any other public corporation. This makes REIT shares very marketable, but not necessarily liquid, since their prices are often as volatile as those of other stocks.

Equity trusts: REITS specializing in investing in real estate.

DIFFERENCES AMONG REITS REITs differ in a number of respects. First, some invest in buildings, shopping centers, warehouses, and many other kinds of properties. These are called **equity trusts,** and they earn income from renting space to tenants. Other REITs do not invest in properties, but instead invest by lending funds to others; that is, they make loans (usually mortgage loans) to builders and developers. These are called **mortgage trusts.** A second difference has to do with the manner in which a REIT finances itself. Some are financed entirely with owners' equity, having no long-term debt whatsoever. Others make extensive use of borrowed funds, which increases their leverage.

Since REITs differ so much in both the kinds of investments they make and how they are financed, they also differ considerably in their expected return and risk characteristics. Some are extremely safe, while others are very risky. Before investing, it is important to research their underlying fundamentals, either by doing the work yourself or asking your broker for a research report and an opinion on which ones seem appropriate for your investment objectives.

THE RETURN FROM A REIT   As mentioned above, a REIT must distribute 90 percent of its realized income as cash dividends. This means your current return on many REITs is fairly high, particularly with mortgage trusts. A small sample of REITs, showing their returns, is given in Table 16.7. This sample indicates the wide variations in debt ratios and also shows the market price and equity per share for each trust. This latter item is similar to the net asset value (NAV) of a mutual fund. In addition to dividends, it is possible to experience capital gains or losses if the market price of the shares increases or decreases. However, a REIT does not offer any direct tax shelters, such as depreciation, and some people see this as a major disadvantage of a REIT.

Of the four REITs shown in Table 16.7, only Federal Realty has investment appeal, based on divided yield and dividend growth. As you see, HRE Properties and MGI Properties have negative dividend growth—a very disturbing situation. At mid-1991 the real estate industry was not doing well.

HISTORICAL EXPERIENCE WITH REITS   The history of REITs clearly illustrates the risks associated with excessive leverage. When the REIT industry began, REITs were the darlings of Wall Street. By borrowing considerable amounts of capital and investing it at slightly higher rates than what they paid on the borrowed funds, they were able to show glowing earnings reports for their shareholders. Moreover, this was a period of growing demand for rental properties, which also strengthened the real estate market. But when interest rates shot up in 1973, and when the severe recession of 1974–1975 hit, the tables turned. Many real estate loans REITs had made wound up in default, and tenants were rou-

TABLE 16.7   ·   A Sample of REITs Traded on the New York Stock Exchange

REIT	Beta Value	Debt Ratio	Equity per Share	Market Price 7/24/91	Dividend Yield	Annual Growth in Dividends	
						Past Five Years	Past Ten Years
Federal Realty	0.80	55%	$17.73	$19	9.7%	+8%	+10%
HRE Properties	0.65	15	20.72	15	10.0	−7	−1
MGI Properties	0.75	33	15.67	10	8.1	−9	−1
Santa Anita Realty	0.70	51	9.82	23	8.6	+2	+4

SOURCE: *The Value Line Investment Survey—Part 3, Ratings and Reports,* May 31, 1991. Copyright © 1991 by Value Line Publishing, Inc.; used by permission.

tinely breaking their lease agreements. As a result, most REITs found themselves in serious financial difficulty as they became unable to meet their own debt obligations. Some failed and no longer exist; many more went through reorganizations and required years to get back in sound financial shape. Following this disaster, REITs were regarded as extremely risky, and as a result the market prices of their shares fell way below their equity value.

The situation is somewhat improved today, although the real estate excesses of the 1980s have led to some disasters. In general, REIT managers pursue more cautious investment and financing approaches, greatly improving the financial condition of REITs. If you feel real estate will offer good returns in the future, and if you are not in a position where tax shelters would be desirable, then REITs might be a good investment for you.

Real Estate Limited Partnerships

Limited partnerships as investment vehicles were introduced and explained in the previous chapter. However, since they are used so frequently in real estate investment, further discussion of them is appropriate here. Before the 1986 Tax Reform Act, about half of all the major commercial-property sales were made by real estate limited partnerships. However, the trend has been downward in recent years.

BLIND POOL VERSUS SINGLE PROPERTY SYNDICATE   Many real estate limited partnerships are **blind pool syndicates,** which means the specific properties to be purchased are not known at the time you make your investment. It's a "pig in the poke," suggesting a fair degree of risk. Many of the large syndications in which you are likely to invest are of this type, and the key is to know the past performance of the general partner, because you are relying considerably upon his or her good judgment. In contrast to blind pools, in **single property syndicates** you know in advance of investing which properties will be purchased.

PUBLIC VERSUS PRIVATE SYNDICATES   **Public syndicates** are large partnerships marketed very much like new distributions of common stock. Stock brokerage firms often sponsor them, and their sales representatives attempt to sell limited partnership interests in the same fashion they sell stocks and bonds. Their commissions are somewhat higher for public syndicates and, accordingly, they tend to be more aggressive in their sales approaches. You usually need a minimum investment of $5,000, but with the growing popularity of IRAs, many now have IRA minimums of $2,000. Public syndicates invest in a wide array of real estate, ranging from row houses in San Francisco to warehouses in New York. Shopping centers and office buildings—both new and existing units—are often their favorite investment targets. Since prices of many of these properties are well in the millions of dollars, about the only way small investors can participate in owning them is through the public limited partnership, or the REIT.

A **private syndicate** is formed by only a few partners. Since it is private, it does not have to be registered with any regulatory agency or file any public reports. Minimum investments here are usually $50,000 and more, which eliminates most small investors. Generally, they are formed to acquire and manage one or several properties.

Blind pool syndicates: Limited partnerships where properties to be acquired are unknown to investors at the time their partnership interests are purchased.

Single property syndicates: Limited partnerships where limited partners know the specific property investment at the time their partnership interests are purchased.

Public syndicate: A large partnership where partnership interests are marketed very much like new distributions of common stock.

Private syndicate: A limited partnership with a few partners.

INVESTMENT POTENTIAL   Since investors in limited partnerships are inactive in their management and operation, they cannot use partnership losses to offset earned or portfolio income. This restriction seriously limits the investment quality of many real estate limited partnerships. Without any particular tax advantages to consider, you should evaluate this investment no differently than you would all other passive investments, such as stocks or bonds. However, evaluation might be more difficult since cash flows from the business, including its eventual liquidation, are difficult to estimate. In today's environment it is probably good advice to avoid all limited partnerships unless you are skilled at interpreting the materials they provide. You can, of course, rely upon a financial adviser; but be careful if that person receives a commission from the partnership in which you invest. At the very least, have the adviser explain (in writing) the return and risks you can expect and why the partnership is suitable for your investment objectives. Investment scams frequently take on the appearance of legitimate business activities, many cloaked in the mystique of the limited partnership. Put simply, you can't be too cautious.

Other Tangible Assets

While many people prefer investing in tangible assets, they are not content investing only in real estate. They may not want the aggravation of owning it directly, or they are not satisfied with the risk and return situation in REITs or real estate limited partnerships. As alternatives, these investors have looked toward precious metals and gems, and some have found their most profitable investments right in activities they most enjoy doing—building their hobbies and adding to their collectibles. And if you are willing to take considerable risks, you might consider commodity futures contracts.

Precious Metals and Gems

Precious metals and gems have appealed to people throughout the ages. Gold and silver are extremely durable and easily fashioned into jewelry or other objects. In addition, their ability to reflect light creates a beauty unmatched by other commodities. Gold is valued for this reason much more than silver, but silver also has many applications in industrial uses. Like gold and silver, gems, such as diamonds, emeralds, and rubies, are much sought after throughout the world. In some respects, precious metals and gems are the all-purpose investments: You can enjoy wearing them, you have a chance of earning a return if their prices increase, and your friends can see how wealthy you are.

GOLD   Gold mania swept the world throughout the late 1970s and early 1980s. Much of it had to do with buying by Middle East nations made rich by steep increases in the price of oil, but even the average person was caught up in it. Almost overnight, every shopping center had a gold store where you could sell coins, jewelry, and anything else that had a trace of gold or silver. Before the bubble finally broke, the price of gold had gone from $36 an ounce in 1970 to $875 an ounce in 1980, but, as Figure 16.4 shows, its price has fallen substantially since then. Moreover, its price is extremely volatile, going up or down as much as $20 an ounce in a single day. Gold is an extremely risky investment, and this must be understood and appreciated before you invest.

Gold bullion: Gold ingots, most weighing 32.15 ounces.

You can invest in gold in a number of ways. One is to own **gold bullion,** but most of this comes in ingots weighing 32.15 ounces. If the price of gold is, say, $400 an ounce, each ingot would be worth $12,860. This puts it out of reach for most investors, and you must also be concerned with storing it and having it certified if you sell it. You can own gold indirectly by buying the common stock of companies that mine gold. Campbell Red Lake Mine is one such company, but there are others. (To achieve adequate diversification, you also can invest in mutual funds that buy the stocks of gold-mining companies. One such fund is Fidelity's Precious Metals and Minerals Portfolio.) Changes in the market prices of the stocks of these companies are closely correlated to changes in the price of gold. Buying gold indirectly by investing in such companies is called a **play on gold.** It has an advantage over owning gold directly in that many of these stocks pay annual dividends, thereby providing a current return.

Play on gold: Investing in gold indirectly, such as buying shares of gold mining companies.

While the above approaches have relative advantages and disadvantages, the most common approaches are either owning gold coins, such as the Canadian Maple Leaf, or buying gold certificates issued by commercial banks and other financial institutions.

Gold coins: A popular gold investment medium; most are one ounce in weight.

Gold Coins.   By far the most popular of the **gold coins** is the one-ounce South African Kruggerand. These can be purchased almost anywhere, and they store nicely in bank safe deposit boxes. (Remember, though, these boxes are not insured against fire and theft.) Because they are coins, their weight and purity are standardized, making them easily transferable. Moreover, because they contain only one ounce of gold, you can determine conveniently the amount you wish to hold in your portfolio. (You can also get them in ½, ¼, and ¹⁄₁₀ ounce sizes.) Gold coins have two big disadvantages: They offer no current income that might be available with gold mining stocks, and they sell at a premium over their intrin-

**Investing for
the Future**

FIGURE 16.4

Gold prices, 1972–
1992; various sources.

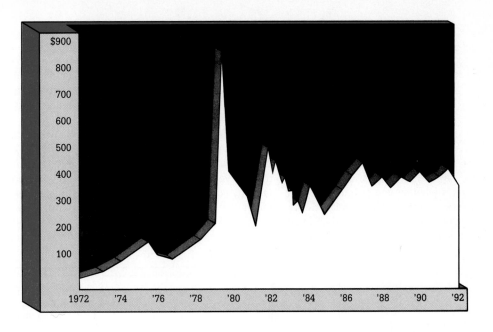

sic gold value. The premium means you buy less actual gold for your investment dollar. The premium varies and tends to decline as the price of gold rises. In effect, it is the price you pay to get the advantages just cited. Commissions to buy coins are typically 3 to 8 percent of the amount purchased, depending on how much you buy and where you buy it. Advisers recommend shopping around, since these costs vary considerably. Also, many states charge a sales tax on each purchase.

Gold certificates: Issued by commercial banks and other financial institutions and backed by a specific gold holding.

Gold Certificates.   Buying **gold certificates** may be the way to own gold if you don't want current income and don't care to handle or look at the metal itself. Many commercial banks sell gold certificates for any amount of gold you care to purchase. The certificate itself merely documents your ownership claim; the actual gold is owned or controlled by the selling institution. You should insist that your gold be stored in an independent warehouse or bank and that it not be lumped together with the seller's other assets. If it is, you run the risk of having no better position than that of a general creditor if the seller fails and goes into bankruptcy. Storage costs usually consist of a one-time charge of ½ percent (or less) of the amount purchased, up to a maximum of around $60. Also, commissions or markups are lower with certificates than with bullion or coins, particularly on large orders.

Some financial institutions allow you to buy a form of gold certificate in much the same manner as you would buy a gold futures contract (futures contracts will be explained shortly). Since these institutions offer a variety of ways to own gold, make sure you understand clearly the type of ownership plan you are using. Also, make sure the institution is a reputable one.

SILVER   In general, silver is very similar to gold as an investment. It can be owned in the same ways and its risk is certainly as great. While gold's price was

Box 16.3
Saving Money

Gold Versus Gold Stocks

So you're convinced gold is ready to make a move. Fine. Now, how do you play your hunch? While there are a number of choices, an important one is whether you care to invest directly in the metal or indirectly by buying an intangible whose value correlates closely to gold. Among the more popular intangibles are the common stocks of gold-mining companies. As the figure below shows, their returns and gold's often move in lock-step fashion. Notice, though, that variations in the stock returns tend to be more pronounced than variations in gold's price. So with the stocks you get a bigger play for your buck. If you guess correctly, you will magnify your return by buying stocks rather than gold itself, such as gold coins or bullion. Unfortunately, if you guess wrong, your losses also will be magnified. An advantage to owning gold-mining stocks is the possibility of earning dividends. Gold itself pays no current return and, in fact, involves holding costs.

Finally, over the entire period shown in the graph, the average return on gold was 1 percent, while the fund's average return was 6 percent. So you were compensated for taking the greater risks with the funds, although you would have been better off had you invested in risk-free U.S. Treasury bills.

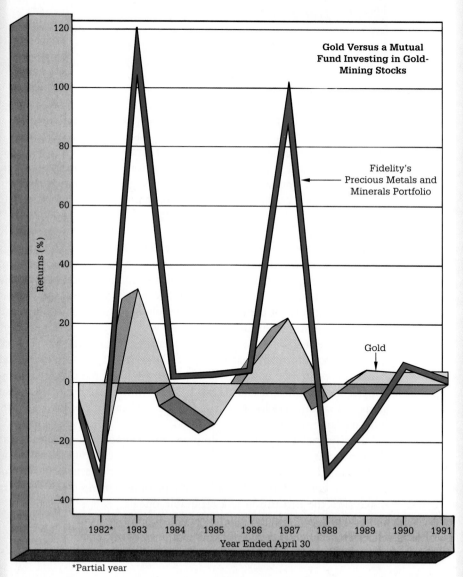

Gold Versus a Mutual Fund Investing in Gold-Mining Stocks

Fidelity's Precious Metals and Minerals Portfolio

Gold

*Partial year

522

Investing for
the Future

rising, silver went from $2 an ounce to over $50 an ounce. Table 13.3 (see Chapter 13) shows that silver has been a very poorly performing asset for the past ten years. Silver is in far greater supply than gold, but much more of it is lost in its industrial uses. Someone has estimated that over 90 percent of all the gold ever mined is still in existence; for silver, the same figure is less than 10 percent. Having industrial applications is both a good and bad feature—good because it increases silver's demand, but bad because substitutes can be found for it. On balance, these applications probably increase its price volatility.

GEMS Diamonds (and other gems) seem to be everybody's best friends—boys' as well as girls'. If the soaring prices of gold and silver didn't impress you, consider this: The wholesale price of a one carat, highest-quality diamond (called "D flawless") went from $1,800 in 1970 to $53,000 in 1980. And how's this for risk: By 1982, its price was down to $14,000! Table 13.3 in Chapter 13 shows that diamonds had an annual average rate of return of 10.5 percent for the 20-year period that ended June 1, 1991. This placed it fifth out of the total 14 investments examined.

It is far beyond the scope of this text to discuss the skills one needs to be an active investor in the gems markets. Simply be forewarned that unless you are appropriately trained, don't be one. If you are convinced precious gems are the best investments for you, then find a reputable dealer and participate in plans that he or she might have to accommodate your interest. For a start, you can consider subscribing to a magazine called *Precious Gem Investor* (P.O. Box 1367, Lafayette, CA 94549). You can also get a free pamphlet from the government, "Gemstone Investing," by writing to the Federal Trade Commission, Room 1301, Sixth St. and Washington Ave., N.W., Washington, DC 20580. In recent years, limited partnerships have been set up to invest in gems, and they offer professional management to appeal to investors. But don't assume that pooling arrangements guarantee a profitable investment. They too have been risky. For example, the stock brokerage firm of Thomson McKinnon established a unit investment trust (called the Jefferson Collection) consisting of very high-quality diamonds. Quality, though, could not overcome a declining inflation rate, and each unit in the trust—offered in December of 1980 at $994—was worth less than $300 five years later. The trust has now been liquidated.

The one gem many of us invest in is the diamond engagement ring. Why not look at it as an investment? By all means, deal with a reputable dealer and get a second opinion of its value, if you can. You might want to stretch the budget to get a significantly better-quality gem. Be sure to use carats as a basis for determining the gold content in a ring or other jewelry item: *18 carat* means 75 percent gold, and *14 carat* means 58 percent gold. The expression *solid gold* is virtually meaningless and indicates only that an item is not hollow. If you collect silver items, they should be sterling, which means 92.5 percent pure.

Hobbies and Collectibles

Have you inherited a U.S. stamp or U.S. coin collection? And if so, have you priced it recently? If not, you may be in for a pleasant surprise. Over the 20-year period that ended June 1, 1991, U.S. stamps ranked sixth in total return (see Table 13.3 again). Markets for all types of collectibles have developed over the years. In addition to coin and stamp collections, people have become interested in antiques of all types. Persian rugs, dolls, railroad sets, beer cans, ceramics, and many more.

Hobbies and collectibles: Popular tangible investments, but with considerable risk and a need for specialized knowledge.

Hobbies and collectibles can be the riskiest of all your investments, particularly if your knowledge of the items is inadequate. Collections often include one-of-a-kind items, and establishing their value may be impossible. And even if you are successful and buy an item that appreciates, say, 50 percent in value in one year, you may find that your transaction costs—commissions and others—will be 30 percent or more. If you have a collection of some type and enjoy buying and selling to improve it, there isn't a great deal of danger of losing much; but if you find yourself buying things simply because you think prices are going up, then your hobby has become an investment, and one that could prove very unprofitable.

Knowledgeable collectors insist you should always buy the very best items you can afford, even if these are small pieces such as a set of china or a fine museum print. As little as $500 can get you started if you follow this approach, but even at this level it is important to know what you are doing. You are unlikely to gain enough background in a wide range of collectibles, so it makes sense to specialize in one or a few areas. Find your "thing" and then visit libraries, museums, galleries, flea markets, garage sales, and any other place that can help you. Understand, though, that the markets for hobbies and collectibles often follow fads and a boom–bust cycle. Today, the baseball card dealer has replaced the gold shop in shopping centers, and the prices of baseball cards and other memorabilia are skyrocketing. A 1952 Mickey Mantle rookie card goes for $6,000, and even 1991 rookie cards are hawked for $25 on a cable shopping network. An autographed item, such as a ball signed by Pete Rose (who often frequents shows and sells thousands of his autograph for $10 and up), might triple in value when it is resold a week or two later. While it is impossible to predict when such euphoric markets will end, you can be assured that this one, in common with all others in the past, will come to an end. And when it does, losses for many speculators will be substantial.

Finally, the federal income tax law does not allow losses from hobby activities, but you must pay taxes on any profits. Considering this disadvantage along with others discussed above, hobbies and collectibles are probably investments to avoid, unless they give you considerable pleasure.

Commodity Futures Contracts

Commodity futures contracts: Contracts that involve future deliveries of commodities, but at prices negotiated today.

If your reason for holding tangible assets is simply to hedge inflation, you might be able to do so in an indirect manner by investing in **commodity futures contracts.** One party in such a contract agrees to accept delivery of a standardized quantity of a commodity at a future date. The second party agrees to make such delivery, and both parties agree on the price at which the exchange will take place. The person taking delivery is called the buyer; with the contract, he or she has a guaranteed price on the particular commodity for the life of the contract. If the market price of the commodity goes above this contract price, the buyer will make a profit; but if the price goes below it, the buyer suffers a loss. It is important to note that the contract is a legal obligation to perform. In contrast, if you buy an option, you can simply discard the option if it proves valueless, and the most you can lose is the cost of the option. The futures buyer's losses are virtually unlimited; that is, they continue to mount as long as the commodity's price falls. The situation works in reverse if you are the seller of a futures contract. You lose when prices go above the contract price and gain when it goes below it.

USE OF MARGIN   Most commodity futures speculators use margin accounts in their trading activities. Table 16.8 shows only a partial list of the large number of commodities available for purchase or sale. The margin requirement is set by the organized commodity exchanges, and the required amount depends upon the commodity in question. The more volatile the commodity's price, the greater the required margin. In general, margins are extremely thin. For example, to trade corn you would need only about $1,500, about 12 percent of its market value in Table 16.8. Notice that if corn increased only $0.30 a bushel, you would double your investment ($0.30 × 5,000 bushels); and if it decreased by $0.30, you would be wiped out, assuming you were the buyer in each case. A price change of $0.30 per bushel of corn has often taken place in a period of time as short as one week, which should alert you to the risks inherent in commodity futures contracts.

INVESTMENT SUITABILITY   Considering the risks involved, with both leverage and price volatility, commodity futures contracts are, in our view, not suitable investments unless you have considerable investment funds (probably over $100,000) and are willing to assume such risks. Even then, you must be willing to put in a reasonable amount of time to understand the mechanics of commodity trading, not to mention understanding trading strategies.

TABLE 16.8 ▪ Some Commodities Traded on Major Commodity Exchanges

(1) Commodity	(2) Contract Size	(3) Unit Price*	(4) Market Value (Money at Risk) (2) × (3)
Grains:			
Corn	5,000 bushels	$ 2.45	$12,250
Soybeans	5,000 bushels	5.50	27,500
Canola	20 metric tons	265.00	5,300
Livestock:			
Feeder cattle	44,000 pounds	0.90	39,600
Pork bellies	38,000 pounds	0.44	16,720
Metals:			
Gold	100 troy ounces	365.00	36,500
Silver	5,000 troy ounces	3.98	19,900
Financial:			
British pound	62,500 pounds	1.69	105,625
U.S. Treasury bonds	8%, $100,000 face value	94,156.00	94,156
S&P 500 Stock Index	500 times Index	380.75	190,375

*Approximate prices at mid-June 1991. Contracts selected are those with closest delivery month.

Investing in Tangibles

A number of commodity-trading limited partnerships have developed in recent years. These allow you to participate in commodities markets and at the same time limit your losses to the amounts you invest. Obviously, these are much more suitable to smaller investors, but their performance records have not been particularly impressive. If you can find one that pursues a cautious, inflation-hedging investment approach—mostly buy positions and not thinly margined—you can get the inflation protection of commodities without the inconveniences of owning them directly. Moreover, such a partnership could invest in a broad range of commodities, providing better diversification than what you might get investing in tangibles on your own. The best source of information is your full-service stockbroker, but be sure you tell him or her that your investment goal is hedging inflation—and not speculating on commodity price movements.

Summary

Investors look toward tangible assets for both return and enjoyment. Real estate is the most popular tangible asset. An income-producing property provides a net operating income (NOI), which is one source of return. Other sources are capital gains and tax savings. Most real estate deals involve considerable borrowing that acts as leverage, which magnifies both risk and return. Investing in real estate also includes investing in land. Because of its risks, land investment is usually more suitable to wealthy investors. Vacation homes have also become popular investments; however, the tax law should be considered in buying or using the vacation home. Many people desire real estate investment but do not wish to own properties directly. They invest in real estate investment trusts (REITs) or real estate limited partnerships.

In addition to real estate, tangible assets include precious metals and gems, and hobbies and collectibles. Gold is by far the most popular precious metal. Silver's price parallels gold's in volatility, and it also can be owned in the same ways. Gem investment is a highly specialized area, requiring considerable expertise, which is also true for hobbies and collectibles. Commodity futures contracts represent possible indirect investments in tangibles. They are available for a wide variety of commodities but are extremely risky because they often involve considerable leverage.

Key Terms

after-tax cash flow (p. 507)

blind pool syndicates (p. 518)

cash flow before taxes (p. 506)

commodity futures contracts (p. 524)

depreciation (p. 506)

depreciation basis (p. 506)

equity trusts (p. 516)

gold bullion (p. 520)

gold certificates (p. 521)

gold coins (p. 520)

hobbies and collectibles (p. 524)

income-producing property (p. 503)

mortgage trusts (p. 517)

net operating income (NOI) (p. 503)

play on gold (p. 520)

private syndicate (p. 518)

public syndicate (p. 518)

real estate investment trust (REIT) (p. 516)

recapture (p. 507)

single property syndicates (p. 518)

"sweat equity" (p. 503)

Problems and Review Questions

1. Explain potential sources of return from an income-producing property, and discuss important topics to consider when you are looking at alternative income-producing properties.

2. Define the following terms: (a) net operating income (NOI); (b) cash flow before taxes; (c) tax shelter; (d) depreciation; (e) after-tax cash flow.

3. Matilda Blakesley is thinking of buying a duplex in an area close to the university she is attending. It is in very run-down condition, but she is sure the seller will assist with financing, allowing her to buy it with only $3,000 as a down payment. Matilda is a sophomore and a hard worker; she plans to fix up the place and re-sell it at the end of her senior year. Discuss Matilda's plan, focusing on potential problems and advantages.

4. Explain various factors that make land investment risky.

5. Why is the location of a vacation home an important factor in your buying decision? Should you buy only in areas that appeal to you personally, or in areas that appeal to other people? Discuss. Also, briefly explain three different residency situations that will affect the federal income tax treatment of a vacation home.

6. What is a real estate investment trust (REIT)? How does an equity trust differ from a mortgage trust? Do REITs pay dividends? Do they offer direct tax shelters to investors? Explain.

7. Explain: (a) blind pool syndicate; (b) single property syndicate; (c) private syndicate; (d) public syndicate.

8. Would you describe the price of gold as stable or volatile? Explain. In what ways can you own gold? Which way do you consider best in your own case?

9. What factors should you consider before you invest in gems or hobbies and collectibles?

10. Explain a commodity futures contract and discuss why it is a risky investment.

Case 16.1
The Pettys' Real Estate Venture

Wilma and Norman Petty, a recently married couple, are in their late twenties. They have two young children who will both be in school next year, and Wilma expects to have much more time available to help with the family's income. However, she cannot work full time, which is proving a barrier to finding a decent position. She and Norm have saved about $10,000 (in total) and have it invested in a money market mutual fund where it currently earns 6 percent before taxes. They are thinking very seriously of using $7,000 of it as a deposit on a fourplex located close to their home. The property is structurally sound but in a somewhat run-down condition. The Pettys think that all it really needs is lots of paint and elbow grease, but there is a chance the heating, plumbing, or electrical systems might require a major improvement. The property is owned by the savings and loan that repossessed it when the previous owner could not make the monthly payments of $720. The S&L would let the Pettys assume the loan of $70,000 at the same interest rate (12 percent), maturity (30 years), and monthly payments. The Pettys are in favor of this loan because it has a fixed rate.

Three of the four apartments are now rented at $200 a month. Wilma is confident the fourth apartment will rent shortly—also at $200 a month—if it is advertised in the newspaper. All utilities, including water and sewerage, are paid by tenants. Wilma will manage and maintain the property, eliminating those expenses, but they expect the following outlays in the first year: (a) potential vacancy losses = 10 percent of gross rentals; (b) advertising, licenses, and permits = $50; (c) insurance = $600; (d) property taxes = $900; and (e) allowance for repairs and major maintenance = 5 percent of gross rentals.

If Wilma and Norm go ahead with the deal, the purchase price of the property will be $77,000—their down payment plus the loan assumption. A reasonable estimate of the land's value is $17,000. They think they will hold the property about three years and then try to sell it for $90,000, working through a realtor who will charge 7 percent commission. They also think the property's NOI will increase 5 percent a year, and they estimate that 97 percent of their monthly mortgage payments is interest and 3 percent is principal. The Pettys are in a 28 percent tax bracket and will probably continue to be in the future. They will depreciate the building over 27.5 years using straight-line depreciation. Finally, the loss limitation rules will not apply in the Pettys' case.

Questions

1 Going through the steps detailed in this chapter, calculate an approximate average rate of return on the property to the Pettys.
2 Calculate approximate average rates of return, assuming the property is eventually sold for: (a) $95,000; (b) $85,000.
3 Given your answers to Questions 1 and 2 and considering other facts in the case, do you feel this is a good investment for Wilma and Norm? Explain, making sure you include risk in the discussion.

Case 16.2 Should Francine Buy a Vacation Condominium?

Francine Lester has been quite successful as a free-lance author in New York. Along with success, though, comes a high tax bracket (28 percent), and Francine thinks she should do something to soften her tax situation. At a recent party, she discussed the problem with one of her friends—Lou Cimino—from whom she usually rents a vacation condo for two weeks each year. Lou felt she ought to buy a condo like his and, as a matter of fact, one right next to his was on the market for $65,000. Lou said that he rented his 60 days last year at $70 a day (this is what Francine paid) and his only expense was a flat fee of 20 percent of rentals that he paid to the rental agent. (This included utilities, association dues, laundry and linen service, and all others.) He was sure this same arrangement would be available on Francine's unit, if she were to buy it. Financing is available on the property (assume it is identical to the data shown in Table 16.1), but Francine would need a down payment of $5,000.

She is very excited about the deal but thinks she should temper her enthusiasm by looking at some cash flow figures. That's where you come into the picture, since Francine knows absolutely nothing about real estate investment. She does not plan to sell the place for some time—if ever—so she is not concerned about growth or fluctuations in the property's market value. She will continue to take her usual two weeks of vacation and feels she can rent it in the same way Lou does; also, she would be active enough in managing the condo that loss limitation rules would not apply. Lou also explained that his unit had a depreciation basis of $45,000 for federal income tax purposes, and that he depreciated it over a 27.5-year period using straight-line depreciation.

Questions

1 Calculate the appropriate cash flows and then explain if the condo investment seems a good deal in Francine's case. (Ignore any allocation of mortgage interest for personal-use days.)
2 Assume Francine decided to spend one extra day at her condo. How much would this day cost? Show your calculations.
3 Francine said she was not concerned about changes in the market value of the condo, but suppose it increased 3 percent in value each year for three years after her purchase. Assuming she could sell it at the end of three years without a realtor's commission, calculate her average annual rate of return on the property. Show your work and discuss your conclusion.

Helpful Reading

Changing Times

Bodnar, Janet. *"Sure Ways to Make a Killing (or Lose Your Shirt)."* May 1991, pp. 53–56.

Giese, William. *"Whatever Happened to Gold Prices?"* April 1991, pp. 69–72.

Money

Wang, Penelope. *"Real Estate at Rock-Bottom Prices."* December 1990, pp. 107–109.

The Wall Street Journal

Angrist, Stanley W. *"Commodity Traders Do Better Than Believed, Study Finds—Only Three-Fourths Lose Money."* August 12, 1991, p. C12.

Asinof, Lynn. *"Caution! Vacation-Home Bargains Ahead."* March 19, 1991, p. C1.

Peers, Alexandria. *"Glory Days Gone, Prices of Folk Art Return to Roots."* April 16, 1991, p. C1.

Tanouye, Elyse, and Stanley W. Angrist. *"Angry Commodity Players Can Get Even."* May 6, 1991, p. C1.

Barron's

Wasik, John F. *"How to Check out a Broker."* January 14, 1991, p. 24.

Welling, Kathryn M. *"Ready to Reclaim Its Luster: Gold Could Be the 'Sleeper' Investment of the Nineties."* July 15, 1991, p. 8.

Helpful Contacts

Commodity Futures Trading Commission (telephone 202–254–3067)

Boards of Trade (some will provide free educational materials):
    Chicago Board of Trade (telephone 312–435–3758)
    Chicago Mercantile Exchange (telephone 312–930–1000)
    New York Mercantile Exchange (telephone 212–938–2973)
    Kansas City Board of Trade (telephone 816–753–7500)

Information and materials on real estate investment may be available from the Board of Realtors in your local area. Check the Yellow Pages of your telephone directory.

Long-Term Planning

These last two chapters examine the topics of retirement planning and estate planning. The placement of these topics at the end of the book does not indicate their relative importance, or when such planning should be undertaken. Instead, it reflects the impact of retirement and estate planning on the later years of the life cycle.

Both retirement and estate planning must be approached early in the cycle. Adequate retirement plans take many years to implement. Furthermore, retirement savings should complement your current investment and tax strategies. None of your plans and goals, particularly those pertaining to retirement, should be considered separate from all others. A book must be read one chapter at a time, but this isn't the way to implement your financial planning. What you need is an integrated approach, in which retirement and estate planning are an integral component of a personal financial plan that leads to financial independence for you and your family.

In furtherance of this goal, you may want to review some of the previous chapters before proceeding. Given the importance of taxes and investments in retirement planning, a review of Chapter 5 on taxes and Chapter 15 on portfolio management should prove helpful. In addition, Chapter 10, "Life Insurance," complements the discussion of estate planning in Chapter 18.

In the last few decades, people have tended to retire earlier and live longer increasing the importance of retirement planning. You probably already recognize the need to plan for your retirement, but not the need for estate planning. You might even think of skipping the final chapter because you believe that this topic concerns only the very rich. That would be a mistake. Estate planning can have a tax impact on families with moderate income as well. More important, estate planning will determine how your wealth will be shared among your beneficiaries. This is an important concern for every family, especially those with dependent children.

Part 5

Retirement and Pension Planning: Planning for Your Long-Term Needs

Objectives

1   To evaluate the features of a company pension plan
2   To analyze alternative company retirement plans
3   To list individual tax-deferred methods of saving
4   To estimate your retirement needs
5   To learn how to establish a personal saving plan for retirement

Most financial planners will advise you to begin planning for retirement as soon as you enter the work force. If you put off retirement planning until your forties and fifties, altering projected retirement benefits during your remaining working years will be much more difficult. In addition, you will have missed most of the tax advantages that come from funding tax-deferred retirement plans.

You probably realize this is good advice, but if you are in your early twenties and retirement is far off into the twenty-first century, you may find it very difficult to follow. Unless you have a crystal ball, forecasting more than five years ahead is usually fruitless. Changes in tax rates, interest rates, inflation rates, and Social Security benefits may all upset well-made retirement plans. For this reason, a retirement plan should not be viewed as something set in concrete. It should change as circumstances change. And the important point to remember is that the sooner you get started, the easier it will be to accommodate that plan to your changing personal and financial environment.

Retirement planning should take into consideration the family's needs and resources over the financial life cycle. Figure 17.1 illustrates a typical family's earnings and expenditures with respect to the age of the primary market worker. During the worker's twenties, thirties, and forties, both income and expenditures will likely increase. Savings accumulated during these early years will have more time to grow and accumulate tax-deferred returns until they are needed in retirement. Unfortunately, this is also the time when the family experiences the significant financial demands of child rearing, culminating with the high cost of a college education. In the fifties, most of the children will have left the household, and there will be a dramatic rise in savings as expenditures drop. Saving will be

533

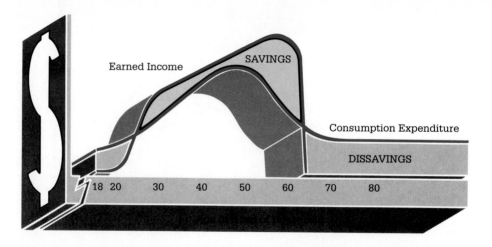

FIGURE 17.1

A typical family's earnings and expenditures over the family life cycle.

easier at this time, but the money set aside will have fewer years in which to accumulate returns.

Earnings for the average market worker begin to decline in the early sixties as work time decreases and leisure time increases. Self-employed individuals may experience no clear division between preretirement and postretirement years. Financially, retirement may be said to occur when expenses begin to exceed earnings. Retirement years are ones of dissaving, when the wealth accumulated over the preretirement years is slowly depleted. The standard of living in retirement will depend largely upon the family's accumulated savings, and therefore on plans begun and actions taken many years before.

When and how much to save are personal decisions. There is not one "right" retirement plan for everyone. In saving for retirement, you are trading off present consumption for future consumption. How much you plan to save will depend on how much weight you place on each of these needs. Your retirement plan may be to consume everything today and leave nothing for tomorrow. As long as you realize that this decision means you will someday have to survive on minimal benefits provided under an uncertain system of Social Security, we have no quarrel with your choice.

In this chapter, we will first examine the traditional ways of saving for retirement. Once you understand how you can save, we address the question of how much you need to save to achieve your goals.

Saving and Investing for Retirement

Is saving for retirement different from other types of saving? Like most questions in personal finance, this one can be answered with both a yes and a no. It is different because in many cases the government permits it to be treated differently. The nation has an interest in seeing that older Americans are financially independent. To achieve this end, it provides special tax status for funds that it believes are earmarked for this purpose. The tax isn't forgiven; it's just deferred until the funds are needed in your later years.

Retirement saving is also different because the funding need is not immediate. This means the savings can be channeled into less liquid investments that possibly penalize short-term withdrawals but pay a high return on long-term holdings.

Other than these two characteristics, saving and investing for retirement are the same as for any other purpose. Accordingly, investments for retirement should satisfy all of the guidelines for investments discussed in previous chapters. Most important, there should be a proper diversification of holdings, and the acceptable risk-return trade-off should depend on the size of your nest egg. Only after you have provided for a needed safety margin in your later years should you consider speculative deals with potentially more rewarding or more damaging outcomes.

Company Pension Plans

Company-sponsored retirement plans have become an increasingly important source of income for retired workers. Unfortunately, since the mid-1980s there is evidence that private pension coverage may have actually declined. Recent estimates by the Bureau of Labor Statistics reveal that in firms with more than 100 workers, 81 percent of all full-time employees were covered by at least one retirement plan. However, in smaller businesses with less than 100 workers, only 42 percent were similarly covered.

ERISA: Federal act regulating funding and coverage guidelines for tax-qualified, employer-sponsored pension plans.

The passage of the **Employee Retirement Income Security Act (ERISA)** in 1974 eliminated much of the uncertainty surrounding the payment of company benefits. ERISA set down certain standards for funding of company-sponsored retirement plans, including guidelines for employee coverage and contributions. When a plan meets all of the government-mandated requirements, it becomes a **qualified retirement plan.** This means that taxes are deferred on employer contributions to the retirement fund and on interest earned by the retirement fund. Taxes do not become due until the benefits of the retirement fund are received by the employee.

Qualified retirement plan: One that satisfies conditions set down in ERISA and therefore qualifies for special tax advantages.

Because "qualified" plans offer significant tax advantages, almost all company plans satisfy the ERISA requirements. To understand the advantages of tax deferral, look at the example in Table 17.1. The comparison is based upon an assumed flat tax rate of 28 percent. In Case One, the monies placed into the fund and the interest on the fund are taxed; in Case Two the tax is applied when the fund matures at the end of the 20-year period. In the first example, $2,000 in compensation is set aside each year for investment, but only $1,440 can be invested after taxes. Given an assumed pretax interest rate of 10 percent, the effective after-tax interest rate reduces to 7.2 percent. After 20 years this non-tax-deferred investment fund will accumulate to $64,683.27. In Case Two, the full $2,000 of compensation can be invested and return a pretax interest rate of 10 percent. When the fund matures at the end of 20 years, taxes become due. Applying the same 28 percent tax rate to the distributions, we find that you are still over $26,000 ahead on the tax-deferred investment. This is the power of tax deferral.

Notice that the current example assumes your marginal tax rate is the same in both your preretirement years and your postretirement years. If your real income declines after retirement, thus placing you in a lower marginal tax bracket, the benefits of tax deferral can be even greater. On the other hand, for the lucky few who might find themselves in a higher marginal tax bracket after retirement, perhaps because of a tax on Social Security earnings, deferral of income taxes may be an unwise choice.

Case One: No Deferral of Taxes			
Year	Contribution After Taxes	Interest Income After Taxes (After-Tax Rate 7.2%)	Ending Balance
1	$1,440	$ 103.68	$ 1,543.68
2	1,440	214.82	3,198.50
3	1,440	333.97	4,972.48
•	•	•	•
•	•	•	•
•	•	•	•
18	1,440	3,593.48	53,502.97
19	1,440	3,955.89	58,898.87
20	1,440	4,344.40	64,683.27
		Taxes due at maturity	(−0−)
		Ending year's balance after taxes	$64,683.27

Case Two: Deferral of Taxes			
Year	Tax-Deferred Contribution	Tax-Deferred Interest Income (Tax-Deferred Rate 10%)	Ending Balance
1	$2,000	$ 100.00	$ 2,200.00
2	2,000	420.00	4,620.00
3	2,000	662.00	7,282.00
•	•	•	•
•	•	•	•
•	•	•	•
18	2,000	9,119.83	100,318.00
19	2,000	10,231.80	112,550.00
20	2,000	11,455.00	126,005.00
		Taxes due at maturity	(−35,281.40)
		Ending year's balance after taxes	$ 90,723.60

A pension is nothing more than a promissory note. If you have a pension, what you have is a promise that you will receive certain payments at retirement. Before the passage of ERISA it was not uncommon to hear of workers nearing retirement losing all of the promised pension benefits they had been depending on. Some firms purposely terminated workers right before retirement so that they would not have to pay pension benefits. Other, better-intentioned firms found they simply could not afford to pay the promised benefits.

ERISA has remedied this situation by requiring that all qualified pension plans be adequately funded and by setting down rules so that workers could not be denied their rights to an expected pension. It has also created the Pension Benefit Guaranty Corporation (PBGC) to insure promised benefits against unexpected loss. However, even after ERISA, it is still possible for an employee to end his or her career without a pension. Furthermore, ERISA does not set standards for minimum benefits. At retirement you may find your benefits are not as generous as you thought. For these reasons, and because the pension plan is often a valuable component of the salary package, it deserves close examination.

Box 17.1
What's New in Personal Finance

PBGC Coverage Limited

Some retirees who thought their retirement benefits were protected by the federal government have been unhappily surprised to find otherwise. When Congress passed the Employment Retirement Income Security Act (ERISA) of 1974, it also created the Pension Benefit Guaranty Corporation (PBGC) to insure pension benefits against loss. PBGC insurance, however, protects only up to $2,250 in retirement benefits per month for all company-sponsored, tax-qualified, defined-benefit plans. Defined-contribution plans, such as 401(k) savings plans, are not covered.

But even those with defined-benefit plans may not always have their benefits guaranteed by the PBGC. Companies can terminate their defined-benefit plans and their responsibility for future defined benefits by purchasing annuities to cover their obligations. The PBGC sets down regulations which govern plan terminations by requiring employers to fund the promised benefits adequately. But what happens when an employer funds the plan with retirement annuities, and then the company that issued the annuities becomes insolvent? It turns out that once an employer receives PBGC approval to terminate a plan, the PBGC no longer insures those benefits.

Jesse and Irma Bell of Sequin, Texas, were receiving a $780.32 monthly pension check as a result of Jesse, 74, having worked 46 years in the oil fields. Those checks ended abruptly in April 1991, when Executive Life, a bankrupt insurer, was taken over by the state of California. Jesse's old employer had converted his pension into an annuity in the now-bankrupt company. Fortunately for the Bells and other Executive Life annuitants, the state of California has been able to continue the annuity payments, but only after a 30 percent cut in benefits.

The PBGC does not guarantee retirement funds in a defined-contribution account. The value of funds invested in defined-contribution plans will depend upon the volatility and stability of the underlying investment. This may surprise many employees who have retirement savings invested in "guaranteed investment contracts" (GICs). A significant percentage, about 60 percent, of 401(k) assets are invested in GICs. The term is misleading: These are not guaranteed by the federal government— although, if the issuer is an insurance company, there may be a state guaranty fund that provides partial protection.

The only institution that fully guarantees the interest and principal on a GIC is the company that issues it. Since this is usually an insurance company, its financial condition can be checked out by using the rating services we discussed in the chapters on insurance, such as Bests, Moody's or Standard and Poor's.

In an attempt to provide greater security for investors, insurance companies have now begun marketing a "participating" or "separate account" GIC. The new GICs are backed by a pool of securities rather than by the general credit of the insurance company. In the event of insurer insolvency, the pension fund may be able to lay claim to the securities in these separate accounts. (In an ordinary GIC, investors have to wait in line with other creditors for the insurer's assets to be distributed in a bankruptcy.)

Even when losses are not insured by the PBGC, they still may not be permanently lost. Administrators of pension plans have a duty to act in the best interest of the participants. If they act negligently by placing these funds in highly risky investments, they can be held responsible for any subsequent losses. The Department of Labor is currently suing several company plan administrators for doing just that. A few of those represent companies that purchased annuities in Executive Life for their employees. Jesse Bell certainly hopes the Department of Labor will prevail and restore his lost benefits. At age 74, he also probably hopes it doesn't take too long.

A careful study of the plan documents listed in Figure 17.2 will provide essential information on the operation of your pension plan. To make sure you do not overlook an important component, you might use the information in the plan documents to complete the checklist in Figure 17.3. To aid you in this task, the following discussion will parallel the checklist's format. If for some reason you do not have enough information to understand and complete this checklist, you should contact your company's personnel office.

537

Participants in qualified plans are entitled to receive certain documents providing important information on the operation of the plan and their particular interest in the plan. In most cases, these documents will be routinely made available. If they are not, you should demand copies of the following:

Summary Plan Description This general overview of how the retirement plan operates should be written in a clear and understandable form. It contains essential information on the structure of the plan, explaining how benefits are calculated, when they may be received, and most importantly, how you might lose them.

Summary Annual Report It provides updated information on the plan and its financial status. If the pension fund depends upon an underlying portfolio of investments, it should indicate how well those investments performed over the previous year.

Personal Benefits Statement This may be included within the Summary Annual Report. It will indicate the total amount of your pension benefits that are currently accrued and vested. Each participant is entitled to receive an updated statement once a year. If you have not received one in the last 12 months the plan administrator (listed in the Summary Plan Description) must provide it within 30 days upon written request.

Statement of Deferred Vested Benefits for Terminating Employees If you leave your current employer, and you have a vested right to benefits, you should receive a statement describing those rights and benefits. Copies of this statement are kept on file by the Secretary of Health and Human Resources. If you lose your copy, or for some reason the firm will not provide you one, a duplicate is obtainable through the Social Security Administration upon written request.

FIGURE 17.2

Qualified plan documents.

Defined-benefit plan: A pension plan that specifies the monthly benefit you will receive at retirement age.

DEFINED-BENEFIT AND DEFINED-CONTRIBUTION PLANS All pension plans can be classified as defined-benefit plans, defined-contribution plans, or some combination of the two.

A **defined-benefit plan** specifies the monthly benefit you will receive when you reach retirement age. Each year the employer contributes to a retirement fund an amount necessary to pay for those promised future benefits. The present contri-

PENSION PLAN CHECKLIST

Plan Type Checklist

My plan is a:
- ☐ DEFINED BENEFIT PLAN.
  - ☐ integrated with Social Security
  - ☐ nonintegrated
- ☐ DEFINED CONTRIBUTION PLAN.
  - ☐ integrated with Social Security
  - ☐ nonintegrated

Contributions Checklist

My pension plan is financed by:
- ☐ employer contributions only.
- ☐ employer and employee contributions.
- ☐ union dues and assessments.

I contribute to my pension plan at the rate of $ _____ per ☐ month ☐ week ☐ hour, or _____ percent of my compensation.

Vesting Checklist

My plan provides:
- ☐ full and immediate vesting.
- ☐ cliff vesting.
- ☐ graded vesting.
- ☐ other (specify).

I need _____ more years of service to be fully vested.

Credited Service Checklist

I will have a year of service under my pension plan:
- ☐ if I work _____ hours in a 12-consecutive-month period.
- ☐ if I meet other requirements (specify).

The plan year (12-month period for which plan records are kept) ends on _____ of each year.

I will be credited for work performed:
- ☐ before I became a participant in the plan.
- ☐ after the plan's normal retirement age.

As of now, (date), I have earned _____ years of service.

My plan's break-in-service rules are as follows:

Retirement Benefit Checklist

I may begin to receive full normal retirement benefits at age _____.

I may retire early at age _____, if I have completed _____ years of service. Apart from the age requirement, I need _____ more years of service to be eligible for early retirement benefits.

The amount of my <u>normal</u> retirement benefit is computed as follows:

The amount of my <u>early</u> retirement benefit is computed as follows:

My Social Security benefit:
- ☐ will not be deducted from my plan benefit.
- ☐ will be deducted from my plan benefit to the extent of _____ percent of the Social Security benefit I am due to receive at retirement.

My retirement benefit:
- ☐ will be paid monthly for life.
- ☐ will be paid to me in a lump sum.
- ☐ will be adjusted to the cost of living.
- ☐ will be paid to my survivor in the event of my death (see Survivors' Benefits).

Disability Benefit Checklist

My plan ☐ does ☐ does not provide disability benefits.

My plan defines "disability" as follows:

To be eligible for disability retirement benefits, I must be _____ years old and must have _____ years of service. I will not be eligible for disability retirement benefits if I become disabled because of:
- ☐ mental incompetence.
- ☐ drug addiction.
- ☐ alcoholism.
- ☐ self-inflicted injury.
- ☐ other (specify).

A determination as to whether my condition meets my plan's definition of disability is made by:
- ☐ a doctor chosen by me.
- ☐ a doctor designated by the plan administrator.

The amount of my disability retirement benefit is computed as follows:

I must send my application for disability retirement benefits to _____ within _____ months after I stop working.

If I qualify for disability benefits, I will continue to receive benefits:
- ☐ for life, if I remain disabled.
- ☐ until retirement age.
- ☐ until I return to my former job.
- ☐ until I am able to work.

Survivors' Benefit Checklist

My pension plan ☐ provides ☐ does not provide a joint and survivor option or a similar provision for death benefits. My spouse ☐ has ☐ has not rejected in writing the joint and survivor option.

By electing the option, my pension benefit will be reduced to _____.

My survivor will receive _____ per month for life if the following conditions are met (specify):

Plan Termination Checklist

My benefits ☐ are ☐ are not insured by the PBGC.

Benefit Application Checklist

My employer ☐ will ☐ will not automatically submit my pension application for me.

I must apply for my pension benefits ☐ on a special form I get from _____ within _____ months ☐ before ☐ after I retire.

My application for pension benefits should be sent to _____

I must furnish the following documents when applying for my pension:

If my application for benefits is denied, I may appeal in writing to _____ within _____ days.

FIGURE 17.3

Your pension plan checklist. (Source: Adapted from *Know Your Pension Plan*, U.S. Department of Labor, 1979.)

Retirement
and Pension
Planning

bution is actuarially determined; that is, it is based upon assumed investment returns and probabilities of survival.

As illustrated in Figure 17.4, workers can expect a defined-benefit plan to replace about 30 percent of their final salary after 30 years of credited service. Such plans covered about 63 percent of workers in medium and large-size firms in 1989. This was considerably down from 87 percent in 1979. This trend is expected to continue as firms attempt to hold down liabilities for future pension payments.

Under a **defined-contribution plan** you are not guaranteed a specific benefit at retirement. Instead, your benefits will depend upon the investment performance of the retirement fund. Employer contributions go into a separate retirement account for each worker, where they accumulate until retirement. The current value of this account should be indicated on the personal benefits statement (see Figure 17.2). About one-half of workers in medium and large-size firms were participants in 1989.

In most defined-contribution plans, the funds accumulated in the retirement account may be converted at retirement to an annuity that generates lifetime income. The cost of the annuity and the income generated by the annuity will depend on financial factors at the retirement date. Sometimes personal benefits statements for defined-contribution plans will contain an example of the monthly benefits that might be purchased with your retirement account. This example is only an illustration and should not be mistaken for a guaranteed monthly benefit.

Defined-benefit and defined-contribution plans each have offsetting advantages and disadvantages. With a defined-benefit plan, you know how much you will receive, but you don't know how much those dollars will be worth. Inflation can severely erode the purchasing power of benefits that currently appear quite respectable. With a defined-contribution plan, you know how much your retirement fund is currently worth, but you don't know how many dollars you will have at retirement. Remember, this will depend upon future contributions and yet-to-be-determined investment returns.

Both defined-benefit and defined-contribution plans can be integrated with the Social Security system. When they are, your company's benefits and contributions may be less than expected. Defined-benefit plans can be written so that benefit payments from the plan are reduced as Social Security benefits increase. Defined-contribution plans sometimes include part of the Social Security tax in calculating the company's contribution.

CONTRIBUTIONS   A few plans require mandatory contributions from employees who wish to participate in the company retirement plan. Those who elect not to participate should find out under what conditions, if any, they may later join. The majority of qualified plans do not require employee contributions. However, many defined-contribution plans permit the employee to make a voluntary contribution to the retirement account.

Employee contributions, whether mandatory or voluntary, are not ordinarily deductible against your current income, although the tax on the investment returns while these funds are in the account is deferred. An exception occurs when an employer provides supplementary savings plans such as a 401(k), discussed later.

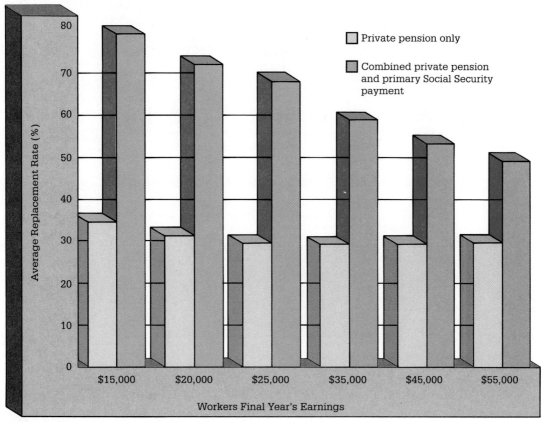

FIGURE 17.4

Defined-benefit pension plans: Average replacement rates including and excluding
Social Security payments, based on 30 years of service, medium and large firms, 1989.
(Source: U.S. Department of Labor, *Employee Benefits in Medium and Large Firms,
1989*, Bulletin 2363, June 1990, p. 83.)

Accrued benefit: Pension
benefits that have been
accumulated because of
previous credited service.

Vested benefits: Pension
benefits that you are
entitled to receive
regardless of future
employment.

VESTING   When you participate in a pension plan, you accrue pension benefits.
The **accrued benefit** is the benefit that a pension plan participant has accumulated to a particular point in time. Some or all of your accrued benefits may be
lost if you leave your present employer. Your rights to your currently promised
benefits will depend upon whether they are *vested*. **Vested benefits** are not for-
feitable for any reason other than death. You may be fired, or you may quit, but
in either case you still retain the right to receive all vested retirement benefits.
   ERISA requires that all employee contributions to a retirement plan must be
immediately vested. However, there may be a specified waiting period before
employer contributions are fully or partially vested. All qualified pension plans
must satisfy one of the vesting schedules in Figure 17.5. Under the cliff vesting,
no vesting need occur before five years of credited service. After the fifth year,
however, all benefits must become fully vested. Graded vesting provides a more
gradual approach, with an increasing portion of accrued benefits vested in years
three through six. In either case, these represent minimum vesting standards.
Many employers allow benefits to vest at a faster pace than is legally required.

Retirement
and Pension
Planning

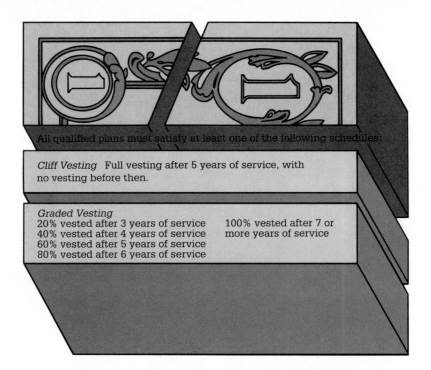

All qualified plans must satisfy at least one of the following schedules:

Cliff Vesting Full vesting after 5 years of service, with no vesting before then.

Graded Vesting
20% vested after 3 years of service
40% vested after 4 years of service
60% vested after 5 years of service
80% vested after 6 years of service

100% vested after 7 or more years of service

FIGURE 17.5

Minimum vesting requirements.

CREDITED SERVICE   It is important that you understand how years of service are defined when determining your vested rights and future benefits. For several reasons, you may have fewer years of credited service than calendar years of employment. Under all plans, you are credited with a year of service only if you have worked a sufficient number of hours within a 12-month period. The required number of hours, typically 1,000, can be found in the Summary Plan Description.

In the Summary Plan Description you will also find a definition for a break in service. Plans generally require that you work at least 500 hours per 12-month period to avoid a break in service. A break in service may delay the vesting of benefits and cause a forfeiture of nonvested benefits. Under federal law, qualified retirement plans cannot terminate nonvested benefits unless the break in service is greater than five years. Furthermore, firms cannot interrupt vesting for maternity or paternity leaves of one year or less.

Normal retirement age: The age at which you are entitled to full retirement benefits.

Early retirement age: The earliest age at which you can retire with reduced benefits.

RETIREMENT BENEFITS   Most plans specify age 65 as **normal retirement age.** At this age, you are eligible to receive the full pension benefits indicated in the plan. Many plans also specify an **early retirement age** at which you can retire with reduced benefits. A common requirement for early retirement benefits is the attainment of age 55 and the completion of ten years of service. The amount by which your benefits will be reduced will depend upon the time interval between the early retirement age and the normal retirement age. You may be given a schedule of reduced payments or a formula for calculating the reduction factor.

The law forbids an employer from requiring you to retire at any age. If the normal retirement age is 65, you have a right to postpone receiving benefits until age 70. Furthermore, the company plan must provide you with additional retirement benefits for years of service beyond normal retirement age.

In a defined-benefit plan, retirement benefits at normal retirement age are computed under a flat benefit method, a unit benefit method, or some combination of the two. With the **flat benefit method,** monthly benefits are equal to either a specific percentage of compensation or a specific dollar payment. Most plans use the **unit benefit method,** where length of service is entered directly into the benefit formula. For example, the formula might state that your monthly normal retirement benefit will be $10 times your years of service. Alternatively, it might employ a percentage formula, such as 2 percent of salary times your years of service.

Regardless of whether the flat or unit method is employed, you will receive better inflation protection when benefits are stated not in specific dollars, but rather as a percentage of your salary. This is so because your salary at retirement should reflect the higher cost of living at that time. Percentage formulas use either the *career average approach* or the *final average approach*. With the career average approach, percentage benefits are based on your average compensation over all years of service. The final average approach bases benefits on a percentage of your average compensation over the last three or five years. Since the final average approach responds more rapidly to an inflationary rise in wages, it is usually preferred.

MEDICAL BENEFITS   You do not qualify for enrollment in the Medicare program until you are age 65. If you presently have health insurance through your employer and you plan to retire before age 65, be sure you have adequate alternative coverage between when you retire and when you and your spouse turn 65. It helps if your employer provides medical benefits for retired workers. In firms with over 100 employees, about 42 percent of participants in retirement plans have their medical coverage at least partially paid for by their previous employer. Such support, however, may not be unconditional. After experiencing significant increases in the cost of medical insurance, many companies have either trimmed back or eliminated medical coverage provided to retired workers. At the present time it is unclear whether promises made by employers concerning medical benefits for retired workers have the same status as promises regarding pension benefits. This is now being decided in the courts.

Regardless of whether your employer subsidizes medical benefits for retired workers, you still may have the right to continued coverage under a group health plan sponsored by an employer with 20 or more workers. Your rights are set down in the Consolidated Omnibus Reconciliation Act of 1985 (COBRA). For 60 days after retiring, you may elect to continue group health coverage. If you make this election, you can extend the group health coverage for another 18 months, after which the group policy may be converted to an individual policy. Under COBRA, the employer does not have to pay for your insurance after you leave employment. However, by continuing coverage under the employer-sponsored plan, you avoid having to satisfy preexisting conditions clauses that might exclude benefit payments under a new insurance plan.

When you do turn age 65, you most likely will qualify for enrollment in the Medicare program. Moreover, for six months after you turn 65, you cannot be

Flat benefit method: Pension benefits are equal to a specified percentage of compensation or a specific dollar benefit.

Unit benefit method: Pension benefits depend directly upon units of credited service.

543

denied private "medigap" insurance because of any preexisting illness. See Chapter 11 for more details on both of these programs.

DISABILITY BENEFITS   Some company retirement plans also include disability income protection. Contributions by the company to the retirement plan may continue during periods of disability. In other situations, the plan may begin paying out monthly benefits at the onset of the disability, regardless of the employee's age. Furthermore, the monthly benefits may be computed under a more generous disability benefit formula. A review of the sections in Chapter 11 on disability insurance will help you determine the quality of this coverage.

SURVIVORS' BENEFITS   ERISA now requires that if you die before your retirement benefits begin, the vested portion of your benefits must be used to provide death benefits for your spouse. It also mandates that married workers automatically be provided a **joint and last survivor annuity** at retirement, unless both spouses elect otherwise. This means that payments will continue as long as either you or your spouse is still alive, although the amount may be reduced after the first death. Federal law requires that monthly payments from the survivor's annuity be more than 50 percent, but less than 100 percent, of the amount paid when both the spouse and the participant are alive. The law also specifies that the benefits cannot be reduced if the surviving spouse remarries. The alternative is a **single life annuity,** for which all payments cease at the pensioner's death. The value of the single life annuity and the joint and last survivor annuity must be actuarially equivalent. That means that the total expected payouts under each annuity option should be the same. Accordingly, since the potential benefit period under a single life annuity is less than a joint and last survivor annuity, the single life option will provide larger monthly benefits.

The choice is a difficult one. Do you select larger monthly payments over your life or lower monthly payments over both your life and your spouse's? Before making the decision, you must understand that the expected total payments are actuarially equivalent. Given life expectancies and interest returns, each of the annuities is worth the same. Accordingly, if both you and your spouse need the cash flow generated by the joint and survivor annuity and you are both in average health, don't gamble on the single life annuity. You may do better under the single life annuity, but the odds are just as good that you will do worse, in which case the surviving spouse may suffer financial hardships.

DISTRIBUTIONS   Distributions from a retirement account may occur for reasons other than just retirement. If you die, become disabled, leave your current employment, or suffer financial hardship, you may be entitled to receive the funds in your retirement plan. The distribution may consist of a single payment, termed a lump-sum distribution, or an annuity, a series of periodic payments. When you receive the distributions, you must pay ordinary income taxes on the proceeds from all tax-deferred accumulations. However, the tax consequences may be postponed further if you roll over the distribution into another tax-deferred retirement account.

If you do take a lump-sum distribution and don't roll it over, all taxes on the benefits will become due at the time of distribution. The lump-sum distribution is eligible, however, for tax-advantageous five-year forward income averaging.

Joint and last survivor annuity: Periodic benefits continue as long as you or your spouse is alive.

Single life annuity: All periodic payments cease at the death of the annuitant.

Under this formula, the tax is based upon the assumption that the distribution would be your only income over a five-year period. For most taxpayers, the use of five-year averaging will reduce the tax on the lump-sum distribution. Of course, choosing an annuity instead of a lump-sum distribution may have even more favorable tax consequences. Those who do take the lump-sum distribution usually have an immediate need for the funds.

An early or late withdrawal of funds from a retirement account may trigger tax penalties in addition to income taxes. In the Tax Reform Act of 1986, Congress imposed a uniform set of penalties on early and late withdrawals from almost all types of group and individual retirement accounts, including those discussed later in this chapter. An early withdrawal is defined as any withdrawal before age 59½. With a few exceptions, such as death, disability, or a lifetime annuity, a 10 percent tax penalty is levied on all early withdrawals.

The penalty on late withdrawals is much worse. Payouts from retirement funds must begin by April 1 of the next calendar year after you reach 70½. In addition, these payouts must be large enough to distribute the fund over your own or your spouse's life expectancy. If you fail to meet the minimum required distribution, there is an onerous 50 percent tax penalty on the difference between the actual distribution and the minimum required distribution.

Other Company Retirement Plans

Companies may offer savings vehicles that differ from the pension format discussed above in one of two ways: One, they may not provide the same type of scheduled contributions or benefits expected of a long-term pension plan; or, two, they may be used to save for needs other than retirement. Such plans are often offered as a supplement to, rather than an alternative to, a typical pension plan. By not tying the employer or the employee into a scheduled set of contributions, they allow each to supplement the basic benefits afforded by the pension plan whenever possible.

ERISA specifies limits on the total amount contributed to company-sponsored retirement plans by both the employer and employee. The guidelines are complicated but generous. Most middle-income taxpayers are not likely to be affected. For example, the combined limit on defined-contribution plans is currently equal to the lesser of 25 percent of employee compensation or $30,000.

PROFIT-SHARING PLANS A **profit-sharing plan** is a type of defined-contribution plan whereby the employer makes contributions into an individual employee's account according to a predetermined formula. Qualified profit-sharing plans must satisfy many of the same rules governing qualified pension plans. Unlike a pension plan, however, the employee may not have to wait until retirement to receive distributions. The plan can be set to pay out after a fixed number of years. One disadvantage for planning purposes is that the firm must contribute only when it earns a profit. Thus, the amount the profit-sharing plan will contain at retirement is highly uncertain.

401(K) SALARY-REDUCTION PLANS In place of, or in addition to, a qualified pension or profit-sharing plan, you may set up a **401(k) salary-reduction plan,**

Profit-sharing plan: A defined-contribution plan where contributions are contingent upon the profitability of the firm.

401(k) salary-reduction plan: A savings plan that permits earners to defer the taxability of income until funds are withdrawn.

which defers a portion of your compensation for retirement. Although you may currently owe Social Security taxes on the earnings, federal income taxes are deferred until you receive the money.

The maximum tax-deferred employee contribution was limited to $8,475 in 1991. It is adjusted upward each year for increases in the Consumer Price Index. The limit is coordinated with those on SEPs and TSAs discussed below. This means that contributions to other plans may reduce your allowable tax-deferred contribution to a 401(k).

Usually the employer provides a choice of investment vehicles into which the funds may be placed while earning tax-deferred returns. Furthermore, many employers offer matching contributions. These contributions, plus the current reduction in income taxes, typically make salary-reduction plans an excellent long-term investment.

EMPLOYEE STOCK OWNERSHIP PLANS (ESOPS) An **employee stock ownership plan (ESOP)** can function in many different ways, but most operate like profit-sharing plans. The difference is that contributions are invested primarily in the employer's stock, and contributions are not necessarily dependent on profits. In addition, all distributions must be made in the form of stock.

ESOP: A savings plan that provides employees benefits in the form of company stock.

An employee stock ownership program is an inappropriate instrument for retirement savings. Because most of the funds are concentrated in the stock of one company, it does not provide any safety through diversification. The value of the fund is likely to swing widely as the company's fortunes change. You could lose both your job and your savings at the same time.

New regulations remedy some of the criticism. Under the Tax Reform Act of 1986, certain employees nearing retirement may elect to place part of their ESOP account in diversified investments.

403(B) TAX-SHELTERED ANNUITIES (TSAS) Only employees of nonprofit institutions are eligible for **403(b) tax-sheltered annuities.** Like the 401(k), they require the employee to enter into a salary-reduction agreement with the employer. Taxes on contributions and returns are deferred until the dollars are withdrawn. The limit on employee contributions is currently $9,500. This will increase as the contribution limit on 401(k) plans rises above $9,500.

403(b) tax-sheltered annuity: A tax-advantaged savings plan for employees of nonprofit institutions.

SIMPLIFIED EMPLOYEE PENSION PLANS (SEPS) A **simplified employee pension plan (SEP)** has advantages for both the employer and employee. For the employer, the paperwork and administrative costs are much less than under a qualified pension plan. For the employee, all amounts deposited in the SEP are immediately vested. As an alternative to a qualified pension plan, the SEP plan permits the employer to set up a tax-deferred individual retirement account for each employee. Into this account the employer can contribute an amount equal to 15 percent of the employee's salary up to a generous annually set maximum. The employee also has the right to make additional tax-deferred contributions. The limit on voluntary contributions is the same as that for 401(k) salary reduction plans.

SEP: An employer-sponsored retirement plan utilizing individual retirement accounts.

Individual Retirement Plans

If you do not have a company retirement plan, or you would like to supplement a company plan through additional private savings, the benefits of tax deferral can also be achieved through non-corporate-sponsored investments. The rules governing early and late withdrawals from individual retirement plans are generally the same as for company-sponsored plans. Distributions before age 59½ incur a 10 percent penalty tax, and insufficient withdrawals after age 70½ suffer a 50 percent tax penalty. The four most common are IRAs, Keoghs, retirement annuities, and home ownership.

IRA: An individual retirement account that qualifies for special tax treatment under IRS regulations.

INDIVIDUAL RETIREMENT ACCOUNTS (IRAS) The **individual retirement account (IRA)** is a trust or custodial account approved by the Internal Revenue Service. In a trust or custodial relationship, the funds are temporarily held by someone other than the investor. However, you as the investor may still retain control over how the funds are managed. The IRS approval indicates that the form of the IRA satisfies the requirements for special tax treatment. It does not suggest anything about the merits of investing in this particular account. Poorly managed IRAs can offer low returns and high risks while still maintaining IRS approval of their tax status.

547

For the majority of Americans, an IRA is probably the most convenient, and most tax advantageous, means to save individually for retirement. Taxes on income earned by funds in the account are deferred until the earnings are withdrawn. Furthermore, for many workers the annual contributions are either partially or fully deductible against current income. This effectively defers taxes on the contribution until it is withdrawn from the account in later years.

Eligibility. Every individual receiving earned income, or alimony, can contribute to an IRA. The maximum annual contribution is restricted to the lesser of earned income or $2,000. For married couples, each may contribute up to $2,000 of earned income, for a combined total contribution of $4,000. You may even open an IRA for a spouse with no earned income, so long as the combined contributions to the regular IRA and the spousal IRA do not exceed $2,250.

Part or all of the IRA may be taken as an adjustment to gross income on your individual tax return. The full amount is deductible for those who are not covered by a retirement plan at work. For those who are, or who are filing a joint return with someone who is, the size of the deduction will depend upon adjusted gross income before the IRA deduction. Singles may deduct the full amount of their contributions when their incomes are less than $25,000. At incomes between $25,000 and $35,000 they are still entitled to a partial deduction. Married couples with combined incomes of less than $40,000 can deduct the full amount. Their IRA deduction is phased out between $40,000 and $50,000. The worksheet for calculating the partial deduction on 1991 federal income taxes is presented in Figure 17.6.

Taxes on deductible IRA contributions are delayed, not forgiven. When contributions are withdrawn, taxes will become due on the portion of the withdrawal resulting from previously untaxed contributions and investment earnings. A deductible IRA contribution can be an excellent tax-advantageous investment for young adults with moderate incomes. They are able to capture both the immediate benefit of the tax reduction and the long-term benefit of tax deferral over the many years until retirement. As was demonstrated in Table 17.1, the benefits of tax deferral can be substantial.

Investments. You cannot invest your IRA funds in life insurance or in collectibles other than gold or silver U.S. coins. Nor can you borrow from the account, use it as collateral for a loan, or engage in investments that put you at risk for more than the value of the IRA. Other than these few rules, how you invest your IRA is a matter of considerable choice. You can place it in CDs, annuities, mutual funds, or real estate, or you can open a self-directed IRA through a brokerage house and organize your own portfolio of stocks and bonds.

The IRA is only one component of your investment portfolio. Where you should invest your IRA will depend on the risk-return trade-off that is acceptable to you, and the diversity and risk in your non-IRA investments. Generally, however, you probably want to consider investments that generate high ordinary income as candidates for inclusion in an IRA. Taxes are deferred on both deductible contributions and investment returns. It makes no sense to use the IRA for investments that generate uncertain tax-postponed capital gains, since taxes are already deferred.

If filing status is:	Enter on line 1:	
Single, or Head of Household	$35,000	
Married-joint return, or Qualifying widow(er)	$50,000	
Married-separate return	$10,000	
1. Amount from above		$_____
2. Adjusted gross income		_____
3. Subtract line 2 from line 1		_____
4. Maximum partial deduction. Multiply line 3 by 20% (.20). If the result is not a multiple of $10, round it to the next highest multiple of $10 (for example, $611.40 rounded to $620). However, if the result is less than $200, but more than zero, enter $200.		$_____

FIGURE 17.6

Worksheet for calculating maximum partial deduction. (Use this worksheet only if the AGI is within phase-out range.)

Keogh plan: A tax-deferred pension account for self-employed individuals.

KEOGH (HR-10) PLANS   If you derive any of your earnings from self-employment, you can set up a **Keogh plan.** Suppose you work by day for a corporation with a qualified corporate pension plan, but by night you run your own business. Part of the earned income from your self-employment may be tax-sheltered for retirement in a Keogh, even though you are already participating in the corporate retirement plan as an employee.

The limits on contributions to a Keogh are more generous than those governing IRAs. You can contribute 20 percent of your net income from self-employment, up to a maximum nontaxable contribution of $30,000. Rules governing withdrawals and related penalties are about the same as for IRAs.

RETIREMENT ANNUITIES   In the early years of the family life cycle, when you have many responsibilities, it is important that you provide an estate for the protection of your survivors. In the later years, when you have fewer family responsibilities, it is more important to protect your family against the possibility that your estate may run out before their deaths. Annuities can provide such assurance.

Annuity contract: A contract that provides for some form of periodic payment.

Accumulation period: The term over which the principal in the contract is building.

Annuity contracts sold by life insurance companies are a convenient means of saving for retirement and of providing security in retirement. Coinciding with these two objectives, annuities have two distinct periods: the accumulation period and the liquidation period.

During the **accumulation period** the principal builds through investments and returns on investments, while benefits are deferred. The annuity contract may allow the buyer to make a single investment (a single premium annuity) or a series of investments during the accumulation period.

Fixed annuity: An annuity in which the principal is guaranteed.

Variable annuity: The value of the annuity is dependent upon the market performance of a specified investment fund.

You can purchase either fixed or variable annuities. The distinction has to do with the preservation of principal during the accumulation period. The value of a **fixed annuity** can only increase, whereas the value of a variable annuity can move both up and down. Typically, the interest rate on fixed annuities is guaranteed for a short period of time, such as a year. After this initial period, the interest rate can be changed at the discretion of the insurance company, so long as it doesn't fall below some guaranteed minimal interest rate, such as 3 percent.

The principal in a **variable annuity** is invested in a portfolio of securities. Therefore, the value of a variable annuity will increase or decrease with the

Liquidation period: The term over which the annuity pays out periodic benefits.

Annuity starting date: The date when the annuity begins periodic payments.

Immediate annuity: Payments begin one period from the current date.

Deferred annuity: Payments are deferred until some later time period.

changing value of the underlying securities. The future worth of the annuity will depend on the portfolio's financial performance. If it does poorly, you could lose some or all of your principal.

When the accumulation period ends, you can typically receive the accumulated cash value in a lump-sum payment or in the form of an annuity. In the **liquidation period** the owner receives the annuity benefit in monthly or annual installments. When you elect the type of payments to be received, you are said to annuitize the contract. The **annuity starting date** is the point in time when the liquidation period begins.

An **immediate annuity** begins payments one period from the date it is purchased. How much income an annuity might purchase is indicated in Figure 17.7. Annuities that defer benefits until some later period are called **deferred annuities.** During the accumulation period, when benefits are deferred, taxes on the investment buildup of principal are also deferred. This makes deferred annuities a tax-advantageous savings vehicle. As with other retirement accounts, income taxes become due when the tax-deferred accumulations are withdrawn. Likewise, there is a 10 percent tax penalty on early distributions before age 59½. The early withdrawal penalty does not apply in cases of death or disability, or when payments are received as an annuity over the life of the annuitant or his or her spouse.

In addition to the penalties levied by the government on early withdrawal, the insurance company may impose a surrender charge in the early years. Some policies contain a bailout provision that permits you to surrender the policy without charges if the rate paid on the annuity falls below some initially guaranteed rate. Together, tax penalties and surrender charges restrict the use of annuities to long-term savings objectives, such as retirement.

This doesn't necessarily mean you are stuck with your current annuity. If you have held the annuity for more than five years, the surrender charges should be low or nonexistent. The typical surrender charge is about 7 percent of the investment in the first year and declines by about 1 percent a year until it reaches zero. In addition, tax penalties can be avoided if you transfer funds from your current annuity into another through what is known as a "1035 exchange." Your new company can help arrange the tax-free transfer. Even with surrender charges, if the previous insurer is paying a low return or is financially unsound, it may be worthwhile to arrange a tax-free reallocation of your funds.

There are many ways you may decide to receive the proceeds from the annuity. You can elect to receive a single life or a joint and last survivor annuity, already discussed in the section on survivor's benefits in qualified retirement plans. Under these options you are assured of receiving benefits no matter how long you (single life annuity) or you and your spouse (joint and last survivor annuity) may live.

Of course, if benefits are based entirely upon survival, the possibility of an early death means you, the annuitant, may never receive the cost of the annuity in expected benefits. For this reason, many annuitants desire a refund feature. This guarantees that payments will continue until they have at least refunded the cost of the annuity. Accordingly, should you die during the guaranteed period, payments would continue to your named beneficiary for the remainder of the guaranteed refund period.

FIGURE 17.7

Single-premium life annuity.

HOW MUCH WILL $100,000 BUY?

Suppose you made a single payment of $100,000 to purchase a single life annuity. The monthly payments were to begin immediately and to last until your death. How much could you expect to receive each month? The table below can help you answer that question.

We compared the cost of several single premium immediate annuities and have listed below the monthly benefits you might expect from a low-benefit annuity and a high-benefit annuity. Using mortality tables, we estimated that the pretax internal rate of return on the high-benefit policy is about 8½ percent, whereas the annual return on the low-benefit policy is a little less than 5 percent.

The wide range in benefits and returns suggests that you should shop carefully and choose wisely.*

Monthly Benefits from a $100,000 Single-Premium Immediate Annuity

Annuity	Starting Age 65	Starting Age 70
High-benefit annuity		
Male	$992	$1,140
Female	856	947
Low-benefit annuity		
Male	790	891
Female	717	794

*A survey of policies can be found in "Single Premium Annuity Quotes," *Life & Health/Financial Services Edition: The National Underwriter Company,* December 16, 1991, p. 14.

The period of guaranteed payments need not coincide with the refund period. Annuities can be written to guarantee any number of payments over 5, 10, 15, or 20 years. Of course, the longer the guarantee period, the smaller will be the annuity payment. A single life annuity with all payments ceasing at death will provide you with the greatest periodic benefit per dollar of cost.

Purchasing an annuity with guaranteed payments does not guarantee that the life insurance company selling the annuity will be around to make those payments. The insurance company is only as secure as its own investments. Given the recent volatility in financial markets, some of those investments may not be as safe as was once thought. This, and the long-term nature of the relationship, make it essential that you check out the financial stability of the company issuing the policy in *Best's Insurance Reports*. As with life insurance, purchase an annuity only from a company with an A+ rating for financial stability.

Retirement annuities receive the same tax treatment as nondeductible IRA contributions, but there is no limit on the amount you may invest. Taxes on investment earnings are deferred until they are withdrawn during the liquidation period.

HOME OWNERSHIP For many people, home ownership is an integral part of their retirement plan. They look forward to having the mortgage paid off and seeing an end to the monthly mortgage payments. Thus, equity in a home, equal to market value less the mortgage balance, represents an important source of savings for the elderly. The Bureau of the Census reports that median net worth in households having a family head aged 65 to 69 was $83,478 in 1988. Moreover, $55,996 of that amount represented equity in a home.

Obviously, owning a home is considered by many an important means of saving for retirement. Interest payments on the mortgage are tax deductible, and you pay no tax on the appreciation in market value until you sell. Furthermore, taxes on the capital gain arising from the sale may be postponed if you reinvest in another home. The real bonus comes when you sell after age 55, because you are then allowed to exclude from capital gains taxes $125,000 of the gains accumulated over the many years of home ownership. This is a once-in-a-lifetime exclusion, so you should consider your financial situation carefully before taking it. It is fully explained in IRS Publication 530, *Tax Information for Homeowners*, and Publication 523, *Tax Information on Selling Your Home*.

Home ownership can be an important source of savings for the future, but there are some potential disadvantages you should be aware of. Markets may rise and fall, and in efficient financial markets the past may be an inaccurate guide to the future. As discussed in Chapter 9, this market did very well in the 1970s as the baby boom generation entered the age of home ownership. What might happen in the twenty-first century, when these same individuals retire and sell homes that are no longer needed, is highly uncertain. In this potential market, those who rely on the equity in a home for financial support in retirement may be very disappointed.

The main point is that you should always attempt to reduce your risks through diversification. Don't rely on home ownership, or any other single investment, as the only source of retirement income. As one component in a comprehensive and diversified savings plan, it is likely to be a very good, tax-advantageous investment.

Having a good chunk of your retirement savings locked up in your home can also be a problem if you need those savings for maintenance expenditures. A reverse mortgage could let you have your savings and your home at the same time. With a **reverse mortgage,** also called an equity conversion loan, the equity in your home serves as collateral for the loan. What makes this loan unique is that repayment of principal and interest is deferred until the house is sold, regardless of when that may be. The loan may provide a line of credit, a lump-sum payment, or, as is the most common option, monthly disbursements. The monthly payout may extend over a fixed number of years or for as long as you remain in the home. When the home is sold, the lender is repaid debt plus interest. The Federal Housing Administration insures reverse mortgages up to about $125,000, thus guaranteeing lenders that the equity will be sufficient to cover the amount owed at sale.

Reverse mortgage: Allows retirees to remain in their home while accessing the home equity for supplemental income.

Establishing a Personal Retirement Plan

We have already examined the various forms your retirement savings might take, but we have not yet answered the question of how much to save. The easy response is that you should save enough to meet your goals. All planning involves a statement of goals and a method for achieving those goals. In retirement planning the goal is a specific standard of living in your later years. Your standard is a personal decision. Do you plan to purchase a pleasure yacht and cruise the high seas, or do you plan to live on handouts from charitable organizations?

Obviously, your goals will depend upon more than mere desires. They will be affected by your present income, your ability and willingness to save, and your expected Social Security benefits. To come up with a viable plan, you might begin by setting a goal and then calculating how much you would have to save to achieve it. If the required savings appear out of line with your present abilities, then revise the goal and repeat your calculations. You should eventually arrive at a goal and a level of current savings that balance your immediate and future needs.

Financial planners often state that retirement planning should be thought of as a three-legged stool, with Social Security, company pensions, and private savings providing each of the essential supporting legs.

Social Security Benefits

Part of your retirement planning will be dependent upon our Social Security system. Because of its uncertain operation, some have accused the system of generating social insecurity. The Social Security taxes you pay each year do not go into an investment fund where they accumulate for your retirement years. The Social Security tax is simply a transfer tax. It transfers income from working Americans to those receiving Social Security benefits.

Because there is no investment fund, and because the government retains the power to tax, the system technically cannot go bankrupt. However, the average age of the population is expected to increase into the twenty-first century. There are currently 5 working persons for each elderly person; by the year 2030 there will be only 2.5 working persons for each elderly person. As this trend continues, the government will confront a difficult choice. It must either increase taxes on the working population or reduce benefits. In anticipation of future problems, some changes are already set to go into effect.

RETIREMENT AGE   Normal retirement age for full Social Security benefits is currently age 65, but the baby boom generation will have to wait a little longer. Beginning in 2003, normal retirement age will increase in installments until it reaches age 67 in 2027.

Additional incentives for delayed retirement should also hold down the cost of benefits. For each year you delay receiving benefits beyond age 65 up to age 71, benefits are increased by 3 percent. Starting in 1990, the percentage increase for a year's delay rises until it reaches 8 percent in 2009.

There are no plans to change the early retirement age of 62. However, benefits at early retirement will eventually fall from 80 to 70 percent of monthly benefits at normal retirement age.

RETIREMENT BENEFITS   In a complicated manner, Social Security benefits are based upon the amount you paid into the system and your age at retirement. The methodology for calculating retirement benefits is contained in Appendix B on the Social Security system. You can save yourself considerable work by having the Social Security Administration estimate your future retirement benefits. How to obtain an estimate of your benefits is also discussed in Appendix B. If you do not yet have a personalized estimate of benefits, you can temporarily use the benchmark estimates in Table 17.2.

TABLE
17.2 • Estimates of
Annual Social Security
Retirement Benefits for
Age 65 Retirement

	Average Annual Social Security-Covered Wages				
	Less than $10,000	$10,000 to $15,000	$15,000 to $25,000	$25,000 to $35,000	$35,000 and over
Worker alone	$6,000	$ 7,560	$ 9,240	$11,400	$12,240
Worker with spouse claiming benefits at age 65	9,000	11,340	13,860	17,100	18,360

Two-earner couples can each qualify separately for a pension, or one may qualify as a dependent on the other's earning record. A dependent spouse at normal retirement age will receive benefits equal to 50 percent of the benefits received by the retired wage earner. Whether you should qualify on your own record or your spouse's will depend on which generates more in retirement benefits.

RETIREMENT TEST   The government would like to reserve benefits for those who are truly retired, so it reduces benefit payments as earnings increase. In 1991, those under 65 and receiving retirement benefits could earn up to $7,080 before Social Security checks were reduced. Between ages 65 and 69 they could earn $9,720 without reduction. For earnings in excess of these annually determined thresholds, Social Security benefits are reduced by $1 for every $3 you earn. Only from age 70 on is there no reduction for earnings.

The retirement test may be necessary to hold down the cost of the Social Security system, but it does have an undesirable side effect. It severely penalizes older Americans who choose to remain in the work force. For each dollar you earn above the threshold, Social Security benefits are reduced by 33 cents. If federal and state income taxes take 17 cents of this dollar, and job-related expenses are another 10 cents, you are left with only 40 cents of each dollar you earn. It is easy to see why only those who really enjoy their work or who really must work continue employment after Social Security benefits begin.

TAXATION OF SOCIAL SECURITY BENEFITS   Before 1984, Social Security benefits were not subject to income taxes. Now, up to half of your Social Security benefits may be taxed if you have significant income from other sources including private pension benefits and asset income. Calculation of the taxable amount is explained in Figure 17.8.

In percentage terms, the method for calculating taxable benefits places the largest tax burden on those achieving middle-income status in retirement. The base-amount exclusion eliminates taxes on benefits for those with low incomes, and the tax on benefits for families with high incomes is limited by the maximum inclusion.

Retirees depending on distributions from tax-deferred retirement accounts can mitigate the effects of the tax on Social Security benefits with proper tax planning. First, avoid unnecessarily large distributions in a single year that may put you above the base amount. Second, it may be worthwhile to distribute the account completely before Social Security benefits begin. In this way the principal in the account will not show up as future income, producing taxable Social Security benefits.

COST-OF-LIVING ADJUSTMENTS   One particularly attractive characteristic of Social Security retirement pensions is that they are periodically increased to offset the rise in the price level. Most private pensions provide for fixed dollar benefits during retirement. Over time these constant dollar benefits will purchase fewer goods and services. Having Social Security as part of your retirement income ensures you will receive at least partial inflation protection.

Estimating and Saving for Your Retirement Needs

What is needed is a simple process that gets you started planning for retirement in your early years, but which can also be refined as you approach retirement,

The taxable portion of your Social Security benefits will be equal to the lesser of:

1. 50% × Social Security benefits

    OR

2. 50% [modified adjusted gross income + 50% (Social Security benefits) − base amount]
    where modified adjusted gross income = gross income + tax-exempt interest
    base amount = $25,000 for individuals and $32,000 for married couples

EXAMPLE

A married couple with income of $30,000, no tax-free interest, and annual benefits of $11,000 would pay income tax on the lesser of:

1. 50% × $11,000 = $5,500

    OR

2. 50% [$30,000 + 50% ($11,000) − $32,000] = $1,750

FIGURE 17.8

Computation of taxable Social Security benefits.

permitting more exact planning as your needs become more apparent. One way of doing this is first to target your retirement needs and then estimate the annual savings necessary to meet that target. Each year, as new information becomes available, it can be incorporated into your retirement planning, and a new savings requirement can be calculated. Although the target may move each year, if you take the indicated steps you should arrive at your retirement goals. In this section we provide two methods for estimating your retirement needs. The first approach simplifies planning by assuming that investment returns and the inflation rate are identical. The second approach involves more complicated computations, but allows you more control over assumed investment returns and assumed rates of inflation.

A SIMPLIFIED APPROACH Younger workers with many years until retirement cannot be certain about economic conditions between now and retirement. They can easily be sidetracked by dwelling on these uncertainties. It is far better to gloss over them with simplifying assumptions, while at the same time building in a safety margin to cover potential misfortunes. This can be accomplished by conservatively assuming that interest rates and inflation rates cancel each other out. Thus, inflation forecasts and complicated financial calculations are eliminated.

Figure 17.9 contains a worksheet that may be used for retirement planning by either a single individual or a household with a single market worker. In households where both spouses have separate retirement plans, and each expects to retire at a different age or date, separate worksheets may be prepared by each market worker. In the current example we are assuming a married couple dependent upon the wages of a single market worker. The market worker plans to retire at age 65, at which time the spouse will be age 63.

Begin your analysis by entering your current salary on line 1. On line 2, estimate the percentage of that salary you would have to replace in order to retain an adequate standard of living during your retirement years. This figure should be based on the assumption that you will not have any work-related expenses, nor

		Sample Data	Your Data
1.	Current salary	$ 50,000	_____
2.	Percentage of current salary you plan to replace	× .60	× _____
3.	Retirement income target	$ 30,000	_____
4.	Minus vested defined benefits	(0)	(_____)
5.	Minus Social Security benefits (see Table 17.2)	($ 17,503)	(_____)
6.	Required supplemental income from investment fund	$ 12,497	_____
7.	Life expectancy (see Table 17.3)	× 26	× _____
8.	Required target investment fund	$324,922	_____
9.	Present target resources		
	Keogh	$ 0	_____
	IRA	$20,000	_____
	Defined-contribution plan	$48,320	_____
	General investments	$25,000	_____
	TOTAL	($ 93,320)	(_____)
10.	Required additions to target fund	$231,602	_____
11.	Years to retirement	÷ 20	÷ _____
12.	Current annual saving needed to achieve target	$ 11,580	_____

FIGURE 17.9

Simplified retirement planning worksheet.

dependent children to support. A good rule of thumb is that you will need about 60 percent of your final salary to retain your current living standard during retirement. If you are planning to have your home fully paid for by then, this percentage may be reduced accordingly.

The retirement income target on line 3 will have to be covered by pension benefits or investment accumulations. To estimate the needed investment fund, first subtract annual pension benefits. Line 4 contains defined-benefit payments from corporate pension plans or independently purchased annuities. Enter only benefits that are vested and accrued—that is, future benefits you would receive at the expected retirement date were you to terminate employment and further contributions today.

Given the nature of the Social Security program, future payments must be highly speculative. If you do not have an estimate provided by the Social Security Administration, you can use one of our estimates listed in Table 17.2. Because we are cancelling out the effects of inflation in the calculations, these may be considered a best estimate of future payments in today's dollars. In the example, Social Security benefits are assumed to equal approximately $17,503. If you or your

Retirement and Pension Planning

spouse are planning on early retirement, reduce Social Security benefits by 7 percent for each year the expected retirement date precedes the normal retirement date under the Social Security program.

After subtracting annual payments under government and nongovernment pension programs, you have the annual income you must generate from investments in defined contribution plans and individual investment accounts.

Table 17.3 contains unisex single and joint life expectancies published by the Internal Revenue Service. The single life expectancy represents the number of years an individual is expected to survive. Of course, 50 percent will live fewer years and 50 percent will live more years. The joint life expectancy is based upon two lives; the expected number of years until both are deceased is the joint life expectancy.

Given a married couple age 65 and age 63 at retirement, their joint life expectancy at that date is 26.0 years. Assuming that supplemental income on line 6 is needed over the joint lives, then 26.0 years can be entered on line 7. Multiplying line 6 by line 7 provides the size of the target retirement fund needed to produce the supplemental investment income.

You may wonder what will happen if you live longer than expected. Remember, we are building a safety margin into our estimates by assuming that investment returns just equal the rate of inflation. You should be able to earn a return that exceeds inflation, so the fund should actually last longer than the stated life expectancy. Alternatively, if you choose to purchase a life annuity at this point, the amount in the investment fund should be more than adequate.

The target investment fund on line 8 will change from year to year as your salary and defined-benefit payments change. But as long as you continue to aim for this moving target, you should reach the appropriate amount at retirement. To find out how much you must devote to retirement savings today, you must subtract the amounts you have already accumulated in defined contribution pension plans, individual retirement accounts, and other savings vehicles that are not reserved to satisfy other purposes. If you then divide the remaining amount on line 10 by the number of years until retirement, you can find the current amount you must devote to additional retirement savings.

If the level of saving indicated on line 12 is greater than you currently wish to undertake, you might instead work backward. Start with your desired level of annual savings, and then estimate how much of your present income this would eventually replace in retirement. This reverse procedure will bring your future goals into alignment with your present level of income and expenditure.

The simplified approach outlined in Figure 17.7 is highly conservative. If you consistently earn a return on your savings that exceeds the rise in the cost of living, the simplified approach to retirement planning will cause you to overfund your retirement needs. To take account of such differences, you must to be familiar with the concepts of present value and future value discussed in Appendix A. If you are unfamiliar with these terms, you can either skip the next section or review the material in Appendix A before proceeding.

AN ADVANCED APPROACH   For those who wish to take the time value of money into consideration—or perhaps observe how sensitive their retirement planning is to the assumed interest rate and inflation rate—the advanced approach outlined in Figure 17.10 is recommended.

TABLE 17.3 ▪ Single and Joint Life Expectancies in Years

Single Life Annuity Life Expectancy (Earnings Multiple)

Age	50	51	52	53	54	55	56	57	58	59	60	61	62	63	64	65	66	67	68	69	70
	33.1	32.2	31.3	30.4	29.5	28.6	27.7	26.8	25.9	25.0	24.2	23.3	22.5	21.6	20.8	20.0	19.2	18.4	17.6	16.8	16.0

Joint Life Annuity Joint Life Expectancy (Earnings Multiple)

Age	50	51	52	53	54	55	56	57	58	59	60	61	62	63	64	65	66	67	68	69	70
50	39.2	38.7	38.3	37.9	37.5	37.1	36.8	36.4	36.1	35.9	35.6	35.4	35.1	34.9	34.8	34.6	34.4	34.3	34.2	34.1	34.0
51		38.2	37.8	37.3	36.9	36.5	36.1	35.8	35.5	35.2	34.9	34.6	34.4	34.2	34.0	33.8	33.6	33.5	33.4	33.2	33.1
52			37.3	36.8	36.4	35.9	35.6	35.2	34.8	34.5	34.2	33.9	33.7	33.5	33.2	33.0	32.9	32.7	32.5	32.4	32.3
53				36.3	35.8	35.4	35.0	34.6	34.2	33.9	33.6	33.3	33.0	32.7	32.5	32.3	32.1	31.9	31.8	31.6	31.5
54					35.3	34.9	34.4	34.0	33.6	33.3	32.9	32.6	32.3	32.0	31.8	31.6	31.4	31.2	31.0	30.8	30.7
55						34.4	33.9	33.5	33.1	32.7	32.3	32.0	31.7	31.4	31.1	30.9	30.6	30.4	30.2	30.1	29.9
56							33.4	33.0	32.5	32.1	31.7	31.4	31.0	30.7	30.4	30.2	29.9	29.7	29.5	29.3	29.1
57								32.5	32.0	31.6	31.2	30.8	30.4	30.1	29.8	29.5	29.2	29.0	28.8	28.6	28.4
58									31.5	31.1	30.6	30.2	29.9	29.5	29.2	28.9	28.6	28.3	28.1	27.8	27.6
59										30.6	30.1	29.7	29.3	28.9	28.6	28.2	27.9	27.6	27.4	27.1	26.9
60											29.7	29.2	28.8	28.4	28.0	27.6	27.3	27.0	26.7	26.5	26.2
61												28.7	28.3	27.8	27.4	27.1	26.7	26.4	26.1	25.8	25.6
62													27.8	27.3	26.9	26.5	26.1	25.8	25.5	25.2	24.9
63														26.9	26.4	26.0	25.6	25.2	24.9	24.6	24.3
64															25.9	25.5	25.1	24.7	24.3	24.0	23.7
65																25.0	24.6	24.2	23.8	23.4	23.1
66																	24.1	23.7	23.3	22.9	22.5
67																		23.2	22.8	22.4	22.0
68																			22.3	21.9	21.5
69																				21.5	21.1
70																					20.6

SOURCE: Internal Revenue Service, Publication 939, Tables V and VI, January 1990.

Retirement
and Pension
Planning

Advanced retirement planning requires that you first estimate the amount of funding you will need at retirement in tomorrow's dollars. Since the initial calculations under both the simplified and the advanced approaches are the same, Figure 17.10 begins with line 6 from the previous worksheet. The required supplemental income listed on line 6 is in current dollars. To find your income needs in future dollars, future rates of inflation must be taken into account. Appendix Table A.1 provides the future value of $1 compounded over various periods, at several different rates of growth. If there are 20 years to retirement and you assume a 5 percent annual rate of inflation, what cost $1.00 today will cost $2.6533 dollars 20 years from now. When you multiply 2.6533 (the future value of $1) by $12,497 on line 6, you will find that in the year you retire you will actually need supplemental dollar income of $33,158.

Action Plan for the Steeles Reviewing Their Retirement Plans

Background   Both Arnold and Sharon should receive Social Security wage earner's pensions when they retire. Furthermore, Arnold has fully vested pension rights at his current job. If he terminated employment today, he could either receive a lump-sum payment of $21,000 or leave the funds in the pension plan for a joint life annuity with survivorship paying $18,000 per year when Arnold reaches age 65, 30 years from now.

The Problem   After reviewing their household budget and balance sheet, the Steeles realize that they have not been saving for retirement. They want to know how much they would need to save each year in order to retire at 60 percent of their present income. The benefit statement from the Social Security Administration indicates that they would receive combined benefits of about $19,000. With Arnold's defined-pension benefits of $18,000, their total retirement income in today's dollars would be about $37,000. That is about $10,000 less than what they would like to have in retirement income.

They would like to know how much they would have to save annually in order to provide for the desired supplemental income. Both Arnold and Sharon have 401(k) plans at work that they have not taken advantage of. Neither plan provides any matching contribution by the employer. They expect a future inflation rate of 4 percent and an after-tax return on their savings of 8 percent.

The Plan   At retirement 30 years from now, if annual inflation averages 4 percent, the required supplemental income in tomorrow's dollars would be $32,434. Arnold and Sharon's joint life expectancy at retirement is about 26 years. Given a net discount rate of 4 percent (8 percent after-tax return minus 4 percent inflation), the required supplemental fund at retirement is $518,385. Assuming an after-tax return of 8 percent, the future value of a $1 annuity at 30 years from now would be $113.28. Therefore, annual savings of $4,576 (= $518,385/ $113.28) would allow the Steeles to satisfy their desired retirement income. Since this is significantly below the contribution ceiling on 401(k) plans, they should be able to use it successfully as a saving vehicle.

	Sample Data	Your Data
6. Required supplemental income from investment fund	$ 12,497	_____
7. Income adjustment		
Number of periods until retirement: 20		_____
Inflation rate: 5%		_____
Future value of $1 (see Appendix Table A.1)	× 2.6533	× _____
Future value of supplemental annual income	$ 33,158	_____
8. Required funding at retirement		
Number of periods of retirement income: 26		_____
Net discount rate: 3% (after-tax interest rate minus the inflation rate)		_____
Present value at retirement of a $1 inflation adjusted annuity due (see Appendix Table A.4)	× 18.4131	× _____
Lump sum needed at retirement to provide annual supplemental income	$610,548	_____
9. Future value of retirement resources		
Years to retirement: 20		_____
After-tax return on investments: 8%		_____
Present retirement resources $93,320		_____
Future value of $1 × 4.6610		× _____
Future value of target resources	434,961	_____
10. Additional savings needed at retirement	$175,587	_____
Future value of $1 annuity to retirement (see Appendix Table A.2)	÷ 45.762	÷ _____
11. Current annual savings needed to achieve target	$ 3,837	_____

FIGURE 17.10

Advanced retirement planning worksheet.

Appendix Table A.4 provides the present value of a $1 annuity payable over various periods. If you multiply the present value of a $1 annuity payable over your retirement years by $33,158, you can find how much you would need to fund this annuity at retirement. Of course, if you want your standard of living to remain constant, what you really desire is an annuity that begins at $33,158 and then is adjusted upward each year for any increase in the cost of living. The present value of an inflation-adjusted annuity can be found by using a net discount rate, which is approximately equal to the rate of inflation minus the rate of interest. For example, if you assume an after-tax return on your investments of 8 percent and a rate of inflation of 5 percent, then the net discount rate is 3 percent.

According to Appendix Table A.4, the present value of a $1 annuity payable for 26 years at a net discount rate of 3 percent is $17.8768. However, this is the present value of an annuity that pays out at the end of each year. What you really need in this example is a payment at the beginning of the year in which you retire, and then 25 future payments, each at the beginning of a subsequent year. An annuity that pays out at the beginning of each period is termed an *annuity due*. The present value of an *n*-period $1 annuity due can be found by taking the present value of an $(n - 1)$-period $1 annuity and adding 1 to it. Accordingly, the present value of a 26-period annuity due at a net discount rate of 3 percent is $18.4131. This is equal to $17.4131 (the present value of a 25-period annuity discounted at 3 percent) plus $1.

Multiplying the present value of a $1 annuity due by the required supplemental income indicates that the lump sum needed at retirement is $610,548. This may be funded by both previously accumulated resources and future savings. Those resources you have already accumulated will continue to earn investment income until they are needed. If you assume that the annual after-tax return on your current resources is 8 percent, then Appendix Table A.1 indicates that $1 of present funding will grow to $4.6610 in 20 years. Therefore, the future value of present resources at retirement will be $434,961 (= $93,320 × 4.6610). Thus, the additional savings needed at retirement will be equal to the difference between future needs and the future value of present resources, or $175,587 (= $610,548 − 434,961).

The future value of a $1 annuity is given in Appendix Table A.2. The value indicates how much you would have in an investment fund after the given number of years, if you deposited $1 in the account each year and the amount deposited earned interest at the indicated rate. For example, the future value of a $1 annual payment made over each of the next 20 years, where these payments earn an annual after-tax return of 8 percent, is $45.762. Dividing $175,587 (the additional savings needed at retirement) by 45.762, you will find that equal annual contributions of $3,837 will cover the shortfall in future funding needs.

You should notice that in this example there is a considerable difference between the required annual savings under the simplified approach and the advanced approach. By assuming resources of $93,320 and then assuming that returns on these resources will beat the rate of inflation by 3 percent over each of the next 20 years, required additional savings are substantially reduced. You are, in effect, assuming that you can provide for much of your retirement needs through real growth in your current portfolio. Of course, should these estimates prove too optimistic, you may have to increase future contributions or else fall short of your target funding.

Summary

Retirement planning involves an explicit consideration of present versus future needs, and an examination of how present resources may be allocated to serve future needs. An important means of saving for retirement is through a company-sponsored pension plan. Other convenient, tax-deferred methods sponsored by employers include profit-sharing plans, salary-reduction agreements, and employee stock ownership plans. Savings may also be channeled through non-company-sponsored plans, such as IRAs and Keoghs. Whatever savings method is used, retirement planning should include a financial goal and a viable savings plan for achieving that goal. The sooner you get started, the easier it will be to alter your plan to meet your changing future needs.

Key Terms

accrued benefit (p. 541)

accumulation period (p. 549)

annuity contract (p. 549)

deferred annuity (p. 550)

defined-benefit plan (p. 538)

defined-contribution plan (p. 540)

early retirement age (p. 542)

Employee Retirement Income Security Act (ERISA) (p. 535)

employee stock ownership plan (ESOP) (p. 546)

fixed annuity (p. 549)

flat benefit method (p. 543)

401(k) salary-reduction plan (p. 545)

403(b) tax-sheltered annuity (p. 546)

immediate annuity (p. 550)

individual retirement account (IRA) (p. 547)

joint and last survivor annuity (p. 544)

Keogh plan (p. 549)

liquidation period (p. 550)

normal retirement age (p. 542)

profit-sharing plan (p. 545)

qualified retirement plan (p. 535)

reverse mortgage (p. 552)

simplified employee pension plan (SEP) (p. 546)

single life annuity (p. 544)

unit benefit method (p. 543)

variable annuity (p. 549)

vested benefits (p. 541)

Problems and Review Questions

1 "Retirement planning should be put off until you can accurately assess your latter-day needs." Do you agree or disagree with this statement? Explain.

2 What does the term *qualified* indicate when describing a pension plan? Why is it important that a pension plan be qualified?

3 What is the difference between a defined-benefit plan and a defined-contribution plan? What are the advantages and disadvantages of each?

4 Why is it important that benefits be vested?

5 What percentage of pension benefits would be vested for an employee with four years of service at age 35 under each of the following vesting standards: *(a)* cliff vesting, and *(b)* graded vesting.

6 Up to what age must the company provide you with additions to your retirement benefits? You cannot be forced into retirement before what age?

7 Which approach for calculating defined benefits responds more rapidly to the effects of inflation: the career average approach or the final average approach? Why?

8 How does a pension plan differ from a profit-sharing plan?

9 Which tax-deferred retirement plans could a self-employed individual take advantage of?

10 How do fixed annuities differ from variable annuities?

11 Why is it unwise to place the majority of your retirement savings into your home?

12 What is normal retirement age for Social Security benefits? How is this expected to change?

13 A 65-year-old retiree earning $10,000 in part-time employment during 1991 would lose what amount in Social Security benefits, according to the retirement test? Suppose the retiree were 64 years of age; what is the potential loss? Suppose the retiree is 71 years of age; what is the potential loss?

14 Are Social Security benefits tax-free? Explain.

15 How much to save today for retirement in the distant future is difficult to determine. How might you simplify the problem?

16   You want to change the mutual fund you have your IRA invested in. How might you change funds without triggering a tax on your withdrawal?

17   When might deferral of taxes on a retirement account be an unwise choice?

18   How does health-care planning before age 65 differ from health-care planning after age 65?

19   Does the nonemployee spouse have any rights to a pension plan participant's defined benefits?

20   Why do the ages 59½ and 70½ have a special significance for qualified retirement plans?

Case 17.1
Steve Deutsch Plans for Retirement

Steve Deutsch's company pension and his expected Social Security benefits are his only sources of retirement income. He would like to retire in ten years at age 62, but he is worried that these programs will not provide enough in early retirement benefits for him to live in his normal style. He figures he would need to generate an additional income of $10,000 from a supplemental investment fund for him to live comfortably in early retirement. He can use either the simplified or advanced approach to project his retirement needs. He expects that the after-tax returns on his investments will average 9 percent, and future inflation will average 5 percent.

Questions
1   What is the target amount he would need in this investment fund?
2   What is his current savings target, given the target investment fund?
3   Where might Steve consider placing these additional funds for retirement?

Case 17.2
Janet Myrnic Considers Changing Jobs

Janet has been offered an executive position at a competing firm. The salary is substantially above what her present employer is paying. Therefore, it is very likely she will accept the offer.

However, before leaving her old job, she would like to review her participation in that company's pension plan and understand her rights. She has participated in the company's defined-contribution plan for the last five years, during which the employer matched each dollar she contributed to the retirement fund. Combined contributions currently total $11,320.

Questions
1   Under graded vesting, what percentage of these benefits must be vested?
2   Suppose the entire amount in Janet's retirement account were fully vested; how much is she definitely entitled to receive in a lump-sum payment at termination of employment?
3   Assuming she leaves some funds in the retirement plan, what document should she receive at termination?
4   What are her investment options if she decides to receive a lump-sum payment?

Helpful Reading

Bucci, Michael. "Contributions to Savings and Thrift Plans." Monthly Labor Review, November 1990, pp. 28–36.

Coates, Edward M., III. "Profit Sharing Today: Plans and Provisions," Monthly Labor Review, April 1991, pp. 19–25.

Kirkpatrick, David. *"Save Until It's Painful: A Beachcombers Life Takes a Lot of Clams."* Time, February 25, 1991, p. 121.

Nelson, Stephen L. *"See How an IRA Affects Your Retirement Savings; An IRA Analyzer Can Tell You How Much You'll Earn."* PC-Computing, January 1991, p. 262.

Nelson, Stephen L. *"This Retirement Planner Helps You Save for the Golden Years; A Worksheet for Both Lotus 1-2-3 and Microsoft Excel."* PC-Computing, June 1991, p. 267.

Ott, David E. *"Survivor Income Benefits Provided by Employers,"* Monthly Labor Review, June 1991, p. 13.

U.S. Department of Labor. *What You Should Know About the Pension Law.* Pension and Welfare Benefits Administration, U.S. Government Printing Office, Washington, DC, 1988.

Wiatrowski, William J. *"Supplementing Retirement Until Social Security Begins."* Monthly Labor Review, February 1990, pp. 25–29.

Wiatrowski, William J. *"New Survey Data on Pension Benefits."* Monthly Labor Review, August 1991, p. 8.

Willis, Clint. *"How to Protect Your Retirement Money."* Time, November 1991, p. 90.

Woods, John R. *"Pension Coverage Among Private Wage and Salary Workers."* Social Security Bulletin, October 1989, pp. 2–19.

Helpful Contacts

American Association of Retired Persons
1909 K Street, NW, Washington, DC 20049
A nonprofit organization engaged in lobbying for the interests of retired individuals. For a list of lenders of reverse mortgages, contact the AARP Home Equity Information Center, 601 E. Street, NW, Washington, DC 20094.

The National Council for the Aging, Inc.
600 Maryland Avenue, SW, Washington, DC 20024. A nonprofit organization providing programs to improve the economic and social conditions of older people. It monitors local employment agencies for older workers.

18

Estate Planning: Dividing Up What's Left

Objectives

1 To understand the purpose of a will

2 To appreciate the need for an attorney's help in writing a will

3 To recognize what may happen if you die without a will

4 To be able to plan for transfers outside the will

5 To discuss the different kinds of trusts

6 To explain the relationship between the federal gift tax and the federal estate tax

Drafting an
Heir-Tight Will

Historians are still not sure who were the real beneficiaries of the will of Daniel Clark, a wealthy merchant who owned a good deal of New Orleans when he died in 1813. Clark left most of his property, valued at $18 million, to his business partners, ignoring the claim of his illegitimate daughter Myra, who under Louisiana law was entitled to half his estate. Myra contested the will, and the battle raged through the Civil War, Reconstruction, and 15 appeals to the U.S. Supreme Court.

Finally, in 1891, the Supreme Court awarded $577,000 to Myra's estate, but by then she'd been dead for six years and had spent more than $600,000 pursuing her case.

"What you leave at your death," wrote Sir Thomas Browne, a 17th-century English physician, "let it be without controversy, else the lawyers will be your heirs." His advice is as true today as it was then. Yet two-thirds of adult Americans are courting such controversy because they don't even

have a will. Only in a will can you dispose of property that is not in joint name or held in trust, provide for a live-in lover, make specific bequests to family and friends, name a guardian for your minor children, and appoint an executor to settle your estate.

SOURCE: Excerpted from Mark Reiter, "Estate Planning: Drafting an Heir-Tight Will." Reprinted from the June 1984 issue of *Money* magazine by special permission; © 1984, Time Inc. All rights reserved.

Death estate: Property and wealth transferred at death.

Upon death, the property you leave is termed your **death estate.** It should be large enough to provide for the care and support of the surviving spouse and children. In Chapter 10 on life insurance, we examined methods for estimating the needed support for survivors, and how that support may be funded through accumulated savings and life insurance. However, all your planning and all your saving may accomplish little if your estate is squandered on legal costs or is transferred to the wrong individual. To make sure this does not happen, you will need some expert advice. Estate planning is not a do-it-yourself project. For small estates the help of an attorney may prove sufficient, but for large estates, especially those over $600,000, the aid of either an accountant or a financial planner specializing in estate transfer should also be enlisted.

Estate planning has two basic objectives: one, to transfer your assets at death in a manner consistent with your wishes, and two, to transfer those assets as intact as possible. The first objective can be achieved through a well-thought-out will. Depending on the amount and nature of your wealth, the second objective can be either very simple or very difficult.

Transferring Your Estate Through a Will

Intestate: To die without a valid will.

As mentioned in the vignette that began this chapter, an overwhelming number of Americans die each year without a valid will. In these situations the deceased is said to have died **intestate.** When this occurs, the state supplies a ready-made will dividing the estate according to that state's laws of intestacy. The division is uniquely determined by each state, but the laws generally follow the format outlined in Figure 18.1.

The chance is very small that the state-mandated distribution of your assets will reflect your own desires. In fact, for many families with minor children, the distribution directed by the state is likely to run counter to the best interest of the family. Typically, under the laws of intestacy a surviving spouse with children

Survivors	Division of Property
Spouse and one child	Spouse and child each receive one-half
Spouse and two or more children	Spouse receives one-third. The other two-thirds is divided equally among the children
Spouse and parents surviving, no children	Spouse receives 50–75% of estate, surviving parents receive the rest
Spouse surviving, no children and parents deceased	Spouse receives 50–100% of estate, surviving brothers and sisters receive remaining balance
Parents surviving, no spouse or children	Parents receive all
Brother(s) and/or sister(s) surviving, no spouse or children, parents deceased	Brother(s) and/or sister(s) receive equal shares

FIGURE 18.1

Possible division of estate under intestate provisions.

receives only one-half to one-third of the estate. The rest is distributed to the children of the deceased. For those who have not yet reached the age of majority, court-appointed trustees will have to manage these funds in the children's interest. The surviving spouse may then be required to gain the agreement of the trustees on how and when these funds may be spent. For most families, this arrangement is undesirable and inconvenient. In addition, the associated administrative and legal costs may use up resources needed to support the surviving spouse and children.

The intentions of the state are good. It ensures that the interest of those least able to defend themselves, minor children, are protected. However, most children don't need protection from their parents. Through the use of a will, we can apportion the estate in a manner that more conveniently and adequately serves the needs of the entire family unit.

The Last Will and Testament

Will: A legal declaration of how you wish your property to be disposed of at your death.

A **will** is a legal declaration of how you wish your property to be disposed of at your death. It should be drawn up only with the supervision of an attorney knowledgeable in estate planning. The presence of an attorney is essential because there are a myriad of reasons for declaring a will invalid and contesting the

Being of Sound Mind
and Sound Software

"Create a legal will in under an hour. No stress, no lawyers."

"Create binding legal documents on any PC!"

". . . the program designed to help you protect your family and your assets."

Do-it-yourself wills can be attractive to personal computer owners. PC users know the power of the PC and the appropriate software to act as an electronic savant doing the owner's bidding. Just think of all the advantages to these programs.

First, there's the privacy of writing a will without having to reveal your wishes to another living soul. Then, there's the peace of mind from knowing you took care of a matter that you have put off for too long. And, finally, there's the satisfaction that for less than $100—and in some cases for much less than that—you can create a legally binding document on a computer and avoid expensive attorney's fees.

But a judge who reviewed the final wills produced by three software packages urges do-it-yourselfers to be careful. Judge George A. Gounaris, a Montgomery County, Ohio, probate judge, said he has seen the heartaches that result when a will maker's intended wishes fail to happen because of a poorly written will.

All three computer-generated wills would hold up in an Ohio probate court, Gounaris said. That wasn't the problem. The judge was concerned about whether each will accurately expressed the wishes of the will maker.

If you do write your own will, then the judge recommends that you have an attorney review it afterwards. He recalled the example of a man who decided to write his own will and that of his wife, all in one document. He included all the nice wording found in wills, and then wrote, "In the event I predecease her, all of my estate goes to my wife. In the event my wife predeceases me, all of her estate goes to me."

The will was correct in every way except that paragraph, Gounaris said.

The law doesn't provide for the inclusion of one person's will in the middle of another will. In effect, it left his wife with no will. She could die intestate, a legal term for having no will.

The software isn't equipped to explain these fine legal points to the user, who might be unaware of the potential hazard. As another example, the judge cited a case in which the will maker left an estranged son a pittance of money and instructions that it be used to buy a hanging rope. The father wanted to make it clear he thought his son should hang himself.

The son refused to take receipt of the bequest and held up the completion of probate indefinitely, to the dismay of the other relatives—not the deceased's intentions at all.

Had the father retained a lawyer to review his do-it-yourself will, perhaps potential problems with the son and probate could have been avoided. "It's not the computer's will," the judge said. "It's not the lawyer's will. It's your will. And you want it right."

SOURCE: Excerpted from Judith L. Schultz, "Being of Sound Mind and Software," *Dayton Daily News*, February 4, 1991, pp. 10–11.

distribution of the estate. For example, unless the will is properly witnessed, according to state-mandated guidelines, you may not have a valid will. Should the will be declared invalid for any reason, the estate will be distributed under the laws of intestacy. Unfortunately, as the case of Daniel Clark illustrates, an improperly written will that does not foreclose future court proceedings may be more costly to your intended beneficiaries than dying with no will at all. With the advice and supervision of an attorney, you should be able to avoid this possibility and still accomplish a desirable division of your assets.

Your estate planning objectives will not be achieved if you simply write a will and then forget it. Review the document periodically, to ensure that it reflects your current familial status and needs. Additionally, be sure to review your will whenever you change your state of residency or your family structure. Don't assume that just because you previously wrote a will with the help of a knowledgeable attorney that it is necessarily still valid. The laws differ among states, and a valid will in one state may be invalid in another.

A person who leaves a valid will is said to die **testate,** and is referred to as either the **testator** or the **testatrix.** The correct suffix depends on whether the person is a male, requiring a *tor* ending, or a female, requiring a *trix* ending. You as the testator or testatrix can accomplish several objectives through the use of will. You can name the executor for your estate. You can choose the guardian for your children. You can specify how your estate should be divided among beneficiaries. And finally, you can create investment trusts to provide for the future support and welfare of the beneficiaries.

NAMING AN EXECUTOR The person named in the will who manages your estate from the time of death until all the assets are distributed is called the **executor** or **executrix.** Because he or she is given extensive powers to handle your affairs and distribute your property according to your wishes, you must pick someone who is exceedingly trustworthy. Furthermore, discuss your choice with your potential executor, explaining what is required and who might provide additional information on the handling of your estate. This information should also be contained in the "letter of last instructions" discussed later. If you die without a will, or the named executor refuses to serve, the court chooses some-one termed the **administrator** or **administratrix** to handle your estate. This choice may not coincide with your own desires.

An executor will normally be paid a fee for services performed, but the person you select may agree to serve free. More important, unless the will specifically states otherwise, the executor will be required to post a bond to cover any poten-tial mismanagement of the estate. This is expensive and will eventually be charged to the estate. Assuming you have picked a trustworthy individual, you may waive the need for posting bond in the will.

SPECIFYING GUARDIANSHIP For those who have children, the will is used to name a guardian in the event both parents die before the children reach the age of majority. As in the case of executor, you should make sure the proposed guardian will accept the assigned role. If you leave surviving children without a named guardian, or the named guardian refuses to serve, the court chooses one. In some cases this assignment provides the incentive for a lengthy and emotional custody battle among relatives. A potentially undesirable outcome is that guardianship of the children may be split. Consequently, brothers and sisters may grow up emo-tionally and physically separated from each other.

DIVIDING THE ESTATE In the will you also indicate how your property should be disposed of. You may divide your estate up into percentage shares or provide for absolute dollar payments for each beneficiary. You may also make a specific **bequest,** also termed a **legacy,** leaving a specific item of property to a particular individual.

Most property is divided up under either a per capita or a per stirpes division. Suppose Arnold and Sharon Steele have two grandchildren by their son, John, as illustrated in Figure 18.2. Furthermore, assume John dies before his parents. At Arnold's and Sharon's subsequent death, how will their property be divided

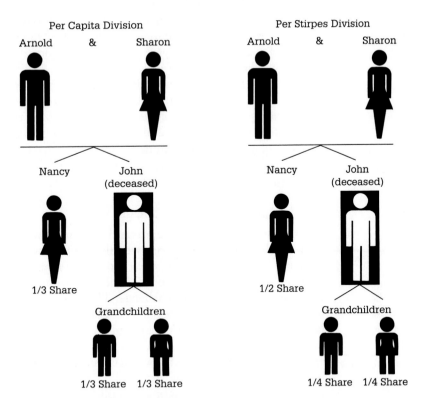

Per Capita Division

Arnold & Sharon

Nancy   John (deceased)

1/3 Share

Grandchildren

1/3 Share   1/3 Share

Per Stirpes Division

Arnold & Sharon

Nancy   John (deceased)

1/2 Share

Grandchildren

1/4 Share   1/4 Share

FIGURE 18.2

Alternative Estate
Distributions.

Per capita division: One in
which the inheritance is
divided equally among
surviving family members.

Per stirpes division: One in
which the inheritance is
divided equally among
branches of the family.

among the grandchildren and the surviving daughter, Nancy? The answer will depend upon whether the Steeles specified a per capita or a per stirpes distribution in their will. In a **per capita division,** all of the survivors would share equally. One-third would go to Nancy, and one-third would go to each of the grandchildren. In a **per stirpes division,** each *branch* of the family would share equally. In this example, Nancy would receive one-half of the property, and each of John's children would receive one-quarter.

The way in which the estate is divided may affect estate taxes, inheritance taxes, and the income taxes of beneficiaries. In addition, there are some potential legal problems that should be considered. First, property cannot be left directly to minor children. If you have minor children, you will have to provide for their continued support through some kind of trust arrangement. An attorney can help you formulate one that reflects your intentions. Second, who is included and who is not included in your will may determine its validity. Under state law you may have no choice but to leave part of your estate to your spouse. Your failure to do so in your will may later provide the basis for contesting the will's validity. If you wish to leave another close relative, such as a child, out of the will, be sure to state so. Otherwise, this person may successfully argue in court that he or she was inadvertently omitted, meaning the present will is invalid. Obviously, a knowledgeable attorney can provide crucial advice on achieving your estate planning objectives.

Changing or Revoking the Will

If you wish to change only a few specific items in the will, you can do so through a **codicil,** which is usually a one-page document indicating the desired changes in the existing will. Like the initial will, the codicil should also be drawn up and witnessed in a manner satisfying state law. Thus, an attorney should also be used when amending an existing will with a codicil.

For matters that require more than a few simple changes, the old will should be revoked and a new will written. The old will can be revoked by expressly stating so in the new will. What most people do not realize is that a previously valid will may be automatically revoked by a change in family status. Marriage, divorce, or the birth of a child can all automatically revoke an existing will. The exact result of this change will, again, depend upon state law. Naturally, you should consult an attorney whenever family arrangements change.

The Letter of Last Instructions

If you desire, you can leave your relatives with a few well-chosen words, but not in the will, as most TV dramas would have you believe. The will is a tool for attaining certain legal objectives; accordingly, it should not be cluttered up with personal comments. Since the will is a legal document, everything in it is subject to legal interpretation and challenge. Therefore, to minimize the possibility of misinterpretation and conflict, unnecessary statements should be omitted. Your last words of wisdom or insult should be contained in the **letter of last instructions.**

In it you might explain why you structured your bequests as you did, what you hoped to accomplish in the specified distribution of your assets, and what you hope your beneficiaries might accomplish in the future.

The letter of last instructions should also have a more practical objective. It should serve as a road map for your survivors, pointing the way to information on your estate. Since a road map is most useful at the beginning of a trip, inform your beneficiaries where it might be found and keep copies at several locations.

The letter of last instructions should contain a list of your assets and the location of important documents, beginning with the location of your will. You may want to keep a copy of the will along with the letter of last instructions. However, the original will should be kept on file at the attorney's office or, where applicable, at the county office with the register of wills and not in your safe deposit box or home. It may take awhile before the safe deposit box may be opened after your death, and wills left at home have been known to disappear.

Be sure to provide information on life insurance policies, death and survivor benefits under pension plans, and your financial holdings. Such readily available information can save the executor considerable time and expense when taking inventory of your estate. Also provide the names of individuals who are familiar with the operation of your estate, such as your stockbroker, accountant, lawyer, and financial planner. The executor may have to rely on their help in the management and distribution of your assets.

Probate

Probate is the name for the court process in which assets are transferred subject to the will or the laws of intestacy. A special court, known as the probate court,

Codicil: An amendment to an existing will, modifying or explaining specific items.

Letter of last instructions: A document providing advice on the management of your death estate and the distribution of your assets.

Probate: A court process in which assets are transferred according to a will or the laws of intestacy.

exists to handle the transferal of death estates. The proceedings in this court may be divided into the seven major steps listed in Figure 18.3.

In the first step the court determines whether a valid will exists. If there is one, the named executor oversees the rest of the process. In the absence of a valid will, the court will appoint an administrator to help manage the probate process.

Lately, many attorneys and financial planners have been strongly critical of the probate process. They have argued that it is too costly and has led to unfortunate delays in the transferal of the death estate, producing a prolonged disruption in the lives of the survivors. Probate costs can average from about 3 to 5 percent of the value of the estate, and it can typically take a year to complete the probate process, with larger estates taking many years. To remedy this situation, two suggestions have been put forth, one for governments and one for individuals. The first proposes a **Uniform Probate Code** for adoption by state legislatures. Some states have already enacted this code, thus reducing some of the cost and delay associated with the probate process. The second suggests that individuals structure their estates so as to avoid probate.

Not all property is distributed through the will and the probate process. Property may be passed outside of the will. Since probate costs are usually equal to a percentage of the assets transferred, even a partial transfer of assets outside the will can result in cost savings. However, this need not result in any tax savings. Estate taxes are based on the value of the gross estate, which will include property transferred both within and outside of the will.

Uniform Probate Code: A code for standardizing the probate process among the states.

FIGURE 18.3

Seven major steps of probate.

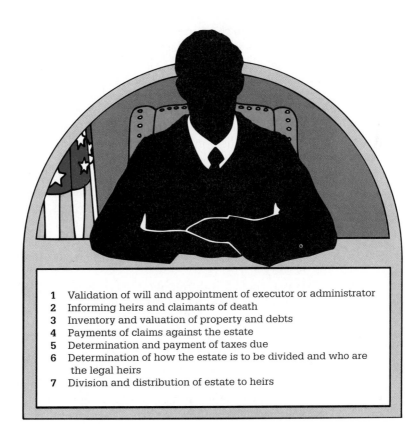

1. Validation of will and appointment of executor or administrator
2. Informing heirs and claimants of death
3. Inventory and valuation of property and debts
4. Payments of claims against the estate
5. Determination and payment of taxes due
6. Determination of how the estate is to be divided and who are the legal heirs
7. Division and distribution of estate to heirs

Transferring Your Estate Outside the Will

One way of transferring property and avoiding probate is to give your assets away while you are still living. Most of us would like to retain control over our property in case of future need, however, so this method isn't always desirable. There are ways in which property may transfer at death, thus leaving us with control while living, and yet still avoiding probate. Joint tenancy, trusts, and contracts are the three most important ways in which this is accomplished. Each has advantages and drawbacks, and none should be entered into just to avoid probate. The indiscriminate use of these estate planning instruments could result in increased tax liabilities, increased estate management costs, and an undesirable distribution of your estate. Accordingly, each should be used with care and forethought, and never as a substitute for a will. Rather, they should be looked upon as individual instruments in your estate planning tool kit.

Joint Tenancy with Right of Survivorship

When property is held under the form of ownership called *joint tenancy with right of survivorship*, it automatically passes at death to the surviving co-owner. It is not distributed through the will and, therefore, avoids probate. In a **joint tenancy,** each owner has an undivided interest in the property, meaning that each has an equal right to make use of and enjoy the entire property.

Married couples are often joint tenants in the ownership of a home. Having a sizable asset such as the home pass outside of probate can result in a significant cost saving. However, on estates large enough to incur estate taxes, a reduction in probate costs should not be a primary objective, because tax liabilities could be much greater. In these situations, the form of ownership for major assets should be discussed with a knowledgeable attorney or tax analyst.

Most estate planners tend to look upon joint tenancy unfavorably, because too many people use it as a substitute for a will. It is not. Even when most of your assets are held in joint tenancy, you still need a will to specify how the property is to be distributed at the death of the surviving owner. Joint tenants who are husband and wife might die simultaneously in an accident; only a will can specify how the jointly held property would then be disposed of.

Joint tenancy can also present problems in life. In some situations a co-owner can dispose of the property without your knowledge or consent, while in others you may need the consent of the co-owner before entering a transaction. This can only make problems worse in troubled marriages or between divorced partners. Furthermore, you should realize that joint tenancy makes your interest in the property liable for claims on the co-owner. When one of the owners is engaged in a business where there are potential liabilities, this tool of estate planning should be avoided.

Married couples with complicated family relationships should also think twice before becoming joint tenants. For example, if both spouses have children from a previous marriage, and all property is held jointly by the couple, the children of the spouse to die first may be left with nothing. The property passes first to the surviving spouse and then probably to the children of the surviving spouse.

Joint tenancy should not be confused with other forms of multiple ownership such as *tenancy in common* or *community property*. **Tenancy in common** is similar to joint tenancy in that each owner shares an undivided interest, even when each owns an unequal share. However, an important difference for estate planning is

Joint tenancy: A form of ownership in which each co-owner has an undivided interest in the property, and the property passes to the co-owner at death.

Tenancy in common: A form of ownership in which each co-owner has an undivided interest in the property, but the property can be individually transferred.

Box 18.2
Saving Money

Medicaid Planning:
The Controversial Side
of Estate Planning

Statistics show that one out of four Americans over the age of 65 will go into a nursing home. But a nursing home can cost $25,000 to $70,000 a year, and the government won't pick up the bill until you have virtually no assets.

Welcome to the world of Medicaid planning, where the primary goal is to shift assets, divert income, and structure finances so that you can get Medicaid coverage without leaving your spouse bankrupt.

It is also one of the more controversial aspects of planning. Medicaid planning has been characterized by many as the province of welfare cheats. The field makes even advocates of senior citizens uncomfortable. The American Association of Retired Persons, for example, deliberately chooses not to advise people on Medicaid planning, which it sees as outside "the spirit of the law," says AARP health lobbyist Tricia Smith.

To qualify for Medicaid, a joint federal-state program for the poor, a person must be 65 years or older (or blind or physically or mentally disabled) and be within the state's income limit. Typically, a Medicaid recipient's assets can't total more than $2,000, although some states set the amount higher.

But not all assets are counted when determining Medicaid eligibility. Consider a couple of hypothetical examples.

John and Mary own a $400,000 house and have put most of their life savings into annuity contracts that produce income payable to Mary. When John enters a nursing home, he qualifies for Medicaid immediately. The reason: The house is a noncountable asset and the spouse gets to keep all of her own income.

Frederic and Martha rent an apartment in Boston but own a $200,000 condominium in Florida. They have $200,000 in stocks and bonds. When Frederic enters a Massachusetts nursing home, he gets no Medicaid until he has exhausted $333,520 of his assets. Why? His assets are all countable, and his wife gets to retain only half of their assets up to $66,480.

Clearly, paying attention to what is countable and where the income goes makes a big difference in who ends up footing the nursing-home bill.

Here's how it works. At the time someone enters a nursing home, a "snapshot" of family assets is taken to determine the spouse's share. With a married couple, the assets that aren't counted typically include the family home and household belongings, a segregated burial account, burial plots, some life insurance policies, and one automobile.

The goal of Medicaid planning is to take advantage of the noncountable assets to shelter assets, to shift income to the healthy spouse, and to either give away assets or put them safely into a variety of trusts that shield them from Medicaid.

One option is to use the family home, says Mr. Budish, a Cleveland Lawyer. For instance, he says, a couple who own a home and have $100,000 in the bank when the husband enters a nursing home might use the following strategy: After establishing and separating the wife's share of assets, the husband could take his $50,000 and pay off the mortgage, put a new roof on the house, and buy a refrigerator. "It protects those funds," says Mr. Budish. "The next day you can go to Medicaid and say, 'I qualify.'"

SOURCE: Excerpted from Lynn Asinof, "Medicaid Planning: Shielding Assets from Uncle Sam," *The Wall Street Journal*, May 23, 1991, p. C1. Reprinted by permission of The Wall Street Journal, © 1991 Dow Jones & Company, Inc. All Rights Reserved Worldwide.

that the property does not necessarily pass to the co-owner(s) at death. Each owner can transfer his or her share in the tenancy in common as desired in both life and death. Thus, ownership will pass through the will the same as individually owned property.

Some states employ the concept of **community property.** This is property acquired during the marriage from the joint efforts of husband and wife. Each is assumed to share equally in the ownership of such assets. Upon the death of either spouse, community property is treated much the same as in tenancy in common. The surviving spouse receives one-half of the property. The other half is disposed of through the will of the deceased spouse or through the laws of intestacy.

Community property: Recognized in some states, it is property acquired during the marriage by the joint efforts of husband and wife.

575

Trusts

Trust: A legal arrangement in which property is held by one party for the benefit of another.

Trustee: The one who controls the property in a trust.

Beneficiary: The one who is to benefit from the trust.

Fiduciary responsibility: A legal responsibility to manage the trust in the best interests of the beneficiary.

Grantor: The one who establishes and funds the trust.

Testamentary trust: A trust that takes effect at death.

Inter vivos or living trust: A trust that takes effect during the grantor's lifetime.

Revocable trust: A trust that can be changed or revoked by the grantor.

Irrevocable trust: A trust that cannot be changed by the grantor once it is established.

A **trust** is an arrangement whereby the right to property is held by one party, the **trustee,** for the benefit of another, the **beneficiary.** The trustee is said to have a **fiduciary responsibility** to the beneficiary. This means that the trustee has a legal obligation to manage the trust in the best interests of the beneficiary. If the trustee does not honor this obligation, he or she may be held liable for any damages suffered by the beneficiary.

The person who establishes and funds the trust is known as the **grantor.** The grantor may arrange for the trust to become operational either at his or her death, or while the grantor is still alive. Each arrangement can play an important role in estate planning.

A trust specified in the will and taking effect at death is called a **testamentary trust.** The most common reason for including a testamentary trust in a will is to provide for the support and care of dependent children. A minor cannot receive the proceeds from an estate directly. When property is left to a minor and the funds are not placed in a testamentary trust, the court will create a trust fund to manage the bequest in the minor's interest. By preempting the court, you can specify who will manage the fund, for what purpose the funds may be used, and when the funds may be paid out.

Since funding for a testamentary trust must be specified in the will, the trust funds are generally liable for both probate costs and estate taxes. An **inter vivos trust** is one established during the grantor's lifetime and is also termed a **living trust.** Funds in a living trust pass outside the will and the probate process, saving probate costs. This occurs because probate includes only those items held in the name of the deceased. The property in a living trust is held in the name of the trust.

Although funds in a living trust escape probate, they still may be taxable as part of the decedent's estate. The deciding factor for estate tax liability is whether the trust fund is *revocable* or *irrevocable*. A **revocable trust** can be changed or revoked by the grantor at any time. In reality the property still remains under the control of the person who established the trust and is therefore part of the deceased's taxable estate. The same is not true for an **irrevocable trust.** The terms of an irrevocable trust cannot be changed after it is established. Thus, the grantor loses all effective future control of the property placed in the trust, which eliminates future estate tax liabilities but creates immediate gift tax liabilities. Naturally, irrevocable trusts should be set up only after considerable forethought.

In a living trust, the grantor, the trustee, and the beneficiary may all be the same person. Setting up a revocable living trust that provides for your own welfare while you are still alive and then for the welfare of your survivors after your death is often suggested in the popular financial literature as an ideal method of avoiding probate. One book on the subject even has tear-out forms for setting up your own living trust.

As discussed previously, estate planning is not a do-it-yourself project. If you are considering setting up a revocable living trust, you would probably be better off if you first discussed the matter with an attorney specializing in estate planning. You might learn that this arrangement has both advantages and disadvantages. Property placed in the trust is not so easily exchanged as property outside the trust. Moreover, if you want an attorney to write the living trust and provide support in funding it, you will find that legal costs exceed those associated with writing a will. Furthermore, even if you have a living trust, you may still need a will. Such things as naming a guardian for your children can be accomplished only through a will.

The trust arrangement in the hands of knowledgeable estate planner is like a scalpel in the hands of a skilled surgeon. It can accomplish the seemingly impossible in appropriately caring for beneficiaries and in minimizing death taxes. However, in the hands of a layperson it may cause nothing but trouble.

Contractual Transfers

Life insurance policies, retirement plans, and bank accounts are all contractual relationships, the benefits of which can be assigned directly to beneficiaries, thus passing outside the will.

In states that have adopted the Uniform Probate Code, a bank account with the designation, "Arnold Steele, payable on death to Sharon Steele," would pass directly to Sharon at Arnold's death. In other states the same type of transfer may be accomplished through a **trustee bank account.** The designation for this type of account would be "Arnold Steele, as trustee for Sharon Steele."

Because no trust is actually created, the terminology used in setting up a trustee bank account is confusing. In the present example, Arnold would not owe Sharon any fiduciary responsibility. Moreover, Sharon would have absolutely no right to the bank account while Arnold is alive. However, at his death, the funds in the account would pass directly to Sharon, thus circumventing probate.

Trustee bank account: A bank account that provides for a contractual transfer of ownership at death.

Death Taxes and Other Related Tax Issues

Death tax: A tax on property either transferred or received at death.

Estate tax: A tax imposed on the property of the deceased before transfer.

Inheritance tax: A tax paid by the beneficiary on property received as an inheritance.

Gift tax: A tax imposed upon gifts transferred during life.

A tax on the property transferred or received upon the death of the owner is known as a **death tax.** There are two types of death taxes: an estate tax and an inheritance tax. An **estate tax** is imposed on the property of the deceased before it is transferred; an **inheritance tax** is levied on the property when it is received by the beneficiary. At the federal level, only an estate tax exists. However, state governments impose either estate or inheritance taxes, and sometimes both.

Most discussions of death taxes also include an examination of gift taxes. This is because an effective estate or inheritance tax presupposes the existence of a tax on gifts. Without a **gift tax,** any estate taxes can be avoided by simply giving away your belongings before you die.

The Federal Gift Tax

In 1976 Congress passed a unified rate schedule that applies identical tax rates to taxable gifts and taxable estates. The rate structure is progressive, with a maximum rate of 50 percent on taxable estates over $2.5 million. When you consider that the income generating this wealth has already been subject to an income tax, the rates do seem high. However, they apply only after generous exclusions and exemptions, and reduction by the unified tax credit on gifts and estates of $192,800. This is enough to completely offset the tax liability on taxable gifts and estates of $600,000 or less.

577

Box 18.3
Simplifying Personal Finance

Living Trust Hoopla
Bears a Close Look

Everyone from attorneys and charitable organizations to do-it-yourself promoters seems to be touting living trusts these days, as a way to avoid the horrors of probate court. But all that hoopla troubles a number of lawyers and others who specialize in estate planning. They express concern that living trusts are being overpromoted and misleadingly marketed in an atmosphere of hype.

A living trust can, indeed, be a useful tool for someone with lots of assets, especially in states with lengthy probate procedures and high costs for settling wills, these estate-planning specialists say. But, they add, the trusts don't cut estate taxes and, if not executed properly, they can result in costly legal fees and years of litigation.

The biggest selling point of a living trust is that nothing passes through probate, the often expensive and time-consuming court process for administering a will. In California, where living trusts have gained tre-

mendous popularity, the typical will takes 18 months to two years to go through probate, say Graydon Calder, a San Diego financial planner specializing in estate planning.

Alexander A. Bove, Jr., a Boston lawyer, says probate costs can run as high as 3 to 5 percent of the assets in the estate. Assets in a living trust can be disposed of more quickly and at a lower administrative cost, he says.

A living trust also avoids the publicity of probate, in which the estate becomes part of public record. And for a person who becomes incapacitated, a living trust is one way to avoid the legal proceedings required to appoint a guardian.

How smoothly a living trust can work is illustrated by the case of John Woods, a San Diego widower who died two years ago of cancer at the age of 80. Mr. Woods had previously transferred his home, bank accounts, stocks held at a brokerage firm, and mutual funds into a living trust with Mr. Calder. When Mr. Wood died, Mr. Calder says it took "only a matter of hours" to distribute the assets in the trust following Mr. Wood's instructions. The cost of the trust: $500. "It would have taken two years to administer the will in probate court," Mr. Calder says.

But living trusts aren't for everyone and every situation. In New York pro-

bate takes only 30 days. Also, you can't place ownership of a co-op apartment in a living trust in New York. In some states, bank and savings and loan officials who aren't familiar with living trusts may be reluctant to refinance property that is titled in the name of a trust, specialists say.

In addition, with a living trust, a person must follow through. A large number of people who pay to set up living trusts fail to place all their major assets in the trusts, limiting the device's effectiveness.

For a married couple with uncomplicated assets, a living trust may not be worth the effort. All jointly owned property, life insurance proceeds, retirement and pension plan money go directly to the named beneficiaries without passing through probate, says William Brennan, CPA partner in Earnst & Young's Washington office. "There are people who are setting up living trusts to save their assets from probate where the money wouldn't have gone through probate anyway."

SOURCE: Excerpted from Earl C. Gottschalk, Jr., "Living Trust Hoopla Bears a Close Look," *The Wall Street Journal*, February 11, 1991, p. C1. Reprinted by permission of the Wall Street Journal © 1991. Dow Jones & Company, Inc. All Rights Reserved Worldwide.

Taxable gifts: The value of gifts less excludable amounts.

To understand how the federal gift tax and the unified credit operate, you must first be able to calculate **taxable gifts,** as illustrated in Figure 18.4. Taxable gifts equal the total value of gifts made during the year less the annual exclusion per recipient, gifts to charitable institutions, amounts paid to medical and educational institutions for services provided the recipient, and amounts given to a spouse.

The annual exclusion per recipient is $10,000. Through the yearly application of this exclusion, a good part of many estates can be transferred tax-free over the donor's lifetime. For example, suppose you have three children and you transfer $10,000 to each one. Accordingly, $30,000 could be transferred each year without incurring a gift tax. Moreover, if you are married, each spouse is entitled to a

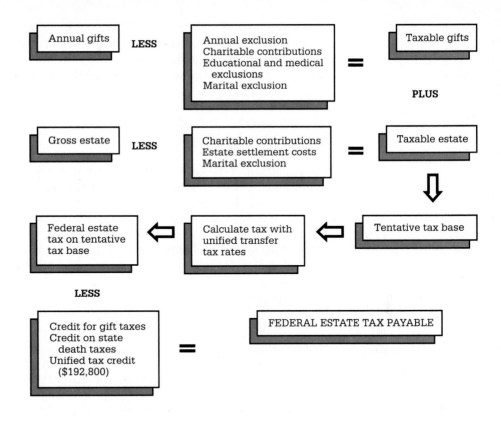

FIGURE 18.4

Taxable transfers.

$10,000 exclusion per recipient, so that in this situation $60,000 in yearly transfers would escape the gift tax.

Even if you have a taxable gift, you will probably not have to pay a gift tax. For example, if the taxable gifts for this and previous years total less than $600,000, then the unified tax credit could be used to offset the entire amount due.

The Federal Estate Tax

Taxable estate: The gross estate less excludable amounts.

Gross estate: Everything owned at death less indebtedness.

Marital exclusion: The value of property transferred to the spouse which is excluded from taxable transfers.

That part of the unified tax credit not used to offset gift taxes may be applied to reduce federal estate taxes on the **taxable estate.** To calculate the taxable estate, you must first begin with an estimate of the **gross estate.** This figure equals the value of everything owned at the moment of death, including life insurance proceeds when the policy is owned by the deceased, less indebtedness. The gross estate is then reduced by the marital deduction, estate settlement costs, and charitable contributions to arrive at the taxable estate.

The **marital exclusion** is equal to the value of the property transferred to the spouse. Since 1982 there has been an unlimited deduction for such transfers, whether by gift or at death. Accordingly, regardless of the size of the estate, the property received by one spouse at the death of the other will transfer free of federal estate taxes.

579

For nonspousal transfers there will be a taxable estate. However, the unused portion of the unified tax credit may eliminate all or most of the tentative estate tax. For example, suppose the last surviving parent is leaving a taxable estate of $500,000, and that this individual made taxable gifts of $200,000. On the combined tentative tax base of $700,000, estate and gift taxes would amount to $229,800. When we subtract from this the unified tax credit of $192,800, federal estate taxes payable are reduced to only $37,000. This is slightly more than 5 percent of the taxable transfers.

However, it is possible that even this minimal tax could have been avoided by transferring part of the estate to the children at the death of the first parent and the remainder of the estate at the death of the second parent. In this manner, $600,000 in transfers could have been excluded at each death, eliminating potential gift and estate taxes on $1,200,000 of taxable transfers.

TRUSTS AND SPOUSAL TRANSFERS Through the use of trusts you can accomplish several important estate planning tasks simultaneously: You can provide for the lifetime support of a surviving spouse, you can determine whether the property used to provide the lifetime support should be included in your own or your spouse's taxable estate, and finally, you can determine who chooses the ultimate beneficiary of the estate at the death of the surviving spouse. The types and characteristics of trusts used for these purposes are summarized in Table 18.1.

Suppose you want to take advantage of the unified tax credit at your death. As explained previously, this would reduce the size of the surviving spouse's taxable estate, possibly eliminating a future estate tax liability. This could be accomplished if you left the property directly to your children. But you hesitate to do this, because you feel the assets might be needed for the support of the surviving spouse. A **bypass trust** (also called a nonmarital trust) could eliminate your dilemma.

Bypass trust: Provides lifetime support for the surviving spouse, but bypasses the death estate of that spouse.

A bypass trust provides for the life support of the surviving spouse. At the death of the surviving spouse the remainder in the trust passes to beneficiaries named by the initial creator of the trust. Since the surviving spouse has no say in who ultimately receives the trust, the trust would not be included in the death estate of the surviving spouse. The property of the trust therefore bypasses the estate of the surviving spouse. The property in the bypass trust is included in the taxable estate of the creator. However, if the taxable estate of the creator is less than $600,000, the unified tax credit will eliminate all tax liabilities.

Alternatively, suppose you want to take advantage of the marital exclusion and provide for the life support of a surviving spouse. In this case, property used to fund the trust would be excluded from the initial spouse's death estate but in-

TABLE 18.1 • Trusts and Estate Planning

	Qualifies for Marital Deduction	Surviving Spouse Has Right to Appoint Beneficiary	Included in Deceased Spouse's Estate	Included in Surviving Spouse's Estate
Marital trusts				
Power of appointment	Yes	Yes	No	Yes
Q-TIP	Yes	No	No	Yes
Bypass trusts (nonmarital trusts)	No	No	Yes	No

cluded in the estate of the last spouse to die. This could be accomplished through a **marital trust.**

A marital trust typically provides the surviving spouse with the power to appoint the ultimate beneficiary. Suppose you want to provide for the future support of a surviving spouse. On the other hand, you are worried your spouse might squander your estate or even remarry and leave the remainder to someone other than your children. Therefore, you might want to deny the surviving spouse the right to appoint the ultimate beneficiaries of the trust. A special kind of marital trust called a **Q-TIP** trust (a qualified terminable interest property trust) would satisfy all your objectives. It denies the surviving spouse the right to appoint beneficiaries, while at the same time qualifying for the marital exclusion.

INTERGENERATIONAL TRANSFERS   An intergenerational transfer is any transfer of property from one generation to another. A transfer of money from parents to children, or from grandparents to grandchildren, would be an intergenerational transfer.

It is possible to make direct transfers and create trusts that skip a generation. For example, a transfer from grandparent to grandchildren while the grandchildren's parents were living would skip a generation. Such transfers would also skip being included in the grandchildren's parents' death estate, and thus avoid a whole generation of death/estate taxes. The **Generation Skipping Transfer Tax (GST)** is meant to close this loophole partially by levying a special tax of 50 percent on generation-skipping transfers. The tax is only applied, however, after a liberal $1 million exclusion.

Federal Income Taxes

Most of us are not wealthy enough to worry about the gift or estate tax. However, the method in which our property is distributed can still be important because it may determine federal income taxes paid by the beneficiaries. In some situations it may be preferable to let the property transfer at death rather than as a gift. For example, suppose Sharon Steele lived in a non-community property state and owned exclusively under her own name some shares of stock with an original cost of $5,000 and a current market value of $15,000. If she sold the shares today, she would have to pay tax on the $10,000 gain in value. However, if she died today, and Arnold received these shares as a death transfer and then subsequently sold the stocks for $15,000, there would be no capital gains tax to pay. This is because the property of the deceased receives a stepped-up cost basis for tax purposes, set by the executor either at the time of death or at an alternative valuation date six months after the death. Thus, if the shares are valued at $15,000 at the time of the death and later sold for the same amount, no capital gains taxes are due.

On the other hand, if Sharon had made Arnold a gift of the stock before her supposed death, there would be a $5,000 cost basis when Arnold sold the stock. The recipient of a gift must assume the donor's cost basis when the property has appreciated in value. The basic rule of thumb is that you let those goods that have appreciated in market value transfer at death rather than as gifts. In this way a new cost basis is established, and potential capital gains taxes are eliminated.

Alternatively, don't bequeath property that has depreciated in value. The beneficiary will not be able to receive the tax benefit from the capital loss. Don't give

Background   Most of the Steeles' major assets, including their home, the cars, and the bank accounts, are owned by Arnold and Sharon in joint tenancy. The other important assets, such as life insurance policies and retirement accounts, have assigned beneficiaries. Given that the terms of ownership of their assets already provide for their disposition upon the death of either Sharon or Arnold, and that they both would feel comfortable with any of their close relatives assuming the role of guardian, the Steeles have not felt the need to draw up a will.

The Problem   Recently, one of Arnold's co-workers, who was not much older than Arnold, suffered a stroke and died. Since he mentioned this news to Sharon, she has been urging Arnold to consult an attorney and have a will drawn up. She now feels they have reached the time in life when they should take a more formal approach to estate planning. However, Arnold still wonders whether the will is worth the cost of the attorney's fee. He has suggested to Sharon they get one of those books with tear-out forms telling you how to write a will without consulting an attorney.

The Plan   The Steeles have erred in not having a will drawn up before now. They should contact an attorney specializing in estate planning immediately and have wills drawn up for both of them. If Arnold wants to save money, he should consider changing the oil in the family cars, rather than writing his own will. The attorney's fee is likely to be much less expensive than the financial mess that would ensue were both Arnold and Sharon to die without a valid will. In the absence of a valid will, the courts would have to pick an administrator for the estate, choose a guardian for the children, and set up a trust fund for their future support. Resolving these matters in the will would cut legal expenses and ease the emotional strain on the surviving children.

If Arnold and Sharon both died intestate, the children would divide the estate equally. However, since both Nancy and John are minors, they could not receive the property directly. Rather, it would be placed in a court-appointed trust and utilized according to terms set down by the court. As each reached the age of majority, Nancy and John would receive whatever amount remained in the trust fund.

Instead of having the court determine how these funds will be managed and used for the support of the children, Arnold and Sharon can decide this by creating a testamentary trust through the will. With a little forethought, they can set up a trust fund that would support the children in much the same way as they do now, not the way the court-imposed trust would do it.

The Steeles will not spend equal amounts on the upbringing of Nancy and John. Families usually provide for their children according to each child's needs, aptitudes, and opportunities. For example, if one child requires special medical care or has a special talent for academics or athletics, the parents might decide to allocate a disproportionate share of the family's resources for the improvement of that child. Through a testamentary trust the Steeles could accomplish much the same. The property could be placed in a single fund that provided for the care and support of both children according to need. Only after the younger child reached the age of majority would what was left be divided equally between the children.

Another important item the Steeles could control in a testamentary trust is the time when each child receives the monies held in trust. The fund need not be dissolved when the child reaches the age of majority, but instead could be delayed until some later age. Furthermore, the entire amount does not have to be paid out at one time. One common provision in testamentary trusts is that only one-half of the value of the trust fund is paid out when the child reaches a specific age. Payment of the other half is delayed for about five years. Consequently, if the child squanders the first payment, he or she gets a second chance to manage the second half more carefully.

Another obvious reason the Steeles need a will is so that they can name a potential guardian for the children. They shouldn't assume that surviving relatives, children, and the courts will all come to a mutually agreeable decision. To avoid misunderstandings and costly litigation, a guardian should be selected. If both the chosen guardian and the children agree with the decision, this person should be named guardian in the will.

While they are at the lawyer's office having the will drawn up, they should also inquire about a **durable power of attorney.** Most of the Steeles' property is held in joint tenancy. Given the family relationships involved, and tax considerations, this form of ownership may be appropriate for them. However, it could present problems were either Arnold or Sharon to become mentally incapable of making financial decisions. The disposition of jointly held property may require the written consent of both tenants.

Durable power of attorney: Allows another to act on your behalf, even if you become incapacitated or disabled.

A *power of attorney* is a written agreement that allows one individual to act on behalf of another. With a power of attorney, another person could act with the same authority over your financial affairs as you would yourself. Even stronger is a *durable* power of attorney, which does not lapse if you become incapacitated or disabled.

The one major drawback of such an arrangement is that it may delegate to your spouse a little more power than is desirable during ordinary times. Accordingly, a knowledgeable attorney may be able to organize your affairs so that the power of attorney does not become operative unless one spouse becomes mentally incapacitated.

With durable powers of attorney and complete wills, the Steeles should be prepared for some of life's worst setbacks.

depreciated property away, either. The best strategy is to take the capital loss yourself. On gifts that have depreciated in value, the cost basis to the recipient is the lower of the cost to the donor, or the fair market value at the time the gift was made. Thus, the recipient of a gift that has depreciated in value since it was purchased by the donor would not be able to take the reduction in value before the property was transferred as a loss for tax purposes.

The type of ownership can also influence income tax liabilities for survivors. If the stocks in the previous example were held in joint tenancy by both Arnold and Sharon, instead of being solely owned by Sharon, then only 50 percent of the shares would have received a stepped-up cost basis at the time of Sharon's supposed death. When a husband and wife enter into a joint tenancy, the assumption is that each owns an undivided interest of 50 percent. Therefore, if Arnold subsequently sold the stock for $15,000, he would pay taxes on only half of the $10,000 capital gain.

You would expect taxes to affect community property in the same way as property in joint tenancy, but they don't. If the stocks in the previous example were acquired during the marriage from the joint efforts of Arnold and Sharon, they would be community property, regardless of whose name they were held in. The entire amount of such community property receives a new cost basis at the death of either partner. In this example, the stocks would have a new cost basis of $15,000 even though they were previously held in Sharon's name.

The exception to this rule proves that the tax code, if nothing else, is meant to be consistent. If property is held in joint tenancy by a husband and wife in a community property state, the community interest is negated, and only 50 percent of the property receives a stepped-up basis.

Funds in qualified retirement plans and individual retirement accounts (see Chapter 17) do not receive a stepped-up basis at death. The deceased is said to have had a zero cost basis in these retirement funds. This means that the funds become fully taxable when withdrawn by the beneficiary.

Inheritance Taxes

The federal government does not impose an inheritance tax. However, 18 states tax inheritances. In all of them, the rates are structured so that the larger the estate and the more distant the relationship to the deceased, the higher is the tax rate. The exact tax rate and the exemption accorded each beneficiary from the tax differ from state to state.

Inheritance tax statutes generally segregates beneficiaries into classes similar to the following:

- Class 1: Spouse
- Class 2: Parents, children, grandparents, lineal descendants
- Class 3: Brothers and sisters, aunts and uncles
- Class 4: Children of brothers and sisters, children of aunts and uncles
- Class 5: All others

Inheritance taxes should play an important role in estate planning by providing an incentive to leave property to closer relatives. Furthermore, because exemptions are low—in one state $5,000 for a spouse—and because rates can be high on large estates, approaching 30 percent, inheritance taxes also provide an incentive for lifetime gifts.

Summary

Estate planning has two primary objectives: first, to transfer your assets at death in a manner consistent with your wishes; and second, to transfer those assets intact insofar as possible. With the advice of professionals, these goals may be accomplished through the use of a will, joint tenancy, revocable and irrevocable trusts, contractual transfers, and gifts. The benefits and disadvantages of each have been examined in this chapter. With proper planning, these methods can be used to minimize the impact on transfers of both death and income taxes.

Key Terms

administrator/administratrix (p. 570)

beneficiary (p. 576)

bequest (p. 570)

bypass trust (p. 580)

codicil (p. 572)

community property (p. 575)

death estate (p. 577)

death tax (p. 577)

durable power of attorney (p. 583)

estate tax (p. 577)

executor/executrix (p. 570)

fiduciary responsibility (p. 576)

Generation Skipping Transfer Tax (GST) (p. 581)

gift tax (p. 577)

grantor (p. 576)

gross estate (p. 579)

inheritance tax (p. 577)

inter vivos trust (p. 576)

intestate (p. 567)

irrevocable trust (p. 576)

joint tenancy (p. 574)

legacy (p. 570)

letter of last instructions (p. 572)

living trust (p. 576)

marital exclusion (p. 579)

marital trust (p. 581)

per capita division (p. 571)

per stirpes division (p. 571)

probate (p. 572)

revocable trust (p. 576)

Q-TIP trust (p. 581)

taxable estate (p. 579)

taxable gifts (p. 578)

tenancy in common (p. 574)

testamentary trust (p. 576)

testate (p. 570)

testator/testatrix (p. 570)

trust (p. 576)

trustee (p. 576)

trustee bank account (p. 577)

Uniform Probate Code (p. 573)

will (p. 568)

Problems and Review Questions

1 What are the basic objectives of estate planning?

2 What does it mean to die intestate? How might your estate be divided if you died intestate?

3 What can be accomplished only through the use of a will? How would these matters be handled in the absence of a will?

4 How may a previous will be revoked?

5 When certain changes occur, it is important that you review your will. What are these changes, and why is it important to review your will when they occur?

6 How does the letter of last instructions differ from the last will and testament? What might be included in one but not the other?

7 For estate planning purposes, what is the difference between *joint tenancy* and *tenancy in common*? When might a husband and wife want to avoid joint tenancy?

8   What is a trust? What obligation does the trustee have?

9   What different types of trusts can be created? Explain how each can affect probate costs and estate taxes.

10 There are two common types of death taxes. What are they, and how do they differ?

11 For an estate tax to be effective, what other type of tax must also exist? Why?

12 Suppose a married couple jointly gave $25,000 to a distant relative during the year. How much of this amount would represent a taxable gift? Under what circumstances would the full amount be nontaxable?

13 Discuss the ways in which a married couple might plan to transfer this estate so as to avoid all federal estate and gift taxes.

14 How is the cost basis of a gift determined for income tax purposes?

15 Discuss how previous ownership of assets by the deceased may affect future income taxes paid by the beneficiaries.

**Case 18.1
Jim and Nancy
Vuduris Purchase
a New Home**

Jim and Nancy recently got married. Each was married before, and each had two children from the previous marriage living with them. Since the new combined family was too large for either of their present homes, they found it necessary to sell the old homes and purchase a single, larger house. They realize that the way in which ownership in the new home is specified will affect their estate planning and future tax liabilities. Accordingly, they plan to consult an attorney before taking title to the new home.

Questions

1   Why are the sale of the old homes and the purchase of a new home important considerations in their estate plan? What types of problems do such transactions create?

2   What are the several ways in which Jim and Nancy might hold ownership in the new home? How might each of these affect future tax liabilities of the survivor at the death of the first?

3   If Jim were to die intestate, how might his ownership in the home be distributed?

**Case 18.2
A Grandchild for
the Trebnicks**

Last night Linda and Gregg received a phone call from their son Matt, telling them their first grandchild had been born, a ten-pound baby girl to be named Marta Trebnick.

The senior Trebnicks have done well over the years. Linda and Gregg invested in some common stocks that have risen enormously in value since they purchased them many years ago. They now have a portfolio of stocks and bonds that is large enough to meet all of their expected retirement needs and then some, but not large enough to make them worry about federal estate taxes. Moreover, they are on a substantial government pension with automatic cost-of-living adjustments.

Given their present financial position, they would like to celebrate the birth by setting up a trust fund to provide for Marta's future college education. They are considering selling some of their stocks that have appreciated in value and placing these funds in the trust.

Questions

1   Given the types of trust funds discussed in this chapter, which one appears most advantageous for the Trebnicks? Explain why.

2   Setting up the trust will have certain tax implications. What are these?

3   Suppose the Trebnicks had an estate large enough to be potentially liable for estate taxes. Would this affect the choice of the most advantageous trust vehicle? How and why?

Helpful Reading

Gordon, Harley. *How to Protect Your Life Savings From Catastrophic Illness and Nursing Homes* (Boston: Financial Planning Institute, 1990).

Mulligan, Michael D. *"Planning for Disabled Children." Best's Review—Life-Health Insurance Edition,* February 1991, p. 75.

Shipley, Chris, and Gregg Keizer. *"You Call All the Shots with a 'Lawyer in a Box; Legal Software,'" PC-Computing* (March 1991), pp. 298–299.

Stewart, C. Jean, and Sandra Honath. *"The Marriage Factor: Estate Planning and Tax Planning During Marriage and Divorce." Best's Review—Life-Health Insurance Edition,* September 1990, p. 57.

Topolnicki, Denise M. *"Why You Might Inherit Less Than You Expect." Money,* November 1991, pp. 47–50.

Weaver, Peter. *"Long-Term-Care Coverage as Inheritance Insurance." Nation's Business,* February 1991, p. 62.

———. *"The Revocable Trust: Better Than a Will." Nation's Business,* July 1990, p. 51.

Time Value of Money Concepts

In Chapter 1 you were introduced to the basic concepts regarding the time value of money. This appendix provides greater detail about these concepts and it also includes present value and future value of $1 tables.

Future Value of a Single Payment

Finding the future value, *FV*, of a sum of money invested today answers the question: "How much will my money grow if I invest it today and leave it in the investment for a specified number of time periods, assuming it earns a specified rate of return each period?" For example, $100 invested for three years and earning 10 percent each year grows to $133.10, as shown below.

$$FV \text{ end of year } 1 = \$100 + 0.10(\$100) = \$110.00$$
$$FV \text{ end of year } 2 = \$110 + 0.10(\$110) = \$121.00$$
$$FV \text{ end of year } 3 = \$121 + 0.10(\$121) = \$133.10$$

The year-by-year solution is long and unnecessary, because there are two much quicker solutions. If you have a calculator, simple use the *FV* of a single payment formula, which is

$$FV = PV(1.0 + i)^n \tag{A1}$$

where *FV* = the future value

     PV = the present value (the amount invested today)
       i = the interest rate per period
      n = the number of periods the *PV* is invested.

In the above example, we have

$$FV = \$100(1.0 + 0.10)^3 = \$100(1.10)^3 = \$100(1.331) = \$133.10$$

The other approach for finding an FV is to refer to a future value (also called compound value) table. These are widely available, and they show the future value of \$1 for various investment periods and rates. Table A.1 illustrates a future value table, and if you go down the left-hand column to period 3 (indicating three holding periods) and across to the 10 percent column, you find the number 1.331. (Of course, this is the same number we have already calculated.) Since this shows the future value of \$1, the final step is to multiply the FV of \$1 by the amount of dollars invested, as we have already done.

Future Value of a Stream of Equal Payments (an Annuity)

Very often an investment program calls for an equal amount invested each period. For example, suppose your budget allows a \$100 investment each year. You are curious about how much you will accumulate at the end of three years, assuming you begin making payments at the end of each of the next three years. This total future value is calculated below:

FV of the payment made at the end of year 1 =
$$\$100(1.10)^2 = \$100(1.21) = \$121.00$$
FV of the payment made at the end of year 2 =
$$\$100(1.10)^1 = \$100(1.10) = \$110.00$$
FV of the payment made at the end of year 3 = $\$100.00$
Total future value = $\$331.00$

Just as in the case of the FV of a single payment, you can use a formula to find the future value of a stream of equal investments—that is, of an annuity. It is

$$FV = \frac{[(1.0 + i)^n - 1.0] \times A}{i} \qquad (A2)$$

where FV, i, and n have the same meaning as before and A = the amount of the annuity.

Substituting the above values, we have

$$FV = \frac{[(1.0 + 0.10)^3 - 1.0] \times 100}{0.10} = \frac{[(1.10)^3 - 1.0] \times 100}{0.10}$$

$$= \frac{(1.331 - 1.0) \times 100}{0.10} = \frac{0.331 \times 100}{0.10} = \frac{33.10}{0.10} = \$331.10$$

There are also future value of an annuity tables that can be consulted for a quick answer. Table A.2 is an example of such a table. To find the answer to the above example, again simply go down to period 3 and across to the 10 percent column to find the answer for the future value of a \$1 annuity invested for three

589

TABLE A.1 • Future Value of $1 at the End of n Periods: $FV = (1.0 + i)^n$

Period	1%	2%	3%	4%	5%	6%	7%	8%	9%	10%	12%	14%	15%	16%	18%	20%	24%	28%	32%	36%
1	1.0100	1.0200	1.0300	1.0400	1.0500	1.0600	1.0700	1.0800	1.0900	1.1000	1.1200	1.1400	1.1500	1.1600	1.1800	1.2000	1.2400	1.2800	1.3200	1.3600
2	1.0201	1.0404	1.0609	1.0816	1.1025	1.1236	1.1449	1.1664	1.1881	1.2100	1.2544	1.2996	1.3225	1.3456	1.3924	1.4400	1.5376	1.6384	1.7424	1.8496
3	1.0303	1.0612	1.0927	1.1249	1.1576	1.1910	1.2250	1.2597	1.2950	1.3310	1.4049	1.4815	1.5209	1.5609	1.6430	1.7280	1.9066	2.0972	2.3000	2.5155
4	1.0406	1.0824	1.1255	1.1699	1.2155	1.2625	1.3108	1.3605	1.4116	1.4641	1.5735	1.6890	1.7490	1.8106	1.9388	2.0736	2.3642	2.6844	3.0360	3.4210
5	1.0510	1.1041	1.1593	1.2167	1.2763	1.3382	1.4026	1.4693	1.5386	1.6105	1.7623	1.9254	2.0114	2.1003	2.2878	2.4883	2.9316	3.4360	4.0075	4.6526
6	1.0615	1.1262	1.1941	1.2653	1.3401	1.4185	1.5007	1.5869	1.6771	1.7716	1.9738	2.1950	2.3131	2.4364	2.6996	2.9860	3.6352	4.3980	5.2899	6.3275
7	1.0721	1.1487	1.2299	1.3159	1.4071	1.5036	1.6058	1.7138	1.8280	1.9487	2.2107	2.5023	2.6600	2.8262	3.1855	3.5832	4.5077	5.6295	6.9826	8.6054
8	1.0829	1.1717	1.2668	1.3686	1.4775	1.5938	1.7182	1.8509	1.9926	2.1436	2.4760	2.8526	3.0590	3.2784	3.7589	4.2998	5.5895	7.2058	9.2170	11.703
9	1.0937	1.1951	1.3048	1.4233	1.5513	1.6895	1.8385	1.9990	2.1719	2.3579	2.7731	3.2519	3.5179	3.8030	4.4355	5.1598	6.9310	9.2234	12.166	15.916
10	1.1046	1.2190	1.3439	1.4802	1.6289	1.7908	1.9672	2.1589	2.3674	2.5937	3.1058	3.7072	4.0456	4.4114	5.2338	6.1917	8.5944	11.805	16.059	21.646
11	1.1157	1.2434	1.3842	1.5395	1.7103	1.8983	2.1049	2.3316	2.5804	2.8531	3.4785	4.2262	4.6524	5.1173	6.1759	7.4301	10.657	15.111	21.198	29.439
12	1.1268	1.2682	1.4258	1.6010	1.7959	2.0122	2.2522	2.5182	2.8127	3.1384	3.8960	4.8179	5.3502	5.9360	7.2876	8.9161	13.214	19.342	27.982	40.037
13	1.1381	1.2936	1.4685	1.6651	1.8856	2.1329	2.4098	2.7196	3.0658	3.4523	4.3635	5.4924	6.1528	6.8858	8.5994	10.699	16.386	24.758	36.937	54.451
14	1.1495	1.3195	1.5126	1.7317	1.9799	2.2609	2.5785	2.9372	3.3417	3.7975	4.8871	6.2613	7.0757	7.9875	10.147	12.839	20.319	31.691	48.756	74.053
15	1.1610	1.3459	1.5580	1.8009	2.0789	2.3966	2.7590	3.1722	3.6425	4.1772	5.4736	7.1379	8.1371	9.2655	11.973	15.407	25.195	40.564	64.358	100.71
16	1.1726	1.3728	1.6047	1.8730	2.1829	2.5404	2.9522	3.4259	3.9703	4.5950	6.1304	8.1372	9.3576	10.748	14.129	18.488	31.242	51.923	84.953	136.96
17	1.1843	1.4002	1.6528	1.9479	2.2920	2.6928	3.1588	3.7000	4.3276	5.0545	6.8660	9.2765	10.761	12.467	16.672	22.186	38.740	66.461	112.13	186.27
18	1.1961	1.4282	1.7024	2.0258	2.4066	2.8543	3.3799	3.9960	4.7171	5.5599	7.6900	10.575	12.375	14.462	19.673	26.623	48.038	85.070	148.02	253.33
19	1.2081	1.4568	1.7535	2.1068	2.5270	3.0256	3.6165	4.3157	5.1417	6.1159	8.6128	12.055	14.231	16.776	23.214	31.948	59.567	108.89	195.39	344.53
20	1.2202	1.4859	1.8061	2.1911	2.6533	3.2071	3.8697	4.6610	5.6044	6.7275	9.6463	13.743	16.366	19.460	27.393	38.337	73.864	139.37	257.91	468.57
21	1.2324	1.5157	1.8603	2.2788	2.7860	3.3996	4.1406	5.0338	6.1088	7.4002	10.803	15.667	18.821	22.574	32.323	46.005	91.591	178.40	340.44	637.26
22	1.2447	1.5460	1.9161	2.3699	2.9253	3.6035	4.4304	5.4365	6.6586	8.1403	12.100	17.861	21.644	26.186	38.142	55.206	113.57	228.35	449.39	866.67
23	1.2572	1.5769	1.9736	2.4647	3.0715	3.8197	4.7405	5.8715	7.2579	8.9543	13.552	20.361	24.891	30.376	45.007	66.247	140.83	292.30	593.19	1178.6
24	1.2697	1.6084	2.0328	2.5633	3.2251	4.0489	5.0724	6.3412	7.9111	9.8497	15.178	23.212	28.625	35.236	53.108	79.496	174.63	374.14	783.02	1602.9
25	1.2824	1.6406	2.0938	2.6658	3.3864	4.2919	5.4274	6.8485	8.6231	10.834	17.000	26.461	32.918	40.874	62.668	95.396	216.54	478.90	1033.5	2180.0
26	1.2953	1.6734	2.1566	2.7725	3.5557	4.5494	5.8074	7.3964	9.3992	11.918	19.040	30.166	37.856	47.414	73.948	114.47	268.51	612.99	1364.3	2964.9
27	1.3082	1.7069	2.2213	2.8834	3.7335	4.8223	6.2139	7.9881	10.245	13.110	21.324	34.389	43.535	55.000	87.259	137.37	332.95	784.63	1800.9	4032.2
28	1.3213	1.7410	2.2879	2.9987	3.9201	5.1117	6.6488	8.6271	11.167	14.421	23.883	39.204	50.065	63.800	102.96	164.84	412.86	1004.3	2377.2	5483.8
29	1.3345	1.7758	2.3566	3.1187	4.1161	5.4184	7.1143	9.3173	12.172	15.863	26.749	44.693	57.575	74.008	121.50	197.81	511.95	1285.5	3137.9	7458.0
30	1.3478	1.8114	2.4273	3.2434	4.3219	5.7435	7.6123	10.062	13.267	17.449	29.959	50.950	66.211	85.849	143.37	237.37	634.81	1645.5	4142.0	10143.
40	1.4889	2.2080	3.2620	4.8010	7.0400	10.285	14.974	21.724	31.409	45.259	93.050	188.88	267.86	378.72	750.37	1469.7	5455.9	19426.	66520.	*
50	1.6446	2.6916	4.3839	7.1067	11.467	18.420	29.457	46.901	74.357	117.39	289.00	700.23	1083.6	1670.7	3927.3	9100.4	46890.	*	*	*
60	1.8167	3.2810	5.8916	10.519	18.679	32.987	57.946	101.25	176.03	304.48	897.59	2595.9	4383.9	7370.1	20555.	56347.	*	*	*	*

TABLE A.2 • Future Value of $1 Annuity: $FV = \left[\dfrac{(1.0 + i)^n - 1.0}{i}\right]$

Number of Periods	1%	2%	3%	4%	5%	6%	7%	8%	9%	10%	12%	14%	15%	16%	18%	20%	24%	28%	32%	36%
1	1.0000	1.0000	1.0000	1.0000	1.0000	1.0000	1.0000	1.0000	1.0000	1.0000	1.0000	1.0000	1.0000	1.0000	1.0000	1.0000	1.0000	1.0000	1.0000	1.0000
2	2.0100	2.0200	2.0300	2.0400	2.0500	2.0600	2.0700	2.0800	2.0900	2.1000	2.1200	2.1400	2.1500	2.1600	2.1800	2.2000	2.2400	2.2800	2.3200	2.3600
3	3.0301	3.0604	3.0909	3.1216	3.1525	3.1836	3.2149	3.2464	3.2781	3.3100	3.3744	3.4396	3.4725	3.5056	3.5724	3.6400	3.7776	3.9184	4.0624	4.2096
4	4.0604	4.1216	4.1836	4.2465	4.3101	4.3746	4.4399	4.5061	4.5731	4.6410	4.7793	4.9211	4.9934	5.0665	5.2154	5.3680	5.6842	6.0156	6.3624	6.7251
5	5.1010	5.2040	5.3091	5.4163	5.5256	5.6371	5.7507	5.8666	5.9847	6.1051	6.3528	6.6101	6.7424	6.8771	7.1542	7.4416	8.0484	8.6999	9.3983	10.146
6	6.1520	6.3081	6.4684	6.6330	6.8019	6.9753	7.1533	7.3359	7.5233	7.7156	8.1152	8.5355	8.7537	8.9775	9.4420	9.9299	10.980	12.135	13.405	14.798
7	7.2135	7.4343	7.6625	7.8983	8.1420	8.3938	8.6540	8.9228	9.2004	9.4872	10.089	10.730	11.066	11.413	12.141	12.915	14.615	16.533	18.695	21.126
8	8.2857	8.5830	8.8923	9.2142	9.5491	9.8975	10.259	10.636	11.028	11.435	12.299	13.232	13.726	14.240	15.327	16.499	19.122	22.163	25.678	29.731
9	9.3685	9.7546	10.159	10.582	11.026	11.491	11.978	12.487	13.021	13.579	14.775	16.085	16.785	17.518	19.085	20.798	24.712	29.369	34.895	41.435
10	10.462	10.949	11.463	12.006	12.577	13.180	13.816	14.486	15.192	15.937	17.548	19.337	20.303	21.321	23.521	25.958	31.643	38.592	47.061	57.351
11	11.566	12.168	12.807	13.486	14.206	14.971	15.783	16.645	17.560	18.531	20.654	23.044	24.349	25.732	28.755	32.150	40.237	50.398	63.121	78.998
12	12.682	13.412	14.192	15.025	15.917	16.869	17.888	18.977	20.140	21.384	24.133	27.270	29.001	30.850	34.931	39.580	50.894	65.510	84.320	108.43
13	13.809	14.680	15.617	16.626	17.713	18.882	20.140	21.495	22.953	24.522	28.029	32.088	34.351	36.786	42.218	48.496	64.109	84.852	112.30	148.47
14	14.947	15.973	17.086	18.291	19.598	21.015	22.550	24.214	26.019	27.975	32.392	37.581	40.504	43.672	50.818	59.195	80.496	109.61	149.23	202.92
15	16.096	17.293	18.598	20.023	21.578	23.276	25.129	27.152	29.360	31.772	37.279	43.842	47.580	51.659	60.965	72.035	100.81	141.30	197.99	276.97
16	17.257	18.639	20.156	21.824	23.657	25.672	27.888	30.324	33.003	35.949	42.753	50.980	55.717	60.925	72.939	87.442	126.01	181.86	262.35	377.69
17	18.430	20.012	21.761	23.697	25.840	28.212	30.840	33.750	36.973	40.544	48.883	59.117	65.075	71.673	87.068	105.93	157.25	233.79	347.30	514.66
18	19.614	21.412	23.414	25.645	28.132	30.905	33.999	37.450	41.301	45.599	55.749	68.394	75.836	84.140	103.74	128.11	195.99	300.25	459.44	700.93
19	20.810	22.840	25.116	27.671	30.539	33.760	37.379	41.446	46.018	51.159	63.439	78.969	88.211	98.603	123.41	154.74	244.03	385.32	607.47	954.27
20	22.019	24.297	26.870	29.778	33.066	36.785	40.995	45.762	51.160	57.275	72.052	91.024	102.44	115.37	146.62	186.68	303.60	494.21	802.86	1298.8
21	23.239	25.783	28.676	31.969	35.719	39.992	44.865	50.422	56.764	64.002	81.698	104.76	118.81	134.84	174.02	225.02	377.46	633.59	1060.7	1767.3
22	24.471	27.299	30.536	34.248	38.505	43.392	49.005	55.456	62.873	71.402	92.502	120.43	137.63	157.41	206.34	271.03	469.05	811.99	1401.2	2404.6
23	25.716	28.845	32.452	36.617	41.430	46.995	53.436	60.893	69.531	79.543	104.60	138.29	159.27	183.60	244.48	326.23	582.62	1040.3	1850.6	3271.3
24	26.973	30.421	34.426	39.082	44.502	50.815	58.176	66.764	76.789	88.497	118.15	158.65	184.16	213.97	289.49	392.48	723.46	1332.6	2443.8	4449.9
25	28.243	32.030	36.459	41.645	47.727	54.864	63.249	73.105	84.700	98.347	133.33	181.87	212.79	249.21	342.60	471.98	898.09	1706.8	3226.8	6052.9
26	29.525	33.670	38.553	44.311	51.113	59.156	68.676	79.954	93.323	109.18	150.33	208.33	245.71	290.08	405.27	567.37	1114.6	2185.7	4260.4	8233.0
27	30.820	35.344	40.709	47.084	54.669	63.705	74.483	87.350	102.72	121.09	169.37	238.49	283.56	337.50	479.22	681.85	1383.1	2798.7	5624.7	11197.9
28	32.129	37.051	42.930	49.967	58.402	68.528	80.697	95.338	112.96	134.20	190.69	272.88	327.10	392.50	566.48	819.22	1716.0	3583.3	7425.6	15230.2
29	33.450	38.792	45.218	52.966	62.322	73.639	87.346	103.96	124.13	148.63	214.58	312.09	377.16	456.30	669.44	984.06	2128.9	4587.6	9802.9	20714.1
30	34.784	40.568	47.575	56.084	66.438	79.058	94.460	113.28	136.30	164.49	241.33	356.78	434.74	530.31	790.94	1181.8	2640.9	5873.2	12940.	28172.2
40	48.886	60.402	75.401	95.025	120.79	154.76	199.63	259.05	337.88	442.59	767.09	1342.0	1779.0	2360.7	4163.2	7343.8	22728.	69377.	*	*
50	64.463	84.579	112.79	152.66	209.34	290.33	406.52	573.76	815.08	1163.9	2400.0	4994.5	72177.	10435.	21813.	45497.	*	*	*	*
60	81.669	114.05	163.05	237.99	353.58	533.12	813.52	1253.2	1944.7	3034.8	7471.6	18535.	29219.	46057.	*	*	*	*	*	*

Time Value of
Money
Concepts

periods at a rate of 10 percent each period. It is 3.31. Multiply the amount of the annuity, $100, by this number to arrive at the correct answer: $331.00.

The above example assumes the annuity payments begin at the end of the first period. However, you might encounter situations where the payments begin immediately. Let's assume that to be the case using the above example again. This change offers no particular problem: Simply assume four holding periods instead of three and then subtract 1.0 from the *FV* coefficient. Referring to Table A.2, the coefficient for four periods at 10 percent is 4.641. Subtracting 1.0 from this gives 3.641, which is the future value of $1 invested for three periods with payments beginning immediately. So $100 invested in this fashion would grow to $364.10, a somewhat larger amount than in the previous illustration. Of course, this answer makes sense because your money is invested one year longer.

Present Value of a Single Payment

To find the present value, *PV*, of a single payment, you just reverse the process of finding a future value. Referring to Equation (A1), you simply rearrange terms to get

$$PV = \frac{FV}{(1.0 + i)^n} \quad \text{or} \quad PV = FV \times \frac{1.0}{(1.0 + i)^n} \tag{A3}$$

Thus, the present value of 133.10 received three years from today is $100.

$$PV = \frac{\$133.10}{(1.0 + 0.10)^3} = \frac{\$133.10}{(1.10)^3} = \frac{\$133.10}{1.331} = \$100$$

Table A.3 shows a present value of $1 table. It is used in exactly the same manner as a future value table. The number in the period 3 row and 10 percent column is .7513, which is 1 divided by $(1.10)^3$. Multiplying .7513 by $133.10 gives $100.

Present Value of a Stream of Equal Payments (an Annuity)

The formula below can be used to calculate the present value of a stream of equal payments to be received beginning at the end of the first period and assuming that each payment is discounted at the discount rate applicable each period.

$$PV = \frac{[1.0 - 1.0/(1.0 + i)^n] \times A}{i} \tag{A4}$$

If you receive $100 at the end of each of the next three periods, the present value of this stream is

$$PV = \frac{[1.0 - 1.0/(1.0 + 0.10)^3] \times \$100}{0.10} = \frac{[1.0 - 1.0/(1.10)^3] \times \$100}{0.10}$$

$$= \frac{[1.0 - (1.0/1.331) \times \$100}{0.10}$$

$$= \frac{(1.0 - 0.7513) \times \$100}{0.10} = \frac{0.24869 \times \$100}{0.10} = \frac{\$24.869}{0.10}$$

$$= \$248.69$$

TABLE A.3 ▪ Present Value of $1: $PV = \dfrac{1.0}{(1.0 + i)^n}$

Period	1%	2%	3%	4%	5%	6%	7%	8%	9%	10%	12%	14%	15%	16%	18%	20%	24%	28%	32%	36%
1	.9901	.9804	.9709	.9615	.9524	.9434	.9346	.9259	.9174	.9091	.8929	.8772	.8696	.8621	.8475	.8333	.8065	.7813	.7576	.7353
2	.9803	.9612	.9426	.9246	.9070	.8900	.8734	.8573	.8417	.8264	.7972	.7695	.7561	.7432	.7182	.6944	.6504	.6104	.5739	.5407
3	.9706	.9423	.9151	.8890	.8638	.8396	.8163	.7938	.7722	.7513	.7118	.6750	.6575	.6407	.6086	.5787	.5245	.4768	.4348	.3975
4	.9610	.9238	.8885	.8548	.8227	.7921	.7629	.7350	.7084	.6830	.6355	.5921	.5718	.5523	.5158	.4823	.4230	.3725	.3294	.2923
5	.9515	.9057	.8626	.8219	.7835	.7473	.7130	.6806	.6499	.6209	.5674	.5194	.4972	.4761	.4371	.4019	.3411	.2910	.2495	.2149
6	.9420	.8880	.8375	.7903	.7462	.7050	.6633	.6302	.5963	.5645	.5066	.4556	.4323	.4104	.3704	.3349	.2751	.2274	.1890	.1580
7	.9327	.8706	.8131	.7599	.7107	.6651	.6227	.5835	.5470	.5132	.4523	.3996	.3759	.3538	.3139	.2791	.2218	.1776	.1432	.1162
8	.9235	.8535	.7894	.7307	.6768	.6274	.5820	.5403	.5019	.4665	.4039	.3506	.3269	.3050	.2660	.2326	.1789	.1388	.1085	.0854
9	.9143	.8368	.7664	.7026	.6446	.5919	.5439	.5002	.4604	.4241	.3606	.3075	.2843	.2630	.2255	.1938	.1443	.1084	.0822	.0628
10	.9053	.8203	.7441	.6756	.6139	.5584	.5083	.4632	.4224	.3855	.3220	.2697	.2472	.2267	.1911	.1615	.1164	.0847	.0623	.0462
11	.8963	.8043	.7224	.6496	.5847	.5268	.4751	.4289	.3875	.3505	.2875	.2366	.2149	.1954	.1619	.1346	.0938	.0662	.0472	.0340
12	.8874	.7885	.7014	.6246	.5568	.4970	.4440	.3971	.3555	.3186	.2567	.2076	.1869	.1685	.1372	.1122	.0757	.0517	.0357	.0250
13	.8787	.7730	.6810	.6006	.5303	.4688	.4150	.3677	.3262	.2897	.2292	.1821	.1625	.1452	.1163	.0935	.0610	.0404	.0271	.0184
14	.8700	.7579	.6611	.5775	.5051	.4423	.3878	.3405	.2992	.2633	.2046	.1597	.1413	.1252	.0985	.0779	.0492	.0316	.0205	.0135
15	.8613	.7430	.6419	.5553	.4810	.4173	.3624	.3152	.2745	.2394	.1827	.1401	.1229	.1079	.0835	.0649	.0397	.0247	0.155	.0099
16	.8528	.7284	.6232	.5339	.4581	.3936	.3387	.2919	.2519	.2176	.1631	.1229	.1069	.0930	.0708	.0541	0.320	.0193	.0118	.0073
17	.8444	.7142	.6050	.5134	.4363	.3714	.3166	.2703	.2311	.1978	.1456	.1078	.0929	.0802	.0600	.0451	.0258	.0150	.0089	.0054
18	.8360	.7002	.5874	.4936	.4155	.3503	.2959	.2502	.2120	.1799	.1300	.0946	.0808	.0691	.0508	.0376	.0208	.0118	.0068	.0039
19	.8277	.6864	.5703	.4746	.3957	.3305	.2765	.2317	.1945	.1635	.1161	.0829	.0703	.0596	.0431	.0313	.0168	.0092	.0051	.0029
20	.8195	.6730	.5537	.4564	.3769	.3118	.2584	.2145	.1784	.1486	.1037	.0728	.0611	.0514	.0365	.0261	.0135	.0072	.0039	.0021
21	.8114	.6598	.5375	.4388	.3589	.2942	.2415	.1987	.1637	.1351	.0926	.0638	.0531	.0443	.0309	.0217	.0109	.0056	.0029	.0016
22	.8034	.6468	.5219	.4220	.3418	.2775	.2257	.1839	.1502	.1228	.0826	.0560	.0462	.0382	.0262	.0181	.0088	.0044	.0022	.0012
23	.7954	.6342	.5067	.4057	.3256	.2618	.2109	.1703	.1378	.1117	.0738	.0491	.0402	.0329	.0222	.0151	.0071	.0034	.0017	.0008
24	.7876	.6217	.4919	.3901	.3101	.2470	.1971	.1577	.1264	.1015	.0659	.0431	.0349	.0284	.0188	.0126	.0057	.0027	.0013	.0006
25	.7798	.6095	.4776	.3751	.2953	.2330	.1842	.1460	.1160	.0923	.0588	.0378	.0304	.0245	.0160	.0105	.0046	.0021	.0010	.0005
26	.7720	.5976	.4637	.3607	.2812	.2198	.1722	.1352	.1064	.0839	.0525	.0331	.0264	.0211	.0135	.0087	.0037	.0016	.0007	.0003
27	.7644	.5859	.4502	.3468	.2678	.2074	.1609	.1252	.0976	.0763	.0469	.0291	.0230	.0182	.0115	.0073	.0030	.0013	.0006	.0002
28	.7568	.5744	.4371	.3335	.2551	.1956	.1504	.1159	.0895	.0693	.0419	.0255	.0200	.0157	.0097	.0061	.0024	.0010	.0004	.0002
29	.7493	.5631	.4243	.3207	.2429	.1846	.1406	.1073	.0822	.0630	.0374	.0224	.0174	.0135	.0082	.0051	.0020	.0008	.0003	.0001
30	.7419	.5521	.4120	.3083	.2314	.1741	.1314	.0994	.0754	.0573	.03374	.0196	.0151	.0116	.0070	.0042	.0016	.0006	.0002	.0001
40	.6717	.4529	.3066	.2083	.1420	.0972	.0668	.0460	.0318	.0221	.0107	.0053	.0037	.0026	.0013	.0007	.0002	.0001	*	*
50	.6080	.3715	.2281	.1407	.0872	.0543	.0339	.0213	.0134	.0085	.0035	.0014	.0009	.0006	.0003	.0001	*	*	*	*
60	.5504	.3048	.1697	.0951	.0535	.0303	.0173	.0099	.0057	.0033	.0011	.0004	.0002	.0001	*	*	*	*	*	*

Time Value of
Money
Concepts

The same answer can be found by referring to a present value of an annuity table, such as the one in Table A.4, and finding the value for $n = 3$ and $i = 10$ percent. This is 2.4869, and multiplying it by the $100 annuity gives $248.69. Figure A.1 shows some applications of FV and PV techniques; exercises to test your understanding of the material follow.

Exercises

1   You receive $500 in graduation presents and plan to invest it for your retirement in 40 years. Assuming you can earn 8 percent interest each year, how much will you have at retirement? (Answer: $10,862.) How much will you have if you could earn 12 percent each year? (Answer: $46,526.)

2   Suppose you cannot make an immediate investment for retirement but can afford $100 each year for the next 30 years with the first payment starting in one year. Assuming a 14 percent investment rate each year, how much will you accumulate at the end of 30 years? (Answer: $35,678.) Suppose your target was to accumulate $50,000; how much must you invest each year? (Answer: $140.14.) Suppose your target was $50,000 but you had only 20 years and could earn only 10 percent each year. What would be your yearly contribution? (Answer: $872.98.)

3   You are thinking of buying a zero-coupon bond. It matures in ten years for $1.000, pays no yearly interest, and current costs $200. You look at other similar bonds and see that they are yielding 16 percent. Since you feel the zero-coupon bond should also yield 16 percent, the most you are willing to pay for it is _____? (Answer: $226.70.) Therefore, should you or should you not buy the bond? (Answer: Should.) Suppose you bought the bond and interest rates fell immediately afterward, such that your bond yielded only 10 percent based on its current market price. How much would its current market price be? (Answer: $385.50.)

4   You are thinking of buying an annuity to provide future income to your spouse in the event of your death. The insurance company selling the annuity offers two alternatives: The first calls for an immediate payment of $10,000, and the other requires annual payments of $1,500 for the next ten years with payments beginning in one year. You are pretty sure you can invest your money at 6 percent interest each year for the next ten years. If this is true, which alternative should you prefer? (Answer: The first, since the present value of the second is $11,040, which is greater than $10,000.) Suppose you could earn 10 percent; now which would be better? (Answer: The second; its present value is $9,217.)

TABLE A.4 ▪ Present Value of an Annuity of $1 per Period for n Periods; $PV = \dfrac{1.0 - \dfrac{1.0}{(1.0+i)^n}}{i}$

Number of Periods	1%	2%	3%	4%	5%	6%	7%	8%	9%	10%	12%	14%	15%	16%	18%	20%	24%	28%	32%
1	0.9901	0.9804	0.9709	0.9615	0.9524	0.9434	0.9346	0.9259	0.9174	0.9091	0.8929	0.8772	0.8696	0.8621	0.8475	0.8333	0.8065	0.7813	0.7576
2	1.9704	1.9416	1.9135	1.8861	1.8594	1.8334	1.8080	1.7833	1.7591	1.7355	1.6901	1.6467	1.6257	1.6052	1.5656	1.5278	1.4568	1.3916	1.3315
3	2.9410	2.8839	2.8286	2.7751	2.7232	2.6730	2.6243	2.5771	2.5313	2.4869	2.4018	2.3216	2.2832	2.2459	2.1743	2.1065	1.9813	1.8684	1.7663
4	3.9020	3.8077	3.7171	3.6299	3.5460	3.4651	3.3872	3.3121	3.2397	3.1699	3.0373	2.9137	2.8550	2.7982	2.6901	2.5887	2.4043	2.2410	2.0957
5	4.8534	4.7135	4.5797	4.4518	4.3295	4.2124	4.1002	3.9927	3.8897	3.7908	3.6048	3.4331	3.3522	3.2743	3.1272	2.9906	2.7454	2.5320	2.3452
6	5.7955	5.6014	5.4172	5.2421	5.0757	4.9173	4.7665	4.6229	4.4859	4.3553	4.1114	3.8887	3.7845	3.6847	3.4976	3.3255	3.0205	2.7594	2.5342
7	6.7282	6.4720	6.2303	6.0021	5.7864	5.5824	5.3893	5.2064	5.0330	4.8684	4.5638	4.2883	4.1604	4.0386	3.8115	3.6046	3.2423	2.9370	2.6775
8	7.6517	7.3255	7.0179	6.7327	6.4632	6.2098	5.9713	5.7466	5.5348	5.3349	4.9676	4.6389	4.4873	4.3436	4.0776	3.8372	3.4212	3.0758	2.7860
9	8.5660	8.1622	7.7861	7.4353	7.1078	6.8017	6.5152	6.2469	5.9952	5.7590	5.3282	4.9464	4.7716	4.6065	4.3030	4.0310	3.5655	3.1842	2.8681
10	9.4713	8.9826	8.5302	8.1109	7.7217	7.3601	7.0236	6.7101	6.4177	6.1446	5.6502	5.2161	5.0188	4.8332	4.4941	4.1925	3.6819	3.2689	2.9304
11	10.3676	9.7868	9.2526	8.7605	8.3064	7.8869	7.4987	7.1390	6.8052	6.4951	5.9377	5.4527	5.2337	5.0286	4.6560	4.3271	3.7757	3.3351	2.9776
12	11.2551	10.5753	9.9540	9.3851	8.8633	8.3838	7.9427	7.5361	7.1607	6.8137	6.1944	5.6603	5.4206	5.1971	4.7932	4.4392	3.8514	3.3868	3.0133
13	12.1337	11.3484	10.6350	9.9856	9.3936	8.8527	8.3577	7.9038	7.4869	7.1034	6.4235	5.8424	5.5831	5.3423	4.9095	4.5327	3.9124	3.4272	3.0404
14	13.0037	12.1062	11.2961	10.5631	9.8986	9.2950	8.7455	8.2442	7.7862	7.3667	6.6282	6.0021	5.7245	5.4675	5.0081	4.6106	3.9616	3.4587	3.0609
15	13.8651	12.8493	11.9379	11.1184	10.3797	9.7122	9.1079	8.5595	8.0607	7.6061	6.8109	6.1422	5.8474	5.5755	5.0916	4.6755	4.0013	3.4834	3.0764
16	14.7179	13.5777	12.5611	11.6523	10.8378	10.1059	9.4466	8.8514	8.3126	7.8237	6.9740	6.2651	5.9542	5.6685	5.1624	4.7296	4.0333	3.5026	3.0882
17	15.5623	14.2919	13.1661	12.1657	11.2741	10.4773	9.7632	9.1216	8.5436	8.0216	7.1196	6.3729	6.0472	5.7487	5.2223	4.7746	4.0591	3.5177	3.0971
18	16.3983	14.9920	13.7535	12.6593	11.6896	10.8276	10.0591	9.3719	8.7556	8.2014	7.2497	6.4674	6.1280	5.8178	5.2732	4.8122	4.0799	3.5294	3.1039
19	17.2260	15.6785	14.3238	13.1339	12.0853	11.1581	10.3356	9.6036	8.9501	8.3649	7.3658	6.5504	6.1982	5.8775	5.3162	4.8435	4.0967	3.5386	3.1090
19	17.2260	15.6785	14.3238	13.1339	12.0853	11.1581	10.3356	9.6036	8.9501	8.3649	7.3658	6.5504	6.1982	5.8775	5.3162	4.8435	4.0967	3.5386	3.1090
20	18.0456	16.3514	14.8775	13.5903	12.4622	11.4699	10.5940	9.8181	9.1285	8.5136	7.4694	6.6231	6.2593	5.9288	5.3527	4.8696	4.1103	3.5458	3.1129
21	18.8570	17.0112	15.4150	14.0292	12.8212	11.7641	10.8355	10.0168	9.2922	8.6487	7.5620	6.6870	6.3125	5.9731	5.3837	4.8913	4.1212	3.5514	3.1158
22	19.6604	17.6580	15.9369	14.4511	13.1630	12.0416	11.0612	10.2007	9.4424	8.7715	7.6446	6.7429	6.3587	6.0113	5.4099	4.9094	4.1300	3.5558	3.1180
23	20.4558	18.2922	16.4436	14.8568	13.4886	12.3034	11.2722	10.3711	9.5802	8.8832	7.7184	6.7921	6.3988	6.0442	5.4321	4.9245	4.1371	3.5592	3.1197
24	21.2434	18.9139	16.9355	15.2470	13.7986	12.5504	11.4693	10.5288	9.7066	8.9847	7.7843	6.8351	6.4338	6.0726	5.4509	4.9371	4.1428	3.5619	3.1210
25	22.0232	19.5235	17.4131	15.6221	14.0939	12.7834	11.6536	10.6748	9.8226	9.0770	7.8431	6.8729	6.4641	6.0971	5.4669	4.9476	4.1474	3.5640	3.1220
26	22.7952	20.1210	17.8768	15.9828	14.3752	13.0032	11.8258	10.8100	9.9290	9.1609	7.8957	6.9061	6.4906	6.1182	5.4804	4.9563	4.1511	3.5656	3.1227
27	23.5596	20.7069	18.3270	16.3296	14.6430	13.2105	11.9867	10.9352	10.0266	9.2372	7.9426	6.9352	6.5135	6.1364	5.4919	4.9636	4.1542	3.5669	3.1233
28	24.3164	21.2813	18.7641	16.6631	14.8981	13.4062	12.1371	11.0511	10.1161	9.3066	7.9844	6.9607	6.5335	6.1520	5.5016	4.9697	4.1566	3.5679	3.1237
29	25.0658	21.8444	19.1885	16.9837	15.1411	13.5907	12.2777	11.1584	10.1983	9.3696	8.0218	6.9830	6.5509	6.1656	5.5098	4.9747	4.1585	3.5687	3.1240
30	25.8077	22.3965	19.6004	17.2920	15.3725	13.7648	12.4090	11.2578	10.2737	9.4269	8.0552	7.0027	6.5660	6.1772	5.5168	4.9789	4.1601	3.5693	3.1242
40	32.8347	27.3555	23.1148	19.7928	17.1591	15.0463	13.3317	11.9246	10.7574	9.7791	8.2438	7.1050	6.6418	6.2335	5.5482	4.9966	4.1659	3.5712	3.1250
50	39.1961	31.4236	25.7298	21.4822	18.2559	15.7619	13.8007	12.2335	10.9617	9.9148	8.3045	7.1327	6.6605	6.2463	5.5541	4.9995	4.1666	3.5714	3.1250
60	44.9550	34.7609	27.6756	22.6235	18.9293	16.1614	14.0392	12.3766	11.0480	9.9672	8.3240	7.1401	6.6651	6.2492	5.5553	4.9999	4.1667	3.5714	3.1250

Problem	Solution
1. Alicia invests $350 today and expects to earn 20% on the investment each year for the next 20 years. How much will she have?	Find the future value, FV, of $1 for 20% and 20 years; 38.337. Multiply 38.337 times $350 to get the answer; it is $13,417.95.
2. Manuel's uncle plans to give him a graduation present of $500 at graduation or $700 three years later if Manuel agrees to complete a graduate program. Considering the value of the gift only, and assuming Manuel could invest at 8% in each of the three years, which is the better alternative?	You can use either future or present value of $1 tables. Using the Manuel former, find the FV for 8% and three years; it is 1.2597. The future value of $500 is $629.85 ($500 × 1.2597). Since this is less than $700, Manuel is better off waiting three years for his uncle's gift. If you use the present value of $1, you find the present value coefficient for 8% and three years; it is 0.7938. You then find the present value, PV, of $700, which is $555.66 (0.7938 × $700). Since the present value is greater than the immediate $500, Manuel should accept the future $700.
3. Gunther's stockbroker is trying to convince Gunther to purchase a security that will be worth $10,000 in 30 years. The cost of the security today is $1,500. Gunther isn't sure whether this is a good or bad investment, but believes he could make a better decision if he knew the approximate rate of return on the investment. What is it?	You can find a rate of return by dividing the future value of an investment by its cost to arrive at a future value of $1 coefficient. Relate this coefficient then to the number of periods and the approximate value of i. You have a coefficient of 6.667 ($10,000/$1,500). Since the number of periods is 30, go across the 30 row until you come as close as possible to 6.667. As you see, that corresponds to an i value of 6%, which is 5.7435. Since 6.667 is somewhat larger than 5.7435, you conclude the rate of return is greater than 6% but far less than 8% (in which case the coefficient would be 10.0620). As a rough approximation, you conclude it is about 6.5%. (You could use more accurate interpolation techniques, but such accuracy is not necessary in many cases. Moreover, for greater accuracy you should use expanded tables or an appropriate calculating device.)

596

Appendix A

Appendix B

The Social Security System

The amount you receive from private disability insurance or a private pension plan may be dependent upon your Social Security benefits. However, even when payments under these plans are not contingent on Social Security benefits, the need for private protection will be dependent upon the size of the governmentally supplied safety net. Your private disability insurance, life insurance, and retirement planning will all depend upon how much you can expect to receive from Social Security.

Fortunately, the Social Security Administration has reversed its previous practice of providing benefit estimates only for those nearing retirement. Social Security now supplies estimates of benefits to all upon request. To receive an estimate of your future Social Security benefits, you need only contact the nearest Social Security office listed in your telephone directory. Ask them to send you Form SSA-7004, known as a "Request for Earnings and Benefit Estimate Statement." A few weeks after returning this form, you should receive a "Personal Earnings and Benefit Estimate Statement." This statement will contain the following information:

- Your total covered earnings from 1937 to 1950
- A year-by-year statement of your covered earnings from 1951 to the present
- Estimates of your retirement benefits at different ages
- Estimates of your survivor and disability benefits
- The number of credits you need to be insured for each type of Social Security, and the total credits you have earned to date

The estimates provided by the Social Security Administration are in today's dollars of purchasing power. This makes it possible for you to judge what standard of living these benefits might support. The actual amount you receive in future dollars will depend upon future inflation, your future labor force experience and, of course, the generosity of some future U.S. Congress.

You should check the earnings statement. It's estimated that one person in 13 has not had covered earnings credited correctly. Old W-2 forms and tax returns can provide proof of historical earnings. A certified copy of any tax return you filed within the last six years can be obtained by sending IRS Form 4506.

The purpose of this appendix is to explain how your Social Security benefits are determined. Because the best we can do here is summarize the calculations and rules for estimating benefits, and because the benefits will change as a result of inflation and changes in the laws, this is only an estimate. The actual benefits you are to receive can be calculated only at the time you are to receive them with the aid of an informed employee of the Social Security system.

The rules governing eligibility and benefits are very complicated. For this reason, you should contact the nearest office of the Social Security Administration when there is the slightest possibility that you may receive benefits. Accordingly, you should check on potential benefits if you:

1. Are unable to work because of an illness or injury that is expected to last a year or longer
2. Are 62 or older or plan to retire
3. Are within three months of age 65 even if you don't plan to retire
4. Experience a death in the family
5. Your spouse or your dependent children suffer permanent kidney failure

Not all individuals in these categories will qualify for benefits. Furthermore, those who do qualify may find benefits reduced or eliminated because of other income received. However, given the likelihood of benefits, it is best to check.

Who Is Covered by Social Security?

The objective of the Social Security system is to provide universal coverage for all workers. If you have held a nongovernment job, you have most likely paid some funds into the system, entitling you and your family to potential benefits. Previously, federal workers were not covered, and nonprofit private and public institutions were permitted to opt out of the system. Since 1984, however, all new federal employees are required to become members, and no additional nonprofit institutions are allowed to leave the system.

For one of several reasons, covered workers, their dependents, and their survivors may all be entitled to benefits from the Social Security system. To be eligible for the entire range of potential benefits, a worker must be "fully insured." This requirement is satisfied when the worker has sufficient *quarters of coverage*. Before 1978, a quarter of coverage was awarded for each calendar quarter in which the worker received $50 or more of covered earnings. After 1978, quarters of coverage were based upon annual earnings. In 1991, a worker was credited with one quarter of coverage for each $540 earned during the year up to a maximum of four quarters in one year. The amounts needed for a quarter of coverage are adjusted each year for the change in the wage level. Values for the intervening years are given in Table B.1.

Fully Insured at Retirement

To receive benefits that are contingent on the covered worker reaching retirement age, the worker must be fully insured at retirement. For workers currently reaching age 62, *fully insured* is achieved with 40 quarters of coverage (ten years of covered wages).

Fully Insured at the Onset of Disability

Only those who satisfy the Social Security Administration's stringent requirements may receive disability benefits. To qualify for Social Security disability, you must have a physical or mental impairment that prevents you from doing any substantial gainful activity, and that is expected to last at least 12 months or is expected to result in death. In 1991, substantial gainful activity was defined as any work that resulted in a monthly income above $500. For disabled workers or families of disabled workers who meet this strict definition, the insured worker must also be both fully insured and disability insured before being eligible for benefits. Monthly disability benefits begin at the sixth month of disability.

The test to determine whether the worker is fully insured at the onset of the disability, is the same as that for retirement except that the age at the onset of the disability is used instead of age 62, and a minimum of six quarters of coverage must exist. For example, if a worker became disabled at age 30, there would be eight complete years between age 21 and age 30. Therefore, this person would need eight complete quarters of coverage to be fully insured.

To be "disability insured," this person must have been recently employed. Those within three years of their twenty-first birthday must have six quarters of

TABLE B.1 • Earnings Needed for One Quarter of Coverage

Year	Dollar Amount
1977	50
1978	250
1979	260
1980	290
1981	310
1982	340
1983	370
1984	390
1985	410
1986	440
1987	460
1988	470
1989	500
1990	520
1991	540
1992	570
1993*	600

*Estimated value for this year.

The Social Security System

coverage within the immediate 12 quarters to be disability insured. Those under 31 must have earned coverage in at least half of the quarters, beginning with the quarter after that in which they turned age 21 and ending with the quarter in which they became disabled. All others must meet what is called the 20/40 test. They must have 20 quarters of coverage in the immediately preceding 40 quarters.

To receive benefits, the worker must be both fully insured and disability insured. As you can see, it is possible to be fully insured, which would entitle you to retirement benefits, without being disability insured. With ten years of covered work you would be fully insured. However, unless five of those years were within the last ten years before the onset of the disability, you would not be disability insured and, consequently, you would be ineligible for disability benefits.

One last point: Those who do not qualify for benefits based on their own earnings history may still qualify based upon a parent's earnings record. This is possible if the disability occurred before age 22.

Fully Insured at Death

In order for survivors of a covered worker to be entitled to the full range of Social Security survivors' benefits, the covered worker must be fully insured at death. The fully insured test at death is the same as for fully insured at disability except that age at death is substituted for age at onset of disability. There must be a quarter of coverage for each year between age 21 and age at death, with a maximum of 40 quarters of coverage and a minimum of six quarters of coverage.

Currently Insured

When determining whether a worker is fully insured, only those quarters of coverage accumulated after age 21 are counted. Accordingly, many young workers who have already spent considerable time in covered employment may not be fully insured. In order to ensure that families of young workers would not be unfairly denied benefits, Congress created another category of insureds called *currently insured*. This status applies only at death. Its purpose is to provide benefits to survivors of young workers even though the covered workers may not be fully insured. For widow(er)s with dependent children and dependent children to be entitled to survivors' benefits, the deceased worker need only be currently insured. Persons are currently insured if they have at least six quarters of coverage during the last 13 quarters before they died, became disabled, or retired.

Calculation of Benefits

Benefit payments are generally related to past earnings of the covered worker. The actual computation of the benefits is an involved, four-phase process that includes the following:

1. Indexing past earnings
2. Calculating average indexed monthly earnings (AIME)
3. Calculating the primary insurance amount (PIA)
4. Calculating the basic monthly benefit

Indexing Past Earnings

A sample worksheet for estimating average indexed monthly earnings is given in Table B.2. The data on the worksheet are for a worker who became disabled in 1991 at age 28. Column 1 includes each year since 1950, or each year between when the covered worker turned 21 and the one before the covered worker became disabled, reached age 62, or died. These years are called the "base computation years." In column 2, earnings in each of these years are listed. If you are making the calculation for yourself and you don't know your previous earnings, you can receive a record of your past covered wages by contacting the Social Security Administration.

The maximum amount of wages covered by Social Security taxes for each of the base computation years is entered in column 3. The needed values can be found in Table B.3. Only wages up to these amounts will count toward the calculation of your Social Security benefits. Therefore, the lesser of the wages in column 2 and column 3 is entered in column 4.

The next step is to multiply the wages in column 4 by the wage index in column 5 (see Table B.4 for wage index values). The Social Security Administration revises this index each year for changes in the national wage level. The purpose of this adjustment is to increase the value of wages earned in the early years so that recent wages, which are more heavily dominated by inflation, do not overly influence the calculation of benefits. The correct index will depend upon the last year of covered earnings. The index-adjusted wage is entered in column 6.

Calculating Average Indexed Monthly Earnings

Before you calculate average earnings, you are allowed to exclude several years in which earnings were low. This prevents a few bad years of earnings from significantly reducing your benefits payments. You may drop one-fifth of the base computation years (disregard any fraction) up to a maximum of five, but no less

TABLE B.2 · Worksheet for Calculating Average Indexed Monthly Earnings (AIME)

1 Base Computation Years	2 Gross Wages	3 Maximum Taxable Wages	4 Covered Wages	5 Wage Index	6 Indexed Wages	7 Indexed Wages in Benefit Computation Years
1985	$26,875	$39,600	$26,875	1.19	$31,981.25	—
1986	31,420	42,000	31,420	1.16	36,447.20	—
1987	36,843	43,800	36,843	1.09	40,158.87	$40,158.87
1988	42,801	45,000	42,801	1.04	44,513.04	44,513.04
1989	48,358	48,000	48,000	1.00	48,358.00	48,358.00
1990	55,396	51,300	51,300	1.00	55,396.00	55,396.00
			Total wages in benefit computation years =			$188,425.91
			Months in benefit computation years =			÷ 48
						$3,925.54
					AIME =	$3,925.00

TABLE B.3 · Maximum Taxable Wages

Years	Amount
1951–1954	$3,600
1955–1958	4,200
1959–1964	4,800
1965–1967	6,600
1968–1971	7,800
1972	9,000
1973	10,800
1974	13,200
1975	14,100
1976	15,300
1977	16,500
1978	17,700
1979	22,900
1980	25,900
1981	29,700
1982	32,400
1983	35,700
1984	37,800
1985	39,600
1986	42,000
1987	43,800
1988	45,000
1989	48,000
1990	51,300
1991	53,400
1992	55,500
1993*	58,900

*Estimated value for this year.

than two. The years that are left, those with the highest indexed earnings, are called the *benefit computation years*.

The final step in calculating average indexed monthly earnings is to sum wages over the benefit computation years in column 7, and divide this value by the number of months in the benefit computation years. The resulting figure rounded to the next lower dollar is average indexed monthly earnings (AIME).

Calculating the Primary Insurance Amount

Once you have calculated AIME, you may next compute the primary insurance amount (PIA). To compute the PIA you need the AIME and a percentage formula published by the Social Security Administration. For example, in 1991 the PIA was equal to 90 percent of the first $370 of AIME, plus 32 percent of the next $1,860 of AIME, plus 15 percent of everything over $2,230 of AIME. Given an AIME of $3,925, the PIA rounded to the next lower dime would be $1,182.40, computed as follows:

$$
\begin{aligned}
90\% \text{ of } \$370 &= \quad \$333.00 \\
32\% \text{ of } \$1,860 &= \quad 595.20 \\
15\% \text{ of } \$1,695 &= \quad \underline{254.25} \\
&\quad \$1,182.45 \\
\text{PIA} &= \quad 1,182.40
\end{aligned}
$$

The level of monthly wages at which the percentage applied changes is called the *bend point*. Each year the bend points are revised to reflect changes in the national wage level. Previous and estimated future bend points are included in Table B.5.

Some workers who receive a pension for noncovered employment and who are also eligible for Social Security retirement benefits must apply a different formula for calculating the PIA. After 1990, the alternative benefit formula reduces the percentage factor on the first bracket from 90 percent to 40 percent.

Calculating the Basic Monthly Benefit

The primary insurance amount is a very important figure, because all monthly benefit payments will be based upon a percentage of the PIA. For example, a fully insured worker retiring at age 65 would receive an initial benefit payment equal to 100 percent of the PIA. Furthermore, the spouse of this pensioner could receive a spousal benefit beginning at age 65 equal to 50 percent of the PIA. Some other basic monthly benefits expressed as a percentage of the PIA are listed in Table B.6. Unless the sum of the individual benefits due family members exceeds the family maximum (see below), monthly benefits payable to each member of the family would generally be based upon the indicated percentage of the PIA.

TABLE B.4 · Wage
Index Factor for Onset
of Death, Retirement,
or Onset of Disability
in Year Indicated by
Column Heading

Year	1993 (Est.)	1992	1991
1993	—	—	—
1992	1.00	—	—
1991	1.00	1.00	—
1990	1.05	1.00	1.00
1989	1.10	1.05	1.00
1988	1.15	1.09	1.04
1987	1.20	1.14	1.09
1986	1.28	1.21	1.16
1985	1.32	1.25	1.19
1984	1.37	1.30	1.25
1983	1.45	1.38	1.32
1982	1.52	1.45	1.38
1981	1.61	1.53	1.46
1980	1.77	1.68	1.61
1979	1.93	1.83	1.75
1978	2.10	1.99	1.90
1977	2.27	2.15	2.06
1976	2.40	2.28	2.18
1975	2.57	2.44	2.33
1974	2.76	2.62	2.50
1973	2.92	2.77	2.65
1972	3.11	2.95	2.82
1971	3.41	3.24	3.09
1970	3.58	3.40	3.25
1969	3.76	3.57	3.41
1968	3.98	3.77	3.61
1967	4.25	4.03	3.86
1966	4.49	4.26	4.07
1965	4.76	4.51	4.31
1964	4.84	4.59	4.39
1963	5.04	4.78	4.57
1962	5.16	4.90	4.68
1961	5.42	5.15	4.92
1960	5.53	5.25	5.02

Adjustments to Monthly Benefits

For numerous reasons, the monthly benefits payable may not be equal to the percentage of the PIA indicated in Table B.6. Several adjustments can either increase or decrease the actual monthly benefit. Below we discuss some of the more common ones.

Cost-of-Living Adjustments

In January of each year, Social Security benefits are adjusted for increases in the cost of living. If the Social Security trust fund is above a stated level, the adjustments are calculated according to changes in the Consumer Price Index; otherwise, the increase is based on the lesser of the rise in the CPI, or in the national wage level.

603

TABLE B.5 · Bend Points for Calculation of Primary Insurance Amount			
Year Worker Retires, Becomes Disabled, or Dies	**90% of First**	**32% of Next**	**15% Over**
1991	$370	$1,860	$2,230
1992	387	1,946	2,333
1993*	408	2,051	2,459

*Bend points estimated for this year.

TABLE B.6 · Basic Monthly Benefits as a Percentage of the Primary Insurance Amount of Fully Insured Worker	
Status	**Percentage**
Retired worker at 65	100
Disabled worker	100
Spouse or divorced spouse of retired worker at 65	50
Spouse of disabled worker with dependent children	50
Child of retired or disabled worker	50
Surviving spouse or surviving divorced spouse of retired worker at 65	100
Sole parent of deceased worker	82.5
Each of two dependent parents of a deceased worker	75
Child of a deceased worker	75
Surviving spouse with dependent children	75

Retirement Age and Reduction for Early Retirement

The retirement age at which unreduced retirement benefits are first available is currently age 65. This is when a monthly pension equal to 100 percent of the primary insurance amount would begin.

Congress has scheduled a change in normal retirement age. It is set to increase two months a year for workers reaching age 62 between 2000 and 2005, remain fixed at age 66 for those reaching age 62 between 2006 and 2016, and then again increase two months a year for those reaching age 62 between 2017 and 2022. For all those reaching age 62 after 2022, normal retirement age will be 67. The effect of the age requirements is illustrated in Table B.7.

Insured workers may elect to retire before reaching normal retirement age. However, monthly benefit payments will be adjusted downward from the PIA for each month early retirement precedes normal retirement age. An eligible worker can now retire at age 62 with 80 percent of the benefits received at the normal retirement age of 65. As shown in Table B.7, this is also scheduled to change over the next few decades, with age 62 benefits for a retired worker eventually falling to only 70 percent of the primary insurance amount.

Increase for Delayed Retirement

Delaying retirement past normal retirement age can result in an increase in monthly benefits for each month retirement is delayed between normal retirement age and age 70. For those who reach 62 between December 1978 and January 1987, the delayed retirement credit is equal to 3 percent for each year, or

Year of Birth	Retirement Age (Years/Months)		Age 62 Benefits as Percent of PIA*	
	Worker/ Spouse	Widow(er)	Worker	Spouse
1937 (same as prior law)	65/0	65/0	80.0	37.5
1938	65/2	65/0	79.2	37.1
1939	65/4	65/0	78.3	36.7
1940	65/6	65/2	77.5	36.2
1941	65/8	65/4	76.7	35.8
1942	65/10	65/6	75.8	35.4
1943	66/0	65/8	75.0	35.0
1944	66/0	65/10	75.0	35.0
1945–1954	66/0	66/0	75.0	35.0
1955	66/2	66/0	74.2	34.6
1956	66/4	66/0	73.3	34.2
1957	66/6	66/2	72.5	33.8
1958	66/8	66/4	71.7	33.3
1959	66/10	66/6	70.8	32.9
1960	67/0	66/8	70.0	32.5
1961	67/0	66/10	70.0	32.5
1962 and after	67/0	67/0	70.0	32.5

*Reduced retirement benefits will continue to be available to workers (and spouses) beginning at age 62 but at a greater reduction. For workers and spouses, the prior-law reduction factors (5/9ths of 1 percent per month for workers and 25/36ths of 1 percent per month for spouses) are retained for the first 36 months of benefits before age 65 and a new factor (5/12ths of 1 percent) is applied for each additional month. For older survivors, reduced benefits continue to be available at age 60 with the monthly reduction adjusted for each age cohort so as to maintain a 28.5 percent reduction at age 60—the same maximum reduction as occurred under prior law.

SOURCE: *Social Security Bulletin*, July 1983, p. 30.

¼ percent for each month retirement is delayed. For those reaching 62 after 1986, the delayed retirement credit is 3½ percent per year, or ⅔ percent per month up to age 70. From then on, the delayed retirement credit is set to increase steadily until 2008, when it reaches 8 percent for each year of delayed retirement.

Adjustment for the Family Maximum

The *family maximum* is the maximum amount that can be paid one family—excluding payments to divorced spouses—in monthly benefits based on one worker's earnings record. There is one family maximum for survivors' and retirement benefits, and another one for disability benefits.

The family maximum for survivors' and retirement benefits is calculated in a manner similar to that for figuring the PIA. However, the bend points and the percentages are unique. Present and estimated values of the bend points are contained in Table B.8.

As can be seen, in 1991 the family maximum was equal to 150 percent of the first $473 of the PIA, plus 272 percent of the PIA in excess of $473 but not in excess of $682, plus 134 percent of the PIA in excess of $682 but not in excess of $890, plus 175 percent of the PIA in excess of $890. For example, given a pri-

605

TABLE B.8 · Bend Points for Computing Family Maximum for Retirement and Survivors' Benefits

Year	150% of First	272% of Next	134% of Next	175% of Excess Over
1991	$473	$209	$208	$890
1992	495	219	217	931
1993*	521	230	229	981

*Estimated values for this year.

mary insurance amount of $1,182.40 in 1991, the maximum that could be paid out in family survivors' benefits was $2,068.40 after rounding to the next lower dime.

$$
\begin{aligned}
150\% \text{ of } \$473 &= \$709.50 \\
272\% \text{ of } (\$682 - \$473)\$209 &= 568.48 \\
134\% \text{ of } (\$890 - \$682)\$208 &= 278.72 \\
175\% \text{ of } (\$1,182.40 - \$890)\$292.40 &= \underline{511.70} \\
&\ \$2,068.40 \\
\text{Family maximum} &= 2,068.40
\end{aligned}
$$

The family maximum for a family with an insured disabled worker is calculated in a different manner. It is equal to the lesser of 150 percent of the PIA, or 85 percent of the AIME, but never less than the PIA. Using the sample calculations for a disabled worker, the maximum family benefit would be equal to 150 percent of $1,182.40 (PIA), or $1,773.60.

When the total basic benefits due a single family exceed the relevant maximum, then benefits paid all family members except the insured worker are reduced proportionately to bring total benefits in line with the family maximum. Total benefits due a disabled worker with a dependent spouse and four children, and a primary insurance amount of $1,182.40, would seemingly total $4,434.00. Table B.9 demonstrates how these benefits would be adjusted for a family maximum of $1,774, and how they subsequently would be adjusted after one child left the household.

TABLE B.9 · Example of Adjustment for Family Maximum

	Original Benefit	Adjusted Benefit (Four-Child Family)	Adjusted Benefit (Three-Child Family)
Insured	$1,182	$1,182	$1,182
Spouse	591	118	148
First child	591	118	148
Second child	591	118	148
Third child	591	118	148
Fourth child	591	118	—
		$1,774	$1,774

Earnings Test

Social Security retirement benefits are for those who have truly retired from the work force. Likewise, benefits for survivors or dependents are for those truly in need. Accordingly, if market wages of persons who are less than 70 years of age exceed an annual exemption, Social Security benefits will be reduced. Actual and estimated values of the annual amount that can be earned without an offset appear in Table B.10. As can be seen, the annual exemption is lower for those below normal retirement age (currently 65). Social Security benefits are reduced by $1 for each $3 above the annual exemption.

TABLE B.10 ▪
Retirement Test

| Year | Annual Exemption | |
	Under 65	65–69*
1991	$7,080	$9,720
1992	7,440	10,200
1993†	7,800	10,720

*Unlimited exclusion after age 70.

†Estimated values for this year.

**The Social
Security
System**

Photo Credits

PART OPENING PHOTOS

Part 1: © Art Stein, Photo Researchers, Inc.
Part 2: © Spencer Grant, Photo Researchers, Inc.
Part 3: © Wil & Deni McIntyre, Photo Researchers, Inc.
Part 4: © Joseph Nettis, 1991, Photo Researchers, Inc.
Part 5: © Wil & Deni McIntyre, Photo Researchers, Inc.

COLOR INSERT 1

Spending, Borrowing, and Saving

Family buying a car: Photo Researchers, Inc.
Woman using credit card: © Mike Kagan, Monkmeyer Press Photo Service
Man opening bank account: © Richard Hackett,
Man using ATM machine: © Shambroom 83, Photo Researchers, Inc.
Family buying a house: © Spencer Grant, Photo Researchers, Inc.

Protecting What You Have

Home damaged by earthquake: © Wil & Deni McIntyre, Photo Researchers, Inc.
Car accident: © Joseph Nettis, 1991, Photo Researchers, Inc.
Nationwide ad: Courtesy Nationwide Life Insurance Company
Private maternity suite: © Lawrence Migdale, Photo Researchers, Inc.
Doctor examining child: © '86 Blair Seitz, Photo Researchers, Inc.
Auto car repair: © Tom Hollymann, 1985, Photo Researchers, Inc.

COLOR INSERT 2

Investing for the Future

Sotheby's auction: © Bill Bachman, Photo Researchers, Inc.
Man reading journal: © Joseph Nettis, 1991, Photo Researchers, Inc.
Stock certificates: © Ken Lax, Photo Researchers, Inc.
Assorted bonds: © Dick Luria/Science Source, Photo Researchers, Inc.
NYSE trading floor: Courtesy New York Stock Exchange, Inc.

Planning for Your Long-Term Needs

Retired couple having lunch: © Lee Snyder, Photo Researchers, Inc.
Retired couple riding bikes: © Blair Seitz, Photo Researchers, Inc.
Woman at Tigers' "Fantasy Camp": © 1991 Andy Levin, Photo Researchers, Inc.
Senior couple camping: © Wil & Deni McIntyre, Photo Researchers, Inc.
Couple drawing up will: © Will & Deni McIntyre, Photo Researchers, Inc.

Index